THE
AMERICAN
WOMAN

1999–2000

Edited by Cynthia B. Costello,

Shari E. Miles, and Anne J. Stone

for the Women's Research & Education Institute

Betty Dooley, President

W. W. NORTON & COMPANY

NEW YORK / LONDON

THE
AMERICAN
WOMAN

1999–2000

A CENTURY OF CHANGE—
WHAT'S NEXT?

First Edition

For information about permission to reproduce selections from this book, write to Permissions,
W. W. Norton & Company, Inc., 500 Fifth Avenue, New York, NY 10110.

The text of this book is composed in 11/13 Bembo,
with the display set in Centaur.
Composition and manufacturing by The Haddon Craftsmen, Inc.

ISBN 0-393-31862-1 (pbk.)

W. W. Norton & Company, Inc., 500 Fifth Avenue, New York, N.Y. 10110
http://www.wwnorton.com

W. W. Norton & Company Ltd., 10 Coptic Street, London WC1A 1PU

1 2 3 4 5 6 7 8 9 0

CONTENTS

AMERICAN WOMEN TODAY: A STATISTICAL PORTRAIT

WOMEN IN CONGRESS

LIST OF TABLES
AND FIGURES

AMERICAN WOMEN TODAY: A STATISTICAL PORTRAIT

ACKNOWLEDGMENTS

THE SEVENTH EDITION OF *The American Woman*, like the first six, has enjoyed a broad base of support from foundations, corporations, and individuals who have made generous financial or in-kind contributions to the Women's Research & Education Institute (WREI) and its work.

The American Woman series was launched with a grant from the Ford Foundation and supported by contributions from other donors. We are extremely grateful to the Ford Foundation both for its past assistance and for providing a grant to help in the preparation of this edition of *The American Woman*. Helen Neuborne and Janice Petrovich, in particular, have earned our gratitude for their support and ongoing advice. Alison Bernstein of the Ford Foundation deserves special thanks for her encouragement of *The American Woman* series.

Special thanks are also due Eli Evans and Lisa Goldberg at the Revson Foundation for their many years of support.

The other funders and persons without whose assistance we could not have prepared this book are the American Express Company, Karen Davis, Denise Ferguson, Matina Horner, and Juanita Kreps. To each we extend our appreciation.

We would also like to acknowledge the support of the AFL-CIO; AT&T; Akin, Gump, Strauss, Hauer and Feld; Allen and Company, Inc.; AMBAC; American Income Life Insurance Company; American Postal Workers Union; Associated Actors and Artistes of America; Association of Flight Attendants; Avon Products Inc.; Chase Manhattan Bank; Chrysler Corporation Fund; Citibank; Coca-Cola Company; Communications Workers of America; DC Comics; Eastman Kodak; Eli Lilly Corporation; Fannie Mae; Fluor Corporation; Guinness America, Inc.; Hoechst Marion Roussel; J. C.

Penney Company, Inc.; Johnson and Johnson; Mary V. Mochary; Merck and Company; Motorola; Pfizer Inc.; Philip Morris; RJR Nabisco Inc.; Ryder System, Inc.; Sara Lee Corporation; Sidney Frank Importing Company, Inc.; Suburban Capitol Markets, Inc.; Time Warner Inc.; UNITE!; United Auto Workers; United Distillers North America; and Warner-Lambert Company.

Members of WREI's board of directors have offered extensive practical help as well as continuing encouragement throughout all the editions of *The American Woman*. Board chair Jean Stapleton has tirelessly spoken about every edition of *The American Woman* in towns and cities across the country. JoAnn Heffernan Heisen, Martina L. Bradford, and Carolyn Forrest have promoted the book enthusiastically in the corporate and labor communities. Thanks to Alma Rangel's initiative, *The American Woman* has reached many African American women's organizations in New York. Matina Horner and Juanita Kreps were especially helpful with respect to funding for the book. Indeed, the WREI staff is grateful to the entire board for its belief in the book and for its moral support.

Our editor at Norton, Patricia Chui, consistently provided constructive advice and guidance for which we are most appreciative. We would also like to thank Mary Cunnane, former vice president of Norton, for her enthusiastic support over many editions of *The American Woman*.

A stellar advisory committee has been generous with wisdom, expertise, and encouragement. Sara Rix, who edited the first three volumes of *The American Woman,* deserves special thanks. Her recommendations for this edition were, as always, right on target. Other book advisory committee members who offered guidance include Miriam Chamberlain, Harriet Harper, Cynthia Harrison, Deirdre Martinez, Jill Miller, Irene Natividad, Margaret Simms, Suzanne Stoiber, and Cindy Taeuber.

We wish to thank the individuals at the Bureau of the Census and the Bureau of Labor Statistics who so generously shared their time and expertise. Howard Hayge of the Bureau of Labor Statistics and Diana Lewis and Eleanor Baugher of the Census Bureau deserve special thanks. Lesley Primmer and Marjorie Sims, president and executive director of Women's Policy Inc., were always generous with information, time, and expertise. Special thanks are also due to Wendy Blum for her wonderful messenger service. The writing and editorial assistance of Sarah Orrick have been invaluable.

No book of this kind could have been produced without the hard work of WREI's entire staff. The editorial team, made up of WREI's former research director Cynthia Costello, WREI executive director Shari Miles, and WREI senior research associate Anne Stone, dedicated many hours to the planning, editing, and preparation of *The American Woman*. Special thanks are also due to Jennifer E. Griffith for a first-rate job in preparing the tables and figures for this book.

Lory Manning, director of WREI's women in the military project, compiled the statistics on military women. Shelby Reardon, WREI's development assistant, helped with the fund-raising efforts that made *The American Woman* possible. Angela Wilbon reviewed chapters and sections for this volume. We would also like to thank Barbara Kivimae Krimgold, former director of WREI's Women's Health Project, for her interest and assistance with this edition of *The American Woman*. WREI's able interns—Emmeline Yu, Katherine Tumlinson, and Dina Warnken—deserve special thanks for their careful review of book chapters and sections.

Finally, I want to underscore that our funders, advisers, reviewers, and independent editors are not responsible for any errors or misstatements that may appear in the book. The views expressed in the book do not necessarily reflect the opinions of anyone other than the authors and editors of *The American Woman*.

BETTY DOOLEY
President
Women's Research & Education Institute

PREFACE

Jean Stapleton

THIS VOLUME IS THE SEVENTH in a series of comprehensive reports on the status of women prepared by the Women's Research & Education Institute (WREI). Published every other year, *The American Woman* assembles the latest available information about women's progress and setbacks in many aspects of their lives. This series has become a reliable almanac, summarizing where American women are and reflecting on where they are going.

Nurturing the series from the first volume's appearance in 1987, the board and staff have made *The American Woman* a vehicle for assessing women's status in the policymaking process and politics, as well as in society. Under the leadership of Betty Dooley, president of WREI, these books have reinforced the organization's persistent contributions to improving the status of American women. This wonderful series offers solid testimony to the effectiveness of WREI's strong leadership.

A brief look backward: The first three editions of *The American Woman* covered a broad array of topics, highlighting, for example, the educational status of women of color, the legacy of the women's movement of the past three decades, and women's status in the military. The Fourth Edition, published in the spring of 1992, hit the mark by covering women's roles as political players—as candidates, officeholders, and voters—in what became a breakthrough year for women in U.S. politics as a record 48 women were elected to the House of Representatives and five to the Senate.

The Fifth Edition of *The American Woman* focused on women and health care at a time when reform of our nation's health care system was prominent on the political agenda. And the Sixth Edition addressed a topic of vital concern to all American women and their families: women and work.

Through chapters on women's employment patterns, affirmative action, work and family, unemployment, and pensions, this edition explored the challenges faced by today's working women.

With the publication of this Seventh Edition, WREI takes a look at where we've come from and where we're headed. The chapters in this volume celebrate women's progress over the twentieth century—much of it the result of women's activism in the feminist and civil rights movements. Many of the changes that have occurred in women's lives—such as women's movement into the labor force, the increase in dual-earner and female-headed households, and the decline in fertility—are probably here to stay. But, as this edition of *The American Woman* reminds us, the rights that women have fought so hard to gain are today hanging by a thread.

We live in a country that defines itself as a "land of opportunity." For far too long, women and people of color were shut out of the opportunities available to others. Today, we can take great pride as a country in the opening up of opportunities—in the employment, educational, and political arenas—for women and people of color. It would be untenable, however, if that progress were to stop now.

As we cross over into the next millennium, it is my hope that we will look back on the last decade of the twentieth century as a time when women's equity was affirmed, not denied. Women cannot afford to be passive about protecting—and indeed advancing—their rights. I believe that the time has come for women to be insistent that our hard-fought-for gains not be taken from us!

A Century of
Change—
What's Next?

Introduction

Cynthia B. Costello

IT HAS ALMOST BECOME trite to use the dawning of a new century as an opportunity to take stock of the twentieth century and make projections about the twenty-first. When it comes to women, however, the exercise is appropriate. Women's lives have undergone tremendous change in the decades since 1900—and probably will continue to do so as we cross over into a new millennium.

Consider these few facts: In 1900, women could not own property. They could not vote. And they could not enter most professions. Families had, on average, seven children. Many women died in childbirth, and many others did not see their own children grow into adulthood.

Today, women can own property. They not only vote but vote in larger numbers than men. Most professions are open to women, although the glass ceiling prevents women from rising to the top in many of them. Women have, on average, two children. Their life expectancy is almost 80—seven years longer than men's.

Of course, challenges remain. And depending on a woman's racial, ethnic, and educational background, the obstacles can be formidable. At both ends of the age spectrum, poverty is pervasive among women. Despite the tremendous gains made by women in such professions as law, medicine, and dentistry, most women continue to work in sex-segregated occupations as clerical workers, nurses' aides, fast-food workers, and the like. And whether women work outside the home or not, caretaking is still primarily "women's work." Without true flexibility in the corporate world, many women find themselves stretched to the point of exhaustion.

This edition of *The American Woman* is the seventh in a biennial series prepared by the Women's Research & Education Institute. This edition explores the progress and setbacks for women over the twentieth century and makes projections about what lies ahead for women in the next century.

The book opens with two essays written by the Honorable Juanita Kreps and her daughter, Sarah Kreps. As the first woman to hold the cabinet position of Secretary of Commerce (and a founding member of WREI's board of directors), Dr. Kreps describes her personal experience with breaking barriers in the academy, the board room, and government. A remarkable woman who has achieved many "firsts" in her own lifetime, Dr. Kreps conveys a keen awareness of the barriers that prevent most women from accomplishing similar feats.

Complementing her mother's essay, Sarah Kreps provides an inside look at what it meant for women of her generation to grow up in the 1960s—a time when doors were starting to open but many remained shut. As the baby-boomer daughter of a feminist, Sarah Kreps contrasts her own experience with that of her mother, pointing to the myriad achievements of her generation of women in politics, industry, and even the military. Yet, Ms. Kreps reminds us, cultural stereotypes continue to undermine the self-esteem of young women and challenge us to confront the "girl-poisoning culture" that surrounds us.

The first chapter in the book, "American Women in a New Millennium," is written by Sara Evans, a noted historian of the women's movement. Dr. Evans traces the ebb and flow of the "second wave of feminism" and the major changes that have shaped women's lives in the second half of the twentieth century. The author reminds us that, in the aftermath of World War II, the Cold War culture reasserted traditional gender roles through the ideology of the "feminine mystique." Yet at the same time, women were moving rapidly into the labor force, initiating social movements for civil rights and world peace, and flooding institutions of higher education.

Dr. Evans profiles the two streams of feminism that joined together to create the "second wave." In 1961, the President's Commission on the Status of Women put women's issues on the national political agenda by recruiting a network of powerful women to develop a set of shared goals and issue a major report. In 1966, many of these same women joined a small group of political, professional, and labor union leaders to found the National Organization for Women (NOW).

A second branch of feminist activism emerged from younger activists in the civil rights movement and the student new left (organized to oppose the Vietnam War). In 1967, these young women began to form consciousness-raising groups, and from 1968 to 1975, the women's liberation movement grew explosively. The early 1970s were dynamic years for the women's movement. Successes included the passage of the Equal Rights Amendment

(ERA) (approved by Congress and sent to the states in 1973); the pro-choice Supreme Court decision in *Roe v. Wade* in 1972; and the passage of Title IX of the Higher Education Act, the Women's Equity Education Act, and the Equal Credit Opportunity Act.

By the mid-1970s, antifeminism had become a strong political force with the mobilization of Phyllis Schlafley's Stop-ERA and anti-abortion forces. The ERA stalled after 1975 and went down to defeat in 1982. With the hostile political climate framed by the Reagan administration, the 1980s nourished a growing backlash against feminism in the media, popular culture, and public policy. At the same time, this decade saw the increased presence of women in positions of public authority.

Dr. Evans traces the signs of feminist remobilization that abounded in the late 1980s and early 1990s as a new generation of women began to realize that rights they had taken for granted could be lost. Furthermore, the testimony of Anita Hill during the 1990 hearings on the nomination of Clarence Thomas to the Supreme Court mobilized thousands of women to run for office and contribute to political campaigns. Dr. Evans concludes that in the decades ahead, women will be challenged to find common ground across different generations and backgrounds in an effort to protect—and, it is hoped, expand—women's rights and opportunities.

Chapter Two, "African American Women in the Twenty-first Century: The Continuing Challenge," focuses on the experiences of African American women in the decades since the Second World War. Dr. Vicki Crawford, an historian of African American history, shows that African American women's tradition of community and social activism has provided the foundation for social change in the black community.

Starting in the mid-1950s, African American women played major roles in the formation of the civil rights movement. Through participation in boycotts, demonstrations, voter registration drives, and other forms of nonviolent direct protest, black women provided leadership and support to the movement. Black women's activism was crucial in the passage of the Voting Rights Act of 1965 banning discriminatory practices in voting—one of the most far-reaching and successful civil rights laws ever passed by Congress.

By the mid-1960s, African American protest had shifted from a southern-based movement to one that focused on the racial and economic disparities in the urban north. Here too, African American women were central participants. With the formation of the National Welfare Rights Organization, poor African American women challenged the discriminatory practices of the welfare system and worked to expand access to benefits for eligible women and children. By the late 1960s, African American women's activism in the civil rights and black nationalist movements had evolved into a distinctive black feminism that articulated the position of African American women at the nexus of race, class, and gender in the United States.

The 1970s was a time of progress and setbacks for African American women. A significant number of educated African Americans entered the ranks of the middle class during this period, and black women experienced record growth in clerical and professional employment. However, by the mid-1970s, black economic progress had stalled and African American women who lacked education and skills—especially those who headed families—faced declining job opportunities, rising unemployment, and increasing poverty. Dr. Crawford concludes that, in the next millennium, African American women will need to draw on their strong activist tradition to meet the challenges of growing rates of urban poverty and the persistence of race, class, and gender inequalities.

In Chapter Three, "Hispanic Women in the United States," Margarita Benitez of the University of Puerto Rico surveys the experience of Hispanic women over the twentieth century. The author reminds us that Hispanic women in the United States have confronted many barriers and challenges—including cultural isolation, low living standards, limited opportunities for education and employment, and persistent stereotypes. Nevertheless, Hispanic women are not a homogeneous group; they come from many different social, cultural, and ethnic backgrounds and bring to this country a rich variety of experiences and characteristics.

Dr. Benitez reports that most Hispanic women (and men) work in low-paid, unskilled, and often temporary jobs. They labor in agriculture and food processing, the service industries, some sectors of manufacturing, and the underground economy. Today, over 40 percent of employed Hispanic women work in technical, sales, and administrative support occupations. Hispanic women are also the main source of domestic servants, waitresses, cooks, and child care workers in the United States.

Education is key to the socioeconomic advancement of Hispanic women. Here too, there is cause for concern. Hispanic dropout rates are alarmingly high, and the schools most Hispanics attend are among the poorest in the country. Still, Hispanic women have made progress in recent years. From 1981 to 1993, the number of B.A. degrees awarded to Hispanic women increased from 11,000 to 25,500.

Dr. Benitez explores the ways in which life in the United States has affected the traditional roles of Hispanic women, and how Latina women have given voice to their experiences through art and literature. And, like the other authors in this volume, Dr. Benitez believes that the empowerment of Hispanic women—through networking, electoral politics, and Latina feminism—holds the key to improving their conditions.

Chapter Four, "Women and the Law: Learning from the Past to Protect the Future," written by Sonia Jarvis, a noted civil rights attorney, traces the history of judicial and legislative decisions that have shaped women's lives over the last hundred years. Ms. Jarvis reminds us that in the nineteenth century, a woman's legal status was largely defined by her marital status. Married women were subject to physical and economic domination by their husbands, with little recourse in the courts, while single or unmarried women with children often faced social ostracism and lived in legal limbo. The status of women under the law began to change once women started to organize. Women's participation in the abolition of slavery and the temperance movement helped prepare them for the suffrage movement, which resulted in the passage of the Nineteenth Amendment in 1920.

Ms. Jarvis traces the judicial and legislative decisions that have opened up opportunities and expanded women's rights over the last 50 years. The civil rights movement, along with a more modern interpretation of the Fourteenth Amendment to the U.S. Constitution, greatly assisted women in establishing their constitutional rights. Over the past 30 years, a number of legal rights for women have been recognized by federal and state courts, including the right to maintain a separate legal identity regardless of marital status; the right to privacy in decisions regarding reproduction, personal autonomy, and marital status; and the right to bodily integrity, regardless of marital status.

Despite the gains made by women since the Second World War, a number of warning signs have emerged in recent years. Certain federal statutes and policies, such as affirmative action, are subject to intense debate and backlash. Cases at the state and federal level continue to challenge a woman's right to control her reproductive process, to gain equal access to educational opportunities, and to be free from discrimination on the basis of sex in the workplace. Ms. Jarvis concludes that women's legal status is surprisingly fragile. If women do not want to see their hard-won gains dissipate at the dawn of a new century, they will need to become more vigilant and politically active.

In Chapter Five, "The American Woman: The Road Ahead," Carol De Vita of the Urban Institute presents a demographic portrait of women's lives over the second half of the twentieth century. Dr. De Vita reports that:

- The average family continues to hover around two children per couple, although racial and ethnic differences in fertility are evident. On average, Hispanic women have the highest number of children (3.0 per woman), followed by black women (2.2), white women (2.0), and Asian women (1.9).
- By 2030, minorities will account for two in five American women, compared with one in four today. All minority groups are growing, but Hispanics are adding the largest numbers. By 2030, the number of Hispanic

women is expected to reach 33 million. Black women will number 24 million, and Asian women, 12 million.

- The aging of the U.S. population is one of the most significant demographic trends facing the nation today. Both the number and share of people age 65 and older will rise dramatically in the next 30 years. Population aging will hold special significance for women. Not only do women outlive men, on average, but they are also the primary caregivers of people in need of assistance.
- Women have made great strides in education, but not all women have shared equally in this progress. In 1995, 88 percent of women age 25 to 34 had graduated from high school—up from 60 percent in 1960. However, 40 percent of white women age 18 to 21 were enrolled in college in 1994, compared with only 25 percent of black women and 16 percent of Hispanic women.
- Notable increases have occurred in women's labor force participation over the last several decades—almost six in 10 adult women were in the workforce in 1995, compared with less than four in ten (38 percent) in 1960. One result is that the dual-worker family has replaced the breadwinner-homemaker model as the most common type of family in the United States.

Lesley Primmer's essay presents the history of the bipartisan Congressional Caucus for Women's Issues. As the former director of the Caucus, Lesley Primmer is well qualified to describe the political ups and downs confronted by the caucus over its twenty-year history.

The Congressional Caucus for Women's Issues (CCWI) was founded in 1977 by 15 of the 18 women then in Congress as a vehicle for advancing a women's legislative agenda. From its inception, the bipartisan women's caucus was headed by two cochairs—one Democrat and one Republican. As one of its first acts, the Congresswomen's Caucus (as it was initially called) mounted a successful three-year extension of the ratification period for the ERA. Another hallmark event of 1977 was the founding of the Women's Research & Education Institute (WREI) to serve as the research and education arm of the caucus.

The caucus's first legislative package was the Economic Equity Act (EEA). Over the years, the EEA has addressed a range of women's concerns, including tax and retirement policies, dependent care, health insurance coverage for dependents, and child support enforcement. One of the caucus's greatest victories was the passage of the Family and Medical Leave Act in 1993 following an eight-year campaign by women both inside and outside of Congress.

Since 1990, the caucus has also led the way in focusing congressional and public attention on deficiencies in women's health care through the Women's Health Equity Act (WHEA). By the end of the 104th Congress (1996), more than two dozen WHEA provisions had become law, and billions of additional dollars had been pumped into women's health research and services.

The status of the caucus changed in 1994, when the new Republican Congress abolished all legislative service organizations (LSOs). Like all the other LSOs, the Congressional Caucus for Women's Issues lost its right to meet as a formal organization, to have office space in the congressional buildings, and to receive membership dues from members of Congress. The CCWI had little choice at the beginning of the 104th Congress but to reorganize as a congressional member organization (CMO). Although limited by the absence of staff and an operating budget, the restructured women's caucus has continued to serve as the primary advocate for women's issues on Capitol Hill, promoting women's health and economic agendas in the 104th and 105th Congresses.

TRENDS TO WATCH

The American Woman's statistical portrait provides the hard numbers that underlie the trends shaping women's experience. This section of the book explores demographics first, followed by a look at education and health. The economic status of American women is examined through the numbers on employment, earnings and benefits, and economic security. Separate sections are devoted to elections and officials, and women in the military.

The lights and shadows of the situation of American women appear in the statistics. Let us mention a few of them.

- Women of every race can expect to outlive their male counterparts. By the time a woman reaches the age of 75, the chances that she is living with a spouse have dropped below one in three. The majority of women over 75 live alone.
- Age at first marriage has been going up steadily for both women and men for a quarter-century; the divorce rate has been gradually declining since the early 1980s.
- The college-educated proportion of women, although still smaller than the comparable proportion of men, has been increasing faster, and in the younger cohorts, the gender gap has closed: the typical American woman between 25 and 34 has more education than her male contemporary.

- Undergraduates of both sexes, but especially women, were a racially more diverse group in 1994 than their counterparts of a decade earlier. The proportion of black women with bachelor's degrees exceeds that of black men, but is still smaller than the comparable proportion of white women.
- More than one in every seven infants born to black mothers are low-birthweight babies, a proportion almost twice that for U.S. babies overall, and the infant mortality rate among babies whose mothers are black is nearly double the overall rate.
- Both white and black women's death rates from heart disease have dropped significantly since 1970, while their death rates from cancer have increased somewhat. Black and white women's lung cancer death rates, which are very similar, increased fivefold between 1960 and 1990.
- Breast cancer is more common among white women than black women, but deadlier for black women. The good news is that the percentage of women over 50 who have recently received a mammogram and clinical breast exam has increased, most dramatically among black women.
- The incidence of AIDS among black and Hispanic women and teenage girls is far out of proportion to their presence in the population as a whole.
- A school-age child is more likely than a preschool child to have a mother in the labor force, but youngsters whose mothers work are in the majority, even among children under six.
- Women are now the majority in some professional and managerial occupations that were largely male until relatively recently. However, there are still very few women in the skilled blue-collar trades.
- The ratio of women's to men's earnings, which had been narrowing for some years, widened slightly after 1993. In 1996, women made 75 cents for every dollar men made, but there are great variations by occupation.
- More education means significantly higher earnings for women as well as for men, and education increases earnings for both more than it used to, but higher education still does not pay off as handsomely for women as for men.
- No more than 70 percent of year-round, full-time workers of either sex have health insurance coverage through their jobs. Half the women workers who have health insurance through their own jobs work for very large employers.
- In 1995, as in 1985, median real income was higher for white families of every type than for their black or Hispanic counterparts.
- Dual-earner couples' median real income rose steadily between 1975 and 1995; it was nearly 20 percent higher at the end of the period. Median income declined for married couples without wives in the labor force and for male-headed families.

- At every age, but especially in adulthood, females are more likely than their male contemporaries to be poor. Black and Hispanic women have by far the highest poverty rates among adults.
- The number of women serving in the U.S. armed forces has increased steadily since the advent of the all volunteer force in 1974, when less than two percent of military personnel were women. Today, more than one in seven are women.

LOOKING AHEAD

The essays, chapters, and statistics in this edition of *The American Woman* show that much has changed for women over the twentieth century. The fact that 59 women with voting rights are serving in the 105th Congress attests to women's progress. (Brief biographies of the women in Congress are included in this volume.) However, it is important to remember that we still have a long road ahead of us: women constitute only about 11 percent of Congress, even though they account for more than half the U.S. population.

Although the year 2000 is in some ways an arbitrary marker, its approach provides an opportunity to project what probably lies ahead for American women. Many women—especially those with adequate incomes and good educations—will continue to thrive, and it is likely that women's representation in better-paying jobs will continue to increase. Those less fortunate because of their race, lower incomes, or other disadvantages will probably continue to fall through the cracks. Whether women's futures are bright or shadowed, in short, depends on the borders where they stand—borders of income, race, occupation, class, and family responsibility.

The future of women, of course, also depends on their political and social activism. If there is one message from this volume, it is that the campaign to protect and expand women's rights and opportunities is an ongoing process. It is our hope that this book will contribute to women's efforts to improve their lives.

Women in This Century: A Personal Perspective

Juanita M. Kreps

DURING THE SECOND HALF of the twentieth century, several major social changes altered women's lives dramatically. More and more women—including married and single women and those with and without young children—joined the labor force. Education and training opportunities for women gradually broadened, and women's lengthening worklife patterns began to resemble those of men. The number of children per family declined, and the proportion of single-parent families headed by women increased.

Early writers on women's changing lifestyles often failed to recognize the long-term significance of these changes, at first questioning whether the growth in the rate of women's employment would continue. It was expected that, after holding routine, low-wage jobs during World War II, women would return to their homes as soon as possible. But women quickly realized that the jobs they held, however menial, provided a necessary supplement to family income—a lesson already familiar to low-income (particularly minority) women. Meanwhile, the availability of jobs then considered "women's work" increased as the economy continued its transition from manufacturing to services. Women's drive for better living standards and employers' readiness to hire them coincided to build a large and stable female workforce.

At the same time, women were no longer content with the traditionally female jobs for which they were often overqualified. Instead, they demanded access to higher-level positions previously available only to men, and admission to the educational institutions that could give them the appropriate credentials. Educators responded, albeit slowly; the goal of graduating significant numbers of women in such areas as science and engineering was elusive, and women's progress through the ranks of industry and most professions was slow.

WHAT WAS IT LIKE TO PURSUE A CAREER DURING THIS ERA?

At midcentury, a woman who chose to study a nontraditional discipline like economics was regarded as a bit odd. I was drawn to the subject during an introductory course in college because it seemed to address the unemployment and poverty that had plagued the nation throughout my youth. After completing a major in the field, however, I decided that a minimal understanding of economics was insufficient for solving social problems but that graduate study might do the trick. While my early idealism and confidence in the practical applications of economics has never been completely shattered, it has taken a beating in the face of repeated recessions and the poverty that persists even in prosperous times.

In graduate school, as the economics department's first woman student, I received the same welcome from professors accorded to the male students; clearly, one female posed no threat to a class of 20 men. The subject appealed primarily to future business executives, financial managers, and college professors and was considered somewhat demanding, even for males. Once I had obtained the appropriate degrees and an academic position, however, resistance surfaced among male students. On one occasion, after I had delivered a lecture at an all-male college, a young man announced that he could not accept the idea of a woman professor of economics. When pressed for an explanation, he pointed out that his mother could not balance her checkbook.

However, this attitude was seldom evident among the professors who awarded the fellowships and teaching assignments; in the 1950s, there were never enough economists to teach the undergraduates. Yet few women were counseled to complete the work required for a Ph.D. And since most women were married and had children, and there was no precedent for considering a second career, our generation rarely questioned the traditional order of priorities. In contrast to today's young women, who expect to compete on an equal basis professionally and who often start their own businesses, we tended to accept the prevailing view that males were better suited to dealing with money matters.

Another factor that slowed our entry into professions will come as no surprise to today's young women: we had no access to day care. Neither corporations nor universities offered help in solving this problem, even when they were actively seeking women employees. Day care centers had not been introduced. Most of us relied on family members or women who came to the home several hours a day, and we took part-time jobs that allowed us to spend most of each day with our children. Even women with advanced degrees and significant professional experience were expected to drop out of the workforce altogether for a number of years; indeed, mothers who were away from their children all day were viewed with some dismay. Nobody believed that a woman could do a full-time job and give her children adequate time and attention. Superwoman did not appear on the scene until much later.

Today's young women have one burden we did not have, however. Society expects them somehow to do both jobs well, and, compounding the problem, women expect it of themselves as well. Their struggle leads women to wonder how our generation survived under the pressure. "When you have three small children, how can you possibly get out of the house and off to work every morning?" they ask. Aside from the (now permissible) jest that having three children was a powerful incentive to leave the house, it is important to emphasize that very few of us did go off to work every morning. And if we did, we often were too tired to enjoy it.

Despite the odds, our careers sometimes flourished at later ages, in part because of growing market pressures that called for the service of women in a range of professions. We also began to challenge discriminatory employment practices, and, with some misgivings, human resource directors (then called "personnel managers") began to allow women and minorities to fill vacancies in formerly all-male positions.

For the most part, however, life in the fast lanes of business, government, and higher education was limited to males throughout the 1960s and 1970s. With the exception of high-level civil service positions and professorships in women's colleges, few women advanced to the top ranks and almost never at the rate of advancement enjoyed by male colleagues with comparable credentials. Study after study found evidence of glass ceilings long after affirmative action was mandated. The corporate brass seemed oblivious to women's executive potential, despite the growing number of eligible women who had passed the age of major family responsibilities and had time and energy to devote to their work.

By the late 1970s, some businesses had started promoting women to better jobs or even electing women directors. After the J. C. Penney Company invited me to become the first woman on their board (a first for me as well), I discovered that their search had been very thorough; they had checked my credentials with every man I had ever worked with. "Think what they must know about me," I worried. "Think what they know about the women they did *not* select," someone suggested, which was not reassuring.

Corporations that closed their doors to women were put on the defensive by women's organizations and occasionally by irate stockholders who protested the absence of women executives or board members. Women in offices and factories were also alert to their employers' policies. I once toured a plant with a group of male board members, walking past women bent over their intricate assembly process. One of them called out: "How does it feel to be the only woman board member?" My response, "Not as good as it will when we have half a dozen," brought smiles from the women but not from the rest of the board.

The discomfort persisted between male executives and women who were moving ahead. We worried that our performance might be found inadequate, jeopardizing the chances for other women. Accusations of tokenism were commonplace; true or not, nothing could be more devastating to one's self confidence. When I left the secretary of commerce position in 1979, a congressman asked whether I was going to become the "token woman on all those corporate boards." It would have been futile to point out that previous board service was largely the basis for my appointment to the Cabinet.

Patricia Roberts Harris, a noted lawyer and former dean of Howard University Law School, served first as secretary of housing and urban development and then as secretary of health, education, and welfare under President Jimmy Carter. The President then chose Shirley Hufstedier as the first secretary of education. The three of us more than doubled the number of female Cabinet officers in the nation's history. During the 1980s and 1990s, the number and range of department-level posts to which women were appointed grew to include secretary of labor, secretary of energy, special trade representative, chair of the Council of Economic Advisors, director of the Office of Management and Budget, ambassador to the United Nations, attorney general, and secretary of state. The enthusiasm that greeted Madeleine Albright's appointment as secretary of state was a recognition of her demonstrated ability and a cause for rejoicing for those of us who never dreamed we would see it happen.

Women whose careers developed during the last half-century are sometimes asked why we were so accepting of the status quo. Knowing the talents women could bring to the higher ranks of education and other nonprofit endeavors, business, law, medicine, and the sciences, why were our expectations so modest? The fact that we recognized reality did not stop us from protesting in the marketplace, universities, and government agencies. But the response was not encouraging.

Teaching economics meant teaching males whose career focus was on industry jobs or further graduate or professional study and who expected women to play the roles their mothers played. Only after the number of women preparing for male-dominated professions increased and the 1960s era made Americans more sensitive to race and gender discrimination, were serious discussions about comparative male and female earnings possible. Even then, the male students showed little concern. They agreed that it was all right for a woman to have a career, as long as she did not neglect her duties at home.[1]

In this unwelcome environment, women students were at first reluctant to speak out. The Vietnam War and the ensuing protests changed the context of the dialogue, with a new emphasis on freedom of lifestyle that extended to women as well as to men. The growth in the number of women entering law and business schools in recent decades proves that women's quiet demeanor during that earlier era masked high aspirations. Today half the graduates of these schools are women, and they clearly expect to compete on an equal basis with men. Equality does not come quickly or easily, however; women made up only three percent of the top ranks of management in the mid-1990s.

The problems of women who have little education and therefore no access to the better jobs are even more difficult to solve. These women have little or no upward mobility, yet often bear financial responsibility for their children. Discontinuing welfare payments for nonworking mothers after two years, on the assumption that these women can earn even poverty-level wages, is a serious threat to already vulnerable families. The economy's recent record of growth promises further job creation for women and men, but only for those who are well prepared for the new labor market.

WHAT HAS CHANGED?

Today's young woman has a far wider range of educational and career options than her mother. There are few fields she cannot enter—indeed, few

---

[1]Underlying men's assumption of total responsibility for supporting their families was their belief that this role was expected of them. It was easy to move from that mind-set to the position that women were, if not intellectually inferior, certainly ill equipped to deal with the harsh realities of the business world. Behold: the pendulum has swung—and some would say too far. A tongue-in-cheek editorial in the *Economist* last year, deploring men's difficulty in holding jobs in the information society, began by declaring, "Apart from being more violent, more prone to disease, more likely to succumb to drugs, bad diet, or suicide—more socially undesirable from almost any point of view, in fact—men, it seems, are slightly more stupid than women."

areas in which women have not reached senior levels. While women were permitted to enter most professions in earlier decades, they were not fully accepted in them. And they certainly were not encouraged to compete with men for leadership roles in their chosen fields. Consequently, women often did not remain active scholars or scientists over the long run.

A woman's expectations today are quite different. She assumes she can go as far as her ability allows, and her male peers recognize that she is a contender for jobs at all levels. Interestingly, some older men in high-level positions seem reluctant to offer women the opportunities, because they see the long hours, frequent travel, and pressures of their own jobs as incompatible with women's family commitments.

So today's young woman will not be shortchanged because she is not capable (there is too much evidence to the contrary) but because she continues to have other heavy demands on her time and energy. The fact that women in lower-level jobs also work hard, sometimes at two jobs out of necessity, is not considered relevant to the requirements of key professional and managerial positions. Nor does there seem to be any significant interest in restructuring work to allow the sharing of duties that would accommodate women to the higher levels of industry or professions.

Directing women into areas of less professional promise, on the basis that family obligations prevent them from giving more-demanding jobs sufficient time and energy, is a serious waste of human resources. We should explore and experiment with a range of societal and workplace measures that might allow women access commensurate with their abilities: part-time careers, better child care facilities, and shared responsibilities at home with the expectation that men, too, can opt out when necessary. If American employers are willing to embrace variations in traditional work patterns, the American woman will finally have a more level playing field in which to practice her chosen profession.

Women in the Next Century: A Personal Perspective

Sarah B. Kreps

THE PAST HALF-CENTURY'S PROGRESS toward equal treatment in the work-place notwithstanding, women in the new century face challenges that are at least as daunting.

As women assume leadership roles in formerly all-male professions, important questions arise about how society will be affected. Will men accept direction by women in these areas? Will women's leadership change the quality of services delivered by corporations and organizations? Can shared responsibility for home and child care be achieved, and will a new division of these functions better serve family needs?

Predictions are difficult because so far we have few instructive cases. A recent study of the growing number of women in the military by the Women's Research & Education Institute found that the public strongly supports women's participation. Another example yet to be evaluated is that of female law enforcement officers. That such professions now appeal to so many women raises interesting questions about how women will approach these new roles and how receptive the public will be to women's integration into formerly all-male occupations and positions.

An equally important set of questions relates to the public perception of the family, its composition, and the roles assumed by different members. The presumption that today's families have the same characteristics as yesterday's families often clouds public-policy debates. Families are assumed to be headed by fathers who provide primary support, with supplementary earnings from mothers who retain responsibility for the care of children and, when necessary, elderly parents. In fact, the proportion of families with two parents has been declining rapidly; the male is not necessarily the major breadwinner; and the care of the elderly and often the children is increasingly provided by nonfamily members.

Yet workplace rules are based on the earlier model, making it particularly difficult for the female-headed household or the single woman to fit into the system. Women make up the bulk of the temporary workforce, for which employers do not provide health, dental, and unemployment insurance coverage. Pension plans are also less likely to extend to those who work part time or intermittently; this imposes an additional burden on women's financial stability.

As the baby-boomer daughter of a feminist, before the word came into wide usage, my life experience to date has differed vastly from that of my mother. She grew up in Appalachia in the midst of the Depression. It was not easy for her to find her way into college and graduate school. I grew up the child of two academics in a university town, with endless educational opportunities. My now 15-year-old daughter's adult life as an American woman in the twenty-first century will be just as different from mine, although it is impossible to predict exactly what those differences will be.

My mother was 30 years old when I, her first child, was born. She has told me that, at the time, people looked askance at a woman who delayed starting a family until that age; it was considered "old." What was she waiting for, anyway? In my mother's case, what she was "waiting for" was to earn a Ph.D. in economics, begin a career, and establish herself professionally before committing to the children she had always wanted. Her wisdom in choosing this path, which went against the grain of the socially acceptable pattern prescribed for young women in the 1950s, surely went unrecognized in that decade.

In one of life's interesting coincidences, my daughter arrived on the scene when I was 30 years old. Needless to say, no one made negative comments about the age at which I began my family. Most of my friends had careers, and those who elected to have children waited until their thirties. Today, as we know, it is not uncommon for women to begin having children at 40 or later. Medical advances of the last two decades have made this a new option for many women who, because of career considerations or fertility problems, have delayed childbearing.

Both my mother's generation and mine respected the gospel that one had to be married before having children. To break that ironclad rule was to invite ignominy, not only on one's self, but also on one's entire family. Most women of my generation can recall the girl in their high school who "got into trouble," and either endured the humiliation of a shotgun wedding or was abruptly whisked out of town to "live with her aunt." If she married, she kept the child; if she did not marry, the child was immediately given up for adoption. The young woman rarely had a say in the matter.

Today, there are more options. Women who are financially independent may choose to bear or adopt children without a husband and, in most communities, without stigma. Married or not, they may choose a child-free life. These choices are made possible by the widespread availability of reliable methods of contraception. My generation was the first to have access to the pill and other effective forms of birth control. Many of us fought for and saw the legalization of abortion in this country while we were in college.

The women of my daughter's generation will take all these rights for granted, assuming *Roe v. Wade* stands. They will have something no previous generation of American women has truly enjoyed—the means to fully control their sexual lives and reproductive health within the dictates of their own consciences. Yet, the specter of AIDS and other sexually transmitted diseases—which undoubtedly will accompany us into the twenty-first century—make it all the more imperative that the next generation of women receive adequate instruction on how to protect themselves. The means are there, and the alternatives—unwanted pregnancy, illness and even death, poverty, and the uncertainties of government assistance for health care and child support—are chilling.

The new generation of American women will grow up with a multitude of female role models I did not encounter as a girl—women whose accomplishments I have applauded as "firsts." The young women of the twenty-first century will not feel the exhilaration, the urge to cheer at the sight of a female physician, attorney, CEO, cleric, astronaut, law enforcement official, military officer, or vice-presidential nominee. They will expect to see women serving as elected officials at every level of government, and in appointed positions such as Supreme Court justice, Cabinet member, and presidential adviser. They will see more female heads of state, including perhaps a woman President. This is the legacy of my mother's generation. Those of us who see how far we have come in the last half-century need to commit to achieving a comparable level of advancement for our own daughters and the young women who follow us into the expanding universe of the twenty-first century.

Inevitably, however, each new generation must face its own barriers, pressures, and challenges. For my daughter's generation, these may be as amorphous as the popular culture that permeates our daily lives. Whereas baby boomers were the first generation to have grown up with television, their children are the first to be saturated by it. My parents have said that I learned how to turn on the television set before I learned how to walk. Nevertheless, as youngsters we had far fewer viewing options, most of which would be considered harmless by today's standards, and we spent far less time in front of the television than children today. It is unlikely that children in the twenty-first century will be less influenced by this medium, as the ever-evolving technology of satellite television and the Internet create seemingly endless communications possibilities.

Even the most conscientious parents of today face enormous difficulties in trying to monitor—or moderate—the influence of the media on their children. The highly profitable powers of television, advertising, and the movie and music industries continue to grow. Their aggressive and ubiquitous presence has already had its effects on those young women who will come of age early in the next century; one cannot expect that these forces will loosen their hold on the captive audience they have targeted since that generation's toddlerhood.

What messages has this generation already been bombarded with throughout childhood and adolescence, and how have those messages affected young women in particular? Will the ways in which the popular media have portrayed women over the last quarter century dominate U.S. (and global) culture in the near future?

These questions provide much food for thought. In her extraordinary work, *Where the Girls Are: Growing Up Female with the Mass Media*, media critic Susan J. Douglas identifies ways that we, as American women, base our self-image on icons thrust on us by the media. Douglas addresses the influence of the popular media on women growing up in the 1950s, 1960s, and 1970s, but her thesis rings true in our daughters' time as well:

> We must reject the notion that popular culture for girls and women didn't matter. . . . American women today are a bundle of contradictions because much of the media imagery we grew up with was itself filled with mixed messages about what women should and should not do, what women could and could not be. . . . These contradictions still exist, and the mass media continues to provide us with stories, images, and whopping rationalizations that shape how we make sense of the roles we assume in our families, our workplaces, our society.

In her recent best seller, *Reviving Ophelia: Saving the Selves of Adolescent Girls,* psychologist Mary Pipher details the impact of our popular culture on today's young women. Her portrayals of girls and their parents, gleaned in counseling sessions, reveal the effects of our "girl-poisoning culture." So although most of us expected our daughters to have an easier time than we did, the author says no, reminding us that "with puberty, girls crash into junk culture." "Girls today are much more oppressed," Pipher writes. "They face incredible pressures. . . . [A]s they navigate a more dangerous world, girls are less protected."

Our daughters' generation, having spent their formative years under the influence of U.S. advertising, television, and movies, may find it difficult to reject that artificial world and develop their own identities. Thus, changing the media's image of women may be no less daunting a task than the challenges our mothers faced in a male-dominated society.

At the same time, the explosion in telecommunications technology holds great promise for American women, as we become less separate from the political and social events of other countries. Women of the twenty-first century will be citizens of the world, with all the privileges and obligations that accompany this emerging form of citizenship. The young American woman of today will have new opportunities to bring her country's tradition of freedom and activism to bear in finding solutions to such global problems as human rights violations, gender violence, famine, disease, and environmental deterioration. And the dissolving barriers in communications and geography will open up new vistas for her ideals, ambitions, and talents.

ONE

AMERICAN WOMEN IN A NEW MILLENNIUM

Sara M. Evans

HIGHLIGHTS

IN THE SECOND HALF of the twentieth century, American women forged dramatically new patterns of labor force participation, marriage and fertility, sexual behavior, and political action. The reverberating aftershocks of these ongoing changes—and the rebirth of a massive feminist movement—will profoundly affect U.S. social, political, and economic life in the twenty-first century.

- Cold War culture, in the aftermath of World War II, reasserted traditional gender roles through the ideology of the "feminine mystique," which consigned women to domestic roles. Yet, at the same time, women were rapidly changing their patterns of labor force and civic participation, initiating social movements for civil rights and world peace, and flooding into institutions of higher education.
- The President's Commission on the Status of Women, established in 1961, put women's issues back on the national political agenda by recruiting a network of powerful women who issued a major report in 1963—the same year that Betty Friedan published *The Feminine Mystique*.
- In 1964, Title VII of the Civil Rights Act was passed, giving women a powerful legal weapon against employment discrimination. Perceiving the need for an organization that could demand enforcement of laws like Title VII, a small group of political, professional, labor union, and political leaders founded the National Organization for Women (NOW) in 1966.
- A second branch of feminist activism emerged from younger activists in the civil rights movement and the student new left. In 1967, young

women broke away from these movements to form consciousness-raising groups and from 1968 to 1975, the women's liberation movement grew explosively.

* The synergy between different branches of feminist activism made the 1970s a very dynamic era. The years between 1968 and 1975 were described by feminist policymakers as the "golden years" because of the number of significant legislative victories: the Equal Rights Amendment (which passed Congress in 1973 and then was sent to the states for ratification), *Roe* v. *Wade* (1972), Title IX of the Higher Education Act, the Women's Equity Education Act, and the Equal Credit Opportunity Act.

* By the mid-1970s, antifeminism had also became a strong political force with the mobilization of Phyllis Schlafley's Stop-ERA and anti-abortion forces. In the face of widespread cultural anxiety about equality for women and changing gender roles, the ERA stalled after 1975 and went down to defeat in 1982 despite an extension of the deadline for ratification.

* The 1980s brought a sharp increase in female poverty as public spending shifted away from social programs and toward the military. The Reagan economic boom after 1983 did not touch the poorest segment of the population who were disproportionately female and minority.

* At the same time, the 1980s witnessed the continued growth of women's presence in positions of public authority (e.g., Supreme Court justice, astronaut, arctic explorer, military officer, truck driver, carpenter, Olympic star, bishop, rabbi).

* Feminism did not die in the 1980s, but rather it entered the mainstream with new levels of community activism, sophisticated political organizations such as EMILY's List, and broad political alliances which placed new issues such as "comparable worth" on many state legislative agendas.

* Signs of remobilization abounded in the late 1980s and early 1990s as a new generation of women began to realize that rights they had taken for granted could be lost. The Supreme Court's *Webster* decision restricting abortion rights—together with the increasingly violent attacks on abortion clinics—drew thousands of new members into NOW and other women's rights organizations.

* The testimony of Anita Hill during the 1990 hearings on the nomination of Clarence Thomas to the Supreme Court catalyzed a new round of national conversation, complicated by deep fissures of race and sex, and mobilized thousands of women to run for office and contribute to political campaigns.

* In the 1990s, American women have achieved new levels of political power at the same time that "family values" have been used to attack welfare mothers, homosexuals, and nontraditional families (which, in fact, far outnumber traditional ones).

• At the dawn of the twenty-first century, American women have come through a massive upheaval and find themselves on entirely different terrain than they occupied even a half-century before. Their task will be to find common ground among women of different generations and backgrounds by renewing the civic resources already developed through two centuries of struggle for equality.

INTRODUCTION

At the end of the Second World War, American women were on the brink of a dramatically new era. They could not have imagined the revolutions that were to occur in women's roles in society and in their own daily lives. The groundwork, certainly, had been well laid in earlier struggles for political rights, in the creation of a massive infrastructure of women's organizations, and in the flow of women into the labor force. But during the last half of the century, an unprecedented upheaval would take place in family, sexuality, and work. It was as if an earthquake had rearranged the meaning and place of gender in U.S. society, an earthquake resulting from deep, long-term pressures of social changes which—like plates in the earth—had built up beyond the breaking point.

As we move into the twenty-first century with this new landscape beneath our feet, we will find that much of the terrain remains familiar and the tremors are still occurring. On the brink of the twenty-first century, we need to take stock of the upheavals in our recent history so that we can think clearly about future possibilities. In 1900, Americans talked about the "century of the child"—marking their new perception of childhood and society's responsibility for children. Today, women around the globe are claiming new economic roles and demanding political rights. We can say with great certainty that women will be a force in the twenty-first century and that their roles in the coming millennium will be pivotal and visible. We know this because of the dramatic changes of recent decades.

Let's pan back to 1945 and the end of World War II. Women were breathless with joy over the victory, eager for the return of fathers, sons, husbands, and brothers, and intensely proud of their contribution to the war effort. As workers in defense industries (symbolized by Rosie the Riveter), as volunteers in the new women's branches of the military, and as preservers of families, businesses, and farms through years of emergency, women knew that their participation had been essential. Wartime opportunities also brought additional new expectations of access and advancement for racial minorities. The era into which women were moving was one of high expectations, dramatic change, and both domestic and international tension.

NOT SO "HAPPY DAYS"

The end of World War II also marked the beginning of the Cold War, a global nuclear standoff between the United States and the Soviet Union. Traditional gender roles (male breadwinners/female housewives) assumed a prominent place in the Cold War culture that evolved over the next 15 years, even though the reality of women's lives diverged sharply from that norm. The postwar era was filled with traditional imagery, repackaged into a consumption-oriented, suburban lifestyle. Rosie the Riveter's androgynous competence yielded quickly to the "New Look" introduced in 1947 by Christian Dior: dropped hems, nipped waists, and a strikingly feminine elegance. This was the era of what Betty Friedan later named the "feminine mystique"—a term that defined women's place in the postwar, family-centered, prosperous, middle-class lifestyle, wedding prewar ideas about homemaking and motherhood to popularized versions of Freudian sexuality.

This return to tradition that dominated popular media might be understood as one way of coping with the dynamics of change in the Cold War era. While Americans enjoyed booming prosperity, they remained fearful of a return to the harsh conditions of the Great Depression. And the very real possibility of global conflict and atomic war made the world a threatening place indeed. As the leader of the "free world," the United States announced policies of containment and massive retaliation to keep the forces of communism from spreading in the Third World. By analogy, the feminine mystique "contained" women in a set of images and a lifestyle that held at bay the very real (and growing) possibilities of female independence (May 1988).

In "How to Be a Woman," a 1951 issue of *Seventeen* magazine told the young woman that she was "a partner of man . . . not his rival, his enemy, or his plaything. Your partnership in most cases will produce children, and together you and the man will create a haven, a home, a way of life for yourselves and the children." The middle ground, then, lay between rivalry or enmity and a family-centered haven. After extolling the "exciting career" of wife and mother, the article gave advice on preventing what apparently was the principal obstacle to such a future: premarital sex (Thompson 1951: 76, 106).

This definition of women effectively depoliticized them to the extent that, in 1952, the Democratic Party abolished its women's division in a powerful demonstration of the dissociation of women and private life from politics (Hartmann 1993). A number of women continued to work within the political parties, pressing behind the scenes for increased representation, but their efforts remained invisible and only marginally effective (Harrison 1980). Similarly, women's growing presence in the labor force was "contained" in a domestic vision. In 1956, *Look* magazine explained away women's growing presence in the labor force: "No longer a psychological immigrant to man's world, she works rather casually, as a third of the U.S. labor force, and less toward a 'big career' than as a way of filling a hope chest or buying a new home freezer. She gracefully concedes the top job rungs to men" (Bergquist 1956: 35).

These ideas seemed "normal" in an era characterized by high rates of family formation (people married at younger ages and in greater numbers than ever before), soaring fertility, and the flowering of a suburban consumer society. Burgeoning suburbs absorbed not only middle- and upper-middle-class but also working-class families as rising incomes placed home ownership within reach of nearly 70 percent of Americans (Burnham 1982).

The suburbs also effected a new racial and economic segregation of U.S. society. While the more affluent whites were moving out of the cities, the rural poor, many of them African American, were moving into them. There they joined communities of ethnic, blue-collar workers who could not afford or did not want the novelty and uniformity of suburbia. Meanwhile, with social scientists glibly predicting the withering of the welfare state, the growing numbers of female-headed households among the urban poor evoked moral condemnation rather than social concern. Single mothers, especially the never-married, had no place in a world that saw itself through the television lens of *I Love Lucy, Father Knows Best,* and *Leave It to Beaver* (Solinger 1992). Television entered five million new homes per year, with a powerful capacity to generate cultural norms and present a homogenized image of white middle-America.

In 1959, Vice President Nixon asserted that U.S. superiority over the Soviets should be measured in terms of household consumer goods rather than nuclear warheads. "Would it not be better to compete in the relative merits of washing machines than in the strength of rockets?" he argued to Soviet Premier Nikita Khrushchev as they lingered over a model kitchen at the American National Exhibition in Moscow. Gesturing to a built-in, panel-controlled washing machine, Nixon boasted, "In America these are designed to make things easier for our women." Kruschev's counterpoint—that Soviet women were proud to be workers and that his people rejected the "capitalist attitude toward women"—fell on deaf ears. Nixon's winning move (as reported in the Western press) was to assert "I think that this attitude toward women is universal. What we want is to make easier the life of our housewives." An entranced press dubbed this exchange "the kitchen debate" ("The Two Worlds: A Day-Long Debate" 1959: 1–4).

Later that day, when they could not agree on an appropriate toast regarding foreign bases or peace, Nixon and Khrushchev settled on drinking "to the ladies" (May 1988: 16–20). Thus, a technology-filled kitchen, with a woman at its center, served as an effective symbol of U.S. superiority.

The fact was, however, that women had begun to assume new roles that raised questions about the nature and structure of the family, work, and sexuality—the very meaning of womanhood and manhood. Even as Nixon and Kruschev sparred over household technology, American women were moving away from the patterns that had given the feminine mystique such a powerful hold on the public imagination.

The baby boom peaked in 1957, and fertility levels began a steep decline. At the same time, the average marriage age began to rise and marriage rates began to fall, suggesting that the headlong rush into domesticity had reversed itself. With twice as many women attending college in 1960 as in 1950, young single women once again represented a significant proportion of young adults—just in time for the introduction of the birth control pill in 1960!

The restlessness of suburban housewives showed up in many ways. Betty Friedan's famous survey of her Smith graduating class uncovered a "problem that has no name," a sense of ennui, frustration, and limited horizons on the part of educated, middle-class housewives. Colleges and universities experienced a new demand from adult women wishing to return to school— some for enrichment, others to complete degrees and embark on careers. In 1960, the continuing education movement started at Radcliffe College and the University of Minnesota in response to this demand (Evans 1979).

Finally, a growing youth culture drew younger women into a world of music (rock and roll), sexual experimentation, and existential angst. Even before the birth control pill became available in 1960, younger women were beginning to create new norms of sexual behavior that challenged the inherited views of chastity and sin and defied the chaste movie star images of Debbie Reynolds and Doris Day and the kittenish child-woman sexuality of Marilyn Monroe. But the popular culture still labeled sexually active young women as "bad" and offered them few supports if they became pregnant. White women could be hidden away in maternity homes, retrained in feminine skills, and redeemed by giving their babies up for adoption. African American women received virtually no prenatal services and experienced increasing vilification linked to racist perceptions of welfare (Solinger 1992).

The rapid entry of women into the labor force also flew in the face of Cold War verities about home and motherhood. In the 1950s, the link between husbands' incomes and female labor force participation began to change. In 1950, the less a man earned, the more likely it was that his wife would be employed. Over the next two decades, however, this pattern gradually changed until, by 1968, the women most likely to work were married to middle-income men. Indeed, married women in middle-income families were entering the labor force faster than any other group (Weiner 1985).

Women who went to work outside the home in the 1950s found that traditionally male fields were either closed to them or offered overtly hostile environments. As a result, women crowded into clerical and service occupations, and their average wages lost ground compared with those of men. In 1955, the average woman's wage was 63.9 percent of the average man's. By 1960, it was only 60 percent. Social scientists began to worry about women's "two roles" and the lack of social services for working women. The United Auto Workers (UAW) Women's Department ran workshops for women leaders and discovered growing resentment of dual pay scales, which paid women less than men for exactly the same work, and company practices that used "protective" legislation to bar women from more lucrative jobs.

SIGNS OF CHANGE

Newsweek worried in 1960 about "Young Wives with Brains: Babies, Yes— But What Else?" (Diamond 1960). But domesticity had never meant passivity. In cities and suburbs, whether or not they worked outside the home, middle- and working-class women engaged in a dynamic round of community-building volunteer activities that belied static images. Suburban housewives, in particular, having left older neighborhoods and extended family networks, had to rely on one another to construct a lifestyle in which they extended mothering roles into the community. Organized domesticity—in the form of PTAs, Girl Scouts, churches, charitable fundraisers, and neighborhood recreation programs—framed the public life of local communities. Not surprisingly, women's reemergence onto the national political scene was through these very networks.

The postwar era also was marked by the emergence of a massive movement for civil rights and racial equality in which women played critical roles. The nature of those roles was highlighted in 1955 when Rosa Parks, secretary of the Montgomery, Alabama, National Association for the Advancement of Colored People (NAACP), was arrested for refusing to move to the back of a segregated city bus. Behind the scenes, African American women in Montgomery had been organizing and planning for some time, and they seized on Parks's arrest as the moment to initiate a boycott of the city bus system.

The story of the Montgomery bus boycott has entered U.S. mythology in a way that tends to obscure the behind-the-scenes work of the Montgomery Women's Political Council. The boycott, called by the local NAACP chapter, was effective because the Women's Political Caucus—an organization of middle-class African American women, parallel to the League of Women Voters in the white community—was able, overnight, to print and distribute literally thousands of flyers at every bus stop in the African American community. Most of the riders were women who rode buses to their jobs as domestics in white neighborhoods. The buses remained empty for months. Women walked and carpooled to work and gathered with others in community churches at night to hear the inspiring rhetoric of Dr. Martin Luther King, Jr., and other civil rights leaders (Robinson 1987).

Another early sign of renewed activism was the emergence of a peace movement that challenged the nuclear arms race in the name of motherhood. Five women who had been active in the Committee for a SANE Nuclear Policy started Women's Strike for Peace (WSP) in 1960 to raise "mothers' issues" about the dangers of nuclear testing to children through the radioactive contamination of milk. They called for a one-day "strike" on November 1, 1961, as a radioactive cloud from a Russian test floated across the United States.

Using female networks in PTAs, the League of Women Voters, peace organizations, and personal contacts, WSP leaders spread the word. Fifty thousand turned out to lobby government officials to "End the Arms Race— Not the Human Race." Sixty-one percent of Women's Strike for Peace activists were housewives, intellectuals, and civic-minded women who were increasingly concerned about the dangers of nuclear war. Inspired by the courageous examples of civil rights activists in the South and drawing on their own histories of involvement during the war years of the 1940s, these women insisted that their point of view as mothers deserved recognition. Leader Dagmar Wilson, conscious that "the housewife was a downgraded person," set out to show "that this was an important role and that it was time we were heard" (Swerdlow 1982: 510).

Even as housewives began to mobilize, professional women were subjected to blatant discrimination and openly accused of failing to be proper wives and mothers. The silence domestic ideology imposed was a source of pain and confusion, especially among educated women who simply could not resolve the contradictory messages about their lives. Professional women in the 1950s faced a lonely struggle. Maria Iandolo New, chief of pediatrics at Cornell University Medical College, still remembers the chastising words of a medical school dean in 1950 in response to her plea that her application be judged on its merits and not dismissed because she had married: "You are an impertinent young lady, and I am more sure than ever that we do not want you in our medical school" (Chira 1993: A:1, 16).

Major law firms routinely rejected female applicants like Ellen Peters, first in her class at Yale Law School in 1954, and Ruth Bader Ginsburg, first at Columbia in 1959, who became the second woman appointed to the Supreme Court. In 1957, Madeline Kunin, a student at Columbia University Graduate School of Journalism, applied for a newsroom job at the *New York Times;* she was offered a job in the cafeteria. She later became governor of Vermont. Many women dropped out when professors announced that "women don't belong in graduate school," and those who persevered hid their pregnancies and paid careful attention to dress and demeanor. In professional settings, male colleagues routinely assumed that the white women they encountered were secretaries and that the African American women were domestics (Chira 1993; Ruddick and Daniels 1977). While most professional women pursued their careers in relative isolation, networks in the Women's Bureau of the Department of Labor, the United Auto Workers Women's Department, religious groups, the YWCA, and other organizations continued to raise issues of women's roles and rights that would prove critical to the revival of feminism.

A new generation raised in postwar affluence flooded colleges and universities in the 1960s. They believed they could "have it all," but had no models for what that might mean. Many recall bitterly how they had no idea what their work should be or how to imagine themselves as adults. Certainly, they knew they were supposed to marry, have children, age gracefully, and enjoy grandchildren, but their actual life choices included college, graduate school, and professional expectations. "In my generation," as Sarah Ruddick put it, "women's work histories were so buried in our love histories as to be barely visible." Unable to write her dissertation while her husband pursued his first academic job, she wrestled with an indescribable "pain of worklessness." "I had learned to think of life as a matter of personal relations, to think about myself as a daughter, wife, friend, and lover. I knew more about myself as a mother, more about babies even before I ever had children, than I knew about myself as a worker." For such women there was "an invisible, almost amorphous weight of guilt and apology for interests and ambitions that should have been a source of pride"—a sense of an invalidated life (Ruddick and Daniels 1977: 129, 145).

While women with graduate degrees were still a small minority, broad changes in behavior were starting to occur as millions of women—and men—made choices that were different from those of their parents. They married older (or not at all) and rejected their parents' pronatalism. As a result, the baby boom vanished precipitously. Married women and women with children continued to enter the labor force in massive numbers. Those who dropped out to bear and raise children devoted fewer and fewer years to child care as an exclusive occupation. A rising tide of older women returned to school to continue and complete educations suspended in the 1950s. Millions, then, knew that something was amiss, that their ideological relegation to private life was increasingly intolerable, but they had no name for the phenomenon that linked their individual experiences and gave form to their collective grievances.

These were the women who in later years talked about the moment when everything "clicked," after which the world looked and sounded and felt different—crystal clear and infuriating (O'Reilly 1972). As feminism rekindled, these women found their ways into consciousness-raising groups, where they felt immediately "at home," and set out, in a thousand different ways, to *do something* to reshape the landscapes of U.S. daily life.

MOBILIZATION

The mobilization of professional women was the first tremor in the quake that set off the second wave of women's rights activism in the twentieth century. That mobilization can be traced to the President's Commission on the Status of Women, established in 1961. Esther Peterson, Kennedy's appointee to head the Women's Bureau, had the idea that a commission, chaired by Eleanor Roosevelt, could reexamine women's place in the economy, the family, and the legal system. The commission, its staff, and seven technical committees were drawn from labor unions, women's organizations, and governmental agencies.

The President's Commission on the Status of Women put women's issues back on the national political agenda by recruiting a network of powerful women to develop a set of shared goals. Lawyers, government officials, union organizers, academics, commission members, and the commission's staff documented in great detail the ongoing realities of employment discrimination, unequal pay, legal inequities, and lack of child care and other social services. They were stunned by their findings. Individually they had all experienced the problems, but the pervasiveness of discrimination and the hardships that accompanied women's "double burden" of household and labor force responsibilities validated that experience and gave them a sense of mission (Freeman 1975).

Two policy changes occurred immediately after the report was published in 1963. The President issued an order requiring the federal Civil Service to hire for career positions "solely on the basis of ability to meet the requirements of the position, and without regard to sex." Congress then passed the 1963 Equal Pay Act, making it illegal to have different rates of pay for women and men for equal (i.e., the same) work (Harrison 1980: 641–42). The pressure for change broadened as governors in virtually every state appointed commissions on the status of women to conduct similar state-level investigations.

Nineteen sixty-three was also the year that Betty Friedan published her book *The Feminine Mystique*. In a brilliant and thoroughly researched polemic, Friedan gave a name to the malaise of housewives and the dilemma of those who did not fit the mold. Popular culture, psychologists, and educators, she argued, defined women out of public life (and paid work) and into a passive and childlike domesticity. Thousands of letters flooded her mailbox as women poured out the stories they had thought no one would ever understand. "My undiluted wrath," wrote one, "is expended on those of us who were educated and therefore privileged, who put on our black organza nightgowns and went willingly, joyfully, without so much as a backward look at the hard-won freedoms handed down to us by the feminists (men and women)." Others turned their anger on themselves in depression and despair. A suburban housewife claimed that she and her female neighbors were depressed and self-destructive. Describing herself as brilliant (with "an I.Q. in the 145–150 range"), a compulsive eater, and occasionally suicidal, she summarized her life: "I 'caught' a husband at 19, married him on my twentieth birthday, quit school pregnant, and now have six children! I am the typical stay-at-home, domineering mother and wife. I love my children yet I hate them, have actually wished them dead" (May 1988: 209, 210, 212).

Congress was surprised when, during the debate on the 1964 Civil Rights Act, Senator Howard Smith of Virginia suggested that the Title VII prohibition against discrimination in employment on the basis of race, creed, and national origin should also include sex. As a longtime supporter of the Equal Rights Amendment (ERA), he was serious in offering the amendment. But as an ardent segregationist, he probably also hoped it would help to kill the bill (Rupp and Taylor 1987). His efforts drew a chuckle from his male colleagues, but Senator Margaret Chase Smith of Maine was not amused. She and Congresswoman Martha Griffiths of Michigan set to work to ensure that the amendment passed, and when it did, women suddenly had a potentially powerful and far-reaching legal tool.

Title VII provided an outlet for the thousands of women who knew that they faced discrimination but previously had no place to file their grievances.

The Equal Employment Opportunity Commission (EEOC) received a flood of complaints against employers (and also against unions). But the bureaucrats were slow to take them seriously. Most, including those at the EEOC, still considered the inclusion of sex a bit of a joke. The *New York Times* referred to it as the "bunny law," on the theory that a Playboy Club might be sued for refusing to hire a male applicant as a bunny/waitress ("Desexing the Job Market" 1965).

The rumbles were beginning to be audible, but women still had no organized force to demand the enforcement of laws like Title VII. At a 1966 conference of state commissions on the status of women, several women gathered in Betty Friedan's hotel room to discuss the situation. When they submitted a resolution to the conference and were told that action of any kind was not permitted, the women decided on the spot that they had to form a new organization. On the last day, Betty Friedan recalled, they "cornered a large table at the luncheon, so that we could start organizing before we had to rush for planes. We all chipped in $5.00, began to discuss names. I dreamed up NOW on the spur of the moment." Thus, the National Organization for Women, NOW, was born with a clear statement of purpose: "To take action to bring women into full participation in the mainstream of American society now, assuming all the privileges and responsibilities thereof in truly equal partnership with men" (Hole and Levine 1971: 84).

NOW challenged the assumptions of the feminine mystique head-on and demanded full and equal access for women to education, work, and political participation. "It is no longer either necessary or possible," NOW's organizers argued in their founding statement, "for women to devote the greater part of their lives to child-rearing . . ." (Freeman 1975: 74). Using the United Auto Workers Women's Department as their headquarters, NOW sparked pickets and demonstrations across the country against sex-segregated want ads and "men only" clubs. They also pressured the government to enforce antidiscrimination laws, especially Title VII. By 1968, the membership insisted on an endorsement of the Equal Rights Amendment (ERA)—which forced UAW women to withdraw until their union changed its position. The issue of abortion precipitated another split, as lawyers who wanted to focus on legal and economic issues left to found the Women's Equity Action League (WEAL).

WOMEN'S LIBERATION

While NOW laid the organizational and legal groundwork for a new push for women's rights, a younger generation of women provided the jolt that challenged society's expectations across the board. Middle-class women, raised in the era of the feminine mystique, had come of age with deeply contradictory expectations. Although they received little social validation for any life choices outside of marriage and motherhood, vast numbers of them attended college nonetheless, preparing for careers. In an expanding economy, they heard, simultaneously, the message "you can be anything" and the warning "if you pursue your own interests too intensely, you may fail as a woman."

For such young women, the civil rights movement offered an environment in which they could begin to challenge dominant ideas and learn the skills of building a movement. The movement advanced a set of ideas that highlighted the radical egalitarianism of U.S. tradition. "The beloved community" of "black and white together" took on lived reality in a movement of sacrifice and suffering. Middle-class women who joined the movement also came to know poor African American women who had always been excluded—on the grounds both of race and of poverty—from the ideal of the feminine mystique. The generosity and courage of women like freedom fighter Fannie Lou Hamor and the harsh conditions of their lives reframed the meaning of womanhood for middle-class young women—both African American and white (Evans 1979).

Similarly, the student new left, inspired by the civil rights movement in the early 1960s, grew into a movement in which young women honed political skills and imbibed a deep belief in participatory democracy. Feminism arose when these movements, which had provided a unique kind of free space for women, also replicated the restrictive stereotypes of the broader culture. Young men unreflectively assumed that the women who could organize and teach and go to jail would also be responsible for cooking and cleaning the freedom house. Visible charismatic leaders most often were men. Women did the bulk of support work like typing. And finally, the experimentation and liberation of the sexual revolution left many women feeling used and confused. They shared the new-left conviction that it was essential to embed their ideals in their daily lives but found that when it came to relationships between women and men, egalitarian ideals did not hold. In the student movement, however, women found a voice with which to name the problem of sexism and the skill to initiate a burst of female activism. Having broken the middle-class rules of female decorum and discovered themselves as political actors, they named the movement's sexism and immediately broadened their analysis to society as a whole (Evans 1979).

The women's liberation movement emerged from several years of conversation and debate within the civil rights and new-left movements. In the fall of 1967, following a rebuff at a national meeting, small groups of women gathered in Chicago, New York, and Seattle. It was a turbulent and utopian moment. The movements that nourished the groups emphasized participation and intense personal engagement. Around these movements, an emerging youthful counterculture challenged the values of commercialism, work, and competitive success. The black power movement, against a backdrop of growing urban violence in black ghettos, argued forcefully that oppressed groups needed to organize and affirm themselves, to develop collective strength. The antiwar movement contested the righteousness of U.S. military goals in Vietnam and the association of manliness with militarism. Everything, it seemed, was up for grabs. Even revolution was possible.

Black power offered a compelling model for women's liberationists whose driving passion was fury at cultural definitions of women as inferior, sexual objects. These women engaged in consciousness-raising, using the prism of their own experience to rethink everything they had been told. It was a brilliant tool that released thousands of women from isolation through the discovery that others shared their experience and the empowering strength of sisterhood. As a New York group, Redstockings, put it,

> We regard our personal experience, and our feelings about that experience, as the basis for an analysis of our common situation. We cannot rely on existing ideologies as they are all products of male supremacist culture. We question every generalization and accept none that are not **confirmed** by our experience.
>
> Our chief task at present is to develop female class consciousness through sharing experience and publicly exposing the sexist foundation of all our institutions ("Redstockings Manifesto" 1970: 113).

The founders of Bread and Roses, a Boston women's liberation group that formed in 1969 (about the same time as Redstockings), recalled:

> When our group started . . . it was a wonderful time to be in the women's movement. It may have been a unique moment. It felt then almost as though whatever stood in our way would be swept away overnight, with the power of our ideas, our simplicity, our unanswerable truth (Popkin 1978: 59).

Consciousness-raising was an intense form of collective self-education. The founders of Bread and Roses continued, "It seems impossible that adults have ever learned so much so fast as we did then. We taught each other sexual politics, emotional politics, the politics of the family, the politics of the SDS meeting" (Popkin 1978: 98). Another Bread and Roses member, Jane Mansbridge, described consciousness-raising as "the feeling that we were, like Columbus, sailing at the edge of the world. Everything was new and intense" (Davis 1991: 143).

Through 1968 and 1969, the women's liberation movement grew at an accelerating rate. No one was keeping a list—and many groups existed without knowledge of others nearby—but the experience in city after city was that groups would form and multiply almost effortlessly. In some places, like New York City, where the movement tended to be highly ideological, this multiplication often looked like sectarian hairsplitting in search of "true" feminism. Yet the energy of the groups' ideas found expression in dozens of mimeographed articles, manifestoes, newsletters, and, by 1969, journals that included *Notes from the First Year* (New York), *Up from Under* (New York), *No More Fun and Games* (Boston), and *Women: A Journal of Liberation* (Baltimore).

The immense creativity unleashed by the women's movement between 1967 and 1975 owed much to the practices of both branches (NOW and the women's liberationists) which encouraged local initiatives and allowed issues and ideas to flow from grassroots experiences. NOW's structure encouraged the creation of task forces at the local and national levels on virtually any topic. The task forces, in turn, issued a string of reports—on sexism in education, legal discrimination, and violence against women—with recommendations for action. Eleanor Smeal recalled how, in the early 1970s in Pittsburgh:

> We were not real philosophical in those days. . . . We became instant experts on everything. On child care. Started our own nursery school. We worked on employment cases. . . . First we started organizing local NOW chapters. Then we organized the state. I went to every village and town, organizing, if you have just one or two people, you can get a chapter going. I organized housewives. Because that's where I was. You have to do what you know. It never occurred to me that we weren't going to get housewives, and we did (Levine and Lyons 1980: 188).

Women's liberation, with its antistructure, antileadership, and "do your own thing" ethos spawned thousands of projects and institutions, as consciousness-raising groups put their words into action.

When NOW called for a "women's strike" on August 26, 1970, in commemoration of the fiftieth anniversary of the passage of the Nineteenth Amendment to the Constitution granting women the right to vote, the national scope of this new movement became visible to activists and observers alike. Its insistence on the politics of personal life was likewise on display as women took action under the slogan "Don't iron while the strike is hot."

Life magazine reported that "in Rochester, NY women shattered teacups. In Syracuse they dumped 50 children in the city hall. In New York City, Boston, and Washington thousands marched and rallied and hundreds more held teach-ins and speech-ins in dozens of other cities. Women's liberation is the liveliest conversational topic in the land, and last week, all across it, the new feminists took their argument for sexual equality into the streets . . ." ("Women Arise" 1970: 16B).

In New York City, between 20,000 and 50,000 women staged the largest women's rights rally since the suffrage movement, totally blocking Fifth Avenue during rush hour. Branches of a movement springing from different roots intertwined in theatrical and humorous actions: guerilla theater in Indianapolis portrayed the middle-class female life cycle, from "sugar and spice" to "Queen for a Day"; Boston women chained themselves to a huge typewriter; women in Berkeley marched with pots and pans on their backs; New Orleans reporters ran engagement announcements under photos of future grooms; and stewardesses carried posters challenging discriminatory airline rules: "Storks Fly—Why Can't Mothers?" (Davis 1991; Nielsen 1982).

MAKING THE PERSONAL POLITICAL

The contagiousness of feminism lay in its ability to touch women at a deeply personal level, giving political voice to issues that had gone unchallenged and bringing new opportunities for action. When *Newsweek* published a cover story on the women's movement, it hired a freelance writer, having rejected versions by one of the few females in its ranks of reporters and editors. The day the cover story reached the newsstands, however, a group of women on the staff called a press conference to announce that they had filed a sex discrimination complaint with EEOC. At that time all but one of *Newsweek's* research staff were women, and all but one of its 52 writers were men (Freeman 1975; North 1970).

Women responded even when the media's presentation of this new movement was decidedly hostile. For example, the epithet "bra burners" was a media fabrication. No bras were actually burned at the Miss America Pageant demonstration in August 1968, though one of the organizers suggested ahead of time to a journalist that they might be. Instead, participants tossed "objects of female torture"—girdles, bras, curlers, issues of the *Ladies Home Journal*—into a "freedom trashcan," auctioned off an effigy of Miss

America ("Gentlemen, I offer you the 1969 model. She's better in every way. She walks. She talks. AND she does housework"), and crowned a live sheep (Evans 1979; Echols 1989: 92–96).

In general, media coverage sensationalized and mocked women's liberation with nicknames like "Women's Lib" and "Libbers."[1] One editor was known to have instructed a journalist to "get the bra-burning and karate up front" (Brownmiller 1975: 27). It did not matter. For a few years, publicity of any sort sufficed to bring women out in droves.

The spectrum of feminist activism that existed by 1969–1971 in many cities made it accessible to middle-class white women of many ages and backgrounds. Working-class women and women of color claimed their space in the movement shortly thereafter. NOW and WEAL chapters (and in 1971, the National Women's Political Caucus) attracted middle-class professional and semiprofessional women who brought experience in discrimination in employment and in the political arena. These were women who were ready to jump in and work systematically in the courts and the legal system. Radical groups drew first on a constituency of new-left activists. But consciousness-raising, as a method of organizing, attracted women who were drawn to the idea of a women's movement but had questions about whether women were really oppressed and in what ways. In such groups, women used their own experience as the basis for exploration and definition. Soon these two organizing modes overlapped as new women, recruited to one or another of these two styles, freely redefined them.

Consciousness-raising groups were seedbeds for what grew into diverse movements around issues ranging from women's health, child care, violence, and pornography to spirituality and music. The groups formed child care centers, bookstores, coffee houses, shelters for battered women, and rape crisis hotlines—new institutions they could wholly own. At the same time, other feminists built enclaves within mainstream institutions—unions, churches and synagogues, and professional associations. Feminism erupted onto the landscape of U.S. life during a time that was already turbulent with social movements, conflict over the Vietnam War, racial strife, and a national crisis over the meaning and inclusiveness of democracy. It challenged Americans to rethink the most fundamental aspects of personal as well as political life, indeed of human identity. As it did so, it mobilized a new kind of political power that could be felt in the bedroom as well as in the courtroom, the boardroom, and the halls of Congress.

---

[1] *The Reader's Guide to Periodical Literature* first listed "Women's Liberation" as a subtopic under "Women" in Volume 29, March 1969–February 1970, with three entries. The next year there were more than 75 entries under "Women's Liberation."

1968 TO 1975: THE GOLDEN YEARS

From the late 1960s through the mid-1970s, lawmakers rushed to appease a newly aroused constituency that potentially represented more than half the voting public.[2] Hearings, votes, and legislative victories came with breathtaking speed, and Congress passed more laws on behalf of women's rights than it had considered seriously for decades.

These victories represented the combined efforts of diverse groups of women, including policy-oriented feminist activists, feminists in key administrative posts and other Washington insider positions, and working women who initiated EEOC complaints and court actions against discriminatory employers and unions. The actions of these women took place amid the roar of the cultural debate on "women's place" in kitchens, bedrooms, and offices.

With the passage of the Equal Pay Act in 1963 and Title VII of the Civil Rights Act in 1964, working women had new legal tools, which they proceeded to employ with vigor. In the EEOC's first year, more than a third of the complaints submitted concerned sex discrimination. Though these complaints, which numbered in the hundreds, were independent from the organized women's movement, they came in response to the same social pressures and expectations and led commissioners like Aileen Hernandez and Richard Graham to articulate the need for a "NAACP for women." Even progressive unions like the United Auto Workers and the International Union of Electrical Workers—with leaders who had been involved in the President's Commission on the Status of Women and had a history of attention to women's issues—found their members restless and willing to use governmental remedies when local leaders did not take them seriously. Unions and corporations alike argued that their denials of access to overtime or higher-paying jobs were required by state protective laws (Hartmann 1993). In turn, courts, prodded by feminist lawyers, began to rule that protective laws were discriminatory and thereby in violation of Title VII of the Civil Rights Act.

The landmark case in this regard began when Lorena Weeks sued Southern Bell Telephone Company for refusing to promote her to a job she had handled many times as a substitute, hiring a man with less seniority instead. When she lost her case in 1967, Marguerite Rawalt of the NOW legal committee offered assistance on appeal. Attorney Sylvia Roberts of Baton Rouge prepared the case with Ms. Rawalt and argued it before the appeals court.

[2]In the 1968 presidential election, for the first time women voted in equal numbers to men. By the 1980s they were, in fact, a majority of voters.

Standing only five feet tall, Roberts marched around the courtroom carrying the equipment required for the job in one hand, while arguing that the weight-lifting restrictions the company placed on women's jobs did not constitute a "bona fide occupational qualification," or bfoq.[3]

The decision handed down in March 1969, in *Weeks v. Southern Bell,* denied the validity of the bfoq exemption for Bell's weight-lifting restrictions and set a new standard of proof. No longer would a demonstration that many, or even most, women could not perform a specific job requirement justify such a restriction. Instead, employers (and states) would have to show that all or "substantially all" women could not perform the required task. The choice of whether to accept a particularly difficult job would rest with the woman, as it already did with men (Davis 1991; Hole and Levine 1971; Weeks 1969).

The *Weeks* decision and similar cases, executive orders forbidding discrimination, and the many EEOC complaints under Title VII began to convince key union leaders and other former opponents of the Equal Rights Amendment (ERA) that the protective laws unfairly prevented women from access to higher-paying jobs (Madar 1982; Haener 1983; Jeffry 1982). By 1970, the ranks of ERA supporters included the League of Women Voters, Business and Professional Women, the YWCA, the American Association of University Women, Common Cause, and the United Auto Workers. Together they formed a coalition that succeeded in mounting a massive two-year campaign that generated more mail on Capitol Hill than the Vietnam War.

The ERA received an official sanction in 1970 in the report of President Nixon's short-lived Task Force on Women's Rights and Responsibilities, appointed to gather information for the President's State of the Union address. Under the leadership of Virginia Allen, the task force produced a sharply worded pro-ERA report, *A Matter of Simple Justice,* which the administration quickly suppressed. Elizabeth Koonz, director of the Women's Bureau in the Department of Labor, finally succeeded in having the report published (after it had circulated underground for several months) in time for the Women's Bureau's fiftieth anniversary conference in June 1970.

Just one month earlier, the ERA had been the subject of the first committee hearing on the issue in decades. The hearing was the result of a NOW demonstration in February during which 20 women from the Pittsburgh chapter, under the leadership of Wilma Scott Heide, disrupted a hearing on the 18-year-old voting age to demand immediate action on the ERA. While

---

[3]Since the Georgia legislature had repealed its weight-limitations law, the company's only defense lay in the Title VII exemption for bfoq.

a thousand women participated in the Women's Bureau conference, Representative Martha Griffiths filed a discharge petition to force the ERA out of committee. By July 20, a constant flow of letters and telegrams to reluctant congressmen had helped Representative Griffiths collect the 218 signatures needed to bring the ERA to the House floor. On August 10 (after a debate in which Representative Emanuel Celler of New York argued that there was "as much difference between a male and a female as between a horse chestnut and a chestnut horse"), the ERA passed the House 350 to 15 (Davis 1991: 121–27; Hole and Levine 1971; Rawalt 1983). By March 22, 1972, both houses of Congress finally had approved the ERA. By the end of the year, 22 of the needed 35 states had ratified it.

Nineteen seventy-two turned out to be a banner year for women's rights legislation in Congress. In addition to the ERA, Congress passed Title IX of the Higher Education Act, which stated "No person in the United States shall, on the basis of sex, be excluded from participation in, be denied the benefits of, or be subjected to discrimination under any education program or activity receiving federal financial assistance." The new law set the stage for the growth of women's athletics later in the decade. The Equal Opportunity Act broadened the jurisdiction of the EEOC and strengthened its enforcement capacity. And working parents received a tax break for their child care expenses. Representative Bella Abzug of New York recalled 1972 as "a watershed year. We put sex discrimination provisions into everything. There was no opposition. Who'd be against equal rights for women? So we just kept passing women's rights legislation" (Milsap 1983: 93–94; Klein 1984).

The secret to this success lay in new alliances among the few women in Congress, Washington insiders of all sorts, and leaders linked to grassroots feminist constituencies. A key organizer of insiders was Arvonne Fraser, a longtime activist in the Democratic Party who worked in her husband's congressional office and managed his campaigns. In 1969, she invited about 20 women to her home to talk about the new women's movement. She had tried to join NOW, but her letter had been returned—probably a result of NOW's disorganization following the withdrawal of support by the United Auto Workers. Like many of her friends, she found women's liberation groups too young and radical, but she easily adopted their small-group organizing strategy. At the first meeting, women decided not to introduce themselves through relationships with men (though many were related to or on the staff of prominent men). They decided to be a discussion group, not a consciousness-raising group. "Many of us realized later," according to Fraser, "that the main difference between the two was in name only" (Fraser 1983: 122).

At a meeting of the Nameless Sisterhood, as the group was called, Bernice Sandler, an academic at the University of Maryland, asked Fraser to organize a Washington chapter of the Women's Equity Action League. The chapter rapidly became a major source of activism on both legal and legislative fronts. For example, the idea for the Women's Educational Equity Act (WEEA) originated with Arlene Horowitz, a secretary on Capitol Hill. When she called Fraser and then Sandler, they were dubious, but as she persisted, they agreed to call a meeting to draft a bill and to ask Representative Patsy Mink of Hawaii to hold hearings. Fraser recalled:

> We met one night in 1972 at George Washington University to draft the bill. Present were Shirley McCune, who was working on sex-equity problems for the National Education Association, and Marguerite Rawalt, who came to ensure that the bill would be consistent with the ERA when it passed. Sandler, Horowitz, I, and a few others rounded out the group. When we came to the authorizing of funds, we laughingly entered $30 million, fantasizing about what that amount of money could accomplish (Fraser 1983: 131).

As the bill, sponsored by Representative Mink and Minnesota Senator Walter Mondale, progressed through Congress, networks went into action to generate publicity and support. Hearings aired the issues. Fraser's longtime political ally, columnist Geri Joseph, wrote a widely reprinted column, "Women's Rebellion Against Dick and Jane," which linked the proposed WEEA to myriad feminist grassroots efforts: a WEAL study on vocational education for girls in Waco, Texas; NOW task forces "around the country poring over children's readers"; and Princeton NOW's widely read study, "Dick and Jane as Victims." Joseph also culled Fraser's own testimony at hearings on the bill to charge that "We have looked at the education of girls as a kind of life insurance, something they need 'just in case'—just in case they can't find a husband or in case they need to support themselves while looking for a husband" (Fraser 1983: 131). Two years later, the Women's Educational Equity Act became law.

During these "golden years," women at the grassroots articulated new dimensions of the discrimination they faced, providing feminist policy activists with more ammunition, waves of new leadership, and a growing number of more specialized organizations. For example, when the National Commission on Consumer Finance initiated hearings on the problem of women and consumer credit in the spring of 1972, policymakers were stunned by the flood of complaints and demands for action. NOW, WEAL, Parents

Without Partners, and the ACLU all conducted investigations on consumer credit and found that the credit industry consistently marked women as "poor risks." If single, they might marry; if married, they might become pregnant. In either case, it was presumed that they would stop working, so their income was not considered a valid basis for credit. Divorced women found that they had no credit record. A married woman's income was commonly not considered in mortgage applications, although some companies would reconsider her application on the basis of a physician's assurance that she was sterilized or taking birth control pills (Davis 1991; U.S. Congress 1973).

Two NOW members, economist Jane Roberts Chapman and attorney Margaret Gates, established the Center for Women Policy Studies in March 1972, with a $10,000 seed grant from Ralph Nader's organization. Later that year, they garnered a $40,000 grant from the Ford Foundation to investigate women and consumer credit (an interest created when "a female employee of the Ford Foundation was turned down on a credit application, and senior staff there became interested in this economic issue") (Chapman 1983: 179). Their research, in turn, both galvanized other networks and produced a systematic body of "expert" information for presentation to legislative hearings and briefings for interested organizations. The result was the passage, in 1974, of the Equal Credit Opportunity Act (ECOA), followed by two years of careful monitoring and pressure to ensure that the Federal Reserve Board's regulations to enforce the ECOA would have the necessary teeth to protect women. Though problems persisted, by the 1980s, women had greater access to credit than ever before (Davis 1991; Gelb and Palley 1987; Card 1985; Chapman 1983).

CONSCIOUSNESS-RAISING AND THE POLITICS OF WORK

This pattern, in which problems, once named, unleashed a wave of individual and organized responses, repeated itself in one arena after another. Under the microscope of consciousness-raising, politics encompassed virtually all of life. One of the first issues, for most women, was that of work. As one study of the impact of consciousness-raising groups concluded:

> Consciousness-raising encouraged women to become breadwinners, to enter into male-dominated professions, to push further ahead in chosen careers, to think beyond the myth of Prince Charming, to demand equal pay for equal work, and to begin to think of women as having the same rights as men not only in the workplace but to work at all (Shreve 1989: 103).

While small groups facilitated the decisions of millions of women to take advantage of crumbling barriers to professional education and occupational advancement, more organized forms of action proliferated among both professional and blue-collar women.

By the early 1970s there were active women's caucuses in most professional associations in the humanities and social sciences. Some focused on obstacles to professional advancement. Others also challenged the intellectual premises of their professions. In 1970, a panel of young feminist historians at the American Historical Association (AHA), including Bread and Roses founder Linda Gordon, accused the profession of ignoring women (or treating them with condescending stereotypes) in the dominant narratives presented in textbooks. It was a turbulent, angry meeting at the usually decorous AHA. The association appointed a commission on the status of women in the historical profession, headed by Professor Willie Lee Rose. The commission's report resulted in the establishment of a standing committee on the status of women. Similar caucuses and committees rapidly emerged in most disciplines (Rossi and Calderwood 1973).

Bernice Sandler initiated one of the most far-reaching challenges to discrimination in colleges and universities after she was denied tenure at the University of Maryland. Discovering that she was far from alone in this experience, Sandler approached WEAL about taking action. In January 1970, WEAL filed a complaint with the U.S. Department of Labor demanding a review of all colleges and universities holding federal contracts, to determine whether they complied with antidiscrimination regulations. Two hundred and fifty institutions were targets for more specific charges of sex discrimination. By the end of the year, more than 360 institutions of higher education were in court because of suits brought by women willing to make public charges against discriminatory employers—both for themselves as individuals and for women as a class.

In response to similar pressures, most professional schools began to pay new attention to their own employment patterns and to drop barriers and quotas designed to limit the enrollment of female students. The proportion of women in law schools and medical schools rose dramatically. By 1990, women earned 40 percent of all law degrees and a third of medical degrees. In turn, the increase in the numbers of women "in the pipeline" laid the basis for an ongoing dynamic of change within many professions.

Among the first to make headlines were women who had been waiting, fully prepared, for ordination. In 1970, two Lutheran denominations approved the ordination of women. In 1972, Sally Priesand became the first female rabbi. Most major denominations experienced turbulence, as "women's liberation" presentations appeared on the agendas of major national meetings (Hyer 1970; Soukup 1970; "Events That Matter" 1970). Episcopalians seated female deputies for the first time in 1970 but denied ordination on the grounds that women were not in the "image of Christ." In 1974, 11 women deacons participated in an "illegal" ordination ceremony, which their church initially declared "invalid." In 1976, after two more years of intense debate and politicking, the Episcopal Church reversed itself on the ordination of women and recognized the earlier ordinations of these rebellious pioneers (Huyck 1981).

Many of the most powerful and visible symbols of women's access to new worlds of public work were highly educated professionals. But far greater numbers of women were affected by the tenacious and courageous challenges by women in the "pink-collar" ghettos of factories and offices. In 1974, clerical workers in Boston and Chicago created a new kind of workplace organization, using the techniques of community organization pioneered by radical activist Saul Alinsky rather than traditional trade union methods.

The story of Women Employed in Chicago provides another illustration of how the branches of the women's movement intertwined. As an undergraduate at Duke University and then a student in social work at the University of North Carolina in the late 1960s, Day Piercy had become intensely involved in community organizing and, for a brief time, was connected to women's liberation groups. After moving to Chicago in 1969, she served as the first staff member of the Chicago Women's Liberation Union (CWLU)—a field placement from the University of Chicago School of Social Work where she was completing her MSW—working out of a small office in the YWCA. After graduation, she convinced the YWCA to hire her "to do rap groups with working-class women." Through this experience she developed a strong interest in day care and, with Heather Booth (a founder of the Chicago Women's Liberation Union), created an action committee for decent child care through the CWLU.

It was the demise of that child care project—in the aftermath of Nixon's veto of federal child care funding—that provoked Piercy to shift her focus toward organizing working women. With Heather Booth and others, she debated the possibilities of using the model of Caesar Chavez's farmworkers union to organize women workers. Piercy recalls thinking that the farmworkers union, which began with civil rights issues and then moved to more traditional forms of collective bargaining, "was totally parallel to feminism in many ways. I began to wonder if you couldn't take those same principles: dignity for women workers, equal opportunity for women, equal pay for equal work . . ." and use them to build a new kind of working women's organization (Piercy 1981).

Women Employed, then, began as a dream shared by two women in their midtwenties who had been active in the women's liberation movement and influenced by civil rights, farmworkers, and Alinsky-style organizing. Both women also had an institutional connection to the YWCA, where Piercy still worked. Aware that labor unions denigrated the idea of organizing women, Booth and Piercy set out "to take the principles of community organizing and apply them in a workplace setting," namely, the Chicago Loop. Among their first recruits were Ann Ladky and Ann Scott from Chicago NOW. Another was Ellen Cassedy, who worked with a Boston group called 9 to 5, started by Karen Nussbaum. After two months of working with the fledgling Women Employed, Cassedy returned to Boston, inspired to change her small group into an organization that could win concrete changes for working women (Cassedy 1981; Booth 1981; Piercy 1981).

Women Employed in Chicago and 9 to 5 in Boston used the techniques of community organizing to bring clerical workers into the women's movement. For example, when Iris Rivera was fired from her job as a legal secretary for refusing to make coffee, Women Employed staged a nationally televised sit-in on February 3, 1977, at her employer's prestigious Chicago law office. Handing out bags of used coffee grounds with leaflets, women from Women Employed explained that even men with law degrees could follow directions for making coffee, starting with "plug in the pot."

While Women Employed and 9 to 5 experimented with new forms of organizing, women in the labor movement also responded to issues raised by the new wave of feminism. The initiative that led to the Coalition of Labor Union Women (CLUW) came from the United Auto Workers (UAW) Women's Department, the only such department in any major union. Throughout the 1950s and 1960s, the UAW Women's Department had served as a tiny enclave where working women could articulate their concerns. They found natural allies in commissions on the status of women and participated in the founding of the National Organization for Women in 1966. The shockwave of the new feminism was felt not only in the UAW but also in other unions whose constituencies embraced the growing female sector of the workforce, including the International Union of Electrical, Radio, and Machine Workers (IUE), which had maintained a more radical tradition through the 1950s; the Communications Workers of America (CWA); the American Federation of Teachers; and the American Federation of State, County, and Municipal Employees. Traditional union divisions not only prevented concerted action but kept female activists in different unions from knowing each other, even when they worked in the same city.

Several CLUW founders recalled the atmosphere of change in the early 1970s, when women were on the move and looking for labor unions to join.

Those who were active in NOW, WEAL, or commissions on the status of women felt the pressure of expectations: "When are you people going to do your part?" An upsurge at the grassroots level no doubt increased the sense of urgency, as female workers resorted to government intervention against both their employers and their unions when protective legislation served as a cover for discrimination. For example, in 1996, the IUE expanded its Civil Rights Department into a Social Action Department to incorporate women's issues. The following year, the union held a national women's conference spotlighting the problem of sex discrimination (Hartmann 1993).

The extreme stratification of the labor movement meant that any organization that crossed union boundaries needed networks outside the union movement itself. A few leaders got to know each other in the aftermath of the President's Commission on the Status of Women, as first state commissions, then NOW and WEAL forged new channels. Others met at the roundtable discussions of women union leaders hosted by Elizabeth Koonz at the Women's Bureau in the early 1970s. Opportunities continued to multiply in the late 1960s and early 1970s, as union women like Olga Madar of the UAW and Addie Wyatt of the Amalgamated Meatcutters Union met during antiwar activities and farmworkers' organizing efforts (Madar 1982; Haener 1983; Wyatt 1983; Miller 1983).

When a founding meeting for CLUW was called in 1974, more than 3,000 women showed up—twice the expected attendance. Joan Goodin described the excitement as "electric." "I remember being hugged in a jammed elevator by a stranger who proclaimed: 'Sister, we're about to put trade union women on the map' " (Goodin 1983: 141–42). Founders were surprised at how exciting it was simply to establish a network among union women. In subsequent years, despite the serious internal divisions that occurred between 1974 and 1977, CLUW became an important training ground in leadership skills as well as a support group for women. For many, active involvement in CLUW translated into leadership roles in local unions (Miller 1983).

CONSCIOUSNESS-RAISING AND THE POLITICS OF LANGUAGE

The storytelling dynamics of consciousness-raising also called attention to language as a prism through which women's lives could be shaped, distorted, or diminished. Once women identified the politics and the power of language, they used it to press for change wherever they were—with dramatic results.

Anne Ladky wanted a job in publishing after graduating from Northwestern University in 1970. After some searching, she landed a position as a writer in the promotion department of Scott Foresman. The carpool she joined in April 1971 to get to her office in the Chicago suburbs was filled with women "who were all reading and talking about the women's movement." Soon the women began to ponder setting up a women's group at work. They also urged Ladky to join the Chicago NOW chapter. "I didn't see myself as a joiner at all, but I was disturbed the longer we talked." Late in 1971, a dozen or so women from different publishing companies began to discuss the possibility of creating a citywide organization, Women in Publishing. The first issue they chose was sexism in publishing. The guidelines they drew up were later published and widely publicized (Ladky 1983). Ladky, inspired by a Midwest Academy Training Session in 1972, conducted by Day Piercy and Heather Booth, went on to become a leader in Women Employed.

In October 1974, the *New York Times Magazine* published excerpts from "Guidelines for Equal Treatment of the Sexes in McGraw-Hill Book Company Publications," an 11-page statement that had been distributed to all editorial employees and 8,000 authors of textbooks, reference works, trade journals, educational materials, and children's books. The guidelines incorporated key feminist ideas about sex roles and individual choice in the mid-1970s, stating: "Men and women should be treated primarily as people, and not primarily as members of opposite sexes." They advised against typecasting men *or* women, either by work responsibilities or level of authority: "Members of both sexes should be represented as whole human beings with *human* strengths and weaknesses, not masculine or feminine ones." They advised writers to avoid stereotypic and simplistic presentations and to deal with men and women on the same terms. (A negative example was: "Henry Harris is a shrewd lawyer and his wife, Ann, is a striking brunette.")

They also warned against patronizing references, "girl-watching," and sexual innuendo, instructing writers to treat women "as part of the rule, not as the exception" (as in the case of a woman doctor). The guidelines addressed the grammar of sexism, through admonitions to avoid the generic use of "man" or male pronouns. Numerous examples included using "fire fighter" instead of "fireman." The guidelines also challenged the double standard of referring to women by their first names while designating men by their full names and titles; identifying women by their roles as wives, mothers, sisters, or daughters, regardless of relevance; such pairings as "man and wife" or "the men and the ladies"; and the practice of never putting women first in order of mention. The disquiet of the *New York Times* editors—who had not adopted such guidelines—was reflected in the subtitle: "The McGraw-Hill Book Company's guidelines for equal treatment of the sexes, in which the average American loses *his* pronoun, Betty Co-ed becomes simply *student,* and boys shall henceforth grow to *adult*hood" (" 'Man!' Memo From A Publisher" 1974.)

By the time publishers began to pay serious attention to the language of sexism, women's liberation had been a major force in the mass media for several years. Feminists communicated among themselves in a startling array of journals and newsletters. By 1975, there were at least two dozen feminist presses and nearly 200 feminist periodicals.[4] In 1970, Florence Howe and Paul Lauter founded the Feminist Press which, under Florence Howe's leadership, has continued to publish both contemporary and historical feminist books for more than 25 years (Tobias 1997). The most prominent bridge between the internal conversations generated by these publications (often within groups of women with specific professional or personal interests) and the broader public was *Ms.* magazine, whose preview edition, enclosed in an issue of *New York Magazine,* appeared at the end of 1972.

Ms. set out to bring a feminist voice to the marketplace of women's magazines, to compete with them on the shelves of grocery stores for the attention of American women. Glossy, slick, professional, run by professional journalists Gloria Steinem and Pat Carbine (the former editors of *McCall's* and *Look*), the first "stand-alone" issue of *Ms.* sold out its 300,000 copies within eight days, generating 36,000 subscriptions and 20,000 letters (Farrell 1991). On the cover, a figure of the Hindu goddess Kali brandished in her ten arms the tools of women's daily lives: an iron, a broom, a telephone, a duster, a frying pay, an auto steering wheel, a clock, a hand mirror, and a typewriter.[5]

In this first issue, Jane O'Reilly wrote about "the click" in "The Housewife's Moment of Truth"; Gloria Steinem explained "sisterhood" as "deep and personal connections of women . . . [which] often ignore barriers of age, economics, worldly experience, race, culture—all the barriers that, in male or mixed society, had seemed so difficult to cross"; Judy Syfer humorously addressed working women's exhaustion in "I Want a Wife"; Letty Cottin Pogrebin explained how to raise children without imposing traditional sex roles in "Down with Sexist Upbringing"; and Cellestine Ware interviewed Eleanor Holmes Norton on "The Black Family and Feminism." Additional articles—on welfare as a women's issue, abortion rights,

[4]Harrison (1975) lists 190 periodicals and 39 "publishers," many of which published one book, catalogue, or journal.
[5]Farrell (1991: 43–44) describes this cover as refusing "to construct a definitive image of the "*Ms.* woman" by combining "the accoutrements of a housewife—the role primarily of a white, middle-class Western woman—[while] the woman herself suggested a Hindu goddess, suggesting that this magazine intended to speak to all women, to transcend differences created by race or class."

lesbian love, how to set up child care centers, and where to complain about job discrimination—covered a significant range of feminist concerns and activities.[6]

Ms. was neither an angry litany of women's liberation manifestos nor a dry policy brief. Instead, it packaged feminism in an optimistic and personalized context. For example, *Ms.* included the traditional women's magazine "how-to" articles but with an altogether new twist. The articles gave advice on how to raise children without imposing stereotypic sex roles, or how to file an EEOC complaint about discrimination on the job. Through *Ms.*, a new form of address entered the popular culture. While many Americans found the term odd, even insultingly strange, *Ms.* defined its title as a "form of address meaning whole person, female" as opposed to objectifying modes of address like "chick," "bitch," and "babe" ("Ms.—form of address . . ." 1972).

While *Ms.* reached tens of thousands overnight, women's liberation found another institutionalized and mainstream outlet in the creation of women's studies programs on campuses across the country. Women's studies began with isolated courses, frequently at free universities or other informal, alternative settings. Soon professors and students also collaborated to teach a wide range of courses about women.

Betty Friedan and Sheila Tobias, associate provost at Wesleyan University, teamed up as visitors during Intersession at Cornell in January 1969 (Friedan 1991). Gerda Lerner taught a women's history course at Sarah Lawrence. In 1970, Sheila Tobias put together a collection of 17 syllabi and bibliographies. Two years later, the Commission on the Status of Women of the Modern Language Association compiled 66 syllabi from about 40 different schools for publication in *Female Studies II*. Nearly half the courses concerned women and literature or cultural criticism, understandable because of the networks closest to the compilers. But they also included descriptions of nine history courses (several on women's social roles, two on the history of women's rights movements), 15 social science courses (e.g., "Sex and Politics," "Linguistic Behavior of Male and Female," "Psychology of Women," "Women in the U.S. Economy"), and 11 interdisciplinary courses (e.g., "Philosophical and Psychological Aspects of Women's Roles," "Women as a Minority Group," "Biology and Society," "Sex Roles in American Society and Politics").

---

[6]Farrell (1991: 47) says that "this, more than any other issue, was Steinem's product. While she used the input from others working on the issue, she made the decisions as to what went into the magazine, and many of the articles were authored by women or men whom she already knew."

As word of the courses spread through movement as well as academic channels, students at many universities were the first to demand women's studies courses, and they frequently participated in teaching experimental and interdisciplinary offerings. Rapidly growing caucuses created a kind of synergy as student demands bolstered the professional aspirations and intellectual agendas of a rapidly growing cohort of academic women. Following on the heels—and in the mold—of newly formed Afro-American or black studies programs, women's studies programs had appeared on hundreds of campuses by the mid-1970s.

CONSCIOUSNESS-RAISING AND THE POLITICS OF THE BODY

Consciousness-raising also meant that feminist deliberation would center on the most intimate, personal aspects of womanhood. Groups analyzed childhood experiences for clues to the origins of women's oppression; they discussed relations with men, marriage, and motherhood; and they talked about sex. Frequently, discussion led to action. For example, in an early meeting of New York Radical Women, several women described their experiences with illegal abortion. For most, it was the first time they had told anyone beyond a close friend or two.

The power of these revelations, however, contrasted sharply with the debates surrounding the proposed liberalization of the abortion law in New York, which were being conducted with clinical detachment. Women's own stories were not in evidence. A group of women—subsequent founders of Redstockings—decided to disrupt a legislative hearing that was scheduled to hear testimony from 14 men and one woman (a nun). When the legislative committee refused to hear the women, they held a public "speak-out" on March 21, 1969, drawing an audience of 300 (Echols 1989; Petchesky 1990). Thousands of women, hearing about such speak-outs, experienced a release from lonely silence. Journalist Gloria Steinem recalled that "For the first time, I understood that the abortion I had kept so shamefully quiet about for years was an experience I had probably shared with at least one out of four American women of every race and group" (Levine and Lyons 1980: 9).

Soon women's liberation groups became the "shock troops" of abortion rights, joining an already active abortion law reform movement (Petchesky 1990). For the most part, they sought to intervene directly, offering services and assistance to women and public education, rather than lobbying for reform. Numerous groups, for example, began to help women seeking illegal abortions find competent doctors. Word of mouth communication usually resulted in a flood of requests. In Chicago, members of the socialist-feminist Chicago Women's Liberation Union began doing counseling and referrals in 1969. Calling themselves Jane, they shifted, in 1971, from making referrals to doing the abortions themselves. Between 1971 and 1973, the abortion collective performed 11,000 illegal abortions, with a safety record that matched that of doctor-performed legal abortions (Kaplan 1995).

At about the same time that Jane was formed, a consciousness-raising group—made up primarily of graduate students and writers for an underground newspaper in Austin, Texas—also shifted its focus to abortion referral. The group built an alliance with local members of the Clergy Consultation Service on Abortion, an organization that maintained close contacts with doctors to ensure high quality services and, by 1973, had referred more than 6,000 women. At a garage sale to raise money for the group, Sarah Weddington, a recent law school graduate, debated with another group member the legality and the risks of their activities and volunteered to do some legal research. That research revealed that outside of Texas, where the law forbade abortion even in cases of rape and incest, legal changes and judicial precedents suggested the real possibility of challenging laws against abortion in court. Thus began the process that resulted in the landmark Supreme Court Case, *Roe* v. *Wade*, in which Sarah Wedding argued her first case at the age of 26 (Weddington 1992).

Sarah Weddington's small group had formed in 1968 initially to discuss a mimeographed pamphlet from a women's health collective in Boston entitled "Women and Their Bodies." The Boston project was one of many working under the umbrella of Bread and Roses, a women's liberation group that saw itself as both socialist and feminist. It began when discussions of sexuality within Bread and Roses, especially regarding Anne Koedt's article, "The Myth of the Vaginal Orgasm," inspired several women to gather information about women's health. Calling themselves the "Doctor's Project," they first created a list of good female gynecologists, then moved on to teach a course and to write "Women and Their Bodies," which found its way to Austin.

Even after the demise of Bread and Roses, the group continued as the Boston Women's Health Collective and revised its pamphlet for publication as a book, *Our Bodies, Ourselves*. That book, still in print after many editions, exemplified the widespread effort among women's groups to empower women in relation to their bodies. They demystified medical "expertise" by giving women direct information, conveyed through personal stories and narratives with an emphasis on the importance of sexual self-determination. Koedt's paper and the enthusiasm elicited in early workshops on sexuality made understanding orgasm and learning to masturbate common items on consciousness-raising discussion topic lists. Indeed, one of the most common memories of such groups was the moment when one woman would confess that she had faked orgasm and then one after another would acknowledge the same (Shreve 1989).

Efforts to increase women's sexual autonomy frequently sparked concerns about the problem of sexual violence as well. One group, Cell 16 in Boston, made headlines with its advocacy of celibacy (which never really caught on) and karate (which did). One of the classic realizations in consciousness-raising groups had to do with the sexual objectification and vulnerability of women in public. Susan Griffin took this subject a step further in a pathbreaking article on rape in 1971: "I HAVE NEVER BEEN FREE OF THE FEAR OF RAPE," she wrote. "RAPE IS AN ACT OF AGGRESSION in which the victim is denied her self-determination. It is an act of violence, which always carries with it the threat of death. And finally, rape is a form of mass terrorism . . ." (Griffin 1971: 36).

The first rape crisis hotline, established in Washington, D.C., in 1972, was followed by the rapid emergence of rape crisis centers across the country. In addition to the initiatives of women's liberation groups, by the mid-1970s, NOW chapters had formed more than 300 local and state rape task forces. Rape crisis centers provided counsel and advice to rape victims, assisted them in dealing with police and medical personnel, set up speakers bureaus, offered self-defense courses and training for professionals, and created support groups for victims (Schechter 1982).

The movement to create shelters for battered women grew from a similar impulse. The first such shelter, Women's Advocates in St. Paul, Minnesota, began as a consciousness-raising group in 1971. When the group members reached the stage of wanting to take action, they started by writing a handbook on divorce and setting up a telephone service to provide legal information. Soon they were flooded with requests for emergency housing. They collected pledges to support the rent on a small apartment and a telephone answering service in 1973, but the demand was so great that members took women into their own homes. By 1974, when Women's Advocates opened, the collective already had 18 months' experience working with battered women. Other shelters grew out of rape crisis hotlines and coalitions of battered women and feminist activists (Schechter 1982; Women's Advocates 1980).

Finally, consciousness-raising led women to explore their own sexuality, to critique the messages of a culture that defined them as sexual objects, and to challenge the heterosexual obsessions of both American popular culture and a male-dominated counterculture. Lesbians found mixed messages in these conversations. On the one hand, they could finally publicly celebrate the power of relationships among women, of sisterhood. On the other hand, their sexuality provoked extreme anxiety and even hostility when they articulated it. Within many NOW chapters, lesbians felt silenced and ostracized. In the emerging gay rights movement, they struggled with male dominance. But within radical feminist groups, lesbians found a new voice. Validated by the notion that the personal is political and by the separatist politics of black power, they began to articulate a specifically lesbian feminist point of view. One of the early, classic pieces, "Woman-Identified Woman," described lesbianism as central to feminism: "It is the primacy of women relating to women, of women creating a new consciousness of and with each other which is at the heart of women's liberation, and the basis for the cultural revolution" (Radicalesbians 1970: 176).

The energy unleashed by the emergence of lesbian feminism was another source of turbulence in the women's movement and broader change in society. For several years, serious tensions persisted between lesbian and straight women. Some separatist groups formed. In 1970, when Kate Millett, author of *Sexual Politics*, was excoriated by *Time* magazine for acknowledging her bisexuality, feminist leaders realized that a united front was important to combat the use of the label "lesbian" to attack and divide the movement. By 1977, even Betty Friedan was willing to acknowledge publicly the crucial role of lesbian leadership in the movement as a whole and to embrace the battle against homophobic prejudice and discrimination as part of the larger struggle for women's rights (Abbott and Love 1972; Bunch 1987).

REACTION: BACKLASH

The revival of feminism at first met little resistance beyond ridicule because it was so new, so surprising. Most Americans were confused, defensive, and sometimes angry. When Bobby Riggs, a 1939 Wimbledon winner, challenged tennis star Billie Jean King to a match, millions tuned in to watch on September 20, 1973. Riggs had hustled the media brilliantly with his taunts against King's campaign for more opportunities and more money for women tennis professionals: "You insist that top women players provide a brand of tennis comparable to men's. I challenge you to prove it. I contend that you not only cannot beat a top male player, but that you can't beat me, a tired old man." Las Vegas bookies set odds of five to two for Riggs, but King won three sets with ease (Wandersee 1988: 153; King 1974; Collins 1973).

A more-organized opposition also emerged as the new movement demonstrated its clout. In 1972, Phyllis Schlafley founded Stop ERA to lobby against the ratification of the Equal Rights Amendment with the message that most women did not want to be "liberated." Similarly, a movement to reinstitute laws against abortion—soon renamed the "pro-life" movement—

emerged rapidly in the wake of the *Roe* v. *Wade* decision. A "new right," with powerful roots in the Republican Party, took up the cultural issues raised by the women's movement, politicizing personal life even further. Where previous conservative movements had focused primarily on anti-communism and hostility to government involvement in the economy, the new right emphasized "family values," opposition to abortion and the ERA, hostility to homosexuality, and antagonism to affirmative action for minorities and women.

By the mid-1970s, the movement itself took on a defensive cast in at least two areas. The National Association for the Repeal of Abortion Laws, founded in 1969, changed its name in 1973 to the National Abortion Rights Action League following the Supreme Court decision in *Roe* v. *Wade*. It grew, however, in response to the emergence of a vehement anti-abortion movement, coining the label "pro-choice" to counter the opposition's description of itself as "pro-life." Far from resolving the issue, *Roe* v. *Wade* had become a rallying point for an emerging new-right coalition that would continue to gain momentum through the 1970s and into the 1980s. Faced with a spreading backlash focused on abortion, ERA, and women's athletics (Title IX didn't resolve anything either) and with a declining economy that made women easy scapegoats, public feminism shifted gradually from offensive to defensive, from ebullient optimism to tenacious persistence.

While policy-oriented feminists hunkered down and honed their skills, the terrain of many feminist organizations became a battleground. Torn apart by a battle between Chicago followers of Mary Jean Collins and NOW President Karen DeCrow (who had narrowly defeated Collins in an election filled with cries of fraud), NOW sat out the fight for women's consumer credit. By 1977, it began to rebuild with the election of Eleanor Smeal and a renewed focus on the Equal Rights Amendment in response to the growing success of the right.

Both the breadth and the internal conflicts of the new feminism became visible in 1977 at the massive International Women's Year Conference in Houston, Texas, and the 50 state conferences that preceded it. State conferences, called to elect delegates for the Houston conference, became areas for battle between feminists and the right wing. Although liberal feminists prevailed for the most part, they were unprepared for the strength of anti-abortion and anti-ERA forces in several states.

The Houston conference, consisting of about 2,000 delegates and 18,000 additional observers, made clear that the women's movement had spread well beyond its original white, middle-class base. Thirty-five percent of the delegates were nonwhite and nearly one in five was low-income. Protestants represented 42 percent of the delegates, Catholics 26 percent, and Jews eight percent (Rossi 1982). In an emotional move, the conference adopted, by significant majorities, a "Plan for Action," with the ERA as its centerpiece and major planks on reproductive freedom and minority and lesbian rights.

The contacts, and conflicts, among differing groups of women made for a powerful experience. A small delegation of 12, including three Native American women, "developed a deep level of intimacy . . . as the hours went on." One of the whites in the group recalled that "we grew to respect each other's opinions and ended up influencing the delegation on issues, such as reproductive freedom and lesbianism, which the Native Americans had previously been against. When the Minorities resolution passed, we all danced in the aisle and cried tears of joy" (Rossi 1982: 178). Other delegates reported stereotype-shattering conversations on coffee breaks. But the planks on abortion and lesbianism, in particular, provoked intense divisions. In a counterconference on the other side of Houston, Phyllis Schlafley's "Pro-Family Rally," the possibility of dialogue did not exist.

Differences of race had become central issues for feminists by the late 1970s. Minority women had always held some leadership positions in organizations like NOW, and earlier articles had challenged the tendency to talk about women as a unified group from the perspectives of women who could not separate their femaleness from their racial, religious, and ethnic identities. When Alice Walker wrote an article for an issue of *Southern Exposure* devoted to southern women, she pondered the question "When . . . did my over-worked mother have time to know or care about feeding the creative spirit?" Virginia Woolf's question about women's creative resources and her assertion of the need for "a room of one's own" was reworked by Walker, who saw the insistence on beauty, "flowers lovingly cultivated by the barest of houses and around the smallest of vegetable patches," as an expressive outlet (Walker 1977: 63). Throughout the 1970s organizations like the National Black Feminist Organization, founded in 1973, and the powerful writings of poets and novelists like Walker, Audre Lourde, and Toni Morrison and lawyers like Florynce Kennedy and Pauli Murray gave new voice to black feminism.

The ERA stalled after 1975. NOW led a massive lobbying effort in the late 1970s to extend the deadline for ratification until 1982 and, under the leadership of Eleanor Smeal, spearheaded a series of state campaigns reminiscent of the struggle for women's suffrage early in the century. Membership in NOW, the National Women's Political Caucus, and other active groups soared for a few years, and a new generation of women were schooled on the battlelines. Yet, it proved impossible to gain the required number of states for ERA ratification, and by the time the clock ran out in 1982, several states had even repealed their ratification.

Subsequent analyses of the struggle highlighted a variety of reasons for the failure of the ERA. Jane Mansbridge pointed to the unintended consequence of allowing the issue of women in the military to become a pivot of the debate. Mary Berry argued that the very process of amending the Constitution is so arduous and requires such a large majority that failure is the likely outcome in most instances. Jane DeHart and Donald Mathews analyzed the ironies of a cultural conflict in which women were prominent on both sides. Women opposed to the ERA were, in their view, often as suspicious of male intentions toward women as were supporters. Their fears, however, did not center on inequality in the public worlds of work, politics, and education. Rather they feared that without the coercion of the state, men would abandon their traditional responsibilities for the family (Mansbridge 1986; Berry 1986; Mathews and DeHart 1990).

In the wake of the ERA's defeat, most national women's rights organizations—NOW, NWPC, NARAL, and others—experienced a sharp contraction of membership. Cuts in government funding combined with membership losses destroyed many feminist groups (Whittier 1995). The conservative ethos of the Reagan administration abruptly reversed the political influence of the women's rights movement. Making effective use of cultural themes initially politicized by feminists—family, sexuality, and reproduction—the new conservatism reshaped the 1980 Republican Party platform, eliminating its longstanding endorsement of the ERA. Once elected, the new administration removed many feminists from positions on commissions and in federal departments, replacing them with appointees hostile to affirmative action and other governmental activism on behalf of women's rights and civil rights.

THE 1980s: THRIVING IN THE DOLDRUMS

Despite an increasingly hostile political and cultural climate, the "second wave" of the women's movement produced aftershocks throughout the 1980s. Feminism flowed into the mainstream even as it became less visible, especially to younger women. By the late 1970s, feminist institutions were grappling with the necessity of becoming more efficient and businesslike. Rape crisis hotlines, battered women's shelters, bookstores, journals and publishers, theater and musical groups, all having passed through the creative burst of volunteer energy that formed them, confronted the nitty-gritty problems of institutional survival. Founders entered new life stages of both family and career and looked for balance after years of total devotion to the movement. The organizations they built needed infrastructure—buildings, budgets, staff with professional skills. The movement, increasingly diffuse, entered a new phase in a changing political and economic climate.

On the surface, the demise of the ERA reflected the apparent dissolution of the second wave. Popular media in the early 1980s discussed the "death of feminism" or, more kindly, "post-feminism" (Bolotin 1982; Salholz 1986). *Elle* wrote, in 1986, that the new generation of women "no longer needs to examine the whys and hows of sexism. . . . All those ideals that were once held as absolute truths—sexual liberation, the women's movement, true equality—have been debunked or debased" (Faludi 1991: 111). In this sense, the 1980s echoed the 1920s, when flappers debunked their suffragist fore-mothers. Dorothy Dunbar Bromley's words from 1927 were prescient:

> "Feminism" has become a term of opprobrium to the modern young woman. For the word suggests either the old school of fighting femi nists who wore flat heels and had very little feminine charm, or the cur-rent species who antagonize men with their constant clamor about maiden names, equal rights, woman's place in the world, and many an-other causes . . . *ad infinitum* (Bromley 1927: 552).

Similar stereotypes governed the perceptions of the vast majority of young people, both male and female. Paula Kamen, writing for the student news-paper at the University of Illinois in the fall of 1988, "quickly learned that taking a stand on anything even remotely construed as a women's issue aroused strange and strong suspicions." When she subsequently interviewed more than 100 women of her own generation, she found that their associ-ations with the word "feminist" were infused with rigid and extreme stereo-types of "bra-burning, hairy-legged, amazon, castrating, militant-almost-antifeminine, communist, Marxist, separatist, female skinheads, female supremacists, he-woman types, bunch-a-lesbians. . . ." She attributed the power of these stereotypes in part to the sense that young feminists were virtually invisible in the 1980s. "During our 'coming of age' years from 1980 to 1990, young feminists didn't seem to exist" (Kamen 1991: 1, 6, 2). Yet these young women experienced athletic opportunities unheard of just a decade before as a result of Title IX, unparalleled access to education and jobs, and curricula, in both schools and organizations like the Girl Scouts, that were explicitly designed to give them a broad perspective on their own potentials and choices.

BACKLASH

Popular media reinforced a sense that the new complexity of women's lives—rather than the inflexibility of the world in which they lived—was the problem. Newspapers and magazines deplored the toll on women trying to meet standards for success as *both* professionals *and* housewives, two full-time jobs. Numerous articles profiled women who dropped out of high-powered, high-paying jobs in order to have time with their children (Faludi 1991). In 1986, *Fortune* magazine published a cover article on "Why Women Are Bailing Out" of successful careers (Taylor 1986). Such coverage laid the groundwork for Felice M. Schwartz's idea, promulgated in the *Harvard Business Review* in 1989, that businesses should offer a "mommy track" for women, on the grounds that most women are "career-and-family" oriented rather than "career primary" (Schwartz 1989). The next year, however, a study of 50 women who left Fortune 500 companies after more than five years found that their primary reason for leaving was the limited opportunity for advancement. It was the "glass ceiling," not a lack of "family friendly benefits," that drove them away (Solomon 1990).

Choices that had been cheered as liberating in the 1970s evoked criticism and dire warnings in the 1980s. In 1973, *Newsweek* had praised the emergence of singleness: "Within just eight years, singlehood has emerged as an intensely ritualized—and newly respectable—style of American life. It is finally becoming possible to be both single and whole" (Waters 1973). By the mid-1980s, another cover story in the same magazine warned single women that their opportunities for marriage may have passed by. "For many economically independent women, the consequences of their actions have begun to set in. For years bright young women single-mindedly pursued their careers, assuming that when it was time for a husband they could pencil one in. They were wrong" (Faludi 1991: 99). This warning was based on a poorly researched, unpublished study that rapidly had become the basis for numerous cover stories and TV special reports in which single women (but not men) emoted about their loneliness and lost opportunities.

Certainly there were more single women, and many of them hoped eventually to marry. The media played expertly on the anxieties of women living out new life patterns without familiar models to show the way. Despite overwhelming evidence of life satisfaction and mental health among working women, whether married or not, many women began to believe that they *should* be lonely and panic-stricken.

Where images of women and men briefly had seemed to be moving in an androgynous direction, the 1980s saw a return to stories in which raw male violence and aggression dominated and women were either absent or depicted as sexualized accessories. Movie star Sylvester Stallone's *Rambo* epitomized the untamed, macho screen image that displaced the "sensitive man," as portrayed by Alan Alda in the TV series "Mash." Similarly, fashion sharpened the contrast between aggressive masculinity and sexualized femininity with a return to cinched waists, high heels, miniskirts, and childlike poufs. In the mid-1980s, feminist author Susan Brownmiller attributed the reemphasis on femininity to "a sociological fact of the 1980s . . . that female competition for two scarce resources—men and jobs—is especially fierce" (Brownmiller 1985: 17). By the end of the decade, fashion photographers were selling clothes with photographs of pale, pinched, and sometimes beaten women.

Yet the fact was that norms had shifted as women shaped new life patterns. By the late 1980s, women were resisting the dictates of fashion by refusing to shift away from suits and other standard office attire toward sexy, frilly, body-displaying designs. The miniskirt bombed but didn't disappear in 1987, as retailers learned that they had to stock a variety of skirt lengths and styles and that there were limits to fashion dictates (Stern 1988; Caminiti 1989).[7] Women's athletics, both amateur and professional, blossomed, offering powerful validation for a strong and active image of the female body (Cahn 1994).

On the home front, hours spent on housework declined for the first time, starting in the late 1970s (Wandersee 1988). For decades, women who worked outside the home had been held to standards of cleanliness and meal preparation established by full-time housewives. Now that most women were employed, those standards began to give way to more realistic expectations. With a remarkable synergy, women's new lives created demands for services—from meal preparation to child care—which in turn created vast numbers of female-dominated jobs.

In the 1980s, however, the increase in female employment was matched by an increase in female poverty. Soon after Ronald Reagan assumed the presidency, the country plunged into the worst recession since the 1930s. It was a brief but devastating period, and when the economy began to grow again, the benefits were not evenly distributed. While two-income professional families generated a new, high-consumption standard of living, recovery from the recession in the early 1980s never trickled down to the very poor. In addition, the Reagan administration made sharp cuts in traditional social programs. The proportion of the population living in poverty had declined from around 20 percent in the 1940s to 12 percent in 1969. By the 1980s, it had climbed again to 24 percent, and most of the poor were women and children.

The realities of life in poor communities also underwent visible change.

---

[7]A decade before, in 1977, John T. Molloy's *The Woman's Dress for Success Book,* which advocated neutral attire for women similar to men's suits, had been on the *New York Times* best-seller list for several months. The miniskirt hung on and made a significant resurgence in the 1990s but never with the kind of dominance it had enjoyed in the early 1970s.

The elimination of immigration quotas led to the largest wave of new immigration in the twentieth century, dominated by economic and political refugees from Asia and Latin America; the proportion of legal immigrants from Europe declined from 90 percent in 1965 to only 10 percent 20 years later. Homelessness was seen on the streets for the first time since the Great Depression. Hospitals for the mentally ill had begun to empty their wards in response to advocates of smaller-scale, community-level programs. But cutbacks in government mental health and housing assistance programs meant that thousands of mentally ill people had literally nowhere to turn (Lamar 1988). A massive influx of drugs wrecked havoc on the fragile fabric of inner-city communities. People began to talk about an "underclass" that seemed permanently locked out of the American dream (Auletta 1982; U.S. Congress 1989).

Thus, a large poor, disproportionately female, and racially diverse segment of the population did not share in the Reagan boom. Ninety-four percent of the new wealth generated in the 1980s went to the richest 20 percent of Americans; half to the top one percent. Those in the middle experienced stagnation or decline, while the poorest, female-headed households, faced desperation (Danziger and Gottschalk 1995). Their plight, however, was frequently discussed in conjunction with alarm about rising rates of unwed motherhood and the cost of welfare. Racist images of "unwed mothers" and "welfare cheats" distanced readers or television viewers from the human reality. Since the vast majority of married women with children now worked outside the home, public support for traditional welfare policies, premised on the notion that women without male support should be home with their children, eroded sharply. With federal encouragement, welfare programs shifted toward state rather than federal control, with an increased emphasis on "workfare," which required recipients to work in order to receive benefits. A contracting economy also fueled the growing hostility to affirmative action and sealed the fate of the ERA.

Mainstreaming Feminism

Backlash was not the dominant reality of the 1980s, however. Indeed, the new hostility to change reflected the fact that, whether as working professionals or homeless "bag ladies," women had become omnipresent in public life. Though too often still tokens in terms of total numbers, they were there nonetheless—in corporate board rooms, on highway crews, at truck stops (driving trucks!), in courtrooms (as judges and lawyers, and also as defendants), in Congress, in the pulpit, and in combat fatigues. The simple appearance of a woman in a position of authority no longer provoked disbelief. And the joint impact of the feminist and civil rights movements meant that many of these newly visible women were women of color.

The list of "firsts" for women grew longer and longer: In 1981, President Reagan named Sandra Day O'Connor to the U.S. Supreme Court. In 1984, the Democratic Party nominated Congresswoman Geraldine Ferraro for vice president. Wilma Mankiller was elected principal chief of the Cherokee Nation of Oklahoma in 1985, the first woman to lead a major Native American tribe. On May 1, 1986, Ann Bancroft reached the North Pole by dogsled. During the 1988 Olympics in Seoul, South Korea, Americans stayed riveted to their televisions as African American track stars Jackie Joyner-Kersee and Florence Griffith Joyner set world and Olympic records. West Point graduated its thousandth woman. Connie Chung and Charlayne Hunter-Gault (the first African American woman to attend the University of Alabama in 1963) anchored network news shows. The Episcopal Church elected an African American, the Reverend Barbara C. Harris, as its first woman bishop.

The first woman astronaut, Sally K. Ride, traveled into space in 1983 aboard the shuttle *Challenger.* By the time of the Gulf War in 1990–91, 11 percent of the armed forces on active duty were female, and many women, though supposedly not "in combat," served in positions that were within range of enemy fire. Women flew helicopters, reconnaissance planes, inflight fueling tankers, strategic transport, and medical airlifts. They also served on naval logistics ships in the Gulf and the Red Sea. Two women were taken as war prisoners, and 15 women died (Defense Manpower Data Center 1989, 1990a, 1990b; Lawrence 1991; Schmitt 1991). There was an irony, of course, in the fact that the ERA was defeated nearly a decade earlier in part because of the argument that it would expose women to precisely such situations.

Women's leadership also continued to grow among community-level activists, who further broadened women's participation in public life. Poor and working-class women brought new issues and definitions of public life into the political arena that cut against the grain of the conservative ethos of the 1980s. In San Antonio, Texas, for example, Communities Organized for Public Service (COPS) created a powerful political base for the Mexican community. Building on the foundation of Catholic churches in the community, it tackled problems ranging from poor schools and housing to unpaved streets and open drainage ditches. The effectiveness of COPS depended to a great extent on the talents of women. As former president Beatrice Cortez put it, "Women have community ties. We knew that to make things happen in the community, you have to talk to people. It was a matter of tapping our networks." The program's success provided a model for dozens of new, frequently female-led, community organizations in Hispanic, African American, Asian American, and white ethnic communities across the country. Community-level activism increased the number of female officeholders as well. From 1969 to the mid-1990s, women increased their representation in state legislatures fourfold. In 1969, only 4.5 percent of state elected officials were women; by 1981, women held 12.1 percent of elected state offices, and by 1997, more than one in five (21.5 percent) state legislators were women. In municipal governments, the proportion of women grew from about 10 percent in 1975 to 23 percent in 1988 (Klein 1984: 30; CAWP 1997; Darcy, Welch, and Clark 1994).

The decades of the 1970s and 1980s also saw the growing influence of women in Congress. For years, the National Organization for Women, the National Women's Political Caucus, and the Business and Professional Women's Club had been pressing for a caucus which could enhance feminists' access to congressional lawmakers (Gertzog 1984). In 1977, they joined forces with 15 of the 18 women then in Congress to found the Congresswomen's Caucus. Key leaders included the first cochairs, Representatives Elizabeth Holtzman (D-NY) and Margaret Heckler (R-MA), along with Representatives Shirley Chisholm (D-NY), Barbara Mikulski (D-MD), Lindy Boggs (D-LA), and Pat Schroeder (D-CO). Helen Meyner (D-NJ) and Barbara Jordan (D-TX) were also pivotal in getting the caucus off the ground. For its first executive director, the caucus hired Betty Dooley—who herself had been a candidate for Congress in Texas and for state legislative office (Gertzog 1984).

The congresswomen decided not to allow the issue of abortion to bar them from uniting around economic equity issues of importance to women. (In 1993, after 24 new, pro-choice women were elected to the House of Representatives, the caucus adopted a pro-choice position.) One of the caucus's first acts was a successful campaign for a three-year extension of the ratification period for the Equal Rights Amendment. Margaret Heckler and Lindy Boggs led the successful fight to provide credit to women. The efforts of the caucus also focused on improving access to federal contracts for women business owners, achieving gender equity in education, and enacting protections against domestic violence.

From the beginning, the caucus founders saw a need for a research arm that could provide members of Congress with information about women's issues. Accordingly, the caucus established the Congresswomen's Caucus Corporation in 1977 (which was replaced a year later by the Women's Research & Education Institute) and named Betty Dooley as the executive director. For twenty years, WREI has provided members of Congress and their staffs with research on topics such as the poverty status of elderly women, women's health, women's employment, and women in the military (Gertzog 1984).

New alliances at state and local levels linked the organizational power of working women with that of elected officials, producing policy initiatives that belied the conservative image of the 1980s. In the 1970s, unions, working women's organizations, and members of the EEOC pondered the gap that persisted between women's and men's wages despite the legal tools of affirmative action and equal pay for equal work. Numerous research projects revealed an underlying cause: the labor market, though less racially segregated after the 1960s, continued to be sharply sex-segregated. In general, women had access to the least-skilled, lowest-paying jobs, few of which could support a family. Not only that, but female-dominated jobs paid consistently less than comparable male-dominated jobs.[8]

As a result, in 1980, Eleanor Holmes Norton, chair of the EEOC, proclaimed comparable worth—a policy designed to rectify the wage gap between traditionally male and traditionally female-dominated jobs—to be the "issue of the 1980s." By the mid-1980s, however, what had looked like a fairly uncomplicated drive for legislative and judicial change had run into a buzz saw of opposition to government intervention into "free markets." Despite active opposition by the Reagan administration, by 1987, more than 40 states and 1,700 local governments had taken major steps toward implementing comparable-worth policies to raise the wages of female-dominated job classes. Such success produced strong backlashes in 1983 and 1984, however, following several key court cases and legislative victories. From that point on, instituting comparable-worth policies was increasingly difficult (Evans and Nelson 1989).

Comparable worth demonstrated the growing credibility and clout of a network of women's policy research institutes that could generate sophisticated data analyses and provide expert testimony for elected and appointed officials. For example, Heidi Hartmann, editor of the National Academy of Sciences study that undergirded most comparable-worth laws, went on to found the Institute for Women's Policy Research.

The receptivity of some corporations to policy-oriented research reflected their conscious need to find ways to attract and sustain an effective

---

[8]The establishment of "comparability" based on measurements of skill, effort, responsibility, and working conditions requires the use of highly technical job evaluation systems (Evans and Nelson 1989: chaps. 2–3).

labor force with substantial numbers of women at all levels, as well as their desire to avoid litigation around discrimination claims.[9] Sexual harassment training became commonplace as companies sought to avoid litigation by changing work cultures. Gender-polarized images, common in popular culture, also appeared in a new guise as management consultants discovered that the characteristics of what they called the "new leader," as opposed to the outmoded "traditional leader," were culturally coded as female. Thousands of workshops on leadership styles encouraged the adoption of "women's leadership," which emphasized change over control, facilitation over giving orders, empowerment over commands, creativity over discipline, and networking over hierarchy (Aburdene and Naisbitt 1992; Rosener 1990; Helgeson 1990).

The rumbling of feminist ideas through mainstream institutions can be traced in religious institutions as well. Whereas many denominations ordained their first female clergy and rabbis in the 1970s, by the 1980s, seminaries were filled with women, and major denominations embarked on inclusive language revisions of liturgies and hymnbooks. "Mankind" and "brotherhood" gave way to "humankind" or "people of faith." Congregations experimented with feminine images of God ("More Hymn Changes" 1987; "Avoiding Sexism" 1987). Synagogues in the 1980s became as accustomed to *bat mitzvahs* for 13-year-old girls as they were to *bar mitzvahs* for boys. Catholic women who organized in the 1970s to press for women's ordination turned in the 1980s to building Women Church, a grassroots network of women who shared liturgy and rituals, celebrated life-cycle events (puberty, menopause, divorce), and wrestled with theological inquiry (Ziegnenhals 1989; Ruether 1985).

These changes occurred against growing resistance, however. Inclusive language revisions of the 1989 Methodist hymnal—carefully calibrated to avoid changing the gender of references to God or the words of especially beloved hymns (e.g., "Onward Christian Soldiers")—were greeted with polls proving that most Methodists preferred male images of God ("In Worship, Methodists Want Tradition" 1990). So were inclusive language translations of the New Testament and Psalms.[10] Protestant denominations also struggled with the ordination of homosexuals (Steinfels 1991; "World-Wide: A Lesbian Minister" 1992). Thus, even as feminist discourse was "nor-

[9]The authors of *Megatrends* found only 300 corporations in 1980 that offered on-site child care. By 1990 they counted 3,500. A staff member of the Conference Board gave an even larger figure for employer-assisted child care in 1990: 7,000 (Aburdene and Naisbitt 1992).
[10]The Vatican refused to allow these translations to be used in Catholic liturgies in the United States (Fox 1994). Newspapers editorialized against the "PC Bible" as well (see, for example, "A PC Bible" 1995).

malized" in certain circles, when the burgeoning feminist theology movement gathered for a national "re-imagining" conference in Minneapolis in November 1993, it provoked explosive confrontations in many denominations (White 1994; Steinfels 1994; Keller 1994; Broadway, 1994).

INSTITUTIONALIZING FEMINISM

While feminist ideas reshaped the mainstream, thousands of explicitly feminist institutions and organizations also persisted through the 1980s. The movement was fragmented, but the fragments themselves exhibited considerable staying power. Institutions founded by consciousness-raising groups in the 1970s—shelters for battered women, rape crisis hotlines, bookstores, health clinics, and others—took on the formal trappings of social service institutions, with boards, directors, accountants, funding from the United Way, or even direct government control. The processes of institutionaliza tion and professionalization meant that staff members were no longer volunteers but professionals, and their time was more focused on service delivery and institutional maintenance than on the broader processes of social change (Ryan 1992; Whittier 1995; Ferree and Hess 1985; Davis 1991).

Women's studies programs similarly became institutionalized at most universities, complete with majors, minors, and tenure-track faculty. Graduate programs produced students whose academic specialty was the study of women. The problem of race moved to center stage as authors like Gloria Anzaldúa, bell hooks, and Barbara Smith forged new, multicultural directions within feminist scholarship (Hull, Scott, and Smith 1981; Anzaldua 1987; hooks 1981 and 1984). The shift in discussions of race, away from a dichotomous focus on black and white, was encapsulated in an anthology, *This Bridge Called My Back: Writings by Radical Women of Color* (1981), which was widely used in women's studies courses throughout the 1980s (Moraga and Anzaldua 1981).[11]

Armed with new knowledge, feminist scholars inaugurated a massive effort to transform the entire curriculum in the humanities and social sciences. With initial funds from the Ford Foundation, faculty development seminars at many universities facilitated the revision of courses with the goal of making them more inclusive, not only of women but also of racial and ethnic minorities. Institutes or centers for research on women sprouted on dozens

---

[11]Racial conflicts also led to serious division. In 1989, the National Woman's Studies Association became embroiled in an internal battle in which charges of racism and elitism were the critical weapons in a struggle for power and control, and the organization was almost destroyed.

of campuses, winning research grants, developing curricula at the graduate level, and forming a national network through the National Council for Research on Women (Chamberlain 1988).

The Ford Foundation was a strong supporter of women's nonprofit organizations during this period—a rarity in the world of foundations. Miriam Chamberlain, a program officer at the Ford Foundation, played a pivotal role in the early 1970s by providing grants to women's research centers across the country. Later on, grants from her program helped sustain several fledgling independent women's public-policy centers. It was Chamberlain who launched the National Council for Research on Women, bringing together a healthy mix of women's research centers and policy organizations under one umbrella.

As with social service organizations, the institutionalization of women's studies led to specialization, professionalization, and fragmentation. Wrestling with the problem of "difference," academic feminists turned to postmodern cultural theories, whose languages were accessible only to highly trained insiders. A proliferation of journals drew academic feminists into specialized, disciplinary conversations, while increasingly theoretical approaches signaled a distressing disconnect between academics and activists.[12]

While academics debated the "social construction" of gender—questioning the meaning of the very category of "woman" in light of differences of class and race—activists continued to speak for women as a group. Though sprung from the same roots, academics and activists no longer spoke the same language.

Yet, the institutionalization of women's studies also gave younger generations a new kind of access to feminism. Throughout the 1980s, despite marginalization and stereotypes, on most campuses student groups intensely debated the meanings of feminism and its implications for life choices. Indeed, women's studies classrooms became a crucial incubator for a new generation of women whose voices gradually became audible in the late 1980s and early 1990s, challenging the fragmentation of the movement (Findlen 1995; Walker 1995).

CONFLICT AND FRAGMENTATION

In the early 1980s, however, feminists were increasingly divided over what their agenda should include. In the battle to tear down barriers to female

---

[12]Academic feminist journals began in the 1970s with *Signs* and *Feminist Studies,* both of which were interdisciplinary. By the late 1980s there were journals of feminist sociology, literary criticism, history, political science, philosophy, and numerous other specialties.

participation in all-male clubs and schools, they debated whether they should embrace coeducation as better for all or preserve all-female schools for their ability to develop women's educational and leadership potentials. Should all laws be written in a gender-neutral way, they asked, or were there occasions when women needed to be treated separately in order to make genuine equity possible? Feminists split, for example, over the issue of maternity leave (linked to the biological fact of bearing a child) versus parental leave, over the problem of sex-neutral divorce laws, which had the consequence of plunging thousands of women into poverty, and over the question of whether restrictions on the growing pornography industry amounted to dangerous (and antisex) repression or an essential prerequisite to female liberty. Indeed, the latter debate, argued most heatedly at a conference at Barnard College in 1982, became known among feminists as the "sex wars" because each side claimed to have the only truly feminist position.

Such debates persisted not only in mainstream and policy oriented settings but also in a flowering of radical feminist cultural institutions in local communities. The annual National Women's Music Festival, founded in 1974, rebounded from financial and organizational disarray in 1982 and, within a few years, took on formal organizational trappings with a producer and a clear division of responsibilities. "Women's music"—with its own stars (Margie Adam, Holly Near, Sweet Honey in the Rock), labels (Olivia Records), and production companies—flourished through the 1980s. Other cultural events and annual demonstrations, such as "Take Back the Night" marches in cities around the country, functioned as public rituals in which radical feminists remained visible to themselves and to society.

Many of these activities also represented a new level of public activity and visibility for an evolving lesbian community. Where lesbian feminism in the 1970s took a decidedly separatist turn, by the 1980s, it was not markedly different from either straight or bisexual feminism or gay male activism. The AIDS epidemic, for example, made separatism—of lesbians from gay men—seem less salient. New forms of activism—from professional lobbying operations to the theatrical exploits of ACT UP and Queer Nation—mobilized a broad community to demand increased medical research and social services for AIDS victims. The spread of AIDS into the heterosexual population shifted the AIDS crisis from the margins of society into the mainstream and prompted a general reassessment of sexual experimentation and a terrifying realization of interdependence. At the same time hostility to feminists ("feminazis," as radio host Rush Limbaugh called them) had, as always, an undercurrent of homophobia, which became more overt through the 1980s as the AIDS crisis forced public discussion of the needs of the homosexual community.

Thousands of grassroots groups, some of them New Age, joined a diffuse women's spirituality movement. Many focused on reviving the mystical notion of the goddess, some on reconnecting with the traditions of Wicca (or witchcraft). Feminists also linked their spirituality to the environment, emphasizing images of Mother Earth and the goddess Gaia. Indeed, environmental activism in opposition to nuclear power plants, deforestation, acid rain, and toxic waste was one of the most visible forms of protest. The evolution of "eco-feminism" represented yet another of the boundary-blurring developments within the women's movement.

The emphasis on maternal values contributed to a revival of feminist peace activism in the tradition of Jane Addams's Women's Peace Party during World War I, the Women's International League for Peace and Freedom in the 1920s and after, and Women Strike for Peace in the 1960s. In the summer of 1983, a Women's Encampment for A Future of Peace and Justice convened for several months in Seneca County, New York. Modeled after the British women's encampment at Greenham Common, the group framed its opposition to nuclear weapons in the context of "a value system which affirms qualities that have traditionally been considered female: nurturing of life, putting others' well-being before one's own, cooperation, emotional and intuitive sensitivity, attention to detail, the ability to adapt, perseverance" (Krasniewicz 1992: 48). Women provided the backbone of a "nuclear freeze campaign" in 1984, urging a freeze on nuclear weapons. Women Against Military Madness (WAMM) joined feminist/pacifist actions across the world in confronting the horror of global holocaust with a female vision of a humane world. The spirit of Frances Willard's Women's Christian Temperance Union found new focus in a powerful lobby as Mothers Against Drunk Driving (MADD), founded in 1980, made alcohol consumption a political issue again. In the name of protecting innocent loved ones, laws against drunk driving were strengthened across the country (Krasniewicz 1992).

The fragmentation of the women's movement and the blurring of its boundaries were caused by both internal and external changes. As feminism spread to encompass a far broader range of American women, as experiments stabilized and became institutionalized, and as women emerged into public life in a dizzying array of roles, the movement lost focus. This change was exacerbated by the political strength of the opposition (symbolized by the defeat of the ERA) and a loss of government funding, which forced many activist institutions into hard times. For some, cultural events and celebrations became a critical means of feminist persistence. It is an interesting paradox that an essentialist, maternalistic, cultural feminism, which emphasized the difference between women and men, continued to attract a following at the same time that women struggled with deep differences among themselves. Soon a new generation of women would reject the idea that difference meant separation or that one had to choose among identities based on race or class or sexual preference.

The emphasis of radical feminists on female difference, in turn, was ironically congruent with the popular culture's stress on gender polarization. Maternal values informing eco-feminism, goddess spirituality, and peace activism echoed many of the same themes of the "women's leadership" workshops being offered to corporate leaders. By the late 1980s, such notions had become part of the mainstream. A best-seller, *The Chalice and the Blade,* offered a sweeping interpretation of history, contrasting societies based on dominance (the blade) and those based on egalitarianism and partnership (the chalice)—the same ideas that management consultants used in workshops that described "women's leadership" as a style more appropriate to the economy of an information society (Eisler 1987).

REMOBILIZATION

Tides of change ran deep in the late 1980s. The end of the Cold War in 1989, with the dismantling of the Soviet empire in Eastern Europe and the overthrow of communist regimes, challenged some basic assumptions of American politics. Americans watched with amazement as people around the world toppled authoritarian governments on both the left and the right. The international surge toward democracy took place alongside—and perhaps even drew strength from—an increasingly internationalized movement for women's rights.

Fifteen thousand women from around the world gathered in Nairobi, Kenya, in the summer of 1985 under the sponsorship of the United Nations for the Second International Women's Conference. (The First International Women's Conference had drawn a much smaller number—3,000 women—to Mexico City.) They debated the implications for women of political participation, economic development, human rights, and sexual exploitation. Ten years later there would be 50,000 women, and a few men, attending the official Third International Women's Conference and the "unofficial" but equally important conference of Non-Governmental Organizations (NGOs) in Beijing in the summer of 1995.

The Beijing conference marked a watershed in the recognition of women's rights around the world. One hundred and eighty-nine countries were represented at the official conference; 7,500 American women registered for the NGO conference. Debates and policy statements on topics such as violence against women, education of girls and women, health care, and access to financial resources demonstrated that governments around the world had finally begun to pay attention to the needs of women and their families. And whereas the press had ridiculed the earlier International Women's Conferences in Mexico City and Nairobi, it recognized the validity of the Third International Women's Conference by reporting the events in a serious manner.

As the movement for women's rights became increasingly international, young women in the United States were becoming aware by the late 1980s that rights they had taken for granted could also be ephemeral. Abortion, though legal for more than 15 years, had remained the most severely polarizing issue in American politics, and a campaign of terrorist violence against abortion clinics that began in the late 1970s and persisted through the 1980s became the most virulent expression of hostility to changes in gender roles and sexuality. On the grounds that abortion was "murder," abortion opponents escalated their tactics to include civil disobedience, taunt-shouting pickets, and terrorist violence. Law enforcement officials estimated conservatively that, by 1990, abortion clinics had experienced eight bombings, 28 acts of arson, 28 attempted bombings or arson, and 170 acts of vandalism (Hairston 1990). Women's rights activists offered much larger estimates (*Facts on Reproductive Rights . . .* 1989). At one clinic, which became the weekly target of picketing and vandalism, the director remembered that time as, ". . . terrible, just awful. . . . Sometimes there were as many as 150 picketers, and they would be, you know, just right up against our front door . . . in people's faces, screaming and yelling . . ." (Morgen 1995: 238).

Anti-abortion forces successfully lobbied for increasingly restrictive state laws—requiring parental notification for minors, for example—and a series of court decisions suggested that the *Roe* v. *Wade* decision was in jeopardy. By the spring of 1989, when NOW called a national demonstration for abortion rights, between 300,000 and 600,000 people showed up for one of the largest demonstrations ever held in Washington, D.C. By July, the Supreme Court confirmed its willingness to severely restrict abortion, and four of its five justices wrote a minority opinion signaling that they would have preferred to overrule *Roe* v. *Wade* altogether. In *Webster* v. *Reproductive Health Services,* the Court upheld a highly restrictive Missouri law, which began with a preamble stating that life begins at conception and went on to prohibit the use of public funds and public facilities for abortions, except to save the life of the mother. Membership in NOW and NARAL soared. Younger women had found their issue. Paula Kamen found that many young women she interviewed in the late 1980s said that "after *Webster,* they suddenly realized how tenuous their rights were and how seriously they must fight for them" (Kamen 1991: 212).

Glimmers of a new assertiveness among younger women in the late 1980s had broadened into the voice of a new, overtly feminist generation by the early 1990s. While feminist publishing had never waned in the 1980s, it suddenly shifted from the margins to the best-seller lists with books like *The Beauty Myth* by 26-year-old Naomi Wolf. This passionate critique of beauty standards reignited conversations (common in consciousness-raising groups two decades before) about women's identities and the commercialization and manipulation of the female body. In 1991, Susan Faludi's *Backlash* challenged the antifeminism of the Reagan era, and Paula Kamen's *Feminist Fatale* explored the ambivalence and ignorance of young women vis-à-vis feminism.

While Kamen lamented the loss of feminism and Faludi documented its suppression, a new sense of solidarity showed up among younger activists. Undergraduates at Mills College initiated a strike on May 3, 1990, when the board announced its decision to make the college coeducational. After two weeks, the decision was reversed. By the mid-1990s a "third wave" of feminists announced their presence with anthologies like *Listen Up: Voices from the Next Feminist Generation* (1995), *Feminism³, The Third Generation in Fiction* (1996), and *To Be Real: Telling the Truth and Changing the Face of Feminism* (1995).

The culture of this emerging generation was assertive, multicultural, and unabashedly sexy. Pop star Madonna was one embodiment of the contradictions and ironies of the cultural images that defined their youth. Younger women loved her brilliant manipulation of image and persona, musical talent, and business acumen—her "in-your-face" attitude. Her muscular body, honed with hours of exercise, clothed with sexy underwear, was hers to use or display as she chose. Cultural critic Camille Paglia argued in the *New York Times,* in 1990, that "Madonna is the true feminist." Challenging what she saw as the "puritanism" of American feminism, Paglia proclaimed that "Madonna has taught young women to be fully female and sexual while still exercising control over their lives. She shows girls how to be attractive, sensual, energetic, ambitious, aggressive, and funny—all at the same time" (Paglia 1990: A39). This sensibility underlay the success of "Riot Grrls" music and *Sassy* magazine, founded in 1988 for girls age 14 to 19. *Sassy*'s frank articles about sex and birth control provoked a Moral Majority boycott, however, which forced many advertisers to withdraw and the magazine to be sold. While it rapidly recovered its readership and by the early 1990s had a circulation of 650,000, *Sassy*'s coverage of sexual issues had been toned down (Kamen 1991). By 1994, it had become just another teen magazine.

It is ironic, though hardly surprising, that the appearance of a new assertiveness on the part of younger women in the late 1980s and early 1990s coincided with a cresting wave of antifeminist attacks. Right-wingers were joined by former feminist activists like Christina Hoff Sommers, Elizabeth Fox-Genovese, and Camille Paglia, who tore into the women's movement for its individualism (Fox-Genovese), puritanism (Paglia), and rage (Sommers) with books like *Who Stole Feminism: How Women Have Betrayed Women*.

The remobilization of women in the 1990s occurred despite a conservative political climate, driven by the persistence of change and the "normalization" of perceptions once seen as extreme. The attack on abortion, for example, energized young women who had begun to take it for granted as a right. Sexual harassment turned out to be another issue about which most women had come to agree, while many older men remained oblivious to the shift in norms. When these perceptions clashed in the high drama of a congressional hearing, thousands of women were suddenly motivated to make themselves heard. And they were.

The Senate confirmation hearings on President Bush's nominee to replace retiring Supreme Court Justice Thurgood Marshall were not expected to provide a flashpoint for feminist resurgence. A civil rights leader who had argued the landmark civil rights cases, Marshall had been the only African American to serve on the Court. His proposed replacement, Clarence Thomas, was a conservative African American and former director of the Equal Employment Opportunities Commission. Civil rights and feminist leaders were strongly opposed to Thomas, who had been an outspoken opponent of affirmative action, but they had little expectation that they could do more than place a few objections on the record.

Then on October 6, 1991, commentary by Nina Totenberg of National Public Radio and an article in *Newsday* suggested that the committee had suppressed testimony alleging that Thomas had engaged in sexual harassment. The next day Anita Hill, an African American law professor from Oklahoma, held a press conference to confirm these charges. Suddenly, the fault lines of race and gender were visible. Men generally shrugged. African Americans perceived racism in the sensationalism that surrounded the charges. Women, by a substantial proportion but in differing degrees by race, were outraged that the testimony had been covered up. On October 8, Democratic congresswomen marched from the House to the Senate and demanded an investigation. Their angry confrontation was high drama for the media. Airwaves were filled with women calling to say, "They just don't get it, do they?" In short order the Senate Judiciary Committee changed its mind and extended its hearings to incorporate public testimony from Anita Hill (Witt, Paget, and Matthews 1993; Phelps and Winternitz 1992).

For three days, the nation stopped to watch hearings in which a committee of eight white men grilled a genteel, African American woman lawyer. Anita Hill's quiet dignity contrasted sharply with her interrogators' palpable discomfort and ineptitude. They made light of this "sexual harass-ment crap," and dwelled on salacious details. Many, many women were not amused. From private homes to political campaigns, the debate, once ig-nited, catalyzed a new wave of activism.

The next year, the number of women who ran for national office rose sharply. It was a lucky coincidence that an unusually large number of seats were open due to retirements and reapportionment. Twenty-two women ran for the Senate in 1992, compared with only eight two years before. The first African American woman to be elected to the Senate, Carol Moseley-Braun of Illinois, was moved by the hearings to challenge Senator Alan Dixon, a Thomas supporter. In Pennsylvania, Lynn Yeakel gave Senator Arlen Specter a run for his money with ads showing him questioning Anita Hill. In a voice-over, Yeakel asked rhetorically, "Did this make you as angry as it made me?" (Witt, Paget, and Matthews 1993: 5).

Grassroots support for women candidates doubled and tripled. Contri-butions to the National Women's Political Caucus, the Women's Campaign Fund, and EMILY's List grew exponentially. Membership in EMILY's list went from 3,000 to 23,000 members in just one year, allowing it to con tribute six million dollars to women candidates—four times what it had raised in 1990.

In 1992, the number of women in Congress doubled. Forty-eight women were elected to the House of Representatives (including Eleanor Holmes Norton, reelected as the nonvoting delegate for the District of Columbia), an increase of 19 over the 29 elected in 1990. Four new women and one incumbent won seats in the Senate. The subsequent election of Kay Bailey Hutchison in the Texas election to fill the unexpired term of Secretary of the Treasury Lloyd Bentsen brought the number of women in the Senate to seven. (The other incumbent woman Senator was not up for reelection.)

The gains for women in Congress were dramatic and significantly in-creased their potential power to enact legislation. However, it is important to remember that even though women doubled their representation in Congress from five to 10 percent, women were still far from reaching par-ity.

Called the "Year of the Woman," 1992 was also the year that women turned out to vote in record numbers for the presidential election, provid-ing Democratic Party candidate Bill Clinton with his margin of victory. The 1992 election was not a simple victory for women, however. The election was marked by controversy over "family values," which the Republicans made central to their campaign. Conservative rhetoric reflected not only male anxiety about changes but also the growing marginalization of women who chose traditional roles. As one study of a midwestern city found, many of the women in the anti-abortion movement were middle-class housewives who had come of age after the golden years of the feminist breakthrough. Most of their peers, whether by choice or necessity, combined motherhood with paid employment, leaving those who chose motherhood as their primary identity and occupation increasingly isolated and defensive. Some blamed feminism and abortion rights for their marginalization (Ginzburg 1989).

Vice President Dan Quayle criticized a popular television character, Murphy Brown, for having a child out of wedlock, igniting a debate about single motherhood, the stigma of illegitimacy, and abortion. His wife, Marilyn Quayle, told the Republican Convention that "most women do not wish to be liberated from their essential natures as women" (Stanley 1992: A20). Republicans criticized Hillary Clinton for remarking, in response to a question about her legal and volunteer work in Arkansas during Bill Clinton's governorship, that she "could have stayed home and baked cookies." *Family Circle* sponsored a contest in which readers were invited to bake and compare chocolate chip cookies using Hillary Clinton's and Barbara Bush's recipes.

The polarized responses to Hillary Clinton were, perhaps, a measure of both the revival of feminism and the ongoing hostility to women's changing roles. She was idolized and vilified for assuming a strong public role in debates on health policy and children's issues. The deficits generated during the Reagan years had made it politically impossible to consider any dramatic expansion of the welfare state, and as Hillary Clinton's health care task force's recommendations went down to defeat in Congress, she shifted to a lower-profile, more "feminine" image.

The 1994 Republican victory, in which Republicans gained majorities in both houses of Congress, was widely portrayed as a revolt of the "angry white males," whose voices were heard in a profusion of radio talk shows. The most popular talk show host, Rush Limbaugh, led the attack on Hillary Clinton and what he viewed as a liberal takeover. "We have lost control of our major cultural institutions. Liberalism long ago captured the arts, the press, the entertainment industry, the universities, the schools, the libraries the foundations, etc" (Limbaugh 1993: 87).

For Limbaugh and others, a galling symbol of this loss was the demise of the last bastions of an all-male military culture, The Citadel in South Carolina and Virginia Military Institute (VMI). Shannon Faulkner entered The Citadel in 1995 in the national spotlight. But two years of litigation and public scrutiny took their toll, and she dropped out after two weeks, to the cheers of her fellow students.[13] By the next year, however, there were several fe-

---

[13]Faulkner had been accepted to The Citadel until officials learned that she was female. That rejection prompted her suit.

male students, and The Citadel joined West Point and Annapolis as a co-educational institution. Phyllis Schlafley, in an impassioned letter to VMI, offered a challenge: "You've lost a major battle. Are you going to be survivors, or are you going to let the enemy wipe you and your kind from the face of the earth, pour salt in the soil that produced you, and drop you down the Memory Hole?" (Schlafley 1996).

Schlafley skillfully deployed the threat to manhood articulated throughout American history whenever women moved forcefully into public life. By 1996, however, those changes had reshaped the lives of women and men alike, and the arguments, though virulent, no longer had the same potency. Debates themselves were more public and took place in more varied arenas.

While the 1994 elections may have been driven by "angry white men"—a midterm election when women's voting participation declined—two years later those men no longer dominated the campaign. Instead, the "gender gap" returned in force, and in 1996, a President's margin of victory was clearly based on the votes of women. As Sonia Jarvis notes in Chapter Four, the gender gap in political party identification has been recognized since 1984 and continues to play an important role in national politics.

TOWARD THE TWENTY-FIRST CENTURY

Politics in this country will never be the same. The personal is political and women have discovered their "voice." Yet, many of the old practices remain, and they will continue to rub uncomfortably against new expectations and possibilities. This is where the energy will come from for future changes.

American women in the new millennium will confront a rough new terrain shaped by the upheavals of the last half-century. The quake has swept through our labor force, our laws, our language, even our bedrooms. The contrasts with the past are striking. Women now make up almost half the paid labor force and can be found in virtually every field. They occupy positions of public authority that would have been unthinkable even in the 1960s: Supreme Court justices, ministers and rabbis, engineers, generals, and airline pilots. Their political clout is growing, through a sophisticated policy infrastructure and a presence in state and local politics.

Family formation is no longer uniform—marriage ages are up and marriage rates are down, fertility remains low, divorce is common, and a high proportion of children are born out of wedlock. Indeed, the definition of "family" has been challenged profoundly by single parents, by gay and lesbian couples, and by reproductive technologies that separate biological from social parenthood, sex from conception, and conception from gestation. Laws now provide defenses against not only employment discrimination but also marital rape and sexual harassment.

As we look toward the twenty-first century, the contradictions of women's lives are likely to continue to fuel their involvement in politics. Women remain caught between a world of work which presumes that there is someone behind every worker who is available to take care of family needs and the ongoing presumption that women assume primary care for children and household. The process of redefining work—through such measures as flextime, shared or part-time jobs with full benefits, parental leave, and on-site child care—has proceeded at a glacial pace. Perhaps as more and more men are drawn into serious engagement with the daily life of their households, they too will see the necessity of policies that affirm the social importance of child care and personal life. In any case, women are likely to be at the center of these efforts.

As a result of longer life expectancies, different generations of women have distinct and sometimes conflicting experiences. Those who fought for access to work and public life face new generations raised with different expectations. Younger women presume that they will combine work outside the home with family responsibilities. The harsh realities of doing so, however, lead some of them to reassert the value of parenting and family, charging that the values of the marketplace have overshadowed something for which they not only remain responsible but which gives them pleasure and meaning. This explains some of the political popularity of "family values" among people who do not, in fact, advocate returning to traditional, patriarchal family norms. At the same time, older women are creating a new life stage in their forties, fifties, and sixties. Vital, healthy, energetic, they face yet another round of discriminatory attitudes and practices based on sex and age.

Will it be possible to reconcile the goals of women who wish to make work more hospitable and tolerable for those who bear heavy family responsibilities, those who wish to maintain a decent safety net for impoverished women and children, and those who want to reclaim the importance of parenting and motherhood? Finding common ground among women of different generations and backgrounds will be the key to creating spaces for experimentation and building working relationships that go beyond demonizing stereotypes.

Women as a group are more favorable to using government as an instrument of social policy. Furthermore, in our still sex-segregated labor force, women are far more likely than men to work in settings—in the health, education, services, and government sectors—where they experience government as a positive and necessary force, rather than as a burden imposing regulation and taxation.

Despite the current suspicion of government, the new century probably will generate a number of decentralized experiments, led by women, to address community problems related to child care, public safety, and health. In their long struggle for access to public life, women often have invented new forms of voluntary association which have given this country an unusually rich civil society. Renewing that civic resource—as both a training ground for leaders and an environment for experiments in public problem solving—is certainly one of the keys to the survival of democracy in the twenty-first century.

TWO

AFRICAN AMERICAN WOMEN IN THE TWENTY-FIRST CENTURY: THE CONTINUING CHALLENGE

Vicki Crawford

HIGHLIGHTS

AFRICAN AMERICAN WOMEN'S historical tradition of community and social activism provided the foundation for social change in the twentieth century. Through individual and collective efforts, African American women continued to address race, class, and gender discrimination as they persisted in the struggle for full inclusion in U.S. society.

- By the mid-1950s, through individual actions and pre-existing networks of support, African American women were playing major roles in the formation of the civil rights movement. Through participation in boycotts, demonstrations, voter registration drives, and other forms of nonviolent direct protest, African American women were important leaders and supporters of the twentieth-century African American freedom struggle.
- By 1964, as the civil rights movement coalesced into increased African American and white activism in the Deep South, African American women were among the organizers and participants in Freedom Summer, which targeted the state of Mississippi as a testing ground for whether the constitutional rights of African Americans could ever be fully realized.
- African American women were central to the intensive voter registration campaign in the summer of 1964 and to the formation of the Mississippi Freedom Democratic Party (MFDP). In the MFDP challenge to the National Democratic Party at its convention in Atlantic City, New Jersey, in 1964, three African American women—Fannie Lou Hamer, Victoria Gray, and Annie Devine—were elected as the party's representatives.
- The passage of the Voting Rights Act of 1965 banning discriminatory prac-

tices in voting was one of the most far-reaching and successful civil rights laws ever passed by Congress. The Voting Rights Act was the result of MFDP organizing and the activities of Freedom Summer in which the activism of African American women was crucial.

- By the mid-1960s, as African American protest shifted its focus from civil rights in the South to the racial and economic disparities in the urban north, poor African American women formed the National Welfare Rights Organization to challenge the discriminatory practices of the welfare system which had limited access and denied benefits to eligible women and children.
- African American women's activism in the civil rights movement and black nationalist movements of the late 1960s evolved into a separate, distinct articulation of their position at the nexus of race, class, and gender in the United States. In the early 1970s, black feminism/womanism grew out of the sexism and racism faced by African American women in civil rights organizations and in the second wave of the women's movement.
- The decade of the 1970s was a time of progress and setbacks for African American women as one sector benefited from the expanding economic opportunities created by earlier civil rights efforts and federal legislation such as the Civil Rights Act of 1964. As a significant number of educated African Americans entered the ranks of the middle class, black women experienced record growth in clerical and professional employment and their employment in private domestic service dropped from 42 to 18 percent between 1950 and 1970.
- By the mid-1970s, African American economic progress had stalled and those women who lacked education and skills faced declining job opportunities and unemployment.
- The growing proportion of African American families headed by single mothers living in poverty has resulted in crippling rates of joblessness as the federal government, under the Reagan administration, attacked the poor and slashed public assistance to women and their families.
- By 1995, 46 percent of all African American families were headed by women and 45 percent of these single-parent households were living in poverty. Black women were nearly three times as likely to live in poverty and twice as likely to be unemployed as white women. Continuing cutbacks in public assistance to the poor were bolstered by neoconservative politicians who resurrected the 1960s culture of poverty analysis to blame the poor for their own predicament.
- The defederalization of Aid to Families with Dependent Children (AFDC) under President Clinton's 1996 "welfare reform" law has radically altered the nation's primary public assistance program by devolving the respon-

sibility of welfare to the states. The impact of this restructuring will have severe long-term consequences for African American women and families.

• In the next millennium, African American women's strong tradition of social and political activism will ground new approaches to collective action as African American women meet the challenge of growing rates of urban poverty and the persistence of race, class, and gender inequalities.

INTRODUCTION

Throughout our nation's history, African American women, in response to race, class, and gender inequalities, have organized to create a remarkable infrastructure for sustaining their communities. The activism of African American women in the post–World War Two era was grounded in the early community mobilization and self-help efforts of their nineteenth century and turn-of-the-century sisters.

From 1890 to 1920, the National Association of Colored Women (NACW) organized hundreds of local chapters to demand suffrage and political and civil rights. In the absence of social welfare programs, African American women's clubs uplifted communities through the creation of viable self-help institutions, including schools, day care centers, kindergartens, and other independent structures. In the first decades of the twentieth century, as African Americans faced legalized segregation and disenfranchisement, African American women organized to protest Jim Crow, lynching, and other forms of discrimination.

The next millennium approaches amid persistent urban poverty, an increasingly inequitable distribution of wealth, and widening racial divisions. The recent retreat from the national commitment to poor families, as evidenced by major changes in the welfare system, will have immense consequences for African Americans in the years ahead. As contemporary African American women face the challenges of the twenty-first century, the leadership tradition of earlier generations of African American women will anchor their activism on behalf of civil and constitutional rights. The next task lies in mobilizing and organizing to resist institutionalized forms of oppression that continue to limit the options of African American women for full participation in U.S. society.

This chapter assesses the role of African American women in the twentieth century. The chapter starts with a reflection on the significance of African American women's leadership in the Civil Rights Movement. As key agents of social change, African American women extended their tradition of protest to the twentieth-century freedom struggle in which they were essential in initiating the social and political transformations which resulted. Standing at the intersection of race, class, and gender, African American women in the post-civil rights era continued to challenge and resist institutionalized structures of domination as they sought opportunities for advancement and self-expression. The emergence of contemporary black feminism/womanism in the early 1970s provided an organizational base and collective voice to address continuing social and economic inequality.

The 1970s brought new opportunities for economic growth. As a result of African American activism and antidiscrimination legislation, African American women's legacy of hard work and self-determination produced some remarkable achievements. The representation of African American women in clerical and professional employment increased significantly. By the mid-1970s, African American women were no longer disproportionately represented in the occupation of domestic service.

As the political backlash against affirmative action and other social programs intensified by the end of the 1970s, African American women and their communities faced diminishing economic opportunities and continuing racial discrimination. The decades of the 1980s and 1990s have brought staggering rates of urban poverty, joblessness, and a growing proportion of families headed by single mothers. The national retrenchment in federal assistance to the poor reflects the ongoing economic oppression of the vast majority of African American women, despite the relative gains of a few. This chapter traces, in broad outline, the major issues and developments in the lives of African American women over the past five decades and speculates about the challenges they are likely to face in the new millennium.

LAYING A FOUNDATION: AFRICAN AMERICAN WOMEN AND THE EMERGENCE OF THE CIVIL RIGHTS MOVEMENT

By the mid-1950s, African American resistance to racial discrimination had coalesced into collective action through boycotts, demonstrations, voter registration drives, and other forms of nonviolent protest. In keeping with the tradition of institution building established by their nineteenth- and early-twentieth-century sisters, African American women emerged as leaders and supporters of the black freedom struggle, which gained momentum as the decade progressed.

Through individual acts of resistance and networks of social support, African American women provided the infrastructure for social change by organizing and mobilizing local communities throughout the South. While African American women were rarely recognized as national leaders and spokespersons for the movement, their activism was critical in mounting a challenge against segregation and disfranchisement.

In the aftermath of the legal assault by the National Association for the Advancement of Colored People (NAACP) against school segregation—resulting in the landmark 1954 *Brown* v. *Board of Education of Topeka* decision reversing the 1896 *Plessy* v. *Ferguson* ruling which had established the separate-but-equal doctrine—African American women and men initiated a nationwide campaign of nonviolent mass action. The success of the Montgomery bus boycott, which launched the civil rights movement in 1955, was due in large part to the strong participation of African American women. When veteran activist Rosa Parks was arrested for refusing to give up her bus seat to a white man, the quick and efficient response of that southern community was made possible by the Women's Political Council (WPC), an organization of middle-class African American educators and business-women.

Formed nine years before the boycott by Mary Fair Burks, a professor at Alabama State College, the WPC already had addressed the discriminatory treatment of African Americans riding public transportation in the early 1950s (Robinson 1987). When Rosa Parks was arrested on December 1, 1955, the stage was set for a full-scale protest against the local transportation authorities. Years of community organizing had paid off.

Furthermore, Mrs. Parks was the ideal symbol around which to mobilize the Montgomery community. A well-known, respected churchwoman and community worker, she had served as secretary of the state NAACP, working with E. D. Nixon, another architect of the boycott. She also had attended one of the summer workshops sponsored by the Highlander Folk School in Tennessee, an institution that cultivated indigenous local leadership in the early 1950s. Other activists—including Septima Clark, Ella Baker, Dorothy Cotton, and Bernice Robinson—also participated in the Highlander training program. There they developed a philosophy of social change that they would draw on in years to come as they organized local communities throughout the South.

Following Rosa Parks's arrest in 1955, the WPC disseminated thousands of leaflets urging African Americans to stay off the buses. The pre-existing infrastructure of the WPC was crucial to the successful two-day effort to mobilize the community's African American residents. Women who were active in the civic organization also held memberships in local churches and various secular organizations in which they were highly influential in creating a web of support for local activism. These contacts made the WPC pivotal to the establishment of the Montgomery Improvement Association (MIA), the organization of local leadership that sustained the 381-day boycott and elected a young pastor, Martin Luther King, Jr., as its president. The important groundwork laid by middle-class women in the WPC drew additional support from rank-and-file domestic workers and others who pooled rides and walked long distances in their refusal to take public transportation.

In the decade between 1955 and 1965, as the African American freedom struggle gained momentum, women in other local communities followed the courageous example of their Montgomery counterparts. Again and again, women filled mass meetings, participated in boycotts, went to jail, and fed, clothed, and housed other civil rights workers. In locales across the South, young high school teenagers and college-aged women joined in the fight against segregation through participation in direct action and desegregation of schools and universities.

White opposition to court-ordered desegregation of the nation's schools resulted in noncompliance and massive resistance across the South. In one of the most violent confrontations to end segregation, nine African American teenagers, later known as the Little Rock Nine, faced white mobs as they attempted to enroll in Central High School in Little Rock, Arkansas, on September 22, 1957. Led by NAACP activist Daisy Bates, who spearheaded the African American community's challenge to local school authorities, the nine students symbolized the collective courage and determination of youth in the struggle to desegregate schools. One of the most compelling images of the civil rights movement was of young Elizabeth Eckford sitting alone on a bench in front of Central High surrounded by a white mob as federal troops and the Arkansas National Guard stood by.

Elsewhere, across the South, countless children and young adults continued to pressure local school authorities as they joined their elders in the struggle for social change. The significance of the Little Rock Nine and the leadership of Daisy Bates lay in the reciprocal roles of youth and older activists in support of civil rights. While courageous parents such as Mae Bertha Carter, Winson and Dovie Hudson, and Unita Blackwell, among others, brought suit on behalf of their children, young people drew increasing attention to movement activities during this phase of the movement.

The intergenerational dimension of civil rights activism was greatly strengthened by the support of older African American women. Drawing on their rich spiritual heritage and long-standing tradition of active church involvement, older women were uniquely situated to mobilize communities and to endorse civil rights activities during the early years when full-scale support was less forthcoming. Within the context of the civil rights movement, women's roles in church communities were politicized even further. Their power and influence were indisputable. The ministry remained closed to them although, in their roles as deaconesses, missionaries, and respected elders, women's organizing skills and networks of support were invaluable to the movement's effectiveness.

ORGANIZING YOUTH: WOMEN AND THE STUDENT PHASE OF THE CIVIL RIGHTS MOVEMENT

Three years after the Montgomery bus boycott, on August 19, 1958, Clara Luper, an Oklahoma public school teacher and NAACP Youth Council leader, led one of the first sit-ins, at the Katz Drug Store in Oklahoma City. Though not as widely publicized as the Greensboro, North Carolina, sit-ins two years later, the Katz sit-in was one of the earliest efforts to organize youth in nonviolent protest (Luper 1979). Activism among students and young adults grew swiftly. In 1960, local students from North Carolina Agricultural and Technical College led another sit-in at a Woolworth's lunch counter in Greensboro, North Carolina, which launched the student phase of the civil rights movement.

By now, long-time activist Ella Baker, who had worked for progressive causes in the 1930s and as a field secretary with the NAACP in the 1940s, was convinced that young adults could play a unique role in the freedom movement then emerging throughout the South. While working for the NAACP as a field secretary and later as director of the New York City branch, Baker witnessed the long, gradual but important process of challenging segregation through the courts. Moreover, in her role as field secretary, she had traveled throughout the South in the 1940s—a dangerous time when mere association with the NAACP was sure to bring harassment and violence.

Baker's work with African American ministers in the predominantly male Southern Christian Leadership Conference (SCLC) influenced her ideas for establishing a youth organization that would be independent from older, more-established civil rights groups such as SCLC and the NAACP. The students, Baker reasoned, could be far more militant and free to take risks.

The only other women to assume similar leadership roles during that time were the NAACP national youth secretary, Ruby Hurley, and field secretary, Daisy Lumpkin. Though men were at the forefront of the regional and national leadership of the NAACP, women were its strength. They typically headed NAACP Youth Councils in which they were highly effective in organizing young adults. In addition, women were central to fundraising and membership drives in local chapters.

Through Baker's experience with the NAACP and SCLC, she developed a radical view of leadership. The highly bureaucratic hierarchy of the NAACP and male clergy in the SCLC both relied on their top ranks, which excluded women, for making executive decisions. As an astute and seasoned organizer, Baker believed that the most effective strategy for sustaining activism among local people would be to develop a decentralized, group-centered approach to leadership which would minimize hierarchy and involve grassroots people in the decisions affecting their lives.

In describing her own approach to activism, Ella Baker once commented that "the kind of role that I tried to play was to pick up pieces or put together pieces out of which I hoped organization might come. My theory is strong people don't need strong leaders" (Cantarow and O'Malley 1980: 53). As Baker saw it, the top-down decisionmaking of SCLC and NAACP was counterproductive to sustaining community mass action. Baker warned that "there is the danger in our culture that because a person is called upon to give public statements and is acclaimed by the establishment, such a person gets to the point of believing that he is the movement. Such people get so involved with playing the game of being important that they exhaust themselves and their time, and they don't do the work of actually organizing people" (Lerner 1972:351).

On April 15, 1960, Baker called together a meeting of young adults to attend a conference at Shaw University in Raleigh, North Carolina. African American and white student leaders came from across the nation. The result was the formation of the radically progressive Student Nonviolent Coordinating Committee (SNCC). An interracial group of young adults, SNCC later spearheaded some of the era's most courageous and effective campaigns for social change. Its emphasis on grassroots organizing and decision making by consensus cultivated leadership among young women.

SNCC was certainly more egalitarian than older civil rights organizations when it came to women's activism, and Ella Baker's impact was far-reaching. A younger generation of women—including Cynthia Washington, Ruby Doris Smith Robinson, Joyce and Dorie Ladner, Diane Nash, and Annelle Ponder—was largely influenced by Baker's ideas. Female activists such as Casey Hayden and Mary King later would draw on Baker's critique of leadership to organize the second wave of the women's movement in the mid- to late-1960s. Older adults also recognized her pivotal role in the development of indigenous leadership.

Fannie Lou Hamer, whose contribution to the struggle was also extraordinary, often commented on the significant role Ella Baker played in bringing progressive social change to the state of Mississippi. A former Mississippi sharecropper who was fired from her job after attempting to register to vote, Fannie Lou Hamer emerged in 1962 as one of the most eloquent and principled leaders of the 1960s era. She was an outspoken critic of racism, an early critic of the United States's involvement in Vietnam, and a champion of the rights of women and the poor.

Born in 1917, as the twentieth child of a sharecropping family in Montgomery County, Mississippi, Mrs. Hamer grew up in extreme poverty and racial oppression. It was not until 1962, when the first SNCC workers arrived in Mississippi, that her dream of a better life was finally realized. Historically, Mississippi was the most resistant state to racial equality, having led the nation after Reconstruction in the disenfranchisement of the state's large African American population. As such, civil rights activists targeted the state as a means of testing whether the constitutional rights of African Americans could ever be fully realized.

In 1964, civil rights organizations working in Mississippi banned together to form the Congress of Federated Organizations (COFO), which launched a full-scale, statewide attack on segregation. Though SNCC had been trying to register African American voters in the state since 1961, fewer than six percent of eligible African Americans were registered. One of COFO's first projects was Freedom Summer, conceived by project organizers as a means of bringing national attention to the racist practices in Mississippi and the fierce resistance to civil rights activities in the state. Freedom Summer was an interracial effort which drew hundreds of students and activists to Mississippi where they spent the summer of 1964 registering potential African American voters.

The architects of Freedom Summer anticipated the violent response that was sure to come from the interracial challenge to local authority. On the eve of the 1964 summer project, the bodies of three civil rights workers— James Cheney, Michael Schwerner, and Andrew Goodman—were discovered in a shallow grave outside of Philadelphia, Mississippi. Despite the horror of these brutal murders, civil rights activists persisted in carrying out the project. The goal of Freedom Summer was to force the federal government to intervene in Mississippi and bring protection to the state's African American residents and other civil rights activists. Moreover, the project organizers planned to establish a political framework that would demonstrate that Mississippi's African American residents desired the franchise, despite charges by white politicians that African Americans were disinterested in voting.

The potential strength of African American voters had been realized a year earlier in a parallel election held in June of 1963, when over 15,000 votes had been cast in a symbolic mock election. Organizers of the 1964 Freedom Summer hoped to build on the momentum of this symbolic act by intensifying voter registration in the months that followed. Another key aspect of Freedom Summer was the highly successful political education of the state's African American residents through Freedom Schools which taught citizenship skills and African American history. These programs were designed to address the deeply rooted psychological constraints African Americans faced living within a system of economic, political, and social repression.

AFRICAN AMERICAN WOMEN AND THE MISSISSIPPI FREEDOM DEMOCRATIC PARTY

The most significant and far-reaching accomplishment in the summer of 1964 was the creation of a radical third political party, called the Mississippi Freedom Democratic Party (MFDP). African American women were central to the establishment of the party, and their involvement would have long-term benefits for increased African American political participation.

Organized in April 1964, the MFDP was an independent, grassroots party created in opposition to the state's all-white Democratic leadership, which had been fraudulently elected through the exclusion of African American voters. At the initial meeting, held in the state capitol in Jackson, over 200 delegates were in attendance. Several were women who served on the party's executive committee. Later, Fannie Lou Hamer, Victoria Gray (Adams), and Annie Devine were elected as the party's three national representatives.

By 1964, these women were all middle-aged, seasoned activists, having organized the movement in their own respective towns and communities. Hamer, Devine, and Gray had helped organize the MFDP, along with Ella Baker and Unita Blackwell. In 1977, Blackwell became mayor of Mayersville, Mississippi—the first African American female mayor in Mississippi.

Perhaps the most effective and inspirational of the three national representatives was Fannie Lou Hamer who made history at the 1964 Democratic National Convention in Atlantic City, New Jersey. The MFDP elected 68 delegates to attend the August convention in order to challenge the unfair seating of the state's all-white delegation. Months of intensive organizing preceded the challenge, which sought to open future Democratic conventions to African Americans.

As a compromise, the MFDP was offered two at-large seats within the national party. The offer resulted in a heated debate within MFDP's ranks, with one faction arguing for its acceptance and the other strongly opposing its acceptance on the grounds that it was a political maneuver designed to prevent disunity within the ranks of the Democratic Party. Fannie Lou

Hamer, Victoria Gray, and Annie Devine voted against the compromise, with Hamer's strong voice questioning the inconsistency between Democratic principles and ideals and the practice of racism and intolerance (Locke 1993).

The significance of the MFDP's challenge was in the demonstration of indigenous leadership. That August, unlettered women and men stood before Congress to assert their impatience with the federal government's apathy toward racism in Mississippi. As the leading voice of the party, Fannie Lou Hamer spoke to the nation in a televised session of the Credentials Committee, during which she described the intolerable conditions in the state. In her compelling testimony, she cited a brutal beating, following an arrest, that left her permanently scarred.

In a last-minute effort to diminish the impact of Mrs. Hamer's powerful testimony, President-elect Lyndon Johnson preempted her speech with an emergency televised news conference. But the full impact of her words had already reached the nation's ears. Unfortunately, Hamer's testimony, though stirring, did not persuade the Credentials Committee to unseat the Mississippi "regulars." Ultimately, President Johnson and other Democratic leaders had politically circumvented support for the MFDP in their offer of a compromise. Johnson feared that recognition of the MFDP might weaken southern support in his upcoming campaign against Republican Barry Goldwater.

Following those incidents, the MFDP delegates returned to Mississippi to challenge the state's representatives to the U.S. Congress. The congressional challenge of 1965 was the MFDP's second attempt to bring national attention to the plight of African Americans in Mississippi. For the first time since Reconstruction, three African Americans ran for Congress. Although they were defeated, the symbolic candidacies of Fannie Lou Hamer, Annie Devine, and Victoria Gray paved the way for the subsequent election of other African Americans to state and local offices.

The activism of the MFDP was crucial in generating support for passage of the Voting Rights Act of 1965 which expanded African American suffrage throughout the South. The act outlawed the racially discriminatory literacy requirement and authorized federal protection to ensure fair elections. The Voting Rights Act was a landmark achievement. Within two years after its passage, the percentage of African Americans registered to vote in Mississippi increased from 6.7 percent to an estimated 60 percent (Parker 1994). Some thirty years later, by the early 1990s, as a result of the groundwork laid by the MFDP, Mississippi exceeded all other states in its record number of African American elected officials (Parker 1994).

THE NATIONAL COUNCIL OF NEGRO WOMEN: A TRADITION OF ACTIVISM

One of the most significant, yet underappreciated, contributions to the civil rights movement was the political activism of the National Council of Negro Women (NCNW), established in 1935 by educator and activist Mary McCleod Bethune. A national organization of over four million African American women working through state and local chapters, the NCNW, by the 1960s, was able to implement a range of community development programs across the South. Its work in Mississippi was particularly instrumental in forging women's support networks, both locally and across the nation.

Under the national leadership of its fourth president, Dorothy Height, the NCNW addressed the special concerns of women and children in the aftermath of Freedom Summer. In 1963, Dorothy Height had been the only woman among the national coalition of civil rights leaders that planned that summer's March on Washington. In the days following the march, she called together an assembly of women representing other national women's groups, asking them to remain in Washington, D.C., to explore organizational strategies for future action.

Height's vision and experience in the movement convinced her of the need to move beyond direct action campaigns to address deeply rooted social issues, specifically those concerning women and children. She remarked:

> As I represented the interests of women in the whole civil rights leadership group, I found that it was very difficult to get people, who were oriented toward laws and practices, to accept the fact that the conditions affecting children, and affecting youth, whether they were services like childcare, or whether they were things related to employment opportunities—this was all a part of civil rights. And, I found that one of the good things was that when women came together, they were very articulate about it. They saw the relationship between decent housing, and schooling, and child care, to employment and job opportunities (Hill 1991: 173).

The race and gender consciousness of Dorothy Height led to the formation of Women in Community Service (WICS), which included representatives from the NCNW, the YWCA, the National Council of Jewish Women, and Churchwomen United. The interracial alliance was established as a base of support for civil rights activism. Later, in 1964, it helped launch Wednesdays in Mississippi, a program that brought African American and white northern women to the state to desegregate public facilities. The following year, the NCNW implemented several community development and self-help projects in rural Mississippi. These efforts were significant in establishing collaboration among women of varying socioeconomic backgrounds as they sought to address the vast poverty of African Americans in the state.

In January 1965, the NCNW held its first workshop in Oxford, Mississippi, bringing together women from around the state who were small farmers and sharecroppers. Height and the NCNW planned to use federal monies flowing from President Johnson's antipoverty programs to create independent, community-based programs among the poor. The group created a program for low-income home ownership, along with a self-help campaign to address hunger in three of the poorest counties in the nation. Seasoned activists Fannie Lou Hamer and Unita Blackwell were among the local women who joined with the NCNW to create economic opportunities for rural families. This collaboration continued the self-help tradition of African American women who were determined to improve conditions within their communities (Carper 1968).

THE NATIONAL WELFARE RIGHTS ORGANIZATION

The mechanization of southern agriculture in the post–World War II years had led to extensive African American migration out of the South. As the southern phase of the civil rights movement shifted northward, by 1966, African American protest revolved around racism and urban poverty in the nation's inner cities. Rising African American insurgency climaxed in urban rioting between 1964 and 1968, as African Americans confronted the economic problems of low wages, unemployment, and discriminatory restrictions that limited access to public assistance.

In the mid-1960s, African Americans were concentrated largely in the nation's urban inner cities, where they suffered a cruel economic fate. Racism and discrimination resulted in unemployment, creating relentless hardship for those who had previously sought to escape the segregated South. While the civil rights movement had been successful in dismantling legal segregation and discrimination in voting practices, the masses of African Americans still remained economically impoverished and subject to de facto forms of discrimination. Nonetheless, the large concentration of African Americans in inner cities offered the potential for a voting bloc, through which African Americans could alter the balance of power in local and state elections.

In the mid-1960s, the National Welfare Rights Organization (NWRO) emerged as a social protest movement among primarily poor African American women. The political climate of the Johnson administration stimulated this grassroots movement's determination to attack the pervasive problem of urban poverty. When President Johnson took office following the assassination of President Kennedy in 1963, he announced a nationwide "War on Poverty" to alleviate the growing disparities between the nation's poor and the economically privileged. Social policies and federal resources were channeled to inner cities, creating an environment in which mobilization and the creation of NWRO could evolve.

A base of support among white liberals, social workers, and civil rights organizers coalesced to form NWRO, whose membership was composed largely of African American women. Between 1966 and 1975, through more than 800 local chapters, NWRO successfully mobilized thousands of poor mothers receiving public assistance in a challenge to the nation's welfare system (West 1981).

Aid to Families with Dependent Children (AFDC) was initially established in 1935 as part of the Social Security Act. It was originally intended to provide cash income assistance to widowed mothers or women abandoned by their husbands so that they could stay home to care for their children. For the first few years of the program, two-parent families were excluded from receiving support unless the father was disabled. Federal rules changed in 1961 to allow states to provide AFDC to children in families in which the father was unemployed, though half of the states elected not to extend support to these families. As such, AFDC remained primarily composed of poor, single mothers and their children.

Though AFDC was guided by a number of federal regulations and requirements, there was room for and great flexibility in its implementation at the state level. Historically, this resulted in wide variations in benefit levels and eligibility requirements from state to state. "In general, southern states which have higher poverty rates, have lower benefits than states in other areas of the country" (McFate 1996: 129). One of the primary objectives of NWRO was to secure support for families that qualified for public assistance but had been discriminated against and denied eligibility in the past. By the 1960s and 1970s, through the activism of NWRO, the racial composition of the AFDC population had changed.

As the complexion of the AFDC rolls changed, so did the public discourse on government assistance to the poor. Now it reflected a racialized, punitive stance among lawmakers and politicians who began to define poverty as a consequence of the moral shortcomings of the poor. Structural problems, such as the absence of child care programs and the unavailability of economic opportunities, were never cited by politicians and public-policy analysts as reasons for the growing proportions of low-income households headed by women.

Instead, lawmakers demonized poor women and children and sought to limit social services to these families. By the early 1970s, AFDC had become the focus of a highly politicized national debate that ultimately increased public antagonism toward the poor. As a result, eligibility requirements for those in need of public assistance were tightened even further and, in some states, severely reduced.

In response to lawmakers' efforts to limit and control AFDC, organizers and leaders of NWRO initially set out to increase aid for poor families and close the gap between the law and its practice by obtaining welfare benefits for as many of the eligible poor as possible (West 1981). Through the activism of NWRO, AFDC caseloads increased from three million recipients in 1960 to 11.4 million in 1975 (Jones 1985).

Under the national leadership of Johnnie Tillmon, a welfare mother of six from Watts, California, NWRO also attacked the unfair characterization of African American women and children. Elected in 1967 as the movement's chair, Tillmon had worked for most of her life in various menial jobs as a maid and laundry worker, making as little as two dollars a day. Following an unexpected illness, she was forced onto public assistance as the only means of supporting her family.

Tillmon's work history belied the false notion of the "lazy, welfare queen." Rather, she epitomized how race, gender, and class could converge to restrict options for employment, providing no alternative but public assistance. Subsistence wages, the absence of a national child care program, and a lack of opportunities for acquiring job skills left poor women economically disadvantaged.

From her experience, and through contact with other mothers receiving government aid, Tillmon recognized that the real goal of poor mothers was self-sufficiency, not wage supplements. In Watts, where she organized one of the first NWRO chapters, Tillmon stressed the importance of job training programs and other services that would help women obtain the skills needed to seek new employment options. While NWRO emphasized the need for a guaranteed income for the poor, Tillmon made clear its purpose was not to replace the fight for jobs, child care, and educational opportunities for poor women.

In the absence of such programs, NWRO managed to bring some change in welfare policies, however. Between 1966 and 1975, the organization mobilized thousands of poor women to confront welfare bureaucracies in state and local governments across the country. In Boston, New York, and other major cities, welfare rights activists staged boycotts, sit-ins, and other demonstrations, demanding higher benefits and a guaranteed income for the poor. Carrying their fight to the courts, the activists played a major role in restructuring the food stamp program and expanding other nutritional and health programs for poor mothers and children.

Most importantly, in the growing public debate over welfare, NWRO served as a vehicle for the politicization of low-income women, through which they could articulate their own analysis of the problems associated with poverty. For the first time, thousands of African American women receiving public assistance attacked the growing myths and stereotypes that stigmatized poor women and children. They criticized the system that limited their options for employment and restricted them to menial jobs at substandard wages.

The tenure of NWRO was short-lived, however. Race and class conflicts eventually split the organization, separating the predominantly African American, female rank-and-file membership from NWRO's national leadership, which was white, male, and middle class. Poor women struggled constantly for more authority and influence in decision making at the national level. Another problem was that, while NWRO had the backing of white liberals and former civil rights activists, it failed to garner enough support from feminist organizations and the traditional civil rights establishment to stay afloat. By 1975, race and class divisions had eroded the nation's first social protest effort by poor women.

THE ROOTS OF BLACK FEMINISM/WOMANISM

Out of the experiences of African American women in the civil rights and black nationalist movements of the late 1960s and early 1970s evolved a politics of black feminism for the twentieth century. In fact, the awareness of the interconnection of race, class, and gender was hardly new; African American women had articulated it nearly a century ago. In particular, the activism of turn-of-the-century club women was deeply rooted in a consciousness of these tripartite structures, as evidenced in their determination to create programs that benefited the entire African American community, across class and gender lines.

By the mid-1960s, the second wave of the women's movement had emerged, as white women active in the civil rights movement began to address gender inequalities within U.S. society. On the basis of their experiences in civil rights organizations notably SNCC—Mary King, Casey Hayden, and others began to draw parallels between the oppression of women and that of African Americans. From the outset, many African

American women felt that the historic differences surrounding race and class foreclosed any serious possibilities for establishing a political alliance with white, middle-class feminists. In 1966, when white female activists in SNCC drafted a position paper on the subordinate status of women in the organization, African American women responded by pointing out that their experiences were quite different.

Cynthia Washington, a SNCC project director in Bolivar County, Mississippi, explained to the position paper's authors that she and other African American women had held key positions of responsibility and authority in SNCC's various southern-based community projects (Washington 1977). She cited examples of African American women's leadership, including the leadership of Ruby Doris Smith Robinson, who played a central role in SNCC's Atlanta office, and Gloria Richardson, who led one of the most effective SNCC campaigns in Cambridge, Maryland. Then there was Diane Nash, a former Fisk University student who pioneered as one of the early freedom riders, traveling throughout the South testing desegregation of interstate transportation terminals. It was Nash who, while pregnant, was arrested and jailed in a Mississippi penitentiary and refused bail.

Washington remarked further that the historic differences in African American and white women's lives lay in the way white women perceived their roles as activists. While white women were demanding independence and more input in decision making, African American women, by contrast, had been thrust into a life of hard work and survival, often with no assistance. What African American women needed, according to Washington, was more support in meeting the demands of work, activism, and child rearing.

Washington also pointed to another problem that would be addressed later by black feminists—the different standards by which African American and white women were viewed by men in SNCC. She stated that while African American women had borne the same organizing responsibilities as men and had gained respect for their skills and abilities, they were somehow defeminized by their male associates, who "seemed to place us in some category other than female" (Washington 1977: 15).

As the women's movement grew and expanded into various ideological streams, African American women, for the most part, continued to address the issue of race. By 1966, when SNCC fell apart, many African American activists turned toward black nationalism, abandoning the strategy of nonviolence and integration for black separatism and self-determination. As the Black Panther Party and other similar organizations emerged, African American women joined the rank and file. From the outset, black nationalist groups were characteristically male dominated, often relegating women to secondary positions. Over time, many women expressed discontent at the male chauvinism within these groups and finally began to withdraw their support.

Meanwhile, a smaller faction of African American women had joined such emergent feminist organizations as the National Organization for Women (NOW) and other predominantly white women's groups. But they were beginning to express frustration and discontent with the racial divisions and narrow, middle-class consciousness they perceived in these circles.

Thus, in response to racial and sexual discrimination, within black and women's groups respectively, African American women began to organize among themselves. They developed a contemporary critique of race, class, and gender that expressed itself politically and intellectually as black feminism—or what they later would describe as "womanism."

The writer Alice Walker first coined the term "womanist" in the opening to her 1983 collection of essays, *In Search of Our Mother's Gardens*. The term expressed African American women's ideological view of women's oppression, which was far more expansive in its challenge to patriarchy than white women's feminism of the time. African American women recognized that their history of resistance against racism alongside African American men required a distinct criticism of male domination, although it did not rule out alliances with men of their race. Sociologist Patricia Hill Collins, for example, articulated the core theme of black feminist consciousness, which Walker sought to capture in her definition of womanism:

> Black women experienced not just racism, but sexism, classism, and other forms of oppression. This struggle in turn fostered a broader, more humanistic view of community that encouraged each individual to develop his or her own individual, unique human potential. Such a community is based on notions of fairness, equality, and justice for all human beings, not just African American women. Black feminism's fundamental goal of creating a humanistic vision of community is more comprehensive than that of other social action movements (Collins 1993: 418).

The growth and development of black feminist consciousness in the early 1970s was reflected in activism, scholarship, and creative expression. The establishment of the National Black Feminist Organization (NBFO) in 1973 provided a political structure for black female consciousness. The works of writers, activists, and artists also generated space for a radical critique and political analysis of the overlapping structures of racism, classism, and sexism.

Among the early, groundbreaking works articulating black feminism was writer and activist Toni Cade's anthology, *The Black Woman*. Published in 1970, the book included an astute analysis of the African American woman's position in an article by Frances Beale entitled, "Double Jeopardy: To Be Black and Female." Other seminal works published during this period included Ntozake Shange's choreopoem, "For Colored Girls who have Considered Suicide When the Rainbow is Enuf' and numerous works of fiction, including Toni Morrison's *The Bluest Eye*. While incarcerated, activist Angela Davis wrote a groundbreaking essay on "Black Women's Roles in the Community of Slaves," followed later by publication of her book, *Women, Race, and Class*.

Gerda Lerner's *Black Women in White America: A Documentary History* (1972) recovered important primary sources and documents which demonstrated African American women's contributions to U.S. society. The groundbreaking collection, *The Afro-American Woman: Struggles and Images* (1978), published by Sharon Harley and Rosalyn Terborg-Penn, was the first volume of essays on African American women.

Several autobiographies by African American women also articulated the themes of black womanism. One was New York Congresswoman Shirley Chisholm's two-part autobiography *Unbought and Unbossed* (1970) and *The Good Fight* (1973). Chisholm was the first African American woman to serve in the House of Representatives and, in 1972, the first African American to bid for the presidential nomination of the Democratic Party. In her autobiographical accounts, Chisholm eloquently documented how the racism and sexism she experienced from male leadership and women's rights groups served to cement a black womanist critique of institutionalized oppression.

The watershed in black feminist/womanist scholarship was the publication, in 1982, of *All the Women Are White, All the Blacks Are Men, But Some of Us Are Brave,* an anthology edited by Gloria T. Hull, Patricia Bell Scott, and Barbara Smith that included the important Combahee River Collective statement on the politics of black feminism. The Combahee River Collective was organized in 1974 by a group of feminist activists in Roxbury, Massachusetts. Their statement became the foundation for a new generation of African American women scholars and activists. In 1977, they wrote that "the most general statement of our politics at the present time would be that we are actively committed to struggling against racial, sexual, heterosexual, and class oppression, and see as our particular task the development of integrated analysis and practice based upon the fact that the major systems of oppression are interlocking" (Smith 1993: 269).

From this point, African American women's studies expanded as an interdisciplinary field in the academy, resulting in a proliferation of black feminist publications which in turn led to works by other scholars and activists including bell hooks, Gloria Wade Gayles, Beverly Sheftall, and Patricia Hill Collins. Within the academy, African American women's history took a leap forward with the establishment of the Association of Black Women Historians in 1979. Darlene Clark Hine, Rosalyn Terborg-Penn, Sharon Harley, Elsa Barkley Brown, and Stephanie Shaw were among the outstanding historians during the 1980s who pioneered in writing the history of African American women.

PROGRESS AND SETBACKS

The decade of the 1970s was a time of increased social and economic opportunities for African Americans. The social protest of the 1960s resulted in the passage of major new federal civil rights legislation. The Civil Rights Act of 1964 banned discrimination in hiring on the basis of race, sex, color, religion, or national origin, making it illegal to discriminate in education and employment. Finally, qualified African American women and men gained access to new education and employment opportunities and jobs in areas previously restricted to them.

African Americans experienced important economic advancements in the early 1970s. "Educational levels and incomes rose, poverty rates fell, Blacks achieved greater access to white-collar jobs, and the Black middle class grew" (Amott and Matthaei 1991: 178). In her study, *Black Women and White Women in the Professions,* Natalie Sokoloff documented that the 1970s was a "particularly remarkable period for black women who experienced a tenfold increased presence in law, medicine, and other prestigious professions" (Sokoloff 1992: 2). The percentage of black women in clerical and service jobs also continued to expand. For example, "between 1950 and 1970, black female clerical employment grew by over half a million, increasing the share of black women workers in these jobs from five percent to 21 percent" (Amott and Matthaei 1991: 179).

Most significantly, these new employment opportunities finally enabled large numbers of African American women to leave the dehumanizing occupation of private domestic service. In 1950, 42 percent of black women were employed as domestic workers; by 1970, that figure had dropped to 18 percent, and by 1980, to five percent (Amott and Matthaei 1991).

While growth in the African American middle class was significant, particularly during the early 1970s, by the middle of the decade, African American economic progress had begun to decline. Paradoxically, as one sector of the African American female population increased its presence in professional and managerial positions, a lack of education and skills left another sector behind.

During the 1980s and 1990s, economic progress among African American professional women continued to expand significantly as it had since the 1970s. This sector of African American women entered higher-paying, career-oriented specialty occupations—a 79 percent increase from 900,000 in 1986 to 1.6 million by 1996 (Department of Labor 1997). Since the 1970s, the number of black women in traditionally male professions—such as law, accounting, medicine, dentistry, and the ministry—has increased, but the majority have remained clustered in traditionally female occupations as registered nurses, elementary school teachers, social workers, and managers and administrators (Higginbotham 1994).

Both African American women and men continue to experience patterns of discrimination in which job ceilings limit their access to various positions within these ranks. As a result, despite the increase among black, female professionals, the number of black women in these positions has remained relatively small: 4.2 percent in 1980 (Higginbotham 1987). Moreover, scholarship on African American professional women documents that the majority of these employees are overly concentrated in the public sector where there has been less discrimination in hiring as a result of affirmative action and other antidiscrimination legislation (Higginbotham 1994). Overall, it is evident that racial and gender discrimination continue to limit African American women's options for employment and advancement. Even African American women with advanced degrees and specialized training still find themselves limited by barriers to occupational progress, in spite of the significant gains over the past thirty years.

Most working black women (60.4 percent in 1996) remained employed in service, technical, sales, and administrative support jobs as cashiers, secretaries, retail sales workers, investigators and adjusters, and data entry operators. Nearly twice as many worked in administrative support jobs as in technical and sales jobs combined—1.7 million as compared with 928,000. These jobs are often contingent in nature, pay low wages, and exclude the full range of benefits associated with managerial and professional positions. In 1996, the leading occupations for black women were nursing aides, orderlies, and attendants; cashiers; and secretaries (see Table II–1).

For another group of African American women, business ownership has opened up some new opportunities. According to the Department of Commerce, black women owned 45 percent of all black-owned businesses in 1992, although these firms had the lowest average earnings of all minority-owned businesses (Department of Labor 1997).

Table II–1 • TEN LEADING OCCUPATIONS FOR EMPLOYED BLACK WOMEN, 1996 (numbers in thousands)

Occupation	Number Employed
Nursing aides, orderlies, and attendants	536
Cashiers	359
Secretaries	290
Supervisors, personal service occupations	268
Retail sales workers, excluding cashiers	191
Janitors and cleaners	176
Cooks	160
Maids	158
Registered nurses	157
Elementary school teachers	151
Social workers	151

Source: Bureau of Labor Statistics, unpublished data from the March 1996 Current Population Survey.

While the 1980s were a time of economic advancement for one segment of African American women, for another they marked the beginning of a steady descent into poverty and unemployment. During the decade of the 1980s, African American families, like other families in the United States, underwent many changes resulting from economic conditions and changing social trends.

One significant occurrence among African American families was the growth of families headed by women. By 1980, nearly half—46 percent of black families—were maintained by women. Over half of these female-headed families had children under age 18. Families headed by women experienced a high incidence of poverty due to limited employment options and low educational attainment. In 1996, black women who worked full-time earned 88 percent of what black men earned, 85 percent of what white women earned, and only 62 percent of what white men earned. Median family income was only 61 percent of what white families earned in 1995. Of nearly half of all black families headed by women, 45 percent of these single-parent households lived in poverty in 1995 and black women were nearly three times as likely to live in poverty and twice as likely to be unemployed as white women who headed families (Department of Labor 1997).

Much controversy fuels the debate around the increase in low-income, African American families headed by women. To be sure, a range of structural problems, including racial and economic discrimination, contributed to this trend. More specifically, families were destabilized by declining rates in African American employment overall, as African American men and women suffered job losses and were unable to find new work. Plant closings in large, urban cities and the shift to overseas production greatly affected the employment patterns of African Americans by the mid-1980s. Between 1975 and 1986, black unemployment averaged 15.2 percent, compared with less than seven percent for whites (Ammott and Matthaei 1991).

Economic hardship no doubt contributed to rising separation and divorce rates among African American families as well. High rates of African American male mortality and incarceration also limited the number of African American men available for marriage. In addition, federal public assistance policies mandated that an unemployed father be absent from the home before families could be eligible for benefits under AFDC. All these factors, compounded by race, class, and gender discrimination, have taken a devastating toll on African American women and their families over the past thirty years.

Conversely, as the number of African American families living in poverty increased, federal assistance to the poor was substantially reduced in the 1980s. Changing budget priorities exacerbated a political precedent set by the Republican administration of President Nixon, which shifted public policy away from government support for poor and low-income families. Previously, under the Democratic administrations of Presidents Kennedy and Johnson, social programs such as the War on Poverty and Great Society increased federal support for the poor, who were disproportionately African American. In contrast, during the 1970s, under President Nixon, many of the programs aimed at alleviating poverty were attacked and dismantled. Nixon's domestic policy agenda blamed the poor for their plight and fueled public antagonism toward those on public assistance.

During this period of regression, public policymakers reverted to an earlier explanation of poverty articulated by social scientists and politicians. New York Senator Daniel Patrick Moynihan's controversial 1965 report, *The Negro Family: The Case for National Action,* written when he worked for the Johnson Administration, stated that the rising rate of African American poverty and the problems associated with it reflected a pathological family structure that was matriarchal and at odds with the traditional two-parent structure of middle-class, white U.S. families.

Moynihan's ethnocentric analysis failed to consider the varieties and differences in family configurations within African American communities. By attributing all the problems of urban poverty to female-headed families, Moynihan and his supporters unfairly blamed African American women for what they called a self-perpetuating "tangle of pathology," which fostered out-of-wedlock births and teenage pregnancy.

Moynihan's thesis was resurrected by neoconservatives in the late 1970s and early 1980s when they sought justification for the retrenchment of social programs. Rather than looking to the structural causes underlying urban poverty—such as the declining number of jobs, the inequitable distribution of wealth, and continuing racism—Moynihan's analysis unfairly characterized poor, African American families and encouraged a frontal attack on African Americans.

DEFENDING OUR NAME: MYTHS AND MISREPRESENTATIONS OF AFRICAN AMERICAN WOMANHOOD IN THE NINETIES

Myths and stereotypes have perpetuated the continuing economic oppression of African American women and their families. Just as African American club women publicly denounced the vilification of African American womanhood at the turn of the century, contemporary African American women have found themselves expending enormous amounts of time and energy correcting and discounting negative images.

The educational and economic progress of African American women in the early 1980s has been explained as a response to government-imposed affirmative action requirements that mandated equal opportunity in the workplace. The widely popularized myth of the "twofer," or double advantage, alleged that African American women's achievements resulted from hiring practices whereby employers sought to fill two requirements—one for minority group participation and one for women—with one person, thereby remaining in compliance with affirmative-action regulations (Fullbright 1987).

Natalie Sokoloff reported that Eleanor Holmes Norton, an African American woman and former chair of the Equal Employment Opportunity Commission, called the "twofer" idea "totally fallacious." Norton, she states, "explained that regardless of what a company or a school might try to get away with, no enforcement agency would give double credit for bringing in a black woman" (Sokoloff, 1992: 2). Sokoloff's study also belied the myth. While black women held 4.9 percent of all professional positions by the 1980s, "they were still the most poorly represented race/gender group in the male-dominated professions. . . . Their numbers in these occupations have been so small that any increase cannot come close to altering the white complexion of the professions overall" (Sokoloff 1992: 97).

The negative misrepresentation of educated African American women was demonstrated dramatically by the 1991 controversy surrounding University of Oklahoma law professor Anita Faye Hill and the nomination of Clarence Thomas to the U.S. Supreme Court. The episode was a watershed in bringing to light African American women's unique status in the United States in relation to race, class, and gender oppression.

On October 11, 1991, Anita Faye Hill appeared before the U.S. Senate Judiciary Committee to defend charges that Clarence Thomas, an African American, Republican nominee to the Supreme Court, had sexually harassed her between 1981 and 1983 when she worked for him at the Equal Employment Opportunity Commission. Her allegations were cause for reconsideration of the Thomas nomination, although the Senate confirmed him by a narrow margin that fall.

The Hill-Thomas controversy played out on national television where, for the first time, a discussion of gender issues in the workplace and racial-sexual stereotypes was subject to full public view. The issue of sexual harassment became the focus of news headlines and raging debates as it resurrected old stereotypes about African American women's oversexuality. What distinguished this case was the conglomeration of race, class, and gender issues that hinged on an African American woman's accusations that an African American man had sexually harassed her.

Historically, the justification for the lynching of African American men had been the alleged sexual attack on white women. When Clarence Thomas charged before national television that he had been the victim of a "high-tech lynching" by news reporters and defenders of Hill, he dramatized the continued victimization of African American women, who had never been afforded protection against this form of sexual violence.

Thomas was supported by some African Americans in spite of his conservatism on a range of political issues. In this case, the race-based support of Thomas invalidated Anita Hill's charges of sexual discrimination, a symbolic representation of African American women's stance at the crossroads of interlocking systems of oppression. Moreover, this case exposed the deeply rooted power relationships, both within and outside of the African American community, that continued to place African American women at the bottom of the social hierarchy.

In response to the public vilification of Anita Hill by the all-white, all-male Senate Judiciary Committee, a group of African American women inserted a full-page statement in the *New York Times* a month later, on November 17, 1991, expressing outrage and support for Hill's courageous stand. In the media blitz surrounding the case, African American women's voices had been the least heard. Three African American professors—

Barbara Ransby, Elsa Barkley Brown, and Deborah King—organized *African American Women in Defense of Ourselves* to counter the distortion of issues at the heart of the controversy.

Later, in a collection of incisive essays on the hearings, African American women scholars wrote of the continuing need for African American women to organize and address the racial and sexual exploitation that confronts them. The collection reminded readers that poor African American women are subject to sexual abuse on a daily basis, rarely receiving the kind of public support that the Yale-educated Anita Hill drew. Moreover, the collection emphasized that while African American women organizers had supported Anita Hill, the tendency to "deify" her should be avoided, given her support for conservative Republican policies that had far-reaching implications for masses of African Americans (Smitherman 1995).

Three years later, in January 1994, a group of African American women in academia again addressed the institutionalization of racism and sexism, as they voiced their concerns about the underrepresentation of African American women in education. Over 2,000 women educators attended a conference at the Massachusetts Institute of Technology. There they drafted an appeal to President Clinton to form a commission to consider race relations, promote African American women's research, and address women of color in academia.

The title of the conference, "Black Women in the Academy: Defending Our Name," took up where African American female opposition to the treatment of Anita Hill left off. This time, African American women—including Angela Davis, Lani Guinier, and former Spelman College President Johnetta Cole—rallied together in support of public-policy initiatives to address poverty, sexism, and racism.

The most vicious negative characterizations of African American women have been directed at poor, single heads of households. The growing conservatism of the Reagan era labeled this group irresponsible, unwilling to work, and the source of all that ails the African American community. The myth of the welfare queen, who sits back and continues to have children while draining the federal dole, gained wide currency during the 1980s.

A CBS Special Report, "The Vanishing Black Family: Crisis in the Black Community," produced by CBS news correspondent Bill Moyers, projected these negative images as it depicted African American teenage parents in southeast Washington, D.C., as representative of all African American families in the United States. Subsequent press coverage and public policies represented a growing chorus of rhetoric aimed at decreasing federal expenditures for the "undeserving poor," who were disproportionately black and female. The welfare system, neoconservatives argued, did not encourage work but was responsible for the breakdown of the family, and particularly for the rising number of out-of-wedlock births.

This steady retreat from federal assistance to the poor culminated in the 1990s "welfare reform" program passed by Congress and signed into law by President Clinton in August 1996 as the Work and Responsibility Act. The new law abolishes Aid to Families with Dependent Children (AFDC), the basic structure for providing income support to poor families with children. Instead, the states are given federal payments, in the form of Temporary Assistance for Needy Families (TANF) block grants, along with broad discretion to spend those funds as they see fit.

One of the law's most radical features is the eradication of the guarantee of federal assistance that was the center of AFDC. Under the old principle of "entitlement," the states were held responsible for providing assistance to eligible families. Under the new block grant system, no family is "entitled" to assistance, and states have the authority to deny aid if they so choose. Those most affected are adolescents, as the act seeks to discourage parenthood among those who are too young to provide for and nurture a child. Recipients over the age of 18 are subject to a lifetime limit of two years of cash assistance, after which they will be required to work, preferably in the private sector (Sawhill 1997).

Opponents of the defederalization of welfare programs speculate that some states may undertake a "race to the bottom" in retracting aid to families in need of assistance, with devastating effects. With the new "reform" legislation, states are free to reduce spending as they see fit or implement waiting lists for families seeking to enroll. Even worse, some states might opt to permanently reduce caseloads and only provide assistance to a new family if an old family leaves (Bane 1997).

The 1996 welfare law will have far-reaching, deleterious consequences for African American families in poverty in the next millennium. The latest figures reveal that one in three black Americans was living in poverty in 1994, compared with fewer than one in ten white Americans. Of the 28 million blacks and whites living in poverty overall, blacks made up almost 40 percent (Rowe and Jeffries 1996). In general, blacks suffer rates of poverty at least two and one-half times those of whites. The racial gap in poverty continues to increase in the absence of jobs and a national child care program and with the persistence of discrimination.

The major structural change in welfare reflects a reversal in the national commitment to children, who are the primary beneficiaries of public assistance. In 1990, the poverty rate for all U.S. children under three was 24 percent, while the poverty rate for African American children under three was 52 percent (*Status of African-American Children* 1992). The task ahead for

African American women is to begin assessing new approaches to ensuring the survival of children and families.

WORKING FOR CHANGE: THE CHALLENGE AHEAD

African American women's strong tradition of community activism will provide a foundation for social and political action in the decades ahead as they extend their leadership roles to a variety of organizational sectors. The leadership models provided by individual African American women heading organizations with broad constituencies illustrate how African American women have used their positions to advocate and advance programs that address race, class, and gender inequities.

During her tenure, from 1978 to 1992, as the first African American woman to head Planned Parenthood Federation of America, Faye Wattleton advocated for the reproductive rights of all women, while fighting for the rights of poor women in particular. Gloria Scott, appointed to serve as the first African American president of the Girl Scouts in 1975, ushered in a whole new era in the organization as she extended the vision of scouting to include more low-income and minority children. Because of her progressive leadership, the Girl Scouts also expanded its agenda to include women's issues, activities for handicapped youth, and programs addressing teenage sexuality.

From her early days as a student at Spelman College in Atlanta, Georgia, Marian Wright Edelman has championed the cause of social justice. In the early 1960s, after graduating from Yale University Law School, she became the first African American woman to pass the bar in Mississippi, where she litigated key school desegregation cases while working for the NAACP Legal Defense Fund. Ms. Edelman helped to establish the first and largest Head Start program in the country, the Child Development Group of Mississippi (CDGM). In 1973, Edelman's advocacy for the rights of children and the poor led her to establish the Washington Research Project, which was later renamed the Children's Defense Fund (CDF) in Washington, D.C. Since that time, she has remained a strong and highly effective leader in advocating for the rights of children.

CDF will face significant challenges in the years ahead. The problem of child poverty has reached immense proportions. Children in the United States, especially minority children, are at greatest risk of being poor. The total number of black children living in poverty increased by 717,000 between 1979 and 1990. This increase was the result of the falling earnings among black parents, the declining effectiveness of government aid in lifting children out of poverty, and the increasing proportion of black children living in female-headed families. "In 1979, 3.8 million black children were in poverty and by 1990, the number had risen to 4.6 million. Nearly half (44.8 percent) of all black children were poor in 1990" (*Progress and Peril* 1993: 28). In 1992, more children were living in poverty than in any other year since 1965 (*The State of America's Children Yearbook* 1994).

Marian Wright Edelman calls for a national agenda for all children in the United States, saying that the crisis transcends racial lines. "The question we must confront," says Edelman, is "the extent to which children can depend on us, and how we organize our society, our government, to help meet children's needs. This question must be considered in contexts that demolish the perception that most of the children needing and getting our help are poor and black. . . . Another is understanding how throughout the history of the United States we have given assistance to families, overwhelmingly white, to help them meet the needs of their children" (Edelman 1987: 27).

Ms. Edelman calls for a partnership between family and government to solve the problem of child poverty. In addition, she advocates community-based, grassroots initiatives to address adolescent pregnancy. In 1984, CDF launched Adolescent Pregnancy Child Watch in collaboration with the National Council of Negro Women, the Association of Junior Leagues, the March of Dimes, and the National Coalition of 100 Black Women. Child Watch trains and helps local volunteers assess the problem of adolescent pregnancy in their communities and find ways to alleviate it. In 1985, CDF implemented a campaign aimed at expanding funding and access to prenatal care for poor and adolescent mothers.

Ms. Edelman has traveled the country extensively in her advocacy for children, and CDF has lobbied and worked tirelessly to sustain a national public education campaign to increase public awareness of the needs of poor families and children. One of the major thrusts of Edelman's activism has been to dispel myths surrounding welfare and teenage pregnancy rates.

CDF has responded to the recent repeal of AFDC and the potential long-range consequences of this action by organizing across race, class, and generational lines. The group recently launched the Black Community Crusade for Children (BCCC), led by a working committee of African American clergy, educators, community leaders, and policymakers. BCCC is mobilizing and building networks of support for children by returning to the civil rights movement's organizing strategies to encourage leadership and advocacy at the local level.

CDF also created the Black Student Leadership Network to prepare college-aged youths to work toward social change for African American children and families. Through the program, more than 400 young adults already have received training in community service and child advocacy at the Ella Baker Child Policy Training Institute. After completing the program, these young adults are placed in community-based Freedom Schools, similar to the ones established in southern communities in the 1960s, where they in turn will educate local residents.

Ms. Edelman recognizes that while these grassroots initiatives will not remedy the problem overnight, they can build effective leadership for social change over time. By necessity, strategies for the next century will entail widening the base of support for family issues and developing a broad, inclusive coalition among diverse groups of individuals and local institutions. As a start, on June 1, 1996, CDF issued a *Stand for Children Day* at the Lincoln Memorial to bring national attention to the issues affecting poor children. The march successfully mobilized a cross section of supporters as the first step in a more intensive fight against the recent retrenchments in federal assistance to the poor.

The ongoing work of the National Council of Negro Women (NCNW) will also be essential to organizing African American women in the twenty-first century. On October 10, 1996, NCNW celebrated the 100th anniversary of the Black Women's Club Movement and inaugurated the National Centers for African American Women which include four components: the Bethune Program Development Center; the Economic and Entrepreneurial Center; the Research, Public Policy, and Information Center; and the Dorothy I. Height Leadership Institute. As NCNW president Dorothy Height reflected on her 40-year tenure and the legacy of leadership established by the organization's founder, Mary McCleod Bethune, she announced that the Leadership Institute will expand on the vision of its foremothers in the twenty-first century by developing new strategies for leadership and social change in the context of contemporary times (*Voices of Vision* 1997).

Across each era in African American history, African American women have responded individually and collectively to address race, class, and gender discrimination. As a broad collective of women's organizations, NCNW holds tremendous power to propel African American women's voices and concerns to the center of the political stage. This influence could be highly effective in electoral politics as well, as African American women run for office themselves or lend support to political candidates who address their concerns and those of African American communities. In addition, the politicization of sororities and other secular organizations on behalf of progressive social change can amass the unharnessed political potential of African American women.

In 1992, a year after the Anita Hill–Clarence Thomas controversy, which brought national attention to sexual harassment and race and gender discrimination in the workplace, an unprecedented number of African American women ran for Congress. In Illinois, a Democrat, Carol Moseley-Braun, was elected to serve as the first African American woman in the Senate. Currently, there are 11 African American women in Congress. In 1992, Cynthia McKinney became the first African American woman elected to Congress from the state of Georgia, where she has been a strong voice on a range of progressive issues.

In spite of these advances by individuals, the leadership potential of African American women has not been fully realized. While African American women indisputably have been the organizers and the strength of mass social movements, male leadership has dominated in all historical contexts, denying African American women access to positions of decisionmaking and authority. Within both the civil rights and the black nationalist movements of the 1960s, African American women struggled to assert their voices but were routinely relegated to less politicized roles. Shirley Chisholm's bid for the Democratic presidential nomination in 1972 was a striking example of strong male resistance to African American women's leadership. In a more recent context, the exclusion of African American women from the 1995 Million Man March called by Minister Louis Farrakhan of the Nation of Islam points to the continuing problem of sexism within the African American freedom struggle.

The subordination of women continues to exist within African American church communities, even though both historically and today, women make up the majority of church membership. In fact, were it not for the women, the mass mobilization of African Americans in the Montgomery bus boycott would not have been possible, nor would the effective organization of local communities. African American women who exercised strong membership in church communities were also historically prominent in secular organizations, in which their activism was a powerful force in sustaining the movement for social change.

In the decades ahead, African American women must continue to challenge male-dominated leadership within their communities and insist on sharing positions of equal authority in the fight for social justice. Their historic experience and understanding of the interlocking structures of race, class, and gender provide a distinctive standpoint essential to shaping future discourse and public policy around a vast range of domestic and global issues. The agenda for the future will call on African American women to expand on the political strategies of the 1950s and 1960s as we continue to organize among ourselves and join in a broad-based, multiracial, working-class coalition to address the problems of the new millennium.

THREE

HISPANIC WOMEN IN THE UNITED STATES

Margarita Benitez

HIGHLIGHTS

THIS CHAPTER DESCRIBES THE CONDITIONS Hispanic women face as they make their way in U.S. society, presents their efforts to break through the barriers of poverty and prejudice, and discusses some of their educational, economic, cultural, and political achievements in recent decades.

- Hispanics are the fastest-growing, and youngest, ethnic group in the nation. Almost 60 percent of the 26.4 million Hispanics living in the continental United States in 1994 were under the age of 30.
- Hispanics are not a homogeneous group. They come from a variety of ethnic, social, and cultural backgrounds. The Hispanic presence in America predates the founding of the United States. Yet Hispanic migration to the United States is an ongoing phenomenon.
- Most Hispanic men and women fill a demand from certain sectors of the U.S. economy for cheap, unskilled, and temporary labor. They work mostly in agriculture and food processing, the service industries, some sectors of manufacturing, and the underground economy.
- The number of Hispanic women in the labor force is expected to grow from four million in 1992 to seven million in 2005. Presently, over 40 percent of employed Hispanic women work in technical, sales, and administrative support occupations. Hispanic women are also the main source of domestic servants, waitresses, cooks, and child care workers in the United States. The question remains whether Hispanic women will be able to break out of the low-wage, dead-end jobs they have today.
- Education is key to the socioeconomic advancement of Hispanic women.

There is much to be done in that field, for Hispanic dropout rates are alarmingly high and the schools most Hispanics attend are among the poorest in the country.

• Still, the stereotype of Hispanic women as undereducated, child laden, and menially employed fails to take into account remarkable strides in education and the advances made by some Hispanic groups and from one generation to the next.

• There has been a significant increase in Hispanic female enrollment at postsecondary institutions across the country. The number of B.A. degrees awarded to Hispanic women has gone from 11,000 in 1981 to 25,500 in 1993.

• A wealth of artistic and literary creations by Hispanic women portray the struggles, conquests, and ambiguities of their lives in the United States. There is also a growing body of scholarly research into the lives of Hispanic women.

• Social, cultural, and political networks have been very important to the advancement of Hispanic women. Dialogue with mainstream U.S. feminism has been impeded, sometimes by the fact that the liberation of white women from housework is often made possible by the subjugation of Hispanic women.

• The increase in Hispanic female elected officials is a national trend, starting at the local level and extending all the way to the U.S. House of Representatives.

AN INTRODUCTION TO HISPANIC ETHNICITY

Hispanic women in the United States have confronted many barriers and challenges, among them cultural isolation, low living standards, limited opportunities for education and employment, and persistent stereotypes. While Hispanic women may face common obstacles in adjusting to life in the United States, they are not a homogeneous group. They bring to this country a rich variety of experiences and characteristics. This chapter describes the conditions Hispanic women face as they make their way in U.S. society, their efforts to break through the barriers of poverty and prejudice, and some of their most significant attainments.

The chapter begins with the causes and origins of Hispanic migration to the United States in order to understand the employment and educational patterns of Hispanic women in this country. It explores how life in the United States has affected the traditional roles of Hispanic women and how Latina women have given voice to their experiences through art and literature. The chapter concludes with a discussion of the empowerment of Hispanic women—through networking, electoral politics, and Latina feminism.

In the United States, "Hispanic" and the more recent "Latino" are umbrella terms that cover many nations, races, and cultures. The original links are the various languages, ancestries, and traditions that run from the Iberian Peninsula through the Americas and the Caribbean, where they blend with strong and diverse indigenous and African strains. Additionally, the population of the Americas has been fed by migratory streams from every continent. Thus, there is no single Hispanic ethnic identifier.

Many U.S. Hispanics maintain strong political, cultural, and economic ties to their countries of origin. Yet their lives in the United States represent a distinct cultural creation. Spanish is the first language for many Hispanics in the United States, but beyond the second generation this is not necessarily the case. While some Hispanics are still bewildered to find themselves classified alongside people from Hispanic cultures they know little about, many are quick to identify themselves as members of the fastest-growing ethnic group in the United States. As the editors of the *Latino Review of Books* point out, "even though each individual Latino group has a different sense of their own nationality and identity, to a large extent, Latinos are finding that their commonalities provide them with a more effective political voice" (Acosta-Belén and Santiago 1995: 4).

"Hispanic" is at present the designation most commonly used in government documents, while "Latino" and "Latina" are the identifying terms of choice among assertive U.S.-born Hispanics. As new generations appropriate a label that did not recognize their distinct cultural identities in its original English form ("Latins"), they lay claim to an emerging panethnic identity that includes the experience of being a minority in the United States. In this article, "Hispanic" refers to all persons of Hispanic origin who live in the continental United States, regardless of where they were born, and "Latino/Latina" refers specifically to the U.S.-born and to their growing cultural and political awareness.

NUMBERS, ORIGINS, AND DESTINATIONS OF HISPANICS IN THE UNITED STATES

According to the Bureau of the Census, there were 6.9 million Hispanics living in the mainland United States (three percent of the total population) in 1960. By 1992, the mainland count had grown to 24.2 million Hispanics (9.5 percent). Another 3.5 million Hispanics lived in the Commonwealth of Puerto Rico. Particularly striking is the 61 percent increase in the Hispanic U.S. population between 1970 and 1980—from 9.1 million (or 4.5 percent of the total population) to 14.6 (or 6.4 percent of the total population). This increase was almost seven times greater than the national population growth rate of nine percent (Bean and Tienda 1987). The number of Hispanic women over 16 years old increased by 70 percent between 1977 and 1988, from 3.9 million to 6.7 million. In 1996, a total of 9.6 million Hispanic women resided in the United States (Bureau of Labor Statistics 1997).

Today, about one out of every 10 U.S. inhabitants is Hispanic. Hispanics as a whole are a remarkably young population: their median age is 26, and almost 60 percent are under the age of 30. In 1996, a third of the Hispanic population in the United States was under 15 years old. If present rates of population growth continue, by 2030, one in five persons in the United States will be Hispanic, and Hispanics will make up 25 percent of the total school population, with Hispanics age five to 18 numbering almost 16 million (President's Advisory Commission 1996).

Among the causes of these marked increases are high fertility rates among Hispanic women (50 percent higher than among white women) and ongoing immigration from Latin America (National Latina Institute for Reproductive Health 1996). It is likely that there were many more Hispanics in the United States in the 1960s and 1970s than were recorded by the Bureau of the Census. Illegal immigrants to the United States and seasonal agricultural workers are largely Hispanic. Mexicans alone are believed to account for 60 percent of illegal immigrants. Over the past three decades, census criteria and methodology for ethnic identification have been developed and refined to address the problem of undercounting among minority populations.

In its 1996 report, *Our Nation on the Fault Line: Hispanic American Education,* the President's Advisory Commission on Educational Excellence for Hispanic Americans stated:

> In 1994, there were 26.4 million Hispanic Americans living in the Continental United States: 64 percent Mexican Americans, almost 11 percent Puerto Ricans, over 13 percent were from Central and South America and the Caribbean, almost 5 percent were Cuban Americans, 7 percent classified as "other." An additional 3.7 million were Puerto Ricans living on the island of Puerto Rico, bringing the nation's total Hispanic American population to over 30 million. Although Hispanic Americans live in every part of the United States, they are more heavily concentrated in Arizona, California, Colorado, Florida, Illinois, New Mexico, New York, Puerto Rico, and Texas (President's Advisory Commission 1996).

Historical, political, and economic factors illuminate the diversity of the Hispanic presence in the United States—its demographics, geographical distribution, and labor force participation. It is sometimes forgotten that this presence predates not only the formation of the United States but also the founding of the British colonies. Spanish explorers arrived in North America early in the sixteenth century, and Spanish missionaries and settlers followed shortly thereafter. Beyond the U.S. Southwest, in areas as remote from each other as Oregon and Louisiana, Spanish words, place names, architecture, and urban design bear witness to Spain's far-reaching influence from the sixteenth to the eighteenth centuries.

When Mexico won independence from Spain in 1821, its national territory included the vast region that eventually became the states of California, Nevada, Texas, Utah, and parts of Arizona, New Mexico, Colorado, Kansas, Oklahoma, and Wyoming. Less than three decades later, the United States waged war against Mexico. Mexico was defeated and forced to relinquish over half of its national territory in the 1848 Treaty of Guadalupe Hidalgo. Thus, the citizens of Northern Mexico became the disenfranchised dwellers of the Southwest Territories of the United States.

Other wars also have augmented the Hispanic populations under the U.S. flag, though not necessarily of their own volition. The 1898 Spanish-American War brought the Philippines, Cuba, and Puerto Rico under U.S. hegemony, where Puerto Rico remains to this day. In this century, U.S. involvement in civil wars, revolutions, and counterrevolutions in Latin America and the Caribbean have had significant migratory aftermaths. The most salient examples are the migrations from Cuba (since 1959), from the Dominican Republic (in the 1960s), from Nicaragua and El Salvador (in the 1970s and 1980s), and from Guatemala (since the 1950s). These Hispanic populations have congregated mostly in Florida, with significant numbers also settling in New York, New Jersey, and Massachusetts. In the past 15 years, there has been a remarkable influx of Central Americans to Washington, D.C. Today, there are clusters of practically every Latin American nationality—most noticeably Colombians, Peruvians, Ecuadorians, Argentineans, and Chileans—throughout the United States.

SHIFTING PATTERNS OF MIGRATION, EMPLOYMENT, AND EDUCATION

Hispanic migration to the United States in this century has been fueled by the political and economic instability of many Latin American countries and by expectations of better wages, per capita income, and living standards. Immigration policies in the United States seldom take into account systematic research and analysis of trends. They are influenced more often by public pressure, anecdotal evidence, and ethnic stereotyping (Portes and Rumbaut 1997; Cornelius 1995). Beneath and beyond official immigration policies are the powerful messages of film and television, the lure of the marketplace, and the interpretations of government policies and breakthrough opportunities transmitted through ethnic grapevines that function informally as transnational information networks.

Immigrants come to a new country driven not just by their own needs but by transnational economic forces and the requirements of the host society. Those requirements play a major role in how immigrants are integrated into the dominant culture. For instance, from the 1880s to the 1950s, Mexican migration to the United States supplied the demands of the agriculture, mining, and railroad industries in the Southwest. Mexicans settled mostly in rural areas, where they lived apart from Anglos and had a low socioeconomic status (Bean and Tienda 1987). Mexican women worked as domestics, laundresses, and seamstresses. These patterns of low-paying employment and residential segregation continued even as Mexican immigrants started to locate in the cities in the 1930s.

Since agriculture was slow to mechanize, significant numbers of Mexican workers were used—and still are used today—for strenuous, low-paying, and seasonal work. Although farm workers traditionally have been mostly male, women and children participated in the backbreaking work of the fields, as well as in efforts to improve working conditions spearheaded by organizations such as the United Farm Workers (UFW). Women such as Dolores Huerta, Lucy Parsons, and Luisa Moreno strove to attain job security, healthy working conditions, better wages, and benefits for workers.

Today, Hispanics fill a demand from certain sectors of the U.S. economy for cheap, unskilled, and temporary labor. They often take menial jobs at the lowest wages their employers can get away with, thereby earning the resentment of unionized workers from earlier migratory groups. Obviously, Hispanics do not choose such working conditions. Rather, those are often the only jobs they can obtain because of the wide gap between high-tech, high-paying jobs and menial, low-paying or part-time work. This polarization is a worldwide phenomenon due to the internationalization of capital investments, also known as the global economy. Internationally, many of the Third World countries are providing cheap labor to substitute for high-wage manufacturing work in the First World countries. In the United States, immigrants in general, and immigrant women in particular, work in low-paying, unskilled occupations, because that is what the economy needs and wants from them. In the present global economy, an economically integrated world system remains segregated by ethnicity and gender.

Thus, most Hispanics, and women especially, work in fields that impede upward mobility. These include agriculture and food processing, the service industries (especially maintenance, domestic work, and custodial services), some sectors of manufacturing, and the underground economy. The decline in U.S. manufacturing has adversely affected the employment of Hispanic women. Whereas in 1960, Puerto Rican women had the highest participation rate in the manufacturing industry of any ethnic group in the United States, at 69.3 percent, by 1990 their share had declined to 16.1 percent (Amott and Matthaei 1996). Chicanas' employment in manufacturing went from 29.1 to 20 percent during the same time period. This drastic decline resulted from the relocation of manufacturing industries from the Mid-Atlantic region to other parts of the United States and overseas (Nieves–Rosa 1997).

The so-called Nannygate scandal in the first year of the Clinton Administration revealed a key paradox in the complex relations between women in minority groups and women in the dominant culture. It became apparent that the success of many accomplished women in the United States relied on the availability of Hispanic nannies to look after their children and homes. Two of these successful women could have become the nation's chief law enforcement officer, but they were tainted by the illegal status of their indispensable Hispanic nannies. It also came to light that some of the most ardent defenders of legislation against illegal aliens had employed them in their homes for years. What the Hispanic nannies thought about Nannygate and how it changed their lives was not recorded.

The continued influx of Hispanic migration has perpetuated the divide between the dominant Anglo culture and the mostly negative ethnic and socioeconomic stereotypes of Hispanics. Although many Hispanics in the United States have achieved economic success and interact with ease in English-speaking circles, Hispanic women tend to be portrayed in the media and public discourse as unassimilated, undereducated, child laden, and menially employed.

While there are elements of truth in that image, it ignores the multiplicity of Hispanic experiences in the United States and the changes occurring within Hispanic communities. Moreover, this image does not consider the swift economic progress of some Hispanic groups, or the educational and economic advancements from one generation to the next, even among seriously disadvantaged Hispanics. Cubans clearly illustrate the first experience, and Puerto Ricans the latter.

As an ethnic group, Cubans make up the most notable success story of Hispanic migration. They have the highest standard of living and achievement of all Hispanic groups. The first waves of immigrants after the Cuban revolution came from the Cuban elite, and many brought professional skills with them to the United States. Also, unlike most migrant groups, Cubans received federal settlement assistance. Yet, until the time of the Mariel boatlift in 1980, most Cuban exiles experienced a downward plunge on the social ladder. This plunge was felt very strongly by Cuban women, many of whom had known leisure and luxury in their homeland. The abrupt loss of their homes, the separation from extended families, the fears for their children in a new, permissive, and often violent society, and the daily pressures of their diminished circumstances were difficult to bear.

The first jobs that Cuban exiles found in the United States were often far beneath the positions they had held in Cuba. Doctors, lawyers, and intellectuals were performing unskilled labor. Many women who had never worked outside the home used their domestic skills to enter the labor market, formally or informally, as seamstresses, beauticians, cooks, housecleaners, and caretakers. Their earnings were low because they often worked part time, in family-run businesses, or from their homes. Yet Cuban women were important to the successful development of the Cuban enclave economy in Miami and surrounding areas. It was women who maintained and strengthened the social and familial bonds of prerevolutionary Cuba, who eased the integration of successive waves of neighbors and relatives, who emphasized education, and who insisted on buying their food, supplies, and services from other Cubans.

Ethnic enclave economies are based on the mutual support networks immigrants establish to survive and progress in a new country. Bonded by the language, customs, and social hierarchies of the old country, as well as by the prejudices of the dominant culture, immigrant groups construct an economic foundation and create employment opportunities by giving business to each other. The success of the Cuban enclave economy is well documented. Cubans are a driving force in Miami business, banking, and construction; in Latin American trade; and in the Florida food, textile, and cigar industries. In several areas, the socioeconomic profile of Cuban women resembles that of white women. They typically are older and better educated than other Hispanic women and have a higher divorce rate. Some scholars contend that the social structures of prerevolutionary Cuba were transplanted to Miami and that later Cuban arrivals from a lower socioeconomic background came to be reunited with their former masters (Bean and Tienda 1987). Nonetheless, Cubans consistently rank higher than all other Hispanic groups in statistical measures of socioeconomic achievement.

Many indicators put Puerto Ricans in the United States, the only Hispanic migrants who are U.S. citizens from birth, at the low end of the socioeconomic spectrum. An estimated 14.2 percent of all U.S. families and 9.4 percent of whites lived below the poverty level in 1991 (Bureau of the

Census 1993). The percentage rose to 28.7 percent for Hispanics and to 39.4 percent for Puerto Ricans. Among female-headed households, 66.3 percent of Puerto Rican families fell below the poverty level. Except for Cubans, the percentage of female-headed households among Hispanic groups hovered between 42.9 percent for families of Central and South American origin and 47.7 percent for families of Mexican origin in 1991 (Bureau of the Census 1993).

Other statistics show more promising trends for Puerto Rican families. A study of Puerto Ricans in the United States, based on the 1990 Census, documented improvements. According to the study, labor force participation by Puerto Rican women rose from 40.3 percent in 1980 to 50.7 percent in 1990. Earnings rose by 20 percent among women and 9.2 percent among men from 1980 to 1990. The median household income per capita increased by nearly 30 percent from 1980 to 1990, the highest increase among any single ethnic group in the United States (Rivera-Batiz and Santiago 1994).

However, the same study shows that not all Puerto Ricans shared in the gains of the 1980s. Those with less than a high school education fell on the economic scale, with first generation and unskilled migrants having an increasingly difficult time. The trend toward economic polarization is also evident within the Puerto Rican community.

The variations found among Hispanic groups suggest that more than a unidimensional socioeconomic profile is needed to understand the complex and changing socioeconomic patterns of Hispanics in the United States.

HISPANIC WOMEN IN THE LABOR FORCE

By 1986, 50 percent of Hispanic women were participating in the paid labor force (Women's Bureau 1994a). The labor force participation rate of Hispanic women age 20 and older ranged from 54.4 percent in 1994 to 55.2 percent in 1996. In January 1997, the participation rate was 57.6 percent. The labor force participation rate for Hispanic males ranged from 82.5 percent in 1994 to 83.0 percent in 1996 (Bureau of Labor Statistics 1997).

Department of Labor statistics show that women have been the primary source of new entrants into the labor force in the past quarter-century. Hispanic women are among the fastest growing groups of working women in the United States. Their total employment increased from 2.1 million in 1983 to 5.1 million in 1996, when there were 61.8 million women in the civilian labor force (Women's Bureau 1994b; Bureau of Labor Statistics 1997). Among Hispanic women, Cubans showed the highest labor force participation rate.

Over 40 percent of employed Hispanic women work in technical, sales, and administrative support occupations. These jobs include sales workers, cashiers, secretaries, receptionists, bookkeepers, and teacher aides. Hispanic women are also overrepresented in the service occupations. They are the main source of domestic servants, waitresses, cooks, and child care workers in the United States. They are also overrepresented in the operator, fabricator, and laborer occupations, where they work mostly as textile sewing machine operators (Women's Bureau 1994b; Bureau of the Census 1997). These are entry-level or dead-end positions that offer few opportunities for financial or professional advancement. Median weekly earnings for Hispanic women were $318 in 1996 (Bureau of Labor Statistics 1997). In addition, the Department of Labor projects that many of the service and manufacturing occupations in which Hispanic women work will grow slowly or decline in the future.

Most official statistics do not record the underground or informal economy—transactions that occur partly or totally outside legal regulation—and the roles Hispanic women play in it. The informal economy, which includes criminal activity, is found in the ghettos, or *barrios,* where minorities live. But it is not limited to these areas, nor is it isolated from the economically powerful. Many social scientists refer to the informal sector as "an integral part of advanced capitalist economies," and identify subcontracting as the means most often used to link the informal and formal economies (Fernández-Kelly and García 1985). They also posit a link between the decline in union membership and the upsurge of the informal economy in advanced industrial societies (Safa 1995). The informal sector offers lower costs and a docile and nonunion workforce with no employee benefits or taxes and limited paperwork.

Studies indicate that within the informal economy there are at least two groups: the workers, who are vulnerable from all sides, and the entrepreneurs and agents (Fernández-Kelly and García 1985). Most women in the informal economy are unprotected workers. They work in sweatshops, back rooms, bars, and brothels and on the streets. Few women are found above the lower echelons of informal entrepreneurship. Entrepreneurs and agents are mostly male. Some run underground operations and some deal with the formal sector. Those who belong to the lower and middle echelons of this group are often from the same ethnic group as the workers.

The informal sector offers the new arrival a place to start and familiar faces. For an illegal immigrant, it is often the only recourse. For some who work in the formal sector, it is a way to make money on the side. The frequent inconsistencies among government mandates and regulations facilitate the expansion of the informal economy (Fernández-Kelly and García 1985).

Most Cuban women have benefited from their involvement in Miami's informal economy. But the experience of most Hispanic women is quite different. Mexican American women in the Los Angeles garment industry, Dominican and Puerto Rican women in New York sweatshops, and sex workers and domestics from every Hispanic ethnic group in the nation all work very hard, get paid very little, and have no recourse to legal protection.

The Department of Labor projects that the number of Hispanic women in the U.S. labor force will grow from four million in 1992 to seven million in 2005 (Women's Bureau 1994b). That would be a 72 percent increase, one of the largest of any ethnic or gender group in the United States. An 80 percent labor force participation rate is foreseen for Hispanic women by 2005 (President's Advisory Commission 1996). The question is, how many Hispanic women will be able to break out of the low-wage dead-end jobs they have today? The 1991 median annual earnings of Hispanic women working full time were $16,244—78 percent of what non-Hispanic women earned in the same occupations. In 1996, median annual earnings for Hispanic women remained in that range—$16,536 (Bureau of the Census 1997).

A major realignment must occur in the labor force distribution and earning patterns of Hispanic women if they are to progress economically and professionally. Yet the global economic trends described previously do not bode well for such a realignment.

Looking at the younger generation, we find that Hispanic teenage girls have a much higher unemployment rate (26.4 percent in 1993) than white female teenagers (14.6 percent). The highest rate is among African American female teenagers (37.2 percent in 1993) (Women's Bureau 1994). Birth rates are also very high among Hispanic teenagers: 106.9 per 1,000 births compared with 40.2 per 1,000 non-Hispanic teen births. Less than half of Hispanic mothers (47 percent) have 12 or more years of schooling, compared with 86 percent for whites and 70 percent for blacks (National Latina Institute for Reproductive Health 1996). It is well known that female-headed households lead all national poverty indicators. In 1994, 46 percent of Hispanic children in female-headed households were living in poverty. Single Hispanic mothers who are young and uneducated are not going to make it very far in the job market.

HISPANIC WOMEN AND EDUCATION

Education is a key to socioeconomic advancement. Statistics and studies consistently point to a strong correlation between schooling and earnings, as well as to an increasing polarization between the earnings of workers with less than a high school education and those of college graduates. For Puerto Ricans, known as the poorest of the poor among U.S. Hispanics, the 1990 poverty rate was 22.3 percent for those with a high school education and 40.1 percent for those without. The 1990 poverty rate was 13.9 percent for Puerto Ricans with some college education, 8.4 percent for those completing college, and 6.4 percent for those with more than a college degree (Rivera-Batiz and Santiago 1994).

Recent studies show that finishing high school is not enough to make a significant difference in job opportunities and earnings. The real difference is seen after college (Nieto 1996–97). The President's Advisory Commission on Educational Excellence for Hispanic Americans reports that the educational attainment of most Hispanics is in a state of crisis. In the two decades between 1973 and 1994, the percentage of Hispanics taking part in preschool programs has held steady at 15 percent, while white preschool enrollment has increased from 18 to 35 percent. The school districts most Hispanics attend are among the poorest and most technologically behind in the country. This means that Hispanic children do not acquire early the skills they need to get ahead. Hispanics also drop out of school earlier than whites and at much higher rates. Forty percent of Hispanic dropouts do not complete eighth grade. The dropout rate for Hispanics 16 to 24 years old is more than three times that of whites (28 percent for Hispanics, eight percent for whites, and 14 percent for African Americans) (President's Advisory Commission 1996).

Hispanics also lag behind whites and African Americans in gains in college enrollment. Between 1973 and 1994, white high school enrollment in four-year institutions of higher education increased from 16 to 33 percent. During the same period, African American enrollment increased from 13 to 25 percent and Hispanic enrollment increased from 13 to 20 percent. In 1993, Hispanics only earned six percent of all associate degrees, four percent of B.A. degrees, three percent of M.A. degrees, and two percent of Ph.D.s. These percentages have barely changed since the 1980s. Only 946 of the 43,261 Ph.D.s awarded in the United States in 1994 went to Hispanics (President's Advisory Commission 1996). Disparities in college completion rates between whites and Hispanics are growing. In 1992, the gap between the proportion of Hispanic and white high school graduates who had completed a college degree was 15 percentage points. In 1996, the gap had grown to 21 percentage points (National Education Goals Panel 1997).

The good news is that Hispanic women have made real strides in educational achievement in recent years. There has been a significant increase in Hispanic female enrollment at postsecondary institutions across the country. Most Hispanic men and women attend two-year colleges, where their rate of completion of associate degrees is similar to that of whites. There also has been a marked upward trend in the number of B.A. degrees awarded to Hispanic females—from 11,000 in 1981 to 25,500 in 1993. This 131.8 percent increase is the second highest in the United States (Asians rated first, with a 201.1 percent increase) (National Center for Education Statistics 1997). Despite this progress, the number of Hispanic women in the educational pipeline is still relatively low when compared with the total population, whites, and other ethnic groups. Thus, while these percentage gains are impressive, concerted efforts will be needed to change current policies and practices so that the educational achievements of Hispanic women may continue.

BEARING WITNESS: THE VOICES OF HISPANIC WOMEN

The harsh facts of migration, prejudice, and poverty—and the many adjustments to life in the United States—have had a profound effect on the traditional center of Hispanic life: the family. Often Hispanic women have been physically separated from their families and migration has posed new demands and challenges for both women and men.

Most Hispanic women in the United States have experienced social and cultural dislocation in practically every aspect of their lives, finding the ways of the old country very different from those of the new, particularly with respect to women's roles. For women, the preservation of Hispanic traditions usually has meant maintaining cultural roles far more restricted and subservient than those of many women in U.S. society. At the same time, to live in the United States does not necessarily bring liberation to Hispanic women. They find few opportunities for economic advancement, endure ethnic and sexual stereotyping, and may experience continual loneliness. On the other hand, possibilities exist for women in the United States that are rare in traditional societies. Among these are privacy, consumer goods, geographical mobility, contraceptive and sexual alternatives, certain forms of state assistance, and state protection against domestic violence.

Latina writers and artists have portrayed in great detail the ambivalence experienced by Hispanic women as they struggle to define their identities, their roots, and their destinations. The reconstruction of memory is a primary theme of their works. Many Latina writings take the form of testimonials. They attempt to recreate the worlds of female ancestors or to speak for their own generation. Latina writers often create girl characters and take them from childhood to adulthood and from the village to the *barrio* to convey the painful shock of departure, alienation, and prejudice that marks their growing up, and the ensuing loneliness that makes them seek affection in disastrous relationships. For the women in these stories, men who insist on traditional relationships are a difficult habit to break, while lovers from other cultures pose their own difficulties. Generational tensions add to the cultural turmoil, as parents and grandparents attempt to hold on to traditional ways while their children struggle to make their way in the brave new world of the United States. These themes appear in the writings of Puerto Ricans Nicholasa Mohr, Esmeralda Santiago, and Judith Ortiz Cofer; Cubans Cristina García and Dolores Prida; Dominican Julia Alvarez; and Chicanas Sandra Cisneros, Denise Chávez, Gloria Anzaldúa, and Ana Castillo, to name only a few.

Many recent Latina works are rich with references to the mythical homeland. It appears as a lost paradise that perhaps never existed but nevertheless offers warm reassurance in the cold winter of an exile's discontent. Many Latina artists, like Chicana painters Amelia Mesa-Baines and Santa Barraza and ceramist Marsha Gómez, draw from the wealth of imagery in pre-Columbian myth as well as the multiracial traditions of their countries of origin. Indeed "origin" is one of the key concepts behind Latina art. The late Cuban conceptual artist Ana Mendieta explored Afro-Caribbean magic and religious ritual and created provocative art works by blending her body with the earth and with water, fire, and blood in a "search for origin" also undertaken by other Latina artists.

Similar themes are present in the work of Puerto Rican painter and sculptor Nitza Tufiño, who was born in Mexico and now lives in New Jersey. Tufiño is involved with public and experimental art. She explores female imagery through the recreation of ancestral designs, the use of masks, and the combination of apparently dissimilar materials and forms.

The world-renowned Mexican muralist tradition is alive and well among such Chicana artists as Diane Gamboa, Yreina Cervantez, Margaret García, and Linda Vallejo. Besides celebrating their cultural traditions and their current lifestyles, these artists present the contradictions between the stated goals of liberty and justice for all in the United States and the plight of Hispanic peoples. In 1981, Barbara Carrasco was asked to paint a mural in downtown Los Angeles to portray the history of the city. She did so from a critical Chicana perspective, depicting racism, violence, and poverty. An uproar ensued, which increased when she refused to tone the mural down, as requested by the funding agency. The mural survived, but it is now in a United Farm Workers building, instead of outdoors in full public view (Shorris 1992).

Latina poets also are having their say and speaking up for the women who preceded them. Chicana poet Lorna Dee Cervantes gives voice to the cultural ambivalence of her generation:

Mama raised me without language.
I am orphaned from my Spanish name.
The words are foreign, stumbling
on my tongue. I see in the mirror
my reflection: bronzed skin, black hair.

I feel I am a captive
aboard the refugee ship.
The ship that will never dock.
El barco que nunca atraca.

In her poem "For Ana Veldford," Cuban poet Lourdes Casal conveys the poignancy of displacement:

This is why I will always remain on the margins,
a stranger among the stones
even beneath the friendly sun of this summer's day,
just as I will remain forever a foreigner,
even when I return to the city of my childhood
I carry this marginality, immune to all turning back,
too habanera to be a neoyorkina,
too neoyorkina to be
—even to become again—
anything else.

Yet for the Puerto Rican poet Aurora Levins Morales, cultural displacement leads to a renewed and joyous consciousness, as expressed in the poem "Child of the Americas" from her collection *Getting Home Alive*:

I am not african. Africa is in me, but I cannot return.
I am not taína. Taíno is in me, but there is no way back.
I am not european. Europe lives in me, but I have no home there.

I am new. History made me. My first language was spanglish.
I was born at the crossroads
and I am whole.

Besides fiction and poetry, personal testimonies and oral histories of the travails of Hispanic women of earlier generations are being gathered and studied as a scholarly labor of love by some of their descendants who grew up to be academics in the United States. The most ambitious of these initiatives is the *Recovering the U.S. Hispanic Literary Legacy Project,* begun in 1990. The project is a major scholarly undertaking to discover, recover, preserve, study, annotate, and disseminate the literature produced by Hispanic communities in North America from colonial times to 1960. It includes diaries, journals, letters, periodicals, and memoirs, as well as traditional literary genres. Researchers are finding that a remarkable number of Hispanic women recorded their thoughts and experiences in writing. The Recovery Project is based at the University of Houston, with work sites at Stanford, SUNY at Albany, Florida International University, and Colorado College.

THE EMPOWERMENT OF HISPANIC WOMEN: NETWORKING, FEMINISM, AND POLITICAL ACTION

Hispanic women's networks have taken a number of forms. Some—including family, neighborhood and old-country groups, religious associations, social clubs, and sewing or reading circles—are rooted in tradition and culture. Others have the specific purpose of helping women to face new circumstances. Both have led to significant social and political action. Many of the latter groups—labor unions, professional associations, mutual aid societies, and tenants' and parents' associations—already existed in the mainstream culture.

Initially, most Hispanic women's associations were directed toward community service, particularly before the New Deal brought significant federal assistance programs for the poor. World War II provided a focus for community activity in support of the U.S. war effort, as well as new occupational opportunities for women. Hispanic women rose to the occasion, working on railroads, in steel mills and factories, and in a number of war-related occupations, including the weapons and aircraft industries (Santillán 1990). After the war, most women returned to more traditional occupations and Hispanic war veterans found themselves relegated to second-class status. The strengths and skills that many women gained during the war were put to use years later in civil rights and political efforts.

The awakening of Hispanics as a political force in the United States began in the postwar period and reached national prominence in the 1960 Kennedy presidential campaign, with the Viva Kennedy clubs that sprouted in the Southwest, Midwest, and Northeast. The civil rights struggles of the 1960s, the antiwar movement, and the climate of political activism of the 1970s brought a new radical dimension to Hispanic self-affirmation. Groups like La Raza Unida Party and the Brown Berets in the Southwest and Midwest, and the Young Lords in the Northeast and Midwest drew their membership from the Latino youth that had grown up in the urban ghettos. While Latinas participated in all these movements, they found—like women in other political and ethnic affirmation movements—that even there they were expected to play traditional women's roles.

The U.S. feminist movement in the 1960s and 1970s was no doubt important for Latina women, but it must be remembered that it was spearheaded by middle-class white women, whose experiences and priorities were quite different from those of Latinas. The socioeconomic inequities between white and Latina women—specifically the undeniable fact that the liberation of white women from housework and child care is often made possible by the subjugation of Latina women—have impeded a more productive dialogue. Nonetheless, feminism has served as a meeting and learning ground for women of various ethnic groups in U.S. society.

In the past decade, there has been an increase in the numbers of Hispanic women elected to political office at many levels. *The 1992 Census of Governments,* released by the Bureau of the Census in 1995, reveals that the percentage of Hispanic women holding public office rose from 18.4 percent in 1987 to 22.6 percent in 1992. Overall, the number of female Hispanic local elected officials increased by 33 percent between 1987 and 1992, whereas their male counterparts increased by three percent (Brischetto 1997). New Mexico is the only state where the proportion of Hispanic elected officials is commensurate with the size of the Hispanic population. Although still out of proportion to the number of Hispanic women in the U.S. population, the increase in Hispanic female political representation is encouraging. Another promising development is the election to Congress of Hispanic women over well-known white men—Puerto Rican Nydia Velázquez (the first Puerto Rican woman in Congress) over New York Congressman Stephen Solarz in 1992, and liberal Democrat Chicana Loretta Sanchez over conservative Republican California Congressman Robert Dornan in 1996.

There are currently four Hispanic congresswomen in the House of Representatives. The other two are Lucille Roybal-Allard from California and Ileana Ros-Lehtinen from Florida, the only Republican among the four. Congresswoman Roybal-Allard is heir to the distinguished political tradition of her father, former Congressman Edward R. Roybal. Congresswoman Ros-Lehtinen is the first Cuban American woman in Congress. These four congresswomen have come together in the spirit of bipartisanship to support legislation on behalf of the rights of women, Hispanics, the elderly, migrants, and the urban poor. They vigorously oppose legislation to make English the official language of the United States and have spoken out against the rising wave of anti-immigrant sentiment in this country.

CONCLUSION

As we close out one century and look toward a new one, it is evident that Hispanic women confront many challenges—among them low income, limited employment opportunities, and educational barriers. Nevertheless, Hispanic women show endurance and initiative. They are rising above great difficulties to make significant gains in educational achievement. They are redefining their past, present, and future through new and daring works of art and literature. And they are grasping political power and using it to work for a broad range of policy changes. As the Hispanic population increases, the voices of Hispanic women in the United States will become even stronger and more influential.

FOUR

WOMEN AND THE LAW: LEARNING FROM THE PAST TO PROTECT THE FUTURE

Sonia J. Jarvis

HIGHLIGHTS

MOST AMERICANS WOULD ASSUME that the legal status of women in the United States today is so well established that it is not subject to significant challenges. However, American women's legal status is surprisingly fragile, as its foundation rests on a handful of cases dating from the mid-1960s and a few federal statutes. How well women fare in securing their rights to personal autonomy, equality in the workplace, and more equitable representation in the political process will depend on their willingness to meet persistent social, economic, and political challenges. This chapter illustrates the evolution of women's legal rights over the past 100 years.

- One hundred years ago, a woman's legal status was largely defined by her marital status. Women were subject to physical and economic domination by their husbands, with little recourse to the courts, while single or unmarried women with children often faced social ostracism and were in legal limbo.
- Limitations on a woman's rights included the inability to establish a legal identity separate from that of her husband, to control her reproductive capacity, to sue or be sued, to own property in her own name, or to pursue a career of her choice.
- Women were completely locked out of the political process. They could neither vote nor hold political office until ratification of the Nineteenth Amendment to the U.S. Constitution, and they were prevented from serving as jurors until the 1960s.
- Women of color faced further restrictions on their legal rights, due to vir-

ulent racism and segregated political, economic, and social circumstances. Poor women suffered further deprivations because of class discrimination.

- The status of women under the law began to change once women began organizing for their political rights and voting for policies that were in their interests. Women's participation in the abolition of slavery and the temperance movement helped to prepare them for the hard work involved in changing public opinion about the suitability of women's economic and political participation. Passage of the Nineteenth Amendment in 1920 was the result of consistent grassroots organizing and political pressure that began as early as 1848.

- Over the past 30 years, a number of legal rights for women have been recognized by federal and state courts, including: the right to maintain a separate legal identity regardless of marital status; the right to privacy in decisions regarding reproduction, personal autonomy, and marital status; and the right to bodily integrity regardless of marital status.

- Women may now sue for damages if subjected to job discrimination on the basis of sex, pursue work in nontraditional fields, and continue working when pregnant.

- Courts have recognized women's right to equal educational opportunities in secondary schools and institutions of higher learning, including access to intercollegiate sports.

- Since the 1960s, women have made real gains in career opportunities and political participation. However, some warning signs are emerging. Certain federal statutes and policies, such as affirmative action, that allowed women to advance are subject to intense debate and backlash.

- Cases at the state and federal level continue to challenge a woman's right to control her reproductive process, to gain equal access to educational opportunities, and to be free from discrimination on the basis of sex in the workplace.

- Women are expressing frustration at hitting a "glass ceiling" to their advancement in the private sector at the same time that many are feeling the stress of their dual roles as workers and family caretakers.

- While the number of women who vote and hold political office has increased steadily since the early 1960s, women's voter participation has fallen over the past two election cycles. Political participation continues to be the key to protecting the gains of the past and preparing for the challenges of the future.

- Since many current legal rights of American women rest on a handful of cases and statutes, women will have to become more vigilant and politically active if they do not want to see their hard-won gains dissipate at the dawn of a new century.

INTRODUCTION

As our nation approaches the end of the twentieth century, the status of women in U.S. society is undergoing tremendous change. In recent years, issues relating to a woman's right to control her reproductive process, affirmative action in the public and private sectors, and equal access to educational opportunities have dominated the public debate. Looking toward the next century, it is clear that legal issues concerning the status of American women—in their personal lives, at school, in the workplace, and at the ballot box—will continue to have a significant impact on women's ability to thrive in the emerging global economy.

This chapter analyzes the most important twentieth-century legal decisions affecting women at the Supreme Court and federal and state legislative levels. It begins with a brief historical note about the status of women at the beginning of the twentieth century as recognized by the courts. As contrasts are drawn between the legal status of women then and now—in the home, at work and school, and within the political process—the progress of the past hundred years becomes more apparent.

The chapter then discusses major recent court cases that illustrate the complexity of the new issues women confront and provide a glimpse of the expected battlefront of the future. This analysis revolves around five areas of interest: women and bodily integrity, women and affirmative action, women and education, women and health, and women and politics. While a legislative or court decision in one area can have a dramatic influence on the life choices of women in another area, for the purpose of this discussion, the decisions are grouped according to their areas of primary impact.

WOMEN AT THE TURN OF THE CENTURY

When the twentieth century dawned, the status of women was defined by their role in the family, lack of access to education and work, and complete exclusion from the political process. Societal expectations of a proper middle-class woman included marriage, homemaking, and child rearing. Only volunteer activities were permissible outside the home, if family circumstances allowed. For women who were poor, members of minority groups, or living on farms, the roles were somewhat different. These women were expected to work in the fields or in menial jobs under horrendous conditions, while remaining fully responsible for home and children.

Under the common law, women lost their economic independence on marriage and were considered subject to the control and discipline of their husbands, the masters of the household. The concept of "unity of the spouses" regarded husband and wife as one person (the husband), with the married woman losing any semblance of a separate legal identity (NOW and Cherow-O'Leary 1987). The husband provided financial support in exchange for the wife's sexual and social companionship and her domestic service. If a husband physically abused his wife, she had no right to charge him with assault or rape, under the theory that once a woman consented to marriage, with its reciprocal duties, there could be no rape, since rape was defined as sex without a woman's consent (Goldstein 1994; Siegel 1996).

As a general rule, most state courts refused to intervene in domestic disputes because they did not want to violate the doctrine of "family privacy." Such intervention occurred only if the couple had separated or the marriage had broken down. A husband who refused to provide financial support for his wife's personal needs generally did not face court sanction. Only if a husband refused to pay a third-party creditor for household "necessaries" would he face the prospect of a court order. But only a creditor could enforce a case under the necessaries doctrine, and most creditors refused to extend credit to married women (NOW and Cherow-O'Leary 1987). A woman's inability to obtain credit in her own name (by law or social practice she had to adopt her husband's name after marriage) was another reflection of the dependent nature of women's roles within marriage. Divorces were difficult to obtain and by no means were automatically granted (Karst 1984).

Thus, many women were isolated within the confines of marriage, as most professions were closed to them by virtue of their gender and lack of education, and the demands of raising large families precluded regular work outside of the home. According to the census, in the early 1900s, the average family included seven children. Contraceptive methods were virtually nonexistent, and abortion (usually an option available only to the wealthy) was eventually banned outright under state law. In short, married women had few legal rights that they could enforce in a court of law. Certainly, they had no right to control their reproductive capacity (Chute 1969).

At the turn of the twentieth century, women who worked for wages generally were single, with no independent means or marriage prospects (NOW and Cherow-O'Leary 1987). Women who had children outside of marriage were ostracized, and their children's illegitimacy became a lifetime burden. (Such children often were unable to inherit from their fathers if their fathers did not acknowledge them.) Women who chose to remain single generally were ridiculed and scorned for rejecting the roles of wife and mother and found themselves isolated within a community or relegated to sex-segregated employment.

Many women did not have access to basic education, as educating women was considered either inconsistent with a woman's wifely duties or a waste of time. Few institutions of higher education even allowed women to attend. The rationale was that the stress of education would damage a woman's "fragile" health and adversely affect her childbearing potential. A few pioneers were able to surmount the obstacles to higher education that prevented them from qualifying for professional careers. But they often were limited to sex-segregated fields or found it difficult to find work in their chosen professions.

For example, in attempting to become a lawyer, Myra Bradwell, a respected legal publisher, unsuccessfully relied on the Fourteenth Amendment to challenge her exclusion from the legal profession. The amendment was added to the Constitution as one of the three post-Civil War amendments intended to protect the rights of African Americans who had been held in bondage as slaves and ultimately were emancipated as a result of the Civil War. During the antebellum period, the position of women in society was directly comparable to the abject status many African Americans suffered under the slave codes (Gunther 1975). Neither enslaved African Americans nor women could hold an elected office, serve on a jury, own or convey property, or file suit in their own names. The Fourteenth Amendment provided, in part, that the "privileges and immunities" of citizenship, as well as the "due process" and "equal protection of the law," would no longer be withheld from African Americans on account of race or previous condition of servitude.

The Supreme Court ruled, in *Bradwell* v. *Illinois* (83 U.S. 130, 141 [1873]), that the Fourteenth Amendment to the U.S. Constitution did not prevent the state of Illinois from forbidding women to practice law, even if they had passed the bar exam (Goldstein 1994). The Court relied upon the concept of "separate spheres" to explain why the Fourteenth Amendment did not protect a woman's right to earn a living in her chosen profession. As one justice noted,

> [T]he civil law, as well as nature herself, has always recognized a wide difference in the *respective spheres and destinies* of man and woman. Man is, or should be, woman's protector and defender. The natural and proper timidity and delicacy which belongs to the female sex evidently unfits it for many of the occupations of civil life. . . . The paramount destiny and mission of woman are to fulfill the noble and benign offices of wife and mother. This is the law of the creator (*Bradwell*, 83 U.S. 141 [J. Bradley, concurring] [emphasis added]).

This constitutional recognition of the separate spheres concept, namely the weaker-sex stereotype, would not be seriously challenged for another 100 years (Cain 1990). It is not surprising that women looked to the sweeping language of the Fourteenth Amendment, which suggested a more expanded definition of liberty and equality, as a means to improve their status as citizens. But, in the *Slaughter-House Cases* (83 U.S. 36 [1872]), the Supreme Court's determination that the equal protection clause only applied to African Americans foreclosed women from seeking constitutional relief under the privileges and immunities clause in *Bradwell* (Cain 1990).

While the Fourteenth Amendment more clearly defined the rights of all citizens when it sought to incorporate African Americans into the body politic, the first half of the twentieth century would pass before women would be in a position to rely on the Supreme Court's more inclusive interpretation of the amendment. The modern interpretation of the amendment recognized the constitutional claims of women and all other racial groups.

Class differences also became more apparent as the nation shifted from an agrarian to an industrial model of production. By the turn of the century, women who were deemed in need of protection from the hazards of work were generally white and middle class. Women who were poor or recent ethnic immigrants received scant legal protection in the workplace as they labored under extremely dangerous conditions in factories and sweatshops. Similarly, women of color, especially in the South and Southwest, were exploited through sharecropping, migrant working conditions, or other forms of peonage. Unskilled minority women workers often found their options limited to temporary jobs or long hours of domestic work.

Most women were barred from the political process by state constitutions that limited voting rights to white males (Jarvis 1992). Women were precluded from voting in all but a handful of local elections. Social reform movements to promote the abolition of slavery and later the temperance movement helped women gain the political experience needed to end their exclusion from the political process. Efforts to achieve voting rights for women began as early as 1848, and many of the early leaders of the women's suffrage movement were also activists in the antislavery movement.

After 1890, when Wyoming became the first state to allow women to vote in presidential elections through a provision in its state constitution, the activism of the suffrage movement intensified. Leaders of the suffragette movement began to adopt more radical tactics in their efforts to secure the vote for women. In addition to hundreds of campaigns at the national, state, and local levels to put the issue of women's suffrage on the ballot, the suffragettes began to organize parades, marches, and picket lines to bring more attention to their cause (National Women's History Project 1995).

EARLY TWENTIETH CENTURY GAINS

Like many other disenfranchised groups, women ultimately needed a constitutional amendment to guarantee them the right to the franchise (Ewing 1958). African Americans received the right to vote through ratification of the Fifteenth Amendment in 1870. Women in general would have to wait until the Nineteenth Amendment, which allowed women the right to vote, was finally ratified on August 26, 1920, and minority and lower-class white women would have to wait even longer, given state election practices that restricted voting by race or one's ability to pay a poll tax.

On securing the vote, women continued to organize for better treatment within marriage and at the workplace (Seigel 1994). Wives became less subject to total loss of control over their own person, finances, and labor. They could hold property, maintain their earnings, and file suit in their own names. Muckraking journalists of the 1920s and 1930s, including such pioneers as Ida B. Wells and Ida Tarbell, helped to expose and reform the dreadful working conditions at many factories and the horrible treatment of children in poor houses and orphanages.

Many states responded by passing laws to regulate working conditions for women. The rationale for passage of laws that set maximum working hours for women was that women's dependent status and physical weakness justified their protection—a theory approved by the Supreme Court in *Muller* v. *Oregon* (208 U.S. 412 [1908]) and *West Coast Hotel Co.* v. *Parrish* (300 U.S. 379 [1937]). On the other hand, many of these state protective laws limited not only the hours but the type of work women could perform.

Despite passage of the Nineteenth Amendment, most minority women still found themselves locked out of the formal political process through enforcement of "Jim Crow" laws, such as the poll tax and the all-white primary. Economic intimidation was also used by white employers to discourage minority women from voting, especially those employed in domestic jobs. However, African American women began to form and participate in social clubs (e.g., the Delta Sigma Theta and Alpha Kappa Alpha sororities) and such organizations as the National Council of Negro Women, the NAACP, and the National Urban League to protest the widespread lynching of minority men and their overall lack of civil rights.

Women supported the entry of the United States into World War II by entering the labor force to replace the young enlisted men. So many women went to work in nontraditional settings during this period that the U.S. workforce was forever transformed. At the same time, more women gained access to educational opportunities available through women's colleges and older universities that slowly began to admit women. And despite the gender-based restrictions women faced in the workplace, some found ways to develop their creative talents in the arts and made significant contributions to the creation of distinctive forms of U.S. literature, music, theater, and film.

During this major transformation of the role of women in U.S. society, women generally did not turn to the court system to secure their social gains. Instead they used the legislative process to improve their situation in the workforce. For example, during the Depression, the Fair Labor Standards Act of 1938 established national standards for a minimum wage (then set at 25 cents), overtime pay, and the employment of children. Later, the Equal Pay Act of 1963 amended the Fair Labor Standards Act by mandating equal pay for men and women performing work requiring equal skill, effort, and responsibility, although it did not apply to female professional or executive employees until 1972.

Prior to World War II, there were few notable Supreme Court decisions that directly addressed the legal status of women. A handful of cases are significant more for how they served as building blocks for the Supreme Court's eventual recognition of women's constitutional rights during the 1960s than for any major advance in the status or treatment of women before World War II. Although the Supreme Court gradually was expanding the modern concept of liberty embodied in the Fourteenth Amendment, women would have to wait until after the modern civil rights movement before they could use the amendment successfully to challenge discrimination on the basis of sex and enforce their rights in court.

For example, in *Meyer* v. *State of Nebraska* (262 U.S. 390 [1923]), the Supreme Court relied on the Fourteenth Amendment to recognize an *individual*'s "right to contract, to engage in any of the common occupations of life, to acquire useful knowledge, to marry, establish a home and bring up children," while in *Pierce* v. *Society of Sisters* (268 U.S. 510 [1925]), the Court upheld the "liberty of *parents and guardians* to direct the upbringing and education of children under their control" (emphasis added). Given that the Court had refused in *Bradwell* to allow a woman to practice her chosen profession and that most states did not allow women to serve as legal guardians of their own children, the Court's use of language in *Meyer* and *Pierce* that was applicable to both men and women was a step forward (Gunther 1975).

During the pre-World War II period, the Supreme Court also changed its position on the treatment of persons with mental handicaps. While the Court, in *Buck* v. *Bell* (274 U.S. 200 [1927]), initially allowed the sterilization of mentally defective institutionalized men and women (stating that "three generations of imbeciles are enough"), it later, in *Skinner* v. *Okla-*

homa ex re. Williamson (316 U.S. 535 [1942]), overturned a state statute requiring compulsory sterilization after a third felony conviction, finding that such classifications invoked "one of the basic civil rights of man. Marriage and procreation [were] fundamental to the very existence of the race." *Skinner* would later become a critical case in the Supreme Court's decisions affecting a woman's right to control her reproductive process.

A narrower interpretation of the applicability of the Fourteenth Amendment prevailed in cases challenging women's need for special protection in the workplace. State protective laws that limited women's job opportunities continued to receive Supreme Court approval until well after the passage of the Civil Rights Act of 1964. For example, in *Goesaert* v. *Cleary* (335 U.S. 464 [1948]), despite an equal protection argument under the Fourteenth Amendment, the majority upheld a Michigan statute that prohibited a female from obtaining a bartender's license unless she was the "wife or daughter of the male owner."

Similarly, state laws based on the view that women required special protection from the burdens of citizenship also continued to receive constitutional approval. In *Hoyt* v. *Florida* (368 U.S. 57 [1961]), the Supreme Court found that a Florida statute that relieved a woman from jury service unless "she herself determines that such service is consistent with her own special responsibilities" as wife and mother did not violate the Fourteenth Amendment, even if it resulted in a woman's conviction by an all-male jury.

THE 1960S THROUGH THE 1980S: A TIME OF CHANGING ATTITUDES

During the 1960s, building on the success of the civil rights movement and the Supreme Court's willingness to re-examine the status of women, the women's movement argued for even greater personal autonomy in the home and at the workplace. This effort first reached the Supreme Court in cases involving legislation, rather than through direct constitutional challenges under a more modern interpretation of the equal protection clause of the Fourteenth Amendment (Gunther 1975).

As such statutes as the Equal Pay Act of 1963 and Title VII of the Civil Rights Act of 1964 (prohibiting discrimination on the basis of race, color, religion, or sex) became law and thus subject to Supreme Court review, women had to test the boundaries of these important new statutory rights on a case-by-case basis. The Court did not resolve the question of whether the Equal Pay Act of 1963 (which amended the Fair Labor Standards Act) was a valid exercise of congressional authority until a decade later in *Corn-*

ing Glassworks v. *Brennan* (417 U.S. 188 [1974]). In that case, male employees of Corning Glassworks who worked the night shift were paid at a higher rate than females who worked the day shift; women who were later able to work the night shift continued to receive a lower rate of pay than their male counterparts. The Court found that the company paid the higher wage differential to male workers because men would not work at the lower rates paid female inspectors and that the continuation of that differential violated the Equal Pay Act.

Similarly, the Court did not consider the statutory validity of Title VII's applicability to women until several years after passage of the Civil Rights Act of 1964, in *Phillips* v. *Martin Marietta Corp.* (400 U.S. 542 [1971]). In that case, the Court held that an employer's refusal to hire women with young children, while hiring men with young children, violated Title VII. However, the Court noted that if an employer could demonstrate that family obligations had a greater adverse impact on women's job performance than that experienced by male employees, gender distinctions could be permissible under a "bona fide occupational qualification" exemption under Title VII.

In fact, women were included within the protection of Title VII only as the result of a last-minute effort to scuttle the entire act by southern legislators who opposed civil rights generally. After the adoption of Title VII, women gained a powerful tool with which to begin redressing many economic inequities at the workplace. Moreover, the Civil Rights Act of 1964—in conjunction with the landmark decision in *Brown* v. *Board of Education* (347 U.S. 483 [1954]), overturning the "separate-but-equal" doctrine in public education—helped to influence the Supreme Court's more liberal interpretation of the constitutional requirements of the equal protection and due process clauses of the Fourteenth Amendment during the 1960s.

Women's reliance upon the Fourteenth Amendment's protection of due process and equal protection of the law has been marked by controversy. As noted, women were not able to use the earlier *Meyer, Pierce,* and *Skinner* cases to change their legal and social status when those cases were first decided. Yet each of the cases represented a significant precedent, relied on by the Supreme Court when it finally recognized a woman's right of privacy in *Griswold* v. *Connecticut* (381 U.S. 479 [1965]).

Griswold, which stipulated that state law prohibiting contraceptives violates the right of marital privacy, was the first major breakthrough in the establishment of women's constitutional rights. *Griswold* remains a controversial decision, with critics charging that the Supreme Court engaged in judicial activism, rather than constructing a reasoned decision based on precedents, to find a "zone of privacy" within the "penumbras" of the Constitution. The Supreme Court's recognition of privacy in family matters in *Griswold* was markedly different from the "family privacy" doctrine used by courts earlier in the century to maintain the dependent position of women within the family structure.

In a subsequent case, *Eisenstadt* v. *Baird* (405 U.S. 438, 453 [1972]), the Court transformed the right of privacy enjoyed by married couples into a right of individual privacy. A physician who was prosecuted for prescribing contraceptives to married and unmarried couples in Massachusetts had his conviction overturned by the Court, which held: "If the right of privacy means anything, it is the right of the individual, married or single, to be free from unwarranted governmental intrusion into matters so fundamentally affecting a person as the decision whether to bear or beget a child."

The Court's adoption of a "zone of privacy" over personal decisions regarding the reproductive process—first in *Griswold* and *Eisenstadt* and later in *Roe* v. *Wade* (410 U.S. 113 [1973]), giving women the freedom to decide whether to terminate a pregnancy—fundamentally altered the legal status of women in ways that are still being explored. To this day, the *Roe* decision exerts a strong impact on the political process and faces persistent legal challenges.

At the very least, the greater control women gained over their reproductive function enhanced their ability to manage their work schedules and career choices. Women began to successfully challenge restrictive and discriminatory laws under the Fourteenth Amendment that affected their status as females, workers, and citizens. For example, in *Reed* v. *Reed* (404 U.S. 71 [1971]), the Court revisited the "special spheres" concept when it overturned an Idaho statute that preferred male relatives over female relatives in the appointment of administrators in probate. In *Frontiero* v. *Richardson* (411 U.S. 677 [1973]), the Court found that differential treatment of male and female military members solely for administrative convenience violated the due process clause of the Fourteenth Amendment.

Similarly, in *Cleveland Bd. of Education* v. *LaFleur* (414 U.S. 632 [1974]), the Court invalidated a school board policy involving mandatory pregnancy leave for female public school teachers as violating the due process clause. In *Taylor* v. *Louisiana* (419 U.S. 522 [1975]), the Court returned to the issue raised in the 1961 *Hoyt* decision when it overturned a Louisiana statute allowing women to be excluded from jury service unless they had filed a written declaration of their desire to serve. Since *Taylor,* the Court has ruled that women may not be excluded from a jury solely because of their sex.

Griswold, Roe, and the cases that followed have been critical to women's ability to secure their rights within private and public institutions. But middle-class women seeking birth control options were not the only beneficiaries of the courts' changing attitudes. Poor women received greater assistance from the government, from the New Deal to the Great Society programs of the 1960s, in the form of direct federal grant programs. These initial grants in aid were supplemented by such welfare programs as food stamps and Aid for Dependent Children. In *Goldberg* v. *Kelly* (397 U.S. 254 [1970]), the Supreme Court recognized a right to a hearing before welfare benefits or other government entitlements could be terminated. In addition, in *Weber* v. *Aetna Casualty & Surety Co.* (406 U.S. 164 [1972]), the Court overturned policies that penalized illegitimate children of a deceased policyholder solely on the basis of the illegitimacy status.

Many women, but especially minority women, were able to move from the poverty rolls to working- and middle-class status by availing themselves of new opportunities presented by training programs and affirmative action initiatives in local, state, and federal government offices. The changing attitudes toward women even influenced such predominately male institutions as the U.S. military, where the adoption of an all-volunteer force encouraged a dramatic increase in the enlistment of women from the 1970s to the mid-1980s.

In some areas, however, the Supreme Court permitted gender biases to stand. The military was allowed to continue to exclude women from the draft and combat assignments (Karst 1984). In *Schlesinger* v. *Ballard* (419 U.S. 498 [1975]), the Court allowed gender-based distinctions in the military promotion system (caused by the combat exclusion) to be maintained. The Court later reasoned, in *Rostker* v. *Goldberg* (453 U.S. 57 [1981]), that prohibiting women from being drafted for combat positions did not violate the equal protection clause, since men and women were not "similarly situated" regarding their eligibility to engage in combat.

Moreover, in *Geduldig* v. *Aiello* (417 U.S. 484 [1974]), the Supreme Court refused to overturn a California statute that excluded pregnancy from disability insurance coverage, finding that the classification excluding pregnancy was not based on gender as such (even though only women were affected by the exclusion). Even Title VII recognized a bona fide occupational qualification exception that would allow women to be excluded from certain jobs because of their sex. In *Dothard* v. *Rawlinson* (433 U.S. 321, 336 [1977]), a female applicant's denial of a prison guard job was approved by the Court, since her ability to maintain order could be "directly reduced by her womanhood."

By the end of the 1980s, women's legal status had changed in many significant ways. One of the most fundamental changes has been in women's increased control over their bodies and personal autonomy. Women's rights are no longer solely a function of their marital status. Divorce has become much easier to obtain, as states now allow one spouse to unilaterally terminate a marriage without the necessity of establishing fault.

Women are no longer considered the "property" of their husbands or subject to physical abuse without legal recourse. They may sue their husbands or boyfriends for rape or physical assault, and they are no longer restricted by law from acting as legal guardians or in other representative capacities. Women may sue or be sued in their individual capacities. In 1975, the Supreme Court recognized in *Taylor* v. *Louisiana* (419 U.S., 522 [1975]) that women have a constitutional right, under the Sixth Amendment, to serve on juries. Women may own and convey property in their own right and enforce their ownership interests against third parties in state or federal court.

Women have the right to bear children with or without the benefit of wedlock and the right to sue for child support if paternity can be established. At least 24 states now prohibit discrimination on the basis of marital status, and a smaller number prohibit discrimination on the basis of sexual orientation. Women have the right to control their reproductive processes subject to the state's limited control over the timing of any procedures to terminate a pregnancy. (States may restrict the availability of abortions after the fetus becomes viable and may require minors to obtain parental consent.)

The greater equality women enjoy has also meant the loss of certain presumptions. Child custody decisions are usually based on the "best interest of the child" standard, rather than the "tender years" presumption that custody of young children automatically should be awarded to the mother.

American women have greater access to higher education than ever before. In many cases, the rates of women attending undergraduate and graduate programs in U.S. universities and colleges have achieved parity with, and in some instances exceeded, male attendance rates. The passage of Title IX of the Education Amendments Act in 1972 (prohibiting education programs that receive federal assistance from discriminating on the basis of sex in all education programs, including athletics) has had a tremendous impact on women's access to equal educational opportunities. While most of the attention has focused on female sports participation, Title IX has had a more significant impact on women's access to equal educational opportunity than is generally realized.

In addition, the Women's Educational Equity Act of 1974 required the Department of Health, Education, and Welfare (now Health and Human Services) to promote nonsexist curricula and nondiscriminatory career counseling and vocational programs and allowed schools to receive grants for upgrading their female athletics programs.

Meanwhile, private single-sex institutions of higher learning still perform an important role for young women who are not interested in attending integrated colleges and universities. Gender biases still persist in educational settings (AAUW 1992), and studies have shown that some young women find it easier to excel in mathematics and science classes in single-sex environments. However, states that have attempted to establish single-sex public schools, for both girls and boys, face legal challenges from women's groups alleging that "separate but equal" sex-segregated public schools violate Title IX (Asimov 1997).

Fewer jobs or professions are foreclosed to women solely on the basis of gender. Since 1972, the Equal Employment Opportunity Commission has had the power to enforce Title VII of the Civil Rights Act of 1964 on behalf of female workers. While the courts have allowed some gender-based workplace restrictions to stand (women are still restricted from serving in combat or joining certain professional sports leagues because of their sex), women are now more accepted in positions requiring physical or technical skills—such as police officers, firefighters, doctors, and astronauts.

Other statutes that have improved the work environment for female workers include the Age Discrimination in Employment Act of 1967 (prohibiting discrimination in the hiring and firing of persons over 40 and under 70), the 1990 Americans with Disabilities Act (requiring reasonable accommodation of an employee's disability), the Nontraditional Employment for Women Act of 1991 (providing training for low-income women in skilled trade jobs), and the 1993 Family and Medical Leave Act (granting unpaid time off to care for a sick child or relative without losing one's job).

Three other laws, passed to overturn Supreme Court cases adverse to females, resulted in positive changes for women workers. These are the Pregnancy Discrimination Act of 1978, the Civil Rights Restoration Act of 1987, and the Civil Rights Act of 1991.

The Pregnancy Discrimination Act of 1978, which prohibits discrimination due to pregnancy and grants short-term disability to pregnant women, amended Title VII to protect a woman's pregnancy status against sex discrimination. In passing the law, Congress was responding in part to the confusion caused by Supreme Court decisions in three cases: *Geduldig* v. *Aiello* (which permitted discrimination in disability eligibility due to pregnancy), *Cleveland Bd. of Education* v. *LaFleur* (which found it unconstitutional to require teachers to take mandatory maternity leave from the time they were five months pregnant until the infant was three months old), and *Turner* v. *Dept. of Employment Security* (423 U.S. 44 [1975]) (which found it unconstitutional to deny unemployment benefits to women who were more than six months pregnant).

The Civil Rights Restoration Act was passed by Congress to overturn the Supreme Court's narrow interpretation of the meaning of "program" subject to Title IX prohibition of sex discrimination in its *Grove City* v. *Bell* (465 U.S. 555 [1984]) decision. At issue in *Grove City* was whether its students' receipt of federal grants, rather than any direct funds received by the college itself, rendered the college subject to Title IX's requirements of nondiscrimination; the Court had determined that institution-wide coverage was not triggered by the student grants. Title IX's prohibition of sex discrimination in any program that received federal funds was strengthened as a result of the Civil Rights Restoration Act.

Similarly, the Civil Rights Act of 1991 overturned a series of adverse Title VII decisions and extended the protection of Title VII to victims of intentional discrimination based on sex, religion, or disability to allow recovery of damages previously limited to victims of racial discrimination.

During its 1989 term, the Supreme Court had significantly limited the reach of Title VII and other civil rights laws in three cases. In *Price Waterhouse* v. *Hopkins* (490 U.S. 228 [1989]), a fractured court could not agree on the appropriate standard in a Title VII case alleging that stereotyped assumptions prevented a woman from becoming a partner. In *Wards Cove Packing Co.* v. *Atonio* (490 U.S. 642 [1989]), employers were granted an easier burden when rebutting employment discrimination claims based on disparate impact. In *Patterson* v. *McLean Credit Union* (491 U.S. 164 [1989]), the Court found that Section 1981 of the Civil Rights Act of 1866 (providing that all persons shall have the same right to make and enforce contracts enjoyed by white persons) did not cover the terms or conditions of employment where ongoing harassment of an African American woman was alleged.

The effect of these three cases was to change the rules governing lawsuits filed on the basis of race or sex discrimination previously established in cases such as *Griggs* v. *Duke Power Co.* (401 U.S. 424 [1971]) and *McDonnell Douglas Corp.* v. *Green* (411 U.S. 792 [1973]). In *Griggs*, the Court unanimously held that Title VII proscribes not only overt discrimination but practices that are fair in form but discriminatory in operation or have a disparate impact. *McDonnell Douglas Corp.* established the order of proof in cases alleging disparate treatment under Title VII. These 1989 cases also signaled the Court's growing hostility to the Civil Rights Act in particular and to the concept of affirmative action in general.

According to recent studies, women have been the real beneficiaries of affirmative action programs in the public and private sectors (Glass Ceiling Commission 1995). Despite the increase in the number of women in management and nontraditional positions, some women have encountered barriers to further advancement because of their sex—the so-called glass ceiling (NCRW 1996). Still other working women have experienced stress trying to balance the demands of work and family in workplaces that are not "family-friendly." With the additions of the broader protections afforded to victims of sex discrimination under the Civil Rights Act of 1991, women now have enhanced legal means to protect their right to be free from discrimination on the basis of sex. On the other hand, the backlash against policies such as affirmative action that have benefited women, beginning with the *Regents of University of California* v. *Bakke* (438 U.S. 265 [1978]) (recognizing the concept of "reverse discrimination" against white males for the first time) and ending with the recently passed Proposition 209 in California (prohibiting the use of affirmative action by the state government) suggests that women may encounter new obstacles to equality in the workplace in the future.

Against this background, it would appear that few open legal questions remain regarding the status of women in U.S. society. However, the continuing need for new laws to overturn the Supreme Court's interpretation of statutes involving women's rights over the past several years suggests that the legal status of women is still subject to significant legal challenge. Whether women should look primarily to the courts or to state and federal legislatures to secure the legal rights they have gained over the past 30 years is open to debate.

EMERGING ISSUES

There are a number of emerging issues that could have a dramatic effect on women's lives and livelihood. Three areas of controversy illustrate the complexity of some of the legal issues women will face in the future: the Violence Against Women Act (VAWA), child custody decisions against working women, and the use of the criminal law process to punish drug-addicted mothers.

VAWA represents the first federal attempt to regulate domestic violence. The constitutional basis for the law is Congress's right to regulate interstate commerce (the "commerce clause"). Two federal courts have reached different conclusions about the constitutionality of VAWA. In *Doe* v. *Doe* (929 F. Supp 608 [D. Conn 1996]), Judge Janet Arterton ruled that VAWA was constitutional as it did not encroach on traditional areas of state law but complemented them by recognizing a social interest in ensuring that persons have a civil right to be free from gender-based violence. Conversely, Judge Jackson Kiser held in *Brzonkala* v. *VA Polytechnic & State University* (935 F. Supp 779 [W.D. Va 1996]) that the law was insufficiently linked to Congress's power to regulate interstate commerce. Judge Kiser also was not convinced that Congress had demonstrated a need for a civil rights remedy under Section 5 of the Fourteenth Amendment, given the adequacy of state laws to stem domestic violence.

Disputes over constitutionality at the lower-court level virtually assure that the Supreme Court eventually will consider whether the commerce clause is a viable basis for the exercise of federal regulation. Congress has relied on the commerce clause to support civil rights laws since the 1960s. In light of the current Supreme Court's deference to state law and its restrictive view of federalism—as reflected in *United States* v. *Lopez* (514 U.S. 549 [1995]), which found the commerce clause an insufficient basis for prohibiting guns in school zones—it is likely that VAWA may be overturned (Goldscheid 1996). Should the Court base its decision on a restrictive reading of the commerce clause, other civil rights laws, including the Civil Rights Act of 1964, also could be in jeopardy.

With respect to child custody decisions, women who take their jobs seriously or who desire to further their education may find that judges penalize them by awarding children to their fathers in custody disputes. For example, a female attorney found that her job as counsel to a Senate Committee was used against her when a judge awarded custody of her children to her former husband who put the children first in *Prost* v. *Greene* (652 A.2d 621 [D.C. App. 1995]). Some view this example as evidence of a growing backlash against professional women. A young mother in Michigan who wanted to go back to school initially lost a custody battle with her child's father, who had argued that his own mother would be a better caregiver than the strangers in the day care center the child's mother had selected. The mother eventually was awarded custody on appeal in *Ireland* v. *Smith* (542 N.W. 2d 344 [Mich. App. 1995]). These are just a few examples of how the once sacrosanct bond between a mother and young children is no longer a given.

Mothers who have serious problems with drug or alcohol abuse also are finding that the criminal justice system can be used against them. In 1980, Jennifer Clarise Johnson became the first woman to be convicted as a criminal for delivering a controlled substance, crack cocaine, to her child who tested positive at birth (Roberts 1991). The difficult problem of addicted mothers would seem to demand a response of treatment rather than punishment. In effect, however, it is another example of how the rights of a fetus are being enhanced at the expense of a woman's right to personal autonomy.

Ultimately, these issues will be addressed by legislation, and the women's vote could prove the deciding factor. Within the political realm, the existence of the so-called gender gap has already begun to influence elections at the national level. How women respond to emerging issues in such areas as abortion rights, affirmative action, and custody decisions will determine the outcome of many current public policy disputes.

RECENT LEGAL DECISIONS, 1995 TO 1997

In the past two years, the Supreme Court has rendered important decisions involving women's rights to pursue protection under Civil War–era statutes and access to equal employment, educational opportunities, reproductive health clinics, and health care. In each instance, the issue at stake has been whether the significant gains in women's legal rights since the advent of the women's movement will continue to be protected by the Supreme Court and state courts or those gains will become subject to retrenchment or indeed outright repeal.

WOMEN AND BODILY INTEGRITY

The Supreme Court recently considered two cases that involve women's constitutional right to freedom from sexual assault or criminal behavior by state or local officials.

In *United States* v. *Lanier* (117 S.Ct. 1219 [1997]), the Court decided that a state court judge who was convicted of rape and sexual assault against five female victims had sufficient notice that sexual assault violates women's constitutional right of privacy and bodily integrity. The judge's conviction was reinstated, and the case has been remanded to the lower court. The significance of this case to women is that it upheld the statute challenged by the judge (Section 242 of Title 18 of the United States Code), that had been the main tool for women assaulted by prison officials, police officers or other law enforcement officials, and other state officials (Women's Legal Defense Fund 1996).

In *Bd. of Cty. Commissioners of Bryan County* v. *Brown* (117 S.Ct. 1382 [1997]), the Court was presented with the issue of whether local county officials were liable for a sheriff's decision to hire a deputy with a bad record who had violated a woman's rights through the excessive use of force. The woman, Jill Brown, was arrested in such a violent manner that she eventually required knee replacement surgery. A jury and the lower court agreed that she was entitled to damages. The Supreme Court concluded that the county was not liable. The Court's reliance on a narrow interpretation of the Civil War–era civil rights statute is consistent with the more conservative direction the Court has been taking recently regarding civil rights cases.

Had the Court upheld the lower court decision, the ability of victims of constitutional violations by local officials to secure damages would have been enhanced (Women's Legal Defense Fund 1996).

WOMEN AND AFFIRMATIVE ACTION

In the summer of 1996, the Supreme Court's six-to-three decision in *Romer* v. *Evans* (116 S.Ct. 1620 [1996]), struck down a Colorado initiative that would have amended Colorado's constitution to prevent the state from enforcing local laws that banned discrimination on the basis of homosexual, lesbian, or bisexual orientation. The Court found that a disqualification of a class of persons from the right to obtain specific protection from the law was unprecedented and was itself a denial of equal protection of the law in the most literal sense. Moreover, the Court held that the proposed amendment was, in effect, a status-based classification of persons, undertaken for its own sake, which the Equal Protection Clause does not permit. Had the Supreme Court approved the Colorado initiative, other states that currently prohibit discrimination on the basis of sexual orientation would have faced similar efforts to overturn their laws.

It is already apparent that *Romer* has implications far beyond the class of persons who were targeted by the initiative. As more states look to the initiative process as a means of bypassing the legislative process, the Supreme Court increasingly will be called on to evaluate the constitutionality of initiatives that seek to restrict the rights of women and minorities. For example, in November 1994, the state of California passed Proposition 187, prohibiting access to public schools, health care, and welfare by noncitizens, despite a 1981 Supreme court decision, in *Plyler* v. *Doe* (454 U.S. 202 [1981]), that the equal protection clause extended to the children of illegal immigrants. The proposition has not been implemented yet due to ongoing legal challenges that ultimately will be resolved by the Supreme Court.

Similarly, in November 1996, California passed Proposition 209, which amends the state constitution to prohibit state affirmative action plans designed to benefit women and minorities. Following California's lead, citizens in Arizona are beginning the process of placing a similar anti-affirmative action initiative on their next statewide ballot. A lower federal court's injunction against California's implementation of Proposition 209 was recently struck down by a three-panel court and clearly is headed for the Supreme Court.

The lower court entered the injunction on the grounds that it unconstitutionally targeted only women and minorities, without bringing other groups with preference programs (for example, veterans and the disabled) within its parameters. Instead of sending the case back to the lower court according to normal practice, the three-judge appellate court ruled that the lower court lacked the authority to overturn the clear will of the people of California. The decision currently is stayed pending appeal to the full Ninth Circuit. The differing interpretations of the constitutionality of anti-affirmative action initiatives means that these issues will be at the Supreme Court level within the next year or two.

Since 1989, the Supreme Court consistently has limited the application of Title VII of the Civil Rights Act in cases challenging discrimination in employment. Passage of the Civil Rights Act of 1991 interrupted that momentum, at least with respect to discrimination on the basis of gender, through its wider provision of damages, including punitive damages for victims of sexual harassment in the workplace.

Women have been the primary beneficiaries of affirmative action programs at the local, state, and federal levels (Glass Ceiling Commission 1995). It would be unfortunate if women were to sit on the sidelines as the debate over affirmative action takes place across the nation.

The Supreme Court has rendered a few recent decisions that involve sexual harassment under Title VII and Title IX. In *Rowinsky* v. *Bryan Independent School District* (80 F. 3d 1006 [5th Cir. 1996]), the Court allowed to stand the lower-court ruling that Title IX of the Civil Rights Act only covers sexual harassment committed by an institution receiving federal funds or its agent and that it does not protect girls (or women) from sexual harassment by fellow male students.

The Court refused to review *Sims* v. *Brown & Root Industrial Services* (889 F. Supp 920 [W.D. La. 1995]), which held that an employer is not strictly liable under Title VII for the actions of a supervisory employee when the company later takes remedial action. In this case, the male supervisor had reduced the female employee's pay when she refused his sexual demands. The supervisor later was fired, and the employee sued the company for stress-related damages caused by the harassment.

The Court also refused to review *McWilliams* v. *Fairfax Cty. Bd. of Supervisors* (72 F. 3d 1191 [4th Cir. 1996]), which ruled that no Title VII cause of action arises for a hostile work environment when both the perpetrator and the target of sexual harassment are heterosexuals of the same sex.

A number of cases recently decided by the Supreme Court have helped to determine the continued effectiveness of Title VII during an era of corporate downsizing and retaliation against former employees. In *Walters* v. *Metropolitan Educational Enterprises* (117 S. Ct. 660 [1997]), the Court decided that part-time and hourly employees, many of whom are women, count as full-time salaried employees for the purposes of coverage under Title VII. The employment relationship is established by an individual's appearance on the employer's payroll. Title VII only applies to companies with 15 or more employees who work a standard workweek. The lower court had found that the definition of employees only applied to full-time workers. Given the increased use of flextime and employees working from home, the Court's ruling reversing the lower court ultimately will benefit female workers.

Similarly, the Supreme Court made an expansive, rather than narrow, ruling in *Robinson* v. *Shell Oil Co.* (117 S. Ct. 843 [1997]), in deciding whether Title VII protects a fired worker from retaliation in the form of negative performance reports provided to a prospective new employer. The Court interpreted the term "employee" under Title VII to include former employees. Thus, in the future, employees may sue for retaliatory postemployment actions by their former employers.

Recent controversies over alleged discriminatory employment practices by companies like Denny's (race), Mitsubishi Motor Company (gender), and Avis (race) clearly demonstrate that the pernicious problem of discrimination on the basis of race and gender continues to plague the U.S. workplace. Allegations of sexual assault and discrimination in such formerly all-male environments as the military and the oil industry are further proof of the Department of Labor's Glass Ceiling Commission conclusion that more work remains to be done to integrate U.S. workplaces (Glass Ceiling Commission 1995).

In the military, allegations of sexual misconduct against female service members at the Navy's Tailhook Conference in 1991 and of widespread sexual assault on female trainees at the Army's Aberdeen Proving Ground Training Center drew national attention. In the oil industry, Texaco agreed to a $176 million settlement in a racial discrimination class action lawsuit and Shell Oil faces a $10 million racial discrimination class action suit.

How businesses and institutions respond to ongoing problems of sex discrimination will have a dramatic effect on women's work environments. One response to the Army's problems at Aberdeen has been congressional hearings on whether training of new recruits should be segregated by sex. (It would be ironic if the alleged actions of sexual misconduct by male senior enlisted members against junior female recruits were used to justify a serious reconsideration of the integration of females in the military.) In the case of Texaco, after tapes of internal meetings allegedly containing racial slurs were released to the press, the company responded to the embarrassing headlines (and threat of a boycott by civil rights groups) by approving the largest class action settlement of its kind. More significantly, Texaco committed resources to institute new internal procedures designed to enhance diversity within the company.

WOMEN AND EDUCATION

A recent decision by the Supreme Court, in *United States* v. *Virginia* (116 S. Ct. 2264 [1996]), suggests that, at least within the context of access to education on the basis of gender, the Court is not prepared to accept the principle of separate but equal public schools. The Court's seven-to-one opinion held that the state's categorical exclusion of women from educational opportunities at the Virginia Military Institute (VMI) denies equal protection to women and that the state's remedy of providing a separate program for women did not cure the constitutional violation. The case involving The Citadel, South Carolina's all-male state military institution, was resolved when the state elected to follow the law as rendered in the VMI case. One possible downside to the Court's reasoning in the VMI case is that the efforts of local school boards to create single-sex inner-city public schools to promote the self-esteem of young girls probably will not pass constitutional scrutiny.

Most popular references to Title IX allude to its impact on female athletes. Progress is clear in terms of the number of women participating in college athletics which has grown from 300,000 in 1972 to over two million in 1997 (Dionne 1997). Yet, parity in college funding of female athletic programs has not been achieved despite the 25 years that have passed since Title IX became law. Supporters of Title IX were relieved when the Supreme Court recently refused to overturn a lower-court decision, in *Cohen* v. *Brown University* (101 F. 3d 155 [1st Cir. 1996]), that found Brown University had violated Title IX in the operation of its intercollegiate athletics program. The lower court ruled in favor of a female gymnast whose program had been cut, finding that women made up 51 percent of the student body while only 38 percent of Brown's athletes were women.

The test of Title IX in the future will be its effectiveness in resolving continuing issues of disparity in education. While more than 50 percent of all college graduates are women, only 17 percent of college faculty members are women. Women still are underrepresented in the technical fields of engineering, mathematics, and science.

WOMEN AND HEALTH

Since the Supreme Court elected not to revisit the constitutionality of the abortion compromise embodied in *Roe* v. *Wade,* legal attacks against a woman's right to reproductive choices have been concentrated at the edges of the abortion decision.

Anti-abortion activists have organized to prevent the approval of RU-486, a pill that combines two drugs to prohibit contraception. Meanwhile, legislative efforts continue to outlaw a late-term abortion method referred to by opponents as the partial-birth abortion. At the state level, Ohio already has passed a law prohibiting postviability abortions, that was enjoined by the court in *Women's Medical Professional Corporation* v. *Voinovich* (911 F. Supp. 1051 [SD. Ohio 1995]). While Utah's restrictions on late-term abortions were overturned by the Tenth Circuit, and the Supreme Court declined to review the decision, it has been the subject of litigation in *Jane L.* v. *Leavitt* (61 F. 3d 1493 [10th Cir. 1995]); cert. denied, 138 L. Ed. 2d 211 [1997]).

At the federal level, Congress is engaged in efforts to further restrict and limit the availability of late-term abortions. If Congress passes a law outlawing third-trimester abortions, it will be the first major legal limitation on the abortion decision since the *Planned Parenthood of S.E. Penn.* v. *Casey* (505 U.S. 833 [1992]) decision allowing restrictions that do not impose an undue burden on women seeking abortions. In that case, Planned Parenthood presented the Court with an opportunity to overrule *Roe*. The Court allowed some modifications to the impact of viability of a fetus on Pennsylvania's right to regulate abortions but maintained the central holding in *Roe* that state regulation may not impinge on a woman's right to privacy. President Clinton has vetoed late-term legislation on two occasions; a third effort to achieve veto-proof margins undoubtedly will be forthcoming.

The Court recently decided *Schenck* v. *Pro-Choice Network* (117 S. Ct. 855 [1997]), a case defining the physical limits a state may maintain to allow women unimpeded access to reproductive health clinics. In the 1994 decision, *Madsen* v. *Women's Health Center* (512 U.S. 753 [1994]), the Supreme Court ruled that local judges have the power to enjoin anti-abortion demonstrators from coming within 36 feet of an abortion clinic without violating their First Amendment rights. In *Schenck*, the Court determined that a fixed 15-foot limitation on protesters' access to clinic entrances or their clients was permissible but that a "floating buffer-zone" around clients of the clinic unduly restricted the First Amendment rights of abortion protesters.

Continued advances in neonatal care (younger neonatal infants can now be saved, thus changing the concept of viability) and further advances involving *in vitro* fertilization (e.g., the separation of the birthing process from procreation, thus limiting right-to-privacy arguments) will further complicate the abortion debate.

Access to health care cases may be expected to revolve around interpretations of the Family and Medical Leave Act of 1993 (FMLA) and the Personal Responsibility and Work Opportunity Reconciliation Act of 1996 (commonly referred to as the welfare reform law). Lower courts are already grappling with issues under FMLA, including whether an employee must invoke the title of the act in requesting leave and whether the act covers time off for a doctor's appointment to determine the extent of an employee's medical problem.

As a result of the welfare reform law, for the first time in 50 years, Congress will no longer guarantee payment of welfare grants in aid to women, children, and the disabled. However, prior to formal passage of welfare reform, states already were allowed to experiment with programs that denied welfare recipients access to health care for themselves or their children by receiving waivers from the federal government. Under the new law, states receive funding in the form of block grants that they may use according to local conditions rather than federal appropriations. Since there is no longer a federal guarantee to provide welfare assistance regardless of local conditions, states may lose their block grants if they fail to meet certain goals within the new law.

For example, a federal appeals court approved New Jersey's "new child exclusion," which means that any child born to a woman on welfare can be excluded from receiving any welfare benefits. That exclusion is also contained within the federal law: states may now force recipients off the welfare rolls within two years if they are not actively seeking work, and no family may receive benefits beyond five years. The Food Stamp Program was drastically reduced, especially with respect to the able-bodied poor. Eligibility for federal housing has been restricted. Benefits to legal aliens also were dramatically reduced, although some are being restored in the face of intense lobbying by Hispanic and other groups with large numbers of legal resident aliens. A major legal challenge to the new federal welfare reform law, which allows these restrictions and other punitive measures directed against the poor, may be expected over the next few years.

WOMEN AND POLITICS

Over the past three decades, women have steadily increased their presence in the political process. In 1969, women made up just 6.6 percent of all statewide elective executive officers (Center for the American Woman and Politics 1994). By 1997, that number had risen to 25.1 percent (Center for the American Woman and Politics 1997). More women than men register to vote, and women now consistently outvote their male counterparts in national and state elections. Nineteen seventy-six was the last presidential year when men outvoted women (Center for the American Woman and Politics 1995). The so-called gender gap in political party identification has been recognized since 1984 and continues to play a role in national politics.

While a record number of women voted in the presidential election of 1992 (the so-called Year of the Woman), female voter participation, while still higher than male rates, showed significant declines in both the midterm elections of 1994 and the presidential election of 1996. Despite all the attention to "soccer moms" in the last election, the percentage of women voting dropped by seven points at the national level. In 1992, 62.3 percent of women of voting age reported voting; in 1996, exit polls showed just 52 percent participation by women (as compared to 48 percent participation by men) a 10-point drop in women's voting rates. Since 1986, the proportion of female voters in midterm elections has exceeded the proportion of male voters. But the rate of women voting in midterm elections has been declining since 1982: the participation rate of women voters in 1994, 44.9 percent, was the lowest since 1974, when the rate was 43.4 percent.

This decline in female voter participation, at precisely the time that retrenchment on abortion, affirmative action, and welfare is occurring at the federal level, does not auger well for the ability of women to protect the gains of the past.

CONCLUSION

Historically, political organizing has been the key to greater equality for women. The Equal Rights Amendment, which sought to prohibit discrimination on the basis of sex as a constitutional provision, failed to receive enough votes in state legislatures to be ratified. As a result, women's legal status is largely protected by a handful of federal statutes and Supreme Court cases, dating from the mid-1960s to the late 1970s, which are now under serious attack.

Current efforts by the Supreme Court and Congress to return more decisionmaking power to the states means that women will not be able to rely on federal legislation to address their social and economic concerns. If women do not participate actively in political decisionmaking at the local, state, and national levels over the next several years, they may find the gains of the past slowly disappearing.

FIVE

THE AMERICAN WOMAN: THE ROAD AHEAD

Carol J. De Vita

HIGHLIGHTS

IN LESS THAN 50 YEARS, our image of the American woman has been transformed from one of full-time homemaker to do-it-all superwoman. How this transition occurred can be traced in large part through social, economic, and demographic trends. These trends also set the stage for the century ahead.

- Women accounted for 137 million Americans in 1997—just over half the population. In the next 20 years, an additional 28 million women will be added, as the total population reaches 323 million.
- Women's fertility—that is, the number of children that a woman will have in her lifetime—is the most important factor in U.S. population growth. About 70 percent of population growth in the early 1990s resulted from natural increase (that is, the number of births exceeded the number of deaths), while 30 percent can be attributed to immigration.
- There are no signs that a future baby boom looms on the immediate horizon. Although the number of births soared during the early 1990s, the increase was created by post-World War II baby-boom women having babies, not a return to large families. The average family continues to hover around two children per couple.
- Racial and ethnic differences in fertility are evident, however. On average, Hispanic women have the highest number of children (3.0 per woman), followed by black women (2.2), white women (2.0), and Asian women (1.9).
- Higher birth rates, combined with immigration, are changing the nation's racial and ethnic mix. More than half (54 percent) of immigrants in the

early 1990s were women, primarily from Asia and Latin America. By 2030, minorities will account for two in five American women, compared with one in four today.

- All minority groups are growing, but Hispanics are adding the largest numbers. By 2030, the number of Hispanic women is expected to reach 33 million, black women will number 24 million, and Asian women, 12 million.
- The aging of the U.S. population is one of the most significant demographic trends facing the nation today. Both the number and share of people age 65 and older will rise dramatically in the next 30 years. The trend will be strongest for minority elders. Between 1995 and 2030, the size of the older minority population is projected to grow by 260 percent, while the older non-Hispanic white population will increase by 80 percent. Minorities will represent 25 percent of older Americans in 2030, compared with 15 percent today.
- Population aging will hold special significance for women. Not only do women outlive men, on average, but they also are the primary caregivers of people in need of assistance. For middle-aged women, this will be a particular challenge. With more than 60 percent of adult women in the labor force, finding the time to help aging parents, raise young children, and meet the demands of the workplace puts a heavy burden on women. Balancing the needs of each generation will be one of the most important public-policy challenges of the next century.
- Women have made great strides in education, but not all women have shared equally in this progress. In 1995, 88 percent of women age 25 to 34 had graduated from high school—up from 60 percent in 1960. However, 40 percent of white women age 18 to 21 were enrolled in college in 1994, compared with only 25 percent of black women and 16 percent of Hispanic women.
- Notable increases have occurred in women's labor force participation over the last several decades: Almost six in 10 adult women were in the workforce in 1995, compared with less than four in 10 (38 percent) in 1960. One result is that the dual-worker family has replaced the breadwinner-homemaker model as the most common type of family in the United States.

INTRODUCTION

If an American woman in 1950 were asked to describe her life, she most likely would have replied that she was married, had children, managed a household, and was involved in social or civic activities that fostered her family's well-being—attending church and PTA meetings; volunteering for the Boy Scouts, Girl Scouts, or local hospital; or participating in the Red Cross, Community Chest, or local charity drive. For most women in the 1950s, life centered around their homes, their families, and their communities.

Like their white counterparts, black women in the 1950s also shaped their lives around home and family. But women of color were more likely to have another dimension to their lives. About 40 percent of black women worked outside the home, compared with 30 percent of white women.

Since the 1950s, women's lives have changed. Their roles and horizons have expanded, and their lives have become more complex. While most American women today are married and have children, their lives differ from their counterparts in the 1950s in significant ways. Most women work in the paid labor force. An increasing number delay entrance into marriage. Many go to college or take time to establish careers before getting married. Many women are divorced, and a significant share will never marry. Many are raising children on their own. An American woman today will tell you that her life is busy and that she has too little time to juggle the responsibilities of home, family, and work.

In less than 50 years, our image of the American woman has been transformed from one of full-time homemaker to do-it-all superwoman. This makeover has been the result of significant social, economic, and demographic trends in U.S. society—forces that have redefined our lives and will shape our futures.

Demography offers a unique compass for charting the years ahead. It provides the "people dimension" for understanding our changing world and the changing lives of women. Although demographic projections cannot predict the future, they can provide a reasonable estimate (at least in the near term) of basic parameters. It is through this lens that we can glimpse a picture of the American woman in the twenty-first century.

DEMOGRAPHIC TRENDS THAT WILL SHAPE THE FUTURE

Three demographic trends will set the parameters for women's lives—and for the population as a whole—in the next century: (1) continued population growth, (2) increasing racial and ethnic diversity, and (3) population aging.

GROWTH IN THE NUMBERS

Women accounted for 137 million Americans in 1997—just over half (51 percent) of all Americans. These numbers are projected to grow. By 2020, an additional 28 million women will be added to the population, and the total U.S. population is projected to reach 323 million (Bureau of the Census 1996b).

The United States is one of the world's fastest growing industrialized countries. During the first half of the 1990s, the U.S. population grew by 1.0 percent per year, adding roughly 2.7 million people annually. Only Australia, New Zealand, and Canada come close to matching U.S. growth rates. The United States, however, far surpasses these nations in the absolute number of people added each year.

While current population projections forecast greater numbers of Americans, the growth rate is expected to slow during the next 50 years. Increasing life expectancy, relatively high birth rates (at least for an industrialized country), and immigration from abroad all contribute to the continued population growth in the United States. The most important factor, however, is women's fertility—the number of children that women, on average, bear in their lifetimes. During the early 1990s, about 70 percent of U.S. population growth resulted from natural increase (that is, the number of births exceeded the number of deaths), while the arrival of new immigrants accounted for roughly 30 percent of net population growth. Women's decisions about their reproductive lives—particularly how many children to have and when to have them—will have a major impact on both population size and the nation's demographic profile in the next century.

INCREASING DIVERSITY

But demographic change is more than increasing numbers. In the years ahead, a larger share of the population will be from racial and ethnic minority groups. In 1997, almost three of every four American women were non-Hispanic white; over the next 30 years, this share is expected to decline to about three in five (see Figure V–1).

Immigration and relatively high fertility rates among most minority groups are expected to add to the size of the minority population. By 2030, over 70 million American women will be of minority backgrounds, compared with 37 million today. The two fastest growing groups will be Asians and Hispanics. Asians will have the most rapid *rate* of growth; Hispanics will add the most *numbers*. Between 1997 and 2030, the share of Asian American women in the population is expected to almost double—adding roughly 7.1 million

Figure V–1 • U.S. FEMALE POPULATION BY RACE AND HISPANIC ORIGIN, 1997 AND 2030 (projected) (percent distributions)

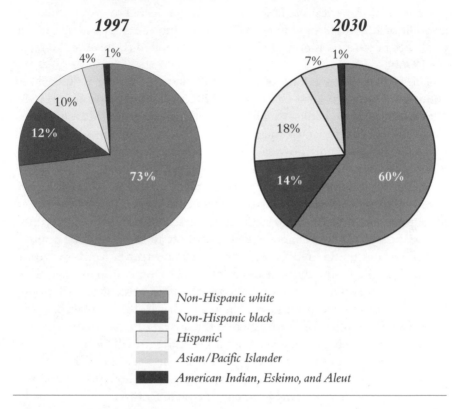

1997

4% 1%
10%
12%
73%

2030

7% 1%
18%
14% 60%

■ Non-Hispanic white
■ Non-Hispanic black
□ Hispanic[1]
▨ Asian/Pacific Islander
■ American Indian, Eskimo, and Aleut

[1]Persons of Hispanic origin may be of any race.

Source: Bureau of the Census, *Population Projections of the United States by Age, Sex, Race, and Hispanic Origin: 1995 to 2050,* 1996, Table 2.

women. Yet Asian American women will continue to represent a relatively small share of the population—less than 10 percent of all women in 2030. In contrast, about 19 million Hispanic women will be added to the population over the next 30 years. By 2030, the number of Hispanic women is expected to reach 33 million and represent 18 percent of all American women.

The number of black women also will grow, reaching 24 million by 2030, but the pace of growth will be slower than for other minority groups. If current trends continue, black women, now the largest minority group in the nation, will become the second largest: Hispanics are expected to outnumber blacks within the next 10 or 15 years. These historic shifts in U.S. racial and ethnic composition are likely to have long-range social and political implications for how we view racial and ethnic issues, how we define racial and ethnic categories, and how the political landscape unfolds.

POPULATION AGING

The aging of the U.S. population is one of the most significant demographic trends facing the nation today. Both the number and share of people age 65 and older will rise dramatically over the next 30 years. The size of this population will grow from 34 million today to roughly 70 million in 2030. One in five Americans will be age 65 or older in 2030, compared with one in eight today. Population aging will hold special significance for women. Not only do women outlive men, on average, but they also are the primary caregivers of people in need of assistance.

One of the driving forces behind this trend is the aging of the baby-boom generation (born between 1946 and 1964). Members of this famed generation have now entered middle age and account for one in three Americans (see Figure V–2). The "senior boom" of the twenty-first century will begin around 2010 and continue to 2030 when the youngest members of the baby-boom generation finally turn age 65. Over the next 30 years, the baby-boom generation will make the gradual transition from middle age into the ranks of the young-old. This inevitable senior boom is likely to reshape our images of older persons, as the health-conscious and age-conscious baby boomers strive to maintain their youth, vigor, and independence.

The most significant aspects of population aging may not occur until *after* 2030, however. In 2031, the first baby boomers will turn 85, and for the next 20 years, the ranks of the oldest-old (age 85 and older) will swell. This is an important demographic marker. The odds of experiencing declining health and a need for assistance increase rapidly after age 85, and the costs associated with care tend to rise as health status declines. The financial implications of an aging population, therefore, may not be fully felt for another 40 years when the baby boomers begin to reach the very oldest stages of life.

Tomorrow's elderly, however, will not be carbon copies of today's older generation. Demographically, they will reflect the growing racial and ethnic diversity of the nation. While the majority of older Americans are (and will continue to be) non-Hispanic white, people of color will represent an increasing share of the older population (see Figure V–3). Indeed, population aging will be most dramatic among minority elders. Between 1995 and 2030, the size of the older minority population is projected to grow by 260 percent—more than triple the current numbers—while the older non-Hispanic white population will increase by roughly 80 percent. Minorities will represent 25 percent of older Americans in 2030, compared with 15 percent today.

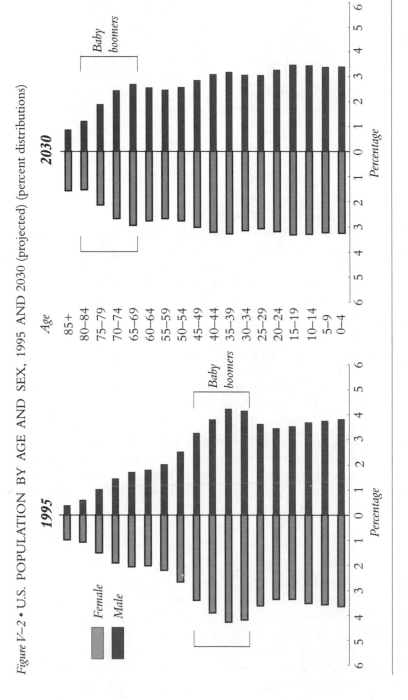

Figure V–2 • U.S. POPULATION BY AGE AND SEX, 1995 AND 2030 (projected) (percent distributions)

Source: Bureau of the Census, *Population Projections of the United States by Age, Sex, Race, and Hispanic Origin: 1995 to 2050*, 1996, Table 2.

Figure V–3 • U.S. POPULATION BY AGE AND RACE OR HISPANIC ORIGIN, 1995 AND 2030 (projected) (percent distributions)

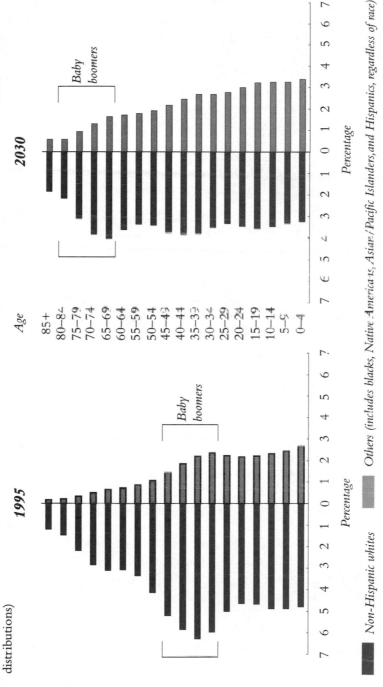

Source: Bureau of the Census, *Population Projections of the United States by Age, Sex, Race, and Hispanic Origin: 1995 to 2050*, 1996, Table 2.

DEMOGRAPHIC DIMENSIONS OF CHANGE

While demography is not destiny, population growth, increasing racial and ethnic diversity, and societal aging are interrelated demographic trends that cannot be easily disentangled, quickly halted, or reversed. These trends reflect decades of cumulative decisions by individuals and society on childbearing, family size, health, mortality, and immigration. Women have been key players in this unfolding drama, and it is the changing lives of women that will continue to shape the demographic future of the United States.

TRENDS IN CHILDBEARING

Children have always been a central part of women's lives. Yet in the last 30 years, norms and expectations about children and families have changed. Childbearing has been delayed, family size has declined, and a larger portion of births have occurred outside of marriage.

Delayed Childbearing

To prepare for the multiple demands of today's changing world, many young women are postponing starting a family until they finish school, start their careers, and become financially independent. This change in behavior has resulted in a change in fertility patterns.

Women in their twenties continue to have the highest number of births, but the peak childbearing ages have shifted from the early twenties to the late twenties. Birth rates for women in their thirties also have shown large increases, but birth rates fall quickly after age 35. By age 40, very few American women have babies. In fact, most women who reach age 40 without having a child are unlikely to do so. Today, nearly 18 percent of women in their early forties are childless, compared with about 10 percent in 1970. The Census Bureau estimates that among today's 30-year-old women, 15 to 20 percent will remain childless (Spain and Bianchi 1996). This increase in childlessness means that more American women will enter old age in the twenty-first century without the potential support of adult children and may look to public and private services to provide for their needs. Preparing for the twenty-first century will require building and strengthening our social supports and service networks, especially for older women without children.

Number of Children

Although childlessness will be more prevalent in the next century, the two-child family continues to be the U.S. norm. American women in the 1990s, on average, have two children. The total fertility rate (TFR), that is the total number of children that a woman will have in her lifetime, has fluctuated between 1.7 and 2.1 since the mid-1970s. In 1995, it stood at 2.0 (National Center for Health Statistics 1997a). In contrast, during the baby-boom era of the 1950s and early 1960s, the TFR ranged from 3.1 to 3.8—nearly one to two children more than the current norm (Bureau of the Census 1975).

Speculation mounted in the late 1980s and early 1990s that a new baby boom had arrived as the number of births climbed upward. Over four million births occurred each year between 1989 and 1993—about the same number as at the height of the original baby-boom era. But this "baby-boom echo," as some demographers call it, was created by baby-boom women having babies, not by a return to large families.

In the early 1990s, the youngest (and most numerous) members of the post-World War II baby-boom generation reached their late twenties and early thirties. Many of these women heard their biological clocks ticking and needed to decide whether they would have children, and if so, how many to have. As these women had babies, they created a mini-baby boom. Although the number of births soared, the TFR never rose above 2.1 during this boomlet. In fact, after 1993, the number of births slipped below the four million mark as baby-boom women began to complete their families. Current fertility measures suggest that there is no surge toward larger families and that couples are not moving far from the two-child ideal that most Americans say they prefer.

Racial and ethnic differences in fertility are evident, however (see Figure V–4). Black women have always had more children than white women, although the difference has narrowed in recent years. In 1995, black women, on average, had 2.2 children each, while white women had 2.0. Asian and Pacific Islander women have the lowest TFR—1.9 children each. Hispanic women, including many immigrants to the United States from countries with higher fertility norms, have the highest TFR—3.0 children each. The higher fertility rates of minority groups, along with immigration, contribute to the changing racial and ethnic mix of the nation. Births to minority women accounted for nearly two in five births in 1995, compared with one in seven in 1960.

Unmarried Motherhood

Perhaps the most controversial and dramatic change in women's childbearing patterns over the past 25 years has been the rise in births to unmarried women. In 1995, nearly one in three births (or a total of 1.3 million babies) was to an unmarried mother (National Center for Health Statistics 1997b). In 1970, only one in ten births occurred out of wedlock. The trend has affected all ages, races, and socioeconomic groups in all regions of the country.

Figure V–4 • TOTAL FERTILITY RATES BY RACE AND HISPANIC ORIGIN, 1960–1995[1]

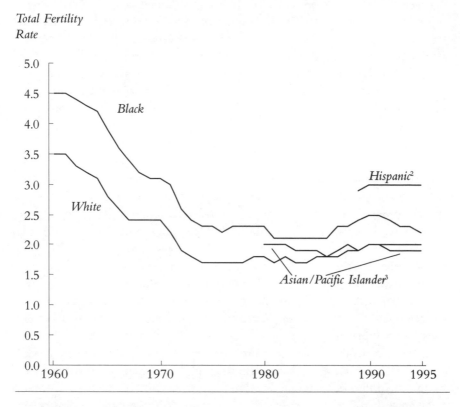

Total Fertility
Rate

[Figure shows curves labeled Black, White, Hispanic[2], and Asian/Pacific Islander[3], with the vertical axis (Total Fertility Rate) from 0.0 to 5.0 and the horizontal axis from 1960 to 1995.]

[1]The total fertility rate is the number of children that a woman, on average, will have in her lifetime.
[2]Persons of Hispanic origin may be of any race. Data for Hispanic women not available before 1989.
[3]Data for Asian/Pacific Islander women not available before 1980.

Source: National Center for Health Statistics, "Report of Final Natality Statistics, 1995," *Monthly Vital Statistics Report* 45, No. 11 (S), June 10, 1997, Tables 4 and 11; and Bureau of the Census, *Historical Statistics of the United States: Colonial Times to 1970*, Part 1, 1975, Table B–11–19.

The trend is not driven by teenagers, however. Over half of all nonmarital births occurred to women in their twenties, while teens accounted for roughly 30 percent of out-of-wedlock births. Two-thirds of the fathers of babies born to teenage mothers were men age 20 or older (Department of Health and Human Services 1995).

While nonmarital childbearing is most prevalent among minorities (70 percent of black babies and 40 percent of Hispanic babies in 1995 were born to unmarried women), the most striking increases have been among white women. One in four white births in 1995 occurred to unmarried women, up from one in 10 in 1980. About one in six Asian births in 1995 was to an unmarried woman (National Center for Health Statistics 1997a).

The United States is not alone in the trend toward single parenting. Canada, France, and the United Kingdom, for example, have experienced similar increases. Between one-quarter and one-third of recent births in these countries are to unmarried women (Bureau of the Census 1996d).

Changing family patterns have had a big impact on the lives of children. Children raised in one-parent homes or in unstable family environments face lower odds of succeeding in school, jobs, and marriage than children from more stable, two-parent households (McLanahan and Sandefur 1994). How well we provide for our children—economically, socially, and education-ally—can make a big difference in how well we succeed as a nation in the next century.

LIVING LONGER

Women tend to live longer than men, not only in the United States but in most countries around the world. This biological advantage affects the composition of the older population of the United States. Today, women represent more than half (55 percent) of the 65-to-69 age group, and almost three-quarters (72 percent) of the oldest age group (85 and older).

Increasing life expectancy is a phenomenon of the twentieth century—the result of modern medicine and improved public health standards. Women have benefited most from these changes. In 1900, men and women could expect to live about the same number of years. The difference between male and female life expectancy at birth was only two years (see Table V–1). But as infant and childhood diseases were conquered and fewer women died from the complications of childbirth, the gender gap in life expectancy began to widen. It hit its widest point in 1979 when women, on average, lived 7.8 years longer than men.

Improvements in life expectancy for women have slowed in recent years, while men's life expectancy has continued to rise. By 1995, the gender gap had closed slightly but still favored women by 6.4 years.

Population projections reflect the narrowing gap in male-female life expectancy and suggest a more balanced sex ratio in the future, especially at older ages. Currently, there are about 69 men for every 100 women age 65 and older. In the 85-and-older age group, the sex ratio is about 39 men for

Table V–1 • LIFE EXPECTANCY AT BIRTH BY SEX, 1900–1995

Year	Life Expectancy at Birth (in years)		
	Total	*Male*	*Female*
1900[1]	47.3	46.3	48.3
1950	68.2	65.6	71.1
1960	69.7	66.6	73.1
1970	70.8	67.1	74.7
1980	73.7	70.0	77.4
1990	75.4	71.8	78.8
1995	75.8	72.5	78.9

[1]Based on 10 states and the District of Columbia (Death Registration Area).

Source: National Center for Health Statistics, "Report of Final Mortality Statistics, 1995," *Monthly Vital Statistics Report* 45, No. 11 (S2), June 12, 1997.

every 100 women. Improvements in male mortality and a narrowing of the gender gap are expected to increase these ratios substantially. By 2030, sex ratios are projected to be about 84 men for every 100 women age 65 and older, and 55 men for every 100 women age 85 and older (Bureau of the Census 1996b).

Racial gaps in life expectancy show few signs of closing, however. The average life expectancy for blacks has remained six to eight years lower than for whites since the 1970s (National Center for Health Statistics 1997b). Life expectancy for black men in 1995 was 65.2 years, compared with 73.4 years for white men. For women, the gap was somewhat smaller, but still significant—73.9 years for blacks and 79.6 years for whites.

Much of the racial difference in life expectancy results from higher mortality at younger ages (National Center for Health Statistics 1997b). Black infants die at more than twice the rate of white and Hispanic babies, and young black males are more than twice as likely to die as young white males. Blacks are more likely to die of AIDS and to be victims of homicide. Unless these trends slow or reverse, the prospects for narrowing the racial gap in life expectancy are not very promising.

Can life expectancy go much higher? International comparisons show that U.S. mortality is not yet pushing up against biological or technological limits. Life expectancy in Japan is now 79.8 years, compared with 75.8 for the United States. Research based on data from Japan and Europe shows that, at the older ages, mortality improvements have been accelerating, not slowing, lending further credence to the idea that U.S. life expectancy can continue to improve (Manton and Vaupel 1995).

But will these added years of life be healthy years? The answer to this question depends, in part, on how one defines health and disability. While more people are living with chronic disabilities, most of these individuals are not incapacitated or bedridden. Many lead active lives, although their disabilities may restrict their activities or require some assistance. Prevention and postponement of disabling conditions can compress the time spent in need of care (Fries, Green, and Levine 1989). Because women live longer than men and because they provide most of the caregiving services for disabled people, women have much to gain from efforts to make life healthier and more productive, as well as longer.

IMMIGRATION TRENDS

Immigration has played an important role in the history of the United States. Not only does it contribute to population growth, but it also adds to the nation's diversity. In the mid-1990s, about 800,000 legal immigrants came to the United States each year (Immigration and Naturalization Service 1996). Three-quarters of these new arrivals were from Asia and Latin America. The number of illegal immigrants is, of course, unknown, but most estimates range from 1.1 million to 2.9 million per year (Acevedo and Espenshade 1992). Most illegal immigrants leave the United States (either through apprehension or voluntary departure), but an estimated 300,000 remain permanently (Warren 1994).

Because immigrants tend to be young adults (in 1995 the average age was 27 for men and 29 for women), new arrivals temporarily counteract the effects of population aging. They also add to the nation's birth rates. About 60 percent of female immigrants in 1995 were of childbearing age (age 15 to 44).

In recent years, women have generally outnumbered men among the immigrant population. Between 1950 and 1979, 54 percent of new arrivals were women. The ratio was more evenly balanced during the 1980s but tilted slightly toward men. By the mid-1990s, however, women had regained the numerical advantage over men (54 percent versus 46 percent, respectively).

The greater share of female immigrants in recent years may be an indirect consequence of the 1986 Immigration Reform and Control Act (IRCA), which allowed illegal aliens to become legal residents if they met certain requirements. Between 1989 and 1994, 2.7 million people qualified and were granted legal resident status. Two-thirds of this group were men. Because legal resident status allows immigrants to sponsor family members to join them in the United States, this provision may have tipped the scales once again to favor women.

In 1995, 68 percent of female immigrants were admitted to the United States under family reunification provisions of the U.S. immigration law, compared with 60 percent of male immigrants. Women were less likely than men to come to the United States for either legal employment or as refugees. About 11 percent of female immigrants and 13 percent of male immigrants were admitted under employment-based preferences, while 14 percent of women and 18 percent of men came to the United States as refugees (Immigration and Naturalization Service 1996).

If current levels and patterns of immigration persist, the U.S. population will continue to grow and become more racially and ethnically diverse. Women contribute to these trends directly, as new arrivals to the country, and indirectly, by the number of children they bear. These personal decisions in the everyday lives of women will be central to determining the nation's future.

SOCIAL AND ECONOMIC DIMENSIONS OF WOMEN'S LIVES

The social and economic changes that have reshaped U.S. society in the past quarter-century have made a deep imprint on women's lives. The women's movement in the 1970s encouraged women's independence and opened new social and economic opportunities. The stagnation (and sometimes decline) of men's wages in the 1970s and 1980s drew many women into the paid labor force. Gradually but decidedly, the traditional aspects of women's lives as wives and mothers expanded to include new roles. In the process, social and economic institutions were transformed.

Marriage

Marriage has not gone out of style for American women. Nearly 60 percent of women age 18 and older are currently married (Bureau of the Census 1996a), and an estimated 90 percent of young women expect to marry at some point in their lifetimes (Norton and Miller 1992). But the share of *currently* married women has declined. In 1970, almost 70 percent of women were married. This apparent movement away from marriage reflects at least two factors: age at marriage and the likelihood of divorce.

Women, as well as men, are waiting longer before getting married. In 1995, the average age at first marriage was 24.5 years for women and 26.9 years for men—the highest average ages recorded in this century. Indeed, 19 percent of women and 28 percent of men in their early thirties have never married (Bureau of the Census 1996a). There is now a prolonged (and accepted) stage of young adulthood when an individual is unmarried—or perhaps cohabiting.

The odds of divorce are much higher today than in the past. Whereas almost half of women who married in the late 1960s and early 1970s have already divorced, only 14 percent of women who married in the early 1940s eventually divorced (London 1991). The share of women currently divorced has tripled since 1970, from three to 10 percent. Compared with the 1960s, marriages have a shorter average duration, and a smaller proportion of a woman's life is spent in marriage, despite gains in life expectancy for both men and women (Espenshade 1985).

While all race and ethnic groups have been affected by changing marriage and divorce patterns, the movement away from marriage has been particularly pronounced among black women (see Figure V–5). Only 40

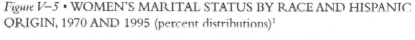

Figure V–5 • WOMEN'S MARITAL STATUS BY RACE AND HISPANIC ORIGIN, 1970 AND 1995 (percent distributions)[1]

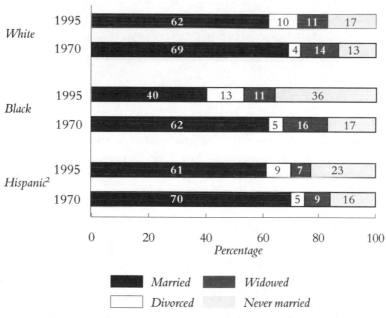

[1]Women age 18 and over.
[2]Persons of Hispanic origin may be of any race.

Source: Bureau of the Census, *Statistical Abstract of the United States 1996*, 1996, Table 58.

percent of black women were married in 1995, compared with 62 percent in 1970. The share of black women who had never married more than doubled between 1970 and 1995. Unlike the 1970s when racial or ethnic differences in marital status were relatively minor, the marital status of black women today contrasts sharply with the marital status of women in other racial and ethnic groups. By 1995, more than half (58 percent) of all black children were being raised by single mothers, compared with 18 percent of white children and 30 percent of Hispanic children (Bureau of the Census 1996a).

The movement away from marriage appears to be slowing—or at least reaching a plateau. Divorce rates stabilized during the first half of the 1990s, and the number of two-parent, married-couple homes with children increased (De Vita 1996). Because young people are waiting longer to get married, presumably they will enter marriage with greater maturity, thereby reducing the risk of divorce. Also, the aging of the baby-boom generation means that a large share of the adult population has passed through the stage of life when the odds of divorce are greatest. Yet, changing attitudes toward men's and women's roles, as well as increasing economic opportunities for women, will continue to redefine marriage and family patterns in the United States. As we move toward the next century, it appears that deferred marriage, divorce, and remarriage are now intrinsic parts of contemporary U.S. life (Castro and Bumpass 1989).

EDUCATIONAL ACHIEVEMENTS

Education has opened new opportunities for women. It also holds the key to their future. Because the demands of the future workplace will require advanced levels of education and the acquisition of technical skills, women who successfully meet these goals are likely to fare well in the years ahead. Women's track record in the educational arena bodes well for their future success.

Each generation of women has achieved a higher level of education than the preceding one (see Table V–2). In 1995, 88 percent of women age 25 to 34 had graduated from high school, up from 60 percent in 1960. Three of every five female high school graduates in 1995 went to college, compared with less than two in five in 1960. One in four women age 25 to 34 is now a college graduate—triple the share reported in 1960. And since 1990, women have earned the majority of bachelor's and master's degrees. For younger women in the 1990s, the gender gap in achieving a college education no longer exists.

Gender differences still persist in professional schools and doctoral pro-

Table V–2 • EDUCATIONAL ATTAINMENT BY WOMEN AGE 25–34
BY BIRTH COHORT, 1960–1995

	1960	*1970*	*1980*	*1990*	*1995*
Birth cohort	1926–35	1936–45	1946–55	1956–65	1961–70
Percentage who graduated from high school	60	73	85	87	88
Percentage of high school graduates who enrolled in college in fall after graduation	38	49	52	62	61
Percentage who are college graduates	8	12	21	23	25
Degrees conferred on women as a percentage of all degrees[1]					
Bachelor's	39[2]	43	49	53	54
Master's	32	40	49	53	55
Doctorates	11	13	30	36	39
Dentistry	1	1	13	31	38
Medicine	6	8	23	34	38
Law	2	5	30	42	43
Business (MBA)	4	4	22	34	36

[1]Data for the 1961–70 cohort are for 1994.
[2]Data are for 1961.

Source: National Center for Education Statistics, *Digest of Education Statistics 1996*, 1996, Tables 259, 262, 263, 265, and 269; and Bureau of the Census, *Years of School Completed by Persons 25 Years and Over, by Age and Sex: Selected Years, 1940 to 1955*, 1997.

grams, however. In 1994, women earned 38 percent of the degrees in dentistry and medicine and 39 percent of the doctoral degrees. Women were somewhat better represented in the legal profession, earning 43 percent of the law degrees. Although women have yet to achieve parity with men in these areas, they have traveled a long way from their starting point. In 1960, fewer than one in 10 professional and doctoral degrees was awarded to women. The women of the baby-boom generation broke these barriers and paved the way for the generations of women that followed.

Women of all racial and ethnic groups have shared in this success (see Figure V–6). Among non-Hispanic whites, the share of bachelor's degrees going to women rose from 46 percent in 1977 to 54 percent in 1994;

Figure V–6 • WOMEN'S SHARE OF BACHELOR'S DEGREES BY
RACE AND HISPANIC ORIGIN, 1977 AND 1994 (in percentages)

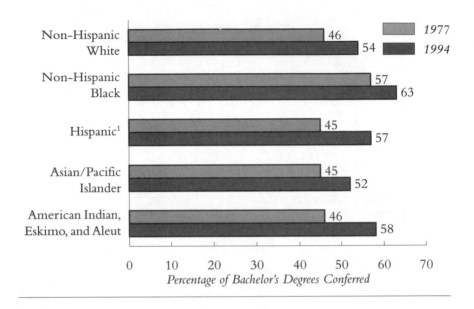

Percentage of Bachelor's Degrees Conferred

---

[1]Persons of Hispanic origin may be of any race.

Source: National Center for Education Statistics, *Digest of Education Statistics 1996,* 1996,
Table 259.

among Hispanics, it rose from 45 to 57 percent. Black women in 1977 already earned a majority of the bachelor's degrees conferred on black students, and they increased this share to over 60 percent by 1994. When given the chance, women can compete and succeed in the educational arena.

Access to higher education is still a struggle, however, for many minority women—and men. In 1994, nearly 40 percent of white women, 25 percent of black women, and 16 percent of Hispanic women age 18 to 21 were enrolled in college (Bureau of the Census 1996d). In contrast, only one in three white men age 18 to 21 was enrolled in college in 1994, and the rates for minority men were even lower—one in five for blacks and one in 10 for Hispanics. Lower college enrollment rates among minorities reflect, in part, the higher share of minority men and women who do not complete high school. They also may reflect the high cost of a college education. In 1996, tuition, fees, and room and board at a four-year, state university averaged $7,500 a year, and about $22,500 a year at a four-year private university (National Center for Education Statistics 1996). Such costs are simply out of reach for many low-income minority families. Although women have made real gains in educational achievement, an important challenge for the nation in the next century will be to increase access to higher education, especially for the growing number of minorities in the population.

LABOR FORCE PARTICIPATION

Working outside the home is no longer only associated with poor or minority women. Women of all income levels, racial and ethnic backgrounds, and family patterns have joined the workforce. The change has been dramatic.

- Almost 60 percent of adult women were in the workforce in 1995, compared with 38 percent in 1960.
- Two of every three married women with preschool-age children worked outside the home in 1995, up from one in three in 1970.
- Three-quarters of married women with school-age children were employed in 1995, up from one-half in 1970.
- About two of every five married women with children held full-time, year-round jobs in 1995.
- The dual-worker family has replaced the breadwinner-homemaker model as the most common type of family in the United States.

From 1940 to the mid-1960s, increases in women's labor force activity were seen mostly among women who were past their prime childbearing years. This was the post-World War II, baby-boom era in the United States and many women saw their roles mainly as wives and mothers. Labor force participation was largely among women who had raised their children or who were financially in need.

As social and economic changes swept the country in the 1960s and 1970s, attitudes and practices changed. Increasing divorce rates meant that more women needed to assume responsibility for their own or their families' economic well-being. Expanding educational opportunities widened career and work options for women. As a result, younger women began to enter the labor force in increasing numbers. Economic pressures, such as high rates of inflation and periodic recessions, drew many married women into the labor force as well.

Women of all racial and ethnic groups have responded to these social and economic forces, as Figure V–7 shows. Black women have always had the strongest attachment to the work force, but labor force participation rates

Figure V–7 • WOMEN'S LABOR FORCE PARTICIPATION BY RACE AND HISPANIC ORIGIN, 1940–1995

Percentage of
Women in the
Labor Force

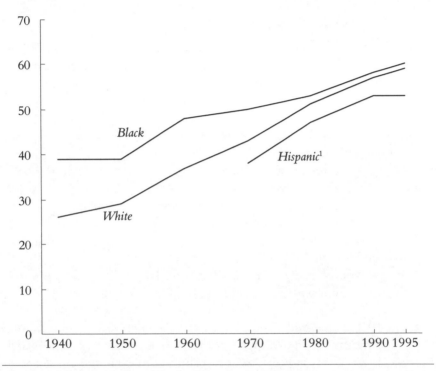

[1]Persons of Hispanic origin may be of any race. Data for Hispanic women not available before 1970.

Source: Bureau of the Census, *1950 Census of the United States,* 1953; *Historical Statistics of the United States: Colonial Times to 1970,* 1975, Table D–42–48; and *Statistical Abstract of the United States 1996,* 1996, Table 615.

for white women have now closed the gap. In 1995, 60 percent of black women were in the labor force, compared with 59 percent of white women. Hispanic women have somewhat lower rates of participation, but even so, 53 percent of Hispanic women were in the paid labor force in 1995.

Women have adjusted to the dual demands of work and family in a number of ways. Many mothers work part time, and some drop out of the labor force temporarily while their children are young. Others seek jobs that allow flexible work schedules. Some husbands and wives work opposite shifts (one at night, one during the day) in order to cover child care or other family needs. Other couples use outside service providers to help them meet their family responsibilities. Working women have found that they must become skilled jugglers of conflicting demands on their time and energy.

The rapid gains in labor force participation that were observed in the 1960s, 1970s, and 1980s have begun to wane. Women's labor force participation continues to rise but at a much slower rate. It is possible that American women's labor force participation rates are reaching an upper limit, but comparisons with other industrial countries suggest that these boundaries can be pushed still further (Bureau of the Census 1996d). Without further accommodations to the family needs of working women, however, the rates are likely to plateau in the years ahead.

Young women are asking "Can I have it all—work, family, marriage, a comfortable and fulfilling future?" The desire to balance work and family is clearly in the forefront of their minds. Although the women who preceded them have set the course, the choices that today's young women make will pave the way to the United States's future.

OUTLOOK FOR THE FUTURE

What lies ahead for the American woman? The answers are as diverse as the women who will create that future. There will be no single image or model lifestyle that will capture the multiple and changing facets of women's lives. Women of different ages, races, and generations will define and shape their worlds to meet their needs.

Yet the challenges that women are likely to face in the next century are already evident in the lives of women today. In many ways, the future is simply a building block on the past. Each generation follows in the footsteps of the last generation—sometimes treading similar ground but often pushing the frontiers further ahead. No doubt American women in the twenty-first century will face conflicts and choices that their predecessors never knew. But if we look ahead about 25 years, we can already see the broad outlines of the demographic future that is likely to unfold.

TODAY'S PRESCHOOLERS

Although it may be hard to imagine today's young toddler as a grown woman, the youngsters who today fill our nurseries, child care programs, and preschools will be the young adults of the next century. Their developmental years are being shaped by computer technologies that their parents are only beginning to explore and understand. As a result, tomorrow's generation of young adults will be increasingly comfortable with technology and find the concepts of instant communication, information on demand, and virtual reality to be commonplace.

As 20- and 30-year-olds in the next century, today's preschoolers will also go through the major transitions that all young women face—leaving their parental homes, perhaps going to college, getting married or starting careers, and having babies. Today's transition to adulthood follows no orderly path, and it is unlikely that future generations will impose order on this time of life. In fact, given the expanding choices and quickening pace of change, the next century's young adults will have more options in constructing their life paths than their parents ever knew or could imagine.

The opportunities arising from such change will be tempered by the socioeconomic circumstances in which children are raised. In today's world, one in four U.S. children under age six is growing up in a family that lives in poverty. Nearly half of all black preschoolers and over 40 percent of Hispanic preschoolers are growing up poor (Bureau of the Census 1996c). For these children, the promises of the future may be harder to grasp and fulfill.

GENERATION X-ERS

Today's high school and college students—collectively known as Generation X—will be the middle-aged women of 2025. As 40- and 50-year-olds, they are likely to be in key decisionmaking positions in the twenty-first century. These women will be tomorrow's business leaders, educators, homemakers, scientists, artists, policymakers, and elected officials. One could even become President of the United States. To make this dream a reality, however, today's Generation X-ers will need to build on the educational opportunities and leadership positions that have opened to women in the past two decades.

While the possibilities may be limitless for some, for the school dropout, teenage mother, or non-English speaker, the path to this bright and exciting future will be strewn with obstacles. Although the women of Generation X will make their own choices, today's middle-aged women can be role models and mentors to help these young women find their way.

BABY-BOOM WOMEN

The most powerful demographic force of the past 50 years has been the baby-boom generation. For the next 50 years, baby-boom women will redefine the U.S. image of old age. In a society that celebrates youth and vigor, growing old can be a daunting prospect. But given their sheer numbers, the response of baby-boom women to this next stage of life will have far-ranging implications for how we perceive and respond to older people.

By 2025, baby-boom women will be in their 60s and 70s. Their current concerns about juggling jobs and babies or breaking the glass ceiling in the workplace are likely to have less urgency. Instead, they will be planning for (or entering into) retirement, facing widowhood, and learning to be grandparents. Issues such as age discrimination in the workplace, pension planning, and retirement income are likely to become the next areas of focus for baby-boom women in the years ahead.

If the past is prologue, then we can already see that the retirement years of baby-boom women will be as varied as their circumstances in middle age. Some will have the social and financial resources to enjoy many comfortable years of retirement. Others, whether because of poor planning or unfortunate circumstances, will be less well off in their older years. In speculating about the future, it would be a mistake to see these women as a homogeneous group, rather than the diverse mix of needs and circumstances that they represent.

WOMEN AT THE THRESHOLD OF RETIREMENT

Finally, the women who were born before the baby-boom generation (1945 and earlier) will be the United States's oldest-old generation. By 2025, they will form the 80-and-older population. Their personal concerns will focus on aging, health, and long-term care issues. This generation of women is likely to be very different from their counterparts today. The 80-something generation of 2025, for example, will enter the oldest ages with far more labor force experience than the current generation of 80-year-old women have had. This past work experience will make the future generation of 80-year-olds much more independent and self-sufficient—at least in terms of decisionmaking—than today's older women. But because tomorrow's 80-something woman is much more likely to have been divorced than her counterpart of today, her financial resources may be less adequate. For many women, the financial consequences of divorce can have long-term, negative effects. The loss of an ex-husband's pension coverage, for example, can create financial hardship in a woman's later years—long after the marriage has ended. The pre-baby-boom generation will be the first generation of women in which substantial numbers have been divorced. Their experiences will help us better understand the long-term consequences of divorce on women as they age.

But the 80-something woman of 2025 will have one valuable asset—her children. This future generation of older women are the mothers of the baby-boom generation—at least those baby boomers who were born in the 1960s, near the end of the baby-boom era. These women have had, on average, 2.6 children each (Bureau of the Census 1983). Only one in 10 is childless (National Center for Health Statistics 1994). In terms of family and social support networks, these women are demographically well endowed. Adult children generally increase the potential range of care options for older women, but they do not necessarily eliminate the need for outside services. As any baby boomer with aging parents will tell you, juggling the demands of work, their own children, and aging parents can be an exhausting and worrisome responsibility. Balancing the needs and lifestyle demands of different generations will be one of the most important public-policy challenges of the next century.

The American woman's future will be shaped by demographic circumstances, by changing social and economic times, and by her own resourcefulness. Although we do not know what lies ahead, demographic trends suggest that a one-size-fits-all model of the future will fall short of capturing the realities of the next century.

Women of different ages, races, ethnic origins, family patterns, and economic circumstances are likely to travel along different paths, but their journeys will cover common ground as they foster family ties, face economic challenges, and make their marks in their communities and the nation as a whole. The challenges of the coming years will be both demanding and diverse for this mosaic of women, but they will best be met through the shared wisdom, common experiences, and courageous steps of every American woman.

AMERICAN WOMEN TODAY: A STATISTICAL PORTRAIT

Section I:
Demographics[1]

This section profiles the U.S. population, with a particular focus on the female population. Included are recent data on age, life expectancy, and the racial and Hispanic/non-Hispanic mix and how it is changing, as well as information on marital status, family characteristics, divorce and fertility rates, and living arrangements. Many of the tables and figures track trends over the past quarter of a century or more. Several also look into the future, projecting some of the key characteristics of the population in the decades ahead (see also Chapter Five).

These are "dry statistics" perhaps, but the realities they reflect both shape and are shaped by the decisions and circumstances of millions of individual women.

- Females outnumber males among non-Hispanics in every racial group, although males outnumber females among persons of Hispanic origin (who may be of any race) (see Table 1–1).
- By 2050, one in four Americans will be of Hispanic origin, and another one in 12 will be of Asian/Pacific Islander descent. Non-Hispanic whites will be a bare majority (see Figure 1–4).
- Women of every race can expect to outlive their male counterparts. Asian/Pacific Islander women have the longest life expectancy of all (see Table 1–4).
- Fertility rates are over 50 percent lower for blacks and over 40 percent

[1]The editors are deeply indebted to Jennifer E. Griffith, who identified and gathered the necessary materials and prepared all the tables and figures in the statistical sections of this edition of *The American Woman*.

lower for whites than they were in 1960. Persons of Hispanic origin have the highest fertility rates (see Figure 1–5).

- Age at first marriage has been going up steadily for both women and men for a quarter-century (see Figure 1–7).
- The divorce rate has been gradually declining since the early 1980s (see Figure 1–8).
- Except among black families, the majority of families are still married-couple families (see Table 1–7).
- Children in two-parent families represent a shrinking proportion of all children in the United States but are still in the majority among whites and Hispanics (see Table 1–9).
- Women begin to outnumber men in the 30-something age group; the older the age group, the larger the preponderance of women (see Figures 1–2 and 1–9).
- By the time a woman reaches the age of 75, the chances that she is living with a spouse have dropped below one in three. The majority of women over 75 live alone (see Table 1–10 and Figure 1–10).

Table 1–1 • POPULATION OF THE UNITED STATES BY RACE, HISPANIC ORIGIN, AND SEX, July 1, 1997 (projected)[1]

Whites who are not of Hispanic origin still predominate in the U.S. population. Females outnumber males in every group shown here except people of Hispanic origin, among whom males have a slight edge.

	Number
White, non-Hispanic	
Females	99,727,000
Males	95,364,000
Black, non-Hispanic	
Females	17,076,000
Males	15,320,000
American Indian, Eskimo, and Aleut, non-Hispanic	
Females	1,008,000
Males	973,000
Asian/Pacific Islander, non-Hispanic	
Females	4,932,000
Males	4,565,000
Hispanic[2]	
Females	14,190,000
Males	14,490,000
All races	
Females	136,933,000
Males	130,712,000

[1]Resident population of the 50 states and the District of Columbia.
[2]Persons of Hispanic origin may be of any race.

Source: Bureau of the Census, *Population Projections of the United States, by Age, Sex, Race, and Hispanic Origin: 1995 to 2050*, 1996, Table 2.

Figure 1–1 • POPULATION OF THE UNITED STATES BY SEX, RACE, AND HISPANIC ORIGIN, July 1, 1997 (projected) (percent distributions)[1]

The proportion of non-Hispanic blacks is slightly larger among females than among males; the proportion of Hispanics is slightly larger among males than among females. In other respects, the distributions of the two sexes are nearly identical.

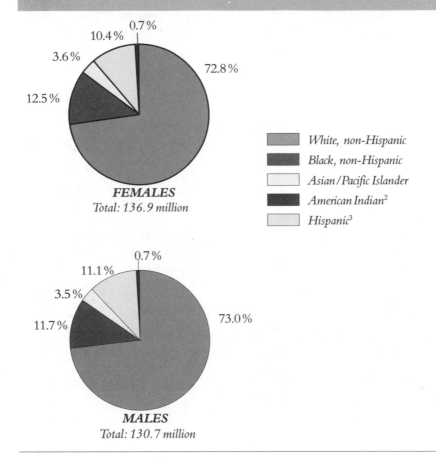

FEMALES
Total: 136.9 million

White, non-Hispanic
Black, non-Hispanic
Asian/Pacific Islander
American Indian[2]
Hispanic[3]

MALES
Total: 130.7 million

[1]Resident population of the 50 states and the District of Columbia.
[2]Includes Eskimo and Aleut.
[3]Persons of Hispanic origin may be of any race.

Source: Bureau of the Census, *Population Projections of the United States by Age, Sex, Race, and Hispanic Origin: 1995 to 2050,* 1996, Table 2.

Figure 1–2 • POPULATION OF THE UNITED STATES BY AGE AND SEX, July 1, 1997 (projected)[1,2]

Males slightly outnumber females in the under-30 age groups, but the balance begins to tip the other way as people move into their mid-thirties. Among Americans who have passed their eightieth birthday, women outnumber men by two to one.

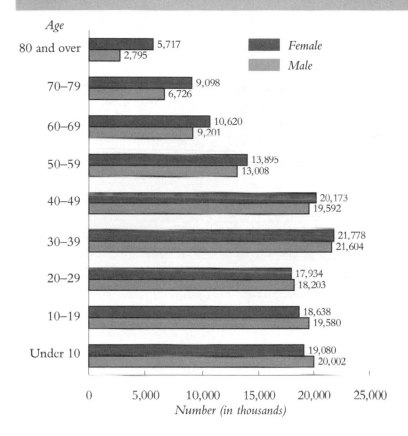

Figure 1–3 • PROJECTED POPULATION OF THE UNITED STATES IN 2050, BY AGE AND SEX[1,2]

> By the middle of the twenty-first century, Americans age 80 or older are projected to account for nearly eight percent of the U.S. population (compared with just over three percent in 1997). Women will predominate in this age group but not to the extent that they do today (see Figure 1–2).

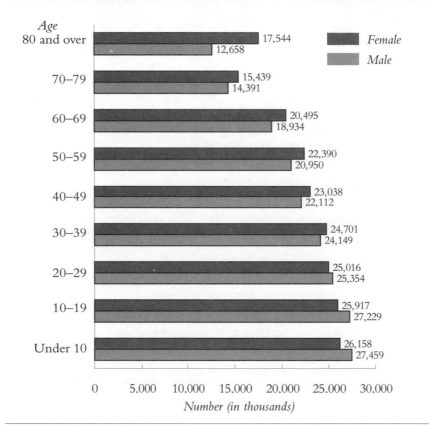

Age

Age	Female	Male
80 and over	17,544	12,658
70–79	15,439	14,391
60–69	20,495	18,934
50–59	22,390	20,950
40–49	23,038	22,112
30–39	24,701	24,149
20–29	25,016	25,354
10–19	25,917	27,229
Under 10	26,158	27,459

0   5.000   10.000   15.000   20.000   25.000   30.000

Number (in thousands)

[1]Resident population of the 50 states and the District of Columbia.
[2]Middle assumptions.

Source: Bureau of the Census, *Population Projections of the United States by Age, Sex, Race, and Hispanic Origin: 1995 to 2050,* 1996, Table 2.

Figure 1–4 • PROJECTED COMPOSITION OF THE POPULATION OF THE UNITED STATES BY RACE AND HISPANIC ORIGIN, 1997, 2000, 2015, 2030, AND 2050

Over the next half-century, whites not of Hispanic origin will still predominate in the U.S. population but with steadily diminishing majorities. People of Asian/ Pacific Islander descent and people of Hispanic origin, by contrast, will see their proportionate shares of the population more than double.

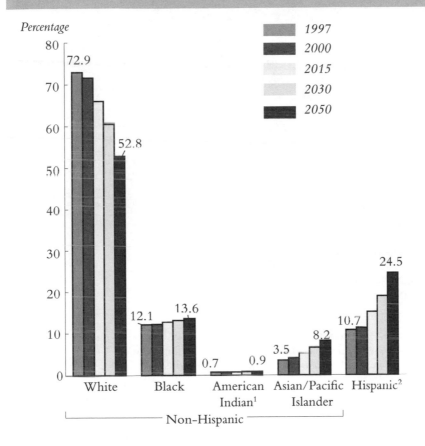

¹Includes Eskimo and Aleut.
²Persons of Hispanic origin may be of any race.

Source: Bureau of the Census, *Projected Population of the United States by Age, Sex, Race, and Hispanic Origin: 1995 to 2050,* 1996, Table 2.

Table 1–2 • THE U.S.- AND FOREIGN-BORN FEMALE POPULATION OF THE UNITED STATES BY RACE AND HISPANIC ORIGIN, 1996 (percent distributions)

The racial and Hispanic/non-Hispanic profile of the foreign-born female population in the United States is quite different from that of the U.S.-born population: Asian/Pacific Islanders and Hispanics (who may be of any race but are usually white) account for much larger proportions, and blacks for a much smaller proportion, of the foreign-born than of the U.S.-born female population.

	Total Female Population	U.S.-Born[1]	Foreign-Born	
			All	Came to U.S. after 1979
White	82.1	83.6	67.3	60.6
Black	13.4	13.9	8.3	9.0
Native American[2]	0.9	1.0	0.4	0.4
Asian/Pacific Islander	3.6	1.6	24.0	30.0
Total percentage	100.0	100.0	100.0	100.0
Hispanic[3]	10.4	7.2	41.7	44.3
Non–Hispanic	89.6	92.8	58.3	55.7
Total percentage	100.0	100.0	100.0	100.0
Percent distribution by nativity	100.0	90.4	9.2	5.4
Total number (in thousands)	135,171	122,639	12,532	7,332

[1]"U.S.-born" persons were born in the United States, Puerto Rico, or an outlying area of the United States, such as Guam or the U.S. Virgin Islands, or were born in a foreign country but had at least one parent who was a U.S. citizen. All other persons are foreign-born. In addition to legally admitted immigrants, the foreign-born include refugees, temporary residents, such as students and temporary workers, and some undocumented immigrants.

[2]American Indian, Eskimo, and Aleut.

[2]Persons of Hispanic origin may be of any race.

Source: Bureau of the Census, *The Foreign-Born Population: 1996,* 1997; and data on the foreign-born from the March 1996 Current Population Survey, <http://www.census.gov/population/socdemo/foreign/96/96tab-1.txt> and <... /96tab-2.txt>, published April 8, 1997, accessed July 7, 1997.

Table 1–3 • MEDIAN AGES OF THE U.S. POPULATION BY SEX, RACE, AND HISPANIC ORIGIN, July 1, 1997 (projected)

Especially when compared with the white non-Hispanic population, the population of Hispanic origin is striking for its youthfulness and for the relatively small difference in the median ages of females and males.

	Median Age in Years	
	Female	Male
Total	36.0	33.8
Non-Hispanic		
White	38.5	36.2
Black	31.3	27.7
American Indian, Eskimo, and Aleut	28.5	26.7
Asian/Pacific Islander	32.2	30.1
Hispanic[1]	27.1	26.2

[1]Persons of Hispanic origin may be of any race.

Source: Bureau of the Census, *Population Projections of the United States by Age, Sex, Race, and Hispanic Origin: 1995 to 2050,* 1996, Table 2.

Table 1–4 • LIFE EXPECTANCY AT BIRTH AND AT AGE 65 BY SEX, RACE, AND HISPANIC ORIGIN, 1997 (in years)

Whether a male or female, an Asian/Pacific Islander baby born in 1997 has a longer life expectancy than a baby of the same sex born into any other racial or ethnic group. An Asian/Pacific Islander woman or man who turned 65 in 1997 also can expect to live longer than her or his counterpart in any other group, although the difference is much smaller. In every group, at birth and at age 65, a female can expect to live longer than her male contemporary of the same race or ethnicity.

| | *Life Expectancy (years of life remaining)* | | | |
| | *At Birth* | | *At Age 65* | |
	Females	*Males*	*Females*	*Males*
All races	79.5	72.7	19.3	15.6
Non-Hispanic				
White	80.2	73.9	19.4	15.8
Black	74.3	64.4	17.6	13.5
Asian/Pacific Islander	85.1	79.7	23.1	18.9
American Indian, Eskimo, and				
Aleut	80.3	71.7	22.6	18.0
Hispanic[1]	82.5	75.0	22.0	18.7

[1]Persons of Hispanic origin may be of any race.

Source: Bureau of the Census, *Population Projections of the United States by Age, Sex, Race, and Hispanic Origin: 1995-2050,* 1996, Tables B–1 and B–2, middle assumptions.

Table 1–5 • LIFE EXPECTANCY AT BIRTH AND AT AGE 65 BY RACE AND SEX, 1900, 1960, AND 1980, AND PROJECTED 2000, 2020, AND 2040

Even in 1900, a female in the United States could expect a longer life than a male of the same age, and a white person of either sex could expect a longer life than her or his black counterpart. If projections hold true, this will still be the case in 2000 and beyond. However, among whites, the female "edge" is beginning to narrow as life expectancy increases faster for males than for females.

	Life Expectancy (years of life remaining)			
	At Birth		*At Age 65*	
	Female	*Male*	*Female*	*Male*
All races				
1900[1]	48.3	46.3	12.2	11.5
1960	73.1	66.6	15.8	12.8
1980	77.4	70.0	18.3	14.1
2000	79.7	73.0	19.5	15.9
2020	81.5	75.5	20.6	17.6
2040	83.3	78.3	21.8	19.3
White				
1900	48.7	46.6	12.2	11.5
1960	74.1	67.4	15.9	12.9
1980	78.1	70.7	18.4	14.2
2000	80.5	74.2	19.7	16.2
2020	82.6	77.1	21.1	18.3
2040	84.8	80.3	22.7	20.4
Black				
1900	33.5	32.5	11.4	10.4
1960	65.9	60.7	15.1	12.7
1980	72.5	63.8	16.8	13.0
2000	74.7	64.6	17.8	13.8
2020	76.5	66.5	18.8	14.8
2040	78.6	69.3	19.8	15.9

[1]Data for 1900 include the years 1900–1902.

Source: National Center for Health Statistics, *Health, United States, 1993,* 1994, Table 27, and Bureau of the Census, *Population Projections of the United States by Age, Sex, Race, and Hispanic Origin: 1995–2050,* 1996, Tables B–1 and B–2, middle assumptions.

Figure 1–5 • U.S. FERTILITY RATES BY RACE AND HISPANIC ORIGIN OF CHILD, 1950–1995[1]

In 1960, the trailing edge of the baby boom years, U.S. fertility rates were close to their highwater mark. Two decades later, they had dropped by more than 40 percent and, after edging up slightly in the late 1980s, they began dropping again. The longstanding difference between white and black rates had nearly disappeared by 1995. Fertility rates for Hispanics (not available for the years before 1989) were much higher than for blacks or whites.

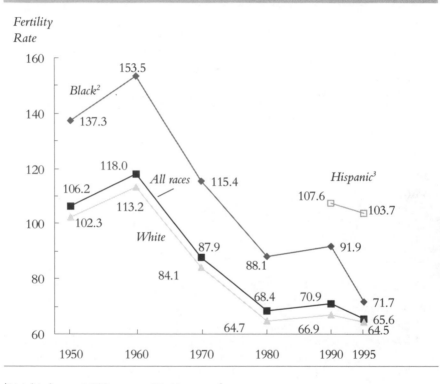

[1]Live births per 1,000 women 15–44 years of age.
[2]"Black and other" for 1950 only.
[3]Persons of Hispanic origin may be of any race.

Source: Bureau of the Census, *Statistical Abstract of the United States: 1980*, 1980, Table 88; National Center for Health Statistics, *Health, United States, 1993*, 1994, Table 4; and *Monthly Vital Statistics Report* 43, No. 11(S), May 25, 1995, Table 5, and 45, No. 3(S)2, October 4, 1996, Table 2.

Table 1–6 • MARITAL STATUS BY SEX, RACE, AND HISPANIC ORIGIN, 1995 (percent distributions)[1]

A larger proportion of men than of women are either currently married and living with their spouses or have never married. This is because the formerly married account for a larger proportion of women than of men: in 1995, more than 20 percent of women overall were either widowed or currently divorced, compared with about 10 percent of men.

Marital Status	All Races		White		Black		Hispanic[2]	
	Women	Men	Women	Men	Women	Men	Women	Men
Married, spouse present	55.1	59.7	58.5	62.4	31.4	40.0	52.9	50.8
Married, spouse absent	4.0	3.0	3.2	2.5	9.0	6.7	7.8	7.1
Widowed	11.1	2.5	11.3	2.5	11.3	3.1	6.6	1.8
Divorced	10.3	8.0	10.1	8.1	12.5	8.5	9.2	6.6
Never married	19.4	26.8	16.9	24.6	35.8	41.7	23.5	33.8
Total number (in thousands)	99,588	92,008	83,219	78,055	12,221	9,921	8,797	8,822
Total percentage[3]	100.0	100.0	100.0	100.0	100.0	100.0	100.0	100.0

[1]Persons age 18 and over.
[2]Persons of Hispanic origin may be of any race.
[3]Percentages may not total 100.0 due to rounding.

Source: Bureau of the Census, *Marital Status and Living Arrangements: March 1995 (Update)*, 1996, Table 1.

Figure 1–6 • CURRENTLY MARRIED AND NEVER MARRIED ADULTS BY SEX, RACE, AND HISPANIC ORIGIN, 1995[1]

Among whites, the currently married outnumber their never married counterparts by 3.5 to one in the case of women and by 2.5 to one in the case of men. Women and men of Hispanic origin are also more likely to be currently married than never married, although the ratios are slimmer than for whites. Among black women and men the never married outnumber the currently married.

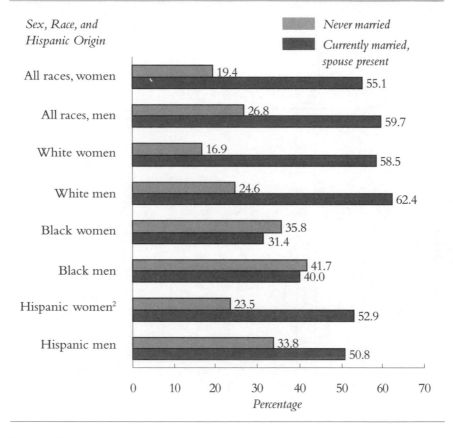

[1]Persons 18 years and over.
[2]Persons of Hispanic origin may be of any race.

Source: Bureau of the Census, *Marital Status and Living Arrangements, March 1995 (Update)*, 1996, Table 1.

Figure 1–7 • MEDIAN AGE AT FIRST MARRIAGE BY SEX, 1970–1994

The typical first-time bride in 1970 was not quite 21 years old. Her 1994 counterpart was nearing her twenty-fifth birthday. The trend toward later marriage has been occurring among both sexes.

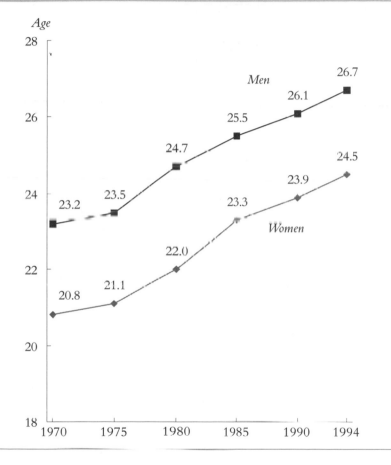

Source: Bureau of the Census, *Marital Status and Living Arrangements: March 1993*, 1994, Table B, and *Marital Status and Living Arrangements: March 1994*, 1996, Figure 2.

Figure 1–8 • THE DIVORCE RATE, 1950–1996

The divorce rate—the number of divorces in a given year per 1,000 persons in the population—has been gradually declining since the early 1980s.

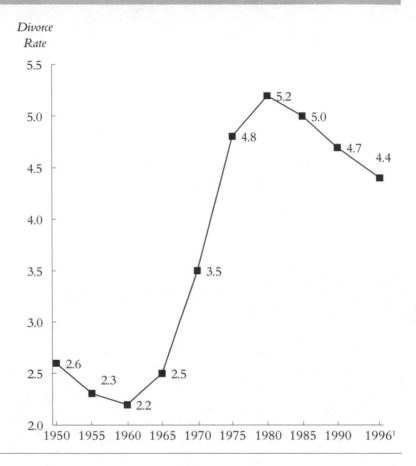

¹For the 12 months ending with July 1996.

Source: Bureau of the Census, *Statistical Abstract of the United States: 1996*, 1996, Table 90; and National Center for Health Statistics, *Monthly Vital Statistics Report* 45, No. 7, February 19, 1997, p1.

Table 1–7 • FAMILIES BY FAMILY TYPE, RACE, AND HISPANIC ORIGIN, 1970, 1980, 1990, AND 1995 (percent distributions)[1]

In 1970, 11.4 percent of U.S. families—or just over one in every 10—were headed by women with no spouse present. Twenty-five years later, the comparable proportion was 18 percent—almost one in every five. The proportion of families headed by men, although still small, doubled over the same period (up from 2.4 percent in 1970 to 5.0 percent in 1995). Except among black families, married couples still predominate, even though their proportion of the total has declined steadily.

Family Type	1970	1980	1990	1995
All races				
Married couple	85.7	81.7	78.6	77.0
Wife in paid labor force	33.6	41.0	45.7	47.0
Wife not in paid labor force	52.0	40.7	32.9	30.0
Male head, no spouse present	2.4	3.2	4.4	5.0
Female head, no spouse present	11.4	15.1	17.0	18.0
Total percentage	100.0	100.0	100.0	100.0
Total number (in thousands)	52,227	60,309	66,322	69,597
White				
Married couple	88.3	85.1	82.8	81.3
Wife in paid labor force	33.6	42.0	47.5	49.3
Wife not in paid labor force	54.7	43.1	35.2	32.1
Male head, no spouse present	2.3	3.0	4.0	4.6
Female head, no spouse present	9.4	11.9	13.2	14.1
Total percentage	100.0	100.0	100.0	100.0
Total number (in thousands)	46,535	52,710	56,803	58,872
Black				
Married couple	65.6	53.7	47.8	46.1
Wife in paid labor force	35.5	32.0	31.4	30.8
Wife not in paid labor force	30.2	21.7	16.3	15.3
Male head, no spouse present	3.8	4.6	6.3	7.1
Female head, no spouse present	30.6	41.7	45.9	46.8
Total percentage	100.0	100.0	100.0	100.0
Total number (in thousands)	4,928	6,317	7,471	8,055

(continued)

[1]Percentages may not total 100.0 due to rounding.

Table 1–7 (continued)

Family Type	1970	1980	1990	1995
Hispanic[2]				
Married couple	—	73.1	69.3	67.6
Wife in paid labor force	—	33.8	35.2	35.6
Wife not in paid labor force	—	39.4	34.2	32.0
Male head, no spouse present	—	5.1	6.9	6.9
Female head, no spouse present	—	21.8	23.8	25.5
Total percentage	—	100.0	100.0	100.0
Total number (in thousands)	—	3,235	4,981	6,287

[2]Persons of Hispanic origin may be of any race. Data by Hispanic origin not available for 1970.

Source: Bureau of the Census, *Money Income of Households, Families, and Persons in the United States: 1990,* 1991, Table 13; *Money Income in the United States: 1995,* 1996, Table 4; and Women's Research and Education Institute, *The American Woman 1997–97,* 1996, Table 1–3.

Table 1–8 • HOUSEHOLDS WITH UNRELATED PARTNERS BY SEX OF PARTNERS AND PRESENCE OF CHILDREN, 1995 (numbers in thousands)[1]

In 1995, nearly five and one-half million households were composed of two adults living together as partners. Over one-third of the households where the partners were of different sexes contained children, as did one-sixth of those with two female partners. Children were rarely present in households where both partners were male.

Household Type	*Number of Households*	*With Children*	
		Number	*Percentage*
Partners of opposite sex	3,668	1,319	36.0
Female householder, male partner	1,593	610	38.3
Male householder, female partner	2,076	1,319	63.5
Partners of same sex	1,760	161	9.1
Both partners female	820	132	16.1
Both partners male	940	28	3.0
Total	5,428	1,480	27.3

[1]Partners over age 18; children under age 15.

Source: Bureau of the Census, *Marital Status and Living Arrangements: March 1995 (Update),* 1996, Table 8.

Table 1–9 • CHILDREN'S LIVING ARRANGEMENTS BY RACE AND HISPANIC ORIGIN, 1970, 1980, 1990, AND 1995 (percent distributions)

Children living in two-parent families represent a shrinking proportion of America's children, whether they are white, black, or of Hispanic origin. Even so, youngsters in two-parent families are still in the majority among white and Hispanic children (75.8 percent and 62.9 percent, respectively). Among black children, on the other hand, they are a distinct minority (33.1 percent in 1995).

Living Arrangements	1970	1980	1990	1995
All races				
Living with two parents	85.2	76.7	72.5	68.7
Living with mother only	10.8	18.0	21.6	23.5
Living with father only	1.1	1.7	3.1	3.5
Other	2.9	3.7	2.8	4.3
Total percentage	100.0	100.0	100.0	100.0
Total number (in thousands)	69,162	63,427	64,137	70,254
White				
Living with two parents	89.5	82.7	79.0	75.8
Living with mother only	7.8	13.5	16.2	17.8
Living with father only	0.9	1.6	3.0	3.4
Other	1.8	2.2	1.8	3.0
Total percentage	100.0	100.0	100.0	100.0
Total number (in thousands)	58,790	52,242	51,390	55,327
Black				
Living with two parents	58.5	42.2	37.7	33.1
Living with mother only	29.5	43.9	51.2	52.0
Living with father only	2.3	1.9	3.5	4.1
Other	9.7	12.0	7.6	10.8
Total percentage	100.0	100.0	100.0	100.0
Total number (in thousands)	9,422	9,375	10,018	11,301

(continued)

Table 1–9 (continued)

Living Arrangements	1970	1980	1990	1995
Hispanic[1]				
Living with two parents	77.7	75.4	66.8	62.9
Living with mother only	—[2]	19.6	27.1	28.4
Living with father only	—[2]	1.5	2.9	4.2
Other	—[2]	3.5	3.2	4.5
Total percentage	—[2]	100.0	100.0	100.0
Total number (in thousands)	4,006	5,459	7,174	9,843

[1]Persons of Hispanic origin may be of any race.
[2]Data not available.

Source: Bureau of the Census, *Marital Status and Living Arrangements: March 1990*, 1991, Table 4; *Marital Status and Living Arrangements: March 1993*, 1994, Table F; and *Marital Status and Living Arrangements: March 1995 (Update)*, 1996, Table 4.

Figure 1–9 • RATIO OF MEN TO WOMEN IN THE POPULATION AGE 65 AND OVER BY AGE, 1995 (number of men per 100 women in a given age group)

The slight preponderance of males to females that exists in the younger population tips the other way in the "30-something" population (see Figure 1–2), and the preponderance of females grows larger as the population ages. Women who live to age 95 or older outnumber their male contemporaries by four to one.

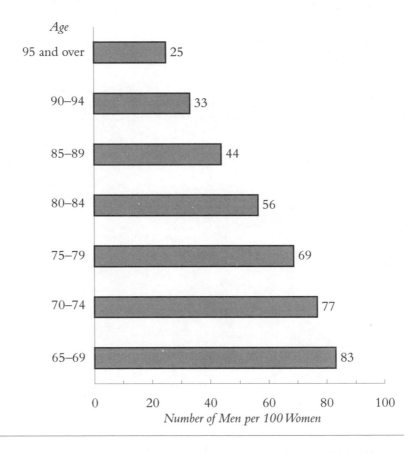

Age

95 and over — 25

90–94 — 33

85–89 — 44

80–84 — 56

75–79 — 69

70–74 — 77

65–69 — 83

0   20   40   60   80   100

Number of Men per 100 Women

Source: Bureau of the Census, *Statistical Abstract of the United States: 1996,* 1996, Table 16.

Table 1–10 • LIVING ARRANGEMENTS OF WOMEN AGE 65 AND OVER BY AGE, RACE, AND HISPANIC ORIGIN, 1995[1] (percent distributions)

> The older a woman is, the more likely she is to be living alone—an unsurprising fact given the dearth of men in the older age groups (see Figure 1–9). In 1995, only one in 10 women over 85 lived with a spouse; more than six in 10 lived alone. Elderly black and Hispanic women were even less likely than their white counterparts to be living with a spouse but much more likely to be sharing a household with others (typically family members).

	Living Alone	Living with Spouse	Living with Others	Total Percentage	Total Number
Age 65–74					
All races	32.0	53.0	15.0	100.0	10,117
White	32.1	55.2	12.7	100.0	8,953
Black	35.3	32.5	32.2	100.0	895
Hispanic[2]	33.3	39.6	27.1	100.0	513
Age 75–84					
All races	50.9	30.4	18.7	100.0	6,122
White	51.8	31.6	16.6	100.0	5,538
Black	46.4	17.2	36.4	100.0	478
Hispanic	37.2	23.7	39.1	100.0	215
Age 85 and over					
All races	61.0	9.7	29.3	100.0	2,025
White	62.7	9.9	27.4	100.0	1,816
Black	50.3	7.0	42.7	100.0	185
Hispanic	31.8	1.5	66.7	100.0	66

[1]Noninstitutional population.
[2]Persons of Hispanic origin may be of any race.

Source: Bureau of the Census, *Marital Status and Living Arrangements: March 1995 (Update)*, 1996, Table 7.

Figure 1–10 • WOMEN AND MEN AGE 65 AND OLDER LIVING
ALONE, 1970, 1980, 1990, AND 1995 (in percentages)[1]

This figure shows the long-term consequences of women's longer life expectancy combined with their propensity to marry older men: a much higher percentage of women than men wind up living alone. In 1995, more than half of all
women over 75 lived alone, compared with less than one-fourth of their male
contemporaries.

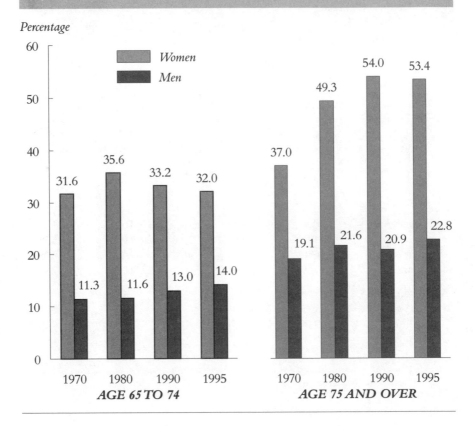

Percentage

[1]Noninstitutional population.

Source: Bureau of the Census, *Marital and Living Arrangements: March 1990*, 1991, Table 7;
Marital Status and Living Arrangements: March 1993, 1994, Table E; and *Marital Status and
Living Arrangements: March 1995*, 1996, Table 7.

SECTION 2:

EDUCATION

The college-educated proportion of women, although still smaller than the comparable proportion of men, has been increasing faster, and in the younger cohorts, the education gender gap has closed: the typical American woman age 25 to 34 has more education than her male contemporary. Since earning power increases with education (see Table 5–6 in the Earnings and Benefits section), these developments should mean greater lifelong economic security (not to mention more interesting lives and jobs) for tens of millions of American women.

Educational attainment lags, however, among women of Hispanic origin, especially the foreign-born. Hispanics' earnings have been declining, and it is hard to escape the conclusion that the educational disadvantage has produced a growing earnings disadvantage.

- Slightly more than one-fifth of all women over age 25 have at least a bachelor's degree. In the over-25 population overall, men are more likely than women to have a college degree, but in the group between 25 and 35, the reverse is true (see Tables 2–1 and 2–2).
- Women are overrepresented among recent recipients of bachelor's and master's degrees (see Tables 2–6 and 2–8).
- The proportion of black women with bachelor's degrees exceeds that of black men but is still smaller than the comparable proportion of white women (see Table 2–1).
- Undergraduates of both sexes, but especially women, were a racially more diverse group in 1994 than their counterparts of a decade earlier (see Table 2–5).
- Foreign-born persons of Hispanic origin—both women and men—tend

to be educationally disadvantaged: nearly 60 percent have not graduated from high school (see Tables 2–3 and 2–4).

- Between the mid-1970s and the mid-1990s, women quintupled their share of dentistry degrees and nearly doubled their share of medical and law degrees. Minority representation increased among the women earning degrees in all three fields (see Table 2–9).
- Women now predominate among the recipients of first professional degrees in veterinary medicine and pharmacy (see Figure 2–4).
- Education was the field of more than one in four of the women who earned doctorate degrees in 1993/94. Few women received doctorates in the physical sciences or engineering (see Figure 2–5).
- The majority of men on college and university faculties are tenured; the majority of women are not. The tenured proportions of female and male faculty have changed very little over time (see Figure 2–6).

Table 2–1 • EDUCATIONAL ATTAINMENT OF WOMEN AND MEN AGE 25 AND OVER BY SEX, RACE, AND HISPANIC ORIGIN, 1996 (percent distributions)

As of 1996, slightly more than one-fifth of all women in the United States who were over age 25 had at least a bachelor's degree; the comparable percentage for men was slightly over one-fourth. The percentage of college graduates is much smaller among black and Hispanics than among whites, but a large majority of black women and men (nearly three-quarters of both sexes) have a high school education or more. Among women and men of Hispanic origin, however, the proportion with a high school education or more is not much over half.

| | Percentage With | | | | |
	No High School	Some High School	High School or More	Bachelor's Degree or More	Number (in thousands)
All races					
Women	8.0	10.4	81.6	21.4	87,984
Men	8.2	9.9	81.9	26.0	80,339
White					
Women	7.6	9.6	82.8	21.8	73,939
Men	8.0	9.3	82.7	26.9	68,795
Black					
Women	8.8	16.9	74.2	14.6	10,429
Men	9.8	15.9	74.3	12.4	8,286
Hispanic[1]					
Women	30.6	16.2	53.3	8.3	7,311
Men	30.0	17.0	53.0	10.3	7,229

[1]Persons of Hispanic origin may be of any race.

Source: Bureau of the Census, *Educational Attainment in the United States: March 1996 (Update)*, 1997, Table 1.

Figure 2–1 • WOMEN AGE 25 AND OVER WITH 12 OR MORE YEARS OF EDUCATION BY RACE AND HISPANIC ORIGIN, 1960–1996 (in percentages)[1]

Between 1960 and 1995, the percentage of women over age 25 with at least a high school education increased most dramatically among black women: as of 1995, nearly three-quarters of black women were high school graduates, up from just over one-fifth in 1960. The drop in the proportion of high school graduates among Hispanic women after 1980 may reflect the low educational levels typical of Hispanic people who have come to the country since then (see Table 2–4).

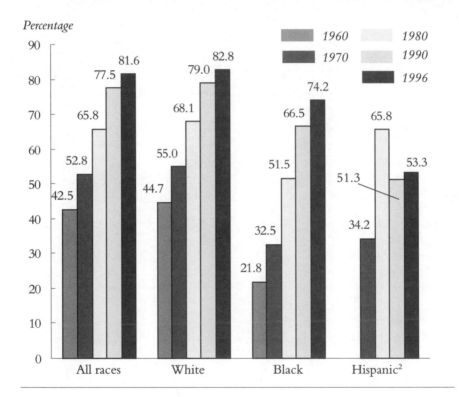

[1]Only 1990 data are available for Asian/Pacific Islanders (A/PI); in that year, 77.2 percent of A/PI women had completed four years of high school or more.
[2]Persons of Hispanic origin may be of any race.

Source: Bureau of the Census, *Statistical Abstract of the United States: 1996,* 1996, Table 242, and *Educational Attainment in the United States: March 1996 (Update),* 1997, Table 1.

Table 2–2 • EDUCATIONAL ATTAINMENT OF WOMEN AND MEN
AGE 25 AND OVER BY AGE, 1996 (in percentages)

Although women's educational attainment falls short of men's in the over-25
population overall, the education gender gap has closed in the age group between 25 and 35. In fact, a woman in this age group is actually more likely than
her male contemporary to be a high school graduate and more likely to have a
bachelor's degree.

	High School Graduate or More		Bachelor's Degree or More	
	Women	*Men*	*Women*	*Men*
Total 25 and over	81.6	81.9	21.4	26.0
25–34	87.9	85.9	27.1	25.9
35–44	88.9	87.0	26.2	26.3
45–54	86.2	86.7	24.0	32.2
55–64	77.3	77.6	15.6	25.2
65 and over	64.5	65.4	10.4	18.9

Source: Bureau of the Census, *Educational Attainment of the United States: March 1996
(Update)*, 1997, Table 3.

Table 2–3 • EDUCATIONAL ATTAINMENT OF U.S.- AND FOREIGN-BORN WOMEN AGE 25 AND OVER, 1996 (percent distributions)

> More than one-third of foreign-born women age 25 and over are not high school graduates, compared with about one-sixth of women who were born in the U.S. or its outlying areas. This phenomenon undoubtedly reflects, at least in part, the relatively low educational levels of foreign-born Hispanics (see Table 2–5).

		U.S.-Born[1]	Foreign-Born	
	Total		All	Came to U.S. after 1979
Not high school graduates	18.4	16.3	35.1	38.5
High school graduates or some college[2]	60.2	62.3	44.0	37.2
Bachelor's degree or more	21.3	21.5	20.8	24.3
Total percentage[3]	100.0	100.0	100.0	100.0
Total number (in thousands)	87,984	78,115	9,870	4,893

[1]"U.S.-born" persons were born in the United States, Puerto Rico, or an outlying area of the United States, such as Guam or the U.S. Virgin Islands, or were born in a foreign country but had at least one parent who was a U.S. citizen. All others are foreign-born. In addition to legally admitted immigrants, the foreign-born include refugees, temporary residents, such as students and temporary workers, and some undocumented immigrants.
[2]Lack a bachelor's degree.
[3]Percentages may not total 100.0 due to rounding.

Source: Bureau of the Census, *The Foreign-Born Population: 1996,* 1997; and data on the foreign-born from the March 1996 Current Population Survey, <http://www.census.gov/population/socdemo/foreign/96/96tab-1.txt> and <... /96tab-2.txt>, published April 8, 1997, accessed July 7, 1997.

Table 2–4 • EDUCATIONAL ATTAINMENT OF U.S.- AND FOREIGN-BORN PERSONS OF HISPANIC ORIGIN AND ASIAN/PACIFIC ISLANDERS, AGE 25 AND OVER, 1996 (percent distributions)

Persons of Hispanic origin (who may be of any race, but are generally white) and Asian/Pacific Islanders account for substantial proportions of the foreign-born in the United States (see Table 1–2). The Hispanic foreign-born tend to be educationally disadvantaged—nearly 60 percent have not graduated from high school and only about seven percent have at least a bachelor's degree.

| | Total (both sexes) | U.S.-Born[1] | Foreign-Born | |
			All	Came to U.S. after 1979
Hispanic				
Not high school graduates	46.9	32.7	58.9	62.3
High school graduates or some college[2]	43.8	55.9	33.7	31.3
Bachelor's degree or more	9.3	11.5	7.4	6.4
Total percentage[3]	100.0	100.0	100.0	100.0
Total number (in thousands)	14,541	6,660	7,880	4,351
Asian/Pacific Islander				
Not high school graduates	16.8	10.2	18.5	19.8
High school graduates or some college[2]	41.5	50.2	39.1	38.2
Bachelor's degree or more	41.7	39.5	42.3	42.0
Total percentage[3]	100.0	100.0	100.0	100.0
Total number (in thousands)	5,677	1,202	4,476	3,010

[1]"U.S.-born" persons were born in the United States, Puerto Rico, or an outlying area of the United States, such as Guam or the U.S. Virgin Islands, or were born in a foreign country but had at least one parent who was a U.S. citizen. All others are foreign-born. In addition to legally admitted immigrants, the foreign-born include refugees, temporary residents, such as students and temporary workers, and some undocumented immigrants.
[2]Lack a bachelor's degree.
[3]Percentages may not total 100.0 due to rounding.

Source: Bureau of the Census, *The Foreign-Born Population: 1996,* 1997; and data on the foreign-born from the March 1996 Current Population Survey, <http://www.census.gov/population/socdemo/foreign/96/96tab-1.txt> and <... /96tab-2.txt>, published April 8, 1997, accessed July 7, 1997.

Table 2–5 • COLLEGE ENROLLMENT OF WOMEN AND MEN BY RACE AND HISPANIC ORIGIN, 1976, 1984, AND 1994 (percent distributions)[1]

The college undergraduates of 1994—especially the women—were a more diverse group than their counterparts of a decade earlier, although non-Hispanic whites still represented a substantial majority of students of both sexes. Non-Hispanic blacks accounted for about one in eight female undergraduates in 1994, a higher proportion than among male undergraduates.

	Women			Men		
	1976	1984	1994[2]	1976	1984	1994[2]
Non-Hispanic						
White	82.4	80.9	73.7	84.4	82.4	75.1
Black	11.5	10.7	12.1	9.0	8.3	9.5
Asian/Pacific Islander	1.7	2.9	5.1	1.9	3.7	6.3
American Indian or Alaskan Native	0.8	0.8	1.0	0.7	0.7	0.9
Hispanic[3]	3.6	4.7	8.0	4.0	4.8	8.1
Total percentage[4]	100.0	100.0	100.0	100.0	100.0	100.0
Total number (in thousands)	4,475	5,535	6,718	4,800	4,860	5,276

[1]Fall enrollment of undergraduates, excluding non-U.S. citizens on temporary visas.
[2]Data for 1994 are preliminary.
[3]Persons of Hispanic origin may be of any race.
[4]Percentages may not total 100.0 due to rounding.

Source: National Center for Education Statistics, *Digest of Education Statistics 1996,* 1996, Table 203.

Figure 2–2 • WOMEN ENROLLED AT ALL LEVELS IN COLLEGES
AND UNIVERSITIES BY AGE, 1970, 1980, 1990, 1994, AND
PROJECTED 2000 (percent distributions)[1]

In 1970, women of the "traditional" undergraduate age—that is, between 18 and
21—constituted well over half of the women enrolled in institutions of higher
learning at all levels; women over 30 accounted for only about one-sixth (16.6
percent). By 1990, the over-30 proportion exceeded one-third. It is projected to
be just below that level in 2000.

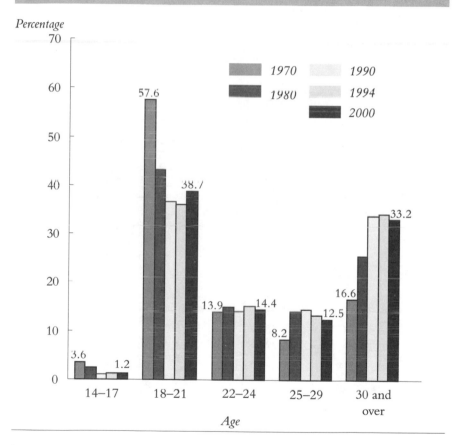

[1]Fall enrollments. Includes undergraduates, students in graduate programs, and students
seeking first professional degrees (i.e., in law, medicine, etc.).

Source: National Center for Education Statistics, *Digest of Education Statistics 1996*, 1996,
Table 171.

Figure 2–3 • WOMEN AND MEN ENROLLED AT ALL LEVELS IN COLLEGES AND UNIVERSITIES BY FULL- OR PART-TIME STATUS, 1970, 1980, 1990, 1994, AND PROJECTED 2000 (numbers in thousands)[1]

In 1970, about two-thirds of the 3.5 million women enrolled in colleges and universities were full-time students. By 1994, the full-time proportion had shrunk to 54.2 percent of the 7.9 million total women enrolled.

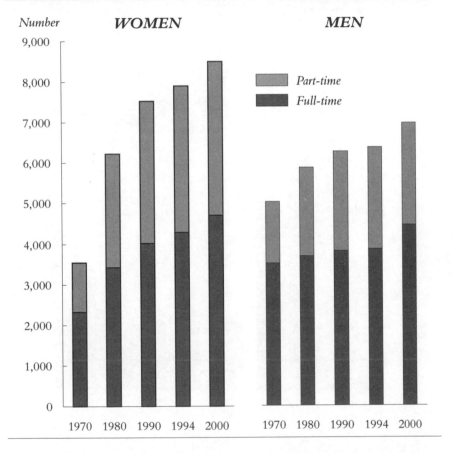

[1]Fall enrollments. Includes undergraduates, students in graduate programs, and students seeking professional degrees (i.e., in law, medicine, etc.).

Source: National Center for Education Statistics, *Digest of Education Statistics 1996,* 1996, Table 171.

Table 2–6 • RECIPIENTS OF POSTSECONDARY DEGREES BY SEX, ACADEMIC YEARS 1973/74, 1993/94, AND PROJECTED 2000/2001

Between 1973 and 1994, women's share of postsecondary degrees at every level increased considerably—spectacularly in the case of first professional degrees, where it quadrupled (from 9.8 percent to 40.7 percent).

Degree	1973/74	1993/94	Percent Change 73/74–93/94	Projected 2000/2001
Associate, total number	343,924	542,449	57.7	549,000
Number of women	155,333	321,459	106.9	334,000
Women as a percentage of degree recipients	45.2	59.3	—	60.8
Bachelor's, total number	945,776	1,169,275	23.6	1,211,000
Number of women	418,463	636,853	52.2	661,000
Women as a percentage of degree recipients	44.2	54.5	—	54.6
Master's, total number	277,033	387,070	39.7	435,000
Number of women	119,191	210,985	77.0	225,000
Women as a percentage of degree recipients	43.0	54.5	—	51.7
First professional, total number[1]	53,816	75,418	40.1	86,100
Number of women	5,286	30,711	481.0	34,500
Women as a percentage of degree recipients	9.8	40.7	—	40.1
Doctoral, total number	33,816	43,185	27.7	46,200
Number of women	6,451	16,633	157.8	19,100
Women as a percentage of degree recipients	19.1	38.5	—	41.3

[1]First professional degrees include dentistry, law, medicine, etc.

Source: National Center for Education Statistics, *Digest of Education Statistics 1996,* 1996, Table 239.

Table 2-7 • TEN MOST POPULAR MAJORS AMONG BACHELOR'S DEGREE RECIPIENTS BY SEX, AND BY RACE AND HISPANIC ORIGIN OF WOMEN, ACADEMIC YEAR 1993/94 (in rank order)[1]

Major Field	Men Total	Women Total	Non-Hispanic Women				Hispanic Women
			White	Black	A/PI[2]	Native American	
Business and management[3]	1	1	1	1	1	1	1
Education	5	2	2	3	9	2	4
Health professions and related sciences		3	3	4	4	4	5
Social sciences	2	4	4	2	2	3	2
Psychology	8	5	5	5	5	5	3
English language and literature	9	6	6	7	8	7	8
Communications	6	7	7	6	10	10	10
Visual and performing arts	7	8	8		6	9	
Biological/life sciences	4	9	9	9	3		7
Liberal arts/general studies		10	10	10		6	
Public administration and services				8		8	
Multi-interdisciplinary studies							6
Foreign languages and literature							9
Engineering	3				7		
Computer and information sciences	10						
Percentage of all degree recipients accounted for by top 10 majors	74.5	81.3	82.0	80.8	80.7	80.8	78.5

[1]Excludes non-U.S. citizens on temporary visas. [2]Asian/Pacific Islander.
[3]Includes business and management, business and office, marketing and distribution, and consumer and personal services.

Source: National Center for Education Statistics, *Digest of Education Statistics 1996*, 1996, Table 260.

Table 2–8 • WOMEN AWARDED UNDERGRADUATE DEGREES IN SELECTED FIELDS, ACADEMIC YEARS 1973/74, 1983/84, AND 1993/94 (in percentages)

Compared with their representation among all students awarded bachelor's degrees in 1993/94, women were heavily overrepresented among degree recipients in fields in which they had been overrepresented 20 years earlier—education, English, and the health professions. But women made significant progress in biological sciences and increased their presence in the engineering field, once almost exclusively male.

Field	*Degrees Awarded to Women as a Percentage of All Degrees Awarded*		
	1973/74	*1983/84*	*1993/94*
Biological sciences	31.2	46.8	51.2
Business	12.8	43.5	47.6
Computer and information sciences	16.4	37.1	28.4
Education	73.5	76.0	77.3
Engineering	1.6	12.8	14.9
English	63.0	66.0	65.8
Health professions	77.4	81.4	82.4
Mathematics	40.7	43.9	46.3
Physical sciences	16.5	27.6	33.6
Psychology	50.4	67.9	73.1
Social sciences	36.4	44.1	46.1
Visual and performing arts	60.2	62.4	60.2
All fields	44.2	50.5	54.5

Source: National Center for Education Statistics, *Digest of Education Statistics 1996*, 1996, Tables 239, 273, 275, 277, 278, 279, 281, 284, 285, 286, 288, 290, and 292.

Table 2–9 • WOMEN AWARDED FIRST PROFESSIONAL DEGREES IN DENTISTRY, MEDICINE, AND LAW BY RACE AND HISPANIC ORIGIN, ACADEMIC YEARS 1976/77 AND 1993/94 (percent distributions)[1]

Between 1976 and 1994, women quintupled their share of dentistry degrees and nearly doubled their share of medical and law degrees. Minority representation—most notably of Asian/Pacific Islanders—increased in all three fields but especially in dentistry and medicine.

	Dentistry		Medicine		Law	
	76/77	93/94	76/77	93/94	76/77	93/94
Non-Hispanic						
White	82.8	65.3	86.7	70.5	90.5	80.5
Black	12.0	7.2	9.5	9.4	5.8	8.7
Asian/Pacific Islander	3.0	19.6	1.9	15.3	1.7	5.4
American Indian or						
Alaskan Native	0.5	0.5	0.2	0.5	0.4	0.5
Hispanic[2]	1.6	7.4	1.7	4.3	1.6	4.9
Total percent[3]	100.0	100.0	100.0	100.0	100.0	100.0
Degrees awarded to women						
Number	367	1,359	2,543	5,764	7,630	17,139
As a percentage of all degrees	7.3	38.8	19.1	37.5	22.5	43.1

[1]Data exclude non-U.S. citizens on temporary visas.
[2]Persons of Hispanic origin may be of any race.
[3]Percentages may not total 100.0 due to rounding.

Source: Women's Research and Education Institute, *The American Woman 1996–97*, 1996, Table 2–4; and National Center for Education Statistics, *Digest of Education Statistics 1996*, 1996, Table 269.

Figure 2–4 • FIRST PROFESSIONAL DEGREES AWARDED IN SELECTED FIELDS BY SEX OF RECIPIENTS, ACADEMIC YEAR 1993/94[1]

Table 2–9 shows that while women made impressive gains in dentistry, medicine, and law, as of 1993/94 men still predominated by a comfortable margin among recipients of degrees in those professions. Women predominated among the recipients of degrees in veterinary medicine and pharmacy. (These may now be seen as "women's professions." As recently as 1984/85, men were the slight majority of D.V.M. recipients and the sexes were represented equally among Pharm.D. recipients.)

Number

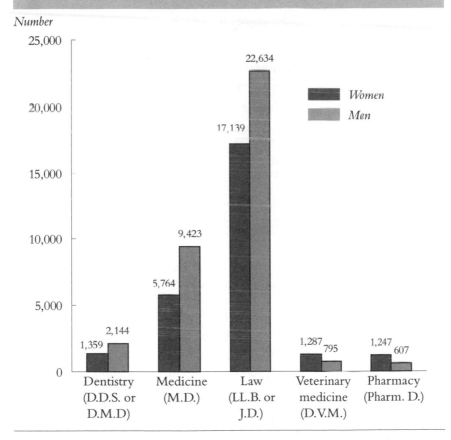

[1]Data exclude non-U.S. citizens on temporary visas.

Source: National Center for Education Statistics, *Digest of Education Statistics 1996,* 1996, Table 269.

Figure 2–5 • DOCTORAL DEGREES AWARDED TO WOMEN AND MEN IN ACADEMIC YEAR 1993/94 BY FIELD OF STUDY (percent distributions)[1]

Education was the field of more than one in four of the women who earned doctorates in 1993/94. Relatively few women were in the physical sciences and even fewer were in engineering.

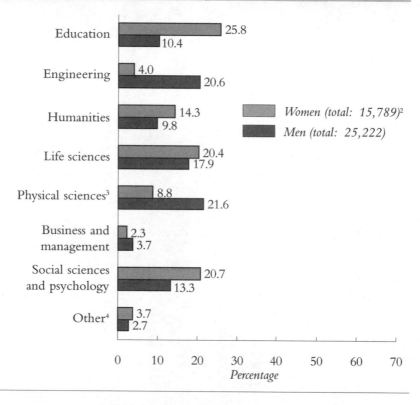

[1]Percentages may not total 100.0 due to rounding.
[2]Overall, about one sixth of the women and one-third of the men awarded doctoral degrees in 1993/94 were non-U.S. citizens on temporary visas. However, in the life and physical sciences and in engineering, the percentages of nonresident aliens were higher.
[3]Includes mathematics, computer science, physics, astronomy, chemistry, and earth, atmospheric, and marine sciences.
[4]Excludes some nonresearch doctorate degrees such as degrees in theology.

Source: National Center for Education Statistics, *Digest of Education Statistics 1996,* 1996, Tables 266 and 293.

Figure 2–6 • FULL-TIME FACULTY WITH TENURE IN PUBLIC AND PRIVATE COLLEGES AND UNIVERSITIES BY SEX, ACADEMIC YEARS 1980/81, 1990/91, AND 1994/95 (in percentages)

The majority of the men on the faculties of both public and private institutions are tenured; the majority of the women are not. Between 1980 and 1995, women made small advances in gaining tenure at private institutions, but so did men—and, unlike women, men gained a bit at public institutions.

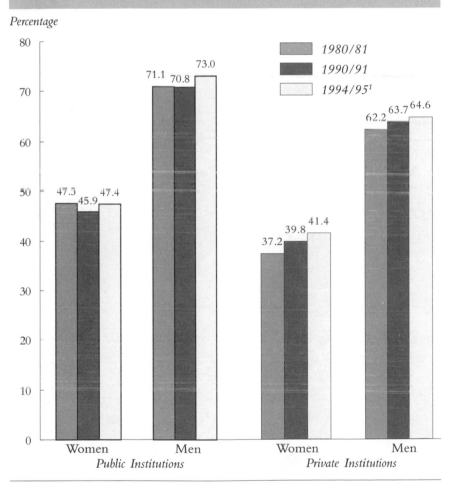

Percentage

[1] 1994/95 data are preliminary.

Source: National Center for Education Statistics, *Digest of Education Statistics 1996*, 1996, Table 235.

SECTION 3:
HEALTH

The spotlight has been on women's health issues in the last decade, and some of the statistics in this section suggest that the attention is beginning to pay off. To the extent that healthier personal behavior along with preventive screening holds the key to conquering the diseases most likely to kill women, it is encouraging that smoking is much less common among young and middle-aged women than it was a generation or so ago. And it is encouraging that a majority of women over 50 have had a fairly recent mammogram and breast exam. Moreover, since black women who get breast cancer are at particular risk of dying from it, and late diagnosis is thought to be one reason, it is certainly good news that middle-aged and older black women are now just as likely as their contemporaries overall to have had the screening that allows early diagnosis of the disease.

Not encouraging, however, are the statistics in this section relating to younger black women who become mothers. They are nearly twice as likely to have low-birthweight babies as U.S. women overall, and their babies are nearly twice as likely to die before their first birthdays.

- Overall, about four in five expectant mothers receive prenatal care in the first trimester; only five percent either have care very late in their pregnancies or have no prenatal care at all. However, these percentages vary considerably by race and ethnicity (see Table 3–4).
- More than one in every seven infants born to black mothers are low-birthweight babies, a proportion almost twice that for U.S. babies overall, and the infant mortality rate among babies whose mothers are black is nearly double the overall rate (see Figure 3–1 and Table 3–5).
- In one decade, the proportion of pregnant girls under age 15 who gave

birth increased by about nine percentage points, and the proportion who had abortions dropped by a similar amount (see Table 3–2).

- Both white and black women's death rates from heart disease have dropped significantly since 1970, while their death rates from cancer have increased somewhat. Black and white women's lung cancer death rates, which are very similar, increased fivefold between 1960 and 1990 (see Table 3–6 and Figure 3–2).
- Smoking is considerably less common in nearly every age group of adult women than it was a generation or so ago. Women over 65 are the exception, although they are still the least likely to smoke (see Figure 3–3).
- Breast cancer is more common among white women than black women, but deadlier for black women; the reverse is true of lung cancer (see Figure 3–4 and Table 3–7).
- The percentage of women over 50 who have recently received a mammogram and clinical breast exam has increased, most dramatically among black women (see Table 3–8).
- The incidence of AIDS among black and Hispanic women and teenage girls is far out of proportion to their presence in the population as a whole (see Table 3–9).

Table 3–1 • FEMALE CONTRACEPTIVE USERS AGE 15–44 BY
RACE AND SELECTED CONTRACEPTIVE METHOD, 1982 AND
1990

Contraceptive use in general grew among American women from 1982 to 1990, with the largest increase (six percentage points) occurring among black women. The proportion of contraceptive users who used condoms increased across the board, but especially among black women (from 6.2 percent in 1982 to 19.2 percent in 1990). However, voluntary sterilization was by far the most common form of contraception among black women.

	All Races		White		Black	
	1982	*1990*	*1982*	*1990*	*1982*	*1990*
Contraceptive users as a percentage of all women age 15–44	55.7	59.3	56.7	59.9	52.0	58.0
Percentage of all contraceptive users who employ method						
Female sterilization	23.2	29.5	22.1	27.7	30.0	41.8
Male sterilization	10.9	12.6	12.2	14.8	1.4[1]	1.5[1]
Birth control pill	28.0	28.5	26.7	28.8	38.0	27.9
Intrauterine device	7.1	1.4	6.9	1 4	9.1	1.4[1]
Diaphragm	8.1	2.8	8.8	2.8	3.5	1.6[1]
Condom	12.0	17.7	12.7	17.0	6.2	19.2

[1]Relative standard error greater than 30 percent.

Source: National Center for Health Statistics, *Health, United States, 1995,* 1996, Table 18.

Table 3–2 • PREGNANCY OUTCOMES BY AGE OF WOMAN, 1981 AND 1991 (percent distribution)

In 1991, more than three in five pregnancies overall resulted in live births, a proportion only slightly higher than the comparable proportion in 1981. What changed most noticeably were the outcomes of teenage pregnancies. The proportion of live births was up and the proportion of abortions was down in both the under-15 and the 15–19 age groups. Among the latter, for example, 54 percent of pregnancies resulted in live births in 1991, compared with not quite 48 percent in 1981.

| | Pregnancy Outcome | | | | | |
| | *Live Birth* | | *Abortion* | | *Miscarriage or Stillbirth* | |
Age	*1981*	*1991*	*1981*	*1991*	*1981*	*1991*
Under 15	35.7	44.4	53.6	44.4	10.7	11.1
15–19	47.8	54.0	39.3	32.6	12.9	13.4
20–24	62.3	60.1	28.5	29.4	9.2	10.5
25–29	67.9	67.8	19.0	19.3	13.1	12.8
30–34	64.8	67.5	18.6	16.2	16.5	16.2
35–39	54.3	60.3	26.0	19.5	19.7	20.2
40 and over	45.5	53.5	38.2	28.7	16.4	17.8
Total	60.9	62.6	26.5	23.7	12.6	13.7

Source: National Center for Health Statistics, *Monthly Vital Statistics Report* 43, No. 11 (S), May 25, 1995, Table 2.

Table 3–3 • ABORTIONS BY WEEK OF GESTATION, 1994

Nearly 90 percent of all abortions in 1994 occurred in the first trimester, that is, before the thirteenth week of gestation.

Week of Gestation[1]	Number of Abortions	Percent Distribution
8 weeks	680,602	53.7
9–10 weeks	297,843	23.5
11–12 weeks	138,148	10.9
13–15 weeks	79,847	6.3
16–20 weeks	54,499	4.3
21 weeks or more	16,476	1.3
Total	1,267,415	100.0

[1]Week of gestation is calculated from last menstrual period.

Source: Centers for Disease Control and Prevention, *Abortion Surveillance· Preliminary Data—United States, 1994* 45, Nos. 51 and 52, January 3, 1997, Table 1.

Table 3–4 • PRENATAL CARE FOR MOTHERS WITH LIVE BIRTHS IN 1993 BY RACE AND HISPANIC ORIGIN (in percentages)

Overall, close to 80 percent of mothers who had babies in the United States in 1993 received prenatal care at least by the end of the first trimester; only about five percent had either no care at all or no care before the third trimester. Breakdowns by race and Hispanic origin, however, show significant differences: women of Cuban and Japanese origin were the most likely to have early care; Native American and Mexican American women were the least likely.

	Percentage of Live Births for Which Mothers Received	
	Late or No Prenatal Care[1]	Early Prenatal Care[2]
All mothers with live births	4.8	78.9
White	3.9	81.8
Black	9.0	66.0
Asian/Pacific Islander	4.6	77.6
Chinese	2.9	84.6
Japanese	2.8	87.2
Filipino	4.0	79.3
Hawaiian and part–Hawaiian	6.7	70.6
Other Asian/Pacific Islander	5.4	74.4
American Indian or Alaskan Native	10.3	63.4
Hispanic[3] total	8.8	66.6
Mexican American	9.7	64.8
Puerto Rican	7.1	70.0
Cuban	1.8	88.9
Central and South American	7.3	68.7
Other Hispanic	7.0	70.0
Black, non–Hispanic[4]	9.0	66.1
White, non–Hispanic	2.7	85.6

[1]No prenatal care or prenatal care began during third trimester.
[2]Care began in the first trimester.
[3]Persons of Hispanic origin may be of any race.
[4]Selected states.

Source: National Center for Health Statistics, *Health, United States, 1995*, 1996, Table 7.

Figure 3–1 • LOW-BIRTHWEIGHT BIRTHS BY MOTHERS' RACE AND HISPANIC ORIGIN, 1993 (low–birthweight births as a percentage of all live births)

Of all infants born in the United States in 1993, just over seven percent were low-birthweight babies; that is, they weighed under 2,500 grams (about 5.5 pounds). Among babies born to black and Puerto Rican mothers, however, the rates were notably higher—in the case of blacks, much higher (13.3 percent). By contrast, low-birthweight babies accounted for fewer than one in 20 infants born to mothers of Chinese origin.

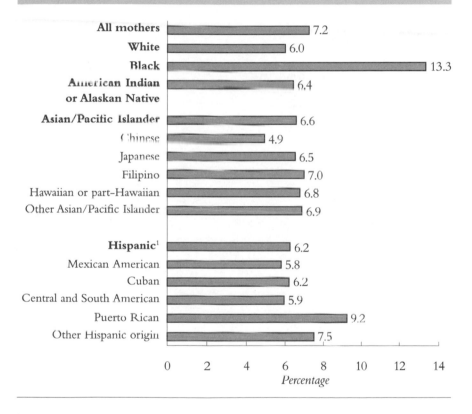

¹Persons of Hispanic origin may be of any race.

Source: National Center for Health Statistics, *Health, United States, 1995,* 1996, Table 11.

Table 3–5 • INFANT MORTALITY RATES FOR BABIES BORN IN THE UNITED STATES 1989–1991 BY MOTHERS' RACE AND HISPANIC ORIGIN (number of infant deaths in the first year of life per 1,000 live births)[1]

The mortality rate among babies of black mothers was nearly double the overall infant mortality rate and exceeded the second highest (American Indian or Alaskan Native) by more than one-third. Mortality rates were lowest among babies whose mothers were of Chinese or Japanese origin.

	Mortality Rate
All races	9.0
White	7.4
Black	17.1
Asian/Pacific Islander total	6.6
Chinese	5.1
Japanese	5.3
Filipino	6.4
Hawaiian and part-Hawaiian	9.0
Other Asian/Pacific Islander	7.0
American Indian or Alaskan Native	12.6
Hispanic total[2]	7.6
Mexican American	7.2
Puerto Rican	10.4
Cuban	6.2
Central and South American	6.6
Other Hispanic	8.2
White, non-Hispanic[3]	7.3
Black, non-Hispanic	17.2

[1]Born between January 1, 1989 and December 31, 1991.

[2]Persons of Hispanic origin may be of any race.

[3]These data apply only to births in those states that specified Hispanic origin as well as race on birth certificates. States that did so included 47 states and the District of Columbia in 1989, 48 states and the District of Columbia in 1990, and 49 states and the District of Columbia in 1991.

Source: National Center for Health Statistics, *Health, United States, 1995,* 1996, Table 20.

Table 3–6 • DEATH RATES FOR SELECTED CAUSES OF DEATH FOR WHITE AND BLACK WOMEN, 1970 AND 1993[1]

Death rates from most of women's leading killers dropped significantly between 1970 and 1993 for both blacks and whites. Notable exceptions were cancer, chronic obstructive pulmonary disease, and HIV/AIDS.

	White Women		Black Women	
	1970	*1993*	*1970*	*1993*
	Death Rate	*Death Rate*	*Death Rate*	*Death Rate*
Heart disease	167.8	99.2	251.7	165.3
Malignant neoplasms (cancers)	107.6	110.1	123.5	135.3
Cerebrovascular diseases (e.g., stroke)	56.2	22.7	107.9	39.9
Unintentional injuries (accidents)	27.2	16.6	35.3	20.1
Pneumonia and influenza	15.0	10.4	29.2	13.5
Diabetes mellitus	12.8	10.0	30.9	26.9
Chronic liver disease and cirrhosis	8.7	4.6	17.8	6.6
Suicide	7.2	4.6	2.9	2.1
Chronic obstructive pulmonary disease	5.3	17.8	—	12.2
Homicide and legal intervention	2.2	3.0	15.0	13.4
Nephritis, nephrotic syndrome, and nephritis (diseases of the kidneys)	—	3.2	—	9.2
HIV/ AIDS	—	1.9	—	17.3

[1]Deaths per 100,000 resident population; rates are age-adjusted.

Source: National Center for Health Statistics. *Health, United States, 1995,* 1996, Table 30.

Figure 3–2 • DEATH RATES FOR BREAST AND LUNG CANCER
FOR WHITE, BLACK, AND HISPANIC WOMEN, 1950–1993 (deaths per
100,000 women in the population, age-adjusted)

Among both black and white women, death rates from lung cancer increased
fivefold between 1960 and 1990, when the rates were 27.5 and 26.5, respectively.
Recently, lung cancer and breast cancer death rates have been identical or nearly
identical among black women, while lung cancer clearly overtook breast cancer
as a killer of white women in the 1980s.

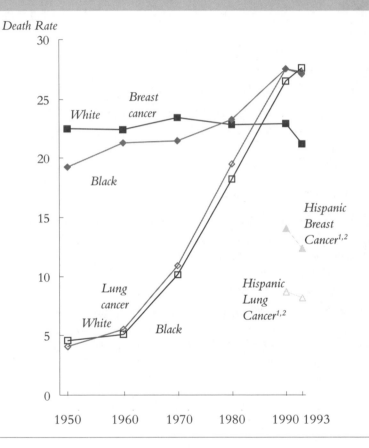

[1]Persons of Hispanic origin may be of any race.
[2]Data for women of Hispanic origin are not available before 1990.

Source: National Center for Health Statistics, *Health, United States, 1995*, 1996, Tables 40
and 41.

Figure 3–3 • WOMEN SMOKERS BY AGE, 1965 AND 1993 (current smokers as a percentage of all women in their age group)

In 1993, smoking was considerably less prevalent in every age group of adult women than it had been in 1965, with the notable exception of the 65-and-older group. In this age group, the proportion of smokers was up slightly.

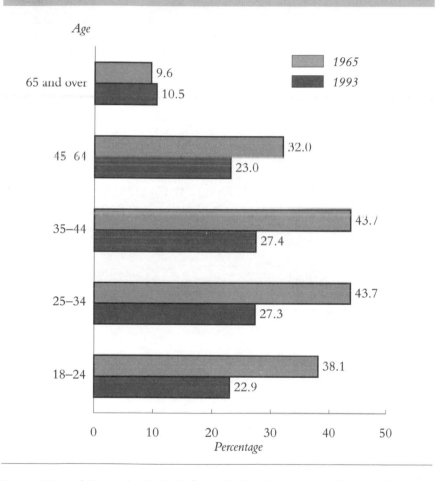

Source: National Center for Health Statistics, *Health, United States, 1995,* 1996, Table 63.

Table 3–7 • INCIDENCE AND DEATH RATES FOR WOMEN FOR SELECTED CANCERS BY CANCER SITE AND RACE, 1993 (per 100,000 women)[1]

Breast cancer, more common among white women than black women, is deadlier for black women. Lung cancer, more common among black women than white women, is deadlier for white women. Cancer of the cervix, one of the most curable cancers if found early, is both more common and more lethal in black women than in white women.

	Incidence[2]			Death Rate		
	All Races	White	Black	All Races	White	Black
Breast	108.3	110.5	100.3	25.9	25.6	31.5
Lung and bronchus	41.7	42.9	45.8	33.5	34.1	32.4
Uterus (except cervix)	21.0	21.9	14.7	3.4	3.1	6.0
Ovary	14.8	15.4	11.0	7.5	7.7	6.3
Cervix	8.2	7.5	11.4	2.8	2.4	6.3

[1]Rates are age-adjusted.
[2]Cancer diagnosed in 1993.

Source: National Cancer Institute, *SEER Cancer Statistics Review, 1973–1993*, 1996, Tables IV–4, XV–3, XV–6, VII–3, XX–3, and V–3.

Figure 3–4 • BREAST CANCER: INCIDENCE AND DEATH RATES FOR WHITE AND BLACK WOMEN, 1992 (age-adjusted)[1]

White women are more likely than black women to get breast cancer. Black women are more likely than white women to die from it. (This anomaly may be related to the availability of preventive care and access to treatment.)

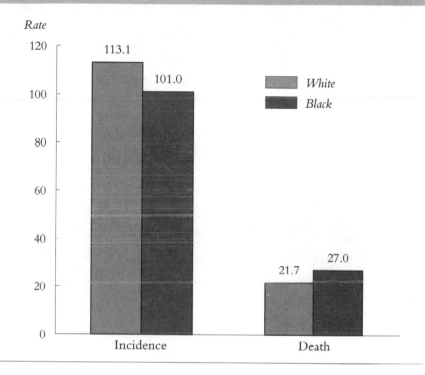

[1]A mortality rate is the number of deaths in a given year per 100,000 persons in the population. An incidence rate is the number of new cases in a given year per 100,000 in the population.

Source: National Center for Health Statistics, *Health, United States, 1995,* 1996, Tables 59 and 41.

Table 3–8 • WOMEN AGE 50 AND OVER WHO HAD A CLINICAL BREAST EXAMINATION AND MAMMOGRAM IN THE PRECEDING TWO YEARS BY SELECTED CHARACTERISTICS, 1992 AND 1994 (in percentages)

Between 1994 and 1996, there were encouraging increases in the proportion of women over 50 who had the screening procedures that are key to the early diagnosis and successful treatment of breast cancer. The most dramatic increase—eight percentage points—was among black women, now as likely as over-50 women in general to have had the breast screening procedures. Still, there is a long way to go, especially among women with little education, low-income women, and women over age 70.

	Percentage Who Had Breast Exam and Mammogram in the Preceding Two Years	
	1992	1994
Total age 50 and over (all races)	51	56
Hispanic origin[1]	47	50
Black	48	56
Less than a high school education	35	42
Low income[2]	32	38
Total age 70 and over (all races)	39	45

[1]Persons of Hispanic origin may be of any race.
[2]Annual family income less than $10,000.

Source: National Center for Health Statistics, *Healthy People 2000 Review, 1995–96,* 1996, Table 16.

Figure 3-5 • AIDS CASES IN FEMALES AND MALES AGE 13 AND OVER BY RACE AND HISPANIC ORIGIN, 1989–1996[1]

AIDS has continued to be far more prevalent among males than among females, but while new male cases declined in each year after 1993 (most noticeably among white males), new female cases increased slightly after 1994.

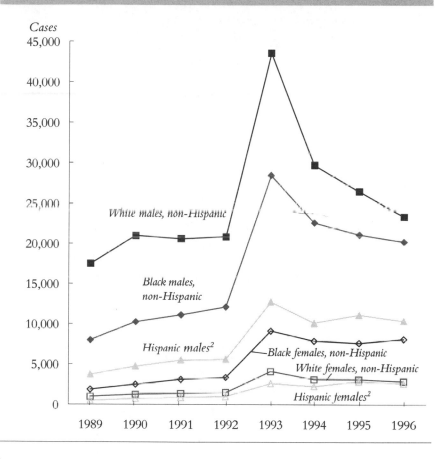

[1]The AIDS case reporting definitions were expanded in 1993.
[2]Persons of Hispanic origin may be of any race.

Source: National Center for Health Statistics, *Health, United States, 1993,* 1994, Table 61, and *Health, United States, 1995,* 1996, Table 56; and Centers for Disease Control and Prevention, *HIV/AIDS Surveillance Report, Year-End Edition* 7, No. 2, 1995, Table 10, and 8, No. 2, 1996, Table 10.

Table 3–9 • NEWLY REPORTED AIDS CASES AMONG FEMALES AGE 13 AND OVER BY RACE AND HISPANIC ORIGIN, 1996

AIDS strikes black and Hispanic women and teenage girls far out of proportion to their presence in the population as a whole. In 1996, non-Hispanic blacks accounted for nearly three in every five (59.1 percent) newly reported AIDS cases among females age 13 and over, although their proportion of all females in this age group was less than one in nine (11.8 percent). The Hispanic proportion of female AIDS cases was more than double the Hispanic proportion of over-13 females in general.

	Percent Distribution of Female AIDS Cases	Percent Distribution of All Females Age 13 and Over
Non-Hispanic		
White	20.9	75.0
Black	59.1	11.8
Asian/Pacific Islander	.6	3.4
American Indian or Alaskan		
Native	.3	0.7
Hispanic[1]	19.1	9.1
Total percentage	100.0	100.0
Total number	13,786	24,590,000

[1]Persons of Hispanic origin may be of any race.

Source: Centers for Disease Control and Prevention, *HIV/AIDS Surveillance Report, Year-End Edition* 8, No. 2, 1996, Table 10; and Bureau of the Census, *Population Projections of the United States by Age, Sex, Race, and Hispanic Origin: 1995 to 2050,* 1996, Table 2.

Section 4:
Employment

The almost 62 million working women in the United States already make up nearly half (46 percent) of the U.S. labor force. By 2005—assuming the experts are correct—that proportion will reach 48 percent, as women's labor force participation continues to grow and men's, which has been slowly ebbing for years, continues to decline.

There's more to the story of America's working women than sheer numbers. On the plus side is evidence that the proportion of women who have good jobs is growing. Thirty percent of today's women workers are either managers or professionals, an increase of eight percentage points since the early 1980s. The proportion of women in these occupations now exceeds not only the comparable proportion of men, but also the proportion of women in service occupations *and* the proportion of women in administrative support occupations. Surely this reflects, in part, the salutary effect that women's educational gains (see Section 2) are having on their job options.

On the minus side are the disturbing data about working women of Hispanic origin. Compared with women workers overall, Hispanic women are much less likely to be in managerial or professional jobs. They have the lowest earnings and the highest unemployment rates. They are the least likely of all women workers to have health insurance through their jobs. In short, the premium the U.S. labor market places on education is bad news for workers—women and men—who lack it.

- Three in every five women are now in the workforce. Women's labor force participation has risen steadily since midcentury (see Figure 4–1 and Table 4–1).
- In 1960, women between 45 and 55 (the baby boomers' grandmothers)

were the women most likely to work: about half were in the labor force in that year. In 2005, the oldest baby-boomer women will be between 45 and 55; their labor force participation rate is expected to be a record-setting 80.7 percent (see Table 4–2).

• While the number of working women overall increased by 71 percent between 1970 and 1995, the number working year round, full time increased by 130 percent (see Figure 4–4).

• Seventy percent of all working women are employed either in the services industry or in wholesale or retail trade. The giants in the services industry are health (including hospitals) and education, which together employ about 15.5 million women (see Figure 4–8 and Table 4–11).

• Women are now the majority in some professional and managerial occupations that were largely male until relatively recently, but there are still very few women in the skilled blue-collar trades (see Table 4–15).

• With the exception of "temps," most of whom are contingent, the majority of workers in so-called alternative or nontraditional work arrangements are not contingent (see Table 4–19).

• Black married women are still more likely to be in the workforce than their white counterparts (see Figure 4–10).

• A school-age child is more likely than a preschool child to have a mother in the workforce, but youngsters whose mothers work are in the majority, even among children under age six (see Figure 4–11).

• The cost of child care is most burdensome for low-income families, even though they typically spend less on care than better-off families (see Table 4–24).

Figure 4–1 • WOMEN IN THE LABOR FORCE, 1948–1996[1]

> This figure and Table 4–1 make plain that the rise in American women's labor
> force participation since midcentury has been steady and incremental, not—as it
> has sometimes been described—"dramatic."

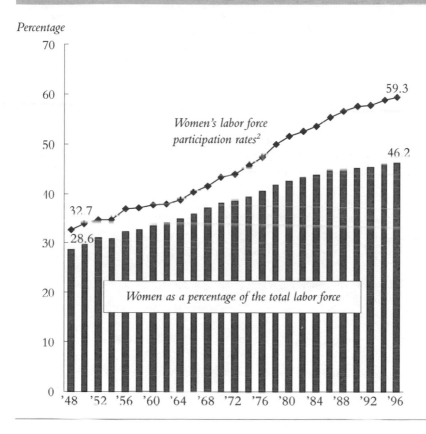

Percentage

[1]Civilians age 16 and over.
[2]Labor force participants as a percentage of all civilian women age 16 and over.

Source: Bureau of Labor Statistics, *Handbook of Labor Statistics,* 1989, Table 2, *and Employment and Earnings,* January 1997, Table 2.

Table 4–1 • WOMEN IN THE LABOR FORCE, 1948–1996[1]

Year	Women's Labor Force Participation Rates[2]	Women as Percentage of Total Labor Force	Year	Women's Labor Force Participation Rates	Women as Percentage of Total Labor Force
1948	32.7	28.6	1974	45.7	39.4
1950	33.9	29.6	1976	47.3	40.5
1952	34.7	31.0	1978	50.0	41.7
1954	34.6	30.9	1980	51.5	42.5
1956	36.9	32.2	1982	52.6	43.3
1958	37.1	32.7	1984	53.6	43.8
1960	37.7	33.4	1986	55.3	44.5
1962	37.9	34.0	1988	56.6	45.0
1964	38.7	34.8	1990	57.5	45.2
1966	40.3	36.0	1992	57.8	45.4
1968	41.6	37.1	1994	58.8	46.0
1970	43.3	38.1	1996	59.3	46.2
1972	43.9	38.5			

[1]Civilians age 16 and over.
[2]Labor force participants as a percentage of all civilian women age 16 and over.

Source: Bureau of Labor Statistics, *Handbook of Labor Statistics,* 1989, Table 2, and *Employment and Earnings,* January 1997, Table 2.

Table 4–2 • WOMEN'S LABOR FORCE PARTICIPATION RATES BY AGE, 1960–1996 AND PROJECTED 2000 AND 2005[1]

In 1960, women between 45 and 55 were the most likely to work: about half were in the labor force in that year. In 2005, if Bureau of Labor Statistics projections hold true, labor force participation will again be highest among women age 45–54. These will be women who were born between 1950 and 1960. Baby boomers all, they break female labor force participation records in every age group they enter, and they are expected to continue that pattern as they move into middle age. The 35–44 age group, which in 2005 will include the last of the boomer women, will run their older sisters a close second. But even after the baby boomers have begun to retire from the scene, women's labor force participation is expected to remain high.

Age	Labor Force Participation Rates[2]						
	1960	*1970*	*1980*	*1990*	*1996*	*2000*	*2005*
Total	37.7	43.3	51.5	57.5	59.3	60.6	61.7
16–19	39.3	44.0	52.9	51.8	51.3	51.2	50.7
20–24	46.1	57.7	68.9	71.6	71.3	70.5	70.7
25–34	36.0	45.0	65.5	73.6	75.2	75.3	76.4
35–44	43.4	51.1	65.5	76.5	77.5	78.7	80.0
45–54	49.9	54.4	59.9	71.2	75.4	78.2	80.7
55–64	37.2	43.0	41.3	45.3	49.6	53.4	56.6
65 and over	10.8	9.7	8.1	8.7	8.6	9.5	10.2
Total number of women in the labor force (in millions)	23.3	31.5	45.5	56.8	61.9	65.8	70.3

[1]Civilian women age 16 and over.
[2]Labor force participants as a percentage of all women in age group.

Source: Bureau of Labor Statistics, *Handbook of Labor Statistics*, 1989, Table 5; "Labor Force Projections: The Baby Boom Moves On," *Monthly Labor Review*, November 1991, Table 3; "The 2005 Labor Force: Growing, but Slowly," *Monthly Labor Review*, November 1995, Table 10; *Employment and Earnings*, January 1997, Tables 2 and 3; and <http://stats.bls.gov>, published February 29, 1997, accessed May 13, 1997.

Table 4–3 • LABOR FORCE PARTICIPATION RATES BY SEX, RACE, AND HISPANIC ORIGIN, 1975, 1990, 1996, AND PROJECTED 2005[1]

Only among white women is labor force participation projected to increase appreciably between 1996 and 2005. Among men of every race, labor force participation is projected to continue declining.

| | *Labor Force Participation Rates[2]* | | | |
	1975	*1990*	*1996*	*2005*
Women				
All races	46.3	57.5	59.3	61.7
White	45.9	57.5	59.1	62.6
Black	48.8	57.8	60.4	58.8
Other	51.3	56.7	58.8	56.7
Hispanic[3]	—[4]	53.0	53.4	53.6
Men				
All races	77.9	76.1	74.9	72.9
White	78.7	76.9	75.8	73.9
Black	71.0	70.1	68.7	65.8
Other	74.8	74.2	68.7	72.3
Hispanic	—	81.2	79.6	76.1

[1]Civilian labor force age 16 and over.
[2]Labor force participants as a percentage of all women in age group.
[3]Persons of Hispanic origin may be of any race.
[4]Data by Hispanic origin not available for 1975.

Source: Bureau of Labor Statistics, *Handbook of Labor Statistics,* 1989, Table 5; "Labor Force Projections: The Baby Boom Moves On," *Monthly Labor Review,* November 1991, Table 3; and <http://stats.bls.gov>, published February 29, 1997, accessed May 13, 1997.

Table 4–4 • LABOR FORCE PARTICIPATION AND UNEMPLOYMENT RATES OF PERSONS OF HISPANIC ORIGIN BY SEX AND ORIGIN, 1996 (numbers are in thousands; rates are percentages)[1]

Women of Hispanic origin are less likely than American women in general to be in the workforce (see Table 4–3), but labor force participation and unemployment among both women and men of Hispanic origin vary considerably by place of origin. People of Puerto Rican origin are the least likely Hispanics of their sex to be in the labor force. Women workers of Mexican origin have the highest unemployment rate.

	Mexican	Puerto Rican	Cuban	Other[2]	Total
Women					
Total number	5,704	1,093	485	2,328	9,610
Labor force number	3,011	529	259	1,329	5,128
Labor force participation rates	52.8	48.5	53.3	57.1	53.4
Unemployment rate	11.0	10.8	8.3	8.7	10.2
Men					
Total number	6,057	925	506	2,116	9,604
Labor force number	4,932	640	378	1,696	7,646
Labor force participation rates	81.4	69.2	74.8	80.2	79.6
Unemployment rate	8.2	8.6	6.4	7.4	7.9

[1]Civilian labor force age 16 and over.

[2]"Other" was derived by subtracting persons of Mexican, Puerto Rican, and Cuban origin from the total Hispanic population and includes persons of Central and South American origin.

Source: Bureau of Labor Statistics, *Employment and Earnings,* January 1997, Table 6.

Table 4–5 • UNEMPLOYMENT RATES BY SEX, RACE, AND HISPANIC ORIGIN, 1951–1996[1]

For years, unemployment rates were consistently higher among women than among men. That is no longer the case. In 1996, among workers overall and among white workers, female and male unemployment rates were identical.

The pattern of much higher unemployment among black women and men than among their white counterparts has proved stubbornly persistent, however. In only one of the years shown here (1976), and only among women, was the ratio of black unemployment to white unemployment less than two to one.

	All Races		White		Black		Hispanic[2]	
Year	Women	Men	Women	Men	Women	Men	Women	Men
1951	4.4	2.8	—	—	—	—	—	—
1956	4.8	3.8	4.2	3.4	—	—	—	—
1961	7.2	6.4	6.5	5.7	—	—	—	—
1966	4.8	3.2	4.3	2.8	—	—	—	—
1971	6.9	5.3	6.3	4.9	—	—	—	—
1976	8.6	7.1	7.9	6.4	14.3	13.7	—	—
1981	7.9	7.4	6.9	6.5	15.6	15.7	10.8	10.2
1986	7.1	6.9	6.1	6.0	14.2	14.8	10.8	10.5
1991	6.3	7.0	5.5	6.4	11.9	12.9	9.5	10.1
1996	5.4	5.4	4.7	4.7	10.0	11.1	10.2	7.9

[1]Civilian workers age 16 and over.
[2]Persons of Hispanic origin may be of any race.

Table 4–6 • VETERANS' UNEMPLOYMENT RATES BY SEX, RACE, AND HISPANIC ORIGIN, 1996

Judging by unemployment rates, being a veteran seems to confer a small advantage in the labor market to women who are black or Hispanic, but the reverse appears to be true for white women. Among male veterans of any of the particular racial or ethnic groups shown here, unemployment rates are lower than among men in that group overall. Still, blacks have the highest unemployment among veterans of both sexes.

	Women		*Men*	
	Veterans	*Overall Civilian*[1]	*Veterans*	*Overall Civilian*[1]
All races	5.9	4.8	3.8	4.6
White	5.3	4.1	3.5	4.1
Black	7.4	8.7	6.8	9.4
Hispanic[2]	6.0	9.2	4.4	6.9

[1]Persons age 20 and over.
[2]Persons of Hispanic origin may be of any race.

Source: Bureau of Labor Statistics, unpublished data from 1996 annual averages of the Current Population Survey, and *Employment and Earnings,* January 1997, Table 5.

Figure 4–2 • UNEMPLOYMENT RATES FOR WHITE, BLACK, AND HISPANIC WOMEN, 1976–1996[1]

As noted in connection with Table 4–5, unemployment rates are typically at least twice as high among black as among white women. Rates for Hispanic women (who may be of any race) are relatively high as well, but until recently have been significantly lower than for black women. In 1996, however, unemployment was higher among Hispanic women than among black women.

Unemployment
Rate

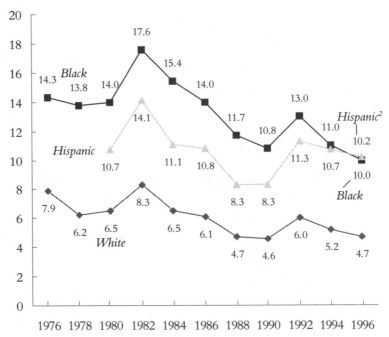

[1]Unemployed women as a percentage of the female civilian labor force age 16 and over.
[2]Persons of Hispanic origin may be of any race. Rates for Hispanic workers are not available before 1980.

Source: Bureau of Labor Statistics, *Handbook of Labor Statistics,* 1989, Table 28, and *Employment and Earnings,* January 1996, Table 5, and January 1997, Table 5.

Figure 4–3 • UNEMPLOYED WORKERS AGE 20 AND OVER BY SEX AND REASONS FOR UNEMPLOYMENT, 1986 AND 1996 (percent distributions)[1]

In both 1986 and 1996, women were considerably less likely than men to be unemployed because of losing a job, and more likely to be looking for work after a time out of the labor force.

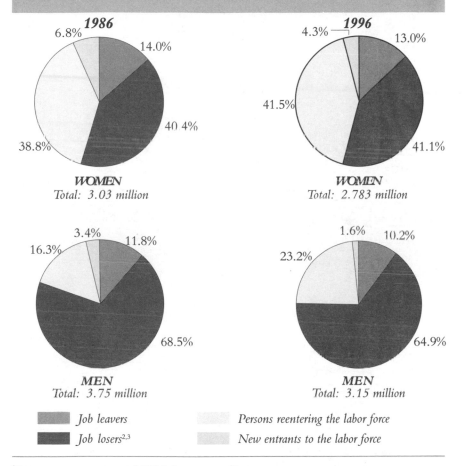

1986

6.8%
14.0%
40.4%
38.8%

WOMEN
Total: 3.03 million

1996

4.3%
13.0%
41.5%
41.1%

WOMEN
Total: 2.783 million

3.4%
16.3%
11.8%
68.5%

MEN
Total: 3.75 million

1.6%
10.2%
23.2%
64.9%

MEN
Total: 3.15 million

■ *Job leavers*   *Persons reentering the labor force*
■ *Job losers*[2,3]   *New entrants to the labor force*

[1]Percentages may not total 100.0 due to rounding.
[2]1996 includes persons who completed temporary jobs.
[3]About 30 percent of the 1996 job losers of both sexes were on temporary layoffs; that is, they expected to get their jobs back. Comparable data for 1986 are not available.

Source: Bureau of Labor Statistics, *Handbook of Labor Statistics,* 1989, Table 37, and *Employment and Earnings,* January 1997, Table 27.

Figure 4–4 • EMPLOYED WOMEN BY YEAR-ROUND, FULL-TIME STATUS, 1970–1995

Between 1970 and 1995, while the number of employed women overall increased by 71 percent, the number employed year round, full time increased by 130 percent. By 1995, 54 percent of all employed women were year-round, full-time workers, up from 40 percent in 1970.

Number
(in thousands)

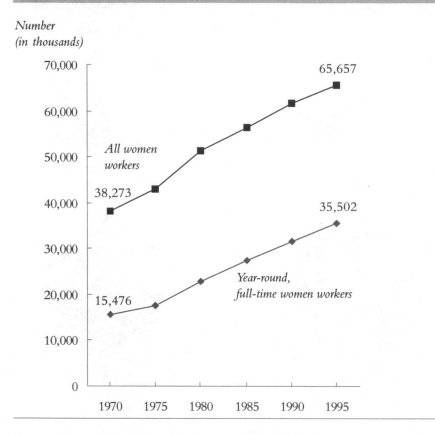

Source: Bureau of the Census, *Money Income of Households, Families, and Persons in the United States: 1991,* 1992, Table B–16, and *Money Income in the United States: 1995,* 1996, Table 10.

Figure 4–5 • WORK SCHEDULES OF WOMEN WITH WORK
EXPERIENCE, 1975 AND 1995

Whether they were on full- or part–time schedules, the working women of 1995
were considerably more likely than their counterparts of 1975 to be working
year round. But it was still the case in 1995 that the majority of women who
worked part time worked for only part of the year.

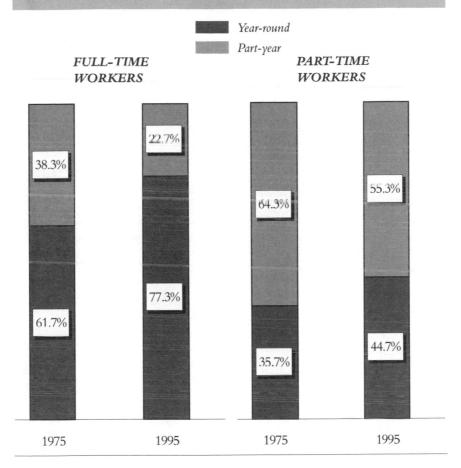

Source: Bureau of Labor Statistics, unpublished data from the March 1976 and March
1996 Current Population Surveys.

Table 4–7 • EMPLOYED WOMEN AND MEN BY FULL- OR PART-TIME STATUS AND RACE, 1996 (percent distributions)[1]

Regardless of race, employed women are much more likely than employed men to work part time. However, black women are less likely than white women to work part time (fewer than one in five compared with more than one in four). Black part-time workers of both sexes (but especially black men) are more likely than their white counterparts to work part time involuntarily.

Work Status	All Races		White		Black	
	Women	Men	Women	Men	Women	Men
Full time[2]	73.7	89.3	72.3	89.4	81.8	88.8
Part time	26.3	10.7	27.7	10.6	18.2	11.2
Voluntary	23.1	8.7	24.7	8.7	13.9	3.2
Involuntary	3.2	2.0	3.0	1.8	4.3	8.0
Total percentage	100.0	100.0	100.0	100.0	100.0	100.0
Total number (in thousands)	55,210	65,729	46,106	56,742	6,717	6,211

[1]Civilians age 16 and over. Excludes employed workers reporting "not at work."
[2]Includes a small number of workers who usually work full time but who were on an involuntary part-time schedule.

Source: Bureau of Labor Statistics, *Employment and Earnings*, January 1997, Table 8.

Table 4–8 • FULL- AND PART-TIME WORKERS BY SEX AND AGE, 1996 (percent distributions)[1]

The age distribution of full-time workers hardly varies by sex—nearly eight in 10 workers of either sex are between the ages of 25 and 55; roughly one in 10 is over 55. The situation is quite different among part-time workers. For example, a male who voluntarily works part time is only half as likely as a similarly employed female to be between the ages of 25 and 55, and nearly twice as likely to be a teenager.

| Age | Full-Time[2] Workers | | Part-Time Workers[3] | | | |
| | | | Voluntary | | Involuntary | |
	Women	Men	Women	Men	Women	Men
16–19	1.9	2.0	16.2	32.2	10.2	12.7
20–24	8.8	8.3	11.8	18.0	17.3	21.0
25–54	79.0	78.3	56.1	23.9	64.8	57.6
55 and over	10.2	11.4	15.9	25.9	7.6	8.8
Total percentage[4]	100.0	100.0	100.0	100.0	100.0	100.0
Total number (in thousands)	42,776	60,762	12,767	5,692	1,758	1,322

[1]Civilians age 16 and over.
[2]Included in the full-time category are a small number of workers who usually work full time but who were on an involuntary part-time schedule when surveyed.
[3]Does not include part-time workers reporting "not at work" when surveyed.
[4]Percentages may not total 100.0 due to rounding.

Source: Bureau of Labor Statistics, *Employment and Earnings,* January 1997, Table 8.

Figure 4–6 • WORKERS HOLDING MULTIPLE JOBS BY SEX, 1970, 1980, 1989, AND 1996[1]

In 1970, when just over four million U.S. workers were multiple jobholders, only 16 percent of them were women. By 1996, the number of multiple jobholders was approaching eight million and the proportion of women among them was upward of 46 percent.

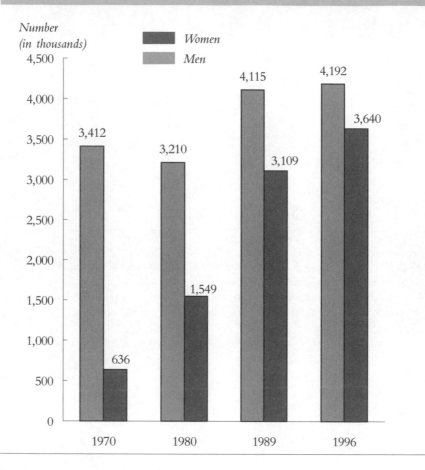

[1]Civilian workers age 16 and over.

Source: Bureau of Labor Statistics, "Multiple Jobholding Up Sharply in the 1980's," *Monthly Labor Review,* July 1990, Table 1, and *Employment and Earnings,* January 1997, Table A–36.

Table 4–9 • CHARACTERISTICS OF MULTIPLE JOBHOLDERS BY SEX, 1996 (percent distributions)[1]

In 1996, women with more than one job were likely to be younger than their male counterparts and more likely than men to have two part-time jobs rather than a part-time job in addition to a full-time job.

	Women	*Men*
Age		
Under 25	16.8	12.8
25–54	75.6	77.5
55 or over	7.6	9.7
Total percentage[2]	100.0	100.0
Race		
White	87.4	87.9
Black	9.0	9.0
Other	3.6	3.1
Total percentage	100.0	100.0
Hispanic (percentage of total)[3]	5.2	6.1
Marital status		
Never married	28.6	24.8
Widowed, divorced, or separated	22.7	10.9
Married, spouse present	48.8	64.3
Total percentage	100.0	100.0
Full- or part-time status		
Primary job full-time, secondary job part-time	48.7	62.2
Both jobs part-time	32.5	12.7
Both jobs full-time	1.9	4.2
Hours vary on primary or secondary job	16.5	20.4
Primary job part-time, secondary job full-time	0.4	0.5
Total percentage	100.0	100.0
Total number (in thousands)	3,640	4,192

[1]Workers age 16 or over.
[2]Percentages may not total 100.0 due to rounding.
[3]Persons of Hispanic origin may be of any race.

Source: Bureau of Labor Statistics, *Employment and Earnings,* January 1997, Table A–36, and "New Data on Multiple Jobholding Available from the CPS," *Monthly Labor Review,* March 1997, Table 4.

Figure 4–7 • WORKERS ON GOODS-PRODUCING AND SERVICE-PRODUCING NONFARM PAYROLLS BY SEX, 1970, 1980, 1990, AND 1996[1]

Employment of both women and men in the goods-producing sector of the U.S. economy grew a little bit between 1970 and 1980 but was essentially flat after 1980 while employment in the service-producing sector continued to grow. As a result, goods-producers accounted for only about 11 percent of employed women in 1996, down from 21 percent in 1970.

Number
(in thousands)

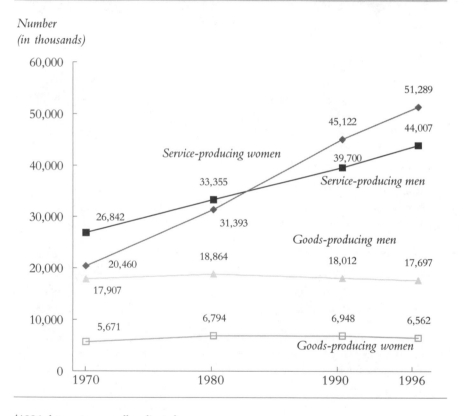

[1]1996 data not seasonally adjusted.

Source: Bureau of Labor Statistics, *Handbook of Labor Statistics,* 1989, Table 68 and Table 73 (as corrected in BLS Bulletin 2340); unpublished data, 1997; and <http://stats.bls.gov:80/cgi-bin/dsrv>, accessed May 15, 1997.

Table 4–10 • EMPLOYED WOMEN AND MEN BY INDUSTRY, 1983 AND 1996 (percent distributions)[1]

The declining importance of manufacturing as an employer of both sexes and the increasing importance of services can be seen clearly in this table. Between 1983 and 1996, services replaced manufacturing as the leading employer of men, accounting for one-quarter of male workers in 1996. The proportion of women employed in services is nearing 50 percent.

	Women		Men	
Industry	*1983*	*1996*	*1983*	*1996*
Agriculture	1.5	1.5	4.8	3.8
Mining	0.4	0.1	1.3	0.7
Construction	1.2	1.4	9.9	10.5
Manufacturing	14.7	11.2	23.7	20.4
Durable goods	7.0	5.6	15.2	13.1
Nondurable goods	7.7	5.6	8.5	7.4
Transportation and public utilities[2]	4.0	4.3	9.2	9.2
Wholesale trade	2.6	2.5	5.5	5.1
Retail trade	19.9	18.8	14.2	15.4
Finance, insurance, and real estate	8.5	8.1	4.8	4.9
Services	42.8	47.7	21.6	25.2
Public administration	4.3	4.4	5.0	4.7
Total percentage[3]	100.0	100.0	100.0	100.0
Total number (in thousands)	44,047	58,502	56,788	68,207

[1]1983 is used here because it is the earliest year for which industry data comparable to 1996 data are available.

[2]In 1983 the Postal Service was moved from "public administration" to "transportation and public utilities."

[3]Percentages may not total 100.0 due to rounding.

Source: Bureau of Labor Statistics, *Employment and Earnings,* January 1984, Table 25, and January 1997, Table 17.

Figure 4–8 • EMPLOYED WOMEN AND MEN BY INDUSTRY, 1996
(percent distributions)[1,2]

The service-producing sector comprises a number of industries. One is the services industry, which of all industrial classifications employs the largest percentage of workers of both sexes. Wholesale and retail trade, employing nearly equal proportions of women and men, ranks second for both sexes. However, these two industries together employed 70 percent of all working women in 1996, compared with 48 percent of working men.

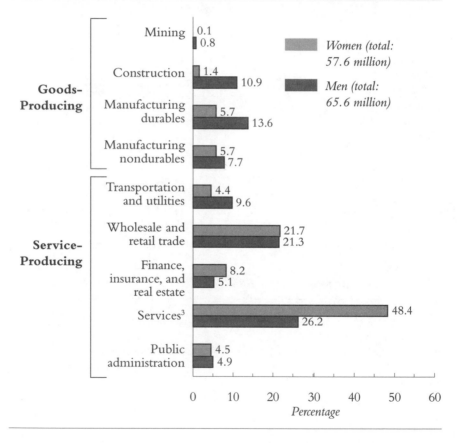

[1]Civilians age 16 and over, excluding workers in agricultural industry.
[2]Percentages may not total 100.0 due to rounding.
[3]Excludes workers in private households.

Source: Bureau of Labor Statistics, *Employment and Earnings,* January 1997, Table 14.

Table 4–11 • EMPLOYMENT IN THE SERVICES INDUSTRY BY SPECIFIC INDUSTRY AND SEX, 1996 (numbers in thousands)

Health (including hospitals) and education are the giants in the services industry; together they employed more than 21 million people in 1996, of whom about 15.5 million were women.

	Total Employees (both sexes)	Percentage Female
Services industry, total	45,043	61.9
Private households	936	89.1
Business, automobile, and repair services The two largest subcategories (each employing about 1.3 million workers, mostly men) are auto repair shops and computer and data processing services. Among other subcategories are building maintenance firms and personnel supply agencies.	8,087	36.8
Personal services (except private household) Subcategories include hotels and motels (the largest, with nearly 1.4 million workers, over half of them women), laundries and dry cleaning establishments, and beauty and barber shops.	3,422	63.2
Entertainment and recreation services Subcategories include theaters and movies, video tape rental stores, and bowling centers.	2,386	44.0
Professional and related services This category, with a predominantly female workforce, accounts for two-thirds of total employment in the services industry. The largest subcategories are:	30,085	69.2
Hospitals	5,041	76.1
Health services (except hospitals) Including, for example, health practitioners' offices and clinics, and nursing and personal care facilities	6,158	79.2

(continued)

Table 4–11 (continued)

	Total Employees (both sexes)	Percent Female
Professional and Related Services *(continued)*		
Educational services Including elementary and secondary schools (6.7 million workers, 75 percent female), and colleges and universities (2.8 million workers, just over 50 percent female)	**10,004**	**68.2**
Social services Including child care centers and family day care homes (together employing 1.3 million workers, 96 percent female)	**3,102**	**80.7**
Other professional services Including, for example, law firms ("legal services," with 1.3 million employees, 56 percent female) and labor unions (59,000 workers, 40 percent female)	**5,781**	**48.3**

Source: Bureau of Labor Statistics, *Employment and Earnings,* January 1997, Table 18.

Table 4–12 • LABOR UNION MEMBERSHIP BY SEX, RACE, AND HISPANIC ORIGIN, 1986 AND 1996 (numbers in thousands)

Over 600,000 more women workers belonged to labor unions in 1996 than in 1986, and the number of union members increased in every group of women shown here. However, because the overall workforce grew faster, union members as a proportion of employed women declined, with the sharpest drop occurring among black women. Among employed men the number as well as the proportion of union members decreased considerably, except among Hispanic males. In their case, the number of union members increased slightly, while the proportion dropped.

	Total Employed[1]		Union Members[2]		Union Members as a Percentage of Total Employed	
	1986	1996	1986	1996	1986	1996
Women						
All races	44,961	53,488	5,802	6,410	12.9	12.0
White	38,410	44,345	4,557	5,016	11.9	11.3
Black	5,257	6,878	1,040	1,138	19.8	16.5
Hispanic[3]	2,648	4,345	367	513	13.9	11.8
Men						
All races	51,942	58,473	11,173	9,859	21.5	16.9
White	45,334	49,961	9,505	8,216	21.0	16.4
Black	5,124	6,031	1,395	1,303	27.2	21.6
Hispanic	4,046	6,455	826	881	20.4	13.7

[1]Wage and salary workers age 16 and over.
[2]Employed members of labor unions or employee associations similar to unions.
[3]Persons of Hispanic origin may be of any race.

Source: Bureau of Labor Statistics, *Employment and Earnings,* January 1987, Table 59, and January 1997, Table 40.

Figure 4–9 • LABOR UNION MEMBERS BY SEX, 1986 AND 1996 (percent distributions)[1]

A result of the trends evident in Table 4–12 is an increased female presence in organized labor. In 1996, about two in five union members were women, up from just over one in three in 1986.

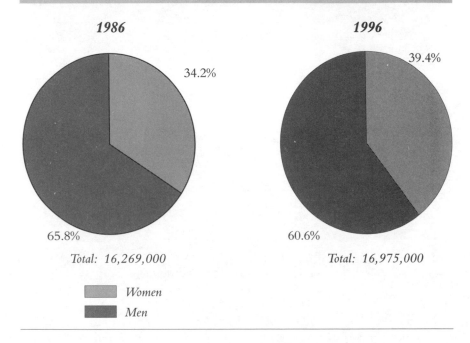

1986

34.2%

65.8%

Total: 16,269,000

1996

39.4%

60.6%

Total: 16,975,000

▢ Women
■ Men

[1]Members of a labor union or an employee association that is similar to a labor union.

Source: Bureau of Labor Statistics, *Employment and Earnings,* January 1987, Table 59, and January 1997, Table 40.

Table 4–13 • EMPLOYED WOMEN AND MEN BY OCCUPATION, 1983 AND 1996 (percent distributions)[1]

In 1983, a woman who worked was more likely to be in an administrative support job than in a managerial or professional job. By 1996, the reverse was true.

	Women		Men	
Occupation	1983	1996	1983	1996
Managerial and professional	**21.9**	**30.3**	**24.5**	**27.5**
Executive, administrative, and managerial	7.9	13.3	12.8	14.6
Professional specialty	14.0	17.1	11.7	12.8
Technical, sales, and administrative support	**45.8**	**41.4**	**19.5**	**19.8**
Technicians and related support	3.3	3.5	2.8	2.7
Sales occupations	12.8	13.0	10.9	11.4
Administrative support, including clerical	29.7	24.8	5.8	5.6
Service occupations	**18.9**	**17.5**	**9.7**	**10.2**
Private household	2.1	1.3	0.1	0.1
Protective service	0.5	0.6	2.6	2.7
Other service	16.3	15.5	7.1	7.5
Precision production, craft, and repair	**2.3**	**2.1**	**19.9**	**18.1**
Operators, fabricators, and laborers	**9.7**	**7.6**	**20.8**	**20.2**
Machine operators, assemblers, and inspectors	7.4	5.1	7.9	7.2
Transportation and material moving occupations	0.7	0.9	6.8	7.0
Handlers, equipment cleaners, helpers, and laborers	1.6	1.7	6.1	5.9
Farming, forestry, and fishing	**1.3**	**1.2**	**5.5**	**4.2**
Total percentage[2]	**100.0**	**100.0**	**100.0**	**100.0**
Total employed (in thousands)	44,047	58,501	56,787	68,207

[1]1983 is used because it is the earliest year for which occupational data comparable to 1996 data are available.

[2]Percentages may not total 100.0 due to rounding.

Source: Bureau of Labor Statistics, *Handbook of Labor Statistics,* 1986, Table 17, and *Employment and Earnings,* January 1997, Table 10.

Table 4–14 • EMPLOYED WOMEN BY OCCUPATION, RACE, AND HISPANIC ORIGIN, 1996 (percent distributions)

Black and Hispanic women are more likely than white women to be in service occupations and less likely to be managers or professionals. But the proportions in administrative support jobs are very similar—about one in four.

Occupation	White	Black	Hispanic[1]
Managerial and professional	**31.5**	**22.8**	**17.4**
Executive, administrative, and managerial	13.9	9.6	8.5
Professional specialty	17.6	13.1	8.9
Technical, sales, and administrative support	**41.9**	**38.4**	**38.4**
Technicians and related support	3.5	3.2	2.7
Sales occupations	13.3	10.6	12.2
Administrative support, including clerical	25.0	24.6	23.6
Service occupations	**16.3**	**25.4**	**25.0**
Private household	1.2	1.9	4.4
Protective service	0.5	1.5	—
Other service	14.6	22.1	20.1
Precision production, craft, and repair	**2.0**	**2.2**	**2.9**
Operators, fabricators, and laborers	**6.9**	**11.0**	**14.3**
Machine operators, assemblers, and inspectors	4.5	7.7	11.0
Transportation and material moving occupations	0.8	1.2	—
Handlers, equipment cleaners, helpers, and laborers	1.6	2.1	2.4
Farming, forestry, and fishing	**1.3**	**0.2**	**1.9**
Total percentage[2]	**100.0**	**100.0**	**100.0**
Total number (in thousands)	48,920	7,086	4,602

[1]Persons of Hispanic origin may be of any race.
[2]Percentages may not total 100.0 due to rounding.

Source: Bureau of Labor Statistics, *Employment and Earnings*, January 1997, Table 10, and unpublished data from the March 1996 Current Population Survey.

Table 4–15 • WOMEN AS A PERCENTAGE OF WORKERS IN SELECTED OCCUPATIONS, 1983 AND 1996[1]

> Women have made considerable headway in many professional and managerial occupations; in some they are the majority. But few women have entered the skilled blue-collar trades.

Occupations	Women as a Percentage of Total Employed	
	1983[2]	1996
Airplane pilots and navigators	2.1	1.4
Architects	12.7	16.7
Auto mechanics	.5	1.2
Carpenters	1.4	1.3
Clergy	5.6	12.3
Computer programmers	32.5	30.8
Data processing equipment repairers	9.3	18.3
Dental assistants	98.1	99.1
Dentists	6.7	13.7
Economists	37.9	54.4
Editors and reporters	48.4	55.7
Financial managers	38.6	54.0
Firefighters	1.0	1.8
Lawyers and judges	15.8	29.0
Librarians	87.3	82.7
Managers, medicine and health	57.0	75.3
Mechanical engineers	2.8	6.9
Physicians	15.8	26.4
Registered nurses	95.8	93.3
Social workers	64.3	68.5
Teachers, college and university	36.3	43.5
Teachers, elementary school	83.3	83.3
Telephone installers and repairers	9.9	13.9
Welders	5.0	5.0

[1]Employed civilians age 16 and over.

[2]1983 is used because it is the earliest year for which the occupational data are comparable to 1996 data.

Source: Bureau of Labor Statistics, *Employment and Earnings,* January 1984, Table 22, and January 1997, Table 11.

Table 4–16 • SELECTED CHARACTERISTICS OF CONTINGENT AND NONCONTINGENT WORKERS, FEBRUARY 1995 (percent distributions)

Contingent workers are more likely to be female, more likely to be black or Hispanic, and typically younger than noncontingent workers. About 32 percent of female contingent workers are under age 25, compared with roughly 14 percent of female noncontingent workers.

	Contingent Workers[1]		Noncontingent Workers	
Sex				
Female	50.4		46.0	
Male	49.6		54.0	
Total percentage[2]	100.0		100.0	
Race				
White	80.9		85.7	
Black	13.3		10.5	
Other	5.8		3.8	
Total percentage	100.0		100.0	
Hispanic[3]	11.3		8.3	
Age	*Female*	*Male*	*Female*	*Male*
16–19	11.7	9.7	4.6	4.0
20–24	20.1	19.6	9.6	9.6
25–34	24.8	27.8	25.7	26.4
35–44	21.4	20.5	28.1	28.0
45–54	13.8	11.4	20.2	19.5
55–64	4.6	7.2	9.4	9.4
65 and over	3.6	3.9	2.5	3.1
Total number (in thousands)	6,034		117,174	

[1]Contingent workers as measured by the Bureau of Labor Statistics using the broadest of three alternative definitions (Estimate No. 3). This definition "effectively included all wage and salary workers who did not expect their jobs to last" plus self-employed persons and independent contractors who had been employed in these arrangements for a year or less and who expected to remain in these arrangements for a year or less.

[2]Percentages may not total 100.0 due to rounding.

[3]Persons of Hispanic origin may be of any race.

Source: Bureau of Labor Statistics, "A Profile of Contingent Workers," *Monthly Labor Review*, October 1996, Tables 1 and 2.

Table 4–17 • CONTINGENCY RATES BY OCCUPATION AND SEX, FEBRUARY 1995

For both women and men, professional specialty occupations (which include, for example, teachers, nurses, and freelance writers) have the highest contingency rates. Contingent workers are rarest in executive, administrative, and managerial occupations and sales occupations.

Occupation	Contingent Workers as a Percentage of All Workers in Occupation[1]	
	Women	*Men*
Executive, administrative, and managerial	3.2	2.3
Professional specialty	7.0	6.6
Technicians and related support	3.6	4.8
Sales occupations	3.4	2.0
Administrative support, including clerical	5.7	6.0
Service occupations	6.5	4.7
Precision production, craft, and repair	4.9	4.5
Operators, fabricators, and laborers	5.7	5.4
Farming, forestry and fishing	4.3	5.9
Total number (in thousands)	3,041	2,993

[1]Contingent workers as measured by the Bureau of Labor Statistics using the broadest of three alternative definitions (Estimate No. 3). This definition "effectively included all wage and salary workers who did not expect their jobs to last" plus self-employed persons and independent contractors who had been employed in these arrangements for a year or less and who expected to remain in these arrangements for a year or less.

Source: Bureau of Labor Statistics, "A Profile of Contingent Workers," *Monthly Labor Review,* October, 1996, Tables 1 and 2.

Table 4-18 • EMPLOYED WOMEN AND MEN IN ALTERNATIVE AND TRADITIONAL WORK ARRANGEMENTS BY OCCUPATION AND SEX, FEBRUARY 1995 (percent distributions)[1]

The occupational distributions of workers in alternative arrangements differ from each other as well as from the distribution of workers in traditional arrangements. Moreover, the occupational distributions of particular types of alternative workers differ by sex. For instance, administrative support workers are by far the single largest group among female "temps" (47 percent), but operators, fabricators, and laborers predominate among male temps (49.5 percent).

	Workers in Alternative Arrangements				Workers in Traditional Arrangements[2]
	Independent Contractors	On Call	Temporary Help Agency	Provided By Contract Firms	
Women					
Executive, administrative, and managerial	11.3	3.4	5.8	5.4	12.9
Professional specialty	20.1	33.0	9.1	31.4	16.8
Technicians and related support	1.0	2.7	3.0	7.6	3.7
Sales occupations	21.3	9.6	3.7	9.7	12.0
Administrative support, including clerical	10.3	14.8	47.0	11.9	26.9
Service occupations	27.7	27.2	9.1	30.8	17.0
Precision, production, craft, and repair	2.9	1.2	3.5	—	2.1
Operators, fabricators, and laborers	3.4	6.9	18.6	3.2	7.6
Farming, forestry, and fishing	2.0	1.2	—	—	1.0
Total percentage	100.0	100.0	100.0	100.0	100.0
Total number (in thousands)	2,714	1,015	624	186	52,373

[1] Percentages may not add to 100.0 due to rounding.
[2] Workers in traditional arrangements are those who do not fall into any of the alternative-arrangement categories.

(continued)

Table 4–18 (continued)

Men	Workers in Alternative Arrangements				Workers in Traditional Arrangements
	Independent Contractors	On Call	Temporary Help Agency	Provided By Contract Firms	
Executive, administrative, and managerial	22.1	2.5	7.3	5.8	14.3
Professional specialty	14.4	10.5	7.3	23.4	12.8
Technicians and related support	1.1	0.5	4.5	6.9	3.1
Sales occupations	17.5	2.5	1.4	0.6	11.4
Administrative support, including clerical	0.7	4.6	11.1	1.9	6.2
Service occupations	2.3	12.2	8.8	26.6	10.5
Precision, production, craft, and repair	27.1	26.3	7.9	20.4	17.2
Operators, fabricators, and laborers	8.0	34.1	49.5	13.3	20.8
Farming, forestry, and fishing	6.7	6.6	2.2	1.3	3.7
Total percentage	100.0	100.0	100.0	100.0	100.0
Total number (in thousands)	5,595	952	557	466	58,678

Source: Bureau of Labor Statistics, "Workers in Alternative Employment Arrangements," *Monthly Labor Review*, October 1996, Table 6.

Table 4–19 • CONTINGENT WORKERS BY WORK ARRANGEMENT
AND SEX, FEBRUARY 1995 (in percentages)[1]

Contingent work and nontraditional work arrangements are not synonymous;
that is, a contingent worker is not necessarily in a nontraditional work arrangement, and a worker in a nontraditional work arrangement is not necessarily contingent. Contingent workers represent a minority of women and men in all the
arrangements shown here except among temporary help agency workers.

	Contingent Workers	
	Women	Men
Workers in nontraditional arrangements		
Independent contractors	5.3	3.1
On-call workers	30.0	40.8
Temporary help agency workers	67.3	65.6
Workers provided by contract firms	18.3	20.4
Workers in traditional arrangements	4.1	3.3

[1]Contingent workers as measured by the Bureau of Labor Statistics using the broadest of
three alternative definitions (Estimate No. 3). This definition "effectively included all wage
and salary workers who did not expect their jobs to last" plus self-employed persons and
independent contractors who had been employed in these arrangements for a year or less
and who expected to remain in these arrangements for a year or less.

Source: Bureau of Labor Statistics, "Workers in Alternative Employment Arrangements,"
Monthly Labor Review, October 1996, Table 11.

Table 4–20 • SELF-EMPLOYED WOMEN AND MEN BY OCCUPATION, 1996

Although their proportions in managerial and professional occupations are similar, in most other respects the occupational distributions of self-employed women and men differ a great deal.

	Self-Employed (numbers in thousands)		Percent Distribution[1]	
	Women	Men	Women	Men
Managerial and professional	**1,194**	**2,152**	**29.9**	**31.8**
Executive, administrative, and managerial	567	1,254	14.2	18.6
Professional specialty	627	898	15.7	13.3
Technical, sales, and administrative support	**1,175**	**1,173**	**29.4**	**17.4**
Technicians and related support	25	48	0.6	0.7
Sales occupations	750	1,068	18.8	15.8
Administrative support, including clerical	400	57	10.0	0.8
Service occupations[2]	**1,043**	**200**	**26.1**	**3.0**
Protective service	1	11	—[3]	0.1
Service, except private household and protective	1,041	189	26.1	2.8
Cleaning and building	109	60	2.7	0.9
Personal services	835	96	20.9	1.4
Precision production, craft, and repair	**128**	**1,534**	**3.2**	**22.7**
Operators, fabricators, and laborers	**122**	**531**	**3.1**	**7.9**
Farming, forestry, and fishing	**330**	**1,170**	**8.3**	**17.3**
Total	3,991	6,759	100.0	100.0

[1]Percentages may not total 100.0 due to rounding.
[2]Includes private households.
[3]Less than 0.05 percent.

Source: Bureau of Labor Statistics, unpublished data from the March 1996 Current Population Survey.

Figure 4–10 • LABOR FORCE PARTICIPATION RATES OF MARRIED WOMEN BY RACE AND HISPANIC ORIGIN, 1976–1996

Of all American married women, those who are black have consistently been the most likely to be in the paid labor force.

Labor Force
Participation
Rate

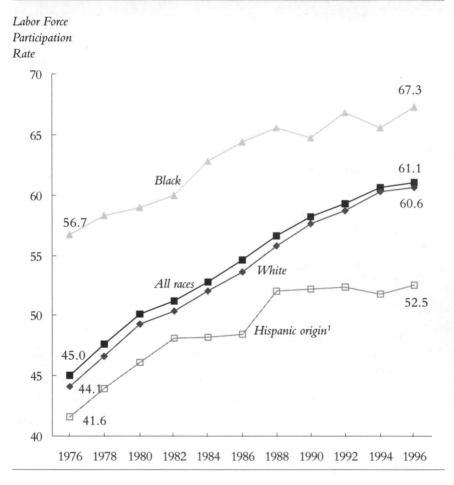

¹Persons of Hispanic origin may be of any race.

Source: Bureau of Labor Statistics, unpublished data from the March Current Population Surveys of 1976, 1978, 1980, 1982, 1984, 1986, 1988, 1990, 1992, 1994, and 1996.

Table 4–21 • CHILDREN WITH WORKING PARENTS BY LIVING ARRANGEMENTS AND AGE OF CHILDREN, 1995[1]

Whether they live with both parents or one parent, children with a stay-at-home parent are in the minority. The only youngsters for whom working parents are not the norm are children under age six who live with their mothers.

		Age of Children		
Children's Living Arrangements	*Total under 18*	*Under 6*	*6–11*	*12–17*
Live with both parents	48,276	16,740	16,359	15,177
Both parents employed				
Number	27,938	8,671	9,507	9,760
Percentage	57.9	51.8	58.1	64.3
Live with mother only	16,477	5,902	5,309	5,266
Mother employed				
Number	9,082	2,620	3,039	3,424
Percentage	55.1	44.4	57.2	65.0
Live with father only	2,461	823	768	870
Father employed				
Number	1,949	652	602	695
Percentage	79.2	79.2	78.4	79.9

[1]Does not include children who live with neither parent.

Source: Bureau of the Census, *Marital Status and Living Arrangements: March 1995 (Update),* 1996, Table 6.

Figure 4–11 • CHILDREN WITH MOTHERS IN THE LABOR FORCE BY AGE OF CHILDREN, 1976–1996 (in percentages)

A child who is old enough to go to school (age six to 17) is more likely than a preschool child to have a mother in the workforce, but youngsters whose mothers work predominate even among children under age six.

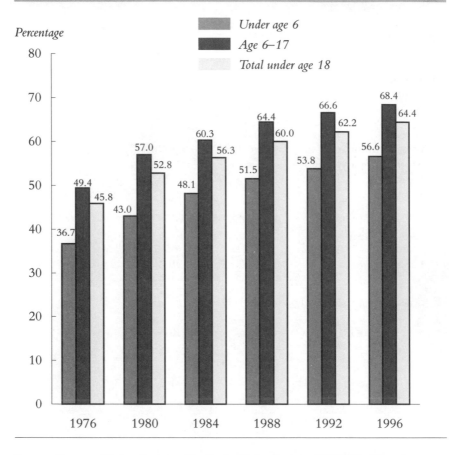

Percentage

Under age 6

Age 6–17

Total under age 18

Source: Bureau of Labor Statistics, *Handbook of Labor Statistics,* 1989, Table 59, and unpublished data from the March 1992 and March 1996 Current Population Surveys.

Figure 4–12 • LABOR FORCE PARTICIPATION RATES OF MOTHERS WITH CHILDREN UNDER SIX BY MARITAL STATUS, 1976–1996

In 1976, only 40.1 percent of mothers with children under six were in the paid workforce. Twenty years later, more than six in 10 were. The increase in labor force participation has been both larger and more consistent among married mothers than among mothers who have never married.

Labor Force
Participation
Rate

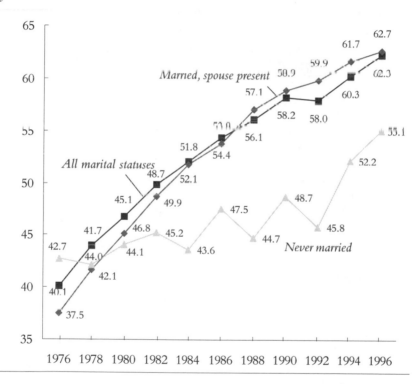

Source: Bureau of Labor Statistics, *Handbook of Labor Statistics,* 1989, Tables 56 and 57, and unpublished data from the March Current Population Surveys of 1990, 1992, 1994, and 1996.

Table 4–22 • EMPLOYED MOTHERS BY FULL-TIME WORK STATUS AND AGE OF CHILDREN, 1976, 1986, AND 1996[1]

Although most employed mothers work full time even if they have very young children, the proportions of full-time workers are consistently higher among mothers whose children are all of school age (six to 17) than among those with younger children.

| | Employed Mothers (numbers in thousands) | | |
Age of Children	1976	1986	1996
Under 3			
Total employed	2,285	4,227	5,222
Percentage full time	67.9	66.3	65.7
Under 6			
Total employed	4,957	7,602	9,592
Percentage full time	68.4	68.8	67.1
6–17[2]			
Total employed	8,769	11,320	13,794
Percentage full time	69.8	73.3	74.5

[1] Women age 16 and over.
[2] No children younger than six.

Source: Bureau of Labor Statistics, *Handbook of Labor Statistics,* 1989, Table 56, and unpublished data from the March 1996 Current Population Survey.

Table 4–23 • CHILD CARE ARRANGEMENTS FOR YOUNG
CHILDREN OF EMPLOYED MOTHERS BY RACE AND HISPANIC
ORIGIN, 1993 (percent distributions)[1]

> Overall, nearly half of all young children with employed mothers are cared for by
> relatives (in some cases by their mothers) while their mothers work. Hispanic
> children are the most likely to be cared for by relatives and the least likely to be in
> organized facilities.

Care Provided by	All Races	White, Non-Hispanic	Black, Non-Hispanic	Hispanic[2]
Relatives	**47.5**	**45.4**	**50.0**	**56.8**
Father	15.9	17.2	8.7	14.9
Grandparent	16.6	14.9	19.7	22.6
In child's home	6.6	5.3	10.6	8.0
In another home	10.0	9.6	9.1	14.7
Other relative	8.8	6.0	18.7	16.0
In child's home	3.3	1.9	7.1	7.9
In another home	5.5	4.1	11.6	8.2
Mother while she works[3]	6.2	7.3	2.8	3.2
Nonrelatives	**21.5**	**22.8**	**15.6**	**19.7**
Babysitter in child's home	5.0	5.1	1.5	7.0
Family day care provider	16.6	17.7	14.1	12.6
Organized facilities	**29.9**	**31.1**	**32.6**	**21.2**
Day care center	18.3	20.0	16.2	10.2
Nursery/preschool	11.6	11.1	16.5	11.0
Other[4]	**1.1**	**0.7**	**1.9**	**2.4**
Total percentage[5]	**100.0**	**100.0**	**100.0**	**100.0**
Total number of children	9,937	7,295	1,161	1,078

[1]Primary care arrangements for children under age five.
[2]Persons of Hispanic origin may be of any race.
[3]Includes mothers working at home or away from home.
[4]Includes preschoolers in kindergarten and school-based activities.
[5]Percentages may not total 100.0 due to rounding.

Source: Bureau of the Census, *Who's Minding Our Preschoolers?* 1996, Table 2.

Table 4–24 • CHILD CARE EXPENDITURES OF FAMILIES WITH
EMPLOYED MOTHERS BY INCOME AND POVERTY STATUS, 1993[1]

The cost of child care is most burdensome for low-income families, even though
they typically spend less on care than better-off families.

Family Income Level and Poverty Status	Number of Families Paying for Child Care (in thousands)	Mean Monthly Child Care Expenses (in dollars)	Percent of Family Income Spent on Child Care
Monthly income			
Less than $1,200	366	205	25.1
$1,200–$2,999	1,295	261	12.0
$3,000–$4,499	1,191	317	8.5
$4,500 and over	1,642	398	5.7
Poverty status			
Below poverty level	319	215	17.7
Above poverty level	4,174	329	7.3
All families	4,493	321	7.6

[1]Children under five years old.

Source: Bureau of the Census, *What Does it Cost to Mind Our Preschoolers?* 1995, Table 3.

Section 5:

Earnings and Benefits

Real median weekly earnings for women who worked full time rose by about 17 percent between 1970 and 1996; real median annual earnings for those who worked year round, full time rose by 21 percent over about the same period. Black women saw the greatest improvement (annual earnings up more than 28 percent); Hispanic women saw the least.

But the narrowing of the wage gap stalled after 1993, as women's median real earnings sagged slightly after years of increasing, and men's median real earnings rose slightly after years of decline. Time will tell whether this will turn out to be a temporary setback or an ominous development.

Lack of health insurance, although still more common among men than women, has increased among both since the late 1980s. Coverage through private insurance is down. Hispanic workers of both sexes are the least likely to have insurance through their jobs; they are also the least likely to belong to a pension plan.

- The ratio of women's to men's earnings, which had been narrowing for some years, widened slightly after 1993. In 1996, women made 75 cents for every dollar men made, but there were great variations by occupation. A female physician earned only about 58 cents to her male counterpart's dollar (see Figure 5–1 and Tables 5–1, 5–3, and 5–4).
- Between 1970 and 1995, real (i.e., inflation-adjusted) annual earnings increased by more than 21 percent for white women who worked year round, full time, and more than 28 percent for their black counterparts (see Table 5–5 and Figure 5–2).
- More education means significantly higher earnings for women as well as for men, and education increases earnings for both more than it used to,

but higher education still does not pay off as handsomely for women as for men (see Table 5–6).

- Women who work year round, full time are slightly more likely than their male counterparts to be in a pension plan through their jobs. Of those workers whose employers do not offer a pension plan, half the women and more than half the men work for small establishments (fewer than 25 employees) (see Tables 5–7 and 5–8).
- No more than 70 percent of year-round, full-time workers of either sex have health insurance coverage through their jobs. Black women and white men are the most likely to have coverage, Hispanic men the least likely. Half the women workers who have health insurance through their own jobs work for very large employers (see Table 5–9 and Figure 5–4).
- Of all women between the ages of 18 and 65 who have private health insurance, about 10 percent have coverage that is unrelated to either their own or a family member's employment, but this proportion jumps to about 19 percent among women in their early sixties (see Figures 5–5 and 5–6).
- People without health insurance accounted for larger proportions of both sexes in 1995 than in 1988. More than one-quarter of the uninsured are adult women—wives, women who head families, or women not living in families (see Figure 5–7 and Table 5–10).

Table 5–1 • MEDIAN WEEKLY EARNINGS BY SEX, AND FEMALE-TO-MALE EARNINGS RATIOS, 1970, 1980, AND 1990–1996[1]

Women's earnings appear to have increased by nearly 350 percent and men's by over 250 percent between 1970 and 1996, but after adjusting for the effect of inflation, these increases translate into a net gain of about 17 percent in women's earnings and a net decline of three percent in men's earnings. Consequently, the wage gap—the ratio of women's to men's weekly earnings—was a good deal narrower in 1996 than in 1970 (75.0 versus 62.3). But the gap is far from disappearing, as Figure 5–1 shows.

	Median Earnings		Ratio of Women's
	Men	Women	to Men's Earnings
Current dollars			
1970[2]	151	94	62.3
1980	312	201	64.4
1990	485	348	71.8
1991	497	368	74.0
1992	505	381	75.4
1993	514	395	76.8
1994	522	399	76.4
1995	538	406	75.5
1996	557	418	75.0
1996 dollars[3]			
1970	574	357	62.2
1996	557	418	75.0
Percent change	-3.0	+17.1	—

[1]Earnings of full-time civilian wage-and-salary workers age 16 and over.
[2]May 1970.
[3]The Consumer Price Index for All Urban Consumers (CPI–U) was used to inflate the earnings series.

Source: Bureau of Labor Statistics, *Employment and Earnings,* January 1979, Table 44; January 1991, Table 54; January 1993, Table 54; January 1995, Table 37; January 1996, Table 37; and January 1997, Table 37; and *Handbook of Labor Statistics,* 1989, Table 41.

Figure 5–1 • MEDIAN WEEKLY EARNINGS BY SEX, 1970–1996 (in constant 1996 dollars)[1,2]

This figure, where earnings are shown in constant 1996 dollars, illustrates what has been happening to the wage gap over time. After narrowing gradually for years, it widened a little after 1993, when men's inflation-adjusted earnings were increasing slightly and women's were not.

1996 Dollars

[1]Earnings of full-time civilian wage-and-salary workers age 16 and over.
[2]The Consumer Price Index for All Urban Consumers (CPI-U) was used to inflate the earnings series.
[3]May 1970.

Source: Bureau of Labor Statistics, *Employment and Earnings,* January 1979, Table 44; January 1991, Table 54; January 1993, Table 54; January 1995, Table 37; January 1996, Table 37; and January 1997, Table 37; and *Handbook of Labor Statistics,* 1989, Table 41.

Table 5–2 • FEMALE-TO-MALE EARNINGS RATIOS BY RACE AND HISPANIC ORIGIN, 1971–1996[1]

The female-to-male earnings ratio—the wage gap—has been consistently narrower among black workers than among their white counterparts, and over the 25 year period shown here has narrowed more among blacks than among whites.

	Ratio of Women's Earnings to Men's Earnings					
	1971	*1976*	*1981*	*1986*	*1991*	*1996*
All races	61.7	62.2	64.6	69.2	74.0	75.0
White	60.7	61.8	63.0	67.9	73.5	73.8
Black[2]	70.7	73.3	76.5	82.7	86.4	87.9
Hispanic[3]	—[4]	—	—	—	89.3	88.8

[1]Based on median weekly earnings of full time civilian wage and salary workers age 16 and over, annual average except for 1971 and 1976, which are for May.
[2]"Black and other" in 1971 and 1976.
[3]Persons of Hispanic origin may be of any race.
[4]Data on median weekly earnings of Hispanic workers by sex were not available for 1971, 1976, 1981, or 1986.

Source: Bureau of Labor Statistics, *Employment and Earnings,* January 1979, Table 44; January 1993, Table 54; and January 1997, Table 37; and *Handbook of Labor Statistics,* August 1989, Table 41.

Table 5–3 • FEMALE-TO-MALE EARNINGS RATIOS BY OCCUPATION,
1986 AND 1996[1]

Between 1986 and 1996, the wage gap narrowed somewhat in most of the occupations shown here but appears to have widened for mechanics and repairers and construction workers (among whom the proportions of women are very small).

	Earnings Ratio	
Occupation	1986	1996
All occupations	69.2	75.0
Managerial and professional specialty	68.2	72.3
Executive, administrative, and managerial	63.6	69.1
Professional specialty	71.4	75.5
Technical, sales, and administrative support	64.5	69.5
Technicians and related support	70.0	76.6
Sales occupations	53.4	59.9
Administrative support, including clerical	70.5	80.0
Service occupations[2]	67.1	76.5
Protective service	72.7	78.1
All other service occupations	81.6	89.5
Precision production, craft, and repair	66.4	66.6
Mechanics and repairers	104.4	89.3
Construction trades	83.1	75.1
Precision production occupations	57.9	61.1
Operators, fabricators, and laborers	67.8	72.7
Machine operators, assemblers, and inspectors	62.9	70.3
Transportation and material moving occupations	77.1	72.0
Handlers, equipment cleaners, helpers, and laborers	83.5	86.0
Farming, forestry, and fishing	85.1	85.0

[1]Earnings of full-time civilian wage-and-salary workers age 16 and over.
[2]Excludes workers in private households.

Source: Bureau of Labor Statistics, *Handbook of Labor Statistics,* August 1989, Table 43, and *Employment and Earnings,* January 1997, Table 39.

Table 5–4 • FEMALE-TO-MALE EARNINGS RATIOS BY DETAILED OCCUPATION, 1996[1]

The female to male earnings ratio—the wage gap—varies greatly by occupation. In the occupations shown here, the gap is widest for physicians—one of the highest-paid occupations and one in which women are still underrepresented—and narrowest for registered nurses, a relatively well-paid occupation in which women are still heavily overrepresented.

Occupation	Percentage Female	Median Earnings (1996 dollars)		Ratio of Women's to Men's Earnings
		Men	Women	
Total, 16 years and over	42.9	557	418	75.0
Managerial and professional	48.8	852	616	72.3
Executive, administrative, and managerial	46.0	846	585	69.1
Financial managers	55.4	979	635	64.9
Managers, marketing, advertising, and public relations	35.9	1,043	674	64.6
Accountants and auditors	56.9	771	561	72.8
Administrators, education and related fields	53.1	956	657	68.7
Professional specialty	51.5	857	647	75.5
Engineers	8.6	963	793	82.3
Physicians	30.8	1,378	802	58.2
Registered nurses	91.5	729	695	95.3
Teachers, college and university	38.0	937	765	81.6
Teachers, except college and university	72.7	723	613	84.8
Lawyers	35.3	1,261	970	76.9

(continued)

[1]Earnings of civilian full-time wage-and-salary workers age 16 and over.

Table 5–4 (continued)

Occupation	Percentage Female	Median Earnings (1996 dollars)		Ratio of Women's to Men's Earnings
		Men	Women	
Technical, sales, and administrative support	61.8	567	394	69.5
Technicians and related support	48.3	650	498	76.6
Health technologists and technicians	77.6	537	470	87.5
Engineering technologists and technicians	18.1	621	542	87.3
Science technicians	36.7	598	443	74.1
Sales occupations	43.4	589	353	59.9
Sales representatives, finance and business services	45.3	727	485	66.7
Sales workers, retail and personal services	55.7	386	259	67.1
Administrative support, including clerical	76.8	489	391	80.0
Secretaries	98.5	—[2]	406	—
Information clerks	88.5	367	343	93.5
Bookkeepers, accounting, and auditing clerks	—[2]	450	396	88.0
Adjusters and investigators	75.0	532	416	78.2
Service occupations	50.2	357	273	76.5
Private household	94.8	—[2]	213	—
Protective service	14.5	562	439	78.1
Police and detectives	12.9	845	—[2]	—
Service, except private household and protective	56.9	304	272	89.5
Food preparation and service occupations	47.3	278	253	91.0
Health service occupations	86.3	342	293	85.7
Cleaning and building services	38.1	321	266	82.9

(continued)

[2]Data not available.

Table 5–4 (continued)

Occupation	Percentage Female	Median Earnings (1996 dollars)		Ratio of Women's to Men's Earnings
		Men	Women	
Precision production, craft, and repair	8.6	560	373	66.6
Mechanics and repairers	4.2	571	510	89.3
Electrical and electronic equipment repairers	12.2	669	542	81.0
Construction trades	1.9	518	389	75.1
Carpenters	1.1	476	—[2]	—
Precision production occupations	20.9	583	356	61.1
Operators, fabricators, and laborers	23.1	422	307	72.7
Machine operators, assemblers, and inspectors	36.2	437	307	70.3
Transportation and material moving occupations	6.4	486	350	72.0
Truck drivers	3.4	485	359	74.0
Handlers, equipment cleaners, helpers, and laborers	17.1	343	295	86.0
Farming, forestry, and fishing	11.7	300	255	85.0

[2]Data not available.

Source: Bureau of Labor Statistics, *Employment and Earnings,* January 1997, Table 39.

Table 5–5 • MEDIAN ANNUAL EARNINGS BY SEX, RACE, AND HISPANIC ORIGIN, 1970–1995 (in constant 1995 dollars)[1,2]

> Using constant dollars allows us to tell whether earnings increases over time have been "real," that is, whether they have increased workers' purchasing power and by how much. In the case of black and white women who worked year round, full time, the increases in annual earnings were not only real but substantial. In the case of Hispanic men, the decrease in annual earnings was steep.

	1970	*1975*	*1980*	*1985*	*1990*	*1995*	*Net Change 1970– 1995*
Women							
All races	19,642	20,349	20,734	22,129	23,113	23,777	+21.1
White	19,971	20,374	20,883	22,373	23,377	24,264	+21.5
Black	16,409	19,625	19,762	20,265	21,035	21,079	+28.5
Hispanic[3]	—[4]	17,439	17,923	18,506	18,273	17,855	+2.4[5]
Men							
All races	33,085	34,597	34,465	34,269	32,274	32,199	-2.7
White	34,034	35,399	35,474	35,496	33,676	33,515	-1.5
Black	23,499	26,323	25,086	24,757	24,619	24,798	+5.5
Hispanic[3]	—	25,525	25,106	24,150	22,313	20,553	-19.5[5]

Columns 2–7 headed *Median Annual Earnings*.

[1]Earnings of civilians age 16 and over who worked year round, full time.
[2]The Consumer Price Index for All Urban Consumers (CPI-U) was used to inflate the earnings series.
[3]Persons of Hispanic origin may be of any race.
[4]Earnings data for 1970 were not available by Hispanic origin of worker.
[5]1975–1995.

Source: Bureau of the Census, *Money Income of Households, Families, and Persons in the United States: 1991*, 1992, Table B–17, and *Money Income in the United States: 1995*, 1996, Table 7.

Figure 5–2 • MEDIAN ANNUAL EARNINGS OF WHITE AND BLACK WORKERS BY SEX, 1970–1995[1,2]

Over the quarter of a century represented in this figure, white men always had by far the highest earnings of all year-round, full-time workers, and black women always had the lowest. However, black women did increase their real (i.e., inflation-adjusted) earnings some while men's earnings were dropping. Only white women gained ground throughout the 25-year period.

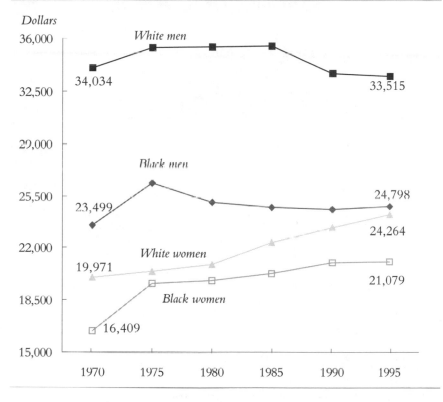

[1]Earnings of full-time civilian wage-and-salary workers age 16 and over.
[2]The Consumer Price Index for All Urban Consumers (CPI-U) was used to inflate the earnings series.

Source: Bureau of the Census, *Money Income of Households, Families, and Persons in the United States: 1991*, 1992, Table B–17, and *Money Income in the United States: 1995*, 1996, Table 7.

Figure 5–3 • MEDIAN ANNUAL EARNINGS BY SEX AND HISPANIC ORIGIN, 1975–1995 (in constant 1995 dollars)[1,2]

While the real (i.e., inflation-adjusted) annual earnings of female year-round, full-time workers as a whole rose over the two decades shown here, the earnings of Hispanic women fell slightly in the second decade. The earnings of Hispanic men dropped over the entire period.

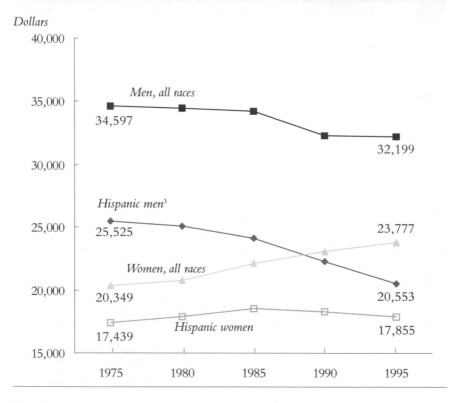

Dollars

[1]Earnings of full-time civilian wage-and-salary workers age 16 and over.
[2]The Consumer Price Index for All Urban Consumers (CPI-U) was used to inflate the earnings series.
[3]Persons of Hispanic origin may be of any race.

Source: Bureau of the Census, *Money Income of Households, Families, and Persons in the United States: 1991*, 1992, Table B–17, and *Money Income in the United States: 1995*, 1996, Table 7.

Table 5–6 • MEAN ANNUAL EARNINGS BY EDUCATIONAL ATTAIN-MENT AND SEX, 1985 AND 1995 (in constant 1995 dollars)[1,2]

In both 1985 and 1995, average annual earnings were higher for men than for women with the same amount of education, and in general, higher levels of education added less to women's earnings than to men's. But men with anything less than a bachelor's degree lost relatively more ground over the decade than their female counterparts. And for both women and men, the earnings edge provided by a bachelor's degree, compared with a high school diploma, was greater in 1995 than in 1985 (for women, it increased from 56 to 75 percent; for men, it increased from 72 to 98 percent). So, although education may not yet pay off as handsomely for women as for men, it definitely does pay off.

	Women		*Men*	
	1985	*1995*	*1985*	*1995*
Total, all levels	24,125	26,593	38,851	40,273
Less than 9th grade	14,777	14,612	23,356	19,625
9–12 (no diploma)	17,445	16,683	27,252	24,029
High school graduate	21,108	21,285	32,367	30,764
Some college (no degree)[3]	24,402	23,771	37,824	36,596
Associate degree[4]	—	28,554	—	37,645
Bachelor's degree or more	33,010	37,275	55,687	60,858
Professional degree[4]	—	60,099	—	113,999

[1]Year-round full-time workers age 18 and over in 1985; year-round, full-time workers age 18 to 65 in 1995.
[2]The Consumer Price Index for All Urban Consumers (CPI-U) was used to inflate the 1985 earnings.
[3]In 1985, "one to three years" of college; associate degrees presumably were included.
[4]Data not available for 1985.

Source: Bureau of the Census, *Money Income of Households, Families, and Persons in the United States: 1985,* 1987, Table 36, and *Money Income in the United States: 1995,* 1996, Table 9.

Table 5–7 • PENSION PLAN AVAILABILITY AND COVERAGE BY WORKERS' SEX AND WORK EXPERIENCE, AND BY RACE AND HISPANIC ORIGIN OF WOMEN, 1995[1]

Among workers in general, women were nearly as likely as men to have a pension plan offered at work but somewhat less likely to be included in the plan. In the case of year-round, full-time workers, however, women were slightly more likely than men to have a plan offered and to be included in the plan.

	Number (in thousands)	Percentage	
		With Pension Plan Offered at Work	Worker Included in Plan
Total[2]			
Men, all races	74,681	53.2	43.3
Women, all races	65,657	52.7	38.9
White	54,925	52.5	38.9
Black	7,952	55.5	40.3
Other	2,780	47.3	33.8
Hispanic[3]	5,220	37.8	26.0
Year-round, full-time			
Men, all races	52,675	61.3	54.1
Women, all races	35,502	64.7	55.1
White	29,131	64.7	55.4
Black	4,812	67.0	55.8
Other	1,559	57.7	47.9
Hispanic	2,773	46.4	37.1
Year-round, part-time			
Men, all races	4,067	30.2	12.6
Women, all races	8,727	37.7	20.9
White	7,715	37.8	21.4
Black	713	39.7	17.4
Other	299	30.1	16.1
Hispanic	646	29.1	15.4

[1]"Pension plan" refers to an employer- or union-provided pension or retirement plan.
[2]Total includes workers who did not work year round.
[3]Persons of Hispanic origin may be of any race.

Source: Bureau of the Census, Current Population Survey, March 1996, <http:// ferret.bls.census.gov/macro/031996/noncash/8_000.htm>, published March 10, 1997, accessed April 24, 1997.

Table 5–8 • PENSION PLAN AVAILABILITY AND COVERAGE BY WORKERS' SEX AND EMPLOYER SIZE, 1995 (percent distributions)[1]

The majority of working women and men who are in a pension plan through their jobs work for employers with 1,000 or more employees (which would include the federal government, the Postal Service, and many other public-sector employers, as well as large private-sector corporations). Less than 10 percent work for employers with fewer than 25 people on the payroll. By contrast, nearly half the women and well over half the men who are not offered a pension plan work for employers with fewer than 25 employees.

Employer Size (number of employees)	Pension Plan Offered, Worker Included in Plan		Pension Plan Not Offered	
	Women	Men	Women	Men
Under 25	8.4	9.9	49.8	57.2
25–99	9.5	11.9	13.9	14.8
100–499	17.3	15.9	11.4	9.7
500–999	8.2	7.3	4.0	3.1
1,000 or more	56.6	55.0	20.9	15.2
Total percentage	100.0	100.0	100.0	100.0
Total number of workers (in thousands)	25,527	32,310	31,075	34,958

[1]"Pension plan" refers to an employer- or union-provided pension or retirement plan.

Source: Bureau of the Census, Current Population Survey, March 1996, <http://ferret.bls.census.gov/macro/031996/noncash/8_000.htm>, published March 10, 1997, accessed April 24, 1997.

Figure 5–4 • WORKERS WITH HEALTH INSURANCE COVERAGE THROUGH THEIR OWN JOBS BY SEX AND EMPLOYER SIZE, 1995 (percent distributions)[1]

Half the women and nearly half the men who have insurance through their own jobs work for employers with 1,000 or more employees (which would include many public-sector employers as well as large private-sector corporations).

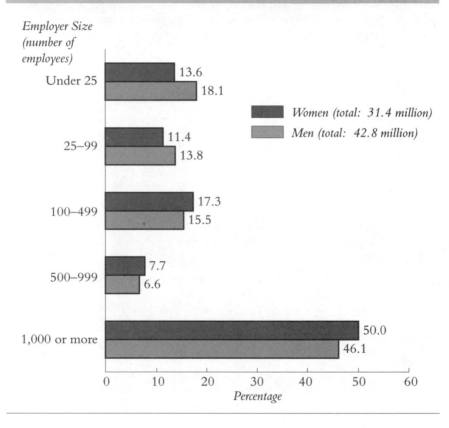

Employer Size (number of employees)

Under 25 — 13.6 / 18.1

■ Women (total: 31.4 million)
■ Men (total: 42.8 million)

25–99 — 11.4 / 13.8

100–499 — 17.3 / 15.5

500–999 — 7.7 / 6.6

1,000 or more — 50.0 / 46.1

Percentage

[1]Workers age 15 and over with employer-provided group health insurance in their own names.

Source: Bureau of the Census, Current Population Survey, March 1996, <http://ferret.bls.gov/macro/031996/noncash/6_000.htm>, published March 10, 1997, accessed April 24, 1997.

Table 5–9 • YEAR-ROUND, FULL-TIME WORKERS COVERED BY HEALTH INSURANCE THROUGH THEIR OWN JOBS BY SEX, RACE, AND HISPANIC ORIGIN, 1995 (numbers are in thousands)[1]

Policymakers count on employers to provide health insurance for most of the population, so it is noteworthy that no more than 70 percent of year-round, full–time workers of either sex have coverage through their jobs. Hispanic workers were the least likely to have coverage. (Some married workers, especially women, who are not insured through their own jobs may be insured through their spouses' jobs; see Figure 5–5.)

	Number Of Workers	*With Health Insurance through Own Jobs*[2]	
		Number	*Percent*
All races			
Women	35,502	23,796	67.0
Men	52,675	36,319	68.9
White			
Women	29,131	19,483	66.9
Men	45,669	31,799	69.6
Black			
Women	4,812	3,336	69.3
Men	4,828	3,088	64.0
Other			
Women	1,559	977	62.7
Men	2,178	1,432	65.7
Hispanic[3]			
Women	2,773	1,529	55.1
Men	4,962	2,581	52.0

[1]Workers age 15 and over.
[2]With employer-provided group health insurance in their own names.
[3]Persons of Hispanic origin may be of any race.

Source: Bureau of the Census, Current Population Survey, March 1996, <http:// ferret.bls.census/gov/macro/031996/noncash/7_000.htm>, published March 10, 1997, accessed April 24, 1997.

Figure 5–5 • WOMEN AND MEN AGE 18–64 WITH PRIVATE HEALTH INSURANCE BY SOURCE OF COVERAGE, 1995 (percent distributions)[1]

Of all women covered by private health insurance for all or part of 1995, the proportion insured through a family member's job was about double the comparable proportion of men. A little over half the women were covered through their own jobs, compared with three-quarters of the men.

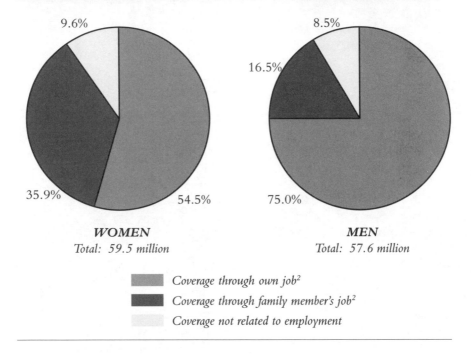

WOMEN
Total: 59.5 million

MEN
Total: 57.6 million

◼ *Coverage through own job[2]*
◼ *Coverage through family member's job[2]*
◻ *Coverage not related to employment*

[1]Persons with coverage for all or part of the year.
[2]Coverage related to current or past employment.

Source: Bureau of the Census, unpublished data from the March 1996 Current Population Survey.

Figure 5–6 • WOMEN AGE 18–64 WITH PRIVATE HEALTH INSUR-
ANCE BY AGE AND SOURCE OF COVERAGE, 1995[1]

Of all women between 60 and 65 who were covered by private health insurance
for all or part of 1995, nearly one in five (18.7 percent) had coverage unrelated to
employment. This almost certainly means that these women—not quite old
enough to qualify for Medicare—purchased individual health insurance policies,
which are typically far more expensive than employer-provided group policies
and often offer fewer benefits. (More than one in seven of all women between 55
and 65 had no health insurance of any kind; see Figure 5–8).

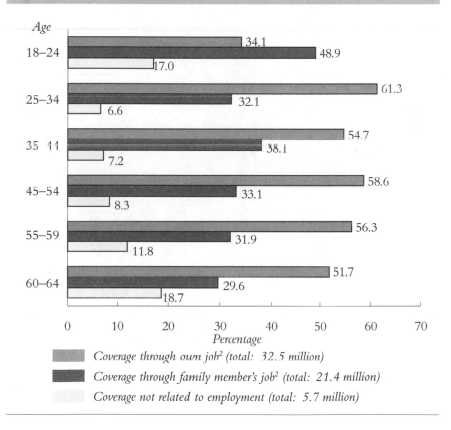

[1]Women with coverage for all or part of the year.
[2]Coverage related to current or past employment.

Source: Bureau of the Census, unpublished data from the March 1996 Current Population
Survey.

Figure 5–7 • HEALTH INSURANCE COVERAGE FOR PERSONS OF ALL AGES BY SEX AND TYPE OF INSURANCE, 1988 AND 1995 (in percentages)[1, 2]

People without health insurance and people covered by Medicaid accounted for larger proportions of both females and males in 1995 than in 1988. The proportions covered by private insurance were smaller in 1995 than in 1988. About 19 million females and 22 million males had no health insurance at all during 1995.

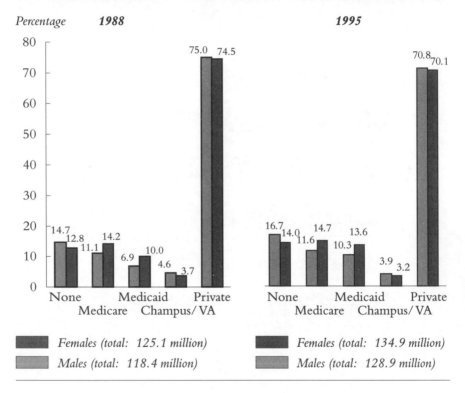

Females (total: 125.1 million)
Males (total: 118.4 million)

Females (total: 134.9 million)
Males (total: 128.9 million)

[1]The "insured" had coverage for all or part of the year; the uninsured had no coverage at any time during the year.
[2]Percentages for each sex total more than 100.0 percent because some insured had coverage from more than one source.

Source: Bureau of the Census, *Poverty in the United States: 1988 and 1989*, 1991, Table 43, and unpublished data from the March 1996 Current Population Survey.

Figure 5–8 • PERSONS WITH AND WITHOUT HEALTH INSURANCE COVERAGE BY SEX AND AGE, 1995

As a rule, males are more likely than females to be uninsured, but the reverse is true among people between 55 and 65. In 1995, more than one in seven of the women in this age group had no coverage of any kind during the entire year.

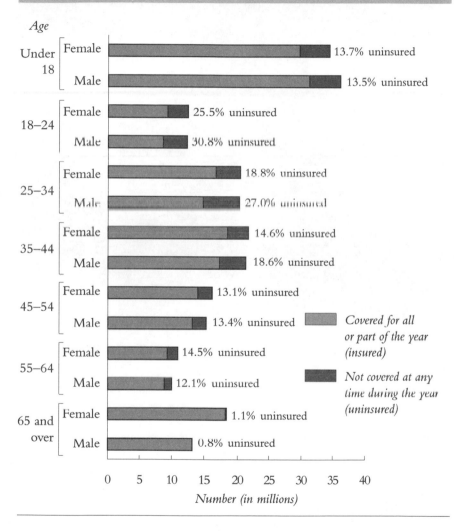

Age

Under 18	Female	13.7% uninsured
	Male	13.5% uninsured
18–24	Female	25.5% uninsured
	Male	30.8% uninsured
25–34	Female	18.8% uninsured
	Male	27.0% uninsured
35–44	Female	14.6% uninsured
	Male	18.6% uninsured
45–54	Female	13.1% uninsured
	Male	13.4% uninsured
55–64	Female	14.5% uninsured
	Male	12.1% uninsured
65 and over	Female	1.1% uninsured
	Male	0.8% uninsured

Covered for all or part of the year (insured)

Not covered at any time during the year (uninsured)

0   5   10   15   20   25   30   35   40

Number (in millions)

Source: Bureau of the Census, unpublished data from the March 1996 Current Population Survey.

Figure 5–9 • WOMEN AND MEN AGE 16–64 WITHOUT HEALTH INSURANCE COVERAGE BY WORK EXPERIENCE, 1995 (percent distributions)[1]

Most people of working age who lack health insurance do work, but working women without insurance are less likely than their male counterparts to work year round, full time, and a larger proportion of uninsured women than of uninsured men are nonworkers.

■ *Worked full time, year round*

■ *Worked, but not full time, year round*

□ *Did not work*

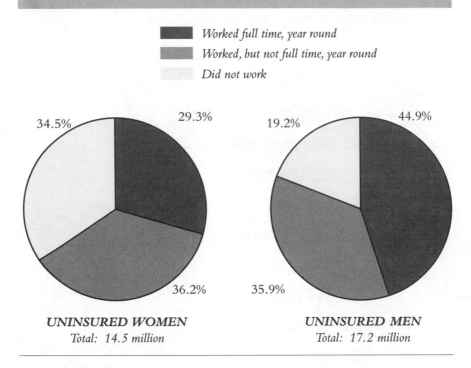

UNINSURED WOMEN
Total: 14.5 million

UNINSURED MEN
Total: 17.2 million

[1]Not covered at any time during the year.

Source: Bureau of the Census, unpublished data from the March 1996 Current Population Survey.

Table 5–10 • PERSONS WITHOUT HEALTH INSURANCE COVERAGE BY FAMILY RELATIONSHIP, 1995 (percent distribution)[1]

More than one in six (15 percent) of the more than 40 million Americans who had no health insurance in 1995 were children under 18; another 8.6 percent were children over 18 who lived with their families. Wives, female householders, and unrelated females (adult women not living in families) together constituted 26 percent of the uninsured.

	Number of Uninsured (in thousands)	Percentage of Uninsured
Persons living in families	**32,315**	**80.0**
Wives	5,594	13.8
Husbands	5,129	12.7
Female householders	2,153	5.3
Children under age 18	6,173	15.3
Children over age 18	3,461	8.6
Other[a]	9,805	24.3
Persons not living in families	**8,074**	**20.0**
Unrelated females	2,890	7.2
Unrelated males	4,801	11.9
In unrelated subfamilies	383	0.9
Total	40,388	100.0

[1]Persons who had no health insurance coverage at any time during the year.
[2]Could include male householders with no spouse present, as well as other relatives.

Source: Bureau of the Census, unpublished data from the March 1996 Current Population Survey.

SECTION 6:

ECONOMIC SECURITY

Dual-earner married couples have been doing better and better financially, as the growth in their median annual income has more than outpaced inflation. The increase has been proportionately largest among black dual-earner couples, although their median real income is still considerably below that of their white counterparts.

For both black and Hispanic families headed by women, median real income was slightly higher in 1995 than it had been 10 years earlier, but that isn't saying much. The poverty rates among these families, especially if they have children, are still shockingly high.

And poverty rates continue to be high among the 7.5 million women over age 65 who live alone. One-fifth of those who are white and half of those who are black or Hispanic have incomes below the poverty threshold; moreover, most of the older black and Hispanic women who are not below the poverty line are perilously close to it.

- Dual-earner couples' median real income rose steadily between 1975 and 1995; it was nearly 20 percent higher at the end of the period. Median income declined for married couples without wives in the labor force and for male-headed families (see Figure 6–1).
- In 1995, as in 1985, median real income was higher for white families of every type than for their black or Hispanic counterparts. However, while income increased for black families of every type except male-headed ones, white families other than dual-earner couples lost ground. Among Hispanic families, only those that were female-headed were better off in 1995 than in 1985 (though not as well off as in 1990) (see Table 6–1).
- Median income for families with children is lower than for families over-

all; still, the income of married couples with children has increased, no doubt because more and more mothers are working (see Figures 6–1 and 6–2).

- At every age, but especially in adulthood, females are more likely than their male contemporaries to be poor. Black and Hispanic women have by far the highest poverty rates among adults (see Table 6–3).

- Overall, two in every five female-headed families with children are poor; among those that are black and Hispanic, over half are in poverty (see Figure 6–3 and Table 6–5).

- The average personal income of men over 65 is nearly double that of their female peers. The women are only half as likely as the men to have earnings or pensions; those women who do have income from those sources receive, on average, much less than men (see Table 6–6).

- Black and Hispanic older women who live alone have, on average, much lower incomes than their white counterparts; nearly half are in poverty, and most of the rest are on the edge of poverty (see Table 6–8).

Figure 6–1 • MEDIAN FAMILY INCOME BY FAMILY TYPE, 1975–1995 (in constant 1995 dollars)[1]

The financial advantage enjoyed by dual–earner married couples is evident. Over the 20-year period shown here, real (i.e., inflation-adjusted) median income increased steadily for couples with wives in the paid labor force. Families headed by women showed a small net increase (six percent). For couples without wives in the workforce and for male-headed families, real income was lower in 1995 than it had been in 1975.

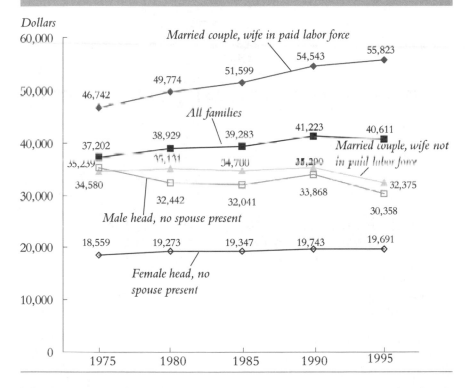

[1]The Consumer Price Index for All Urban Consumers (CPI-U) was used to inflate the earnings series.

Source: Bureau of the Census, *Consumer Income,* 1977, Table D; *Money Income of Households, Families, and Persons in the United States: 1985,* 1987, Table 9; *Money Income of Households, Families, and Persons in the United States: 1991,* 1992, Tables B–6, B–11, and 13; and *Money Income in the United States: 1995,* 1996, Table 4.

Table 6–1 • MEDIAN INCOME OF WHITE, BLACK, AND HISPANIC FAMILIES BY FAMILY TYPE, 1985, 1990, AND 1995 (in constant 1995 dollars)[1]

> Both white and black dual-earner couples saw their purchasing power increase between 1985 and 1995, but Hispanic dual-earner couples saw a net decrease. Between 1990 and 1995, real median income declined for Hispanic families of every type.

	Median Income		
	1985	*1990*	*1995*
White			
All family types	41,290	43,044	42,646
Married couple	44,760	47,027	47,539
Wife in paid labor force	52,394	55,091	56,409
Wife not in paid labor force	35,844	35,892	33,060
Female-headed, no spouse present	22,414	22,770	22,068
Male-headed, no spouse present	34,262	35,646	31,461
Black			
All family types	23,775	24,980	25,970
Married couple	34,800	39,393	41,307
Wife in paid labor force	43,202	46,685	48,533
Wife not in paid labor force	21,428	23,709	25,507
Female-headed, no spouse present	13,179	14,138	15,004
Male-headed, no spouse present	23,251	25,475	25,172
Hispanic[2]			
All family types	26,949	27,321	24,570
Married couple	31,541	32,644	29,861
Wife in paid labor force	39,845	40,552	39,370
Wife not in paid labor force	24,242	24,683	21,219
Female-headed, no spouse present	12,453	13,892	13,474
Male-headed, no spouse present	28,006	26,520	22,257

[1]The 1995 CPI-U inflator was used to adjust the 1985 and 1990 median incomes.
[2]Persons of Hispanic origin may be of any race.

Source: Bureau of the Census, *Money Income of Households, Families, and Persons in the United States: 1985,* 1987, Table 9; *Money Income of Households, Families, and Persons in the United States: 1990,* 1991, Table 13; and *Money Income in the United States: 1995,* 1996, Table 4.

Figure 6–2 • MEDIAN INCOME OF FAMILIES WITH CHILDREN BY FAMILY TYPE, 1975–1995 (in constant 1995 dollars)[1]

Median income for families with children is lower than for families overall (see Figure 6–1); still, inflation-adjusted income increased appreciably for married couples with children between 1975 and 1995 and slightly for female-headed families with children. (It is no coincidence that labor force participation by mothers has increased greatly over roughly the same period; see, for example, Figure 4–12.)

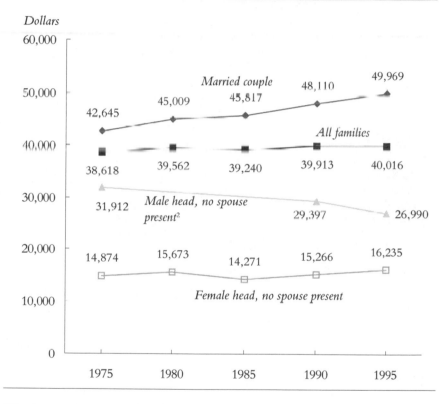

[1] The Consumer Price Index for All Urban Consumers (CPI-U) was used to inflate the earnings series.

[2] Data not available for 1980 and 1985.

Source: Bureau of the Census, *Money Income of Households, Families, and Persons in the United States: 1991*, 1992, Table B–12, and unpublished data from the March 1996 Current Population Survey.

Table 6–2 • SOURCES OF INCOME FOR WOMEN AGE 15–64 BY RACE AND HISPANIC ORIGIN, 1995[1]

Some 78 million women in the age group 15–64 had personal income from at least one source in 1995; the overall average (mean) amount was $18,255. Wages and salaries were by far both the most common and the largest source of women's income, regardless of race or Hispanic origin. However, the amount of income that white women averaged from this source (and from every source shown on this table except AFDC) exceeded that of black and Hispanic women.

| | Women with Income from Source | | Mean Income from Source (in dollars) |
	Number (in thousands)	Percentage	
Total with income[2]			
All races	78,017	100.0	18,255
White	64,473	100.0	18,645
Black	10,104	100.0	15,696
Hispanic origin[3]	6,689	100.0	13,562
Wage and salary			
All races	60,980	78.2	19,212
White	50,668	78.6	19,455
Black	7,668	75.9	17,280
Hispanic origin	5,003	74.8	15,212
Self-employment[4]			
All races	4,137	5.3	10,217
White	3,753	5.8	10,373
Black	256	2.5	7,250
Hispanic origin	228	3.4	7,116

(continued)

[1] The income shown is personal income. For a woman who lives alone, or who is the sole support of a family, personal income constitutes her household's entire income.
[2] Totals include all women who had personal income from any source in 1992. However, not every source of income is detailed in this table.
[3] Persons of Hispanic origin may be of any race.
[4] Excludes farm self-employment, from which 526,000 women had income in 1995.

Table 6–2 (continued)

	Women with Income from Source		Mean Income from Source (in dollars)
	Number (in thousands)	Percentage	
Unemployment compensation			
All races	2,720	3.5	2,564
White	2,241	3.5	2,610
Black	369	3.7	2,440
Hispanic origin	258	3.9	2,132
AFDC			
All races	3,365	4.3	3,896
White	1,958	3.0	3,994
Black	1,249	12.4	3,597
Hispanic origin	701	10.5	4,726
Interest			
All races	44,747	57.4	987
White	39,779	61.7	1,019
Black	3,119	30.9	566
Hispanic origin	2,212	33.1	624
Child support			
All races	4,873	6.2	3,416
White	3,990	6.2	3,623
Black	746	7.4	2,369
Hispanic origin	351	5.2	2,966

Source: Bureau of the Census, March 1996 Current Population Survey, <http://ferret.bls. census.gov/macro/031996/perinc/12_007.htm>, published November 18, 1996, accessed April 24, 1997.

Table 6–3 • POVERTY RATES FOR PERSONS BY SEX, AGE, RACE, AND HISPANIC ORIGIN, 1995

At every age, but especially in adulthood, females are more likely than their male contemporaries to be poor. Women who are white, black, Asian/Pacific Islander or of Hispanic origin are more likely than men of the same race or ethnicity to be in poverty. However, blacks and Hispanics of either sex are more likely than their white or Asian/Pacific Islander counterparts to be poor.

	Females		Males	
	Total Number (in thousands)	*Percentage in Poverty*	*Total Number (in thousands)*	*Percentage in Poverty*
Total	134,880	15.4	128,852	12.2
Age				
Under 18	34,445	21.2	36,111	20.4
18 and over	100,425	13.4	92,741	9.0
18–24	12,441	21.7	12,402	15.0
25–44	42,333	13.1	41,663	8.9
45–64	27,252	9.9	25,416	7.6
65 and over	18,398	13.6	13,260	6.2
Race and Hispanic origin				
White	83,754	11.1	78,830	7.8
Black	12,378	28.1	9,993	16.3
Asian/Pacific Islander	3,477	13.4	3,267	11.7
Hispanic[1]	9,046	28.2	9,085	21.4

[1]Persons of Hispanic origin may be of any race.

Source: Bureau of the Census, *Poverty in the United States: 1995*, 1996, Table 2, and unpublished data from the March 1996 Current Population Survey.

Table 6–4 • POVERTY RATES FOR UNRELATED INDIVIDUALS BY SEX AND AGE, 1995[1]

In a family-oriented society, the often marginal economic situation of people who do not live in families may be overlooked. Most of these "unrelated individuals" live alone. Whether they are female or male, their poverty rates are higher than the average for their sex (see Table 6–3).

	Females		Males	
	Total Number (in thousands)	*Percentage in Poverty*	*Total Number (in thousands)*	*Percentage in Poverty*
Under 18	127	99.7	99	94.9
18–24	2,371	38.1	2,450	31.6
25–34	3,402	16.2	5,533	14.5
35–44	2,399	11.9	3,974	14.1
45–54	2,385	19.4	2,578	17.2
55–59	1,045	28.0	834	21.0
60–64	1,069	26.9	662	22.8
65 and over	7,896	23.8	2,659	14.3
75 and over	4,566	24.7	1,209	15.7
Total	20,694	23.5	18,790	18.0

[1]Unrelated individuals are persons who live alone or with nonrelatives.

Source: Bureau of the Census, March 1996 Current Population Survey, <http://ferret.bls.census.gov/macro/031996/pov/1_001.htm>, published November 18, 1996, accessed April 24, 1997.

Figure 6–3 • POVERTY RATES FOR FAMILIES BY FAMILY TYPE AND PRESENCE OF CHILDREN, 1995

Whatever their type, families with children are more likely to be in poverty than families of the same type without children, but the difference is most dramatic among female-headed families: those with children are nearly four times as likely to be poor as those without children.

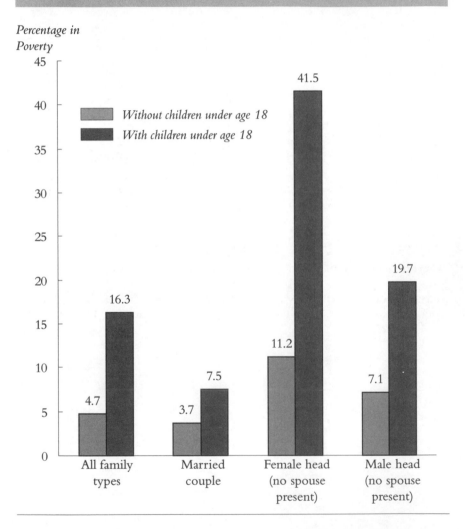

Source: Bureau of the Census, *Poverty in the United States: 1995,* 1996, Table C–3.

Table 6–5 • POVERTY RATES FOR WHITE, BLACK, AND HISPANIC FAMILIES BY FAMILY TYPE AND PRESENCE OF CHILDREN, 1995[1]

Poverty rates among black and Hispanic families of every type exceed the rates for comparable white families. However, when it comes to married couples with children, poverty is most pervasive among Hispanics.

| | *Percentage in Poverty* | | | |
| | *All Family Types* | *Married-Couple Families* | *Families with* | |
			Female Head[2]	*Male Head*[2]
White				
All families	8.5	5.1	26.6	12.9
Families with children	12.9	7.0	35.6	18.4
Families without children	4.0	3.4	8.1	6.2
Black				
All families	26.4	8.5	45.1	19.5
Families with children	34.1	9.9	53.2	23.4
Families without children	11.3	6.6	19.0	14.0
Hispanic[3]				
All families	27.0	18.9	49.4	22.9
Families with children	33.2	22.6	57.3	32.9
Families without children	12.1	10.9	17.8	11.1

[1]Related children under age 18.
[2]With no spouse present.
[3]Persons of Hispanic origin may be of any race.

Source: Bureau of the Census, *Poverty in the United States: 1995*, 1996, Table C–3.

Table 6–6 • SOURCES OF INCOME FOR PERSONS AGE 65 AND OVER BY SEX, 1995[1]

In 1995, on average, older men had nearly double the personal income of older women. A few of the reasons: the women received, on average, much smaller Social Security checks than the men, although women were slightly more likely than men to get Social Security. The women were only half as likely as the men to have income from earnings, and those women who did have earnings averaged less than half of what the men earned. The women were only half as likely as the men to have a pension; women who did have a pension received, on average, a little over half of what men with pensions received.

| | Persons with Income from Source | | Mean Income from Source (in dollars) |
	Number (in thousands)	Percentage	
Total with income[2]			
Women	17,990	100.0	12,973
Men	13,092	100.0	23,967
Earnings			
Women	2,096	11.7	10,940
Men	2,863	21.9	25,959
Social Security			
Women	16,776	93.3	6,971
Men	11,962	91.4	9,376
Supplemental Security Income (SSI)			
Women	991	5.5	2,905
Men	317	2.4	3,224
Survivors' benefits			
Women	1,414	7.9	6,756
Men	190	1.5	11,816
Pensions			
Women	3,887	21.6	6,470
Men	6,090	46.5	11,589

(continued)

[1]The income shown is personal income. For an individual who lives alone or is the sole support of a family, personal income would constitute the household's entire income.
[2]Totals include all persons who had income from any source in 1995. However, not every source of income is detailed in this table.

Table 6–6 (continued)

| | Persons with Income from Source | | Mean Income from Source (in dollars) |
	Number (in thousands)	Percentage	
Interest			
Women	11,541	64.1	3,004
Men	9,153	69.9	3,254
Dividends			
Women	3,177	17.7	3,310
Men	2,893	22.1	3,649
Rents and royalties			
Women	1,692	9.4	3,816
Men	1,556	11.9	3,019

Source: Bureau of the Census, March 1996 Current Population Survey, <http://ferret.bls.census.gov/macro/031996/perinc/12_009.html>, published November 18, 1996, accessed April 24, 1997.

Table 6–7 • SOURCES OF INCOME FOR WHITE, BLACK, AND HISPANIC WOMEN AGE 65 AND OVER, 1995[1]

In 1995, black older women were nearly as likely as their white contemporaries to have income from current earnings or from pensions based on their own previous earnings, and received, on average, larger pensions than white women. However, black women were substantially less likely than white women to have income from the other sources shown here, with one exception—SSI, government assistance for the elderly or disabled poor. Least well-off, on average, were Hispanic older women, nearly one-quarter of whom received SSI.

| | Women with Income from Source | | Mean Income from Source (in dollars) |
	Number (in thousands)	Percentage	
Total with income[2]			
White	16,135	100.0	13,319
Black	1,503	100.0	9,603
Hispanic[3]	788	100.0	8,225
Earnings			
White	1,884	11.7	10,982
Black	164	10.9	10,265
Hispanic	62	7.9	8,270
Social Security			
White	15,236	94.4	7,055
Black	1,277	85.0	6,127
Hispanic	676	85.8	5,778
Supplemental Security Income (SSI)			
White	653	4.0	2,721
Black	244	16.2	2,866
Hispanic	191	24.2	3,427

(continued)

[1]The income shown is personal income. For a woman who lives alone or is the sole support of a family, personal income constitutes her household's entire income.
[2]Totals include all women who had income from any source in 1995. However, not every source of income is detailed in this table.
[3]Persons of Hispanic origin may be of any race.

Table 6–7 (continued)

	Women with Income from Source		Mean Income from Source (in dollars)
	Number (in thousands)	Percentage	
Survivors' benefits			
White	1,289	8.0	6,801
Black	107	7.1	5,301
Hispanic	34	4.3	4,848
Pensions			
White	3,552	22.0	6,313
Black	288	19.2	8,133
Hispanic	97	12.3	6,756
Interest			
White	10,947	67.8	3,043
Black	444	29.5	1,798
Hispanic	209	26.5	1,274
Dividends			
White	3,102	19.2	3,330
Black	42	2.8	1,508
Hispanic	38	4.8	4,002
Rents and royalties			
White	1,593	9.9	3,865
Black	72	4.8	3,042
Hispanic	32	4.1	1,400

Source: Bureau of the Census, Current Population Survey, March 1996, <http://ferret.bls.census.gov/macro/031996/perinc/12_009.htm>, published November 18, 1996, accessed April 24, 1997.

Table 6–8 • WOMEN AGE 65 AND OVER WHO LIVED ALONE BY RATIO OF INCOME TO POVERTY LEVEL, RACE, AND HISPANIC ORIGIN, 1995 (in percentages)

Overall, just under one-fourth of the more than 7.5 million women over 65 who lived alone in 1995 had household incomes below $7,309, the 1995 poverty level for a single person over 65. Half of the total had incomes of less than $10,964—1.5 times the poverty level. Two-thirds of the total had less than $14,618—twice the poverty level. Nearly half of black and Hispanic older women who lived alone were poor; most of the rest were on the edge of poverty.

	Race and Hispanic Origin			
Women Age 65 and Over Who Lived Alone	*All Races*	*White*	*Black*	*Hispanic*[1]
Percentage with income below				
100 percent of poverty	23.6	21.0	48.1	49.3
125 percent of poverty	38.2	35.3	64.8	71.6
150 percent of poverty	49.9	47.4	72.8	79.7
200 percent of poverty	66.7	65.0	83.2	89.8
Total number (in thousands)	7,540	6,798	642	275

[1]Persons of Hispanic origin may be of any race.

Source: Bureau of the Census, *Poverty in the United States: 1995,* 1996, Tables 1 and 2.

Figure 6–4 • HOME OWNERSHIP RATES BY AGE OF HOUSE-
HOLDER, 1985 AND 1995

Home ownership rates in 1995 were lower in the under-55 age groups and higher
in the over-55 age groups than they had been a decade earlier.

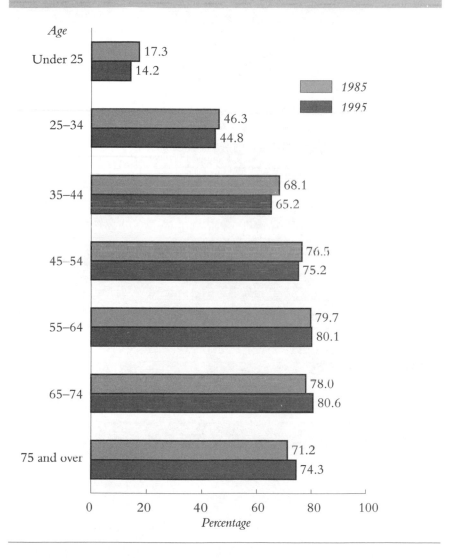

Source: Bureau of the Census, *Household and Family Characteristics: March 1985,* 1986,
Table 22, and *Household and Family Characteristics: March 1995,* 1996, Table 16.

Figure 6–5 • HOME OWNERSHIP RATES BY FAMILY TYPE AND PRESENCE OF CHILDREN, RACE, AND HISPANIC ORIGIN, 1995

Home ownership was the norm in 1995 for black and Hispanic married couples (with children and overall) and for white families of every type except female-headed families with children.

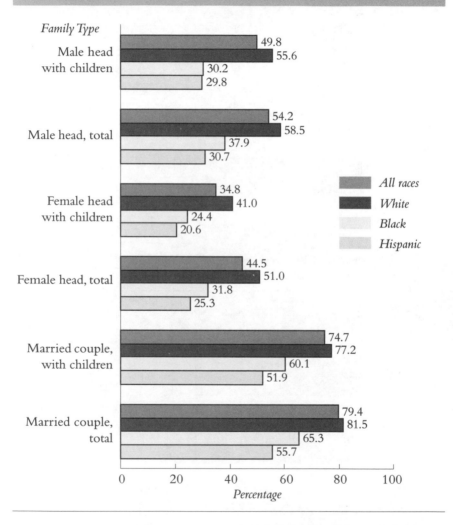

Source: Bureau of the Census, *Household and Family Characteristics: March 1995,* 1996, Table 16.

Table 6–9 • THE HOUSING COST BURDEN BY HOUSEHOLD TYPE
AND TENURE, SELECTED AGE GROUPS, 1995[1]

In proportion to their income, renters pay more for their housing than owners
do. The typical woman renter who is over 65 spends more than half her income
on housing.

	Housing Costs as a Percentage of Income[2]	
	Owners	Renters
Two-or-more-person households		
Married couples, all ages	15.9	24.2
Age 25–29	18.2	22.5
Age 30–34	19.3	22.9
Age 35–44	18.1	23.5
Age 45–64	14.1	23.1
Age 65 and over	14.1	35.6
Female householders, all ages	22.3	48.2
Age 65 and over	15.6	52.9
Male householders, all ages	19.5	32.6
Age 65 and over	14.8	41.0
One-person households		
Female householders, all ages	22.0	45.3
Age 65 and over	24.3	55.5
Male householders, all ages	18.1	26.8
Age 65 and over	18.1	43.3

[1]The age group refers to the age of the person identified as the householder. In the case of
married couples, this is usually—but not necessarily—the husband.
[2]Median housing costs; median income.

Source: Bureau of the Census and Department of Housing and Urban Development,
American Housing Survey for the United States in 1995, 1997, Tables 3–20, 3–21, 4–20, and
4–21.

SECTION 7:

WOMEN IN THE MILITARY[1]

In the next few years, several matters should keep the national debate over the roles of women in the military interesting. Women's growing seniority means that more women will be serving in operational positions with a lot of visibility, such as commanding officers of ships and aviation squadrons, and command sergeant majors and master chief petty officers. And more women will be promoted to the more senior flag and general officer ranks. Currently, three women hold three-star rank—two lieutenant generals (one Marine Corps, one Army) and a vice admiral (Navy).

Argument will continue over whether women should be assigned to ground combat roles in the Army and Marine Corps, especially now that women are no longer barred from combatant positions in the air or on the seas. And those who object to the expanded roles that women are playing in today's armed forces will continue their efforts to roll back some of the gains.

- The number of women serving in the U.S. armed forces has increased steadily since the advent of the all volunteer force in 1973, when less than two percent of total military personnel—1.6 percent of enlisted personnel and 3.8 percent of officers—were women. Today, the proportion of women in both the enlisted and officer ranks exceeds one in seven (see Table 7–1 and Figure 7–1).
- The services continue to attract many black women, who now account for more than one-third of enlisted women and nearly 14 percent of

[1]Captain Lory Manning, USN, (Ret.), director of WREI's women in the military project, compiled this section.

women officers (see Table 7–1). African Americans are among the handful of women who have so far reached the rank of general in the Army and Air Force (and the Navy has recently selected an African American woman for promotion to rear admiral) (see Table 7–2).

- As women gain seniority, their presence in the top three enlisted pay grades and in the rank of colonel (Army, Air Force, Marine Corps) and captain (Navy)—the rank just below the one-star ranks of brigadier general and rear admiral, respectively—has been growing (see Table 7–2 and Figure 7–2).

- Women's roles in the military have changed dramatically. In the early 1970s, women could choose from only a limited number of occupational fields, mostly in health care, administration, and communications/electronics. In 1997, few occupations are closed to women. They serve in aviation as combat pilots, navigators, and mechanics, and aboard ships in every capacity from gunner to chaplain. Still closed to women are occupations and fields involving ground combat and submarine warfare (see Figures 7–3 to 7–5).

- More than one in 10 of the 1997 graduates of every service academy were female; at the Coast Guard Academy, the proportion was one in five (see Table 7–3).

- In the past century, more than 600,000 women have served in the U.S. military services during wartime or have been deployed for military actions or peacekeeping missions. Until fairly recently, most of the military women who served with combat forces were nurses, who not only saw the horrors of combat up close but were often in harm's way themselves. Only in recent years have women other than nurses served in large numbers in combat zones or been deployed as a matter of course to participate in military and peacekeeping actions (see Table 7–4).

Table 7–1 • ACTIVE DUTY SERVICEWOMEN BY BRANCH OF
SERVICE, RANK, RACE, AND HISPANIC ORIGIN, April 30, 1997

As of April 30, 1997, women in the military (including the Coast Guard) numbered 195,290—13.4 percent of total personnel. The Air Force has the highest percentage of women and the Marine Corps the lowest. The Army has the highest percentage of black women; the Marine Corps has the highest percentage of women of Hispanic origin. The repeal in 1994 of the law that barred the permanent assignment of women to combatant ships should increase the percentage of women in the Navy over the next few years. As more ships are converted to accommodate women, more women can be recruited.

Service and Rank[1]	Number of Women	Women as a Percentage of Total Personnel	Percent Distribution of Women[2]			
			White	Black	Hispanic	Other
Total armed forces						
Enlisted	164,056	13.4	53.7	34.1	6.7	5.6
Officers	30,630	13.4	77.5	13.6	3.1	5.8
Army						
Enlisted	58,667	14.8	40.6	47.1	5.5	6.7
Officers	10,239	13.2	69.3	20.6	3.7	6.4
Navy						
Enlisted	41,701	12.2	55.3	30.2	9.4	5.1
Officers	7,676	13.7	81.6	9.4	3.7	5.2
Marine Corps						
Enlisted	8,131	5.3	57.3	24.7	12.3	5.6
Officers	761	4.2	81.9	10.4	4.9	2.9
Air Force						
Enlisted	52,978	17.4	65.4	25.2	4.9	4.6
Officers	11,954	16.0	81.4	10.8	2.0	5.9
Coast Guard						
Enlisted	2,579	9.6	73.3	14.1	7.1	5.5
Officers	604	8.5	82.1	6.0	4.5	7.5

[1]Officers include warrant officers.
[2]Percentages may not total 100.0 due to rounding.

Source: U.S. Department of Defense, Defense Manpower Data Center, unpublished data, April 30, 1997.

Figure 7–1 • ACTIVE DUTY SERVICEWOMEN IN THE DEPARTMENT OF DEFENSE SERVICES BY OFFICER/ENLISTED STATUS, 1972–1997 (in percentages)[1]

Since 1972, the year before the beginning of the all volunteer force, the percentage of enlisted women has grown more than eightfold, and the percentage of women officers has more than tripled. Both are expected to keep growing.

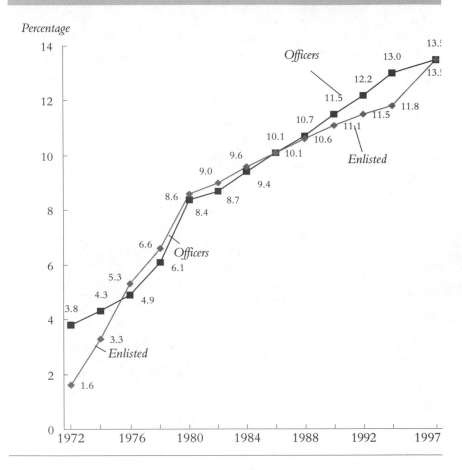

[1]Does not include the Coast Guard, which is part of the Department of Transportation.

Source: U.S. Department of Defense, Defense Manpower Data Center, unpublished data, April 30, 1997.

Table 7–2 • ACTIVE DUTY SERVICEWOMEN BY PAY GRADE GROUPING AND BRANCH OF SERVICE, April 30, 1997[1]

> Women are still underrepresented in the senior enlisted and officer ranks. However, it takes 15 to 20 years to reach these ranks, so the situation should gradually improve over time.

Service and Pay Grade Grouping	Number of Women	Women as a Percentage of Total Personnel
Army		
Officers, total	10,239	13.2
General (O7–O10)	5	1.6
Senior (O6)	266	7.3
Midgrade (O4–O5)	2,823	12.8
Junior (O1 O3, W1 W5)	7,145	12.5
Enlisted, total	58,667	13.7
Senior (E7–E9)	5,679	7.4
Midgrade (E5–E6)	17,744	14.1
Junior (E1 E4)	35,244	14.1
Navy		
Officers, total	7,676	13.7
Flag (O7–O10)	6	2.7
Senior (O6)	243	7.4
Midgrade (O4–O5)	2,531	14.1
Junior (O1–O3, W1–W5)	4,896	14.1
Enlisted, total	41,701	12.2
Senior (E7–E9)	2,419	6.6
Midgrade (E5–E6)	12,473	9.1
Junior (E1–E4)	26,809	16.1

(continued)

[1]Excludes women selected for, but not yet actually serving in, each pay grade grouping as of April 30, 1997.

Table 7–2 (continued)

Service and Pay Grade Grouping	Number of Women	Women as a Percentage of Total Personnel
Marine Corps		
Officers, total	761	4.2
General (O7–O10)	1	1.3
Senior (O6)	11	1.8
Midgrade (O4–O5)	156	3.1
Junior (O1–O3, W1–W5)	593	4.8
Enlisted, total	8,131	5.3
Senior (E7–E9)	655	4.9
Midgrade (E5–E6)	1,899	5.3
Junior (E1–E4)	5,577	5.3
Air Force		
Officers, total	11,954	16.0
General (O7–O10)	5	1.8
Senior (O6)	221	5.6
Midgrade (O4–O5)	3,468	13.3
Junior (O1–O3, W1–W5)	8,260	18.7
Enlisted, total	52,978	17.4
Senior (E7–E9)	4,398	10.8
Midgrade (E5–E6)	15,281	13.2
Junior (E1–E4)	33,299	22.6
Coast Guard		
Officers, total	604	8.5
Flag (O7–O10)	0	0
Senior (O6)	5	1.5
Midgrade (O4–O5)	98	5.4
Junior (O1–O3, W1–W5)	501	10.1
Enlisted, total	2,579	9.6
Senior (E7–E9)	120	3.5
Midgrade (E5–E6)	860	7.8
Junior (E1–E4)	1,599	6.0

Source: U.S. Department of Defense, Manpower Data Center, unpublished data, April 30, 1997.

Figure 7–2 • WOMEN IN SENIOR ENLISTED AND OFFICER PAY
GRADES BY BRANCH OF SERVICE, SELECTED YEARS, 1972–1997
(in percentages)

A key yet usually overlooked measure of women's status in the military is their growing seniority. These charts depict women as a percentage of the three senior enlisted pay grades and of O6—the officer pay grade immediately below brigadier general/rear admiral. The percentages of women in these pay grades are expected to continue growing over the next 10 years.

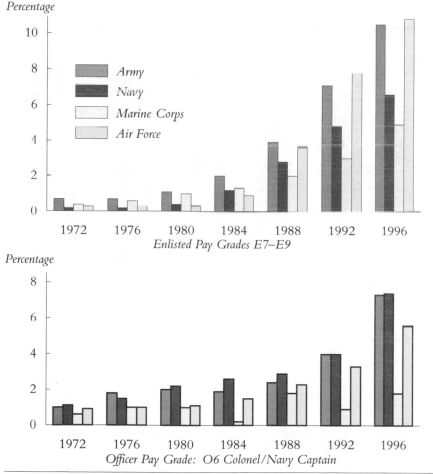

Source: U.S. Department of Defense, Manpower Data Center, unpublished data, April 30, 1997.

Figure 7–3 • POSITIONS AND OCCUPATIONS CURRENTLY OPEN TO ACTIVE DUTY WOMEN BY BRANCH OF SERVICE, 1997 (in percentages)[1]

The term "occupation" refers to an occupational specialty; the term "position" refers to a particular job in a given unit. For example, the occupation of hospital corpsman is open to Navy women, but the position of hospital corpsman aboard a submarine is closed to them. The major fields closed to women include infantry, armor, special forces/SEAL, and submarine warfare. All are associated with ground combat except submarine warfare, which remains closed due to "habitability" (i.e., close living quarters) aboard submarines.

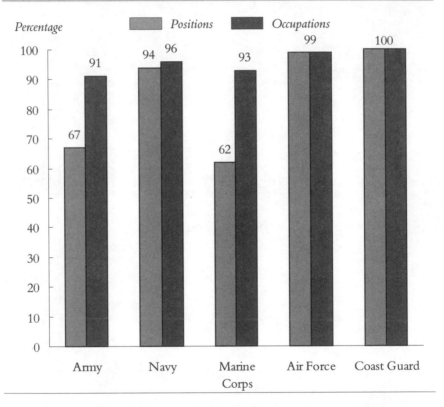

[1]The most recent major changes with respect to the occupations and positions open to military women were made in 1994.

Source: U.S. Department of Defense, Office of the Assistant Secretary of Defense, Public Affairs News Release No. 449-94, July 29, 1994.

Figure 7–4 • OCCUPATIONAL PROFILE OF ACTIVE DUTY ENLISTED PERSONNEL IN THE DEPARTMENT OF DEFENSE SERVICES BY SEX, 1997 (percent distributions)[1,2]

Most women on active duty in 1997 entered the service before the major changes to the combat restriction laws and policies that were made in the early 1990s took effect. That explains, to an extent, the disproportionate numbers of women in health care and support and administration. It will be interesting to see if the proportions change now that women entering the service have more options.

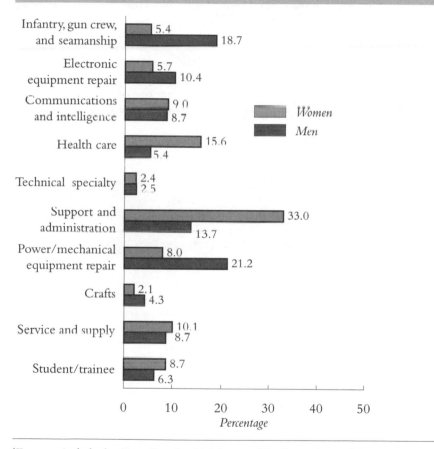

[1]Does not include the Coast Guard, which is part of the Department of Transportation.
[2]Percentages may not total 100.0 due to rounding.

Source: U.S. Department of Defense, Defense Manpower Data Center, unpublished data, June 30, 1997.

Figure 7–5 • OCCUPATIONAL PROFILE OF ACTIVE DUTY OFFICERS IN THE DEPARTMENT OF DEFENSE SERVICES BY SEX, 1997 (percent distributions)[1,2]

> The striking of the combat restriction laws that banned women from serving on combatant ships and aircraft should raise the number of women officers in the tactical operations field somewhat, although the proportions of men and women in this field will not be equal as long as women cannot serve in infantry, artillery, and commando units or aboard submarines. The main reason the percentage of women officers in health care so greatly exceeds that of men is that the services' Nurse Corps are still mostly female.

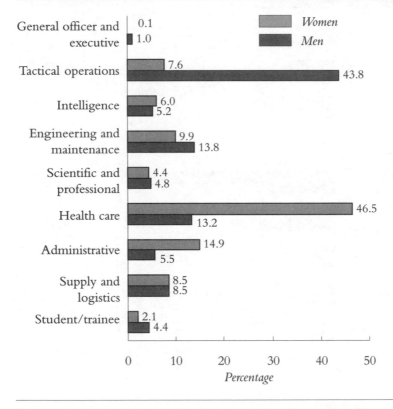

General officer and executive — Women 0.1, Men 1.0
Tactical operations — Women 7.6, Men 43.8
Intelligence — Women 6.0, Men 5.2
Engineering and maintenance — Women 9.9, Men 13.8
Scientific and professional — Women 4.4, Men 4.8
Health care — Women 46.5, Men 13.2
Administrative — Women 14.9, Men 5.5
Supply and logistics — Women 8.5, Men 8.5
Student/trainee — Women 2.1, Men 4.4

Percentage

[1]Does not include the Coast Guard, which is part of the Department of Transportation.
[2]Percentages may not total 100.0 due to rounding.

Source: U.S. Department of Defense, Defense Manpower Data Center, unpublished data, June 30, 1997.

Table 7–3 • WOMEN GRADUATES OF U.S. SERVICE ACADEMIES, 1980, 1990, AND 1997

The first women to attend the service academies graduated in 1980. Since that time the number of women graduating in each class has gradually increased.

Service Academy	Women as a Percentage of Graduates			Number of Women in Class of 1997
	Class of 1980	Class of 1990	Class of 1997	
Air Force	10.9	10.4	15.1	119
Coast Guard	9.2	12.6	20.8	35
Military (West Point)	6.8	9.8	10.6	95
Naval	5.8	9.7	12.1	114

Source: Unpublished data provided by each service academy, June 1993 and May 1997.

Table 7–4 • WOMEN WHO SERVED IN SELECTED U.S. MILITARY AND PEACEKEEPING ACTIONS, 1898 TO MARCH 1997[1]

In the past century, more than 600,000 women have served in the U.S. military services during wartime or have been deployed for military actions or peace-keeping missions. The 1,500 women who served in the Spanish American War were nurses recruited by the Army (they did not have military status, but served under civilian contract). Most of the women who served during World War I were Army or Navy nurses, but some were women recruited by the Navy and the Marine Corps for secretarial and communications jobs. Military nurses have served in combat zones in every war, but only in recent years have military women other than nurses served in large numbers in combat zones or been deployed as a matter of course to participate in military and peacekeeping actions.

	Number of Women
Spanish American War	1,500
World War I	33,000
World War II	400,000
Korea	120,000
Vietnam	7,000
Grenada	170
Panama	770
Desert Storm	41,000
Somalia	1,000
Haiti	1,200
Bosnia	5,000

[1]The numbers are not strictly comparable. The numbers for the Spanish-American War, World War I, World War II, and the Korean War include all women who served on active duty during those eras. The number for the Vietnam War includes only those women who served in theater, that is, those eligible to wear Vietnam Campaign Service medals. The numbers for military actions in Grenada, Panama, and the Persian Gulf, and peacekeeping actions in Somalia, Haiti, and Bosnia include only those women (both active duty and reserve) who were deployed to these areas during the action.

Source: Women in Military Service for America Memorial Foundation, Inc., *Statistics on Women in the Military* (factsheet), 1997.

SECTION 8:

ELECTIONS AND OFFICIALS

Voter turnout in the 1996 election was very low—the lowest in at least six presidential elections. Nevertheless, as in every presidential election since 1980, women were a political force to be reckoned with, not only because there are more women than men of voting age (see Figure 1–2 in the Demographics section), but also because women were more likely than men to vote. This was the case among whites, blacks, and people of Hispanic origin; however, black and Hispanic women and men were less likely than their white counterparts to vote—in the case of Hispanics, much less likely.

Women not only have clout in the voting booth, but they have also gained clout in public office. Although their representation in elected positions still falls far short of parity, in 20 years women have more than doubled their presence in state legislatures and in elected statewide positions, and they have tripled their presence in city halls. Progress for women at the federal level has been slower, but at least women members of Congress are now more than a token few, even in the Senate.

- Beginning in 1980, women have been more likely than men to vote in every presidential election. However, turnout in the 1996 election was lower than usual for women as well as men (see Table 8–1).
- Women's greater likelihood to go to the polls does not hold true in the age groups over 55. Although the gap has narrowed some since 1976, especially among people age 55 to 64, men over 55 have been consistently more likely than women to vote (see Table 8–2). (Even so, female voters outnumber male voters in the over-55 population, simply because women considerably outnumber men in that population.)
- Women have made the most progress in elective office at the state level,

where they hold one in four statewide elected executive positions and more than one in five seats in state legislatures. Women's share of congressional seats is about one in nine (see Table 8–3).

• Women in appointive federal judgeships are no longer a rarity. In just six years, the number of female full-time federal judges increased by 65 percent. The number of federal district court judges doubled (see Table 8–4).

Table 8–1 • VOTER PARTICIPATION IN NATIONAL ELECTIONS BY SEX, RACE, AND HISPANIC ORIGIN, PRESIDENTIAL ELECTION YEARS, 1976–1996 (in percentages)[1]

Beginning with the election of 1980, women have been more likely than men to vote in a presidential election. However, among both sexes voter turnout in the 1996 election was very low.

| Year | All Races | | White | | Black | | Hispanic[2] | |
	Women	Men	Women	Men	Women	Men	Women	Men
1976	58.8	59.6	60.5	61.5	49.9	47.2	30.1	33.9
1980	59.4	59.1	60.9	60.9	52.8	47.5	30.4	29.2
1984	60.8	59.0	62.0	60.8	59.2	51.7	33.1	32.1
1988	58.3	56.4	59.8	58.3	54.2	48.2	30.1	27.4
1992	62.3	60.2	64.5	62.6	56.7	50.8	30.9	26.8
1996	55.5	52.8	57.2	54.8	53.9	46.6	29.3	24.2

[1] Persons who reported having voted as a percentage of the population age 18 and over.
[2] Persons of Hispanic origin may be of any race.

Source: Bureau of the Census, *Voting and Registration in the Election of November 1976,* 1978, Table 2; *Voting and Registration in the Election of November 1980,* 1982, Table 2; *Voting and Registration in the Election of November 1984,* 1986, Table 2; *Voting and Registration in the Election of November 1988,* 1989, Table 2; *Voting and Registration in the Election of November 1988,* 1989, Table 2; *Voting and Registration in the Election of November 1992,* 1993, Table 2; and *Voting and Registration in the Election of November 1996,* forthcoming in 1998, Table 2.

Table 8–2 • VOTER PARTICIPATION IN NATIONAL ELECTIONS BY SEX AND AGE, PRESIDENTIAL ELECTION YEARS, 1976–1996, (in percentages)[1]

Politicians respect "senior power" for very good reason—people between 55 and 75 are the age group most likely to vote. However, turnout is proportionately lower among women over 55 than among men.

Age	1976 Women	1976 Men	1980 Women	1980 Men	1984 Women	1984 Men	1988 Women	1988 Men	1992 Women	1992 Men	1996 Women	1996 Men
18–19	38.8	34.6	34.5	33.9	37.6	32.5	34.4	29.9	39.5	36.2	32.5	27.8
20–24	45.3	43.7	43.9	40.4	44.6	41.0	39.7	35.8	47.2	42.1	36.1	30.7
25–29	53.9	51.6	52.4	50.0	53.3	48.2	46.0	41.2	52.8	46.8	43.7	36.5
30–34	58.9	58.2	59.6	56.7	61.1	56.1	54.1	50.2	58.5	53.6	47.7	43.7
35–44	64.1	62.5	66.0	62.7	64.9	62.0	63.3	59.1	65.7	61.5	56.8	52.9
45–54	67.9	67.9	67.6	67.3	68.0	67.0	66.6	66.6	69.2	68.2	63.6	61.0
55–64	67.9	71.8	70.2	72.6	71.5	72.7	68.9	69.8	71.4	71.9	67.5	68.1
65–74	63.0	70.9	66.7	72.7	70.2	73.9	71.5	75.0	71.8	76.2	68.1	72.6
75 and over	50.1	62.9	52.9	65.7	57.2	68.3	57.5	70.2	60.8	71.4	—[2]	—[2]
75–84[3]	—	—	—	—	—	—	—	—	64.3	74.0	63.5	70.4
85 and over[3]	—	—	—	—	—	—	—	—	48.8	59.4	45.9	58.5

[1] Persons who reported having voted as a percentage of the population age 18 and over. [2] Data not available for 1996. [3] Data for this age group not available for years before 1992.

Source: Bureau of the Census, Voting and Registration in the Election of November 1976, 1978, Table 1; Voting and Registration in the Election of November 1980, 1982, Table 1; Voting and Registration in the Election of November 1984, 1986, Table 1; Voting and Registration in the Election of November 1988, 1989, Table 1; Voting and Registration in the Election of November 1992, 1993, Table 1; and Voting and Registration in the Election of November 1996, forthcoming 1997, Table 1.

Table 8–3 • WOMEN IN ELECTIVE OFFICE, SELECTED YEARS, 1977–1997

Between 1977 and 1997, the number of women in the U.S. House of Representatives nearly tripled and the number in the U.S. Senate more than quadrupled. Women's presence increased in state legislatures, in statewide elected positions, and in mayoralties, as well. Still, if the goal is representation in elective office commensurate with women's proportion in the population as a whole, there remains a long way to go.

| Elected Officeholders | Women as a Percentage of All Officeholders | | | | | | Number of Women |
	1977	1981	1985	1989	1993	1997	1997
Members of Congress	3.7	4.3	4.7	5.8	10.1	11.2[1]	60
House[2]	4.1	4.8	5.3	6.7	10.8	11.7[1]	51
Senate[3]	2.0	2.0	2.0	2.0	7.0	9.0	9
Statewide executive officials[4]	9.9	10.5	13.3	14.3	22.2	25.1	81
State legislators[5]	9.1	12.1	14.8	17.0	20.5	21.5	1,597
Mayors of cities with populations over 30,000[6]	6.2	8.4	9.6	12.7	18.0	20.6	203

[1]As of January 1997, before the resignation of Representative Susan Molinari in August 1997.

[2]Excludes nonvoting delegates. As of January 1997, two women were delegates, representing the District of Columbia and the Virgin Islands.

[3]Excludes women appointed to the Senate.

[4]As of July 1997. Tabulation includes some women who were appointed to fill elective cabinet-level positions. It excludes officials in appointive cabinet-level positions, officials elected to executive posts by state legislatures, members of the judicial branch, and elected members of university boards of trustees and boards of education.

[5]As of May 1997.

[6]As of March 1997.

Source: Center for the American Woman and Politics (CAWP), *Women in the U.S. Congress 1917–1997 Fact Sheet,* January 1997; *Statewide Elective Executive Women 1969–1997 Fact Sheet,* July 1997; *Women in the State Legislatures Fact Sheet,* May 1997; and *Women Mayors and Presidential Appointments,* March 1997.

Table 8–4 • WOMEN ON THE FEDERAL BENCH, 1991 AND 1997[1]

In just six years, the number of women in the full-time federal judiciary increased by 65 percent. Women are now more than a token presence on the federal bench.

| | Women | | | |
| | 1991 | | 1997 | |
	Number	As a Percentage of All Active Judges	Number	As a Percentage of All Active Judges
Supreme Court	1	11.1	2	22.2
Circuit courts[2]	19	12.2	30	18.6
District courts[3]	54	9.7	107	17.2
Bankruptcy courts	39	13.3	56	16.8
U.S. magistrates (full-time)	59	18.2	89	21.4

[1]As of September 1991 and May 1997, respectively.
[2]Includes the Temporary Emergency Court of Appeals.
[3]Includes territorial courts; Claims Court; Court of International Trade; Special Court, Regional Rail Reorganization Act of 1973; and Judicial Panel on Multidistrict Litigation.

Source: Administrative Office of the United States Courts, *Annual Report on the Judiciary Equal Employment Opportunity for the Twelve-Month Period Ended September 30, 1991*, 1991, and unpublished data, May 1997.

WOMEN IN CONGRESS

The Congressional Caucus for Women's Issues: Twenty Years of Bipartisan Advocacy for Women

Lesley Primmer

INTRODUCTION

THE 1994 MIDTERM ELECTIONS turned over control of Congress to the Republican Party for the first time since 1955. With a pledge to reform the workings of Congress, the House Republican leadership pushed through a package of rules changes to reshape the institution. Among the first victims of the new rules were the 28 legislative service organizations (LSOs), including the Congressional Caucus for Women's Issues (CCWI).

The elimination of the LSOs on the first day of the 104th Congress was the culmination of a 15-year effort to control the several dozen House caucuses that had come into existence during the 1960s and 1970s. Although for years the women's caucus remained above the fray—and was even cited as a model caucus by the LSOs' chief opponent in 1995—it suffered the same fate as the other caucuses.

News reports of the caucuses' demise have proved to be exaggerated, however, at least with respect to the women's, black, Hispanic, and Asian/Pacific Island caucuses. The organizations are down but not out. Today, stripped of their funding, staff, and office space, each group continues to function as an informal House caucus, working on behalf of Americans who historically have been underrepresented in Congress.

In 1997, the Congressional Caucus for Women's Issues celebrated its twentieth anniversary. Although it has lost its staff and office, the approximately 51 congresswomen who make up the caucus have maintained their commitment to putting partisan differences aside and working together to advance issues in Congress that are important to women and families.

FOUNDING OF THE WOMEN'S CAUCUS

In 1977, 15 of the 18 women then in Congress founded the Congresswomen's Caucus. In its early days, the caucus held biweekly breakfast meetings to exchange ideas and information about shared legislative interests. In her book, *Champion of the Great American Family,* former Representative Patricia Schroeder (D-CO), the caucus's longest serving cochair, describes the organization's early days as "more of an ongoing tea party than a convincing legislative caucus."

From its inception, the bipartisan women's caucus was headed by two cochairs—one Democrat and one Republican. The first cochairs were former Representatives Elizabeth Holtzman (D-NY) and Margaret Heckler (R-MA). Representative Schroeder succeeded Holtzman in 1980, when Holtzman decided to run for the Senate. Representative Olympia Snowe (R-ME), now a Senator, assumed the Republican cochair position after Heckler lost her House seat in 1982.

As one of its first acts, the organization mounted a successful campaign for a three-year extension of the ratification period for the Equal Rights Amendment (ERA). Other policy concerns of the new caucus included domestic violence, gender bias in education, and improved access to credit and federal contracts for women business owners.

One issue the congresswomen did not address was abortion. The founding members had agreed that they would work on issues that united them, not those that divided them. The abortion issue, perhaps more than any other, was one that divided them. It was not until 1993, after 24 new women were elected to the House—all of them pro-choice—that the caucus went on record in support of reproductive choice.

Another hallmark of 1977 was the founding of the Women's Research & Education Institute (WREI). Established to serve as the research and education arm of the caucus, WREI grew into one of the most respected women's think tanks in Washington. Although the two organizations severed their formal ties in 1985, WREI continues to serve as a link between the women's research community and Washington policymakers.

THE CAUCUS OPENS ITS DOORS TO MEN

One of the most significant changes in the Congresswomen's Caucus came in 1981, when it decided to open its membership to men. The change ushered in a period of growth that transformed the caucus from one of the smaller LSOs into one of the largest. At its peak in 1992, the caucus's membership was 170.

Although some congresswomen had being saying for a long time that men should be allowed to join, the decision was largely forced on the caucus by the adoption of new House rules governing LSOs. The rule changes were prompted by a Better Government Association report raising serious concerns about the intermingling of corporate and public money by the caucuses.

The new House rules prohibited LSOs from accepting any funds other than membership dues paid from the official expense accounts of members of Congress. At the time, the Congresswomen's Caucus received a significant share of its support from subscriptions to its monthly newsletter, *UPDATE,* as well as from WREI, its nonprofit research and education institute.

The Congresswomen's Caucus faced the same dilemma as the Congressional Black Caucus and Congressional Hispanic Caucus: how to continue their organization with no outside money and only a small pool of potential members to draw on for support. There were, after all, only 21 women in the House in 1981.

All three caucuses made the same decision: to solicit support from the largest caucus in the House—the white males. The Congresswomen's Caucus became the Congressional Caucus for Women's Issues (CCWI). The women members elected themselves to the Executive Committee, which became the policymaking structure of the caucus; the new male members made up the general membership.

While the inclusion of men was essential to CCWI's economic survival, it brought significant political advantages as well. During the 103rd Congress (1993–94), the caucus's membership included 42 of the 48 women in the House, the Speaker of the House, the Majority Leader, the Majority Whip, and a number of powerful committee and subcommittee chairs.

LSOs UNDER ATTACK

The 1981 caucus reforms muffled the criticism of legislative service organizations somewhat but did not silence it. A decade later, CCWI and the other LSOs came under attack on the House floor. The chief LSO critic, Representative Pat Roberts (R–KS), proposed abolishing all the LSOs.

Roberts's proposal, introduced as an amendment to the annual legislative branch spending bill, prohibited members of Congress from using their official expense allowances to support the caucuses. The Congressman had done his homework, combing the regular expenditure reports filed by LSOs with the House. During the floor debate, he waited patiently as representatives of the LSOs defended their caucuses. After each had described the valuable work of a particular caucus, Roberts opened his file and asked the member to explain questionable expenditures for food, travel, or gifts—expenditures that were prohibited for individual members but not for LSOs.

Undeterred by the criticism heaped on the other caucuses, Representative Mary Rose Oakar (D–OH) took to the floor to praise the Congressional Caucus for Women's Issues. She spoke proudly of the bipartisan organization's work on women's health, particularly in securing Medicare coverage for mammograms. "We could not have done that if we had not convened together," she concluded. When she finished, Roberts kept his file closed and simply agreed that the women's caucus had done fine work, calling it a model for the other LSOs. "If all caucuses would be run as well as the women's caucus, we would not have near the problems we have," he said.

The House rejected the Roberts amendment by voice vote, leaving the caucuses intact—at least for the time being.

ACTIVISM AND INFORMATION

Over the years, the Congressional Caucus for Women's Issues has had two main functions: to advocate for women and families and to serve as an information clearinghouse on women's issues in Congress.

In its advocacy role, the caucus has created its own agenda while pushing Congress to be more responsive to women's concerns. In an effort to focus on the range of issues affecting women and their families, caucus members introduced several omnibus legislative packages during the 1980s and 1990s. These initiatives formed the core of the caucus's agenda. The congresswomen also worked in coalition with other House caucuses and outside organizations to pass important civil and women's rights initiatives.

The caucus's first legislative package was the Economic Equity Act (EEA). First introduced in 1981, the EEA marked a shift in the public's view of women's issues away from divisive issues, such as the ERA and abortion, to bread–and–butter issues, such as poverty and economic security. Over the years, the EEA has addressed a range of concerns, including tax and retirement policies, dependent care, health insurance coverage for dependents, and child support enforcement.

The issue of temporary leave for workers with newborns or seriously ill family members also dominated the caucus agenda for many years, beginning with the introduction of the first family leave legislation by Representative Schroeder in 1985. The eight-year-long campaign ended in 1993 when President Clinton signed the Family and Medical Leave Act—the first public bill signing of his new presidency.

In 1990, CCWI led the way in focusing congressional and public attention on deficiencies in women's health care. At the time, many large, federally funded medical research studies were being conducted entirely on male subjects. In addition, an internal NIH women's advisory committee had concluded that only a small fraction of the institute's sizable budget was being used for research on women's health. After enlisting support from Health Subcommittee Chair Henry Waxman (D-CA), the caucus asked the General Accounting Office (GAO) to investigate the matter.

The women's health research issue exploded in June 1990 when the GAO reported its findings to Waxman's subcommittee. Although NIH had a policy of encouraging the inclusion of women in medical research studies, the GAO confirmed that little had been done to enforce the policy or even to advise the research community about it. Caucus cochairs Schroeder and Snowe used the Waxman hearing to unveil plans to introduce an omnibus legislative package to improve women's health. The first two initiatives in the package called for the establishment of a NIH Office of Research on Women's Health and the inclusion of women, wherever appropriate, in NIH-funded research studies.

Modeled after the Economic Equity Act, the Women's Health Equity Act (WHEA) proved an even more successful catalyst for legislative action. By the end of the 104th Congress (1996), more than two dozen WHEA provisions had become law and billions more dollars had been pumped into women's health research and services.

In addition to its advocacy work, CCWI became a key source of information about women's issues in Congress for both members of Congress and the public. For many years the organization produced two regular publications: a weekly legislative report for caucus members and a monthly publication, *UPDATE,* that the members could give to their constituents. The caucus also published fact sheets on timely policy topics and an annual summary of legislative action on women's issues.

The caucus's most successful period came during the 103rd Congress (1993–94) when 66 measures of direct benefit to women and families were signed into law—breaking all previous records for legislative accomplishment on women's issues in a single Congress.

CAUCUS REAPS 1992 ELECTION YEAR BENEFITS

The 1992 elections, dubbed by many as the "Year of the Woman," tripled the number of women in the Senate and increased the number of women in the House by three-quarters. The newly elected women were activists. Some had made their decisions to run for Congress while watching Anita Hill testify against her former boss, Supreme Court nominee Clarence Thomas, before the Senate Judiciary Committee in October 1991. Most had campaigned on women's equity issues and came to Congress ready to follow through on their promises. Even before they were sworn in, the 24 newly elected female House members (21 Democrats and three Republicans) called a press conference to announce a four-point agenda for women and families that included reproductive choice, family leave, full funding for Head Start, and the application of civil rights laws to Congress.

At the first Executive Committee meeting in 1993, CCWI voted to end its 15-year silence on abortion and to take a position supporting a woman's right to reproductive choice. During the 103rd Congress, the congresswomen led the fight for coverage of the full range of reproductive health services, including abortion, in health care reform; for protected access to abortion clinics; and for repeal of abortion funding restrictions for poor women, federal workers, and residents of the District of Columbia. Only on repeal of the Hyde amendment—barring the use of federal Medicaid funds to pay for abortions for poor women—were the congresswomen unsuccessful.

The prevailing issue during the 103rd Congress was health care reform, and the caucus worked to shape a bill that addressed women's needs. In addition to reintroducing the Women's Health Equity Act, CCWI worked with national women's organizations to develop a set of principles to ensure equitable treatment for women in whatever health care reform legislation Congress ultimately considered.

The first challenge was to convince the White House that fair treatment of women's health was not only the right thing to do, but politically "doable." Early in the 103rd Congress, CCWI members met with First Lady Hillary Clinton, who was leading the effort to enact health care reform legislation. To the congresswomen's delight, the First Lady was supportive of their goals. Referring to the caucus's unsuccessful attempts to meet with Presidents Reagan and Bush, Representative Schroeder told reporters after the meeting, "We've been waiting for 12 years for someone in the White House to come."

Following the release of the Administration's health care reform proposal, the congresswomen were invited to the White House to discuss their concerns with the President. With abortion coverage already included in the proposal, the congresswomen's main concern was the need to provide adequate coverage for key preventive health services, such as mammograms and pelvic exams.

In the end, the congresswomen won the battle but lost the war. As the 1994 elections approached, a highly successful public relations campaign by the insurance industry doomed prospects for health care reform during the 103rd Congress. However, each of the major health care bills had required the inclusion of comprehensive women's health services in basic benefit packages. Mammogram screenings and Pap tests, family planning services, and services for pregnant women—which were understood to include abortion—would all have been covered.

Another major CCWI accomplishment during the 103rd Congress was passage of the Violence Against Women Act (VAWA), to make homes and streets safer for women by expanding domestic violence and sexual assault services. VAWA was introduced by caucus cochair Pat Schroeder and signed into law as part of the 1994 omnibus crime bill. Extensive lobbying by the congresswomen—both Democrats and Republicans—was necessary to force consideration of this comprehensive legislative approach.

Other important victories included the approval of more than $500 million for breast cancer research and new efforts to improve gender equity in education and federal contracting. According to Representative Schroeder, the caucus's accomplishments during the 103rd Congress "should finally put to rest the question 'What difference does having more women in Congress make?' "

Still, in the eyes of some political analysts, the women's caucus lacked the political muscle of another House caucus to which it frequently was compared—the Congressional Black Caucus (CBC). On several occasions during the 103rd Congress, the CBC had brought the House leadership to its knees by threatening to withhold votes unless its concerns were accommodated. CBC's willingness to vote as a block to advance its mission was a powerful weapon the women's caucus did not possess.

Unlike the CBC, which had a single Democratic chair and a membership roster that included only one Republican, the women's caucus was bipartisan to its core. Initiatives proposed to the caucus for action were first approved by the bipartisan cochairs. Generally, the disapproval of either chair was sufficient to bury an issue before further action could be taken.

While the caucus would never be an arm-twisting organization capable of lining up its members to vote in a prescribed way, during the 103rd Congress, a handful of women's votes supplied the margin of victory on a number of key policy issues. In the Senate, the freshman Democratic women supplied the deciding votes to end consideration of a bill to restrict product liability awards. Women in the House also played a crucial role in the passage of the assault weapons ban, providing the two-vote margin of victory.

NEW WOMEN'S CAUCUS LEADERS

While CCWI's conversion to a pro-choice organization greatly broadened its legislative agenda, the caucus took another step during the 103rd Congress that set in motion significant structural change. It became clear at the first caucus meeting of the new Congress that a growing number of members wanted a change in the group's leadership. Representative Schroeder had served as cochair since before Ronald Reagan assumed the presidency in 1981, and Representative Snowe had joined her not long after, in 1983.

Although no one had challenged Representatives Schroeder or Snow during the Reagan and Bush years, 1993 was the dawn of a new era for the caucus. The anticipation of working with a Democratic President made many Democratic women eager to lead the effort to translate election year gains into legislative victories for women.

The election of officers was the first item on the agenda for the January 1993 meeting. When no challenge was offered, several congresswomen moved to reelect the existing slate of officers. As latecomers arrived, however, the displeasure of some members became apparent.

In an effort to resolve the matter, the Executive Committee agreed to establish a task force to review and revise the organization's bylaws. Representative Maxine Waters (D-CA) volunteered to chair the task force. The only reform the caucus specifically discussed that day was a limit on the terms of officers.

The new bylaws were approved midway through the second session, although they were not scheduled to take effect until the 104th Congress. As expected, the bylaws placed a two-year limit on the terms of caucus officers. They also created two vice chair positions—one Democratic and one Republican—with the idea that those who assumed these positions would be groomed to become cochairs.

AN END TO LSOs

What no one foresaw as the new bylaws were being written was the possibility that the caucus as they knew it would soon cease to exist. Following the surprise takeover of the House by the Republican Party in the 1994 midterm elections, chief LSO opponent Representative Pat Roberts was put in charge of a leadership task force to determine the fate of the caucuses. A bipartisan group of members fought to save the LSOs, which also included such Republican organizations as the Republican Research Committee and the moderate House Wednesday Group. However, in an effort to consolidate power in the Speaker's office, the Republican leadership backed Roberts's proposal that *all* LSOs be abolished.

In January 1995, the women's caucus lost its six-member staff, its office space on the fourth floor of the Rayburn House Office Building, its $250,000 budget, and its ability to use a separate letterhead. What the leadership could not take away was the right of members of Congress to meet as informal caucuses. In fact, such groups, known as congressional member organizations (CMOs), had existed for years, although their activities were severely limited by a lack of staff and operating budgets. The CCWI had little choice at the beginning of the 104th Congress but to reorganize as a CMO, more akin to the organization as founded in 1977 but with virtually no options for growth.

The loss of its staff and budget meant an end to the caucus's weekly and monthly publications and other information services. With the encouragement and support of the congresswomen, three former caucus staff members established a nonprofit organization called Women's Policy, Inc. (WPI) to carry on this key aspect of the former LSO's work. The new organization's board included the caucus cochairs in the 104th Congress—Representatives Nita Lowey (D-NY) and Constance Morella (R-MD). Since June 1995, WPI has published a weekly newsletter detailing legislative action on issues important to women and families. The organization also published a special report on the Women's Health Equity Act and a detailed summary of women's issues in the 104th Congress.

CAUCUS PUSHES FORWARD IN 104TH CONGRESS

The restructured women's caucus has continued to serve as the primary advocate for women's issues on Capitol Hill. In the 104th Congress, as it had for more than a decade, the caucus laid out its own agenda while working to make legislation pending before the House more responsive to the needs of women and families. The caucus cochairs, task force chairs, and members testified at hearings, circulated letters to their colleagues, and worked against attempts to reverse many of the legislative gains of the past two decades. While the record of the 104th Congress on women was a mixed one, it was far more successful than many would have predicted at the outset.

CCWI members reintroduced their two trademark legislative packages—

the Women's Health Equity Act and the Economic Equity Act. Despite a Congress focused largely on deficit reduction and gaining the upper hand in the 1996 elections, the bipartisan efforts of the congresswomen produced some important legislative gains in improving the health and economic standing of women.

Funding for research on women's health issues fared well, both at the National Institutes of Health (NIH) and at the Department of Defense (DOD). Strong bipartisan advocacy from the caucus was critical in securing $137 million for DOD's breast cancer research and prevention effort. Addressing another growing concern of women's health advocates, Congress directed the Environmental Protection Agency (EPA) to develop a screening program for detecting estrogen-mimicking chemicals in the environment.

Health insurance reform legislation—one of the most important domestic policy initiatives of the 104th Congress—included WHEA provisions to prohibit insurance companies from discriminating on the basis of genetic information or evidence of domestic violence.

Major policy initiatives on immigration reform and welfare reform were amended to exempt domestic violence victims from some of the harsher provisions. The immigration bill also included a WHEA provision outlawing female genital mutilation in the United States.

The welfare bill included a section toughening the nation's child support enforcement system. The provision had been developed by CCWI in the previous Congress, and a strong bipartisan push from the congresswomen secured its inclusion in each of the welfare reform proposals approved by the 104th Congress, including the one that became law in August 1996.

The caucus also rallied behind the 27-year-old Title X family planning program after the House Appropriations Committee voted to eliminate it and restored funding by a relatively narrow 20-vote margin.

On other reproductive rights issues, the caucus was less successful. The 104th Congress was described by reproductive rights advocates as the most anti-choice Congress in history. With a record 52 votes on reproductive issues, the anti-abortion majority in the House proved unbeatable in nearly every instance. In addition, drastic reductions in international family planning programs have jeopardized efforts to reduce unintended pregnancies and protect the health of women and families in the developing world.

The battle to secure full funding for programs under the Violence Against Women Act was one of the hardest won bipartisan victories for the caucus and also one of the sweetest. In all, the bill authorized $1.67 billion over six years for domestic violence and sexual assault programs. When it came time to appropriate funds for VAWA programs, however, budgetary concerns prevailed. In Fiscal Year (FY) 1996, the two funding bills for these programs provided only $75 million, little more than a quarter of the full amount authorized by law.

Republican congresswomen, led by Representatives Connie Morella (R–MD) and Susan Molinari (R–NY), appealed to their leadership for an increase in funds. Representative Nita Lowey (D–NY) used her position on the House Appropriations Committee to offer amendments to restore VAWA funding. Faced with a strong challenge to their funding bill and eager to avoid a floor fight over funding for violence against women, House and Senate Appropriations Committee members responded by increasing funding to $228 million. The following year (FY1997) VAWA funding increased again by nearly $100 million, exceeding the amount authorized by the original 1994 law.

LOOKING AHEAD

The 105th Congress continues to be a time of transition for the caucus. With the departure of Representatives Schroeder and Cardiss Collins (D–IL), the last of the caucus's founding members are gone. And consistent with its new bylaws, the caucus has elected new cochairs—Delegate Eleanor Holmes Norton (D–DC) and Representative Nancy Johnson (R–CT). In 1997, in both his inaugural address and his State of the Union address, President Clinton called on Congress to join him in finding bipartisan solutions to the nation's problems. Chastened by an unprecedented gender gap in the 1996 elections (with women voting for President Clinton and Democratic congressional candidates in record numbers), the 105th Congress seems more likely to seek compromise than confrontation on issues important to women.

Despite the elimination of legislative service organizations in 1995, the Congressional Caucus for Women's Issues has 20 years' experience in turning bipartisan support for women's rights into solid legislative accomplishments. Women the world over continue to benefit from the organization's efforts.

Women in the 105th Congress

The 1996 elections slightly increased women's ranks in Congress. In the Senate, the election of Susan Collins (R–ME) and Mary Landrieu (D–LA) and the retirement of Nancy Kassebaum (R–KS) produced a net gain of one in the Senate, for a total of nine women—three Republicans and six Democrats. In the House of Representatives, the number of women—excluding nonvoting delegates—increased from 48 to 51 (reduced to 50 by the retirement in 1997 of Susan Molinari [R–NY]). Of these, 35 are Democrats and 15 are Republicans.

Eleven of the women representatives and both women delegates are African American—in fact, African Americans are considerably better represented among the women in Congress than among the men. Four women representatives are of Hispanic origin—one Cuban American, one Puerto Rican, and two Mexican Americans.

Maine became the second state to have elected women to both its Senate seats. The first, California, has not only two women in the Senate but also eight women in the House—the largest number of women in any state's delegation. Altogether, women in the 105th Congress represent 23 states plus the District of Columbia and the U.S. Virgin Islands, both of which have elected women as their delegates to Congress (delegates have no vote).

The majority of the women in the 105th Congress held elective office before running for Congress. A number served on city councils or county commissions or boards. More than 40 percent were in their states' legislatures, which have traditionally served as "incubators" of congressmen and are clearly playing the same role in developing future congresswomen. Only 11 percent of today's federal legislators are female, but women's share of state legislative seats, which began increasing years before women's share of congressional seats edged up, currently exceeds 20 percent. It is a "leading indicator" of the Congress of the future.

WREI is pleased to include, in this Seventh Edition of *The American Woman,* brief biographies of the women serving in the 105th Congress. The biographies are followed by a list of the members of the Congressional Caucus for Women's Issues, which is cochaired by Representative Nancy Johnson (R–CT) and Delegate Eleanor Holmes Norton (D–DC).

Senator Barbara Boxer (*Democrat, California*) was elected to the Senate in 1992, following 10 years as a member of the House of Representatives. She sits on the Committee on Appropriations, the Committee on Environment and Public Works, and the Committee on Banking, Housing, and Urban Affairs. She also sits on the Committee on the Budget.

During her tenure in the House, Senator Boxer led the fight for federal funding of abortions for women who were victims of rape or incest. In both the House and the Senate, she has championed the Family and Medical Leave Act and the Violence Against Women Act. She also has worked to draw attention and resources to women's health issues, such as breast cancer.

Born in Brooklyn, New York, in 1940, Senator Boxer has a B.A. in economics from Brooklyn College. She is married and the mother of two adult children. Before coming to Congress, she was for six years a member of the Marin County Board of Supervisors.

Representative Corinne Brown (*Democrat, Third District, Florida*), who was first elected to Congress in 1992, serves on the Veterans' Affairs Committee and the Transportation Committee. Her legislative priorities include education, aging, economic development, and women's issues.

Congresswoman Brown holds B.S. and M.A. degrees from Florida A&M University and an education specialist degree from the University of Florida. She served as a member of the faculties at Florida Community College of Jacksonville, the University of Florida, and Edward Waters College. Representative Brown was born in 1946 in Jacksonville, where she still resides.

Representative Julia Carson (*Democrat, Tenth District, Indiana*) was elected to the House in 1996. She is a member of the Banking and Financial Services Committee and the Veterans' Affairs Committee.

In 1972, Congresswoman Carson successfully ran for the Indiana House of Representatives; after two terms in the House, she was elected to the Indiana Senate, where her concerns included health care, child support, and the plight of the poor.

Congresswoman Carson, who was born in 1938, has two children. She resides in Indianapolis.

Representative Helen Chenoweth (*Republican, First District, Idaho*) was first elected to the House in 1994. She serves on the Agriculture Committee, the Veterans' Affairs Committee, and the Resources Committee, where she chairs the Subcommittee on Forests and Forest Health. Her priorities include balancing the budget, lowering taxes, and shrinking the size of government.

Born in eastern Kansas in 1938, Representative Chenoweth served as state executive director of the Idaho Republican Party from 1975 to 1977. She went on to serve as chief of staff to then-Congressman Steve Symms.

Delegate Donna Christian-Green (*Democrat, At Large, U.S. Virgin Islands*) is the fourth person and the first woman to be elected delegate to the House of Representatives from the U.S. Virgin Islands. She serves on the Resources Committee.

Delegate Christian-Green is a physician whose medical career spanned more than 20 years and ranged from private family practice to serving as Acting Commissioner of the U.S. Virgin Islands Department of Health. Since 1995, Delegate Christian-Green has served as a trustee of the National Medical Association.

Delegate Christian-Green was born in 1945. She earned a B.S. from St. Mary's College in Notre Dame, Indiana, and received her M.D. from the George Washington University School of Medicine in Washington, D.C.

Representative Eva Clayton (*Democrat, First District, North Carolina*) was first elected to the House in November 1992, in a combination general and special election, to fill the seat left vacant by the death of her predecessor. She is not only the first woman elected to Congress from North Carolina but also the first woman to be elected president of a Democratic "freshman class." A member of the Agriculture Committee and the Budget Committee, Congresswoman Clayton is an advocate for rural health care, housing assistance, and job training.

Representative Clayton was born in 1933 in Savannah, Georgia. Before coming to Congress, she served as a member of the Warren County Board of Commissioners. She is married and has four children and two grandchildren.

Senator Susan M. Collins (*Republican, Maine*) was elected to the Senate in 1996. She serves on the Labor and Human Resources Committee, the Special Committee on Aging, and the Governmental Affairs Committee, where she is the first woman to hold the position of chair of the Subcommittee on Investigations.

Her career before her election to the Senate included serving as staff director for the Senate Subcommittee on the Oversight of Government Management and as Maine's Commissioner of Professional and Financial Regulation under Governor John R. McKernan.

Born in 1952 in Caribou, Maine, Senator Collins earned a degree in government from St. Lawrence University. She resides in Bangor.

Representative Barbara Cubin (*Republican, At Large, Wyoming*) was first elected to the House in 1994. She is a member of the Commerce Committee and the Resources Committee, where she chairs the Subcommittee on Energy and Mineral Resources. She also serves as a Deputy Whip in the Republican leadership.

Before coming to Congress, Representative Cubin served in both the houses of Wyoming's legislature. She is a graduate of Creighton University and is pursuing a master's degree in business administration. A fifth-generation Wyomingite, Representative Cubin is married and has two children in college.

Representative Patricia Danner (*Democrat, Sixth District, Missouri*) was first elected to Congress in 1992. She is a member of the Committee on Transportation and Infrastructure and the International Relations Committee.

Before her election to the U.S. House, Congresswoman Danner served for 10 years as a member of the Missouri Senate. During her tenure in the state senate, she worked on legislation to enhance federally funded technical programs by providing tuition waivers for displaced homemakers. She also authored Missouri's Extended Day Child Care Act, which provided funds for after-school child care services.

Congresswoman Danner, who was born in 1934 in Louisville, Kentucky, earned her B.A. from Northeast Missouri State University. She is married and has four children.

Representative Diana DeGette (*Democrat, First District, Colorado*), first elected to Congress in 1996, is a member of the Commerce Committee, serving on the Subcommittee on Health and Environment and the Subcommittee on Finance and Hazardous Materials.

A graduate of Colorado College, Congress-woman DeGette earned a law degree from New York University Law School. She practiced law in Denver for 15 years, specializing in civil rights and employment litigation, and served two terms in the Colorado House of Representatives, where she focused on protecting women's reproductive rights and domestic violence laws.

Congresswoman DeGette, who was born in 1957, resides in Denver. She is married and has two daughters.

Representative Rosa DeLauro (*Democrat, Third District, Connecticut*) was first elected to Congress in 1990. A member of the Appropriations Committee, she serves on its Subcommittee on Labor, Health and Human Services, and Education. She also currently serves as Chief Deputy Minority Whip. Representative DeLauro has made improving the delivery of health care a priority during her tenure in Congress, sponsoring legislation to increase funding for research on women's health.

Congresswoman DeLauro, who was born in New Haven, Connecticut, in 1943, has been in public service for much of her lifetime. She was the first woman to serve as executive assistant to the mayor of New Haven and was chief of staff to U.S. Senator Christopher Dodd (D-CT). Before her election to the House, she was the executive director of EMILY's List.

Representative Jennifer Dunn (*Republican, Eighth District, Washington*), who was first elected to Congress in 1992, serves on the House Ways and Means Committee. Her policy priorities include women's health as well as tax relief for small business and the middle class. From 1981 to 1992—before her election to Congress—Representative Dunn was chair of the Washington State Republican Party.

Congresswoman Dunn was born in Seattle in 1941. She holds a B.A. from Stanford University. She is the mother of two children.

Representative Jo Ann Emerson (*Republican, Eighth District, Missouri*), first elected to Congress in 1996, is the first Republican woman from her state to serve in the U.S. House of Representatives. She serves on the Agriculture Committee, the Small Business Committee, and the Transportation and Infrastructure Committee.

Before coming to Congress, Representative Emerson was senior vice president of public affairs for the American Insurance Association. She also served as deputy director of communications for the Republican National Committee.

Representative Emerson, who was born in Bethesda, Maryland, in 1950, graduated from Ohio Wesleyan University. The widow of former Congressman Bill Emerson, she has two daughters and two stepchildren.

Representative Anna Eshoo (*Democrat, Fourteenth District, California*) was elected to her first term in Congress in 1992. She sits on the Commerce Committee.

While a 10-year member of the San Mateo County Board of Supervisors, Congresswoman Eshoo was responsible for securing funds for California's first freestanding nursing facility for AIDS patients. In Congress, she has played an active role in women's health issues, introducing legislation to guarantee insurance coverage of breast reconstructive surgery following a mastectomy.

Representative Eshoo, who was born in New Britain, Connecticut, in

1942, has an A.A. from Cañada College in Redwood City, California. She is the mother of two children.

Senator Dianne Feinstein (*Democrat, California*) was first elected to the Senate in November 1992 to complete the unexpired term of Pete Wilson (R-CA), who had been elected Governor of California. She was reelected in 1994 to her first full six-year term. Senator Feinstein sits on the Judiciary Committee, the Rules and Administration Committee, the Foreign Relations Committee, and the Joint Library Committee.

Senator Feinstein was Mayor of San Francisco from 1978 to 1988. Before that, she was a member of the San Francisco Board of Supervisors. She was born in San Francisco in 1933 and received her B.A. from Stanford University. She is married and has one child and three stepchildren.

Representative Tillie Fowler (*Republican, Fourth District, Florida*) was first elected to the House of Representatives in 1992. She is a member of the National Security Committee and the Transportation and Infrastructure Committee.

She began her career of public service on the staff of former Representative Robert Stephens, Jr. (D-GA), and then served as general counsel in the White House Office of Consumer Affairs during the Nixon Administration. Before her election to Congress, she was a member of the Jacksonville City Council for seven years and was the council president for two years.

Congresswoman Fowler was born in 1942 in Milledgeville, Georgia. She holds both a B.A. and a law degree from Emory University. She is married and has two daughters.

Representative Elizabeth Furse (*Democrat, First District, Oregon*) was first elected in 1992 to the House, where she is a member of the Commerce Committee. Her legislative concerns include domestic violence prevention, budget priorities, reproductive choice, and sustainable development.

Representative Furse was born in Nairobi, Kenya, in 1936 and was raised in South Africa. She came to the United States as a young woman and became a U.S. citizen in 1972. She received her B.A. from Evergreen State College in Olympia, Washington. She is married and has two children.

Representative Kay Granger (*Republican, Twelfth District, Texas*) was elected to Congress in 1996. She is the first Republican woman from Texas to serve in the U.S. House of Representatives, where she is a member of the Budget Committee, the Oversight Committee, and the Transportation and Infrastructure Committee.

Her legislative priorities include balancing the federal budget, strengthening defense, and lifting government regulation on small business.

Before her election to Congress, Representative Granger served three terms as Mayor of Fort Worth; before that, she served two years on the City Council and seven years on the Zoning Commission. She received her B.S. and an Honorary Doctorate of Humane Letters from Texas Wesleyan University. She is the mother of three grown children and lives in Fort Worth.

Representative Jane Harman (*Democrat, Thirty-sixth District, California*), first elected to the House in 1992, sits on the Committee on National Security and the Select Intelligence Committee.

Representative Harman worked in Washington during the 1970s as legislative director to then-Senator John Tunney (D-CA) and as chief counsel and staff director of the Senate Judiciary Subcommittee on Constitutional Rights. She also served in the Carter Administration as deputy secretary to the Cabinet and as special counsel to the Department of Defense.

Born in New York City in 1945, Congresswoman Harman is a graduate of Smith College and Harvard University Law School. She is married and has four children.

Representative Darlene Hooley (*Democrat, Fifth District, Oregon*) was elected to the House in 1996. She is a member of the Banking and Financial Services Committee and the Science Committee.

A former teacher, Congresswoman Hooley became a neighborhood activist in the mid-1970s, advocating for safe playgrounds. She was elected in 1976 to the West Linn City Council, where she served for four years. She was then elected to the state legislature, where she authored landmark welfare reform legislation and pay equity legislation. In 1987, Representative Hooley was appointed to fill a vacancy on the Clackamas County Board of Commissioners. She was subsequently elected and several times reelected to the board.

Representative Hooley, who was born in 1939, received her B.S. from Oregon State University. She lives in West Linn.

Senator Kay Bailey Hutchison (*Republican, Texas*) was first elected to the Senate in June 1993 to fill the unexpired term of Lloyd Benson (D-TX), who had been appointed U.S. Secretary of the Treasury. In November 1994 she was reelected.

Senator Hutchison is a member of the Appropriations Committee as well as the Commerce, Science, and Transportation Committee, and the Rules and Administration Committee. She also serves as Deputy Majority Whip.

Before coming to the Senate, Senator Hutchison was Texas state treasurer—the first Republican woman to be elected to a statewide office in Texas. She served in the Texas House of Representatives and as vice chair of the National Transportation Safety Board in the Ford Administration.

Raised in La Marque, Texas, Senator Hutchison is a graduate of the University of Texas at Austin and the University of Texas School of Law. She is married.

Representative Eddie Bernice Johnson (*Democrat, Thirtieth District, Texas*) was first elected to the House in 1992. She sits on the Science Committee and the Transportation and Infrastructure Committee.

Before her election to Congress, Representative Johnson was a business entrepreneur, professional nurse, and health care administrator. When she was elected to the Texas House of Representatives, she became the first African American woman since 1935 to be elected to public office in Texas. She left the legislature in 1977 to become the regional director of the Department of Health, Education, and Welfare during the Carter Administration. In 1986 she was elected to a seat in the Texas Senate, which she held until her election to Congress.

Representative Johnson is a graduate of Texas Christian University and earned an M.P.A. from Southern Methodist University. She was born in 1935 in Waco, Texas, and is the mother of one child.

Representative Nancy Johnson (*Republican, Sixth District, Connecticut*) was first elected to Congress in 1982. In 1988, she became the first Republican woman to be named to the Ways and Means Committee, and she chairs its Subcommittee on Oversight—the first woman to chair a Ways and Means subcommittee. Currently cochair of the Congressional Caucus for Women's Issues, Congresswoman Johnson has spent much of her congressional career advocating for women in the areas of health care, child care, welfare reform, and reproductive rights.

Representative Johnson was born in Chicago, Illinois, in 1935. She received her B.A. from Radcliffe College and served as a civic leader and adjunct professor before embarking on her political career. Before her election to Congress, she served three terms in the Connecticut Senate. She is married and has three children.

Representative Marcy Kaptur (*Democrat, Ninth District, Ohio*) was first elected to Congress in 1982. She sits on the Appropriations Committee.

In the House, Congresswoman Kaptur has long advocated for U.S. workers and small businesses, particularly those with female entrepreneurs, as well as for tighter restrictions on trade and tougher lobbying restrictions on top-level federal officials.

Born in 1946 in Toledo, Ohio, Representative Kaptur earned her B.A. from the University of Wisconsin and her M.A. in urban planning from the University of Michigan. She practiced as an urban planner for 15 years before seeking office and was a doctoral candidate at the Massachusetts Institute of Technology in urban studies. She also served as an urban adviser during the Carter Administration and as the first deputy director of the National Cooperative Consumer Bank.

Representative Sue Kelly (*Republican, Nineteenth District, New York*) was first elected to the House in 1994. She is a member of the Banking and Financial Services Committee, the Small Business Committee, and the Transportation and Infrastructure Committee. Her legislative priorities include greater opportunities for small business owners, an end to the capital gains tax, and a balanced budget.

Before coming to Congress, Representative Kelly worked as an educator, small-business owner, patient advocate, rape crisis counselor, and community leader. She is a graduate of Denison University and has a master's degree in health advocacy from Sarah Lawrence College.

Congresswoman Kelly was born in 1936 in Lima, Ohio. She is married and has four children and one grandchild.

Representative Barbara Kennelly (*Democrat, First District, Connecticut*) has served in Congress since 1982. She is one of three women on the Ways and Means Committee and is the ranking minority member of its Social Security Subcommittee. She is also the vice chair of the Democratic Caucus.

Congresswoman Kennelly has championed welfare reform, tax policies that help families, and long-term care insurance. She served as a member of the U.S. Commission on Interstate Child Support and has long advocated improved child support enforcement.

Before her election to Congress, she served as Connecticut's Secretary of State and as a member of the Hartford Court of Common Council.

Born in 1936 and raised in Hartford, Connecticut, Representative Kennelly earned her B.A. from Trinity College in Washington, D.C., and her M.A. from Trinity College in Hartford. Now a widow, she has four children.

Representative Carolyn Cheeks Kilpatrick (*Democrat, Fifteenth District, Michigan*) was elected to the House in 1996. She sits on the Banking and Financial Services Committee, the House Oversight Committee, and the Joint Library Committee.

She came to Congress after serving 18 years in the Michigan legislature. Earlier, she taught in the Detroit public schools.

Representative Kilpatrick spent her undergraduate years at Ferris State University and Western Michigan University, and earned her M.S. in education administration from the University of Michigan. A native of Detroit, she has a son and a daughter.

Senator Mary L. Landrieu (*Democrat, Louisiana*) was elected in 1996 to the Senate, where she sits on the Committee on Agriculture, Nutrition, and Forestry, the Committee on Energy and Natural Resources, and the Committee on Small Business.

In 1979, Senator Landrieu became the youngest woman ever to serve in the Louisiana legislature, where she earned a reputation as an advocate for women and children. After two terms in the Louisiana House, she was elected Louisiana treasurer.

Senator Landrieu, who was born in 1955, is a graduate of Louisiana State University in Baton Rouge. She is married and has one child.

Representative Sheila Jackson Lee (*Democrat, Eighteenth District, Texas*), first elected to the House in 1994, sits on the Judiciary Committee and the Science Committee.

Before coming to Congress, Representative Jackson Lee was a member of the Houston City Council. Earlier she served as an associate municipal court judge. She is a graduate of Yale University and holds a J.D. from the University of Virginia Law School. She is married and has two children.

Representative Zoe Lofgren (*Democrat, Sixteenth District, California*) was elected to the House in 1994. Congresswoman Lofgren is a member of the Judiciary Committee and the Science Committee. Before her election to Congress, she served on the Santa Clara County Board of Supervisors.

Representative Lofgren is a graduate of Stanford University and received her law degree from the University of Santa Clara Law School. Following her graduation from college, she worked on the Watergate hearings with then-Congressman Don Edwards (D-CA), who preceded her as Representative from the Sixteenth District.

Congresswoman Lofgren is married and has two children.

Representative Nita Lowey (*Democrat, Eighteenth District, New York*) was first elected to the House in 1988. She is a member of the Appropriations Committee and serves on two of its subcommittees: the Subcommittee on Foreign Operations, Export Financing, and Related Programs and the Subcommittee on Labor, Health and Human Services, and Education.

Congresswoman Lowey is an advocate of biomedical and breast cancer research, women's preventive health programs, aid to Israel, worker retraining initiatives, tough anticrime legislation, and educational reform.

Born in 1937 in the Bronx, New York, Representative Lowey graduated from Mount Holyoke College. She is married and the mother of three grown children.

Representative Carolyn Maloney (*Democrat, Fourteenth District, New York*) was first elected to Congress in 1992. She is a member of the Banking and Financial Services Committee and the Committee on Government Reform and Oversight, as well as the Joint Economic Committee.

Representative Maloney has a strong interest in women's and children's issues. During her 10 years on the New York City Council before coming to Congress, she offered a comprehensive legislative package to increase the availability and affordability of child care services. In Congress, she has advocated on behalf of children in the child welfare system.

Born in Greensboro, North Carolina, in 1948, Congresswoman Maloney is a graduate of Greensboro College. She is married and has two daughters.

Representative Carolyn McCarthy (*Democrat, Fourth District, New York*) was elected to the House in 1996. She sits on the Committee on Education and the Workforce and the Small Business Committee. Her legislative priorities include gun control, health care reform, environmental protection, and targeted tax cuts for working families.

Representative McCarthy, who was born in 1944, is a graduate of Glen Cove Nursing School. She is a lifelong resident of Mineola, who became politically active after her husband was killed and her son was gravely injured by an assault weapon on a Long Island Railroad commuter train.

Representative Karen McCarthy (*Democrat, Fifth District, Missouri*) was elected to Congress in November 1994. She serves on the Commerce Committee and its subcommittees on Energy and Power and on Telecommunications, Trade, and Consumer Protection.

Before her election to Congress, Congresswoman McCarthy was in the Missouri legislature, where she chaired the Ways and Means Committee. She received her B.A. from Kansas University, her M.A. in English from the University of Missouri at Kansas City, and her M.B.A. from the University of Kansas.

Representative Cynthia McKinney (*Democrat, Fourth District, Georgia*), first elected to the House in 1992, is the first African American woman to be elected to Congress from Georgia. She sits on the Banking and Financial Services Committee and the International Relations Committee. Her legislative priorities in the 105th Congress include women and children's issues, ending corporate welfare, and arms control.

Born in 1955 in Atlanta, Congresswoman McKinney is a graduate of the University of Southern California. She is presently a doctoral candidate in international relations at Tufts University. Before her election to Congress, she was a professor of political science at Agnes Scott College in Decatur, Georgia.

Representative Carrie Meek (*Democrat, Seventeenth District, Florida*), who was first elected to the House in 1992, is the first African American elected to Congress from Florida since reconstruction. She is a member of the Appropriations Committee.

Congresswoman Meek came to Congress following a dozen years of service in the Florida legislature, where she served in both chambers. During her last term in the Florida State Senate, she chaired the Appropriations Subcommittee on Education.

In Congress, Representative Meek has championed legislation to provide retirement security to domestic workers, such as household workers, gardeners, and nannies. She also has worked to improve low-income individuals' access to such government services as housing and education.

Congresswoman Meek was born in 1926 in Tallahassee, Florida. She is a graduate of Florida A&M University and holds an M.A. from the University of Michigan. She has three children.

Senator Barbara Mikulski (*Democrat, Maryland*) was first elected to the Senate in 1986. She is the first Democratic woman elected to a Senate seat that had not previously been held by the woman's husband. A first-term member of the House when she won her Senate seat, she is also the first Democratic woman to have served in both the House and the Senate.

Senator Mikulski is the ranking minority member of two subcommittees: the Subcommittee on Veterans' Affairs, Housing and Urban Development, and Independent Agencies of the Appropriations Committee and the Subcommittee on Aging of the Labor and Human Resources Committee. A leader on women's health issues, Senator Mikulski won enactment of legislation requiring licensing of clinical laboratories to ensure proper analysis of Pap smears and access to mammograms for low-income women.

Born in Baltimore in 1936, Senator Mikulski earned her B.A. from Mount Saint Agnes College in Baltimore and her M.S.W. from the University of Maryland. She began her career in public service as a social worker in Baltimore and entered politics with her election to the Baltimore City Council.

Representative Juanita Millender-McDonald (*Democrat, Thirty-seventh District, California*) began her service in Congress in 1996, after winning a special election to fill an open seat, and was reelected in November 1996. She is a member of the Small Business Committee and the Transportation and Infrastructure Committee.

Before her election to the House, Congresswoman Millender-McDonald served in the California legislature, where she made education reform one of her top priorities. Earlier, she was a member of the Carson City Council. She began her professional career as a teacher.

Born in Birmingham, Alabama, Representative Millender-McDonald resides in Carson. She is married and has five adult children and one grandchild.

Representative Patsy Mink (*Democrat, Second District, Hawaii*) was first elected to Congress in 1964 and served until 1977. She returned to the House in 1990, when she was elected to complete the unexpired term of Daniel Akaka (D-HI), who had been appointed to the Senate.

Representative Mink sits on the Budget Committee and the Committee on Education and the Workforce. She has been a leader on welfare issues, sponsoring legislation to provide education and other supportive services to help welfare recipients become self-sufficient. An advocate for women's health issues, she introduced the Ovarian Cancer Research Act.

Congresswoman Mink was born in 1927 in Paia, Hawaii. After earning a B.A. from the University of Hawaii and a J.D. from the University of Chicago, she served in Hawaii's House and later in its Senate. While she was out of Congress after 1977, she served as Assistant Secretary of State for Oceans and International, Environmental, and Scientific Affairs in the Carter Administration. She is married and has one daughter.

Representative Constance Morella (*Republican, Eighth District, Maryland*) was first elected to the House in 1986. She sits on the Science Committee and chairs its Subcommittee on Technology. She is also a member of the Government Reform and Oversight Committee.

Congresswoman Morella has been a leader on women's issues, championing legislation to increase research on and prevention of AIDS in women. She also has been on the forefront of the fight against domestic violence, winning enactment of several bills addressing this issue. In the 104th Congress she served as cochair of the Congressional Caucus for Women's Issues.

Born in Somerville, Massachusetts, in 1931, Representative Morella received her A.B. from Boston University and her M.A. from the American University in Washington, D.C. She served for eight years in the Maryland General Assembly. Before entering politics, she was a professor of English at Montgomery College. She is married and has raised nine children.

Senator Carol Moseley-Braun (*Democrat, Illinois*), who was elected to the Senate in 1992, is the first African American woman to serve in the Senate. She sits on the Banking, Housing, and Urban Affairs Committee and is the ranking minority member of its Subcommittee on International Finance. She is also a member of the Finance Committee and of the Aging Committee.

Senator Moseley-Braun is a graduate of the University of Illinois in Chicago and earned her law degree from the University of Chicago. Following law school, she worked as a prosecutor in the U.S. Attorney's office. In 1978, she was elected to the Illinois legislature, where she earned a reputation as a leader in the field of education. In 1987, she was elected Cook County recorder of deeds. Senator Moseley-Braun, who was born in 1947 in Chicago, is the mother of one child.

Senator Patty Murray (*Democrat, Washington*) was elected in 1992 to the Senate, where she sits on the Labor and Human Resources Committee, the Appropriations Committee, and the Budget Committee. She is also a member of the Veterans' Affairs Committee and the Ethics Committee.

Before coming to Congress, Senator Murray served in the Washington State Senate, where she championed legislation to provide family leave to parents of terminally ill children. She is a strong advocate for families and children, supporting family and medical leave, abortion rights, and tax relief for the middle class.

Senator Murray, who was born in 1950, is a native of Seattle. She earned her B.A. from Washington State University. She is married and has two children.

Representative Sue Myrick (*Republican, Ninth District, North Carolina*) was first elected to the House in 1994. A member of the Rules Committee, she has championed small-business issues. She also serves as Sophomore Class Liaison to the Republican leadership in the House.

Before coming to Congress, Congresswoman Myrick served as Mayor of Charlotte, North Carolina. Born in 1941 in Tifflin, Ohio, she is a graduate of Heidelberg College. She is married and has five children and seven grandchildren.

Representative Anne Meagher Northup (*Republican, Third District, Kentucky*) was first elected to the House in 1996. She is a member of the Appropriations Committee.

Before her election to Congress, Representative Northrup served for nine years in the Kentucky House of Representatives, where she supported increased fiscal responsibility, free enterprise, and small-business concerns.

Born in 1948, Congresswoman Northup earned her B.A. in economics and business from St. Mary's College. She is married and is the mother of six children.

Delegate Eleanor Holmes Norton (*Democrat, At Large, District of Columbia*), who was first elected to Congress in 1990, is the nonvoting delegate from the District of Columbia. The first woman elected to represent the District in the House, Delegate Norton serves on the Government Reform and Oversight Committee where she is the ranking minority member of the District of Columbia Subcommittee. She is also a member of the Transportation and Infrastructure Committee. Delegate Norton is a champion of civil rights issues and of the economic and political independence of the District of Columbia.

Born in the District of Columbia in 1937, Delegate Norton is a graduate of Antioch College. She holds both an M.A. and an L.L.B. from Yale University. A professor of law at Georgetown University before her election to Congress, she also served as chair of the Equal Employment Opportunity Commission during the Carter Administration.

Representative Nancy Pelosi (*Democrat, Eighth District, California*) was first elected to Congress in 1987. She sits on the House Appropriations Committee, where she is the ranking minority member of the Appropriations Subcommittee on Foreign Operations and Export Financing. She also serves on the Select Committee on Intelligence.

Congresswoman Pelosi has focused much of her attention on funding for AIDS research and prevention and on increasing prenatal care for low-income families. She is also the author of legislation to preserve the supply of housing for low-income families and to establish programs to alleviate homelessness among individuals with AIDS.

Born in 1940 in Baltimore, Maryland, Representative Pelosi earned her B.A. from Trinity College in Washington, D.C. She later served as state chair of the California Democratic Party. She and her husband have five children.

Representative Deborah Pryce (*Republican, Fifteenth District, Ohio*), was first elected in 1992 to the House, where she sits on the Rules Committee. She has a strong interest in family and child welfare issues.

Before her election to Congress, Representative Pryce served as a judge on the Franklin County Municipal Court. She is a graduate of Ohio State University and has a law degree from Capital University in Columbus, Ohio. Born in 1952 in Warren, Ohio, she is married and has two children.

Representative Lynn Rivers (*Democrat, Thirteenth District, Michigan*) was elected to the House in 1994. She sits on the Budget Committee and the Science Committee.

Congresswoman Rivers began her public service as a member of the Ann Arbor school board, of which she was president for three years. Before her election to Congress, she served one term in the Michigan legislature.

Representative Rivers, who was born in 1956 in Au Gres, Michigan, has a B.A. from the University of Michigan and a J.D. from Wayne State University Law School. She and her husband live in Ann Arbor with their two daughters.

Representative Ileana Ros-Lehtinen (*Republican, Eighteenth District, Florida*), who was first elected to the House in a special election in 1989, is the first Hispanic woman to be elected to Congress. She is a member of the Government Reform and Oversight Committee and the Committee on International Relations.

Congresswoman Ros-Lehtinen, who was born in Havana, Cuba, in 1952, obtained her A.A. from Miami-Dade Community College and her B.A. and M.S. degrees from Florida International University. She is married and has two daughters.

Representative Marge Roukema (*Republican, Fifth District, New Jersey*) was first elected to the House in 1980. She sits on the Banking and Financial Services Committee, where she chairs the Subcommittee on Financial Institutions and Consumer Credit, and is also a member of the Committee on Education and the Workforce. She has been active on a variety of women's issues, including family and medical leave, welfare reform, and child support enforcement.

Congresswoman Roukema was born in 1929 in Newark, New Jersey. She holds a B.A. from Montclair State College in New Jersey. Before coming to Congress, she was a secondary school teacher. She is married and has two children.

Representative Lucille Roybal-Allard (*Democrat, Thirty-third District, California*), first elected to the House in 1992, is the first Mexican American woman to be elected to Congress. She filled the seat vacated by the retirement of her father, Edward Roybal (D-CA). She is a member of the House Banking and Financial Services Committee and the Budget Committee.

Congresswoman Roybal-Allard has played a major role in highlighting health issues relating to Latinas, enacting the Violence Against Women Act, and protecting small-business programs for women and minorities. Before her election to Congress, she served in the California Assembly, where she was active on women's issues, authoring and winning passage of legislation requiring the courts to take an individual's history of domestic violence into consideration during child custody hearings.

Representative Roybal-Allard, who was born in Los Angeles in 1941, received her B.A. from California State University at Los Angeles. She is married and has two children.

Representative Loretta Sanchez (*Democrat, Forty-sixth District, California*) was elected to the House in 1996. She is a member of the Committee on Education and the Workforce and the Committee on National Security.

Representative Sanchez earned a bachelor's degree in economics from Chapman University and holds an M.B.A. in finance from American University. Before coming to Congress, she was a businesswoman in Santa Ana, specializing in assisting public agencies with financial matters. Congresswoman Sanchez, who was born in 1960, lives in Anaheim.

Representative Louise Slaughter (*Democrat, Twenty-eighth District, New York*) was first elected to the House in 1986. She is a member of the Rules Committee.

Representative Slaughter has fought for programs to provide educational opportunities to homeless children, to broaden the safeguards for victims of domestic violence, to expand the funds available for women's health research, and to protect against genetic discrimination in health insurance.

Born in Harlan County, Kentucky, in 1929, Congresswoman Slaughter received both a B.S. and an M.S. from the University of Kentucky. She entered the Monroe County legislature in New York in 1975 and went on to serve in the New York Assembly before she ran successfully for Congress. She is married and the mother of three grown children.

Representative Linda Smith (*Republican, Third District, Washington*) was first elected to the House in 1994. She is the first person in her state's history to qualify for the general election ballot as a write-in candidate.

Congresswoman Smith sits on the Committee on Resources and the Committee on Small Business and serves as vice chair of the latter's Subcommittee on Tax, Finance, and Exports.

Before coming to Congress, Representative Smith served in both houses of the Washington legislature. She was born in La Junta, Colorado, in 1950 and operated a tax consulting business for 14 years. Congresswoman Smith is married and has two grown children and six grandchildren.

Senator Olympia J. Snowe (*Republican, Maine*) was elected to the Senate in 1994, after eight terms in the House of Representatives.

Senator Snowe sits on the Budget Committee, the Armed Services Committee, the Commerce, Science, and Transportation Committee, and the Small Business Committee.

While in the House, Senator Snowe served for many years as cochair of the Congressional Caucus for Women's Issues. She focused her energies on a successful effort to establish the Office of Research on Women's Health at the National Institutes of Health, thus ensuring that women's health problems are included in medical research. She also has been a leader on international family planning issues.

Senator Snowe, who was born in Augusta, Maine, in 1947, received her B.A. from the University of Maine. She began her political career in 1973 when she was elected to the Maine legislature to fill the seat vacated by her late husband. She has since remarried.

Representative Debbie Stabenow (*Democrat, Eighth District, Michigan*) was elected to the House in 1996. She sits on the Agriculture Committee and the Science Committee.

Representative Stabenow served in both houses of the Michigan legislature before coming to Congress. Born in Michigan in 1950, she was raised in Clare, Michigan, and received her bachelor's and master's degrees from Michigan State University. She lives in Lansing and has two children.

Representative Ellen O. Tauscher (*Democrat, Tenth District, California*) was elected to the House in 1996. She sits on the Science Committee and the Transportation and Infrastructure Committee. Before running for Congress, she cochaired Senator Dianne Feinstein's successful Senate campaigns in 1992 and 1994.

Congresswoman Tauscher, who was born in East Newark, New Jersey, in 1951, received her B.S. in Early Childhood Education from Seton Hall University. She is married and has one daughter.

Representative Karen Thurman (*Democrat, Fifth District, Florida*) was first elected to the House in 1992. She sits on the Ways and Means Committee.

Congresswoman Thurman is a supporter of reproductive rights and is working to broaden women's issues to areas beyond health care and jobs. Before her election to Congress, Representative Thurman served on the Dunnellon, Florida, City Council and was the city's Mayor from 1979 to 1981. She also served for 10 years in the Florida Senate, where she chaired the Agriculture Committee. Born in Rapid City, South Dakota, in 1951, Representative Thurman is a graduate of the University of Florida. She is married and has two children.

Representative Nydia Velázquez (*Democrat, Twelfth District, New York*), who was first elected to Congress in 1992, is the first Puerto Rican woman elected to the House of Representatives. Congresswoman Velázquez sits on the Banking and Financial Services Committee and the Committee on Small Business.

Before coming to Congress, Representative Velázquez worked as a liaison between the Puerto Rican government and the Puerto Rican community in New York, where she organized efforts to increase AIDS education and to register voters. She also was the first Hispanic woman to be elected to the New York City Council, where she served from 1984 to 1986. As a member of Congress, she is continuing her work on women's and poverty issues.

Born in Puerto Rico in 1953, Representative Velázquez received her B.A. from the University of Puerto Rico and her M.S. in political science from New York University.

Representative Maxine Waters (*Democrat, Thirty-fifth District, California*) was first elected to the House in 1990. She sits on the Judiciary Committee and the Banking and Financial Services Committee, where she serves as the ranking minority member of the Subcommittee on General Oversight and Investigations. Congresswoman Waters has been a leader on the issue of AIDS in the African American community. She also has been a vocal advocate of increased investment in programs and services in the nation's urban areas.

Before coming to Congress, Representative Waters served for 15 years in the California Assembly, where she was the first woman in the state's history to be elected chair of the Democratic Caucus. She was born in St. Louis, Missouri, in 1938 and holds a B.A. from California State University at Los Angeles. She is married and has two children.

Representative Lynn Woolsey (*Democrat, Sixth District, California*), first elected to the House in 1992, is the first former welfare mother ever elected to Congress.

Congresswoman Woolsey is a member of the Committee on Education and the Workforce and of the Budget Committee. She has been a leader on welfare reform and children's issues.

Before her election to Congress, Representative Woolsey was a member of the Petaluma, California, City Council, and she was also the city's Vice Mayor. In these positions, she was successful in her efforts to expand low- and moderate-income housing, and led the fight to build the first emergency family shelter for homeless families in Sonoma County.

Representative Woolsey, who was born in Seattle, Washington, in 1937, has four children. She is a graduate of the University of San Francisco.

Congressional Caucus for Women's Issues[1]

Nancy L. Johnson (R-CT), cochair
Eleanor Holmes Norton (Del-D-DC), cochair
Sue W. Kelly (R-NY), vice chair
Carolyn B. Maloney (D-NY), vice chair
Corrine Brown (D-FL)
Julia Carson (D-IN)
Helen Chenoweth (R-ID)
Donna Christian-Green (Del-D-VI)
Eva Clayton (D-NC)
Barbara Cubin (R-WY)
Pat Danner (D-MO)
Diana DeGette (D-CO)
Rosa DeLauro (D-CT)
Jennifer Dunn (R-WA)
Anna G. Eshoo (D-CA)
Tillie Fowler (R-FL)
Elizabeth Furse (D-OR)
Kay Granger (R-TX)
Jane Harman (D-CA)

Darlene Hooley (D-OR)
Eddie Bernice Johnson (D-TX)
Marcy Kaptur (D-OH)
Barbara B. Kennelly (D-CT)
Carolyn Cheeks Kilpatrick (D-MI)
Sheila Jackson Lee (D-TX)
Zoe Lofgren (D-CA)
Nita M. Lowey (D-NY)
Carolyn McCarthy (D-NY)
Karen McCarthy (D-MO)
Cynthia A. McKinney (D-GA)
Carrie P. Meek (D-FL)
Juanita Millender-McDonald (D-CA)
Patsy T. Mink (D-HI)
Constance A. Morella (R-MD)
Sue Myrick (R-NC)
Nancy Pelosi (D-CA)
Deborah Pryce (R-OH)
Lynn Rivers (D-MI)
Ileana Ros-Lehtinen (R-FL)
Marge Roukema (R-NJ)

[1]As of September 8, 1997.

Lucille Roybal-Allard (D-CA)
Loretta Sanchez (D-CA)
Louise M. Slaughter (D-NY)
Linda Smith (R-WA)
Deborah Ann Stabenow (D-MI)

Ellen Tauscher (D-CA)
Karen L. Thurman (D-FL)
Nydia M. Velazquez (D-NY)
Maxine Waters (D-CA)
Lynn Woolsey (D-CA)

REFERENCES

THE AMERICAN WOMAN 1999–2000: A CENTURY OF CHANGE—
WHAT'S NEXT?

Chapter One   American Women in a New Millenium

Abbott, Sidney, and Barbara Love. *Sappho Was a Right-on Woman: A Liberated View of Lesbianism.* New York: Stein and Day, 1972.

Aburdene, Patricia, and John Naisbitt. *Megatrends for Women.* New York: Villard Books, 1992.

Anzaldua, Gloria. *Borderlands: La Fontera.* San Francisco: Spinsters/Aunt Lute, 1987.

"A PC Bible." *The Wall Street Journal,* September 5, 1995.

Auletta, Ken. *The Underclass.* New York: Random House, 1982.

"Avoiding Sexism." *The Christian Century* 104 (April 22, 1987): 376.

Bergquist, Laura. "New Look at the American Woman." *Look,* October 16, 1956, 35–54.

Berry, Mary. *Why ERA Failed: Politics, Women's Rights, and the Amending Process of the Constitution.* Bloomington: Indiana University Press, 1986.

Bolotin, Susan. "Voices from the Post-Feminist Generation." *The New York Times Magazine,* October 17, 1982.

Booth, Heather. Interview with the author. Chicago, July 15, 1981.

Broadway, Bill. "Re-imagining Foments Uproar Among Presbyterians." *The Washington Post,* June 4, 1994.

Bromley, Dorothy Dunbar. "Feminist New Style." *Harper's,* October 1927, 552–53.

Brownmiller, Susan. *Against Our Will: Men, Women and Rape.* New York: Simon & Schuster, 1975.

Brownmiller, Susan. *Femininity.* New York: Fawcett Columbine, 1985.

Bunch, Charlotte. *Passionate Politics: Feminist Theory in Action. Essays, 1968–1986.* New York: St. Martin's Press, 1987.

Burnham, Walter Dean. "The Eclipse of the Democratic Party." *Society* 21 (July–August 1982): 5–11.

Cahn, Susan. *Coming on Strong.* New York: Free Press, 1994.

Caminiti, Susan. "What Ails Retailing: Merchants Have Lost Touch with Older Customers." *Fortune,* January 30, 1989, 61, 64.

Card, Emily. *Staying Solvent: A Comprehensive Guide to Equal Credit for Women.* New York: Holt, Rinehart, 1985.

Cassedy, Ellen. Interview with the author. Bryn Mawr, Pennsylvania, July 11, 1981.

Center for the American Woman and Politics (CAWP). National Information Bank on Women in Public Office, Eagleton Institute of Politics, Rutgers University, 1997.

Chamberlain, Miriam K. *Women in Academe: Progress and Prospects.* New York: Russell Sage Foundation, 1988.

Chapman, Jane Roberts. "Policy Centers: An Essential Resource." In *Women in Washington: Advocates for Public Policy,* edited by Irene Tinker. Beverly Hills, CA: Sage Publications, 1983.

Chira, Susan. "Standing Out in the Crowd." *The New York Times,* August 2, 1993.

Collins, Bud. "Billie Jean King Evens the Score." *Ms.,* July 1973, 37–43.

Danziger, Sheldon, and Peter Gottschalk. *America Unequal.* New York: Russell Sage Foundation, 1995.

Darcy, Robert, Susan Welch, and Janet Clark. *Women, Elections, and Representation.* Second edition. Lincoln: University of Nebraska Press, 1994.

Davis, Flora. *Moving the Mountain: The Women's Movement in America Since 1960.* New York: Simon and Schuster, 1991.

Defense Manpower Data Center. *Distribution of Active Duty Forces by Service, Rank, Sex, and Ethnic Group.* Washington, DC, unpublished data, September 30, 1989.

———. *Distribution of Active Duty Forces by Service, Rank, Sex, and Ethnic Group.* Washington, DC, unpublished data, September 30, 1990a.

———. *Distribution of Active Duty Forces by Service, Rank, Sex, and Ethnic Group.* Washington, DC, unpublished data, April 30, 1990b.

"Desexing the Job Market." *The New York Times,* August 21, 1965.

Diamond, Edwin. "Special Science Report: Young Wives." *Newsweek* 55, March 7, 1960, 57–60.

Echols, Alice. *Daring to Be Bad: Radical Feminism in America.* Minneapolis: University of Minnesota Press, 1989.

Eisler, Riane Tennenhaus. *The Chalice and the Blade: Our History, Our Future.* Cambridge, MA: Harper & Row, 1987.

Evans, Sara. *Personal Politics: The Roots of Women's Liberation in the Civil Rights Movement and the New Left.* New York: Knopf, 1979.

Evans, Sara M., and Barbara J. Nelson. *Wage Justice: Comparable Worth and the Paradox of Technocratic Reform.* Chicago: University of Chicago Press, 1989.

"Events That Matter." *The Christian Century* 87 (December 2, 1970): 1443.

Facts on Reproductive Rights: A Resource Manual. NOW Legal Defense and Education Fund, Fact Sheet No. 11, 1989.

Faludi, Susan. *Backlash: The Undeclared War Against American Women.* New York: Crown Publishers, 1991.

Farrell, Amy Erdman. *Feminism in the Mass Media: Ms. Magazine, 1972–1989.* Unpublished Ph.D. dissertation. University of Minnesota, 1991.

Ferree, Myra Marx, and Beth B. Hess. *Controversy and Coalition: The New Feminist Movement.* Boston: Twayne, 1985.

Findlen, Barbara. *Listen Up. Voices from The Next Feminist Generation.* Seattle, WA: Seal Press, 1995.

Fox, Thomas C. "Rome's Lengthening Shadow." *The New York Times,* November 14, 1994.

Fraser, Arvonne S. "Insiders and Outsiders: Women in the Political Arena." In *Women in Washington: Advocates for Public Policy,* edited by Irene Tinker. Beverly Hills, CA: Sage Publications, 1983.

Freeman, Jo. *The Politics of Women's Liberation: A Case Study of an Emerging Social Movement and Its Relation to the Policy Process.* New York: McKay, 1975.

Friedan, Betty. *The Feminine Mystique.* New York: Norton, 1963.

———. *It Changed My Life: Writings on the Women's Movement.* New York: Dell, 1991.

Gelb, Joyce, and Marian Lief Palley. *Women and Public Policies.* Princeton, NJ: Princeton University Press, 1987.

Gertzog, Irwin N. *Congressional Women: Their Recruitment, Treatment, and Behavior.* New York: Praeger, 1984.

Ginzburg, Faye. *Contested Lives: The Abortion Debate in an American Community.* Berkeley: University of California Press, 1989.

Goodin, Joan M. "Working Women: The Pros and Cons of Unions." In *Women in Washington: Advocates for Public Policy,* edited by Irene Tinker. Beverly Hills, CA: Sage Publications, 1983.

Griffin, Susan. "Rape: The All-American Crime." *Ramparts,* 1971, 26–35.

Haener, Dorothy. Interview with the author. Detroit, January 21, 1983.

Hairston, Julie. "Killing Kittens, Bombing Clinics." *Southern Exposure* 18, No. 2 (1990): 14–18.

Harrison, Cynthia E. "New Frontier for Women: The Public Policy of the Kennedy Administration." *Journal of American History* 67 (December 1980): 630–35.

———. *Women's Movement Media: A Source Guide.* New York: Bowker, 1975.

Hartmann, Susan M. "Allies of the Women's Movement: Origins and Strategies of Feminist Activists in Male Dominated Organizations in the 1970s: The Case of the International Union of Electrical Workers." Paper presented at the 1993 Berkshire Conference on the History of Women, Vassar College, Poughkeepsie, NY, June 1993.

Helgeson, Sally. "The Pyramid and the Web." *The New York Times,* May 27, 1990.

Hole, Judith, and Susan Levine. *Rebirth of Feminism.* New York: Quadrangle Books, 1971.

hooks, bell. *Ain't I a Woman: Black Women and Feminism.* Boston: South End Press, 1981.

―――. *Feminist Theory: From Margin to Center.* Boston: South End Press, 1984.

Hull, Gloria, Patricia Bell Scott, and Barbara Smith. *All the Women are White, All the Blacks Are Men, But Some of Us Are Brave: Black Women's Studies.* Old Westbury, NY: Feminist Press, 1981.

Huyck, Heather Ann. "To Celebrate a Whole Priesthood: The History of Women's Ordination in the Episcopal Church." Unpublished Ph.D. dissertation. University of Minnesota, 1981.

Hyer, Marjorie. "Presbyterian Women Asked to Ponder: What Time Is It?" *The Christian Century* 87 (September 2, 1970): 1047–48.

"In Worship, Methodists Want Tradition." *The Washington Post,* June 16, 1990.

Jeffry, Mildred. Interview with the author. Detroit, December 1982.

Kamen, Paula. *Feminist Fatale: Voices from the Twentysomething Generation Explore the Future of the Women's Movement.* New York: Donald I. Fine, 1991.

Kaplan, Laura. *The Story of Jane: The Legendary Feminist Underground Abortion Service.* New York: Pantheon, 1995.

Keller, Catherine. "Inventing the Goddess: A Study in Ecclesiastical Backlash." *The Christian Century* (April 6, 1994).

King, Billie Jean, with Kim Chapin. *Billie Jean.* New York: Harper & Row, 1974.

Klein, Ethel. *Gender Politics: From Consciousness to Mass Politics.* Cambridge, MA: Harvard University Press, 1984.

Krasniewicz, Louise. *Nuclear Summer: The Clash of Communities at the Seneca Women's Peace Encampment.* Ithaca, NY: Cornell University Press, 1992.

Ladky, Anne. Interview with the author. Chicago, April 18, 1983.

Lamar, Jacob V. "The Homeless: Brick by Brick." *Time,* October 24, 1988, 4.

Lawrence, William P. "Clearing the Way for Women in Combat." *The Washington Post,* July 28, 1991.

Levine, Suzanne, and Harriet Lyons with Joanne Edgar, Ellen Sweet, and Mary Thom. *The Decade of Women: A Ms. History of the Seventies in Words and Pictures.* New York: Paragon, 1980.

Limbaugh, Rush. *See, I Told You So.* New York: Pocket Books, 1993.

Madar, Olga. Interview with the author. Detroit, December 10, 1982.

"Man! Memo from a Publisher." *The New York Times Magazine,* October 20, 1974: 38, 104–8.

Mansbridge, Jane. *Why We Lost the ERA.* Chicago: University of Chicago Press, 1986.

Mathews, Donald, and Jane DeHart. *Sex, Gender and the Politics of ERA: A State and the Nation.* New York: Oxford University Press, 1990.

May, Elaine Tyler. *Homeward Bound: American Families in the Cold War Era.* New York: Basic Books, 1988.

Miller, Joyce. Interview with the author. New York City, February 7, 1983.

Milsap, Mary Ann. "Sex Equity in Education." In *Women in Washington: Advocates for Public Policy,* edited by Irene Tinker. Beverly Hills, CA: Sage Publications, 1983.

Molloy, John T. *The Woman's Dress for Success Book.* Chicago: Warners Books, 1977.

Moraga, Cherrie, and Gloria Anzaldua. *This Bridge Called My Back: Writings by Radical Women of Color.* Watertown, MA: Persephone Press, 1981.

"More Hymn Changes." *The Christian Century* 104 (April 15, 1987): 352.

Morgen, Sandra. "It Was the Best of Times, It Was the Worst of Times: Emotional Discourse in the Work Cultures of Feminist Health Clinics." In *Feminist Organizations: Harvest of the New Women's Movement,* edited by Myra Marx Ferree and Patricia Yancey Martin. Philadelphia: Temple University Press, 1995.

"Ms.—form of address meaning whole person, female." *Ms.* Preview issue, Spring 1972, 113.

Nielsen, Georgia Painter. *From Sky Girl to Flight Attendant.* New York: ILR Press, 1982.

North, Sandie. "Reporting the Movement." *Atlantic,* March 1970, 105–6.

O'Reilly, Jane. "The Housewife's Moment of Truth." *Ms.* Preview issue, Spring 1972, 54–59.

Paglia, Camille. "Madonna I: Animality and Artifice." *The New York Times,* December 14, 1990.

Petchesky, Rosalind Pollak. *Abortion and Woman's Choice: The State, Sexuality, and Reproductive Freedom.* Revised edition. Boston: Northeastern University Press, 1990.

Phelps, Timothy M., and Helen Winternitz. *Capitol Games: The Inside Story of Clarence Thomas, Anita Hill, and a Supreme Court Nomination.* New York: Harper Perennial, 1992.

Piercy, Day. Interview with the author. Chicago, July 16 and 19, 1981.

Popkin, Ann Hunter. "Bread and Roses: An Early Moment in the Development of Socialist-Feminism." Unpublished Ph.D. dissertation. Brandeis University, Boston, 1978.

Radicalesbians. "Woman-Identified Woman" (1970). Reprinted in *Out of the Closets: Voices of Gay Liberation,* edited by Karla Jay and Allen Young. New York: New York University Press, 1972, 1992.

Rawalt, Marguerite. "The Equal Rights Amendment." In *Women in Washington: Advocates for Public Policy,* edited by Irene Tinker. Beverly Hills, CA: Sage Publications, Inc., 1983.

"Redstockings Manifesto." *Notes from the Second Year* (1970): 113.

Reuther, Rosemary. *Women Church: Theology and Practice of Feminist Liturgical Communities.* San Francisco: Harper & Row, 1985.

Roberts, Jane Chapman. "Policy Centers: An Essential Resource." In *Women in Washington: Advocates for Public Policy,* edited by Irene Tinker. Beverly Hills, CA: Sage Publications, 1983.

Robinson, Jo Ann Gibson. *The Montgomery Bus Boycott and the Women Who Started It: The Memoir of Jo Ann Gibson Robinson,* edited with a foreword by David G. Garrow. Knoxville: University of Tennessee Press, 1987.

Rosener, Judy B. "Ways Women Lead." *Harvard Business Review* 68 (November–December 1990): 119–25.

Rossi, Alice. *Feminists in Politics: A Panel Analysis of the First National Women's Conference.* New York: Academic Press, 1982.

Rossi, Alice, and Ann Calderwood. *Academic Women on the Move.* New York: Russell Sage Foundation, 1973.

Ruddick, Sara. "Work of One's Own." In *Working It Out: 23 Women Writers, Artists, Scientists, and Scholars Talk About Their Lives and Work,* edited by Sara Ruddick and Pamela Daniels. New York: Pantheon, 1977.

Ruether, Rosemary Radford. *Women-Church: Theology and Practice of Feminist Liturgical Communities.* San Francisco: Harper & Row, 1985.

Rupp, Leila, and Verta Taylor. *Survival in the Doldrums: The American Women's Rights Movement, 1945 to the 1960s.* New York: Oxford University Press, 1987.

Ryan, Barbara. *Feminism and the Women's Movement.* New York: Routledge, 1992.

Salholz, Eloise. "Feminism's Identity Crisis." *Newsweek* 107 (March 31, 1986): 58–59.

Schechter, Susan. *Women and Male Violence: The Visions and Struggles of the Battered Women's Movement.* Boston: South End Press, 1982.

Schlafley, Phyllis. "Open Letter to VMI Alumni." *The Eagle Forum.* Alton, Illinois, June 11, 1996.

Schwartz, Felice N. "Management Women and the New Facts of Life." *Harvard Business Review* 67 (January–February 1989): 65–76.

Schmitt, Eric. "War Puts U.S. Service Women Closer than Ever to Combat." *The New York Times,* January 22, 1991.

Shreve, Anita. *Women Together, Women Alone: The Legacy of the Consciousness Raising Movement.* New York: Viking, 1989.

Solinger, Rickie. *Wake Up Little Susie: Single Pregnancy and Race Before Roe v. Wade.* New York: Routledge, 1992.

Sommers, Christina Hoff. *Who Stole Feminism: How Women Have Betrayed Women.* New York: Simon and Schuster, 1994.

Soukup, Erwin M. "Episcopal Convention: Violence the Villain." *The Christian Century* 87 (November 18, 1970): 1391–92.

Stanley, Alessandra. "Marilyn Quayle Says the 1960s Had a Flip Side." *The New York Times,* August 20, 1992.

Steinfels, Peter. "Lesbian Ordained Episcopal Priest." *The New York Times,* June 6, 1991.

———. "Presbyterians Try to Resolve Long Dispute." *The New York Times,* June 17, 1994.

Stern, Aimee. "Miniskirt Movement Comes Up Short." *Adweek's Marketing Week,* March 28, 1988, 2.

Swerdlow, Amy. "Ladies Day at the Capitol: Women Strike for Peace Versus HUAC." *Feminist Studies* 8 (Fall 1982): 493–520.

Taylor, Alex III. "Why Women Managers Are Bailing Out." *Fortune,* August 18, 1986, 16–23.

Solomon, Jolie. "The Invisible Barrier Is Crystal Clear to Many." *The Wall Street Journal,* April 20, 1990.

"The Two Worlds: A Day-Long Debate." *The New York Times,* July 25, 1959.

Tobias, Sheila. *Faces of Feminism: An Activist's Reflections on the Women's Movement.* Boulder, CO: Westview Press, 1997.

Thompson, Alice. "How to Be a Woman." *Seventeen,* July 1951, 76, 106.

U.S. Congress. Joint Economic Committee Hearings. *Economic Problems of Women.* 93rd Congress, 1st session (July 12, 1973). Washington, DC: U.S. Government Printing Office, 1973.

———. *The Underclass.* May 25, 1989. Washington, DC: U.S. Government Printing Office, 1989.

Walker, Alice. "In Search of Our Mothers' Gardens." *Southern Exposure* 4, No. 4 (1977): 60–64.

Walker, Rebecca. *To Be Real: Telling the Truth and Changing the Face of Feminism.* New York: Anchor Books, 1995.

Wandersee, Winifred. *On the Move: American Women in the 1970s.* Boston: Twayne, 1988.

Waters, Harry. "Games Singles Play." *Newsweek* 82 (July 16, 1973): 52–58.

Weddington, Sarah. *A Question of Choice.* New York: Putnam's Sons, 1992.

Weeks v. Southern Tel. & Tel. Co. (CA-5, 3-4-69) 408 F. 2d rev. & rem. S.D. Ga 277 F. Supp. 117.

Weiner, Lynn Y. *From Working Girl to Working Mother: The Female Labor Force in the United States, 1820–1980.* Chapel Hill: University of North Carolina Press, 1985.

White, Gayle. "Reacting to Re-Imagining." *Atlanta Journal Constitution,* May 21, 1994.

Whittier, Nancy. *Feminist Generations: The Persistence of the Radical Women's Movement.* Philadelphia: Temple University Press, 1995.

Witt, Linda, Karen M. Paget, and Glenna Matthews. *Running as a Woman: Gender and Power in American Politics.* New York: Free Press, 1993.

Women's Advocates. *Women's Advocates: The Story of a Shelter.* St. Paul, MN: Advocates, 1980.

"Women Arise." *Life* 69 (September 4, 1970): 16B–24.

"World Wide: A Lesbian Minister." *The Wall Street Journal,* November 5, 1992.

Wyatt, Addie. Interview with the author. Chicago, June 15, 1983.

Zahava, Irene. *Feminism³: The Third Generation in Fiction. Boulder, CO: Westview Press, 1996.*

Zeigenhals, Gretchen E. "Meeting the Women of Women-Church." *The Christian Century* (May 10, 1989): 492–94.

Chapter Two   African American Women in the Twenty-first Century: The Continuing Challenge

Amott, Teresa, and Julie Matthaei. *Race, Gender and Work: A Multicultural Economic History of Women in the United States.* Boston: South End Press, 1991.

Bane, Mary Jo. "Welfare as We Might Know It." *The American Prospect* 30 (January–February 1997): 47–53.

Cantarow, Ellen, and Susan O'Malley. *Moving the Mountain: Women Working for Social Change.* Old Westbury, NY: Feminist Press, 1980.

Carper, Jean, editor. *Operation Daily Bread Report.* New York: National Council of Negro Women, Inc., 1968.

Collins, Patricia Hill. "Feminism in the Twentieth Century." In *Black Women in America: An Historical Encyclopedia,* edited by Darlene Clark Hine. New York: Carlson Publishing, 1993.

Edelman, Marian Wright. *Families in Peril: An Agenda for Social Change.* Cambridge, MA: Harvard University Press, 1987.

Fulbright, Karen. "The Myth of the Double-Advantage: Black Female Managers." In *Slipping Through the Cracks: The Status of Black Women,* edited by Margaret C. Simms and Julianne Malveaux. New Brunswick, NJ: Transaction, 1987.

Higginbotham, Elizabeth. "Black Professional Women: Job Ceilings and Employment Sectors." In *Women of Color in U.S. Society,* edited by Maxine Baca Zinn and Bonnie Thornton Dill. Philadelphia: Temple University Press, 1994.

Hill, Ruth Edmonds, editor. *The Black Woman Oral History Project.* Westport, CT: Meckler Publishing, 1991.

Jones, Jacqueline. *Labor of Love, Labor of Sorrow: Black Women, Work and the Family from Slavery to the Present.* New York: Basic Books, 1985.

Lerner, Gerda. *Black Women in White America: A Documentary History.* New York: Vintage, 1972.

Locke, Mamie. "Is This America? Fannie Lou Hamer and the Mississippi Freedom Democratic Party." In *Women in the Civil Rights Movement: Trailblazers and Torchbearers, 1941–1965,* edited by Vicki Crawford, Jacqueline Rouse, and Barbara Woods. New York: Carlson Publishing, 1993.

Luper, Clara. *Behold the Walls.* Oklahoma City, OK: Jim Wire, 1979.

McFate, Katherine. "Struggling to Survive: Welfare, Work and Lone Mothers." In *The American Woman, 1996–97,* edited by Cynthia Costello and Barbara K. Krimgold. New York: Norton, 1996.

Parker, Frank. *Turning Point: The 1964 Mississippi Freedom Summer.* Washington, DC: Joint Center for Political and Economic Studies, 1994.

Progress and Peril: Black Children in America. Washington, DC: Children's Defense Fund, 1993.

Robinson, Jo Ann Gibson. *The Montgomery Bus Boycott and the Women Who Started It.* Knoxville: University of Tennessee Press, 1987.

Rowe, Audrey, and John Jeffries, editors. *The State of Black America, 1996.* New York: National Urban League, Inc., 1996.

Sawhill, Isabel. "Welfare Reform: Analysis of the Issues." <http://www.urban.org/welfare/overview.htm>, accessed 1997.

Smitherman, Geneva, editor. *African-American Women Speak Out on Anita Hill–Clarence Thomas.* Detroit, MI: Wayne State University Press, 1995.

Sokoloff, Natalie. *Black and White Women in the Professions: Occupational Segregation by Race and Gender, 1960–1980.* New York: Routledge, 1992.

Smith, Barbara. "Combahee River Collective." In *Black Women in America: An Historical Encyclopedia,* edited by Darlene Clark Hine. New York: Carlson Publishing, 1993.

The State of America's Children Yearbook. Washington, DC: Children's Defense Fund, 1994.

"Status of African-American Children Under Three Living in Poverty." *Child Poverty News and Issues* 2 (1992). <http://cpmcnet.columbia.edu/news/child-pov/news0004.html>.

Voices of Vision: African-American Women on the Issues. Washington, DC: National Council of Negro Women, 1997.

Washington, Cynthia. "We Started from Different Ends of the Spectrum." *Southern Exposure* 4 (Winter 1977): 14–20.

West, Guida. *The National Welfare Rights Movement: The Social Protest of Poor Women.* New York: Praeger, 1981.

Women's Bureau. *Black Women in the Labor Force.* Washington, DC: U.S. Government Printing Office, 1997.

Chapter Three Hispanic Women in the United States

Acosta-Belén, Edna, and Carlos E Santiago. "Merging Borders: The Remapping of America." *The Latino Review of Books* 1 (Spring 1995): 2–11.

Amott, Teresa, and Julie Matthaei. *Race, Gender, and Work: A Multicultural Economic History of Women in the United States.* Boston: South End Press, 1996.

Bean, Frank D., and Marta Tienda. *The Hispanic Population of the United States.* New York: Russell Sage Foundation, 1987.

Brischetto, Robert. "Women Lead the Modest Jump in Hispanic Political Representation." *Hispanic Business Magazine,* Homepage Archives, January 17, 1977.

Bureau of the Census. *The Hispanic Population in the United States: March 1992 (revised).* Washington, DC: U.S. Government Printing Office, 1993.

————. *Household Data Annual Averages, 1997.* Unpublished data, Washington, DC, 1997.

Bureau of Labor Statistics. *Labor Force Participation Rate, May 1997.* Unpublished data, Washington, DC, 1997.

Cornelius, Wayne A. "The Latin American Presence in the United States: Can Scholarship Catch Up With the Immigration Backlash?" *Latin American Studies Association Forum* 26, No. 4 (1995): 4–6.

Fernández-Kelly, M. Patricia, and Anna M. García. "The Making of an Underground Economy: Hispanic Women, Home Work, and the Advanced Capitalist State." *Urban Anthropology* 14, Nos. 1–3 (1985): 59–89.

National Center for Education Statistics. *The Condition of Education 1996.* Washington, DC: U.S. Government Printing Office, 1997.

National Education Goals Panel. *The National Education Goals Report: Building a Nation of Learners 1996.* Washington, DC: U.S. Government Printing Office, 1997.

National Latina Institute for Reproductive Health (NLIRH). *Status of Latina Health in the United States and Puerto Rico.* Washington, DC: NLIRH (January 1996): 1–5.

Nieto, Sonia. "Barriers to Latino Education." *The Latino Review of Books* 2, no. 3 (winter 1996–97): 48–49.

Nieves-Rosa, Limarie. "Puerto Rican Women in the United States: Struggles, Survival, and Self-Empowerment." Unpublished research paper, spring 1997.

Portes, Alejandro, and Rubén G. Rumbaut. *Immigrant America: A Portrait.* Second Edition. Berkeley: University of California Press, 1997.

President's Advisory Commission on Educational Excellence for Hispanic Americans (President's Advisory Commission). *Our Nation on the Fault Line: Hispanic American Education.* Washington, DC: White House Initiative in Educational Excellence for Hispanic Americans, 1996.

Rivera-Batiz, Francisco, and Carlos Santiago. *Puerto Ricans in the United States: A Changing Reality.* Washington, DC: National Puerto Rican Coalition, 1994.

Safa, Helen I. *The Myth of the Male Breadwinner: Women and Industrialization in the Caribbean.* Boulder, CO: Westview Press, 1995.

Santillán, Richard. "Midwestern Mexican American Women and the Struggle for Gender Equality: A Historical Overview, 1920s–1960s." In *Mexican-American Women: Changing Images,* edited by Juan García. Perspectives in Mexican American Studies, University of Arizona, 1990.

Shorris, Earl. *Latinos: A Biography of the People.* New York: Norton, 1992.

Women's Bureau. *1993 Handbook on Women Workers: Trends and Issues.* Washington, DC: Department of Labor, 1994a.

———. "Women of Hispanic Origin in the Labor Force." *Facts on Working Women.* Washington, DC: Department of Labor, 1994b.

Chapter Four   Women and the Law: Learning from the Past to Protect the Future

Age Discrimination in Employment Act of 1967. 29 U.S. Code Sections 621–634.

American Association of University Women (AAUW). *How Schools Shortchange Girls.* Washington, DC: AAUW, 1992.

Americans with Disabilities Act of 1990. 42 U.S. Code Sections 12101–12213. Public Law 101–336.

Asimov, Nanette. "State Closer to Single-Sex Public Schools." *San Francisco Chronicle,* July 14, 1997.

Cain, Patricia A. "Feminism and the Limits of Equality." *Georgia Law Review* 24 (summer 1990): 803–47.

Center for the American Woman and Politics (CAWP). *Statewide Elective Executive Women: 1969–1994 Fact Sheet,* April 1994. New Brunswick, NJ: CAWP, April 1994.

———. *Sex Differences in Voter Turnout Fact Sheet,* July 1995. New Brunswick, NJ: CAWP, July 1995.

————. *Statewide Elective Executive Women 1997 Fact Sheet.* New Brunswick, NJ: CAWP, January 1997.

Chute, Marchette G. *The First Liberty: A History of the Right to Vote in America, 1619–1850.* New York: Dutton, 1969.

Civil Rights Act of 1964. 42 U.S. Code Section 2000 et seq. Public Law 88–352.

Civil Rights Restoration Act of 1987. Public Law 100–259.

Civil Rights Act of 1991. 42 U.S. Code Section 1981–1981a. Public Law 102–166.

Dionne, E. J., Jr. "Get With the Program: Women's Sports Matter." *The Washington Post,* May 14, 1997.

Educational Equity Act of 1974. 20 U.S. Code Section 1866.

Equal Pay Act of 1963. 29 U.S. Code Section 206(d) et seq. Public Law 88–38.

Ewing, Cortez A. *American National Government.* New York: American Book, 1958.

Fair Labor Standards Act of 1938. 29 U.S. Code Section 201 et seq. 52 Stat. 106.

Family and Medical Leave Act of 1993. 29 U.S. Code Sections 2601–2611. Public Law 103–03.

Glass Ceiling Commission. *Good for Business: Making Full Use of the Nation's Human Capital.* Washington, DC: U.S. Government Printing Office, 1995.

Goldscheid, Julie. "Will a Vital New Women's Right be Withdrawn?" *National Law Journal* (August 26, 1996): A20–A21.

Goldstein, Leslie Friedman. *Contemporary Cases in Women's Rights.* Madison: University of Wisconsin Press, 1994

Gunther, Gerald. *Cases and Materials on Constitutional Law.* Mineola, NY: Foundation Press, 1975.

Jarvis, Sonia R. "Historical Overview: African Americans and the Evolution of Voting Rights." In *From Exclusion to Inclusion: The Long Struggles for African American Political Power,* edited by Ralph Gomes and Linda Faye Williams. New York: Greenwood Press, 1992.

Karst, Kenneth L. "Woman's Constitution." *Duke Law Journal* (June 1984): 447–508.

National Council for Research on Women (NCRW). "Affirmative Action: Beyond the Glass Ceiling and the Sticky Floor." *Issues Quarterly* 1, No. 4 (1996): 1–28.

National Women's History Project (NWHP). "Women Win the Vote." Windsor, CA: NWHP, 1995.

Nontraditional Employment for Women Act of 1991. Public Law 102–235 (amending the Job Training and Partnership Act).

NOW Legal Defense and Education Fund and Renee Cherow-O'Leary (NOW). *The State-By-State Guide To Women's Legal Rights.* New York: McGraw-Hill, 1987.

Personal Responsibility and Work Opportunity Reconciliation Act of 1996. Public Law 104–193 (amending eight limited states code sections 1612 and 1641).

Pregnancy Discrimination Act of 1978. 42 U.S. Code Sections 654–666 (amending Title VII of the Civil Rights Act of 1964). Public Law 95–555.

Roberts, Dorothy E. "The Genetic Tie." *University of Chicago Law Review* 62 (winter 1995): 209–73.

———. "Punishing Drug Addicts Who Have Babies: Women of Color, Equality, and the Right of Privacy." *Harvard Law Review* 104 (May 1991): 1419–81.

Title VII of the Civil Rights Act of 1964. 42 U.S. Code Section 2000e et seq.

Title IX of the Education Amendments of 1972. 20 U.S. Code Sections 1681–1688. Public Law 92–318.

Siegel, Reva B. "The Modernization of Marital Status Law: Adjudicating Wives' Rights to Earnings, 1860–1930." *Georgetown Law Journal* 82 (September 1994): 2127–210.

———. "The Rule of Love: Wife Beating as Prerogative and Privacy." *Yale Law Journal* 105 (June 1996): 2117–207.

Violence Against Women Act of 1994. 42 U.S. Code Section 13981 (Title IV of Public Law 103–322).

Women's Legal Defense Fund (WLDF). *Annual Preview of Supreme Court Cases Vital to Women,* 1995–96. Washington, DC: WLDF, 1996.

Chapter Five   The American Woman: The Road Ahead

Acevedo, Dolores, and Thomas J. Espenshade. "Implications of a North American Free Trade Agreement for Mexican Migration into the United States." *Population and Development Review* 18, no. 4 (December 1992): 729–44.

Bureau of the Census. Current Population Reports, Series P23-180. *Marriage, Divorce, and Remarriage in the 1990s.* Washington, DC: U.S. Government Printing Office, 1992.

———. Current Population Reports, Series P20-491. *Marital Status and Living Arrangements: March 1995 (Update).* <http://www.census.gov/prod/2/pop/p20/p20-491.pdf>, published 1996a.

———. Current Population Reports, Series P25-1130. *Population Projections of the United States by Age, Sex, Race, and Hispanic Origin: 1995 to 2050.* Washington, DC: U.S. Government Printing Office, 1996b.

———. Current Population Reports, Series P60-194. *Poverty in America, 1995.* Washington, DC: U.S. Government Printing Office, 1996c.

———. *Historical Statistics of the United States: Colonial Times to 1970, Part 1.* Washington, DC: U.S. Government Printing Office, 1975.

———. *1980 Census, General Social and Economic Characteristics.* Volume PC80-1-C1. Washington, DC: U.S. Government Printing Office, 1983.

———. *Statistical Abstract of the United States: 1996.* Washington, DC: U.S. Government Printing Office, 1996d.

———. *U.S. Census of Population: 1950.* Vol. 4, *Special Reports,* Part 1, Chapter A, "Employment and Personal Characteristics." Washington, DC: U.S. Government Printing Office, 1953.

Castro Martin, Teresa, and Larry L. Bumpass. "Recent Trends in Marital Disruption." *Demography* 26, No. 1 (February 1989): 49.

Department of Health and Human Services. *Report to Congress on Out-of-Wedlock*

Childbearing: Executive Summary. Hyattsville, MD: U.S. Government Printing Office, September 1995.

De Vita, Carol J. "The United States at Mid-Decade." *Population Bulletin,* 50, no. 4. Washington, DC: Population Reference Bureau, March 1996.

Espenshade, Thomas J. "Marriage Trends in America: Estimates, Implications and Underlying Causes." *Population and Development Review* 11, no. 2 (June 1985): 193–245.

Fries, James F., Lawrence W. Green, and Sol Levine. "Health Promotion and the Compression of Morbidity." *The Lancet,* March 4, 1989.

Immigration and Naturalization Service. *Immigration to the United States in Fiscal Year 1995.* Washington, DC: U.S. Government Printing Office, March 1996.

McLanahan, Sara, and Gary Sandefur. *Growing Up with a Single Parent.* Cambridge, MA: Harvard University Press, 1994.

Manton, Kenneth G., and James W. Vaupel. "Survival After the Age of 80 in the United States, Sweden, France, England, and Japan." *The New England Journal of Medicine* 333, No. 18 (November 2, 1995): 1232–35.

National Center for Education Statistics. *Digest of Education Statistics 1996,* Washington, DC: U.S. Government Printing Office, November 1996.

National Center for Health Statistics. "Cohabitation, Marriage, Marital Dissolution, and Remarriage: United States, 1988." *Advance Data from Vital Statistics,* no. 194 (1991). 1–3.

———. "Report of Final Natality Statistics, 1995." *Monthly Vital Statistics Report* 45, no. 11, Supplement (June 10, 1997a).

———. "Report of Final Mortality Statistics, 1995." *Monthly Vital Statistics Report* 45, no. 11, Supplement 2 (June 12, 1997b).

———. *Vital Statistics of the United States, 1992.* Vol. 1, *Natality.* Hyattsville, MD: Public Health Service, 1994.

Spain, Daphne, and Suzanne Bianchi. *Balancing Act: Motherhood, Marriage, and Employment Among American Women.* New York: Russell Sage Foundation, 1996.

Warren, Robert. "Estimates of the Unauthorized Immigrant Population Residing in the United States, by Country of Origin and State of Residence: October 1992." Paper presented at the California Immigration 1994 Seminar, Sacramento, CA, April 1994.

AMERICAN WOMEN TODAY: A STATISTICAL PORTRAIT

Section 1: Demographics

Bureau of the Census. Current Population Reports, Series P20, no. 450. *Marital Status and Living Arrangements: March 1990.* Washington, DC: U.S. Government Printing Office, 1991.

———. Current Population Reports, Series P20-478. *Marital Status and Living Arrangements: March 1993.* Washington, DC: U.S. Government Printing Office, 1994.

———. Current Population Reports, Series P20-484. *Marital Status and Living*

Arrangements: March 1994. Washington, DC: U.S. Government Printing Office, 1996.

————. Current Population Reports, Series P20-491. *Marital Status and Living Arrangements: March 1995 (Update).* <http://www.census.gov/prod/2/pop/p20/p20-491.pdf>, published December 1996.

————. Current Population Reports, Series P20-494. *The Foreign-Born Population: 1996.* <http://www.census.gov/prod/2/pop/p20/p20-494.pdf>, published March 1997.

————. Current Population Reports, Series P25-1130. *Population Projections of the United States by Age, Sex, Race, and Hispanic Origin: 1995 to 2050.* Washington, DC: U.S. Government Printing Office, 1996.

————. Current Population Reports, Series P-60, no. 174. *Money Income of Households, Families, and Persons in the United States: 1990.* Washington, DC: U.S. Government Printing Office, 1991.

————. Current Population Reports, Series P60-193. *Money Income in the United States: 1995 (With Separate Data on Valuation of Noncash Benefits).* Washington, DC: U.S. Government Printing Office, 1996.

————. Current Population Survey, March 1996. <http://www.census.gov/population/socdemo/foreign/96/96tab-1.txt>, published April 8, 1997.

————. Current Population Survey, March 1996. <http://www.census.gov/population/socdemo/foreign/96/96tab-2.txt>, published April 8, 1997.

————. *Statistical Abstract of the United States: 1980.* Washington, DC: U.S. Government Printing Office, 1980.

————. *Statistical Abstract of the United States: 1996.* Washington, DC: U.S. Government Printing Office, 1996.

National Center for Health Statistics. *Health, United States, 1993.* Hyattsville, MD: Public Health Service, 1994.

————. *Monthly Vital Statistics Report* 43, no. 11(S) (May 25, 1995).

————. *Monthly Vital Statistics Report* 45, no. 3(S)2 (October 4, 1996).

————. *Monthly Vital Statistics Report* 45, no. 7 (February 19, 1997).

Women's Research and Education Institute. *The American Woman 1996–97*, edited by Cynthia Costello and Barbara K. Krimgold. New York: Norton, 1996.

Section 2: Education

Bureau of the Census. Current Population Reports, Series P20-493. *Educational Attainment in the United States: March 1996 (Update).* <http://www.census.gov/prop/2/p20/p20-493u.pdf>, published July 1997.

————. Current Population Reports, Series P20-494. *The Foreign-Born Population: 1996.* <http://www.census.gov/prod/2/pop/p20/p20-494.pdf>, published March 1997.

————. Current Population Survey, March 1996. <http://www.census.gov/population/socdemo/foreign/96/96tab-1.txt>, published April 8, 1997.

————. Current Population Survey, March 1996. <http://www.census.gov/population/socdemo/foreign/96/96tab-2.txt>, published April 8, 1997.

————. *Statistical Abstract of the United States: 1996.* Washington, DC: U.S. Government Printing Office, 1996.

National Center for Education Statistics. *Digest of Education Statistics 1996.* Washington, DC: U.S. Government Printing Office, 1996.

Women's Research and Education Institute. *The American Woman 1996–97*, edited by Cynthia Costello and Barbara K. Krimgold. New York: Norton, 1996.

Section 3: Health

Bureau of the Census. Current Population Reports, Series P25-1130. *Population Projections of the United States by Age, Sex, Race, and Hispanic Origin: 1995 to 2050.* Washington, DC: U.S. Government Printing Office, February 1996.

Centers for Disease Control and Prevention. *Abortion Surveillance: Preliminary Data—United States, 1994* 45, nos. 51 and 52 (January 3, 1997).

————. *HIV/AIDS Surveillance Report Year-End Edition* 7, no. 2 (1995).

————. *HIV/AIDS Surveillance Report Year-End Edition* 8, no. 2 (1996).

National Cancer Institute. *SEER Cancer Statistics Review, 1973–1993: Tables and Graphs.* Bethesda, MD: National Cancer Institute, 1996.

National Center for Health Statistics. *Health, United States, 1993.* Hyattsville, MD: Public Health Service, 1994.

————. *Health, United States, 1995.* Hyattsville, MD: Public Health Service, 1996.

————. *Healthy People 2000 Review, 1995–96.* Hyattsville, MD: Public Health Service, 1996.

————. *Monthly Vital Statistics Report* 43, No. 11(S) (May 25, 1995).

Section 4: Employment

Bureau of Labor Statistics. "A Profile of Contingent Workers." *Monthly Labor Review* 119, no. 10 (October 1996): 10–21.

————. Current Population Reports, Series P20-491. *Marital Status and Living Arrangements: March 1995 (Update).* <http://www.census.gov/prod/2/pop/p20/p20-491.pdf>, December 1996.

;————. Current Population Reports, Series P-60, no. 180. *Money Income of Households, Families, and Persons in the United States: 1991.* Washington, DC: U.S. Government Printing Office, 1992.

————. Current Population Reports, Series P60-193. *Money Income in the United States: 1995 (With Separate Data on Valuation of Noncash Benefits).* Washington, DC: U.S. Government Printing Office, 1996.

————. Current Population Reports, Series P70-52. *What Does It Cost to Mind Our Preschoolers?* Washington, DC: Bureau of the Census, 1996.

————. Current Population Reports, Series P70-53. *Who's Minding Our Preschoolers?* Washington, DC: Bureau of the Census, 1996.

————. Current Population Survey, March 1976. Unpublished data, Washington, DC.

————. Current Population Survey, March 1978. Unpublished data, Washington, DC.

————. Current Population Survey, March 1980. Unpublished data, Washington, DC.

————. Current Population Survey, March 1982. Unpublished data, Washington, DC.

————. Current Population Survey, March 1984. Unpublished data, Washington, DC.

————. Current Population Survey, March 1986. Unpublished data, Washington, DC.

————. Current Population Survey, March 1988. Unpublished data, Washington, DC.

————. Current Population Survey, March 1990. Unpublished data, Washington, DC.

————. Current Population Survey, March 1992. Unpublished data, Washington, DC.

————. Current Population Survey, March 1994. Unpublished data, Washington, DC.

————. Current Population Survey, March 1996. Unpublished data, Washington, DC.

————. Current Population Survey, annual averages, 1996. Unpublished data, Washington, DC.

————. *Employment and Earnings* 31, no. 1. Washington, DC: U.S. Government Printing Office, January 1984.

————. *Employment and Earnings* 34, no. 1. Washington, DC: U.S. Government Printing Office, January 1987.

————. *Employment and Earnings* 40, no. 1. Washington, DC: U.S. Government Printing Office, January 1993.

————. *Employment and Earnings* 43, no. 1. Washington, DC: U.S. Government Printing Office, January 1996.

————. *Employment and Earnings* 44, no. 1. Washington, DC: U.S. Government Printing Office, January 1997.

————. <http://stats.bls.gov/>, published February 29, 1997.

————. *Handbook of Labor Statistics.* Washington, DC: U.S. Government Printing Office, 1989.

————. <http://stats.bls.gov>, accessed May 15, 1997.

————. "Labor Force Projections: The Baby Boom Moves On." *Monthly Labor Review* 114, no. 11 (November 1991): 31–44.

————. "Multiple Jobholding Up Sharply in the 1980's." *Monthly Labor Review* 113, no. 7 (July 1990): 3–10.

————. "New Data on Multiple Jobholding Available From the CPS." *Monthly Labor Review* 120, no. 3 (March 1997): 3–15.

————. "The 2005 Labor Force: Growing, but Slowly." *Monthly Labor Review* 118, no. 11 (November 1995): 29–44.

————. "Workers in Alternative Employment Arrangements." *Monthly Labor Review* 119, no. 10 (October 1996): 31–45.

Section 5: Earnings and Benefits

Bureau of Labor Statistics. *Employment and Earnings* 26, no. 1. Washington, DC: U.S. Government Printing Office, January 1979.

———. *Employment and Earnings* 38, no. 1. Washington, DC: U.S. Government Printing Office, January 1991.

———. *Employment and Earnings* 40, no. 1. Washington, DC: U.S. Government Printing Office, January 1993.

———. *Employment and Earnings* 42, no. 1. Washington, DC: U.S. Government Printing Office, January 1995.

———. *Employment and Earnings* 43, no. 1. Washington, DC: U.S. Government Printing Office, January 1996.

———. *Employment and Earnings* 44, no. 1. Washington, DC: U.S. Government Printing Office, January 1997.

———. *Handbook of Labor Statistics*. Washington, DC: U.S. Government Printing Office, 1989.

Bureau of the Census. Current Population Reports, Series P60, no. 156, *Money Income of Households, Families, and Persons in the United States. 1985*. Washington, DC: U.S. Government Printing Office, 1987.

———. Current Population Reports, Series P-60, no. 180. *Money Income of Households, Families, and Persons in the United States: 1991*. Washington, DC: U.S. Government Printing Office, 1992.

———. Current Population Reports, Series P60-193. *Money Income in the United States: 1995 (With Separate Data on Valuation of Noncash Benefits)*. Washington, DC: U.S. Government Printing Office, 1996.

———. Current Population Reports, Series P-60, no. 171. *Poverty in the United States: 1988 and 1989*. Washington, DC: U.S. Government Printing Office, 1991.

———. Current Population Survey, March 1996. <http://ferret.bls.census.gov/macro/031996/noncash/6__000.htm>, published March 10, 1997.

———. Current Population Survey, March 1996. <http://ferret.bls.census.gov/macro/031996/noncash/7__000.htm>, published March 10, 1997.

———. Current Population Survey, March 1996. <http://ferret.bls.census.gov/macro/031996/noncash/8__000.htm>, published March 10, 1997.

———. Current Population Survey, March 1996. Unpublished data, Washington, DC.

Section 6: Economic Security

Bureau of the Census. Current Population Reports, Series P-20, no. 411. *Household and Family Characteristics: March 1985*. Washington, DC: U.S. Government Printing Office, 1986.

———. Current Population Reports, Series P20-488. *Household and Family Characteristics: March 1995*. <http://www.census.gov/prod/2/pop/p20/p20488.pdf>, published October 1996.

————. Current Population Reports, Series P60-105. *Consumer Income*. Washington, DC: U.S. Government Printing Office, 1977.

————. Current Population Reports, Series P-60, no. 156. *Money Income of Households, Families, and Persons in the United States: 1985.* Washington, DC: U.S. Government Printing Office, 1987.

————. Current Population Reports, Series P-60, no. 174. *Money Income of Households, Families, and Persons in the United States: 1990.* Washington, DC: U.S. Government Printing Office, 1991.

————. Current Population Reports, Series P-60, no. 180. *Money Income of Households, Families, and Persons in the United States: 1991.* Washington, DC: U.S. Government Printing Office, 1992.

————. Current Population Reports, Series P60-193. *Money Income in the United States: 1995 (With Separate Data on Valuation of Noncash Benefits).* Washington, DC: U.S. Government Printing Office, 1996.

————. Current Population Reports, Series P60-194. *Poverty in the United States: 1995.* Washington, DC: U.S. Government Printing Office, 1996.

————. Current Population Survey, March 1996. Unpublished data, Washington, DC.

————. Current Population Survey, March 1996. <http://ferret.bls.census.gov/macro/031996/perinc/12__007.htm>, published November 18, 1996.

————. Current Population Survey, March 1996. <http://ferret.bls.census.gov/macro/031996/perinc/12__009.htm>, published November 18, 1996.

————. Current Population Survey, March 1996. <http://ferret.bls.census.gov/macro/031996/pov/1__001.htm>, published November 18, 1996.

Bureau of the Census and Department of Housing and Urban Development. *American Housing Survey for the United States in 1995.* Washington, DC: U.S. Government Printing Office, 1997.

Section 7: Women in the Military

U.S. Department of Defense. Defense Manpower Data Center. Unpublished historical population data, Arlington, VA, provided August 1997.

————. Defense Manpower Data Center. Unpublished data, Arlington, VA, April 30, 1997.

————. Defense Manpower Data Center. Unpublished data, Arlington, VA, June 30, 1997.

————. Office of the Assistant Secretary of Defense for Public Affairs. Public Affairs News Release no. 449-94, July 29, 1994.

Women in Military Service for America, Inc. *Statistics on Women in the Military* (factsheet). Washington, DC, February 23, 1996.

Section 8: Elections and Officials

Administrative Office of the U.S. Courts. *Annual Report on the Judiciary Equal Employment Opportunity Program for the Twelve-Month Period Ended September 30, 1991.* Washington, DC: 1991.

————. Unpublished data, May 1997.

Bureau of the Census. Current Population Reports, Series P-20, no. 322. *Voting and Registration in the Election of November 1976.* Washington, DC: U.S. Government Printing Office, 1978.

————. Current Population Reports, Series P-20, no. 370. *Voting and Registration in the Election of November 1980.* Washington, DC: U.S. Government Printing Office, 1982.

————. Current Population Reports, Series P-20, no. 405. *Voting and Registration in the Election of November 1984.* Washington, DC: U.S. Government Printing Office, 1986.

————. Current Population Reports, Series P-20, no. 440. *Voting and Registration in the Election of November 1988.* Washington, DC: U.S. Government Printing Office, 1989.

————. Current Population Reports, Series P20-466. *Voting and Registration in the Election of November 1992.* Washington, DC: U.S. Government Printing Office, 1993.

————. Current Population Reports, Series P20. *Voting and Registration in the Election of November 1996.* Washington, DC: U.S. Government Printing Office, forthcoming in 1997.

Center for the American Woman and Politics (CAWP), National Information Bank on Women in Public Office, Eagleton Institute of Politics, Rutgers University. *Statewide Elective Executive Women, 1969–1997 Fact Sheet.* New Brunswick, NJ: CAWP, July 1997.

————. *Women in the State Legislatures Fact Sheet.* New Brunswick, NJ: CAWP, May 1997.

————. *Women in the U.S. Congress 1917–1997 Fact Sheet.* New Brunswick, NJ: CAWP, January 1997.

————. *Women Mayors and Presidential Appointments.* New Brunswick, NJ: CAWP, March 1997.

NOTES ON THE CONTRIBUTORS

Margarita Benitez is a professor of humanities at the University of Puerto Rico and vice president for Interuniversity Collaboration at Equity Research, a Washington-based educational consulting firm. She holds a Ph.D. in Spanish literature from Columbia University and often writes about issues affecting higher education, the status of women, Hispanics in the United States, and Puerto Rican culture, as well as literary topics. From 1985 to 1994, Dr. Benitez was chancellor of the University of Puerto Rico at Cayey, where she initiated the Women's Studies Project.

Vicki Crawford is an associate professor of history at the State University of West Georgia, where she specializes in African American history and the history of the civil rights movement. Prior to her present position, Dr. Crawford was on the faculty in the Department of African American Studies at the University of North Carolina at Charlotte and in the Department of Women's Studies at the University of Massachusetts-Amherst. Dr. Crawford is a joint editor of *Women in the Civil Rights Movement: Trailblazers and Torchbearers, 1941–1965* and author of other articles on women in the civil rights movement. She is currently working on a manuscript on African American women in the Mississippi civil rights movement while leading workshops and participating in curriculum revision projects on the inclusion of the history of the civil rights movement in secondary school curricula. Dr. Crawford received her Ph.D. in American studies from Emory University.

Carol J. De Vita has written extensively on demographic change and its implications for public policies. Her monographs, *The United States at Mid-Decade, New Realities of the American Family,* and *The Baby Boom—Entering Mid-life,* have received widespread recognition in the media and among public policymakers. Dr. De Vita holds a B.A. in American history from the University of North Carolina at Chapel Hill, an M.A. in demography from Georgetown University, and a Ph.D. in social welfare policy from Brandeis University. She is a member of Northwestern University's Council of 100—a group of professional women who serve as role models and mentors to undergraduate women. Dr. De Vita is a senior research associate at the Urban Institute in Washington, D.C.

Betty Dooley, president of the Women's Research & Education Institute (WREI), has been with WREI since its beginning in 1977. An early Texas feminist, she was active in state politics before moving to Washington, D.C. In 1964, Ms. Dooley was a candidate for the U.S. House of Representatives from the Sixteenth District of Texas. She served for several years as director of the Health Security Action Council, an advocacy organization based in Washington, D.C. that worked for comprehensive national health insurance. Ms. Dooley is a charter member of the National Council for Research on Women, a member of the Women's Health Advisory Board at Duke University, a member of the Secretary of Labor's Advisory Committee on Employment and Training for Veterans, and a board member of the Center for Cross-Cultural Research on Women at Oxford University.

Sara M. Evans is Distinguished McKnight University Professor of History at the University of Minnesota. Born in a South Carolina Methodist parsonage in 1943, she became involved in the civil rights movement in the 1960s and has been an activist in, and a historian of, the contemporary feminist movement since its inception. Her publications include *Personal Politics: The Roots of Women's Liberation in the Civil Rights Movement and the New Left, Wage Justice: Comparable Worth and the Paradox of Technocratic Reform* (with Barbara J. Nelson), and *Born for Liberty: A History of Women in America*.

Sonia R. Jarvis is a civil attorney practicing in Washington, D.C., who has specialized in civil rights and discrimination cases. She is currently research professor in communication at the George Washington University's School of Media and Public Affairs, where she has been conducting research on the interaction of race, media, and politics since the civil rights movement. Prior to this position, Ms. Jarvis was the executive director of the National Coalition on Black Voter Participation, Inc., a national nonprofit voter registration organization that pursued voting rights for minority voters. She has also held visiting professor positions at Rutgers University's Eagleton Institute of Politics and Harvard University's Kennedy School of Government. She has lectured at Catholic University's Columbia School of Law and Georgetown University Law Center. Ms. Jarvis is vice president of legislative affairs for the Black Women's Agenda and has served on the screening committee of the Women's Legal Defense Fund. She received both a B.A. in political science and a B.A. in psychology from Stanford University, and a J.D. from Yale Law School.

Juanita M. Kreps is vice president and James B. Duke Professor Emerita at Duke University. She has served as U.S. Secretary of Commerce and as director of numerous corporate boards, including AT&T, Chrysler Corporation, Citicorp, Eastman Kodak, J. C. Penny Company, and United Airlines. Dr. Kreps, who has also served as a member of the board of the New York Stock Exchange, is a charter member of the board of the Women's Research & Education Institute (WREI).

Sarah B. Kreps is a freelance editor and writer whose special interests include women's health issues and women in the arts. Prior to writing feature articles and profiles for various publications in Fairfield, Connecticut, she worked in marketing and public relations at Clairol, Inc., in New York City. Ms. Kreps has planned public relations projects for Resolve, Inc., a national support group for infertile couples, and edited the textbook, *Marketing Analysis and Decision Making: Text and Cases with Spreadsheets*. She received her B.A. in French language and literature from the University of North Carolina at Chapel Hill and spent a postgraduate year in France on a French government scholarship.

Lesley Primmer is the cofounder and president of Women's Policy, Inc., an organization established in 1995 to carry on the informational and policy work of the Congressional Caucus for Women's Issues. One of the first actions of the 104th Congress was to defund legislative service organizations, including the Women's Caucus. Ms. Primmer has worked on public policy issues affecting women for the past 15 years. Prior to founding Women's Policy, Inc., she served as executive director of the Congressional Caucus for Women's Issues from 1989 until the caucus's office was forced to close its doors in January 1995. Ms. Primmer has also served as legislative representative for Planned Parenthood Federation of America and as legislative director to former Representative, now Senator Olympia Snowe (R–ME). Ms. Primmer came to Capitol Hill in 1981 as a WREI fellow on women and public policy. She has an M.A. in women's studies from George Washington University.

Jean Stapleton, chair of WREI's board of directors, is an actress who has starred in many plays, motion pictures, and television productions. She has long been committed to the women's movement. She was a commissioner of the National Women's Conference in Houston, Texas, and a leading proponent of the Equal Rights Amendment. Ms. Stapleton was deeply involved in the successful effort to have Val-Kil, the home of Eleanor Roosevelt, declared a national historic site.

About the Women's Research & Education Institute

Betty Dooley, *president*
Shari Miles, *executive director*
Anne J. Stone, *senior research associate*
Lory Manning, *Women in the Military Project director*
Jennifer E. Griffith, *research associate*
Shelby T. Reardon, *development assistant*
Angela M. Wilbon, *accounting associate*

THE WOMEN'S RESEARCH & EDUCATION INSTITUTE (WREI) is an independent nonprofit organization in Washington, D.C. It was established in 1977.

WREI gathers, synthesizes, and analyzes policy-relevant information on issues that concern or affect women and serves as a resource for federal and state policymakers, advocates for women, scholars, the media, and the interested public.

In addition to preparing *The American Woman*, a biennial series of which this volume is the seventh, WREI's projects include:

- Congressional Fellowships on Women and Public Policy. By means of the fellowship program, which is open to graduate students with strong academic skills and a proven commitment to equity for women, WREI enhances the research capacity of congressional offices, especially with respect to the implications of federal policy for women. Now in its eighteenth year, the fellowship program identifies and trains new leaders and has given scores of promising women hands-on experience in the federal legislative process.
- Women in the Military. This project, which WREI first undertook in 1989, monitors the status of women in the U.S. armed forces and gathers and disseminates research findings and data about military women and the issues that concern them.

Biennial conferences serve as important vehicles for sharing and disseminating information. The most recent of these involved women in the uniformed civilian services, such as firefighting and police, as well as military women.

- Hire A Vet, She's a Good Investment. This five-year-old project aims to improve civilian career opportunities for women leaving the armed forces, both by making employers aware that women veterans represent a pool of skilled and committed workers and by helping employers to find women veterans with the right skills and experience for their jobs.
- Women's Health. Women's health and policies to improve it have been concerns of WREI for many years. They were the focus of the Fifth Edition of *The American Woman 1994–95,* as well as of *Women's Health Insurance Costs and Experiences,* and other WREI publications. The objective of WREI's latest health-related project, *The Health of Mid-Life Women in the States,* is to identify the states where critical health issues related to mid-life women are most conscientiously and effectively addressed.

BOARD OF DIRECTORS

Jean Stapleton, *chair*
Martina L. Bradford
Esther Coopersmith
Mary Ann Dirzis
Evelyn Dubrow
Barbara J. Easterling
Elizabeth Ehrenfeld
Denise Ferguson
Carolyn Forrest
Beba Gaines

Margaret M. Heckler
Dorothy Height
Joann Heffernan Heisen
Matina Horner
Juanita Kreps
Alma Rangel
Lisa Rickard
Annette Strauss
Diane E. Watson

INDEX

Page numbers in italics refer to tables and figures.

ABOUT THE EDITORS

Cynthia B. Costello is an independent consultant and former research director for the Women's Research & Education Institute (WREI) where she served as senior editor for the Fifth and Sixth Editions of *The American Woman*. Dr. Costello's previous positions include director of research at the American Sociological Association, director of employment policy at Families USA Foundation, and director of the Committee on Women's Employment at the National Academy of Sciences. She is the author of *We're Worth It! Women and Collective Action in the Insurance Workplace* and a number of policy reports on employment, health care, and income security issues, including *Managed Care: Opportunities and Risks for Mid-Life and Older Women*. She holds a B.A. in sociology from the University of California and a Ph.D. in sociology from the University of Wisconsin. Dr. Costello lives in Bethesda, Maryland, with her husband, Peter Caulkins, and their son, Michael.

Shari E. Miles is executive director of WREI. Dr. Miles joined the WREI staff in 1992 as director of the Fellowship Program, a leadership and training program for graduate students interested in women's public policy issues. Earlier, Dr. Miles was, herself, a WREI public policy fellow in the office of Representative Ronald V. Dellums (D-CA). She has also directed a crisis intervention service for women and assisted homeless women in the transition to independent living. Dr. Miles is a member of the board of the National Council for Research on Women and a member of the Howard University African American Women's Institute Committee. She holds a B.A. in psychology from the University of Colorado at Boulder and a Ph.D. in personality psychology from Howard University. Her publications include *Resource Guide on African American Women* and a co-authored chapter, "Black Women in Psychology: Past and Present," in *Bringing Cultural Diversity to Feminist Psychology: Theory, Research, and Practice*. She lives in Washington, D.C., with her husband, Miguel A. Sapp.

Anne J. Stone is senior research associate at WREI, where she has authored and co-authored policy analyses on various subjects, including the federal budget, women's employment, and women in the military. She has also worked on the six previous editions of *The American Woman* and was coeditor of the Fourth and Fifth Editions. Ms. Stone lives in Washington, D.C., with her husband Herbert Stone. They have two grown daughters and two granddaughters.

MODERN DIPLOMACY

THE ART AND THE ARTISANS

EDITED BY
ELMER PLISCHKE

Elmer Plischke is professor at the University of Maryland, adjunct professor at Gettysburg College, and adjunct scholar at the American Enterprise Institute.

Library of Congress Cataloging in Publication Data

Main entry under title:
Modern diplomacy.

    (AEI studies ; 247)
    Bibliography: p.
    1. Diplomacy—Addresses, essays, lectures.
I. Plischke, Elmer, 1914–   II. Series: American
Enterprise Institute for Public Policy Research.   AEI
studies ; 247.
JX1662.M56   327'.2   79–17677
ISBN 0–8447–3350–4

AEI Studies 247

Printed in the United States of America

War, it was said, was the extension of diplomacy by other means. Modern weapons make recourse to war suicidal. It is thus not a question of giving diplomacy a chance. Diplomacy is the only chance we have.

DREW MIDDLETON

It is often said, tritely but truly, that diplomacy is our first line of defense.

HUGH S. GIBSON

The day-to-day effort to promote the national interests of the United States through our relations with other nations around the globe is the job of the Department of State. Yet it seems to me that the men and women to whom we entrust this critical task and the work they accomplish are too little known by the American people whose interests they serve.

JOHN F. KENNEDY

Coddled and pampered behind this formidable barrier of international law and custom, untouchable by the police, beyond the reach of the tax collector and the customs inspector, the diplomatic corps, one might suppose, would be the world's greatest breeding ground for adult delinquents.

CHARLES W. THAYER

CONTENTS

INTRODUCTION

Diplomatic historian Thomas A. Bailey has called diplomacy "a first line of defense," and columnist Drew Middleton has dramatically described it as "the only chance we have" in this nuclear age.[1] Some have claimed that diplomacy is the principal alternative to war; others have suggested that it is the only productive means by which nations can effectively work together to maintain peace and promote both their individual interests and their mutual welfare. If diplomacy has any of these qualities, it must be vital to the functioning of each state within the society of nations and to the vitality and stability of the international community as a whole.

Because the goals and actions of states are inherently competitive, the conduct of their relations with one another may be critical as well as challenging and exciting. Each government has a particularized view of its own purposes and desires, so the means by which it implements its foreign policy are of widespread and compelling concern. The very nature of the international community and its manner of functioning require diplomatic interaction to be a continuum; the essentials remain constant, though the style must be flexible to accommodate changing needs. And because communication, consultation, and negotiation are essential to the interdependence of the states of the world, diplomacy is indispensable to both the interrelations of governments and the performance of the global system.

Diplomacy may be regarded as a science or an art, as a craft, a practice, an institution, or a process. A number of serious analysts,

---

[1] Thomas A. Bailey, *The Art of Diplomacy: The American Experience* (New York: Appleton-Century-Crofts, 1968), p. 148 (also see p. 71); Drew Middleton, "Notes on Diplomats and Diplomacy," *New York Times Magazine* (October 30, 1955), p. 60.

particularly planners and decision makers at the vortex of the foreign relations mechanism, are presently focusing attention on the scientific aspects of diplomacy. This is demonstrated in part by the movement from the so-called intuitive to the scientifically devised decision, by an emphasis on the systematic aspects of administrative or bureaucratic management, and by the modification of diplomatic practice to take advantage of relevant technological developments such as improved methods of transportation and communications and automated facilities for information coordination, documents management, and international capability assessment.

Nevertheless, such scientific aspects have by no means supplanted the art of diplomacy, which continues to be essential in the field— that is, at the actual point of personal contact, consultation, persuasion, and negotiation. "The business of diplomacy," according to Sir Duff Cooper, "is the carrying out of policy," whereas "the art of diplomacy is the manner of carrying it out";[2] the latter depends largely on the capacity of the practitioner. Headquarters operations can scarcely replace or obviate diplomat-to-diplomat relations, and this reality imbues the diplomatic emissary and the diplomatic profession with a unique mandate in world affairs.

Like other social processes, diplomacy is ever changing. Modifications may be gradual or sudden, enduring or transitory, substantial or tangential, explicit or subtle. Diplomacy expands to encompass the growing complex of individual national and corporate concerns. Technological and scientific achievements create new problems that must be resolved, and improving methods of international transportation and communication reorient public attitudes and modes of interaction. Changing national and international status, instruments and processes utilized to institutionalize interrelations, and national desires, together with inflated expectations, impel modification of practices and procedures to accommodate them. These and other developments—in the late twentieth century as in earlier generations—augment the requirements, enrich the possibilities, and orchestrate the contemporary evolution of diplomacy.

This anthology of essays—the products of statesmen, diplomats, and academicians—provides a spectrum of descriptive and analytical commentary on selected aspects of modern diplomacy and its practitioners.[3] Although the focus is universal, some selections relate spe-

---

[2] "The World Still Needs the Diplomat," *New York Times Magazine* (July 25, 1948), p. 5.

[3] Brief descriptive commentary on the literary treatment of various aspects of diplomacy and diplomats is provided in the essay prefacing the bibliography at the end of this volume.

cifically to U. S. practice, and most of the contributions are written by Americans. Those who prefer a castigation of U. S. diplomacy and its emissaries or an apologia for the weaknesses of the profession and its members are likely to be disappointed.

The perspective is broad, viewing diplomacy as a fundamental process of interstate contact and action in the international environment. The treatment differs, therefore, from the more common study of policy relations and traditional diplomatic history. It also differs from the perception of diplomacy as primarily intergovernmental concern with the political, economic, and social relationships of nations, such as power politics and geopolitical equilibrium, transnational rule making and the developing international code of legal precepts, international integration and institutionalization, comparative policy analysis, and the like.

The essays selected are concerned, rather, with the concept, nature, scope, and development of diplomacy. They also deal with the changing status of diplomacy in the contemporary world and with a number of identifiable dimensions of current diplomatic practice such as democratic, open, personal (both summit and ministerial), multilateral, parliamentary, and crisis diplomacy. The selections on diplomats are devoted to their general roles and titles, to an analysis of their essential qualities, and to the juxtaposition of professionals/nonprofessionals and careerists/noncareerists. These selections also deal with certain aspects of traditional diplomatic functions, such as day-to-day activities, policy formulation, representation, reporting, and negotiation. A few essays focus upon other subjects—the issue of precedence and protocol, the normalization of diplomatic relations, and a historical profile of U.S. diplomats.

Despite the claim of Ambassador Hugh S. Gibson that "the American people have long looked on diplomacy as a mysterious activity on another plane,"[4] it is an uncontested axiom that Americans should be informed concerning the foreign relations and diplomatic process of their country, perhaps more than ever in this age of national fragmentation, functional pluralism, international interdependence, and nuclear weaponry. This volume of generally short and sometimes comparative essays recounts some of the most salient aspects of the diplomatic art and its artisans. It is intended to stimulate understanding and to assist in enlightening those interested in the past development, current practices and problems, and future prospects of what Dean Acheson has dignified as the "corpus diplomaticum."

---

[4] *The Road to Foreign Policy* (Garden City, N.Y.: Doubleday, Doran, 1944), p. 33.

1

Nature and Development
of Diplomacy

*Modern diplomacy is . . . a continuing and exhausting study of whole
societies and of their inter-relationships. It requires a knowledge of
the history and culture, of the political, economic, technological
and social forces at work in the society in which the diplomat resides.
It requires a careful evaluation of the direction in which these
forces will move within that society and of the effect they will have
on relations between that society and other societies, in particular
his own.*

Foy D. Kohler, "History and the Diplomat"

*The art of diplomacy consists of making the policy of one government
understood and if possible accepted by other governments. Policy
is thus the substance of foreign relations; diplomacy is the process
by which policy is carried out.*

James Rives Childs, *American Foreign Service*

The essays selected for this chapter are important background for the
study and understanding of diplomacy and its practitioners. The first,
"Diplomacy—Contemporary Practice," by the diplomat and scholar
Hermann F. Eilts, offers a general overview of diplomacy, touching
on its definitions, purposes, participants, mechanisms, and manifestations in the international milieu. Those with a taste for history will
find particularly useful the section of Eilts's analysis entitled "Evolution of Diplomacy"; others will find the article a balanced survey of
the diplomatic process. "Diplomacy—Political Technique for Implementing Foreign Policy," by Charles O. Lerche, Jr., and Abdul A.
Said, is a concise functional synthesis of the subject as it relates to

1

the broader field of foreign policy in international relations. It describes distinct techniques—coercion, persuasion, adjustment, and agreement—and it suggests four fundamental conditions for the successful functioning of the diplomatic process. In "Diplomacy/Diplomat—Derivation of the Concepts," Sir Ernest M. Satow presents brief interpretations of and etymological commentary on diplomats and diplomacy. In a related vein, Elmer Plischke's "Diplomacy—Search for Its Meaning," examines in greater depth the nature of diplomacy and its relation to other fields of human knowledge and to state practice. It also reviews the contemporary literature on diplomatic practice, drawing a clear-cut distinction between diplomacy and foreign policy.

Charles W. Thayer's "Titles of Diplomats" is an introduction to the confusion of ranks and titles of ambassadors, ministers, and members of their missions in contemporary diplomatic practice. A brief survey of U. S. use of ranks and titles is also included in Chapter 5. The final essay in this chapter, "Normalization of Diplomatic Relations," by Warren Christopher, emphasizes how well normal diplomatic relations serve American interests by maintaining open channels of communication.

Some of the subjects touched on or discussed briefly in these pages are elaborated later in this volume. Readers interested specifically in the history of diplomacy may wish to refer to "Transition from the Old to the New Diplomacy," by Sir Harold Nicolson (Chapter 2), and to "Profile of United States Diplomats: Bicentennial Review and Future Projection," by Elmer Plischke (Chapter 5).

Selections in Chapter 2 focus on significant changes that characterize contemporary diplomacy. Chapters 3 and 4 deal with various manifestations of modern diplomacy. Chapters 5 and 6 are concerned with the artisans—assessing the qualities that characterize the able diplomat, discussing the career Foreign Service, and commenting on the issue of professionalism. The final chapter examines some of the basic functions of diplomats in contemporary world affairs.

Diplomacy—Contemporary Practice

Hermann F. Eilts

Every profession suffers its problems of distorted image. My own—diplomacy—is no exception. Of the criticisms sometimes leveled against it, one stands out as most in need of correction. It was first expressed three hundred and fifty years ago in a descriptive aphorism which . . . I give you in its original Latin form:

Legatus est vir bonus peregre missus ad mentiendum Respublicae causa.

Latinists among you will readily recognize the calumny. Should your Latin be a bit rusty this morning, rendered into English the phrase reads, "An ambassador is an honest man sent to lie abroad for the good of his country."

This cutting aphorism, whose thrust has persisted—alas—ever since, originated with one Sir Henry Wotton, a distinguished British diplomat in the service of King James I. In 1604, while en route to Venice to assume an assignment as English Ambassador, he transitted Augsburg, where he was the house guest of a friend. When leaving, Wotton, in response to his host's request that he sign the guest book, jestingly inscribed these lines, and promptly forgot all about them. Eight years later, one Jasper Scioppius—a well-known muckraker of his time—managed somehow to unearth and publish them. Their publication aroused great furor throughout Europe and was seized upon by continental enemies of King James to disparage that monarch's diplomacy. For Sir Henry they earned the severe disapproval of his sovereign. In vain did he point out that they were intended to be no more than a "merriment" and that the verb "lie" had a dual

Source: Lecture, U.S. Army War College, Carlisle Barracks, Pennsylvania, August 31, 1973.

meaning. King James would not be assuaged. He failed to see the joke. On the contrary, the incident had caused him considerable embarrassment throughout Europe. Apart from this, he icily pointed out, there was no such double meaning in his errant ambassador's original Latin inscription.

For a time, the hapless Wotton was in royal disfavor. But being one of the more skillful contemporary English diplomats, his sovereign soon again had need for his skills and reinstated him to a position of trust. Shortly before the end of his career, a much wiser Wotton also redeemed himself to his profession. When asked by a young diplomatist on how one's adversaries might best be puzzled, his reply was succinct: "Tell the truth." Wotton's counsel was—and remains—pithy on two counts. First, it underscores the importance of credibility to the process of diplomacy and to the diplomat engaged in it. Second, he was absolutely right, as I can attest from personal experience, in his judgment that the truth is often greeted by foe and friend alike with utter disbelief, incredulity and, on occasion, even with profound suspicion.

My purpose this morning, in the brief time allotted to me, is to give you what might be called a brief anatomy of diplomacy—its origins, evolution, practice in the United States and at least some of its operational dynamics. In doing so, I ask you to envisage diplomacy as an institution rather than focussing on any of its day-to-day substantive manifestations.

By way of introduction a definition of diplomacy seems desirable. According to *Funk & Wagnalls New Standard Dictionary of the English Language*, diplomacy is "the art or science that has to do with the transaction of business between sovereign states by means of accredited agents and according to international law; the method or procedure employed in the management of international negotiations." While the thrust of that definition is adequate, it is considerably too restrictive. It suggests, first of all, that only accredited agents conduct diplomacy. Such is only partially the case today. Moreover, the language of the definition suggests, perhaps inadvertently, that diplomacy is limited to the conduct of business between two states or that it needs be bilateral. In point of fact, while bilateral diplomacy remains prominent in our day and age, multilateral diplomacy, i.e., the conduct of business among a group of states, is today also widespread. Starting with the Congress of Westphalia in 1648, multilateral diplomacy has steadily developed in many forms and forums. The United Nations and the numerous regional coalitions which exist today are cases in point. Today, indeed, some states, conscious of the high cost of maintaining resident missions abroad, are considering conducting all their diplomacy through established multilateral channels.

Still another definition offered by an eminent British writer on the subject, the late Sir Ernest Satow, views diplomacy " . . . as the application of intelligence, tact and sound judgment to the conduct of official relations between governments of independent states." Some wags have suggested this may be more of a pious hope than a proven fact. In a later edition of Satow's work, "sound judgment" was inexplicably removed from the definition. The need for that mental commodity remains, in my view, as strong as ever.

Diplomacy is conducted in a number of modes. These range from exchange of views, negotiation, arbitration, conciliation, mediation to adjudication. Of this spectrum, the first two, exchange of views and negotiation, unquestionably loom largest; at least ninety percent, if not more, of all diplomatic transactions embrace one or both of these modalities. The reason for this is obvious. They allow the participating parties maximum control of their efforts. In all other diplomatic modes, a third party is introduced and tends to restrict—at least to some extent—the disputants' maneuverability.

The military concept of "roles and missions" is not common to diplomatic practice. In the United States, to be sure, each ambassador, before departing to assume his post, is charged by the President or the Secretary of State, acting for him, to undertake certain tasks in connection with relations between the United States and the country to which he is accredited. Occasionally, depending upon the nature of outstanding problems, such a charge may be specific; more often it is general in nature. This is often referred to as the "ambassador's mission." In a broader sense, however, the mission of a diplomat as derived from his functions might be set forth as follows:

> First, to attempt to identify a mutuality of interest between states in order to encourage joint or common policies;
>
> Second, failing the above, to develop a parallelism of interest between states in order to encourage complementary policies or at least nonconflicting policies;
>
> And, third, lacking a mutuality or a parallelism of interest, to manage disagreement between states so that it remains short of armed conflict.

Evolution of Diplomacy

The origins of diplomacy go back far into antiquity. Chinese, Indian, Egyptian and Mesopotamian records predating our Christian era record the sending and receiving of envoys between political entities in order to make arrangements for peace or attempt to resolve disputes. These represented practices followed between states with a high level of civilization. Professor Ragnar Numelin of Copenhagen, in a seminal book entitled *The Beginnings of Diplomacy*, carries the concept beyond such civilized groupings and traces the origins of diplomacy to the sociological roots of intertribal relationships. I am reminded that among the primitive and constantly feuding tribes of south Arabia, who are among the few carry-overs of traditional tribal society, a relatively well-ordered system of customary law still exists on the handling of envoys from opposing tribal groups. Admittedly, it may not always be followed, but failure to do so invokes general social disapproval and even ostracism for the culprit or group.

Modern diplomacy has evolved relatively rapidly in the last seven centuries. Several milestones mark its progress. The first worthy of note took place in Europe in the twelfth and thirteenth centuries. Already during this period, officials were designated by princes and other leaders to conduct special missions in their behalf at the courts of peers. These officials were known variously as nuncios (a term used today only for Vatican diplomats, but one which enjoyed much wider usage in medieval times), legates, procurators, syndics and ambassadors. There were nuancial differences among these groups of officials, but essentially they had two duties: The first was a relatively simple one. They were messengers charged with conveying factually and accurately, and as rapidly as circumstances allowed, the views of the sending prince and, conversely, bringing back a response. The second, known as *plena potestas*, or full powers, was of far greater significance. It envisaged a projection of the prince in the person of his emissary in order to enable the latter to negotiate and, indeed, to conclude agreements in his master's behalf. Full powers, incidentally, which exist in diplomatic practice to this day, have altered over the years. Initially, in an age when communications were slow and unreliable, they constituted authority for both the negotiation and conclusion of agreements. Today, in an era of rapid communications, full powers are exchanged after the emissary has negotiated the agreement and obtained his government's approval for an initialled text. Such full powers are now limited to authorizing signature in behalf of each of the contracting governments.

A second milestone in the development of diplomacy took place in the Italian city-states of the fourteenth and fifteenth centuries. Beginning with Mantua, one after another of these states began to send resident missions abroad, to courts outside and inside the Italian city-state system. Their example was followed by the European sovereigns. The purpose of such resident missions was clear. They enabled continuous monitoring of events in a rival state and, where necessary, insured a continuing dialogue between states.

A third milestone was the Congress of Vienna, held in 1815 after the defeat of Napoleon Bonaparte. Apart from establishing a concert of Europe and redistributing territories seized by Napoleon, the statesmen assembled at Vienna recognized the need to regularize diplomatic relations among them. Accordingly, a codicil was signed by the plenipotentiaries assembled there setting forth a general outline of proper diplomatic practice and rank-ordering for the first time the heretofore diffuse categories of diplomatic agents. This codified system has lasted, with only minor modification, into our own century.

Following World War II, largely as a result of the large number of new states that achieved independence, another look had to be taken by the international community at the subject of diplomacy. As early as 1958 the International Law Commission of the United Nations drew up a draft diplomatic convention setting forth optimum duties and responsibilities for diplomatic agents. Three years later, with some modifications, this instrument became the Vienna Convention on Diplomatic Relations.* (In 1963 a parallel instrument on Consular Relations was concluded at Vienna.) The United States signed the Vienna Convention, but did not ratify it until last year [1972]. It is now part of the law of the land.

United States Diplomacy

Let us now turn from the general subject of diplomacy to a more specific consideration of American diplomacy. The United States has been an actor in the international arena for about two hundred years. The Department of State, established in 1789, was the first executive department of the Federal Government. It was responsible for the dispatch of American diplomatic agents to a number of countries. Even then, however, the practice of sending such emissaries was not new to Americans. Fifteen years earlier the Committee of Public Safety, which had been established at the outbreak of the War of Independence, had already sent some representatives abroad. The most notable of these, of course, was Benjamin Franklin.

Throughout much of the nineteenth century United States business with foreign governments focussed on commercial matters and

---

* EDITOR'S NOTE: For the text of this convention, see Appendix A.

7

was handled by consuls. These were in many instances merchant consuls, whose official work was subsumed in their business activities. In the larger states of Europe and some South American countries, small diplomatic legations were maintained to handle political matters. For many decades, incidentally, ministers plenipotentiary, who headed legations, were the principal American diplomatic officers. Not until 1893 was the first American ambassador sent abroad. Initially, such ambassadors were sent only to larger countries, while ministers continued to represent the United States in smaller ones. Following World War II, however, more and more legations were elevated to embassy status as a gesture of goodwill toward foreign states regardless of their size and importance. The presence of embassies became national prestige symbols. Today there are no longer any American legations abroad. I well recall, however, that my initial foreign service some twenty-five years ago in Tehran and later in Jidda was in legations. In both instances, these offices were elevated to embassy status as part of a general upgrading of our diplomatic missions abroad.

Principles of Diplomacy

In its two-century-old history United States diplomacy has developed a series of fundamental principles. Some preceded World War II, others grew out of the Nation's postwar experience. Distilled into their essence, I would identify five such pre-World War II principles which persist to this day. (At any earlier point in American history, others—e.g., the Monroe Doctrine—might have been adduced, but these have been superseded or amalgamated into broader ones.) These may be listed as follows:

1. The equality of states and the rule of law in international relations.
2. The peaceful settlement of international disputes.
3. Noninterference in the internal affairs of other states.
4. Freedom of access to international markets.
5. Democratic style.

A few words should be said about these principles. United States foreign policy has sometimes been described as a fusion of the principles of Theodore Roosevelt and St. Francis of Assisi. Consciously and unconsciously, it has sought to blend pragmatism and national assertiveness with a strong sense of morality. All of these qualities, as well as many others, are characteristic of American society.

* * *

Instruments of Diplomacy

The instruments of diplomacy need next be assayed. These fall into two general categories: accredited and nonaccredited. The first comprises resident diplomatic and consular missions abroad, ambassadors-at-large, special presidential emissaries or missions, occasional cabinet officers and the chief of state or head of government himself. Of cabinet officers, the Secretary of State is the principal such instrument, but other cabinet officers are occasionally also involved. The second category consists of private American citizens without formal diplomatic status.

From the beginning of its history the United States has employed special missions to conduct aspects of its diplomacy. These were often sent to countries where it had no resident diplomatic mission. Even after such resident missions were established, special missions continued to be utilized and are to this day. In general terms, their purpose is to handle specially designated matters in which a degree of expertise is required that is not normally assumed to be present in the resident mission. Alternatively, they are intended to emphasize the importance the President attaches to a particular problem and its resolution. Such special missions may continue for some time.

The Secretary of State is, of course, a frequent traveler. In the course of such travels, he conducts foreign policy. His participation elevates the level of discussion. Other cabinet officers, though they may not normally be involved in the foreign policy process, are sometimes involved. Examples are the Secretary of Defense on problems involving international military relationships, the Secretary of Interior on matters involving desalination, the Secretary of the Treasury in matters involving international currency parity and balance of payments problems.

The senior-most diplomatic instrument that the Nation can engage is, of course, the chief of state. In the past twenty years, summit diplomacy has become increasingly common. The President, on visits abroad, or other chiefs of state or heads of government visiting him in Washington conduct diplomacy. A perusal of the joint communiques following President Nixon's visits to Moscow and Peking and Soviet leader Brezhnev's visit to the United States illustrates the breadth of presidential involvement. Accustomed as we are to this phenomenon, it is a trifle amusing to look back only fifty years when President Wilson planned to leave the country in order to attend the Paris Peace Conference. Grave constitutional reservations were raised by some American legal authorities as to whether a serving President had the authority to leave the country.

In the somewhat shadowy area of nonaccredited agents, it has not been uncommon for American Presidents or Secretaries of State to ask one or another private individual well known to him and who happens to be traveling abroad to take certain soundings. This is perfectly natural. It may provide the President or Secretary of State with an additional, fresh source of information or impressions and supplement the formal reporting of resident diplomatic missions. At the same time such private agents can sometimes create embarrassment not only for the resident ambassador in that country, but also for the national conduct of American foreign policy. Most such private agents work fairly closely and well with American Ambassadors. A few tend deliberately to ignore American representatives abroad and freewheel. The potential danger in such freewheeling is obvious. They risk creating wrong and unhelpful impressions in the minds of foreign governments as to United States purposes and intentions. Still, a nonaccredited private individual, if carefully chosen and briefed, can be a useful means of informally conveying views.

While I am on the subject of the instruments of diplomacy, a word should be said on the organization of a United States diplomatic mission abroad. The embassy, the core of the official American representation, consists of the chief of mission, the deputy chief of mission and five sections of varying size depending upon the country involved: political, economic, administrative, consular and public affairs. There may be additional attached sections, such as the Defense Attache's office, Treasury, Labor, Agricultural, FAA [Federal Aviation Administration] and other attaches. Such sections are organic to the mission in this sense. While they are separate agencies reporting to their home offices and assigned by the latter, they come into the country as part of the "suite" of the ambassador and are entitled to the privileges and immunities accorded to him and his staff. In a somewhat different category are the associated missions, such as Military Assistance Advisory Groups, Agency for International Development, Peace Corps, etc. Such associated agencies, while subject to the ambassador's general supervision and control in accordance with presidential directives, come into a foreign country by virtue of specific agreements arrived at between the United States and that country as to their functions, privileges and immunities. Also worth noting is the fact that some non-Department of State officials, such as Agricultural and Treasury attaches, are often regionally accredited.

When visiting a country other than that where they are normally resident, they are subject to the American Ambassador in that country.

The principal USIA [United States Information Agency, now the International Communication Agency (ICA)] officer has a somewhat unique status. As the ambassador's Public Affairs Officer, he is an integral member of the ambassador's staff. As director of the USIS mission he heads a separate but associated mission.

For . . . military officers who may one day be involved in a Defense Attache's office or a MAAG, one additional point deserves mentioning. Like the ambassador, the Defense Attache and the head of the MAAG, together with his three service chiefs, are frequently subject to a diplomatic process known as *agréation*. This means that their names, biographies, career history and other personalia are first submitted to the host government for approval. Only after such is received is the assignment made. In recent years, the United States has by reciprocal arrangement dropped this advance approval procedure in the case of defense attaches and MAAG chiefs. In a good many countries, however, some formal or informal *agrément*, as the foreign government's approval is called, continues.

Unique in American diplomatic practice is the concept of the country team. Chaired by the ambassador and/or his deputy, it consists of his principal staff officers and the heads of the various attached missions. Pursuant to presidential directive, the ambassador is charged with supervisory authority over the totality of the United States effort in a particular country. The country team does not involve collective responsibility since the ambassador cannot divest himself of this specific presidential charge. It is nevertheless an attempt at collective counsel and coordination to avoid duplication of effort and to make maximum use of personnel and other resources. Much more deserves to be said about the country team, but time precludes me from doing so.*

Arsenal of Diplomacy

Closely related to instruments is the arsenal of diplomacy. In military terms, what is the weaponry or firepower that can be brought to bear in the conduct of diplomacy? It is a truism that all diplomacy is conducted in the shadow of power—military, economic, technological, psychological. It must take into account parity or disparities of power

* EDITOR'S NOTE: Additional comments on the country team may be found in Ellis O. Briggs's essay, "A Day with the Ambassador," in Chapter 7.

and it must somehow solve the problem of how national power, in its diffuse and often sprawling manifestations, can be focussed on a particular problem in order to achieve United States purposes.

As might be expected, the diplomatic arsenal embraces both formal and informal means. Of these, *communications* is the most frequently used. Four general forms of communication may be noted: one, the trial balloon or public statement. The first, usually in the form of an unattributed semiofficial public statement, is intended to take soundings on reactions on a contemplated course of action. The second, the official public statement, issued through the media as general guidance, is intended to signal to foreign governments the parameters of United States policy on a particular problem.

A second form of communication, and perhaps the most common in the diplomatic reservoir is *oral exchanges*. These are conducted between members of a resident diplomatic mission or special mission and appropriate foreign office officials. One step higher are written exchanges beween governments. These range from *aide memoires* through third and first person notes to presidential letters. The form used depends upon the nature of the subject and the degree of interest in it on the part of the leaders of the states involved.

A brief explanatory word might be useful about the presidential letter. When judiciously and sparingly used the presidential letter is an extremely useful diplomatic weapon. It signifies the interest of the highest level of the Government of the United States in a problem. By the same token, its high status can be a source of weakness. If used too frequently its value tends to be depreciated. Well over a decade ago a former American Ambassador, now out of government, observed in a message to Washington that "Presidential letters around here are getting to be like Confederate currency." What he meant was that they were being used so frequently in the country to which he was accredited that they were being taken for granted.

Also worth noting is that presidential letters, by their very nature, engage the personal prestige of the chief of state. There is no further recourse to a higher authority. If disagreement persists, one or another of the chiefs of state must give way or the problem remains unresolved. In such instances, they sometimes limit the ability of American diplomats abroad to resolve problems. Occasionally, too, drafted as they are by officials who may not have a day-to-day knowledge of a particular country and its chief of state, they are insensitively drafted and raise new problems rather than resolve old ones. If drafters are mindful of all these potential problems, nevertheless, the presidential letter has its distinct value.

Still another communications device is the *treaty or executive agreement*. Treaties require ratification following receipt of the advice and consent of the Senate. Executive agreements, usually made in accordance with an already approved treaty or United States legislation, need no such approval on the grounds that authority for pertinent executive action already exists. Treaties rank alongside domestic legislation as part of the law of the land; executive agreements, on the other hand, are primarily statements of executive policy.

Another weapon of United States diplomacy is *foreign aid*. This takes the form of what is now called security assistance (formerly military assistance), development assistance, technical assistance and humanitarian assistance. They are self-descriptive and no elaboration seems necessary.

The *security commitment* is yet another element in the arsenal of diplomacy. This may take the form of treaties, such as the NATO and SEATO treaties or of executive agreements consistent with domestic legislation. Examples of the latter are the three bilateral agreements of cooperation concluded with Turkey, Iran and Pakistan in 1959 in the context of the earlier Joint Congressional Middle East Resolution. A more limited security commitment may also take the form of a unilateral presidential statement indicating United States interest in the political independence and territorial integrity of a country. Such unilateral statements, usually of a general nature, are consistent with the United Nations Charter.

An additional weapon in the arsenal of diplomacy are such *punitive measures* as sanctions, embargoes, boycotts, credit restrictions, etc. More symbolic are such actions as suspending diplomatic relations, closing consulates (as in Rhodesia), withdrawal of the ambassador for a period of time, etc. Some disagreement exists as to the value of such punitive measures. Certain it is that they signal disapproval to an offending government. Yet against this must be weighed the consequences of severing communications at the very time dialogue between two states is most needed.

Still another punitive measure, though used with great reluctance, is the use of military force. I will say more about the latter when I speak of the dimensions of diplomacy.

Some Dimensions of Diplomacy

A final word needs be said about some contemporary dimensions of diplomacy. There has been much talk of late about a so-called "new" diplomacy. The term really means two separate things. In the substantive field, when there is a major change in United States foreign policy, such as the Nixon Doctrine or the President's policy of détente with the Soviet Union and China, the innovation may appropriately be called "new" diplomacy in the sense that policy has altered from what it was previously.

Institutionally, however, the term "new" diplomacy means something quite different. It describes the enormous increase during the past quarter of a century in the scope of diplomacy. The point is graphically illustrated by a partial listing of some relatively new dimensions of United States diplomacy in peace and war. Each such dimension, incidentally, has certain characteristics unique to it. Specific United States diplomatic actions may sometimes straddle two or more of these dimensions.

In the bipolar world in which we have so long lived, *East-West diplomacy* probably deserves pride of place. It represents the adversary relationship between the Soviets and the People's Republic of China on the one hand and the United States. In the past, it has often been characterized by a considerable bluntness of language. The parties often seem to be speaking at rather than to each other. Soviet and PRC notes are heavily laced with Marxist ideology, with each side accusing the other of being responsible for generating crises. The efforts of resident diplomatic missions have been directed largely at routine matters and at probing, carefully and cautiously, whether there might be areas where more substantive agreement is possible. Once such an area appears to have been identified, it is often handled by a special mission. Negotiations tend to be protracted with maximum jousting for advantage. Both the SALT agreement and the Nuclear Nonproliferation Treaty are cases in point. To be sure, the development of a United States–Soviet and United States–PRC détente has softened the previous harshness of diplomatic communications between these parties. Détente has not, however, entirely removed it. Some thaw has indeed taken place, but communications still tend to reflect a high degree of mutual distrust. Flash tensions still characterize United States–Soviet relationships.

Another characteristic of East-West diplomacy has been its heavy emphasis on information gathering, a reflection of prevailing distrust between the parties. You will recall that a year or so ago the United Kingdom expelled some one hundred thirty so-called Soviet diplomats on charges of espionage. The Soviets cried foul! The British, they implied, were not playing the game! Despite their protest, however, they recognized their vulnerability. They had indeed overdone it, and their retaliatory actions were relatively moderate. The story is told that Sir Alec Douglas-Home, the British Foreign Secretary, shortly afterwards commiserated with Mr. Gromyko, the Soviet Foreign Minister, that it must be very difficult to conduct foreign policy when so much of it had to be done by secret KGB agents. Mr. Gromyko, a normally impassive gentleman, allegedly showed his annoyance.

A second new dimension is *United Nations diplomacy*. Utilizing legislative procedures, this has often been called a parliamentary type of diplomacy. It seeks to develop an international consensus on a particular problem, to the extent such a thing exists, in the form of a resolution. The limitations of this type of diplomacy are obvious. In the Security Council, the veto power of the five permanent members prevents the passage of any resolution unacceptable to one or another of them. In the General Assembly, while passage of a resolution is not subject to the veto, a resolution is binding only on those members who have accepted it, not on others. Notwithstanding these patent limitations, the United Nations has sometimes served as a useful device to defuse explosive tensions. It has been less successful in solving international problems. When operating in the economic, technical and/or humanitarian sphere, moreover, the United Nations has been a useful multilateral forum which some of the smaller states find especially congenial.

Coalition diplomacy represents a third new dimension. I use the term not simply to apply to the United States multilateral alliance structure, but also to its bilateral alliances with Japan, Korea and others. Two aspects of coalition diplomacy deserve to be highlighted. Initially at least, it had a heavy military emphasis. This was soon found to be inadequate, and a political dimension was added. The latter, redundant in some respects to bilateral relationships already existing between members, stressed the importance of "consultation" among coalition members. While few would deny the importance of consultation, it is not always an easy thing to achieve. In effect, the consultative process of coalition diplomacy has established a series of "special relationships" which have created the expectation that the United States will not act until and unless it has discussed its proposed actions with alliance partners. The latter have made crystal clear that simply being informed of United States actions, either shortly before they take place or afterwards, is insufficient. They want to be consulted sufficiently in advance to have the opportunity to comment and thus, hopefully, influence proposed American actions. Given the diversity of interests among alliance partners, consultation is viewed by some as running the risk of tying the Nation's hands in policy initiatives. The present administration, as you know, has sometimes been charged by critics at home and abroad with inadequate consultation with friends and partners. In my judgment, this charge needs [to] be weighed against the likelihood that some of the President's initiatives might have been hamstrung or might have been leaked if the self-admitted obligation of consultation had too literally been followed. We have yet to find the happy medium between adequate recourse to the consultative process and freedom to take innovative foreign policy measures in no way designed to harm the interests of American treaty partners.

Since World War II *economic diplomacy* has been a prominent new dimension in the art. It has assumed many forms: encouraging foreign trade and investment, establishing monetary stability as was envisaged in the Bretton-Woods and subsequent Smithsonian agreements, stockpiling of raw materials, regulating the export of strategic material to potentially hostile states, and commodity agreements. And, of course, correcting the chronic deficit of recent years in the United States balance of trade, now seemingly about to be rectified, has been a major subject of economic diplomacy. Although the United States has entered some commodity agreements, largely at the strong insistence of commodity producers, it has generally been reluctant to do so. As a consumer nation, it has feared that such commodity agreements hamper free market operations.

Closely related to the above, but possessed of an identity of its own, is *development diplomacy*. The military, or at least the United States Air Force, calls this "nation-building," i.e., assisting in the economic, political and social development of the less developed nations of the world. One is not dealing here with large international trade or investment problems, but with the difficult task of finding ways and means of encouraging a nation to pull itself up by the bootstraps. Both economic and security considerations are usually pertinent and the effort needs be carried on in what is often a still unstable political environment. Material assistance, but more importantly, sound technological and military advice, are essential ingredients of this effort. It frequently tends to be a particularly sensitive one. The independence of the states involved is usually of relatively recent vintage. Not unnaturally, therefore, a high suspicion quotient exists on the part of local officials about real or imagined foreign interference. The comments of Professor Howard Wriggins of Columbia, which most of you have read, on the problem of involvement are especially germane in this category.

Irrespective of criticism from many quarters, *coercive diplomacy* is another dimension of the art. In a sense, there is nothing new about this. Gunboat diplomacy, as it was called at the turn of this century, was common, but has now been generally eschewed. At the same time, the concept has assumed some new forms and exists today in both macro and micro configurations.

In a macro sense, it may be said to involve the occasional confrontations between the United States, on the one hand, and the Soviet Union and/or Communist states on the other. President Kennedy's warning to the Soviets in 1962 that the United States would take military action unless the Communist side stopped what it was doing in Laos is a case in point. They heeded the warning, desisted and the Geneva Conference on Laos ensued. While the Geneva agreements on Laos proved to be demonstrably ineffective, the President's firm action on that occasion caused the Soviets to desist. The Cuban missile confrontation between the Soviet Union and the United States, also in 1962, is another example. The President's demand in that instance was greater. He not only asked that the Soviets desist, but that they roll back some of the things they had done, including disestablishing the Soviet missile bases in Cuba. Failure to do so, the President warned, would prompt the United States to act militarily to achieve its purpose and a naval "quarantine" was established to prevent Soviet vessels bearing military cargoes from proceeding to Cuba. Again, the Soviets disengaged from the confrontation posture that had developed. More recently, the President's action in December, 1972, in mining Haiphong harbor and bombing Hanoi was an example of coercive diplomacy.

Coercive diplomacy in a micro sense is illustrated by the landing of United States forces in Lebanon in 1958 and in the Dominican Republic in 1962. In each of these cases, American troops were deployed in an attempt to assist the government of a particular country in preventing interference by other countries. While these interventions have been much criticized, there is no gainsaying the fact that they were undertaken at the request of the threatened government and ultimately permitted the democratic processes in that country to determine what governmental changes should be made. In the case of both Lebanon and the Dominican Republic, governments were elected in the wake of United States intervention which were not necessarily those most favored by the United States.

In recent years much emphasis has been placed on *public diplomacy*. In essence this represents an effort to develop a people-to-people relationship and to make United States foreign policies better understood abroad. Though largely in the hands of USIA, this effort requires the assistance of all elements of a diplomatic mission.

A final new dimension worth noting is *ecological and techno-*

logical diplomacy. There is a growing transnational concern about the need to prevent further damage to our environment. At the same time, a growing international realization exists that there is a need for regulation of various outstanding technocratic problems. Overlooked in the welter of political, economic and military developments that "make the headlines" are the large number of purely technocratic meetings, sponsored by the United Nations or individual countries, that take place constantly. In the coming month of September, some forty-six such international meetings are scheduled to take place all over the world. They will deal with everything from the preservation of polar bears, wildlife, the regulation of maritime satellites and dozens of other subjects. Though these meetings are usually unheralded, it is only fair to say that their overall contribution to the mosaic of international understanding is commendable.

In wartime, two basic dimensions of diplomacy are identifiable: supportive and settlement. *Supportive diplomacy* is the effort that the United States makes to elicit the cooperation of those states that are not directly involved in the conflict in which we find ourselves engaged. Its purpose is to urge such states to provide active or passive assistance. *Settlement diplomacy*, as its name implies, is the wartime effort made with those countries involved in the conflict, directly or indirectly, to seek to negotiate a ceasefire and peace.

You will appreciate, I am sure, that the above dimensional listing is at best skimming over the surface.* Volumes could be—and in some cases have been—written on each of these diplomatic dimensions. You will also realize that one thing comes out rather clearly from this listing. With the scope of diplomacy so widened, it calls for an exceptionally wide spectrum of technical skills. The professional diplomat, try as he may, is hardly qualified to negotiate meaningfully in all of these spheres. The Department of State, like other foreign offices, has in recent years enlarged itself in an effort to cope with the various new dimensions of its work. Increasingly, however, some special expertise is required. This in turn means the co-opting of official assistance, expertise from all government departments, and occasionally from private industry, to assist in the task. The role of the Department of State and the professional diplomat, in many of these dimensions, is limited to that of coordinator of the United States effort and insuring that it is consistent with the totality of American foreign policy.

* * *

---

* EDITOR's NOTE: See Chapter 4 for additional comments on the dimensions of diplomacy.

Diplomacy—Political Technique for Implementing Foreign Policy

CHARLES O. LERCHE, JR., AND ABDUL A. SAID

In one sense all foreign policy techniques are, or ought to be, political. No matter what a state may do in the execution of its purposes, its orientation and goal are always political in that it seeks the maximization of its value system. Yet in practice the word "political" is applied more narrowly to those methods that involve direct government-to-government relations. The contacts that governments have with each other and the manner in which this intercourse is carried on are generally subsumed under the name of diplomacy.

The Nature of Diplomacy

Diplomacy, considered as a technique of state action, is essentially a process whereby communications from one government go directly into the decision-making apparatus of another. It is the one direct technique of state action, in that it exerts its diplomatic power upon the crucial personnel of the other government or governments. If the operational purpose of policy is to secure the agreement of other states to national designs, it is only by diplomatic means that such assent can be formally registered and communicated. In this sense, diplomacy is the central technique of foreign policy.

Diplomacy is both a full-fledged technique in its own right and the instrument by which other techniques are often transmitted. A state can act diplomatically in a purely political context, using only the methods and resources of the diplomatic instrument, or it may implement economic, psychological, or even military action by diplomatic maneuvering. Although the operating requirements of pure diplomacy

SOURCE: Charles O. Lerche, Jr., and Abdul A. Said, *Concepts of International Relations*, 2nd ed. (Prentice-Hall Inc. Englewood Cliffs, New Jersey, 1970), pp. 79–83.

and what we might call "mixed" diplomacy differ to some extent, their fundamental rationale remains essentially the same.

The actual procedures of diplomacy are many, ranging from such highly formal devices as notes, *aides-memoires*, and *communiqués* to more informal and almost casual conversations. At bottom, diplomacy is a method of negotiating between sovereignties, and although the elaborate ritual and protocol that surround the practice may sometimes seem pretentious and time-consuming, their roots lie in the nature of the task. By diplomatic means a state transmits its position on an issue to another state and receives the other state's response. Whatever changes may take place in the respective positions are registered diplomatically, and the eventual elaboration of whatever relationship develops also lies in the hands of diplomats.

The Functions of Diplomacy

We can distinguish several distinct functions of diplomacy. Which of these the working diplomat may be called upon to perform depends on the nature of the policy his government is following.

First, diplomacy is to a major extent a technique of *coercion*. Coercive moves made by other means are communicated diplomatically, and the narrower framework of pure diplomacy contains significant resources of pressure. In many cases, rupture of diplomatic relations has a coercive element, as does exclusion of the target state from international conferences or organizations. Coercion may also be applied in negotiation by an ultimatum, by establishment of a rigid time limit for the conclusion of an arrangement, or by the registration of a formal or informal protest or complaint. In the past few decades, "pragmatic" dictators have added an element of psychological coercion to diplomacy by eliminating the courtesy and good manners traditional to the art, and conducting relationships in an atmosphere of vilification and intensive emotion. This procedure has had its undeniable advantages.

Second, diplomacy is a technique of *persuasion*. The advancement of arguments and the proffering of a *quid pro quo*, both persuasive devices, are within the exclusive province of diplomatic technique. In terms of our discussion of the forms of capability, diplomacy is the most frequently used and best suited of all state techniques for application of the influence component of state capability. While the actual line between coercion and persuasion is often vague, and the two approaches frequently blend into one another, there is a real difference in both motivation and atmosphere, and most diplomatic initiatives are at least initially cast in a persuasive form.

Third, diplomacy is uniquely a procedure of *adjustment*. It is admirably suited to the task of enabling two states to modify their positions on an issue in order to reach a stable relationship. Its directness of communication, its potentially noncoercive nature, and its subtlety and flexibility all contribute to its usefulness. States may prosecute their differences and intensify their conflicts by a great variety of methods, but they may reduce tensions between themselves only by diplomatic means. However, the adjustment function of diplomacy is effective only if both parties are amenable to negotiation; nothing in the diplomatic instrument can overcome a state's unwillingness to change a policy.

Finally, diplomacy is a technique for reaching *agreement*; indeed, it has been said that diplomacy is the art of negotiating written agreements. Formal written agreements are the most binding strictures on international commitment offered by world politics, and can be brought into existence only by diplomatic procedures. We must note that agreement may involve coercion, persuasion, or adjustment, and that no agreement is possible unless both parties wish it. On the other hand, even a strong interest in formalizing an understanding would be pointless if instruments and procedures for reaching one were not available. Here diplomacy comes usefully into its own.

Success and Failure in Diplomacy

What are the characteristics of good diplomacy? More directly, what are the marks of the policy of a state that is making good use of diplomatic technique? Conversely, what is wrong with the normal practice of diplomacy in the contemporary world that has given the diplomat such an apparently small role in the conduct of international politics?

There is little disagreement about the requirements for success in diplomacy. The essentials of the diplomatic art have been well-known for centuries, and the actual practice of its masters furnish us with clear guidelines. We may here reduce the vast literature into four basic operative requirements.

1. *The diplomat must have a clear understanding of the situation in which he is operating.* He must be sensitive to the forces at work in his problem area, and must also be quite clear about his own purposes and the ultimate implications of his policy with respect to long-range goals. Last, he must have a clear understanding of the points of view, interests, and goals of other states, because without such empathy he will be virtually powerless.

2. *The diplomat must be fully aware of his real action capability.*

He must appreciate how much coercive capacity his government will support him with, and how much influence he may enjoy at that particular moment. He dare not attempt initiatives that lie beyond his capability, nor should he content himself with less than full exploitation of the resources appropriate to his objectives.

3. *The diplomat's approach must be flexible.* He must be prepared for unforeseen developments or for withstanding the consequences of analytical error by having some alternate policies and approaches in reserve, by having an unpublicized "fallback" position available, and by being consistently eclectic in methodology. He distinguishes as much as possible between abstract "principle" and concrete interest, and remains firmly committed to the latter while being quite flexible on the former.

4. *The diplomat is eager to compromise within limits of non-essentiality.* A clear priority system is essential to a diplomat because only in this way can he determine what issues are subject to bargaining and which are not. Priorities also suggest quantitative criteria to guide him in determining how extensively he may compromise without giving away matters of importance in return for lesser concessions. In theory, a good diplomat should always be willing to give up a position of lower priority to secure one of higher rank; although subject to drastic modification in practice, this rule does have great importance in diplomatic maneuvering. The criterion of a good diplomatic bargain is less how much is given up than how much is won, for only the prize can determine whether the price was too high.

Diplomacy in the contemporary era has not proved able to cope adequately with the dilemmas of politics. Its inadequacy has been so obvious that some critics have been moved to speculate on "the end of traditional diplomacy." In practice, since the end of World War II, the four roles we have formulated have been honored more often in the breach than in the observance. Situations are analyzed far too often in ideological and nationalistic terms, and too seldom realistically. It is currently unfashionable to admit that one's opponent has any point of view, let alone one meriting consideration. Capability factors are grossly misinterpreted, especially in the military realm. Flexibility, thanks to ideology and nationalism, is usually a lost cause, and compromise is normally rejected as striking a bargain with sin.

In these circumstances, diplomacy cannot flourish, and current practice has involved either ill-concealed and blatant attempts at coercion or nonpurposive propaganda. Real negotiation, persuasion, and adjustment of positions culminating in agreement have been accidental phenomena instead of the normal procedures of states in the system. Deep popular involvement in foreign policy by means of absolutist and emotional sloganizing, common in both large and small states, has seriously impeded the force of diplomacy by depriving it of the necessary "elbow room" in which to maneuver.

Some recent hopeful signs, however, augur a revival of diplomatic activity in the true sense. The height of the cold war era had been marked by constant advocacy of absolute solution to problems. More than two decades of struggle have had their effect; absolutist positions are advanced somewhat less seriously, and responsible and increasingly prudent governments are willing at least to entertain the possibility of partial solutions. With this frame of mind becoming more common, the opportunity for diplomacy to work its harmonizing and adjusting effect becomes somewhat brighter. The future will undoubtedly see relatively greater reliance on diplomacy and possibly a much more favorable record of its success.

Diplomacy/Diplomat—Derivation

of the Concepts

Sir Ernest M. Satow

Diplomacy is the application of intelligence and tact to the conduct of official relations between the governments of independent states, extending sometimes also to their relations with vassal states; or, more briefly still, the conduct of business between states by peaceful means.

* * *

The diplomat, says Littré, is so called, because diplomas are official documents (*actes*) emanating from princes, and the word diploma comes from the Greek δίπλωμα (διπλόω, I double), from the way in which they were folded. A diploma is understood to be a document by which a privilege is conferred: a state paper, official document, a charter. The earliest English instance of the use of this word is of the year 1645.

Leibnitz, in 1693, published his *Codex Juris Gentium Diplomaticus*, Dumont in 1726 the *Corps universel Diplomatique du Droit des Gens*. Both were collections of treaties and other official documents. In these titles *diplomaticus, diplomatique,* are applied to a body or collection of original state-papers, but as the subject-matter of these particular collections was *international* relations, "corps diplomatique" appears to have been treated as equivalent to "corps du droit des gens," and "diplomatique" as "having to do with international relations." Hence the application also to the officials connected with such matters. *Diplomatic body* now came to signify the body of ambassadors, envoys and officials attached to the foreign missions residing at any seat of government, and *diplomatic service* that branch of the public service which supplies the *personnel* of the permanent mis-

SOURCE: *A Guide to Diplomatic Practice*, 4th ed., edited by Sir Nevile Bland (London: Longmans, Green, 1957), pp. 1–4.

sions in foreign countries. The earliest example of this use in England appears to be in the *Annual Register* for 1787. Burke, in 1796, speaks of the "diplomatic body," and also uses "diplomacy" to mean skill or address in the conduct of international intercourse and negotiations. The terms *diplomat, diplomate, diplomatist* were adopted to designate a member of this body.[1] In the eighteenth century they were scarcely known. Disraeli is quoted as using "diplomatic" in 1826 as "displaying address" in negotiations or intercourse of any kind (*New English Dictionary*). *La diplomatique* is used in French for the art of deciphering ancient documents, such as charters and so forth.

The words, then, are comparatively modern, but diplomatists existed long before the words were employed to denote the class. Machiavelli (1469–1527) is perhaps the most celebrated of men who discharged diplomatic functions in early days. D'Ossat (1536–1604), Kaunitz (1710–1794), Metternich (1773–1859), Pozzo di Borgo (1764–1842), the first Lord Malmesbury (1764–1820), Talleyrand (1754–1838), Lord Stratford de Redcliffe (1786–1880) are among the most eminent of the profession in more recent times. If men who combined fame as statesmen with diplomatic reputation are to be included, Count Cavour (1810–1861) and Prince Bismarck (1815–1898) enjoyed a world-wide celebrity.

"Diplomatist" ought, however, to be understood as including all the public servants employed in diplomatic affairs, whether serving at home in the department of foreign affairs, or abroad at embassies or other diplomatic agencies. Strictly speaking, the head of the foreign department is also a diplomatist, as regards his function of responsible statesman conducting the relations of his country with other states. This he does by discussion with their official representatives or by issuing instructions to his agents in foreign countries. Sometimes he is a diplomatist by training and profession; at others he may be a political personage, often possessed of special knowledge fitting him for the post. In the Netherlands it is not unusual for a member of the Foreign Service to be appointed Minister for Foreign Affairs and, after serving his term, to return to the Service.

When we speak of the "diplomacy" of a country as skilful or blundering, we do not mean the management of its international affairs by its agents residing abroad, but their direction by the statesman at the head of the department. Many writers and speakers are disposed to put the blame for a weak or unintelligent diplomacy on

---

[1] Callières, whose book was published in 1716, never uses the word *diplomate*. He always speaks of "un bon" or "un habile négociateur." EDITOR'S NOTE: see bibliography for citation to Callières.

the agent, but this mistake arises from their ignorance of the organisation of public business. The real responsibility necessarily rests with the government concerned, though this must not be taken as absolving the agent from all responsibility whatsoever: if his reports, or his advice, are misleading, and his government falls into error as a result, the blame must lie largely on him.

Diplomacy—Search for Its Meaning

Elmer Plischke

Everyone presumes to understand the meaning and nature of diplomacy; yet, even a random sampling of definitions produces a confusing array of interpretations. Thus, diplomacy is called "the management of international relations by negotiation," "the use of accredited officials for intergovernmental communication," "the art or science that has to do with the transaction of business between sovereign states by means of accredited agents and according to international law," "the business or art of conducting international intercourse," and simply "the manner in which international relations are conducted." It also is held to be one of four fundamental alternative procedures for implementing foreign policy, the others being economic, psychological, and military in nature.

More precisely, diplomacy has been described as "a first line of defense" or as "both the art and the science by which each state attempts to achieve success in its foreign policy short of forcing conclusions by armed conflict," and in this sense it "may be said to stop where war begins, and it starts where war ends." In this same vein, "diplomacy together with strategy are complementary aspects of the single art of politics—the art of conducting relations with other states so as to further the 'national interest.'" In the popular mind it "denotes primarily guile, stealth, a penchant for making 'deals,' inimical to the national interest, and an overall indifference to moral-ethical principles in the relationships among nations."

When delineating fields of human knowledge and activity, problems of language—or what Winston Churchill referred to as "termi-

SOURCE: "The Optimum Scope of Instruction in Diplomacy" by Elmer Plischke in Monograph 13, *Instruction in Diplomacy: The Liberal Arts Approach* (April 1972) of the American Academy of Political and Social Science, pp. 1–3, 8–15, 18–21.

nological inexactitude"—often obfuscate both conceptualistic refinement and pragmatic apperception. The word diplomacy is sometimes conceived succinctly as "the business of the diplomat," but this has the obvious weakness of requiring definition of the word diplomat, and to say that he is one who engages in diplomacy resorts to sterile circumlocution. Diplomacy is regarded by some as the aggregate interrelations of nations—often, as noted later, with certain qualifications—but, in view of such inclusiveness, the interpretation is equally unscientific and misleading. Clearly, the general dictionary definition of diplomacy as tact, politeness, skill, and discernment or propriety in human relations—or even Webster's designation as "artful management in securing advantages without arousing hostility"—though useful in general English expression, is useless as a description of diplomacy as a field of learning.

Its meaning may be somewhat restricted when used in its adjectival sense in such expressions as diplomatic credentials, diplomatic privileges and immunities, and diplomatic power, as distinguished from military and other aspects of power relationships. On the other hand, applicability tends to be broader in such expressions as diplomatic agents, diplomatic endeavors, and diplomatic success or achievement. The concept is employed in its widest connotation in "diplomatic history," which generally concerns the gamut of official relations of nations and is rarely limited to the "history of diplomacy" as a precise process or institution.

The term diplomacy has many meanings and tends to be defined by the individual user to suit his particular purposes. Nevertheless, it is essential to seek its etymological, lexicographical, theoretical, functional, and academic interpretations. The method of refinement may be both positive, denoting what diplomacy is, and negative, determining what it is not. Logic, semantics, philosophical conceptualization, and pragmatic application need to be blended in the process of reviewing all rational possibilities, assessing their validity, and electing among them. Furthermore, diplomacy needs to be distinguished from other concepts including foreign relations, foreign policy, various specific aspects of diplomatic practice, individual diplomatic functions such as negotiation, and the like.

* * *

Primary Interpretations of Diplomacy

Based on breadth of inclusion or generality, combining the conceptualistic and empirical approaches, and proceeding from the more comprehensive to the more specific, six primary delineations have been made of the field of diplomacy. These equate the concept respectively with international relations or world affairs, foreign relations, the conduct of foreign relations, the implementation of foreign policy, official communications among governments, and negotiation. Each of these interpretations embraces but exceeds the aggregate of those which follow it in the sequence.

International Relations. Often the concept of diplomacy is regarded as coterminous with international or world relations, including the more limited international affairs of given geographic areas (such as inter-American relations), at prescribed times (such as the period since World War II), or respecting specific functional subjects (such as imperial expansion, East-West relations, disarmament, transnational conflict resolution, and a host of others). In this sweeping sense, although elements of intergovernmental method may be viewed as encompassed within the field, most attention is paid to events and their causes, substantive policy, political consequences, and similar matters. In many cases even the most rudimentary awareness of procedures and references to techniques for policy implementation are lacking or, at best, are regarded as of only passing concern.

While diplomacy has been called "a term [which] customarily refers to the whole process of the political relations of states" and "is most commonly employed as a method of international politics," it is rarely defined explicitly as international relations as a whole. On the other hand, its pragmatic usage in this broad sense is widespread in general volumes on international relations, world affairs, and diplomatic history. Understandably, this is especially characteristic of that literature which reflects the international perspective and which, consequently, approaches the field from the point of view of the family of nations, as compared with those writings, exclusive of the diplomatic histories, that reflect the focus of the individual national state.

Foreign Relations. The scope of foreign relations consists of two distinct, though closely related, components; namely, foreign policy and the conduct of foreign relations. Often these concepts are confused, and sometimes the terms foreign policy and foreign relations are used interchangeably. The equation of diplomacy with the conduct of foreign relations has evoked little intellectual or academic controversy, but some analysts question whether, as a matter of principle, diplomacy should be conceptualistically identified with foreign policy, and yet, it is not unusual for these two terms to be employed interchangeably in practice.

No specific instances have been found in the literature wherein diplomacy is overtly defined as the totality of foreign relations. Nevertheless, pragmatically such usage is fairly widespread. It is interesting to note, however, that in foreign relations literature—as distinguished from that dealing with general international relations—the volumes themselves are rarely entitled "foreign relations," but are more likely to bear the captions "diplomacy" or "foreign policy."

Conduct of Foreign Relations. This conceptualization, which also may be called the conduct of diplomacy, excludes the element of substantive foreign policy. Views differ, however, as to whether the conduct of diplomacy, while encompassing the effectuation of foreign policy, and therefore embracing the making of subsidiary, particularly methodological, policy in the field, also comprehends the making of fundamental substantive policy centrally by the home government. This exclusion may be regarded as founded on logic but scarcely comports with practical usage in the literature. However, for purposes of precise discrimination, were a distinction to be made between the conduct of diplomacy and the conduct of foreign relations, the former might be deemed to exclude central policy-making, whereas the conduct of foreign relations would not.

In any case, the thrust of this third connotation focuses solely on "process" and "method," which in some delineations are reduced to "technique" or "procedure." Thus, by way of illustration, in this guise diplomacy has been defined as "the formation and execution of foreign policy on all levels," as "the whole process of foreign affairs, from policy decisions through execution," and as "the making and execution of foreign policy." Such usage is fairly widespread in the literature.

Implementation of Foreign Policy. This interpretation of diplomacy excludes both substantive foreign policy and policy-making, but embraces policy execution both centrally at the national capital and in the field. A good many published definitions contained in the literature fall into this category. Illustrative are such specifications as: "the primary method by which foreign policy is carried out," "the normal means of conducting international relations," "the business of conducting relations among governments," and "an instrument and procedure by which nation-states conduct their political affairs and other business among themselves while at peace." Literary usage is as widespread as the employment of such formalized definition.

However, a more limited variant of this interpretation also is recognizable in the literature. Restricted to "implementation of foreign policy in the field," when exercised by professional diplomatic personnel, it generally is designated classical or traditional diplomacy and often appears to be the preferred connotation of professional diplomats. This characterizes the older conceptualization of diplomacy and is confined to the customary functions of the acknowledged diplomat. It dissociates the function of the career practitioner accredited to foreign governments or international gatherings from policy implementation by political leaders and other noncareerists—which George F. Kennan regards as "diplomacy by dilettantism"—through those nontraditional techniques which often are associated with the "new diplomacy."* Surprisingly, formalized definitions depicting this particular category, and still transcending the more limited function of negotiation, are virtually nonexistent in the literature. Nevertheless, this interpretation permeates a good deal of the literature which treats of diplomacy as a profession and which has been produced by professionals, especially of an autobiographical and memoir nature.**

Communications. This category of interpretation, in essence, embraces official communications among governments and nations—both oral and written, indirect as well as direct. It may be interpreted generously or narrowly, but cannot properly be delimited solely to the physical communications system, in which sense, in any case, it is not inclined to be used synonymously with diplomacy. It may be equated with international intercourse, which, if regarded as involving the traditional diplomatic functions such as representation, reporting, conferring, and negotiation, may be viewed as duplicating a substantial number of the functions embodied within the previous category. There are subtle differences, however. Thus, the execution of foreign policy may be viewed as entailing program establishment and management overseas, which exceeds the most liberal interpretation of communications. On the other hand, the latter, broadly conceived, embraces certain types of policy enunciation and the manipulation of its propagation in relation to intended targets, which may not be held by some practitioners and analysts to fall within the purview of policy implementation.

So far as usage is concerned, while the literature rarely confines

---

* EDITOR'S NOTE: For a complete discussion of "New Diplomacy" and its contrasts with traditional diplomacy, see Chapter 2.
** EDITOR'S NOTE: For bibliographies of the biographies of U.S. diplomats and consuls, see Boyce and Boyce, *American Foreign Service Authors*; Plischke, *American Diplomacy*; and Plischke, "Bibliography of Autobiographies, Biographies, Commentaries, and Memoirs," listed in the bibliography below.

analysis of the diplomatic process to communications, a few definitions stress this relationship. By way of illustration, the *International Encyclopedia of the Social Sciences* ascribes two meanings to diplomacy, the narrower of which is restricted to "the process by which governments, acting through official agents, communicate with one another." This limited definition, confining communications to accredited officials, mistakenly excludes other important communications links between states. A similarly circumscribed interpretation reduces diplomacy to "the system of reciprocal permanent representation . . . to expedite through official channels any issue requiring negotiation or consultation. . . ." However, somewhat broader delineations are more common, defining diplomacy as "the art of maintaining intercourse," "a system of formal communication," and "the regular channel through which states communicate with one another." It is only rational to regard diplomacy as involving communication among governments and nations, but the issue is whether it is equally reasonable to delimit diplomacy entirely or even largely to this function.

Negotiation. The final, and in certain respects most restricted, interpretation of diplomacy equates it with negotiation. Harold Nicolson and a good many others define it simply as "the art of negotiation," which Robert B. Mowat enjoins with "representation," and Frederick H. Hartmann . . . expands to "discussion and negotiation." This emphasis is understandable because of the centrality of negotiation to the diplomatic process, but it scarcely suffices to characterize diplomacy adequately.

Such restriction results, in all likelihood, not so much from the intent of its delineators to confine the field solely to negotiation as normally conceived, but rather to provide a succinct definition stressing what may be regarded as its primary and distinguishing function; or, perhaps, because the meaning of negotiation is conceived as sufficiently resilient to comprehend much of the gamut of traditional diplomatic activities. The resolution of this difficulty, therefore, requires definition of the concept, negotiation, as well as diplomacy. In any case, diplomacy concerns the method, not the object, of negotiation, and while it may be formally defined as negotiation, it is questionable whether diplomacy should be equated solely with this function.

* * *

Although Samuel Johnson may declare that "definitions are hazardous" and Ezra Pound may warn: "It is only after long experience that most men are able to define a thing in terms of its own genus," it is necessary to seek some understanding of the meaning of diplomacy, both conceptualistically and for academic purposes.

Diplomacy is deemed to be an art, a science, a craft, a process, a practice, a function, and an institution—and it is all of these. The *Encyclopaedia Britannica* claims it to be more an art than a science, and yet certain of its activities may be practiced in a scientific fashion, and surely one of the main deficiencies of the field is that it has been accorded inadequate intellectual and managerial scientific treatment and too little systematic study. Perhaps its quality as an art, one author suggests, may best be elucidated by professional diplomats writing from their own experience. Nevertheless, it would seem that its interpretation in this fashion is more appropriately reflective of its essentials as a function than of the qualities of its practitioners.

To avoid juxtaposing its qualities as either an art or a science, or both, as well as exposing such deficiencies as may result from defining it as a craft, there may be advantage to regarding it more liberally as a process or practice, and for certain purposes as a function or an institution. Whatever eventuates, and however interpreted, it must be realized that its genus may reflect, and reveal, the perspective and predisposition of its user.

Reduced to its basic essentials, diplomacy may be defined succinctly as *the political process by which political entities, generally states, conduct official relations with one another within the international environment.* With the proliferation of the institutionalization of international affairs by other than classical diplomatic processes, and with the engagement in interrelations by political institutions other than states—such as international and supranational organizations, emergent political entities, and the Vatican—diplomacy can no longer be said to be confined solely to the conduct of the international affairs or foreign relations of established national states.

To fix the scope more definitively and refine its three elements of definition more precisely, diplomacy may be defined more fully as follows:

> Diplomacy is the political process by which political entities (generally states) establish and maintain official relations, direct and indirect, with one another, in pursuing their respective goals, objectives, interests, and substantive and procedural policies in the international environment; as a political process it is dynamic, adaptive, and changing, and it constitutes a continuum; functionally it embraces both the making and implementation of foreign policy at all levels, centrally and in the field, and involves essentially, but

is not restricted to the functions of, representation, reporting, communicating, negotiating, and maneuvering, as well as caring for the interests of nationals abroad.

Some would go beyond applying the concept of diplomacy to political institutions, and include quasi-public agencies and private individuals, on the grounds that they engage in practices and functions similar to those pursued by national states and international organizations. Whereas a number of techniques, qualities, and processes may in certain respects be indistinguishable, such nonpolitical entities are unable to qualify even substantially under the full spectrum of functions, activities, and procedures involved in any normal connotation of diplomacy, and many of their practices would be regarded as extra-diplomatic. There is merit, therefore, in such precision which, while acknowledging similarities, recognizes dissimilarity.

If the inclusion of quasi-public agencies and private individuals within the general concept of diplomacy is argued and accepted, it becomes illogical to exclude the application of the term to all similar practices among private individuals, corporations, and institutions internally as well as internationally, including interstate (among the fifty constituent states), federal-state, internal intergovernmental, labor-management, business, police-community, and a host of other interrelationships. In other words, the official/nonofficial dichotomization appears to be as valid as the international/noninternational. Failure to recognize these distinctions tends to confuse rather than to clarify.

In any case, were the scope of diplomacy to be expanded beyond the relations of political entities officially functioning within the international environment, new concepts, or at least semantic distinctions, would need to be developed—such as official versus nonofficial, public versus private, and international versus noninternational diplomacy. Many would contend that the normal meaning of diplomacy has been and should continue to be equated with official, public, international diplomacy, and that the employment of the adjectives in such designation is redundant. Assuming that the remaining types of relations require differentiating delineations, perhaps such appellations as nonofficial or unofficial or nongovernmental negotiations and private foreign relations are minimally essential even in the sphere of conceptualization.

* * *

Titles of Diplomats

Charles W. Thayer

Diplomatic titles* have always been confusing and are becoming more so. The head of an embassy has the title of "ambassador extraordinary and plenipotentiary" but he is simply called "ambassador." The "extraordinary" was added many years ago by thrusting ambassadors in an effort to promote themselves above their colleagues. In self-protection the latter simply followed suit, thereby producing a stalemate. "Plenipotentiary" means the envoy has full powers to negotiate normal diplomatic problems. Should an ambassador be called upon to sign a treaty he must get special "full powers."

A legation is a second-class embassy. In its earliest days the United States maintained only legations but as it grew in importance began raising these to embassies. Today only in a few very small countries do we still have legations. The head of a legation has the title "envoy extraordinary and minister plenipotentiary." He is called "minister" for short. Just to complicate matters, an ambassador from the Vatican is a nuncio and a minister is an internuncio. The treaties the Vatican concludes are not treaties but concordats.

Americans usually address their own ambassador or minister as Mr. Ambassador or Mr. Minister but to a third person he is referred to as "the ambassador," *never* "the Mr. Ambassador." Foreigners addressing American and Americans addressing foreign ambassadors or ministers usually say "Your Excellency" or to third persons, "His Excellency."

Traditionally the ambassador's deputy is called a counselor. When

---

* EDITOR's NOTE: For commentary on the historical development of U.S. usage concerning diplomatic ranks and titles, see Elmer Plischke, "Profile of United States Diplomats," in Chapter 5.

SOURCE: *Diplomat* (New York: Harper, 1959), pp. 122–24.

the ambassador is out of the country, the counselor becomes acting ambassador but his title is "chargé d'affaires, *ad interim*" meaning "temporarily in charge of affairs." He automatically loses the title as soon as the ambassador returns. With the twentieth-century inflation of titles, in some countries the second in command is a minister and in others a minister-counselor. In Foreign Service jargon he is called "D.C.M." or deputy chief of mission. Nowadays embassies may have several counselors: e.g., political, economic or even administrative counselor.

Under the counselors come the diplomatic secretaries, to be carefully distinguished from their secretaries. Their titles are first secretary, second secretary, or third secretary. Though there used to be fourth secretaries, they too have fallen victims to title inflations. Private secretary, though often a key position, is not generally recognized as a diplomatic rank and hence does not rate inclusion on the Diplomatic List.

Parallel to these diplomatic officers are the attachés, military, naval and air, and frequently agricultural, labor, treasury, and commercial, and more recently in a few posts scientific attaché. These seldom are regular career diplomats and almost invariably are career civil servants of the corresponding departments in Washington.

Ambassadors of some countries occasionally appoint their sons, nephews, or other outsiders to the post of attaché which is a diplomatic rank and is included on the list. The practice has in the past been forbidden by the State Department as a precaution against nepotism. An exception to the ban on attachés has recently been made for representatives of government agencies who prefer not to advertise their affiliations.

To confuse the uninitiated still further, these diplomatic ranks have little or no significance, except to protocol officers, receptionists and wives, beyond specifying where one sits at an official dinner or marches in a state funeral. To the career diplomat, but not always to his wife, what is important is his class in the Foreign Service, since this determines his salary. Presently there are ten career classes: career ambassador, career minister, and Classes No. 1 down to Class 8 for beginners. It is curious that, whereas American Civil Service salaries increase with the number of your class, in the Foreign Service they diminish. There is no special significance to this phenomenon.

* * *

Normalization of Diplomatic Relations

WARREN CHRISTOPHER

I think it is important to understand why it is generally in the interest of the United States to exchange diplomats with other governments and, where possible, to exchange ideas, goods, and people as well.

* * *

We live . . . in an interdependent world. And in one way or another, we find our fate and our futures tied increasingly to those of other peoples. If we cannot communicate easily with them, we cannot effectively promote our own interests or build new bonds of common interest.

This brings me to my central point: We believe that diplomatic relations help us to discharge our basic duty to protect the interests of our government and our citizens. By keeping open a channel of communication with other countries, we best serve our long-range objective of encouraging the growth of democratic institutions.

We do not look at the normalization of relations as an end in itself. Rather, diplomatic relations, once established and maintained, enable us to communicate with other governments directly, to state our views and listen to theirs, to avoid misunderstandings and to exert influence. In short, they help us to accomplish more than we can without them.

Let me put the American attitude toward diplomatic relations in a historical perspective.

History of Recognition

In 1792 the French king was replaced by a popular government. The U.S. envoy in Paris wrote to Thomas Jefferson, our first Secretary of

SOURCE: Address, Occidental College, Los Angeles, Department of State Release, June 11, 1977.

State, to ask how to behave with the new government. He received a straightforward answer:

> "It accords with our principles to acknowledge any government to be rightful which is formed by the will of the nation substantially declared. . . . With such a government every kind of business may be done."

Jefferson's answer was interpreted over time to mean that the United States would generally deal with the government effectively in power. This became the policy of our government until late in the 19th century. But in the 20th century our practice became less certain and exceptions were introduced.

Woodrow Wilson introduced a substantial exception by insisting that the United States should not have normal diplomatic relations with governments that came to power in violation of their own constitutions. Wilson's exception proved too rigid in practice and it rather quickly succumbed to the stress of reality. But Wilson's was not the last exception.

When the Chinese Communists established the People's Republic of China in 1949, we were again distracted from our earlier policy. During the Chinese civil war the United States had supported the Nationalist side. After the Communists took power, we were faced with the problem of recognizing rival claims. President Truman reacted in this way:

> "We shall refuse to recognize any government imposed upon any nation by the force of any foreign power. In some cases it may be impossible to prevent forceful imposition of such a government. But the United States will not recognize any such government."

The weakness of Truman's exception is that, like Wilson's, it could prevent us from ever establishing relations with a government that we believe came to power wrongfully.

A few years later, when troops from the People's Republic of China entered the Korean war, Secretary of State Dulles stated his own limitation: "It has been the practice of the United States," he declared, "to recognize de facto governments when the latter are: (1) in control of the machinery of government; (2) are not confronted with active resistance in the country; and (3) are willing and able to live up to their international commitments." This formulation tends to ignore the reality that we, in our own national interest, may want diplomatic relations with governments precisely to urge them to live up to their international obligations.

Perhaps attractive on their face, these exceptions introduced in the 20th century have not always served the national interest. The premise of our present policy is that diplomatic relations do not constitute a seal of approval. Winston Churchill explained it best: "The reason for having diplomatic relations is not to confer a compliment, but to secure a convenience."

Realities of Recognition

We maintain diplomatic relations with many governments of which we do not necessarily approve. The reality is that, in this day and age, coups and other unscheduled changes of government are not exceptional developments. Withholding diplomatic relations from these regimes, after they have obtained effective control, penalizes us. It means that we forsake much of the chance to influence the attitudes and conduct of a new regime. Without relations, we forfeit opportunities to transmit our values and communicate our policies. Isolation may well bring out the worst in the new government.

For the same reasons, we eschew withdrawal of diplomatic relations except in rare instances—for example, the outbreak of war or events which make it physically impossible to maintain a diplomatic presence in another capital.

If we continue to withhold diplomatic relations, this hesitancy invites confusion and can become the center of a touchy political issue. Eventual establishment of diplomatic relations then comes, wrongly, to be considered as a form of approval. In short, it means that someday, when we seek to normalize relations, we will be painting on a dirty canvas.

Indeed, efforts to restore relations once broken often encounter special difficulties. Inevitably, constituencies in both countries develop an emotional investment in the absence of relations. Financial claims and counterclaims pile up, and there is a backlog of issues which might have been resolved if normal relations had existed. Faced with this legacy of problems, the process of restoring relations must be approached with great care and deliberation.

* * *

In sum, we believe normal diplomatic relations are an asset to promote other objectives, an asset we cannot deny ourselves, without incurring substantial cost. As Churchill put it: "When relations are most difficult, that is the time diplomacy is most needed."

There is no certainty that two nations will be able to resolve their

disputes by talking about them. But without effective communications, without some form of dialogue, the odds are high that there
will be no progress at all. This is true . . . among individuals. So it
is among nations, as well.

2

Changing Diplomatic Practice

We are also coming to realize that foreign operations in today's world call for a total diplomacy.... American ambassadors can no longer be content with wining and dining, reporting, analyzing, and cautiously predicting. They must act as administrators and coordinators, responsible for the effective operation of all United States Government activities in the countries of their assignment.
CHESTER B. BOWLES, "Total Diplomacy"

Diplomacy, which was once a relatively simple process, has now become vastly complicated, not only because of the growing number of complex problems we face in the world, but also because of the constantly increasing number of states with which we have to deal.
FRANCIS O. WILCOX, Preface to *U.S. Diplomats and Their Missions*

"Changing Diplomatic Practice" concerns the evolution and nature of modern diplomacy. The five essays contained in this chapter have a number of observations in common on the reasons for the change from the older, classical diplomacy of earlier centuries: growth of the international community and therefore of the volume of its diplomacy, increased global complexity and interdependence, and the emergence of more open and multipartite negotiations, to name but a few. The authors, however, differ in their assessment of the origins of this metamorphosis, of its cost, and of its benefits.

Harold Nicolson, in "Transition from the Old to the New Diplomacy," sees the new or "American" brand of diplomacy as an attempt to superimpose upon international affairs the philosophy and practice of a liberal democracy's domestic affairs. He discerns serious defects in the new diplomacy, including the principle of equality of states, the concept of open negotiations, and the loss of certainty and continuity in the diplomatic process. Although Nicolson is pessimistic about the existing state of diplomacy, he envisions a more "consistent, convincing and reliable" method in America's diplomatic future once the lessons of experience have been adequately assimilated.

Elmer Plischke's "The New Diplomacy" examines the nature of the change, its manifestations, and its continuity. He systematically analyzes recent phenomena such as the increased volume and speed of diplomatic communications, the democratization of diplomacy, the escalation of various types of diplomatic activity, and the growth of multilateralism. He also deals with the enlargement of the diplomatic community, which is explored in greater depth in his essay, "Proliferating International Community and Changing Diplomatic Representation," at the end of this chapter. It is his contention that the new diplomacy is largely the result of this substantial increase in the number of states, the rapid improvements in communication and transportation, and the needs of the times.

Robert J. Pranger recognizes these factors in the metamorphosis and expands upon a number of them, but he views another phenomenon as its cause. In "Contemporary Diplomacy at Work," he attributes the change from the old diplomacy to the new to the growing complexity and sophistication of the world community and to the resulting interdependence, especially economic, of its constituent nations and peoples. He asserts that the new diplomacy represents the diplomat's means of coping with this new world of complexity and interrelationships, but cautions that the envoy's transition to the new diplomacy will not be complete until he also becomes the public's educator in the realm of international affairs.

Dag Hammarskjöld speaks out in favor of the new diplomacy in "New Diplomatic Techniques in a New World." He claims that multilateralism is the necessary concomitant of the world's increasing interdependence and that the contemporary diplomat must represent not only his own country's interests, but those of the other nations involved in the global community as well. Unlike Nicolson, Hammarskjöld lauds the move toward open diplomacy, asserting that the constraint of secrecy exacted by the old diplomacy is inconsistent with the new age of multilateralism. The following chapter examines whether Nicolson's or Hammarskjöld's perception of open diplomacy more closely approximates reality.

Transition from the Old to the New Diplomacy

Harold Nicolson

I have dealt hitherto with three samples of diplomatic method, namely the Greek method, the Italian method and the French method. In this my last lecture, I shall consider what might perhaps be called 'the American method', but what I prefer—since the Americans have not as yet discovered their own formula, to call—'The Transition between the Old Diplomacy and the New.'[*]

By the French method I mean the theory and practice of international negotiation originated by Richelieu, analysed by Callières, and adopted by all European countries during the three centuries that preceded the change of 1919. I regard this method as that best adapted to the conduct of relations between civilised States. It was courteous and dignified; it was continuous and gradual; it attached importance to knowledge and experience; it took account of the realities of existing power; and it defined good faith, lucidity and precision as the qualities essential to any sound negotiation. The mistakes, the follies and the crimes that during those three hundred years accumulated to the discredit of the old diplomacy can, when examined at their sources, be traced to evil foreign policy rather than to faulty methods of negotiation. It is regrettable that the bad things they did should have dishonoured the excellent manner in which they did them.

In drawing attention to the virtues of the French method I am not of course proposing to scrap all existing machinery and to return

---

* EDITOR'S NOTE: For additional commentary on this subject, see Harold Nicolson, "The Faults of American Diplomacy," *Harper's Magazine*, vol. 210 (January 1955), pp. 52–58.

SOURCE: *The Evolution of Diplomatic Method* (New York: Macmillan, 1954), pp. 72–79, 84–93, Chichele Lectures, Oxford University, 1953.

to the system of the eighteenth or nineteenth centuries. The conditions on which the old diplomacy was based no longer exist. Yet there seems no reason why we, in recognising the faults of the old system, should ignore the many merits that it possessed. I am not, I repeat, suggesting that the old diplomacy should be reintroduced or even imitated: I am suggesting only that we should consider it objectively and with some realization that, as a method of negotiation, it was infinitely more efficient than that which we employ today.

Let me therefore consider five of the chief characteristics of the old diplomacy.

In the first place Europe was regarded as the most important of all the continents. Asia and Africa were viewed as areas for imperial, commercial or missionary expansion; Japan, when she arose, appeared an exceptional phenomenon; America, until 1897, remained isolated behind her oceans and her Doctrine. No war, it was felt, could become a major war unless one of the five Great European Powers became involved. It was thus in the chancelleries of Europe alone that the final issue of general peace or war would be decided.

In the second place it was assumed that the Great Powers were greater than the Small Powers, since they possessed a more extended range of interests, wider responsibilities, and, above all, more money and more guns. The Small Powers were graded in importance according to their military resources, their strategic position, their value as markets or sources of raw material, and their relation to the Balance of Power. There was nothing stable about such categories. Places such as Tobago or Santa Lucia, at one date strategically valuable, lost all significance with the invention of steam. At one moment Egypt, at another Afghanistan, at another Albania, would acquire prominence as points of Anglo-French, Anglo-Russian, or Slav-Teuton rivalry: at one moment the Baltic, at another the Balkans, would become the focus of diplomatic concern. Throughout this period the Small Powers were assessed according to their effect upon the relations between the Great Powers: there was seldom any idea that their interests, their opinions, still less their votes, could affect a policy agreed upon by the Concert of Europe.

This axiom implied a third principle, namely that the Great Powers possessed a common responsibility for the conduct of the Small Powers and the preservation of peace between them. The principle of intervention, as in Crete or China, was a generally accepted principle. The classic example of joint intervention by the Concert of Europe in a dispute between the Small Powers was the Ambassadors Conference held in London in 1913 at the time of the Balkan Wars.

That Conference, which provides the last, as well as the best, example of the old diplomacy in action, prevented a Small-Power crisis from developing into a Great-Power crisis. I shall consider it under my next heading.

The fourth characteristic bequeathed by the French system was the establishment in every European country of a professional diplomatic service on a more or less identical model. These officials representing their Governments in foreign capitals possessed similar standards of education, similar experience, and a similar aim. They desired the same sort of world. As de Callières had already noticed in 1716, they tended to develop a corporate identity independent of their national identity. They had often known each other for years, having served in some post together in their early youth; and they all believed, whatever their Governments might believe, that the purpose of diplomacy was the preservation of peace. This professional freemasonry proved of great value in negotiation.

The Ambassadors, for instance, of France, Russia, Germany, Austria and Italy, who, under Sir Edward Grey's chairmanship, managed to settle the Balkan crisis of 1913, each represented national rivalries that were dangerous and acute. Yet they possessed complete confidence in each other's probity and discretion, had a common standard of professional conduct, and desired above all else to prevent a general conflagration.

It was not the fault of the old diplomacy, by which I mean the professional diplomatists of the pre-war period, that the supremacy of Europe was shattered by the First World War. The misfortune was that the advice of these wise men was disregarded at Vienna and Berlin, that their services were not employed, and that other non-diplomatic influences and interests assumed control of affairs.

The fifth main characteristic of the old diplomacy was the rule that sound negotiation must be continuous and confidential. It was a principle essentially different from that governing the itinerant public conferences with which we have become familiar since 1919. The Ambassador in a foreign capital who was instructed to negotiate a treaty with the Government to which he was accredited was already in possession of certain assets. He was acquainted with the people with whom he had to negotiate; he could in advance assess their strength or weakness, their reliability or the reverse. He was fully informed of local interests, prejudices or ambitions, of the local reefs and sandbanks, among which he would have to navigate. His repeated interviews with the Foreign Minister attracted no special public attention, since they were taken for granted as visits of routine. In that his conversations were private, they could remain both rational and courteous; in that they were confidential, there was no danger of public expectation being aroused while they were still in progress. Every negotiation consists of stages and a result; if the stages become matters of public controversy before the result has been achieved, the negotiation will almost certainly founder. A negotiation is the subject of concession and counter-concession: if the concession offered is divulged before the public are aware of the corresponding concession to be received, extreme agitation may follow and the negotiation may have to be abandoned. The necessity of negotiation remaining confidential has never been more forcibly expressed than by M. Jules Cambon, perhaps the best professional diplomatist of this century. 'The day secrecy is abolished,' writes M. Cambon, 'negotiation of any kind will become impossible.'

An ambassador negotiating a treaty according to the methods of the old diplomacy was not pressed for time. Both his own Government and the Government with whom he was negotiating had ample opportunity for reflection. A negotiation that had reached a deadlock could be dropped for a few months without hopes being dashed or speculation aroused. The agreements that in the end resulted were no hasty improvisations or empty formulas, but documents considered and drafted with exact care. We might cite as an example the Anglo-Russian Convention of 1907, the negotiation of which between the Russian Foreign Minister and our Ambassador in St. Petersburg occupied a period of one year and three months. At no stage during those protracted transactions was an indiscretion committed or a confidence betrayed.

Such, therefore, were some of the distinctive characteristics of the old diplomacy—the conception of Europe as the centre of international gravity; the idea that the Great Powers, constituting the Concert of Europe, were more important and more responsible than the Small Powers; the existence in every country of a trained diplomatic service possessing common standards of professional conduct; and the assumption that negotiation must always be a process rather than an episode, and that at every stage it must remain confidential.

I trust that my preference for professional to amateur methods of negotiation will not be ascribed solely to the chance that I was myself born and nurtured in the old diplomacy. I am fully conscious of the many faults that the system encouraged. The axiom that all negotiation must be confidential did certainly create the habit of secretiveness, and did induce men of the highest respectability to enter into commitments which they did not divulge. We must not forget that as late as 1914 the French Assembly was unaware of the secret clauses of the Franco-Russian Alliance or that Sir Edward Grey (a man of scrupulous integrity) did not regard it as wrong to conceal from the Cabinet the exact nature of the military arrangements reached between the French and British General Staffs. Confidential negotiations that lead to secret pledges are worse even than the televised diplomacy that we enjoy today.

Nor am I unaware of the functional defects which the professional diplomatist tends to develop. He has seen human folly or egoism operating in so many different circumstances that he may identify serious passions with transitory feelings and thus underestimate the profound emotion by which whole nations can be swayed. He is so inured to the contrast between those who know the facts and those who do not know the facts, that he forgets that the latter constitute the vast majority and that it is with them that the last decision rests. He may have deduced from experience that time alone is the conciliator, that unimportant things do not matter and that important things settle themselves, that mistakes are the only things that are really effective, and he may thus incline to the fallacy that on the whole it is wiser, in all circumstances, to do nothing at all. He may be a stupid man or complacent; there are few human types more depressing than that of Monsieur de Norpois or the self-satisfied diplomatist. He may be of weak character, inclined to report what is agreeable rather than what is true. He may be vain, a defect resulting in disaster to all concerned. And he often becomes denationalised, internationalised, and therefore dehydrated, an elegant empty husk. A profession should not, however, be judged by its failures.

I have seen it stated that the transition between the old diplomacy and the new began one hundred years before the revolution of 1919. According to this theory, the change is to be ascribed, not to President Wilson's egalitarianism or to Mr. Lloyd George's faith in diplomacy by conference, but to the influence of three factors which had for long been operative but which exercised their maximum effect after the close of the Napoleonic wars. The first factor was the desire for colonial expansion; the second, intense commercial competition; and the third, the increased speed of communications. Each of these three did assuredly exercise an influence on the evolution of diplomatic method, but that influence was neither as quick nor as deep as has been contended.

* * *

No, it was not the telephone that, from 1919 onwards, brought about the transition from the old diplomacy to the new. It was the belief that it was possible to apply to the conduct of *external* affairs, the ideas and practices which, in the conduct of *internal* affairs, had for generations been regarded as the essentials of liberal democracy.

It was inevitable, after the First World War, that some such experiment should be made. On the one hand, the ordinary citizen, being convinced that the masses in every country shared his own detestation of war, attributed the breach of the peace to the vice or folly of a small minority, which must in future be placed under democratic control. On the other hand, when the Americans arrived as the dominant partners in the coalition, they brought with them their dislike of European institutions, their distrust of diplomacy, and their missionary faith in the equality of man.

President Wilson was an idealist and, what was perhaps more dangerous, a consummate master of English prose. He shared with Robespierre the hallucination that there existed some mystic bond between himself and 'The People'—by which he meant not only the American people but the British, French, Italian, Rumanian, Jugo-Slav, Armenian, and even German peoples. If only he could penetrate the fog-barrier of governments, politicians and officials and convey the sweetness and light of his revelation to the ordinary peasant in the Banat, to the shepherds of Albania, or the dock-hands of Fiume, then reason, concord and amity would spread in ever widening circles across the earth. He possessed, moreover, the gift of giving to commonplace ideas the resonance and authority of biblical sentences, and, like all phraseologists, he became mesmerised by the strength and neatness of the phrases that he devised. During the long months of the Paris Peace Conference, I observed him with interest, admiration and anxiety, and became convinced that he regarded himself, not as a world statesman, but as a prophet designated to bring light to a dark world. It may have been for this reason that he forgot all about the American Constitution and Senator Lodge.

I have no desire at all to denigrate President Wilson, who was in many ways inspiring and inspired. He assumed a weight of responsibility greater than any single human being is constituted to support, and he was tragically crushed. Yet if we read again the tremendous sermons that he delivered during 1918 we shall find in them the seeds of the jungle of chaos that today impedes and almost obliterates the processes of rational negotiation. Let me, therefore, remind you, for a moment, of some of the Fourteen Points, the Four Principles, the Four Ends, and the Five Particulars.

The first of the Fourteen Points of January 8, 1918, provided that in future there should be nothing but 'open covenants of peace openly arrived at', and that 'diplomacy should proceed always frankly and in the public view'. On reaching Paris, President Wilson quickly decided that by 'diplomacy' he had not meant 'negotiation', but only the results of that negotiation, namely treaties. He also decided that the phrases 'openly arrived at' and 'in the public view' were relative only and contained nothing that need deter him from conducting prolonged secret negotiations with Lloyd George and Clemenceau, while one American marine stood with fixed bayonet at the study door, and another patrolled the short strip of garden outside. I can well recall how startled I was, on first being admitted to the secret chamber, to discover how original was the President's interpretation of his own first rule. Today, being much older, I realize that the method he adopted was the only possible method which, in the circumstances, could have led to any result.

The general public, however, were not similarly constrained to test the validity of the President's pronouncements against the hard facts of international intercourse. They continued to assume that by 'diplomacy' was meant both policy and negotiation, and to conclude that, since secret treaties were demonstrably evil things, negotiation also must never be secret but conducted always 'in the public view'. This is perhaps the most confusing of all the fallacies that we owe to President Wilson.

In the second of the Four Principles of a month later, the President announced that the system of the Balance of Power was now for ever discredited and that subject populations must be granted their independence, irrespective of the wishes of other States. In the Four Ends of the following July he foreshadowed the creation of a League of Nations which would establish, to quote his words, 'the reign of law, based upon the consent of the governed and sustained by the organised opinion of mankind.' He failed to realize that the public is bored by foreign affairs until a crisis arises; and that then it is guided by feelings rather than by thoughts. Nor did he foresee that it would be impossible to organize the same opinion in every country simultaneously, or that the conscience of mankind, as a means of sustenance, might prove inadequate when faced by a dictator controlling all means of information. In the Five Particulars on September 27 he pronounced that the rule of justice which America must achieve would be one that 'plays no favourites and knows no standards but the equal rights of the several peoples concerned'. This commandment was subsequently misinterpreted to signify that not the rights merely, but also the opinions and the votes of even the tiniest country were of a validity equal to that of a Great Power. Egalitarianism was thus for the first time extended to imply equality among nations, an idea which does not correspond to reality and which creates mixed ideas.

If read as a whole, the successive pronouncements made by President Wilson during those months of 1918 constitute a magnificent gospel. They embody conceptions which no man should either ignore or disdain. The misfortune was that the public imagined that what was intended as a doctrine of perfectability was in fact a statement of American intentions. Thus when America repudiated her own prophet, a regrettable dichotomy was created between the realists and the idealists in every country. The former concluded that the whole of the Wilson doctrine was sentimental nonsense, and the latter floated off into vague imaginings that what they wanted to happen was likely to occur. As the latter were in the majority, the practical politician found himself in an invidious position. It was the endeavour to reconcile the hopes of the many with the doubts of the few that brought such seeming falsity to foreign policy in the twenty years between 1919 and 1939.

The Covenant of the League of Nations was none the less a very sensible document which, had it been applied with consistent strength, might well have established something like the rule of law among nations. The Secretariat created at Geneva by Lord Perth was a truly remarkable innovation, which, had general confidence been maintained, might have provided the world with a machine far preferable to that of the old diplomacy. The trouble was that this fine experiment was based upon a view of human nature which, had it been a correct view, would have rendered any League unnecessary. The ordinary peaceful citizen came to suppose that violence could be restrained by reason: it was not until it was too late that he understood that it could only be restrained by force. The old systems of authority, such as the Balance of Power, the Concert of Europe, and the discipline of the Great Powers, had been discredited; the new theory of reason proved incapable of controlling the unreasonable; in place of the old methods of stability, a new method of the utmost instability was introduced.

You may be thinking that in devoting so much space to the new ideas of 1919, I am transgressing my own principle and confusing policy with negotiation, theory with practice. You may argue that, even after President Wilson had sought to apply to international relations the principles of American democracy, the diplomatists continued undismayed to weave the old tapestry of alliances and combinations, of big or little *ententes*, of pacts and conventions. Yet you will agree, I think, that two important changes were in fact introduced into diplomatic method in the period that followed the war of 1914–1918. The first was the refusal of the American legislature to ratify a treaty negotiated and signed by their own chief executive in person. That assuredly was an innovation of the utmost significance and one that dealt a heavy blow to the sanctity of contract and the reliability of negotiation. The second was the increasing practice of indulging in the method of diplomacy by conference. By that I do not mean merely the several *ad hoc* conferences, such as Spa, Cannes, Genoa, Lausanne, Stresa and so on: some of these were necessary and some were not. I am referring rather to the permanent state of conference introduced by the League system and later by United Nations. These conferences do little to satisfy the vague desire for what is called 'open diplomacy'; but they do much to diminish the utility of professional diplomatists and, in that they entail much publicity, many rumours, and wide speculation—in that they tempt politicians to achieve quick, spectacular and often fictitious results—they tend to promote rather than allay suspicion, and to create those very states of uncertainty which it is the purpose of good diplomatic method to prevent.

The defects, or perhaps I should say the misfortunes, of the new diplomacy are today magnified for us as if on some gigantic screen. The theory that all States are equal, even as all men are equal, has led to lobbies being formed among the smaller countries (as for instance between the Asians and the Latin-Americans), the sole unifying principle of which is to offer opposition even to the reasonable suggestions of the Great Powers. The theory that 'diplomacy should proceed always frankly and in the public view' has led to negotiation being broadcast and televised, and to all rational discussion being abandoned in favour of interminable propaganda speeches addressed, not to those with whom the delegate is supposed to be negotiating, but to his own public at home.

You will have observed that in these lectures I have made but slight reference to the diplomacy of the Soviet Union. Mr. W. P. Potjomkin, in his history of diplomacy, assures us that the Russians possess one powerful weapon denied to their opponents—namely 'the scientific dialectic of the Marx-Lenin formula'. I have not observed as yet that the dialectic has improved international relationships, or that the Soviet diplomatists and commissars have evolved any system of negotiation that might be called a diplomatic system. Their activity in foreign countries or at international conferences is formidable, disturbing, compulsive. I do not for one moment underestimate either its potency or its danger. But it is not diplomacy: it is something else.

This may be a sad conclusion. But it is not my final conclusion.

It would, in my view, be an error to take as an example of modern diplomatic method the discussions that are conducted in the Security Council and the Assembly of United Nations. We may resent the wastage of time, energy and money: we may regret that, in transferring to external affairs the system of parliamentary argument, a more efficient type of parliament should not have been chosen as a model: we may deplore that the invectives there exchanged should add to the sum of human tension and bewilderment. Yet it would be incorrect to suppose that these meetings are intended to serve the purpose of negotiation: they are exercises in forensic propaganda and do not even purport to be experiments in diplomatic method. Such negotiation as may occur in New York is not conducted within the walls of the tall building by the East River: it is carried out elsewhere, in accordance with those principles of courtesy, confidence and discretion which must for ever remain the only principles conducive to the peaceful settlement of disputes.

It is not therefore either diplomacy by loud-speaker or diplomacy by insult, that we need consider, since these contain a contradiction in terms. It is whether the changes inspired, rather than introduced, by President Wilson in 1919 do not repeat and emphasize the defects of previous systems and render more difficult what must always remain the chief aim of diplomacy, namely international stability. Woodrow Wilson, with his academic intelligence and missionary spirit, did not realize that foreign affairs are *foreign* affairs, or that a civilisation is not a linotype machine but an organic growth. He believed that the misfortunes of mankind were due to the faults of statesmen and experts and that 'the people' were always right: he did not realize that, although it may be difficult to fool all the people all the time, it is easy to fool them for a sufficient period of time to compass their destruction. Thus if we examine the diplomatic method which I do not think it unfair to call the 'Wilsonian', or 'the American' method, we shall find that it omits many of the merits of the several systems that I have examined in these lectures and exaggerates many of their faults.

The chief fault of democratic diplomacy as practised by the Greek City States was its uncertainty. Not only were their diplomatic missions composed of delegates who betrayed each other, but the final decision rested with an Assembly whose members were ignorant, volatile, impulsive and swayed by emotions of fear, vanity and suspicion. No negotiator can succeed unless reasonable certainty exists that his signature will be honoured by his own sovereign. If either the conduct or results of negotiation are subject to irresponsible intervention or repudiation on the part of an Assembly, or even a Congressional Committee, then uncertainty is spread. My first criticism therefore of the American method is that it weakens certainty.

The fault of the method practised and perfected by the Italians of the Renaissance was that it lacked all continuity of purpose and represented a kaleidoscope of shifting combinations. It may be, for all I know, that the President, the State Department, the Pentagon and the Foreign Affairs Committee of the Senate, are unanimous regarding the aim to be achieved: but they are not unanimous as to the means to be adopted. The variability of the diplomatic method employed suggests opportunism rather than continuity: this is an unfortunate impression, a Machiavellian impression, for a great good giant to convey.

The French system possessed the great merit of creating a centralised authority for the formation of foreign policy and a professional service of experts through whom that policy could be carried out. The misfortune of the American system is that no foreigner, and few Americans, can be quite positive at any given moment who it is who possesses the first word and who the last: and although the Americans in recent years have been in process of creating an admirable service of professional diplomatists, these experts do not yet possess the necessary influence with their own government or public. The egalitarian illusions of the Americans, or if you prefer it their 'pioneer spirit', tempts them to distrust the expert and to credit the amateur. I am not just being old-fashioned when I affirm that the amateur in diplomacy is apt to be suspicious. 'Gullibility,' as Sir Edward Grey once said to me, 'is in diplomacy a defect infinitely preferable to distrust.'

Now that the old disciplines of Pope and Emperor, the old correctives of the Concert of Europe and the Balance of Power, have been dispensed with, it is regrettable that the authority exercised by the United States is not more consistent, convincing and reliable. Yet I am not pessimistic about the evolution of their diplomatic method. I know that the Americans possess more virtue than any giant Power has yet possessed. I know that, although they pretend to deride the lessons of history, they are astonishingly quick at digesting the experience of others. And, I believe that the principles of sound diplomacy, which are immutable, will in the end prevail, and thus calm the chaos with which the transition between the old diplomacy and the new has for the moment bewildered the world.

The New Diplomacy

ELMER PLISCHKE

In both its conceptual and pragmatic versions, diplomacy—like most human institutions—is a dynamic process and changes with the times. In the twentieth century, especially at the time of World War I and again following World War II, the course of history engendered substantial modifications in diplomatic practice, and these resulted in the emergence of "the new diplomacy," distinguishing it from the conventional or "classical" method of conducting foreign relations.

The term diplomacy, generally regarded by analysts as a *method* of interrelations, is variously defined as "the art or science that has to do with the transaction of business between sovereign states by means of accredited agents and according to international law," as "the management of international relations by negotiation," and as "the business or art of conducting international intercourse." In addition to being described by Metternich as "the art of avoiding the appearance of victory," and by the diplomatic historian Thomas A. Bailey as "a first line of defense," in a similar vein—apposing diplomacy to military force—it has been called "both the art and science by which each state attempts to achieve success in its foreign policy short of forcing conclusions by armed conflict," and in this sense it "may be said to stop where war begins and it starts where war ends."

Diplomacy is ascribed many meanings and tends to be interpreted and employed by the individual user to suit his particular purposes. For this survey it is defined as the political process by which members of the family of nations conduct official relations within the international environment. It encompasses both the making and implementation of foreign policy—centrally and in the field—in the

SOURCE: "The New Diplomacy: A Changing Process," *Virginia Quarterly Review*, vol. 49 (Summer 1973), pp. 321–45.

pursuance of national goals, foreign policy objectives, and national interests. It involves but is not necessarily restricted to the traditional functions of representing, reporting, communicating, and negotiating, as well as caring for the interests of nationals abroad. It is not properly equatable with the substance or essence of foreign policy.

Whereas in the past diplomacy was readily conceived as a unified, easily comprehensible subject, today consideration of the process, to facilitate discriminating among its components and applications, requires distinguishing various categories based on differing criteria. For example, distinctions sometimes are founded on fundamental cultural and national characteristics, differentiating between Occidental and Oriental, Western and Communist, and totalitarian and democratic forms of diplomacy, between that of developed and developing nations, and among African, Anglo-Saxon, Arab, Asian, European, Latin American and other geo-biological forms. Similarly, alliance and bloc diplomacy is compared with that of neutralist powers. To a large extent, such ascriptions, evoked to establish qualities of change in defining the new diplomacy, are associated less with distinguishable methods of procedure than with the participants—grouped either geographically or functionally—or with the subjects of treatment and concern.

More fundamentally, the literature is replete with allusions to particular brands of diplomatic practice that bear relationship to historical development. Sir Harold Nicolson, well-known British diplomatist, in "The Evolution of Diplomatic Method" (1954), for example, refers to the Greek, Roman, Italian (fifteenth and sixteenth centuries), French (seventeenth to nineteenth centuries), and the American (twentieth century) systems of diplomacy. Reviewing United States historical experience, for illustrative purposes, early American practice acknowledges such forms as "colonial," "revolutionary age," "transcontinental," and "golden era" diplomacy. During the nineteenth century, the substantively-oriented notions of "expansionist" or "manifestly-destined diplomacy," "dollar diplomacy," and "open-door diplomacy," together with such procedurally-related forms as "gunboat diplomacy" and "shirtsleeve diplomacy," crept into United States practice and consciousness.

Beginning with World War I, however, the general conceptualization also came to denote fundamental changes in diplomatic style—which Nicolson brands the "American method." Commencing with Woodrow Wilson emphasis came to be attributed to a "new diplomacy"—characterized as consisting primarily of "parliamentary diplomacy" practiced in the international organization such as the League of Nations, the "personal diplomacy" of political leaders, and "open diplomacy." Nicolson regarded this new version essentially as a new kind of "democratic" or "democratized" diplomacy, portrayed by increased responsiveness to the people, less government confidentiality, a greater degree of legislative control, and popularization in the sense of reposing less emphasis on formal protocol and procedure, together with heavier reliance on "conference diplomacy." Following the many top-level meetings and conferences of the principal European leaders during the 1930's and the World War II conclaves of the President with the British Prime Minister, the Soviet Premier, and other world leaders, some writers came to emphasize "summit diplomacy" in the evolvement of the new diplomacy. Since World War II additional qualities and refinements have emerged, such as intensified diplomacy at the ministerial and technical levels, multi-forum diplomatic relations, and total diplomacy.

All of the basic forms—democratic, conference, parliamentary, open, and personal diplomacy—contribute to the new diplomacy as perceived by Nicolson and others. Furthermore, the introduction of nuclear weaponry and the Cold War produced still other types, which have been called "nuclear," "Cold War," "crisis," and "preventive diplomacy." One also encounters such additional specifications as "corridor," "low profile," "hostage," and even "instant" diplomacy. Many of these, however, are obviously less valid as significant types of diplomatic method than as reflections of the times, geopolitical power relationships, or the subjects of concern. The use of additional adjectives renders the potential list of such mutations virtually endless.

In view of these developments, in any case, current perception of "the new diplomacy" is quite different from that of the 1920's, when the expression first came into use. Its most obvious distinguishment is from pre-World War I "traditional" or "classical" diplomacy, characterized essentially by direct representation and largely bilateral negotiation by professional diplomats or appointees commissioned to serve specifically in a diplomatic capacity. It goes without saying, however, that every age experiencing substantial innovation may conceive of its modification as constituting the "new diplomacy," and the version of today varies from that of the era of World War I, while that of the future is likely to differ as materially from current practice.

The evolving nature of contemporary diplomacy flows from a number of tangible causes. Among the more important are substantial changes in the composition of the family of nations, the nature of interstate concerns, the technology of communications, the objectives of the diplomatic process, and the relationships of governments to peoples.

The most apparent of these is the enlargement of the society of states, resulting in a quantitative magnification of diplomatic practice. Whereas only a dozen countries, largely European, engaged in diplomatic relations at the commencement of the modern state system in the mid-seventeenth century, the number of participants has since increased more than tenfold. Some of this growth has occurred in cycles. One of these materialized in the late eighteenth and early nineteenth centuries when the United States and fifteen of her Latin American neighbors achieved independence by 1825, doubling the society of nations and extending the diplomatic arena to the Western Hemisphere. Another though smaller spurt occurred in the mid-nineteenth century as China and Japan, a number of Central American states, and Liberia were added to the diplomatic community. A major expansionist wave followed World War I, principally in the Baltic, Southeast Europe, and the Middle East, enlarging the number to approximately sixty-five states. By far the most impressive independence boom, however, took place after the Second World War, when some seventy-five new members emerged into the family of nations within a quarter of a century, principally in the Arab world, Africa, Asia, and the Pacific. Such increase in the number of participants naturally has necessitated considerable amplification of diplomatic contact and negotiation.

A second reason for major change is the qualitative proliferation of functional international interests. With the shrinkage of world horizons, the industrial revolution and resulting dependence on the flow of trade, the achievements of scientific discovery, and the growing interaction of states on cultural, economic, financial, social, and technological affairs, governments have come to deal diplomatically with one another on a comprehensive spectrum of problems, some of which were previously left to private individuals, or concerning which there was little need to bargain.

Whereas in the early nineteenth century diplomatic relations were generally restricted to limited types of issues, states now negotiate with one another on a multitude of matters, ranging, for example, from alliances to atomic waste, from outer space and seabed resources jurisdiction to pollution, from disarmament to cell biology and unifying technical nomenclature. In recent years international consultation and deliberation centering on law creation, peaceful settlement of disputes, and crisis management have also increased, and currently interrelations entail virtually every subject in which the modern government harbors any public international interest. This broadening of the substance of international affairs naturally has augmented not only the functional quality, but also the very degree of diplomatic contact, and has necessitated the devisement of new diplomatic forms and forums.

Another of the factors influencing the development of modern diplomacy is the technical revolution in the fields of transportation and communication. Distant points are within hours rather than days or weeks, and long-range consultation now is virtually instantaneous via radio, trans-oceanic cable, and the "hot-line." The President, the Secretary of State, or a special emissary may attend a conference abroad, or undertake a good-will or negotiating mission, and reach virtually any foreign capital in a few hours of flying time. A resident emissary overseas is able to return to Washington as rapidly for consultation, and by telegraph he may cable the Department of State and receive information or instructions in not much more time than is necessary to prepare the responding message. Direct contacts are established via telephone, telegram, or "teleconference," by means of cable, radio, or television, and are even being bounced off space satellites. Negotiators in foreign capitals and at the conference table, therefore, are able to maintain intimate contact with policy makers in their national capitals.

These developments have tended to produce such important changes in contemporary diplomacy as greater disposition to maintain tighter control over policy formulation and the conduct of negotiations by foreign offices and heads of governments, more frequent multilateral gatherings, and increased personal involvement of the President and Secretary of State or the appointment of special presidential emissaries to delicate mediatory, trouble-shooting, and peace-keeping missions. Because modern telecommunications facilities enable governments to address large numbers of people with facility and frequency, mass-communications media also have come to be widely employed to influence the people both at home and abroad more directly and extensively in the conduct of foreign relations.

In earlier times the objectives of diplomacy focused primarily on such basic issues as peace-making, territorial disposition and boundaries, commerce and navigation, immigration and citizenship, extradition, and a limited number of other political and economic issues. Diplomats were dispatched primarily to align policy, resolve difficulties, achieve agreements, and promote amiable relations. In the

1930's and following World War II, the diplomatic process, in some cases, came to be perverted, however, as to these objectives were added the promotion of ideological pretensions and conflict, at times deliberately calculated to induce strained relations, enervate governments, and undermine national stability and international equilibrium. Diplomats have been supplemented with, replaced by, or at times actually converted into propagandists, espionage agents, and subverters. Public affairs media, trained political agitators, and revolutionaries have been employed by some political régimes to weaken or topple other governments and divide their peoples. Whether one agrees with Sir Harold Nicolson or not that diplomacy "by loud speaker" and "by insult" are contradictions in terms, during the Nazi period and the Cold War such innovations came to supplement and at times replaced the traditional activities of the diplomat.

Lord Vansittart, another eminent British diplomatist, especially critical of this desecration of diplomatic practice by Fascist and Communist states, claimed that previously espionage, propaganda, and subversion were not usually engaged in by embassies, although they were often the victims of it. The objectives sought—whether ideologically motivated or adopted for purposes of wielding national power in the international arena—currently are sometimes designed less to persuade governments for purposes of agreement than to seduce or coerce peoples of other lands to revile their countries, their national institutions, and their leaders. This development left its unfortunate and retrogressive mark upon the diplomacy of the mid-twentieth century.

A fifth major cause of change emanates from the emergence of a more "democratic" perception of international relations. Formerly the conduct of foreign affairs was entrusted to selected members of a small élite dispatched to promote the policies determined by national governments. In democracies, theoretically, the will of the people was intended to be represented by political leaders and policy was expected to be determined in the best interests of the polity. In the twentieth century, as part of the democratization of national states and their intergovernmental processes, the people are persuaded to become more involved, directly as well as indirectly—to express their views more freely, to arrive at their own conclusions, and to influence policy and negotiations through the media, mass meetings and demonstrations, national legislatures, and the ballot box.

"Democratized diplomacy"—sometimes also called "popular diplomacy"—denotes an increase in the influence over foreign relations of representative bodies, greater openness (if not of negotiations under way, then at least of the nature of foreign policy and diplomatic end-products), and multipartite deliberations in which policy statements and negotiatory arguments are addressed to peoples as well as to fellow negotiators. It also signifies liberalization of the decision-making process, utilization of representatives of the people as primary negotiators, and appeals for popular support of policy positions and diplomatic exchanges. It is epitomized by an insistence in the name of the people not only on a "right to know," but also some "right to participate," or at least an augmented "right to articulate."

In short, the diplomatic process is less the preserve of states and governments, and is brought more immediately into the concerns of peoples, without clearly distinguishing the legitimate need of the individual citizen to be properly advised and represented as a member of the body politic from his individual or collective overt influence upon the operational management of foreign affairs in his own behalf. The "public," however it may be conceived, therefore, not only plays the rôle of prescribing the outer limits of foreign policy and relations and of holding the political leadership and the diplomat ultimately accountable for their stewardship, but also becomes more vigorously entwined in the process.

A final major cause of change—so far as the United States is concerned—results from its rise to a position of international paramountcy following World War II and its assumption of responsibility for worldwide interests and leadership. Having become an epicenter of international power, the United States found itself actively engaged diplomatically in every corner of the globe and in all manner of issues and crises. It also became a joiner, participating in virtually every international conference and international organization not restricted to the Soviet bloc, the uncommitted powers, and certain limited areally-focused arrangements. The result has been a wholesale magnification and complication of its diplomatic relations.

These developments have produced fundamental changes in diplomatic practice—not only in degree, but also in kind—not merely in the magnitude of intergovernmental transactions, but in the very quality of the diplomatic process as well. Among the more significant results—aside from the burgeoning of both traditional and multilateral diplomacy and greater openness respecting policy and the results of negotiations—are the growth of multiple diplomacy through utilizing combinations of forums and techniques and the broadening of the range of diplomatic participants to embrace both the highest ranking officials and a remarkable array of technical experts. Needless to say, the consequences of these and related changes have also engendered a host of new problems.

Modern diplomats must be prepared to handle issues which encompass almost all aspects of human life, because virtually every feature of contemporary existence possesses some international dimensions. Systematic review of this aspect of contemporary diplomacy would be monumental and warrants volumes of analysis. Even when surveyed simply in terms of some of the more obvious quantifiable factors—such as the number and size of diplomatic missions, the flow of messages between them and foreign offices, the production of diplomatic documentation, and the amount of conference and treaty participation—the degree of expansion is staggering.

For example, whereas the United States maintained diplomatic relations with only five countries in 1800, and forty-one in 1900, this grew to approximately sixty-five by the time of World War II and has since doubled, numbering more than 130 in the early 1970's. In addition, special methods are employed for dealing with emerging states and other countries with which Washington does not maintain regular diplomatic relations, such as the "liaison mission" to the People's Republic of China, to which must be added many representational and observership missions to the United Nations and other international agencies. While United States consular missions have declined in number since 1930, they still amount to approximately 300. All told, therefore, American diplomatic and consular representation currently is handled by some 450 field missions. These are supplemented by dozens of economic, military, presidential emissary, and other "special" missions that crisscross the globe.*

Other major powers are similarly represented diplomatically, but many of the smaller states are unable to provide the financial and personnel resources to man comparable massive diplomatic programs. If 135 independent countries were represented by diplomats accredited to each other's capitals and sent missions to fifteen of the major international organizations, the aggregate quantity of diplomatic establishments required would exceed 20,000 throughout the world.

Technological advancements in communications have facilitated the massive expansion of diplomatic exchanges among foreign offices and field missions. In the early days of American diplomacy they were customarily transmitted by courier or ordinary mail. Now they are

---

* EDITOR'S NOTE: These trends have continued; in 1978 the United States maintained more than 140 regular resident diplomatic missions and the number of consular establishments declined to approximately 115.

handled by a complex facility employing telegraphic, teletype, and airgram equipment, radio hookups, encoding and decoding mechanisms, couriers, and traditional diplomatic mail-pouch service, in addition to the ordinary mails. In 1965 the Department of State announced the establishment of a computer-based terminal system to handle its worldwide flow of cables. Switchboards operated within the Department service continental and overseas telephone, cable, and wireless calls, keeping Washington in direct contact with even the most remote outposts.

The current volume of diplomatic communications business is prodigious. The Department of State handles millions of messages each year for itself and related agencies. These include thousands of diplomatic notes, more than 100,000 dispatches, and tens of thousands of instructions to American diplomats abroad. Included also are one and one-half million telegrams, or approximately 4,000 per day. Dean Rusk has reported that, during his eight years as Secretary of State, some 2,100,000 cables—or more than a quarter of a million per year—went out over his signature alone, and these did not include the messages of the Agency for International Development, the Peace Corps, and other administrative agencies for which he bore responsibility.

The expansion of the diplomatic activity of the Department of State is also reflected in the magnitude of its overall documentation. By 1970 the total quantity of departmental resources amounted to more than 357,500 cubic feet of records. Of this massive reservoir, some 167,000 cubic feet of documents were located in the Department and its overseas missions, while the remainder were deposited for refinement and preservation in The National Archives, such transfer normally occurring at the end of thirty years. Illustrating growth, after World War II departmental records increased at the rate of approximately 1,250 cubic feet in a single year, and currently this volume of documentary production is advancing at an even greater rate. Moreover, since the mid-1860's the Department of State has published more than 250 volumes of diplomatic documentation entitled "Foreign Relations of the United States," originally compiling a single volume annually, but recently producing at the rate of eight to ten volumes per year, which, at a projected average of one thousand pages per volume, amounts to nearly 100,000 pages of systematically printed documentation each decade—in addition to policy statements, press releases, special studies, and other published materials.

The expansion of foreign-relations activity is further attested to by the growth of international treaty-making. Whereas 4,834 such instruments were negotiated and registered with the League of Nations in the quarter century between 1920 and 1945, averaging 195 per year, this grew to approximately 7,500 during the first two decades following World War II, amounting to 375 per year, published in more than 530 volumes of the United Nations Treaty Series.

The United States has become a party to an increasing number of treaties and agreements over the years, averaging less than two per year in the early nineteenth century; but since 1939, these have jumped to almost 190 annually, and in one year they nearly reached the peak of one new treaty or agreement each day.* The subjects encompassed within them have also proliferated with the broadening of the international interests of governments to include a great many cultural, humanitarian, economic, scientific, social, and technical subjects not previously involved.

The experience of other countries parallels that of the United States, and the consummation of each treaty and agreement necessitates weeks if not months and sometimes years of policy formulation, conferral, negotiation, and action to devise and approve agreed endproducts. These are augmented by the dozens of resolutions and other determinations of international agencies. Such expansion has led Dean Rusk to allude to "the explosion of international law since 1945," and another international publicist to conclude that more international law has come into being since World War II than was developed during the entire preceding history of mankind.

Concomitant with this enormous growth of diplomatic activity in the contemporary world is the tightening of direct management over affairs abroad by the Department of State and other foreign offices, so that—it is often alleged—the diplomat has degenerated into merely the eyes, the ears, and the mouthpiece of his government, and he is said to possess less discretionary authority and policymaking responsibility than was previously the case. The facts are that he is busier than ever and that he may influence policy making substantially depending on his credibility and circumstances. Furthermore, national bureaucracies—which are not only in instantaneous contact with the diplomat and possess information not always fully available to him, but also view issues from a broader perspective and are better qualified to determine national policy priorities—are bound to manage more closely their diplomacy in the field. The issue, despite

---

* EDITOR'S NOTE: As of 1978 the United States was party to some 6,575 treaties and agreements, and in recent years it has signed approximately 400 new treaties and agreements annually.

the criticism by the professional of his declining rôle, therefore, is less a proposition of returning to the good old days of nineteenth-century diplomacy than a matter of the degree to which the diplomat contributes effectively to the current process of managing foreign affairs.

A great deal of diplomatic business is conducted *among* as well as *between* governments. Widespread international conferencing has become a hallmark of contemporary diplomacy. "In the conduct of foreign relations," reports the Department of State, "perhaps no greater change has occurred in the past half-century than the increased emphasis on multilateral diplomacy and the employment of the international conference as a medium for co-operative action among governments."

The multipartite diplomatic gathering was a rarity prior to the birth of the United States, usually confined either to arranging a settlement at the end of hostilities or to developing precepts of international law. Conferencing—as a diplomatic technique—came to be widely used only as late as the nineteenth century, but even then it was primarily bilateral, with the general, comprehensive conclave remaining highly exceptional until the Hague Conferences at the turn of the century.

The United States attended only one hundred international conferences to 1900—averaging less than one per year, and, of the forty-two most important international assemblages between 1776 and 1914, it attended only six, in addition to a few inter-American meetings—and none of these took place prior to the 1880's. American conference participation has grown progressively, and since World War II the United States has been attending virtually every major gathering in which it has a conceivable interest of consequence and from which it is not logically excluded by the participants. Current United States conference attendance amounts to an annual average of 350 to 400, and in 1972 the Department of State projected some 475 conferencing participations, the preponderant majority of which were multipartite, and most of which involved sessions of established international organizations and their subsidiary agencies.*

At the close of the First World War, British diplomat Lord Maurice Hankey, who personally attended nearly five hundred in-

---

* EDITOR'S NOTE: In recent years, the United States has attended an average of between 800 and 900 international conferences per year, and in 1978 this numbered more than a thousand.

ternational meetings in an official capacity, became one of the most articulate exponents of multilateralism, which, in "Diplomacy by Conference" (1946), he virtually equated with the "new diplomacy." Conceptualistically, the international conference is that form of diplomatic deliberation which involves conferment around the discussion table, with the parties functioning collectively through a common forum of either individual *ad hoc* gatherings, occasional or regularized meetings, or sessions of deliberative organs and agencies of international organizations.

"Parliamentary diplomacy," a currently prevailing mutation described as "institutionalized conferencing," is normally applied within permanent political mechanisms founded on agreed constitutive acts. In this guise much international conferencing implies discussions within fixed and continuing forums, their plenary sessions frequently being public, or at least in the limelight, and forensic exposition often is freely manifested and decisionmaking is reduced, but usually only ostensibly on important political issues, to a formalized voting process. Such parliamentary diplomacy, still rare in the nineteenth century, is currently practiced within the United Nations, the Organization of American States, and many of the other nearly seventy-five multipartite public international organizations in which the United States participates.*

Many of these provide not only forums for discussion and negotiation within their established organs, but also the site and facilities for informal and sometimes unofficial diplomatic contact in their corridors and at the coffee table. Major international organization centers, such as the United Nations, the North Atlantic Treaty Organization, and the European Communities have come to serve as the principal sites of a great deal of ordinary traditional diplomacy, especially among the smaller powers which cannot afford, in terms of both qualified emissaries and embassy facilities, to be represented by regular resident missions in the capitals of all other states. At times, however, important bilateral negotiations of major powers also are undertaken in such "neutral" locations, as was the case with the settlement of the Berlin blockade of 1948.

Dean Rusk has indicated that, as Secretary of State, he spent two or three weeks each year in New York at the beginning of General Assembly sessions, during which time he and other foreign ministers engaged freely in high-level diplomatic discussions. Such conferring, he concludes, generated "a kind of corporate sense among

---

* EDITOR'S NOTE: Chapter 4 provides more comprehensive commentary on multilateral diplomacy.

65

the world's foreign ministers." Much the same type of direct, traditional diplomacy is pursued by regular diplomats at such conferencing locations, which, therefore, have become the principal dual centers of both multilateral and bilateral diplomacy.

Some analysts, especially professional practitioners such as Sir Harold Nicolson and Lord Vansittart, have denounced parliamentary diplomacy as a *non sequitur*, being neither genuine parliamentarianism nor authentic diplomacy. However, former American Foreign Service Officer Charles W. Thayer, though deploring "diplomacy by ballot" and regarding parliamentary diplomacy as lacking the "quality of reality," nevertheless concedes that "it is a form of diplomacy no matter how odd." Professor Hans J. Morgenthau decries what he calls "the vice of the majority decision," juxtaposed with genuine negotiation as a diplomatic technique.

On the other hand, Dean Rusk, representing the views of a great many supporters of international institutionalization, states that the dozens of international organizations, with their permanent bodies which represent the governments of the world "in congress assembled," add "a major new dimension to modern diplomacy." With 133 members in 1972 and about one hundred items considered at each session of the General Assembly, he adds, this means that 13,300 votes are cast in the plenary meetings of each Assembly, in which the United States has some sort of stake. He also intimates that he would be surprised if more than 20 per cent of these votes are based on instructions from home governments, in part because many states do not have foreign offices prepared to follow the enormous agenda of the United Nations system and lack the funds for effective communications to cope with fast-moving parliamentary situations.

Of related importance is the development of what may be designated "multiple diplomacy," which has been ascribed a number of meanings. Previously mentioned is the existence of available international organization sites which provide alternative forums in which bilateral discussions and negotiations may unobtrusively take place on matters not necessarily central to the business before the multilateral agency. Even matters related to the functions of a particular international organization may be raised in optional forums, such as the General Assembly or the Security Council. Or it may be introduced into two or more international organizations having overlapping or competing jurisdictions and interests. So far as the functions of program development, regulatory control, or simply policy coalescence on non-critical issues are concerned, usually questions of jurisdiction and competence are readily resolvable, but where they are not, secondary diplomacy needs to be undertaken to determine the responsible or acceptable primary forum.

When important political and security problems, international conflicts, and crises are involved, the ready availability of alternative diplomatic machinery may have serious disadvantages. Often a subsidiary dispute results, respecting which forum or diplomatic process should be utilized for settling the primary issue, and sometimes this secondary aspect may become equally difficult to resolve. If the stakes are high and important national interests are concerned, governments naturally press for the use of that forum which is most likely to offer it the greatest opportunity to achieve its objectives. Such diplomatic alternatives vary from restricted negotiations among the governments most directly involved, through such a forum with a single or small number of "neutral" participants, to various multipartite diplomatic agencies. On occasion, an uninvolved state also may initiate action to bring the matter before a particular forum, usually one in which it has an interest and a voice, and sometimes such initiation contravenes the expressed desires of one or another of the participants most directly involved in the problem or crisis. Such third-party action may be resented as diplomatic intervention, further exacerbating the original issue.

Over the years, complex networks of potentially competing negotiatory and peace-keeping diplomatic facilities have been established, providing a range of alternative readily available forums. These embrace adjudication by the International Court of Justice and a few other judicial tribunals, arbitration within the framework of the Permanent Court of Arbitration, multipartite conciliation by the United Nations, the Organization of American States, and other agencies, and arbitration and conciliation within regularized bilateral arrangements (such as those provided for the United States by the forty-six Kellogg Treaties of 1928 and their predecessors, the twenty-five Root arbitration treaties of 1908 and twenty-one Bryan cooling-off pacts of 1913).

All of these forums supplement ordinary, direct negotiation or *ad hoc* processes mutually acceptable to the parties. Although most differences and conflicts still are dealt with by such traditional diplomacy among the states concerned, the alternative multilateral and bilateral mechanisms generally available today may serve a useful purpose, but their very existence provides disputants with potentially competing options and national views frequently differ as to the "proper" diplomatic facility or procedure to handle a given matter.

Furthermore, while the availability of pre-existing diplomatic machinery may be advantageous in moments of diplomatic crisis, as Professor Inis L. Claude, Jr., has put it in an essay on multilateralism, the collective forum, such as the United Nations, "should not itself undertake to serve as an agency of conciliation" because this necessitates taking sides and may be viewed as multilateral intervention, but rather it "should encourage and facilitate diplomatic negotiation" among the disputants.* This does not mean that, when diplomatic relations are strained or severed, the multipartite forums may not in some cases afford a ready avenue for handling those matters the parties are willing to accommodate within them, but their availability is clearly not guaranteed, and may not even constitute a mutually acceptable, remedy.

Another kind of multiple diplomacy is characterized by the employment of a multiplicity of forums and techniques in dealing with a particular situation which, if projected to the fullest possible extent, has been called total diplomacy. At the time of the Cuban missile crisis, for example, the United States utilized such measures as a massive endeavor to inform the world of the facts in the situation, bilateral exchanges through the American and Soviet embassies in Washington and Moscow, summit communication by means of written messages flowing between President John F. Kennedy and Premier Nikita S. Khrushchev, indirect communication through others including the United Nations Secretary General, private and collective meetings with representatives of the American republics in Washington and within the Organization of American States, high-level contact with certain North Atlantic powers deputed to a corps of presidential special emissaries, and discussion within the aegis of the United Nations. Careful attention was paid to deciding which process or forum was to be utilized for what purpose, and determining which were to be employed simultaneously and which sequentially—and for the latter, the sequence to be pursued.

Another characteristic of the new diplomacy is the broadening of the range of diplomatic participation, by complementing the rôle of the traditional resident emissary and the professional diplomatist with greater involvement of political principals, on the one hand, and of

---

* EDITOR'S NOTE: See Professor Claude's analysis of multilateral diplomacy in Chapter 4.

specialists and technical experts, on the other. "Personal diplomacy," as noted earlier, also has come to be regarded as one of the primary characteristics of the new diplomacy, and involves increased participation of chiefs of state, heads of government, foreign ministers, and other officials of cabinet rank. When this is of the highest order—that is, when it transcends the ministerial level—it is called "diplomacy at the summit." Although the expression "summit diplomacy" was first used journalistically in the 1950's, as a form of state practice it is as old as history itself. Although employed in the United States since the days of President Washington, it has been broadened in scope, and currently encompasses presidential foreign policy-making and enunciation, personal presidential communications, the use of presidential personal representatives or special agents, visits of world leaders to the United States, presidential visits and tours abroad, and summit meetings and conferences.*

Each of these forms of diplomacy at the summit has its uses and limitations, and no recent President seems to be able to escape their attractions completely. Nevertheless, because of differing perspectives and temperaments, Presidents vary materially in how they employ them. While the modes of summit diplomacy may serve fruitful purposes and personalization may prove to be individually gratifying, Presidents need to avoid what former diplomat George Kennan calls diplomacy by dilettantism, and they need to exercise restraint to avoid what Dean Rusk has called the temptations flowing from the chemistry of the office which seem inexorably to entice them to the summit. The functioning of the President as Diplomat-in-Chief, a practice now entrenched as an acknowledged component of the new diplomacy—although widespread, time-tested, and above all newsworthy—is no guaranteed panacea for all international problems or a magic cure-all for international malady.

Like the President, the Secretary of State also engages personally in international conferencing and other diplomatic activities to a far greater extent than was the case prior to World War II. Foreign ministers not only exercise the traditional function of dealing with foreign ambassadors in national capitals, but they also head delegations to many international conferences and sessions of international organizations, and undertake more frequent, widespread travel for discussions with high level officials throughout the world.

The Secretary of State, for example, has become a peripatetic personal participant, heading American delegations to the most im-

---

* EDITOR'S NOTE: Summit diplomacy is treated more comprehensively in Chapter 4.

portant inter-American conferences, the four-power Council of Foreign Ministers, and other diplomatic gatherings. Because much contemporary international organization machinery has been established at the ministerial level, the Secretary of State regularly attends the sessions of such agencies as the United Nations General Assembly, the Councils of the North Atlantic Alliance and the Southeast Asia Treaty Organization, and the Organ of Consultation of the inter-American system. Foreign Ministers also represent their governments regularly in the sessions of the Council of Europe, the European Communities, Western European Union, and the League of Arab States.*

The personal involvement of the Secretary of State abroad was exceptional prior to World War II, and in the 1890's, when needed for negotiations, two Secretaries—John W. Foster and William R. Day—resigned in order to undertake such missions. Elihu Root was the first Secretary to attend an international conference outside the United States, when he went to Rio de Janeiro in 1906 for the Third Inter-American Conference, to contribute to the opening ceremonies but not to negotiate. Robert Lansing served as a member of President Woodrow Wilson's five-man delegation to the Paris Conference at the end of World War I, Frank B. Kellogg sailed to Europe in 1928 to sign the Peace Pact personally, and Cordell Hull participated in half a dozen negotiations abroad, including the Moscow Foreign Ministers Meeting in 1943, preluding the first Big Three wartime summit conference.

More recently, Edward R. Stettinius, occupying the office for only seven months, spent more than half of that time in negotiations, James F. Byrnes was engaged 350 of his 562 days as Secretary in international conferences, and Dean Acheson attended approximately twenty-five conferences and similar negotiations in four years. John Foster Dulles achieved an unprecedented fifty conference negotiations and traveled 560,000 miles in little more than six years, and Christian Herter spent eighty of his first 115 days as Secretary away from Washington, including nine weeks in Geneva conferring on the Berlin question in 1959.

Dean Rusk made fifty-two trips abroad, for approximately twenty-five consultations, meetings, and conferences, traveling nearly 600,000 miles, and devoting more than 375 days en route and at the discussion table, which amounts to more than one of his eight years in office. Adding the days spent in similar discussion in Washington, New York, Honolulu, and elsewhere in the United States, as well as

---

* EDITOR'S NOTE: Commentary on ministerial diplomacy is included in Chapter 4.

in preparation and reporting time, the conclusion is inescapable that the contemporary Secretary of State dedicates a major portion of his energy to serving personally as a ranking diplomat-at-large, which tempers both the office and the diplomatic processes.

Since World War II, other cabinet members also have assumed increasing diplomatic capacities. Ministers of defense, commerce, and finance particularly, but also others, have come to engage in representation, discussions, and negotiations dealing at the higher echelons with financial, trade, security, and other matters. For example, the Secretary of the Treasury regularly attends sessions of the International Bank and Monetary Fund and in currency negotiations, and the Secretary of Defense accompanies the Secretary of State to meetings of the North Atlantic Alliance and other collective defense arrangements.

Another innovation in recent times is the increasing participation of experts, specialists, and technicians in diplomatic practice, either as members of diplomatic teams or as primary negotiators. In the first capacity they serve as advisers and in other staff capacities, or they function as principals in the subsidiary levels of diplomatic forums, such as international conference committees, technical drafting service, and the like. In the second capacity some assume a central rôle in negotiations on technical as distinguished from political or diplomatic matters. Because the scope of international concerns has broadened so enormously and encompasses so many highly specialized subjects—such as child welfare, crop generic resources, crystallography, infestation, large dams, penology, type faces, and many others—a great deal of contemporary diplomacy centering on them must be left to the experts. Such technical, at times esoteric, issues can only be dealt with effectively by knowledgeable specialists, and the diplomatic need is met, to some degree, by having specialists in the professional diplomatic service, but mainly by appointing experts to specific diplomatic assignments.

In summary, diplomacy is a dynamic institution, designed to facilitate interstate relations and promote the national and international aims of nations—be they fundamental goals, vital interests, or concrete policy objectives. It functions, *ipso facto*, at the epicenter of the international cosmos as a means of aligning correlative interests and accommodating differences. Constituting an interrelational method in an inherently competitive and sometimes adversary milieu—and not besought as an end in itself—diplomacy cannot be expected to achieve the impossible. The degree of its success necessarily varies in direct proportion to the negotiability of competing policies and the reasonableness of national goals.

Most analysts concede that there is no genuine alternative to diplomacy, or as columnist Drew Middleton has put it: "Diplomacy is the only chance we have." It serves an essential and continuing purpose and, to remain effective, it needs to mutate in response to changing circumstances and requirements. The conditions under which the old diplomacy of the nineteenth century operated have long since ceased to exist, and "the diplomatic methods appropriate to" that period, according to Henry A. Kissinger, "proved unequal to the situation after 1918." Persistent longing for a return to the older, classical form of international relations—really little different from expecting diplomacy to be any less astatic than history itself—is illusory if not visionary. Even Harold Nicolson, for decades one of the staunchest critics of the new diplomacy, came to avow "that the principles of sound diplomacy—which are immutable—will in the end prevail, and thus calm the chaos with which the transition between the old and the new has for the moment bewildered the world."

The true test of statesmanship lies in neither outright rejection nor slavish endorsement of innovation and change which, in any case, may be inevitable, but rather in molding the process of diplomacy to blend the best of both the old and the new to produce the better— or at least the most livable—results. Whatever emerges as a new diplomacy in any era, nevertheless, will itself be mutable, will change with the times, and unfortunately is likely never to approximate the status of perfectibility.

Contemporary Diplomacy at Work

ROBERT J. PRANGER

Perhaps the most critical issue facing the United States and the other nations of the world in the years ahead concerns the capacity of political institutions to cope with global issues. Historically, nations have always had to deal with challenges to their security and economic well-being; what distinguishes the post-World War II era from earlier ones are the scope of these challenges and the catastrophic consequences we may endure if they cannot be met. Yet as challenges take on new forms, it is important to ask whether institutions must change as well.

In a book entitled *Renaissance Diplomacy*, Garrett Mattingly wrote the following: "During the transition from medieval to modern times, in diplomacy as in some other fields, formal institutions changed less than might have been expected. It was the objects of policy and the vision of society which changed." This quote is, I believe, especially relevant to our times. Since antiquity, rulers have delegated powers to agents and sent them to other lands to represent the interests of the tribe, feudal manor, city-state or nation state. Diplomacy was and is the art of persuasion, of accommodating the interests of two or more political entities so as to avoid unrestrained competition for scarce resources. Yet interstate relations have undergone both qualitative and quantitative revolutions in recent years, and what is of interest is the manner in which these changes have affected the work and character of diplomats today. Regarding these changes I shall deal with the following topics: (1) the qualitative and quantitative expansion of diplomacy in the international community and of American foreign relations within this community; (2) the evolving role of the Department of State and diplomatic services; (3) the

SOURCE: "Diplomacy at Work," unpublished manuscript, 1978.

emergence of multilateral diplomacy through international organizations and conferences; (4) the relations between executive and legislative branches in today's American diplomacy, including congressional assertion of its powers in this area; and (5) some reflections on the role of the modern American ambassador amidst all this complex, working diplomacy.

Quantitative and Qualitative Expansion of Diplomacy Today. The ambassador who embarks today upon an assignment to another nation's capital or to any of an increasing number of multilateral forums must still concern himself or herself with the traditional questions of peace and war, protection of one's own citizens in foreign lands, fishing and navigation rights, and trade. The challenges to a nation's interests may not have changed much over the decades, but the manners in which they now manifest themselves have. Questions pertaining to adequate supplies of food, energy, and water, for instance, may now involve scores of nations and regional organizations. This is especially evident when one considers for a moment international trade and the way in which our goals and interests have expanded in conjunction with technological advances in transportation and communications.

Because trade has become such a critical factor for the welfare of all nations, and because our trading partners have increased so dramatically in numbers as well as intensity of relations, we have found it preferable to negotiate reduction of tariffs and other barriers to trade in multilateral settings such as GATT [General Agreement on Tariffs and Trade]. This, in turn, has required the United States to negotiate with regional economic and political groupings, be they formal or informal, such as the European Economic Community. Interrelated with these trade negotiations are the more general issues being discussed in the "North-South Dialogue" between industrially developed and less-developed countries. This "dialogue" may take the path of general principle, but it can become very specific as well, as in the twenty or so commodity areas now under negotiation between the United States and other nations, ranging from copper to wheat and including the vital realm of petroleum products.

Other contemporary challenges to national interests have been dealt with through negotiations to prevent the further proliferation of nuclear weapons and to regulate the export of critical nuclear fuels and reprocessing technologies. The Strategic Arms Limitation Talks have sought to control the development of atomic threats to the physical security of all states, and treaties have been signed to avert the militarization of outer space, the seabeds, and the Antarctic. Most recently, international terrorism and violations of human rights have served as topics of discussion among diplomats both in the capitals of the world and at the United Nations. Many of these negotiations have taken on a permanent character, as nations grapple with new developments and challenges.

In dealing with this complicated multitude of issues, the diplomat has been fortunate to be able to take advantage of another revolution of the modern era—the revolution in communications and transportation. As Professor Elmer Plischke of the University of Maryland notes in his 1973 work on "The New Diplomacy":

> The current volume of diplomatic communications business is prodigious. The Department of State handles millions of messages each year for itself and related agencies. These include thousands of diplomatic notes, more than 100,000 dispatches, and tens of thousands of instructions to American diplomats abroad. Included also are one-and-one-half million telegrams, or approximately 4,000 per day. Dean Rusk has reported that, during his eight years as Secretary of State, some 2,100,000 cables—or more than a quarter of a million per year—went out over his signature alone, and these did not include the messages of the Agency for International Development, the Peace Corps, and other administrative agencies for which he bore responsibility.

This plethora of communication, which also includes prodigious use of the telephone, may be a mixed blessing. Having to contend with this information explosion on any given embassy workday can provoke some nostalgia for earlier years of American diplomacy, such as described by Dean Acheson in *Present at the Creation*, when President Harrison and Secretary of State Blaine "wrote to each other in longhand almost every day, largely about appointments and minute points of draftsmanship in the Bering Sea seal fisheries treaty."

Modern transportation has made its own impact on the quantitative and qualitative expansion of our diplomacy. The art of summitry is immeasurably aided by jet travel, to say nothing of what may happen as heads of state and their cabinets "beat the sun" on supersonic aircraft. From 1970 to 1974 President Nixon made twelve trips abroad, while President Ford took seven such trips in 1974–1975. The indefatigable Henry Kissinger logged twenty-three such journeys in two years alone, 1975 and 1976. Meanwhile, according to Department of State count, during the 1970–1977 period, state and official summit visits to Washington from other countries numbered 222. The current administration has its share of summiteers: During 1977, his first year in office, President Carter visited Europe and embarked on a six-nation trip after Christmas; Vice President Mondale made two trips abroad; the peripatetic Andrew Young made seven such trips; and the First Lady visited seven Latin American countries. Secretary of State Vance picked up where his predecessor left off, taking some ten trips abroad in less than one year.

In the process of all this quantitative and qualitative expansion of our diplomacy, we have seen an increasing number of treaties and agreements consummated between ourselves and others. During 1977 alone the United States signed approximately twenty new treaties and entered into nearly 500 new agreements with other nations and international organizations. This adds up to more than one formal commitment a day, a staggering figure when one considers that from 1889 to 1939 this country averaged but twenty-nine agreements and treaties a year. Since 1960 the United States has signed a number of multipartite treaties, covering such diverse issues as diplomatic and consular affairs, the testing and proliferation of nuclear weapons, human rights, and the hijacking of aircraft. Noteworthy bilateral treaties negotiated in recent years include those dealing with the Panama Canal, the limitation of strategic arms, and the release of American prisoners in Mexican jails, among many others.

What all these treaties signify is the expansion of U.S. foreign concerns, in both number and subject matter. While admittedly two world wars made it imperative for the United States to draw itself intimately into the affairs of the community of nations, recent recognition of the growing interdependence of nations for their livelihood and physical security has served to reinforce this activist trend in American diplomacy. It is within such a world—one more complex and sophisticated in terms of threats and interests of allies and adversaries alike—that today's diplomat must ply his trade. It is a more demanding world, both for the diplomat and for the traditional institutions through which conflicting interests must be resolved.

Let us now consider how this world has affected the State Department and its diplomats.

The Evolving Role of the Department of State and Diplomatic Services. Since the earliest days of the United States all matters of foreign relations have been handled by the Department of State and its diplomatic and consular services, with the exception of issues related to defense, trade, and finance. But even in these latter areas, diplomats had to be kept abreast of policies. It is a fairly recent phenomenon that more and more agencies and departments of government have acquired interests and a physical presence in U.S. diplomatic missions abroad. When the first Hoover Commission published its report in 1949, forty-six of the fifty-nine major federal agencies in Washington were found to be involved to some extent in foreign affairs. The 1975 report on the organization of U.S. foreign policy prepared by the Murphy Commission brings home this point about the complexity of the international activities of U.S. domestic bureaucracies in a more contemporary setting. Aside from the traditional concerns of the Departments of State, Defense, Treasury, and Commerce, the formulation of foreign policy today often involves the participation of the Office of Management and Budget, the Arms Control and Disarmament Agency, the Agency for International Development, the newly created Department of Energy, and a host of other offices.

This unprecedented expansion of American interests abroad has inevitably resulted in problems of communication between agencies and coordination of their policies. While recent administrations have sought to remedy this condition, it is obvious to anyone who has served as an ambassador that much still needs to be done. Greater coordination of policy must be accomplished not only in Washington, but also within the embassy, and among embassies and consulates abroad. Centralization in the State Department of responsibility for nonmilitary matters may be one possible solution, but we must bear in mind how this will affect the character and qualifications of career diplomats in the years to come. Even if this centralization is accomplished, however, new problems of coordination are likely to arise as additional significant functions are undertaken, unless they are also placed within the aegis of the Department of State. If U.S. foreign activities were to be reduced to three types—namely, diplomatic-consular missions, military operations, and participation in international organizations—with clear delineation of the responsibility of the Department of State and diplomatic service, some of the confusion and lack of coordination might be eliminated. Should the specialized and technical concerns of various agencies become the province of diplomats, however, the traditional methods for training future envoys will have to adapt to these new challenges.

One of the ironies of modern times, and one which will surely tax the stamina of any diplomat, is the increasing prevalence of summit, or personal, diplomacy. While personal diplomacy has always been a feature of international negotiation, two factors have served to expand its application in recent years. One is the revolution in transportation mentioned earlier, the other is the manner in which many modern international institutions have been created. For in-

77

stance, it is incumbent upon any secretary of state to attend the opening session of each General Assembly of the United Nations and to make yearly appearances before the NATO Council of Ministers meeting. Nor is this something unique to American diplomacy; foreign ministers must attend an endless series of conferences and meetings within the context of the Council of Europe, the Common Market, the Western European Union, the Organization of American States, the League of Arab States, and the list goes on.

Contrast this with the period preceding World War II, when such highly personalized diplomacy by senior officials was not unknown, but also not commonplace. When, for instance, in the 1890s the personal involvement of individuals with the stature of secretaries of state was felt to be necessary in certain negotiations, two secretaries—John W. Foster and William R. Day—*resigned* their offices to undertake such missions.

Today such personal missions by cabinet ministers to foreign capitals are no longer the exception but the rule. James F. Byrnes, for instance, spent 350 of his 562 days as Secretary of State attending international conferences. While those were admittedly difficult times, one has only to recall the travels of a very recent secretary of state to realize how much the work of diplomats has changed. In this regard, it might be interesting to recall how Cyrus Vance, before taking office, sought to dispel any notions that he would become as seasoned a foreign traveler as his predecessor. Yet in his first ten months as secretary of state, Mr. Vance made ten trips overseas.

It is important to remember, however, that as the scope of this highest level of diplomacy has expanded, so too have the other levels. I think it is fair to say that international issues today have in common a complexity unimaginable a few decades ago and a frightening potential for disrupting domestic and international affairs. It has consequently become apparent that the diplomat of earlier times—one schooled in the arts and letters, the generalist—can no longer cope with many of these issues without competent and highly trained experts at his side at the conference table. Increasingly "technical experts" are included in delegations to international conferences and embassy staffs. They provide the specialized knowledge needed to fathom the complexities of international finance and trade, affairs of multinational corporations, the technical aspects of pollution, nuclear waste disposal, and a multitude of other issues. Benjamin Franklin, one of the earliest U.S. envoys, was perhaps the quintessential generalist, yet one could hardly expect even him, were he with us today, to be an expert in nuclear physics, international finance, marine science, and the economics of commodity trading, all at the same time.

Since a good deal of this technical diplomacy is carried on under the aegis of international organizations and conferences, this is a good point at which to discuss the emergence of multilateral diplomacy.

The Emergence of Multilateral Diplomacy through International Organizations and Conferences. Contrary to general impression, based largely on the rejection of the Versailles Treaty and refusal to join the League of Nations, whose covenant President Wilson helped to negotiate at the Paris Peace Conference at the end of World War I, the United States has been and is a "joiner." Except for the League, the United States has participated in virtually all major multipartite intergovernmental organizations in which it had any conceivable interest and from which it was not excluded by others. Not only has the United States been an active participant in the development of international agencies; often, especially in recent times, it has been the initiator. The United Nations itself exemplifies U.S. leadership.

The contemporary sweep of American participation in international organizations is not fully appreciated. During the decade ending with the termination of World War II, the United States was a member of more than three hundred international organizations. These varied in significance from the United Nations to the Cape Spartel Light arrangement, and included about four-fifths of the most important international public agencies in existence in 1945.

Currently there are some 225 to 250 multipartite and bipartite official intergovernmental organizations, and states have the opportunity to affiliate with a broad range of permanent diplomatic institutions. The United States participates in approximately seventy-five multipartite agencies, including the United Nations, as well as in the International Court of Justice, fourteen U.N. specialized agencies (plus the International Labor Organization until November 1977), more than twenty additional global organizations, at least half a dozen regional banks and related financial institutions, approximately ten inter-American and other regional organizations (including NATO and Manila Pact), plus various commodity and other agencies.

As impressive as these membership figures are—on the world scene Americans seem to be as big "joiners" as they are domestically —U.S. financial support is equally extensive. The United States contributes some $400 to $500 million annually to the United Nations system, accounting for approximately 25 percent of its budgets and assessments (exclusive of the International Bank and other financial agencies). United Nations budgets rose from roughly $19 million in 1946 to $400 million in 1977, and the Secretary General requested a 20 percent increase for the next two years. At present more than half the members of the United Nations are minimum contributors, jointly supporting only 1.68 percent of the regular budget but wielding a majority of the General Assembly's votes.

Needless to say, the United States has considerable diplomatic as well as monetary investment in these multilateral involvements. Such complex diplomacy has been the subject of recent comment at the highest levels of American foreign policy making. In September 1976, Secretary of State Kissinger, addressing the U.N. General Assembly, posed a dual equation. He assured the world of American resolve to vindicate mankind's positive goals and help nations frame a nobler international community. But he also warned that the task was being impeded by resurgent nationalism, erosion of moral and political cohesion, politicization and confrontation in multipartite forums, escalation of peremptory demands, stridency of rhetoric, rigid ideologies, appeals to hatred, and resorts to tests of strength. The very states that have most to gain from consensual and cooperative ventures, he added, have most to lose from retrogression of the diplomatic process.

During 1977 the Carter administration adopted a somewhat more conciliatory tone and posture in the United Nations. But it expressed concern over such growing problems as politicization of debate, creeping diffusion of power, structural and functional growth and management complexity, and proliferation of membership and votes.

Department of State estimates of U.S. annual attendance at sessions of agencies of international organizations and international conferences stand at some nine hundred separate meetings and conferences during 1977, and the number seems on the rise. In general, multilateral diplomacy has increased substantially since World War II, and it is the preferred forum for much contemporary diplomacy. Yet much of our foreign relations activity is still handled by our embassies on a bilateral basis, and this has also increased in quantity and complexity since 1945.

Aiding and abetting this expansion of our bilateral and multilateral diplomacy has been the democratic ethos in the United States with its strong emphasis on the right of the complex, pluralistic society to influence its foreign policy. Chief among those representing this pluralism has been the Congress and its persistent demands for a greater voice in diplomacy in recent years.

Executive-Legislative Cooperation and Conflict. Separation of powers is one of the fundamental principles of the American governmental system. The Constitution of the United States contains no specific distribution clause, but the intent of the framers respecting basic legislative, executive, and judicial authority is clear. Yet the separation is far from absolute. While a corollary of separation of powers is the doctrine of checks and balances, it has been deemed important that Congress and President make a special point of cooperating in foreign affairs wherever possible.

Cognizant of the significance of cooperation between the two ends of Pennsylvania Avenue in the conduct of American diplomacy, Secretary of State Cordell Hull stated on January 29, 1944:

> Under our system of Government, the safeguarding and promotion of the nation's interests is a joint responsibility of the Executive and Legislative. Neither can be effective without the other, and the two together can be effective only when there exists between them mutual trust and confidence. In peace and in war, the two branches of the Government are joint trustees of the country's feelings.

Congress enjoys extensive powers in determining the bounds within which the President may exercise his foreign relations authority. Even more effective is the prerogative of Congress to refuse to pass the legislation necessary to implement a President's foreign policy or to execute treaty provisions. The separation of powers, together with checks and balances and coordinate legislative and executive authority over foreign relations, may therefore invite a constant struggle between the President and Congress, especially the Senate. American diplomatic history is replete with examples of such disagreement and contestation.

On the other hand, the record of accommodation between President and Congress on matters of diplomacy is better than is generally believed. Between 1789 and 1965 the Senate approved almost 90 percent of the treaties submitted to it; it approved 72 percent without qualification. In turn, the Senate rejected only a little more than one percent of the treaties submitted; another 10 percent were withdrawn. Of course these rejections included the League of Nations Covenant. Attempts have been made, as in the famous Bricker Amendment proposal of the early 1950s, to change the Constitution to provide for popular approval of treaties; the matter is far from dead.

There is also the problem of presidential use of executive agreements. Actually, in quantitative terms most executive agreements are based on prior legislation enacted by both houses or with congressional approval, such as aid and assistance agreements. The major problem arises from executive pacts—consummated by the President on the basis of his constitutional authority as "Diplomat in Chief"—which have to do with political matters.

Some recent conflicts between executive and legislative branches in the conduct of U.S. diplomacy have been the following: the 1973 congressional override of a presidential veto on the War Powers Act; the 1974 congressional override of a veto of the Freedom of Information Act; the 1975 Jackson-Vanik amendment to the foreign trade bill to permit freer emigration of Soviet Jews to Israel, resulting in repudiation by the U.S.S.R. of its trade agreement with the United States; the 1975 congressional passage, over White House objections, of an arms embargo on Turkey as reaction to Turkey's occupation of parts of Cyprus during the crisis that began in 1974; and in 1976, over Secretary Kissinger's demurrer, a policy requiring the executive to reduce or terminate U.S. security assistance to governments that violate international standards of human rights.*

Some of these congressional restrictions may have transgressed the vague boundaries between executive and legislative authority in U.S. foreign relations. At the very least, some may be politically unworkable or very awkward, as former President Ford observed about the War Powers Act and as President Carter indicated in the wake of the disturbances in Zaire's Shaba province. Certain observers even fear that Congress will run amuck, bringing endless anarchy in the complex diplomacy of the United States, or even legislative usurpation. Ironically, congressional hyperactivity in foreign policy seems more likely to create paralysis on important issues than to produce any "takeover" by the Congress.

Leaving aside matters of grave constitutional principle and plain political sense, which no doubt create difficulties in U.S. foreign relations, I think that intensified congressional interest in how U.S. diplomacy works is a good thing. As American society inevitably demands a greater voice in how foreign policy is to be made, it needs better information and guidance from its elected representatives. To the extent that Congress is involved in this process of popular education in modern diplomacy—and it will be increasingly as the multitude of pluralistic interests in the society want some share of decisions on international questions that affect them directly—it is essential that it be closely involved in the process by which this diplomacy operates. Perhaps through such closer involvement, Congress may also communicate back to its constituencies the importance of

---

* EDITOR'S NOTE: Other issues in executive-legislative relations that peaked in 1979 include legislation to implement the Panama Canal Treaty and Senate approval of the SALT II Pact.

thinking in national as well as special interest terms when it comes to foreign policy issues.

Given all this complexity in modern diplomacy—ranging from sheer quantitative diplomatic interactions to the intricacies of contemporary legislative-executive relations—where does the modern ambassador fit?

Some Reflections on the Role of the Modern American Ambassador. As I have tried to show, contemporary diplomacy is quite different from the image most people have in their minds. While the goals of the United States have not changed much in the last thirty years, the manner in which they are pursued has. This is largely the result of the way challenges to national interests manifest themselves today. Technological advances have contributed both to these challenges of diplomacy and to the means of meeting them.

Perhaps we should look at diplomacy as a sailor would look at an iceberg. Popular perceptions deal only with the tip, with the more visible personages on the world stage such as the President, the Secretary of State, and the ambassador. Beneath them lies a vast body of individuals and institutions, which today extend ever more deeply into virtually every level of society. In circumstances of such complexity, what type of person should the modern American ambassador be? A generalist or an expert? A politician or a professional diplomat?

The recent attention given to the manner in which ambassadorial appointments are made signifies widespread recognition of the critical and diverse functions an ambassador is called upon to perform as a representative of his government. Today's ambassador must embody an extraordinary range of qualities—he or she must be adept at negotiation, capable of understanding and articulating complex interests, imaginative in the creation of policy, perceptive and understanding of other nations' goals, and at ease at social functions and on the lecture circuit. Such an individual must also receive the support of a competent and dedicated staff of experts in any of a large number of technical fields. Yet, while diplomacy may become more technocratic, the role of the generalist will remain essential, and indeed, may take on new meaning.

Before concluding with some thoughts on the nature of the modern diplomat and his role in shaping and executing foreign policy, one other element in the complex process whereby policy is fashioned must be considered. It has great bearing on how we describe the ideal American ambassador of the future. This is the phenomenon of "popular," or democratic, diplomacy. Most, if not all, of the factors mentioned that characterize the work of today's diplomat have to some degree helped foster greater public awareness of the existence of other nations and the risks and challenges inherent in relations among nations. The rapid expansion of trade and the efforts to break down the barriers to freer movement of peoples, ideas, and goods; the revolutionary advances in communications and transportation such as television and the jet airplane; the increasing interdependence of all nations, capitalist and communist, industrial and agricultural, rich and poor; and the ever-present dangers of war and its potential for catastrophe—all of these factors have contributed to the democratization of foreign policy.

Today as never before we witness the increasing involvement of diverse public and private interests in the formulation and execution of policy. In a complex pluralistic society such as the United States, it is essential that our foreign policy reflect the values and ideals of our Judeo-Christian ethic. It must also be faithful to the Constitution and to the democratic process we all esteem. Yet, we must ask ourselves, what are the proper limits to popular influence on policy?

Whereas formerly the conduct of foreign affairs was entrusted to an elite diplomatic corps responsible solely to the head of state, in recent times we have seen such traditional modes of diplomacy as being in conflict with our ideals. Just in the last few decades, the role of Congress in foreign affairs has undergone a tremendous expansion. The legislative branch is no longer content to set the broad parameters within which the executive formulates and implements policy. As this congressional role becomes more comprehensive, Presidents have found it useful to utilize members of Congress and representatives of organized labor and the scientific community in delegations to international conferences and assemblies. Heads of delegations to many negotiations now must spend more of their time before congressional committees, some of which are not content to exercise their powers of oversight, but instead seek to influence the course of negotiations and the tactics employed by U.S. diplomats at the negotiating table.

The danger in all of this is that the diplomacy that the executive must conduct at home, among its constituents and those special interests that seek to influence policy, will deflect more and more attention away from the leadership role it was elected to perform. The diplomat of today and the future will have to contribute to finding a viable formula whereby compromise can be struck between the interests and values of individual citizens and their spokesmen, and the goals of American society as a whole. Diplomacy on the homefront will take on greater importance as the stakes and price of policy increase. In matters of national defense, the stakes are high indeed, and the consequences of failure are just as great. Problems of pollution, of adequate food and raw materials, and of international commerce will also entail great risk and sacrifice if they are to be managed.

Thus the diplomat must put on another hat, so to speak, and participate in the education of the public and in discussions of goals and means of diplomacy, both with the Congress and with special interest groups. Diplomacy abroad will have to be preceded by diplomacy at home, and this brings me to my final point. What type of person should this modern American ambassador be? A politician or a professional diplomat?

It seems to me he or she must be a little of both. The role that today's ambassador must play demands the skills of a negotiator and some knowledge of the issues to be faced. Yet since the world we live in is so complex, the issues an ambassador must deal with are many and increasingly technical. At the same time, the ambassador must be a symbol of U.S. democratic institutions and ideals.

It is unrealistic to expect our chief diplomats to embody the tremendous concentration of skills within that iceberg over which they preside. Rather, I believe it would be far better for us to be represented abroad by individuals who are both generalists and politicians, who are knowledgeable and competent in dealing with the complex issues *and* personalities of our times, yet who also possess the necessary skills for managing the iceberg and advocating the interests of this country before foreign and domestic audiences.

New Diplomatic Techniques in a New World

Dag Hammarskjöld

* * *

Diplomacy as a professional activity is certainly one of the most ancient and conservative. There has always been a need for negotiation between nations and the technique and psychology of such negotiations have, at least until recently, undergone no great changes through all the centuries. I guess that the emissaries of Egypt or Greece or Rome had to approach their problem in very much the same way as the emissaries of Napoleon's France, Bismarck's Germany and Queen Victoria's Great Britain.

However, I do not think that it is an exaggeration to say that the world with which modern diplomacy has to deal differs from the world of the 19th Century in those respects which interest us here more than the world of the 19th Century differed from its predecessors.

May I give you a little example which seems to me to throw considerable light on what has happened to us in this field. In 1783, Benjamin Franklin signed on behalf of the United States of America a treaty of friendship and commerce with the King of Sweden. The first part of the 22nd Article of that treaty reads in translation as follows:

> "In order to favor even further trade between the two sides, it is agreed that in case of war between the two nations, which we pray to God to avert, a period of nine months after the declaration of war shall be given to all tradesmen and all citizens on both sides so as to give them time to withdraw with everything they own, or to sell the same property

SOURCE: Address, Foreign Policy Association, New York, October 21, 1953; "New Diplomatic Techniques in a New World: Perspective—Publicity—Public Opinion," *Vital Speeches of the Day*, vol. 20 (December 1, 1953), pp. 107–9.

wherever they like to do so, it being forbidden in any way to hamper such activities and, even more so, to detain the said persons during this period of nine months. On the contrary, they shall be given passports for the time which they consider necessary for their return home. But in case within the said period anything is taken from them or they are subjected to any harm by one of the two sides, their people or citizens, full and satisfactory compensation shall be paid to them."

War in the period of the enlightenment was, indeed, very different from what it has since become. At the time to which my quotation belongs one could still speak of war as merely the ultimate resource and extension of diplomacy. Although there were wars even then that occasionally got out of hand and became great wars, war generally was a limited military action, fought for limited objectives without weapons of mass destructive power by small professional armies when other means of diplomatic action had failed to arrive at a settlement. Under such conditions, normal civilian life was only moderately disturbed.

For many reasons arising from the development of the modern state, whether it be a democracy of the masses or a dictatorship of the masses, and of our industrial civilization, general war in the Twentieth Century means total war, fought not only by mass armies but the entire civilian population.

From the first world war, through the second, and into the age of the hydrogen bomb, the technique of war has been revolutionized in a way which now brings with it destruction of vast areas, death to millions upon millions of the civilized population, and economic and financial ruin with effects lasting over long periods after the fighting stops. All this does not mean that our ancestors in Benjamin Franklin's time were necessarily more civilized than we, but that the technique of war today presents a new problem to civilized man. To the diplomat of the middle of the Twentieth Century, war is something that must be averted at almost any cost.

But technological development has altered the basis for diplomatic action also in another respect which should be just as obvious to everybody but seems sometimes to be forgotten. Just as the diplomat of today must rule out war as an instrument of policy, so he must recognize that in the new state of interdependence between nations war anywhere becomes the concern of all. The intricate web of relationships which now exist have as part of their basis the new means of communication which have overnight made our world so much smaller than it was in previous generations. We are all very conscious of the fact that it is now but a question of hours for military forces to reach distant parts of the globe and that the old considerations of strategy based on geographic separation no longer count for much.

News also reaches us from all corners of the globe almost as quickly as if we had been eye-witnesses. We are parties to an action practically at the very moment it is undertaken. The nerve signals from a wound are felt at once all through the body of mankind.

But in this rough mapping out of the diplomat's world of today we must go further and deeper. His relationship to his own people has also changed. This has come as a fruit of broader education, of a development of the democratic system and of the revolutionary growth of the mass media of communication. The diplomat may still confer behind closed doors, but he will be met by reporters and photographers when he comes out. His words will reach everybody by press and film and radio and television. His personality will be known to vast numbers for whom in other times he would have been only a name, or less than a name.

These last considerations lead me on to the final, least tangible, but perhaps most important new factor in diplomacy: mass public opinion as a living force in international affairs. Of course, this public opinion has as its background the new mass media of communication, but as a psychological phenomenon and a political factor it is not sufficiently explained by this background. It is the expression of a democratic mass civilization that is still in its infancy, giving to the man in the street and to group reactions a new significance in foreign policy.

Is it possible to envisage the making of foreign policy and the tasks and techniques of diplomacy in the same way for a situation such as the one just described as for previous stages in history? The reply must be, No. The diplomat who works bilaterally on a national basis without the widest perspective, without recognition—and a proper handling—of the publicity aspect of his work, or without giving to public opinion its proper place in the picture, has little place in our world of today.

A first and major change in diplomatic techniques that is called for by developments, is the introduction of what might be described as the multilateral element. I do not mean to suggest that bilateral diplomatic contacts and negotiations have lost their old importance, only that they prove insufficient. In a world of interdependence means must be devised for a broadening of the approach so that the interests of a group of nations or of the community of nations are given their necessary weight.

Negotiations and conferences with several nations represented are, of course, as old as history, but what must be considered as new, in such a conference of today, is when the diplomatic representative speaks not only for his own country, but also shares responsibility for the interests of the other nations represented around the conference table. I have myself, before coming to the United Nations, seen such a development of community viewpoints at various conferences in Europe. On occasions which traditionally would have consisted simply of interlocking bilateral contacts and reactions, this development has added something essential to the picture, meeting a need of today and making the results transcend what would have come out of the conference, had everybody approached it in the traditional way.

A further element in the development of the multilateral approach may be found in the international Secretariat. The concept of an international civil service directly responsible to the whole community of nations was first developed in the League of Nations. It has been carried further in the United Nations, where the Secretariat has wider responsibility, negotiating rights, and powers of initiative, than in the League or in any previous international organization.

The much-debated independence of the international civil service being created in the United Nations Secretariat and in the secretariats of the specialized agencies and various regional organizations has a vital significance here. If this independence should be jeopardized and national influences come to dominate the Secretariats, this evolutionary development of the multilateral approach would receive a serious setback and international organization would be gravely weakened in its capacity to meet the demands of interdependence upon the policies of all governments. I feel that the best defence for the independence of the administrations of the international organizations lies in a fuller understanding of the very special and new needs for such administrations in the kind of a world we live in today.

When I speak here, in the first instance, of the secretariats as representative of the multilateral element in international negotiations, I have done so because they demonstrate in the most obvious way what is new in the picture. However, it goes without saying that their status and their duties only reflect the tasks of international organization as such. Everybody working inside or with the United Nations also carries the responsibility for making it a multilateral diplomatic instrument transcending nationalism and bilateralism, in the approach to political problems.

* * *

A characteristic of the new diplomacy, developing on the multilateral basis or with multilateral aims, is that it has to operate in daylight to an extent unknown in the diplomacy of a traditional type. The importance of publicity for good and for bad in international diplomacy may be studied with the greatest profit in the international organizations. It has been said that one should never forget that the United Nations operates in a glass house. I would add that in our world of today it could not operate properly under any other conditions; in fact, in my view, it should operate in a glass house in order to serve its purposes. Multilateral diplomacy is by its very nature such that the old secrecy has lost its place and justification.

But there should be no mistakes. Publicity is right and necessary in multilateral diplomacy. However, it also represents a danger. Open diplomacy may, as a prominent delegate to the United Nations recently pointed out, easily become frozen diplomacy. This comes about when open diplomacy is turned into diplomacy by public statements made merely to satisfy segments of domestic public opinion or to gain some propaganda advantage elsewhere.

Considerations of national prestige also enter into the picture. Legislators and members of parliaments in our democracies have long been used to the give and take of debate on state and national issues, to the compromises that are fashioned every day in the legislative process, to accepting defeat as well as victory in voting as part of the normal course of politics. Neither the diplomats who practice multilateral diplomacy on the public stage nor the Governments they represent are yet fully acclimated to this new aspect of international relations. Nor, it must be said, is public opinion itself. Too often, any modification of national positions once taken publicly, or acceptance of sensible compromise, is shunned out of fear that it will be labelled appeasement or defeat.

At this point the diplomat of today has to face public opinion in its contemporary significance for international affairs. It may seem to him that this opinion being more or less the master of his masters, is the most important single factor in his planning of the implementation of international policy. And, of course, it is a factor of singular importance. No diplomat can depart too far from what is accepted or acceptable to public opinion in those quarters which give weight to his arguments. But it does not follow from this that he should simply let himself be guided by anticipated reactions of the public. A diplomacy that gives full weight to recognized or anticipated public opinion may in a decisive way also give direction to this opinion.

In the modern world of mass media and publicity no diplomat

trying to respond to the demands of the situation can be only a servant. He must to some extent and in some respects also be a leader by looking beyond the immediate future and going underneath the superficial reactions, be they expressed by ever so powerful news organs catering for what are believed to be the wishes of the broad masses—wishes which may in reality be as loosely attached to the man in the street as the suits which he decides to wear this year. It is part of the diplomat's responsibility not only to lead public opinion toward acceptance of the lasting consequences of the interdependence of our world. He must also help public opinion to become as accustomed to the necessity for give and take and for compromise in international politics as it has long been on questions of state and local concern.

I had promised to speak about diplomatic techniques. In fact, I have talked almost as much about the substance of modern diplomacy. The two things cannot be separated. The technique must be adjusted to the substance and to some extent it is the very substance of diplomacy. No diplomat is likely to play the multilateral game well unless he believes in the need for and value of a multilateral approach. No diplomat will adjust himself to the new type of publicity—which is unavoidable in all official activities but is of special importance in multilateral diplomacy—unless he has the courage of his own actions. No diplomat is likely to meet the demands of public opinion on him as a representative in international policy unless he understands this opinion and unless he respects it deeply enough to give it leadership when he feels that the opinion does not truly represent the deeper and finally decisive aspirations in the minds and hearts of the people.

The ultimate test of a diplomacy adequate to our world is its capacity to evoke this kind of response from the people and thus to rally public opinion behind what is wise and necessary for the peace and progress of the world.

Proliferating International Community and Changing Diplomatic Representation*

Elmer Plischke

Since World War II, the community of nations has been integrating in the United Nations, the International Bank and Monetary Fund, the Common Market, and dozens of other global and regional agencies. At the same time, it is fragmenting into a growing number of smaller and smaller states.

This splintering trend is so strong that it has led to the emergence in recent years of an independent country of less than 7,000 people occupying an isolated Pacific islet no larger than George Washington's estate, Mount Vernon; a Caribbean republic whose entire population would not fill the Rose Bowl, and whose first envoy to the Organization of American States was a hired foreign national, who wielded the same voting power as the United States; and a tiny Asian kingdom that appoints ambassadors to only two other governments, but is a full-fledged member of the United Nations since 1971.

* * *

Many people still do not realize that the major powers today are flanked at international gatherings by delegations from such new countries as Bahrain, Bhutan, Comoro, Djibouti, Grenada, the Maldives, Nauru, Qatar, Sao Tome, the Seychelles, Surinam, and Tonga. Nor is it well known that self-government has been discussed in the United Nations for exotic places like Brunei, Ifni, and Macao, as well as the Cayman, Cocos, Tokelau, and a good many other tiny islands.

If current trends continue, two in every five of the world's na-

* Editor's Note: For a more comprehensive treatment of this subject, see Elmer Plischke, *Microstates in World Affairs: Policy Problems and Options* (Washington, D.C.: American Enterprise Institute, 1977).

Source: "Microstates: Lilliputs in World Affairs," *The Futurist* (Washington, D.C.: World Future Society, Feb. 1978), vol. 12, pp. 19–25.

MICROSTATES

NATIONS WITH POPULATIONS UNDER 300,000. ALL BUT THREE (NAURU, TONGA, AND VATICAN CITY) ARE MEMBERS OF THE UNITED NATIONS.

Country	Location
Bahamas	Caribbean
Bahrain	Mideast
Barbados	Caribbean
Cape Verde Islands	Africa
Comoro Islands	Africa
Djibouti (Afars & Issas)	Africa
Equatorial Guinea	Africa
Grenada	Caribbean
Iceland	Europe
Maldives	Asia
Nauru	Oceania
Qatar	Mideast
Sao Tome and Principe	Africa
Seychelles	Asia
Tonga (Friendly Islands)	Oceania
United Arab Emirates	Mideast
Vatican City (Holy See)	Europe
Western Samoa	Oceania

EDITOR'S NOTE: Since this list was compiled, Dominica and St. Lucia (Caribbean), the Solomon, Gilbert, and Tuvalu (Ellice) Islands (Oceania) gained independence and may be added. In addition, Antigua and St. Christopher (Caribbean) together with Brunei and New Hebrides (Oceania), as well as others, are at the threshold of independence, and the list is likely to continue to grow during the 1980s and 1990s. All of these are microstates, and most are under 100,000 in population.

tions could be microstates—under 300,000 in population—and some 50 could be submicrostates—with less than 100,000 people.

The number of countries comprising the community of nations increased progressively during the past two centuries. Its growth pattern reflects waves of expansion, usually accelerating following periods of widespread revolt and major wars. Never before, however, has there been an independence boom like that which followed World War II.

When the United States was born, it established diplomatic relations with the eight major powers—England, France, the Netherlands, Portugal, Prussia, Russia, Spain, and Sweden. By 1830, following the revolt of Brazil, Mexico, and other Latin American colonies, the diplomatic community tripled. In 1900 it numbered about 45 and, despite the dissolution of the Eastern European empires at the end of World War I, by 1940 it had increased to only 64.

Since then, under the aura of what President Kennedy called "a world-wide declaration of independence," the number of countries has mushroomed to more than 155. Not only were the twentieth-century Belgian, British, Dutch, French, Portuguese, and Spanish empires liquidated, but more than a billion and a quarter people occupying nearly 14 million square miles of territory were also transformed into nearly 95 new countries.

At present less than .03% of the world's landed domain, with under .05% of its population, remains nonindependent. The independence race peaked in the 1960s, but it continues, evidenced by the creation of 20 new states in the 1970s.

Of the territories considered for self-government by the United Nations, several are likely prospects in the next few years. Aside from Namibia and Rhodesia in Southern Africa, these are expected to include the Gilbert and Ellice Islands in the Pacific, and Belize, French Guiana, Antigua, St. Lucia, Guadeloupe, and the Netherlands Antilles and other islands in the Caribbean area. [See editor's note appended to the table of microstates above.]

From a longer range perspective, according to the Department of State, it is possible that approximately 50 miniature states—each under 100,000 in population—may emerge as independent entities in the foreseeable future. This could mean a world community of more than 200 members, or a tripling of its size since World War II.

One result of this fragmentation is a drastic change in the composition of the global community. Aside from the United States, only Brazil, China, Japan, and the Soviet Union, together with two postwar creations—India and Indonesia—exceed 100 million in population. About 70 other countries, a majority of which existed before World War II, have populations between 5 million and 100 million.

The trend in the proliferation of smaller states differs substantially. In 1940, Luxembourg and Vatican City were the only minute members of the society of nations, and more than two-thirds exceeded five million inhabitants. Today, approximately 80—or more than half of the countries of the world—fall below this population level. This means that one of every two is smaller than metropolitan Chicago. Of these, 35 are under one million, so that one in five is less populous than metropolitan New Orleans. Eighteen fall below the 300,000 level and are therefore smaller than Columbia (South Carolina) or Lancaster (Pennsylvania).

Because the preponderant majority of the 50 potential states considered for self-government by the United Nations are also small in population, it is not inconceivable that the global community could soon have 130 members with a population under five million. More than three of every ten would be microstates, and about 50 submicrostates would have a population smaller than the enrollments at the University of California or the attendance at the Super Bowl.

By comparison, one-fourth of U.S. states now have larger populations than would half of the independent countries of the world, and 110 American cities are more populous than would be one of every four sovereign states. This trend toward fragmentation and smallness is transforming the global political system.

* * *

When the United States gained independence, its diplomatic requirements were modest and could be met by accrediting small missions to a few foreign governments and dispatching envoys to an occasional international conference. Today the newborn nation is confronted with the formidable possibility of sending missions to more than 155 foreign capitals, to dozens of world-wide and regional intergovernmental conferences and meetings, and to the United Nations, its 15 specialized agencies, and a variety of regional institutions like the European Communities and the Organization of American States. In terms of both human and financial resources, this is well beyond the capability of many countries—especially the microstates.

Diplomatic nonrepresentation, though general and widespread, is most acute for newer and smaller nations. Significantly, more than half of those with less than five million people maintain missions to less than 10 other countries. Compared with the overall average of 45—which falls short of one-third of potential—the average for states with fewer than one million people amounts to only eight missions, and, except for Vatican City and Iceland, the microstates sustain virtually no regularized diplomatic representation abroad, averaging less than one mission per micro-entity. As nations continue to proliferate, the degree of nonrepresentation is bound to increase, particularly in the interrelations of the less populous countries.

Enormous disparity between actual and possible representation characterizes contemporary diplomatic relations. The 6,400 missions in existence in 1975, for example, amounted to merely 27% of potentiality. On the other hand, if each independent government were to commission an ambassador to every other country today, nearly 24,500 embassies would be accredited to 157 capitals throughout the world. Should each government also send resident missions to 15 international organizations, the total number of diplomatic establishments would approximate 27,000.

Projecting future potential, if the global society expanded to 200 members, and each government accredited envoys to all others, the diplomatic community could number nearly 40,000 missions. Moreover, were each of them to average 10 members, the population of the diplomatic fraternity would mushroom to 400,000.

Although such massive diplomatic proliferation is illusory, the foreseeable problems are still sufficiently serious to suggest either retarding or stopping the movement for independence, or encouraging the use of workable alternatives to traditional bilateral representation, or both. In view of the historic attraction of self-determination and independence, and the vigorous decolonization momentum within the United Nations, there is little question that fragmentation will continue for some time.

Optional methods of diplomatic interchange are available, however, to bridge the gulf between the desire of nations to maintain adequate bilateral relations and their ability to do so. Theoretically, smaller nations are able to deal diplomatically with foreign governments through the unilateral representation provided by other, usually larger, states. Such one-way diplomacy may be occasional, with an emissary deployed on a special or itinerant assignment. This facilitates some mutual communication, but permanent arrangements are normally regarded as better suited to the production of more positive results.

A second method of augmenting diplomatic exchange, called multiple representation, involves the commissioning of a single emissary simultaneously to two or more foreign nations. In such cases the envoy, although he may be formally accredited to more than a single government, usually has his official residence in an assigned capital and proceeds to the other countries from time to time. While three dozen nations utilized this practice in recent years, generally the newer and smaller states, which would appear to have most to gain, fail to take advantage of it.

Another alternative invokes third-country substitution. Guardianship representation is common for states at war or those whose diplomatic relations are severed, and it is also used when micronations arrange to have friendly governments manage their foreign affairs, as is the case with Nauru and the European principalities like Monaco. Although incorporated for decades in the diplomacy of such countries as Luxembourg, this technique is not widely utilized. It would seem, however, that a good many small nations might find it to their advantage to engage a friendly, nearby country to conduct their official representation to a wider circle of governments, but this requires mutuality of interests, reliable communications, and an exceptional degree of trust.

A fourth and somewhat similar device for overcoming limited diplomatic resources is for two governments to appoint a single envoy and staff to represent them both to another country. Such joint representation is rarely resorted to in current relations. Nevertheless, in the event of extensive creation of insular and other small states in the future, some of the new governments might decide that such joint representation could increase appreciably their diplomatic outreach at relatively little cost.

Two additional and closely associated methods of amplifying intergovernmental contact entail multiple bilateral representation at some neutral location. The site may be the capital of a third country. States that do not have resident missions in each other's territory are able to deal with one another, on an ad hoc or continuing basis, through their respective envoys stationed in one of the capitals in which they both have established missions.

It is not inconceivable that smaller countries could forge networks of interrelations with substantial numbers of other states, large and small, in major diplomatic centers like Washington, Brussels, Cairo, London, New Delhi, Paris, Rome, and Tokyo, or in neutral capitals like Bern and Vienna. These centers of large-scale, if not universal, representation would offer a broad spectrum of official contact and serve as convenient foci for multiple direct diplomacy. Even though this means of consultation is widely used informally, smaller states might undertake to formalize the process and thereby extend their diplomatic communities.

On the other hand, small nations may prefer to deal with others bilaterally through ordinary and special missions accredited to a major international organization, especially if its headquarters is located in or near the capital of a power to which many states uniformly send emissaries. The United Nations (New York and Geneva), its specialized agencies such as the Food and Agriculture Organization (Rome) and UNESCO (Paris), the European Communities and NATO (both at Brussels), and other regional institutions, including the Council of Europe (Strasbourg), the League of Arab States (Cairo), the Organization of African Unity (Addis Ababa), and the Organization of American States (Washington), are among the more likely diplomatic centers for this purpose.

As small states perceive sufficient need and develop the requisite competency for doing so, they are inclined to expand their traditional bilateral exchange and their participation in the United Nations system. However, most of the smaller nations, including the microstates, and especially the diminutive, isolated islands, may encounter insurmountable difficulty in broadening their diplomatic horizons. Lacking motivation, qualified manpower, or financial resources, they may be induced or obliged to resort to substitute diplomatic practices.

Enhancing representational levels may well have to be deliberately facilitated by such organizations as the United Nations, agencies like the European Communities or the British Commonwealth of Nations, and the governments of major diplomatic powers, including the United States. In the course of time, this could become a common, if not primary, means of handling the disparate diplomacy of a substantial majority of miniature states and, if so, the traditional diplomatic process will experience fundamental change.

In an era of continuing international fragmentation and national miniaturization, the diplomacy of small nations poses serious policy and pragmatic problems—not only for the microstates, but also for the United States and other large powers, and for the global community as well. Smaller countries are confronted with such critical issues as whether to live with negligible representation, to expand their diplomatic relations as liberally as possible, or to aspire to universality, and which diplomatic processes they will develop to accommodate their needs and their expectations. They also must determine whether and how to systematize their efforts. Because no particular representational alternative or combination is apt to be equally acceptable to all, future international affairs will be burdened, as never before, with a pattern of diplomatic interchange that is characterized by diversity, complexity, fluidity, and uncertainty—if not inadequacy.

* * *

If the international community and the United Nations continue to proliferate, allowing more and more microstates to participate as legal equals, in time some of the options now available for reform and stabilization of global relations will be foreclosed by the flow of events. Continued crystallization of the current community of nations and its multipartite mechanism may render corrective action impossible, and future generations will be destined to live and cope with the anomalous macro-system of micro-entities that the age of Lilliputs has engendered.

3

Democratic and Open Diplomacy

In ordinary circumstances voters cannot be expected to transcend their particular, localized and self-regarding opinions. . . . In their circumstances, which as private persons they cannot readily surmount, the voters are most likely to suppose that whatever seems obviously good to them must be good for the country, and good in the sight of God.

I am far from implying that the voters are not entitled to the representation of their particular opinions and interests. But their opinions and interests should be taken for what they are and for no more. They are not—as such—propositions in the public interest.

WALTER LIPPMANN, *The Public Philosophy*

Open covenants of peace openly arrived at, after which there shall be no private international understandings of any kind, but diplomacy shall proceed always frankly and in the public view.

* * *

When I pronounced for open diplomacy, I meant, not that there should be no private discussions of delicate matters, but that no secret agreements should be entered upon, and that all international relations, when fixed, should be open, aboveboard, and explicit.

WOODROW WILSON, *First of Fourteen Points and Letter to Secretary of State*

As the title of this chapter suggests, "Democratic and Open Diplomacy" deals with two distinct yet intimately related elements of the new diplomacy. Both components have been the subject of widespread controversy and literary analysis.

The first three essays address the question: How and to what extent do, or should, a nation's people influence the conduct of its foreign relations? In his pioneering essay "Requisite for the Success of Popular Diplomacy" published in the aftermath of World War I, Elihu Root discusses the thesis that the people in a democracy such as the United States, who are ultimately responsible for the control and conduct of foreign affairs, have an obligation to become knowledgeable respecting diplomacy. Even after half a century, Root's counsel and analysis remain valid. President Harry S. Truman, in "The People and American Foreign Relations," endorses the principle that in a democratic system foreign relations decisions are the result of the democratic process and denote "the collective judgment of the people," and he concludes that American foreign policy is founded on "an enlightened public opinion."

Monteagle Stearns views democratic diplomacy from a different angle. In "Diplomacy vs. Propaganda," he examines the value of vigorous and supportive public opinion as an added weapon in the diplomatic arsenal. He contends that the diplomat can strengthen his bargaining position at the conference table by learning the art of harnessing the channels of propaganda to sway popular opinion to his support.

The last four essays in this chapter deal with a related issue: To what extent and in what manner should diplomatic relations be exposed to public scrutiny and to what degree are foreign relations information and documentation made publicly available? Reflecting the common view, Andrew Berding and Hugh S. Gibson acknowledge Woodrow Wilson's dictum of 1918 that the results of diplomatic negotiation should be made known to the people. But they disagree on the matter of openness during the policy making and negotiating stages. In "Quiet vs. Unquiet Diplomacy," Berding advances the view held by many exponents of the media interests that negotiation should ordinarily be open to immediate examination in a democratic society. In "Secret vs. Open Diplomacy," Hugh Gibson, an experienced career diplomat representing the traditional view of the professionals, deplores the practice of negotiation "in the marketplace," asserting instead that "real diplomacy" consists of "negotiating in private and making the results public." Thus, although a degree of consensus exists concerning the release of diplomatic end-products, the issue of public scrutiny and hence influence during the negotiating process itself remains moot. William D. Blair, Jr., focusing on "Communication: The Weak Link," comments on some of the reasons for secrecy in an open society, including such forces as tradition and inertia.

Much of the difficulty of resolving the secrecy vs. openness issue, he finds, is attributable to a faulty communication process, and he adds that "the fault lies with the medium, not with the message."

The final essay, on "Availability of Diplomatic Information and Documents," by William M. Franklin, describes in historical context the policy and practice of the American government, especially the Department of State, in making information and records available to the public. He discusses three processes—by systematic and ad hoc publication, by granting access to official files and the transfer of departmental documentation to the National Archives, and by providing copies of papers and other materials on request, especially under the Freedom of Information Act. He contends that the Department of State is improving and expediting each of these "mechanisms." But what needs to be added is that the United States government pursues the most liberal national policy and program in the modern world for the systematic publication of, and for providing access to, its diplomatic documentation.

Requisite for the Success
of Popular Diplomacy

ELIHU ROOT

The control of foreign relations by modern democracies creates a new and pressing demand for popular education in international affairs. When the difficult art of regulating the conduct of nations toward each other, in such a way as to preserve rights and avoid offense and promote peaceful intercourse, was left to the foreign offices of the world the public in each country could judge policies by results, and, in the various ways by which public opinion expresses itself, could reward or punish the success or failure of government. To perform that particular function it was not very important that the public should be familiar with the affairs out of which success or failure came. That condition, however, is passing away. In the democratic countries generally, the great body of citizens are refusing to wait until negotiations are over or policies are acted upon or even determined. They demand to know what is going on and to have an opportunity to express their opinions at all stages of diplomatic proceedings. This tendency is due partly to a desire to escape from certain well recognized evils in diplomacy as it has been practiced. It is due in part doubtless to the natural disposition of democracies to revert to the conditions which existed before the invention of representative government and thus to avoid the temporary inequalities involved in delegations of power to official representatives however selected.

The new condition has undoubtedly been accelerated by the great war [World War I] and its lessons. We have learned that war is essentially a popular business. All the people in the countries concerned are enlisted in carrying it on. It cannot be carried on without their general participation. And whoever wins the war all the people

SOURCE: "A Requisite for the Success of Popular Diplomacy," *Foreign Affairs*, vol. 1 (September 1922), pp. 3–10.

of all the countries involved suffer grievous consequences. There is a general conviction that there has been something wrong about the conduct of diplomacy under which peoples have so often found themselves embarked in war without intending it and without wishing for it and there is a strong desire to stop that sort of thing. Democracies determined to control their own destinies object to being led, without their knowledge, into situations where they have no choice.

The demand for open diplomacy and contemporaneous public information, although in its application there is frequently an element of mere curiosity or news gathering business, nevertheless rests upon the substantial basis of democratic instinct for unhampered self-government. It is incident to the awakening sense of opportunity which, among the unskilled majority, has followed the exercise of universal suffrage, the spread of elementary education, and the revelation of the power of organization. The change is therefore not to be considered as temporary but as a step in the direct line of development of democratic government, which, according to the nature of democracies, will not be retraced. The new conditions and such developments as may grow from them, are the conditions under which diplomacy will be carried on hereafter. Of course, as in all practical human affairs, limitations and safeguards will be found necessary, but the substance will continue, and public opinion will be increasingly not merely the ultimate judge but an immediate and active force in negotiation.

The usefulness of this new departure is subject to one inevitable condition. That is, that the democracy which is undertaking to direct the business of diplomacy shall learn the business. The controlling democracy must acquire a knowledge of the fundamental and essential facts and principles upon which the relations of nations depend. Without such a knowledge there can be no intelligent discussion and consideration of foreign policy and diplomatic conduct. Misrepresentation will have a clear field and ignorance and error will make wild work with foreign relations. This is a point to which the sincere people who are holding meetings and issuing publications in opposition to war in general may well direct their attention if they wish to treat the cause of disease rather than the effects. Given the nature of man, war results from the spiritual condition that follows real or fancied injury or insult. It is a familiar observation that in most wars each side believes itself to be right and both pray with equal sincerity for the blessing of heaven upon their arms. Back of this there must lie a mistake. However much ambition, trade competition, or sinister personal motives of whatever kind, may have led towards the warlike

103

situation, two great bodies of human beings, without whose consent war cannot be carried on, can never have come to two diametrically opposed genuine beliefs as to the justice of the quarrel without one side or the other, and probably both, being mistaken about their country's rights and their country's duties. Here is the real advantage of the change from the old diplomacy to the new. Irresponsible governments may fight without being in the least degree mistaken about their rights and duties. They may be quite willing to make cannon fodder of their own people in order to get more territory or more power; but two democracies will not fight unless they believe themselves to be right. They may have been brought to their belief by misrepresentation as to facts, by a misunderstanding of rules of right conduct, or through having the blank of ignorance filled by racial or national prejudice and passion to the exclusion of inquiry and thought; but they will fight not because they mean to do wrong but because they think they are doing right. When foreign affairs were ruled by autocracies or oligarchies the danger of war was in sinister purpose. When foreign affairs are ruled by democracies the danger of war will be in mistaken beliefs. The world will be the gainer by the change, for, while there is no human way to prevent a king from having a bad heart, there is a human way to prevent a people from having an erroneous opinion. That way is to furnish the whole people, as a part of their ordinary education, with correct information about their relations to other peoples, about the limitations upon their own rights, about their duties to respect the rights of others, about what has happened and is happening in international affairs, and about the effects upon national life of the things that are done or refused as between nations; so that the people themselves will have the means to test misinformation and appeals to prejudice and passion based upon error.

This is a laborious and difficult undertaking. It must be begun early and continued long, with patience and persistence, but it is the very same process as that by which all the people of the great democracies have learned within their own countries to respect law and to follow wise and salutary customs in their communities, and to consider the rights of others while they assert their own rights, and to maintain orderly self-government.

It so happens that our own people in the United States have been peculiarly without that kind of education in foreign affairs. Not only have we been very busy over the development of our own country and our own institutions, but our comparatively isolated position has prevented the foreign relations of the old world from becoming matters of immediate vital interest to the American people, and they have not been interested in the subject. Naturally enough a great part of our public men have neglected to study the subject. The great body of Americans in office would study questions of transportation and tariff and internal improvements and currency because their constituents were interested in these subjects; but there was no incentive for them to study foreign affairs because their constituents were indifferent to them. The conditions are now widely different. Our people have been taught by events to realize that with the increased intercommunication and interdependence of civilized states all our production is a part of the world's production, and all our trade is a part of the world's trade, and a large part of the influences which make for prosperity or disaster within our own country consist of forces and movements which may arise anywhere in the world beyond our direct and immediate control. I suppose that the people of the United States have learned more about international relations within the past eight years [1914–1922] than they had learned in the preceding eighty years. They are, however, only at the beginning of the task.

The subject is extensive and difficult and a fair working knowledge of it, even of the most general kind, requires long and attentive study. Underlying it are the great differences in the modes of thought and feeling of different races of men. Thousands of years of differing usages under different conditions forming different customs and special traditions have given to each separate race its own body of preconceived ideas, its own ways of looking at life and human conduct, its own views of what is natural and proper and desirable. These prepossessions play the chief part in determining thought and action in life. Given two groups of men, each having a different inheritance of custom and tradition, each will have a different understanding of written and spoken words, of the reasons for conduct and the meaning of conduct, and each will to a very considerable degree fail to understand the other. Neither can judge the other by itself. If the instinctive occidental reformer and the instinctive oriental fatalist are to work together they must make biological studies of each other. Add to these differences the selfish passions which have not yet been bred out of mankind and there inevitably follow in the contacts of international intercourse a multitude of situations which cannot be solved by the men of any one nation assuming that the rest of the world is going to think and feel as they themselves do and to act accordingly.

The organization of independent nations which has followed the disappearance of the Holy Roman Empire is in the main the outgrowth of that progress in civilization which leads peoples to seek the liberty of local self-government according to their own ideas. Whatever may be the form of local governments there can be no tyranny so galling as the intimate control of the local affairs of life by foreign rulers who are entirely indifferent to the local conceptions of how life ought to be conducted. National independence is an organized defense against that kind of tyranny. Probably the organization of nations is but a stage of development but it is the nearest that mankind has yet come towards securing for itself a reasonable degree of liberty with a reasonable degree of order.

It is manifest that the differences of thought and feeling and selfish desire which separate nations in general have to be dealt with in particular in the multitude of controversies which are sure to arise between them and between their respective citizens in a world of universal trade and travel and inter-communication. The process of such adjustment without war is the proper subject of diplomacy. During some centuries of that process many usages have grown up which have been found necessary or convenient for carrying on friendly intercourse, and many of these have hardened into generally accepted customs in manners or in morals which no longer require to be discussed but which every nation has a right to assume that other nations will observe. Many rules of right conduct have been accepted and universally agreed upon as law to govern the conduct of nations. In England and America these rules of international law are authoritatively declared to be a part of the municipal law of the country enforceable by the courts. In this way the nations founded upon differences have been gradually rescuing from the field of difference and controversy, and transferring up to the field of common understanding and agreement, one subject after another of practical importance in the affairs of the world. The process is in the direction of that unity of thought and feeling, the absence of which hitherto has caused the failure of all schemes and efforts for the unity of mankind. The study of international relations means not only study of some particular controversy but study of this long history of the process of adjustment between differing ideas and of the prejudices and passions and hitherto irreconcilable differences which have baffled adjustment and which affect the relations and probable conduct of the nations concerned. All these are in the background of every international question and are often of vital importance to its right understanding.

The process I have described has created a community of nations.

That community has grown just as communities of natural persons grow. Men cannot live in neighborhood with each other without having reciprocal rights and obligations towards each other arising from their being neighbors. The practical recognition of these rights and obligations creates the community. It is not a matter of contract. It is a matter of usage arising from the necessities of self-protection. It is not a voluntary matter. It is compelled by the situation. The neighbors generally must govern their conduct by the accepted standards or the community will break up. It is the same with nations. No nation whose citizens trade and travel, that is to say, no nation which lives in neighborhood with other nations need consider whether or not it will be a member of the community of nations. It cannot help itself. It may be a good member or a bad member, but it is a member by reason of the simple fact of neighborhood life and intercourse. The Bolshevik rulers of Russia are illustrating this. They have been trying to repudiate all the obligations resulting from their country's membership in the community of nations, and one result is that intercourse is impossible.

This great fact of the community of nations is not involved at all in any question about the "League of Nations" or any other association of nations founded upon contract. The "League of Nations" is merely a contract between the signers of the instrument by which they agree to super-add to the existing usages, customs, laws, rights, and obligations of the existing community of nations, certain other rights and obligations which shall bind the signers as matter of contract. Whether a country enters into that contract or not, its membership of the community of nations continues with all the rights and obligations incident to that membership.

A self-respecting democracy which undertakes to control the action of its government as a member of this community of nations, and wishes to respond fairly and fully, not only to the demands of its own interests, but to the moral obligations of a member of the community, is bound to try to understand this great and complicated subject so that it may act not upon prejudice and error but upon knowledge and understanding.

There is one specially important result which should follow from such a popular understanding of foreign affairs. That is, a sense of public responsibility in speech and writing, or perhaps it would be better stated as a public sense of private responsibility for words used in discussing international affairs. More fights between natural persons come from insult than from injury. Under our common law, libel was treated as a crime, not because of the injury which it did to the person libeled, but because it tended to provoke a breach of the peace. Nations are even more sensitive to insult than individuals. One of the most useful and imperative lessons learned by all civilized governments in the practice of international intercourse has been the necessity of politeness and restraint in expression. Without these, the peaceful settlement of controversy is impossible. This lesson should be learned by every free democracy which seeks to control foreign relations.

It cannot, however, be expected that every individual in a great democracy will naturally practice restraint. Political demagogues will seek popularity by public speeches full of insult to foreign countries, and yellow journals will seek to increase their circulation by appeals to prejudice against foreigners. Hitherto these have been passed over because the speakers and writers were regarded as irresponsible, but if the democracy of which the speakers and publishers are a part is to control international intercourse that irresponsibility ends, and it is the business of the democracy to see to it that practices by its members which lead directly towards war are discouraged and condemned. Offenses of this character are frequently committed in this country by political speakers and sensational newspapers and because we are a great nation the expressions used become known in the other countries concerned and cause resentment and bitter feeling. What especially concerns us is that these are very injurious offenses against our own country. Such public expressions by our own citizens bring discredit upon our country and injure its business and imperil its peace. They answer to the description of crime in the old indictments as an act "against the peace and dignity" of the State. They will practically cease whenever the American public really condemns and resents them so that neither public office nor newspaper advertising or circulation can be obtained by them. That will come when the American public more fully understands the business of international intercourse and feels a sense of the obligations which it incurs by asserting the right to control the conduct of foreign relations.

The People and American Foreign Relations

Harry S. Truman

In this country, where the facts are readily available, we have a special obligation to inform ourselves concerning world affairs and important international issues

This is vitally important if our country is to carry out the responsibilities of world leadership that it has today. For, in this nation, foreign policy is not made by the decisions of a few. It is the result of the democratic process, and represents the collective judgment of the people. Our foreign policy is founded upon an enlightened public opinion.

The importance of public opinion in the United States is not always understood or properly evaluated. Public opinion in a country such as ours cannot be ignored or manipulated to suit the occasion. It cannot be stampeded. Its formation is necessarily a slow process, because the people must be given ample opportunity to discuss the issues and reach a reasoned conclusion. But once a democratic decision is made, it represents the collective will of the nation and can be depended upon to endure.

Those who rule by arbitrary power in other nations do not understand these things. For this reason, they do not realize the strength behind our foreign policy.

The major decisions in our foreign policy since the war [World War II] have been made on the basis of an informed public opinion and overwhelming public support.

For example, in 1945, the people of our country were almost unanimously in favor of our participation in the United Nations. The

Source: Address delivered in Chicago, July 19, 1949, *Department of State Bulletin*, vol. 21 (August 1, 1949), pp. 145–46.

Senate reflected that public sentiment when it approved the Charter by a vote of 87 to 2.

In 1948, after almost a year of discussion and debate, it was clear that a substantial majority of the people of this Nation approved our participation in the European Recovery Program. The Congress translated that approval into legislative action by a vote of approximately four to one.

*   *   *

These momentous decisions are the decisions not of the government alone, but of the people of the United States. For this reason, it is clear that this country will steadfastly continue, together with other nations of like purpose, along the path we have chosen toward peace and freedom for the world.

The formation of foreign policy on the part of the democratic nations may be a slow and painful process, but the results endure.

It is only in the totalitarian states, where all decisions are made by a few men at the top, that foreign policies can be reversed or radically altered in secrecy, or changed abruptly without warning. Between totalitarian states, disagreements can suddenly become open conflicts, and allies can change into enemies overnight. The democratic nations, by contrast, because they rely on the collective judgment of their people, are dependable and stable in their foreign relations.

*   *   *

Diplomacy vs. Propaganda

MONTEAGLE STEARNS

* * *

The evolution of so-called democratic diplomacy after the First World War introduced, or, more correctly, recognized, the ultimate influence of public opinion on international relations. The achievements of diplomacy became, in this process, more and more reliant upon public sanction, or its interpretation by press and parliament. Today the diplomatist finds himself subject to two distinct, and invariably conflicting, disciplines: his concessions and demands are regulated by public opinion at home and abroad.

While it is altogether proper that diplomacy should be held strictly accountable to the public, and, in fact, could scarcely hope to avoid accountability under our Constitution, it must be recognized that there is a considerable time-lag between private and public awareness of international problems. If, as a rule, the public is ultimately right, it is often immediately wrong. The tendency of public opinion to polarize around categorical positions, then to swing back toward the center after a period of collective consideration, places the diplomatist in an awkward and somewhat ambiguous position when important decisions must be made quickly. He must either accept the views of the public as a basis for negotiation, or risk eventual disavowal.

The public therefore exercises a determining influence over negotiations in two ways: it may adopt an attitude of such intransigence that negotiation is not feasible; or it may disavow diplomatic commitments after the fact.

SOURCE: "Democratic Diplomacy and the Role of Propaganda," *Foreign Service Journal*, vol. 30 (October 1953), pp. 24–25, 62, 64.

The Power of the Public

The power of the public to discourage or veto diplomatic commitments has been demonstrated often and in diverse circumstances. It is by no means confined to the nations of the west, where the growth of representative institutions and the erosion of European monarchy after 1918 made some such circumscription of diplomatic prerogatives inevitable. Near and Far Eastern statesmen, increasingly aware of the value of public opinion as a lever in negotiations, have sought to engage, and often manipulate, public sympathy in support of their policies, even at the risk of finding themselves prisoners of public sentiment if those policies should change. Thus, in 1948 the Anglo-Iraqi Treaty of Alliance was repudiated in the streets of Baghdad, while the Palestine question, Kashmir, the nationalization of Iranian oil and the Anglo-Egyptian dispute over Suez are all areas where passionate public interest has reinforced—one is tempted to say, crystallized—official intransigence, thereby reducing the margin for diplomatic decision.

There is, in truth, scarcely a nation in the world today where diplomacy can operate *in vacuo*. Treaties, which once initiated international obligations, now tend simply to confirm them. The significance of this fact for the practice of diplomacy is unmistakable, for if diplomacy cannot be adapted to the changing conditions of international society it may be ground to death between irreconcilable absolutes. The same historical processes that have deprived diplomacy of so much of its grace and elegance, transforming it from an art into a profession, may, in their inexorable course, reduce it further to a formality. Diplomacy is essentially pragmatic, and we live in an age of presumption. The danger is pointed out by George Kennan when he speaks of "the legalistic-moralistic approach to international problems." Yet, in the face of this danger, diplomacy must make its own adjustment. It seems abundantly clear that this adjustment must be in the field of public relations, and that it is here that the functional relationship between diplomacy and propaganda asserts itself.

* * *

Groping toward unseen objectives, armed with untested implements, the propagandist has devised a jargon that covers his uncertainty with a veneer of business-like assurance. He makes "plans," which are directed at "targets" and embody "themes" and which are eventually "finalized." He aims not at the masses but at "prime movers" and he has not only objectives but "tasks" (distinguished from objectives by indentation) which, if they cannot immediately be

112

finalized, must be "implemented" or at least "firmed-up." Toward this end he employs both "tactics" and "strategy," being careful to draw a distinction between "long-term" and "short-term" objectives.

Borrowed Vocabulary

This vocabulary, borrowed in about equal measure from the military and academic worlds, is applied, often with great indiscrimination, to precise and delicate political situations. The result is unrealistic and speculative assessment of the role that propaganda may properly be expected to play in such situations. . . .

* * *

The conclusion is to me irresistible that the inadequacies of our propaganda, like the confinement of our diplomacy, have been exaggerated by the false distinctions that we have drawn between the purposes of public as opposed to diplomatic persuasion. We have permitted—indeed encouraged—the growth of parallel instrumentalities, arguing that the integrity of each must be preserved. Yet the results are absurdly impractical. It is as though two woodsmen, one equipped with an axe, the other with a saw, undertook to cut down a tree working simultaneously at different levels.

In our obstinate devotion to administrative integrity we have blurred questions of immediate initiative and ultimate responsibility. Our propaganda assumes a posture of independence, pursues its own indeterminate course and then, with guilty opportunism, seeks to share the approbation accorded a diplomatic success while disclaiming responsibility for failure. His status in perpetual doubt, the propagandist must forever be scurrying about in a ferment of activity. The virtues of silence and contemplation are unknown to him. They do not constitute "effectiveness" and would be regarded with hostility by any Congressional Committee worthy of the name.

The diplomatist for his part flounders in the crosscurrents of public opinion. He views propaganda with skeptical apprehension. He reviews its objectives dutifully but is resigned to the conviction that they are hopelessly unreal, and, in any event, no affair of his. To the diplomatist propaganda is a bargaining point or an embarrassment. It is rarely a means.

These attitudes notwithstanding, propaganda and diplomacy need each other today as never before. Each may be too weak to stand alone. The truly awesome complexity of international problems and the turbulent, irrational and contentious atmosphere surrounding them has imposed responsibilities upon diplomacy that the old machinery is not equipped to support. It devolves upon propaganda to clarify or neutralize this atmosphere in the interests of intelligent negotiation. Yet, if propaganda is to exercise a constructive function, it must be subordinated to diplomatic action, accepting the precise, if often limited, objectives of professional diplomacy. It cannot be expected that propaganda will change the world; that it will make people more receptive by making them more American; that it will serve as a cheap but comfortable substitute for policy; that it will sell America, or, for that matter, that it will sell anything. Propaganda will do none of these things: it will only explain what this industrious, young and infinitely hopeful nation is trying to accomplish in the world, for itself and for others.

However our propaganda may be administered, whether within or without the Department of State, the conjunction of diplomacy and propaganda is an inescapable necessity. Their inherent mutuality has, I suggest, been ignored too long.*

---

* EDITOR'S NOTE: This is the first of three articles on the subject.

Quiet vs. Unquiet Diplomacy

Andrew Berding

Three days after he came into office in January 1961, Secretary of State Dean Rusk issued a statement that the "value of the diplomatic channel depends on its privacy."

He added: "We fully recognize the need of the public to be adequately informed on the conduct of foreign affairs. This right, however, cannot extend to the immediate and full disclosure of every exchange between one of our ambassadors and a high official in the government to which he is accredited."

Three months later President Kennedy showed himself keenly perturbed over newspaper articles which had revealed the preparation for the refugees' landing in Cuba. He then met at the White House with a small group of newspaper and radio representatives to ascertain whether any possibility existed for voluntary press censorship of articles likely to damage our national security.

All this was curiously reminiscent of a previous Democratic Administration some four decades before. Then, President Woodrow Wilson, appalled by the disclosure of secret wartime treaties by Britain and France allocating in advance the spoils of war, called, in the first of his famous Fourteen Points, for "Open covenants of peace, openly arrived at, after which there shall be no private international understandings of any kind, but diplomacy shall proceed always frankly and in the public view."

When Mr. Wilson left for the Paris Peace Conference in 1919 he promised to conduct no secret negotiations and to sign no secret treaties. But promise is not always pursued in practice.

After he had been in Paris a while, American Marines stood

Source: *Foreign Affairs and You: How American Foreign Policy Is Made and What It Means to You* (Garden City, N.Y.: Doubleday, 1962), pp. 156–67.

115

guard outside his office as he found it necessary to negotiate in secret with Lloyd George and Clemenceau. He had already, in fact, clarified what he meant by open diplomacy. "When I pronounced for open diplomacy," he wrote to Secretary of State Robert Lansing in June 1918, "I meant, not that there should be no private discussions of delicate matters, but that no secret agreements should be entered upon, and that all international relations, when fixed, should be open, aboveboard, and explicit."

The argument of secrecy versus openness in negotiations is nothing new. "Open negotiations," said Louis XIV of France, "induce negotiators to flaunt their own prestige and to fight for the dignity, the interests and the positions of their sovereigns with undue obstinacy and prevent them from giving consideration to the frequently superior arguments of the occasion."

The American professional diplomat, whether serving overseas or in the State Department, almost always favors secret diplomacy. He believes that public diplomacy subjects negotiators to the snap judgments and emotions of people with imperfect understanding of the complexity and delicacy of the issues being worked out. He sees over his shoulders various non-governmental organizations pressuring the government to accept their particular views. He envisages Congress "getting too much into the act." He notes propaganda speeches and statements being made that will spoil any chance of agreement. He foresees public positions being taken that will tie the negotiators' hands. He fears that the negotiators will be labeled appeasers if they make those concessions in return for counterconcessions without which true agreement is impossible. He sees unrealistic expectations building up in the public. He sees an unhealthy acceleration given to negotiations that should be conducted patiently over perhaps a long time. This impulse might either conduce to the reaching of unwise accords or to the foolish breaking off of negotiations.

Every one of these views has an element of validity. Yet both the trend and the facts of present-day life are against them. The trend since the last war [World War II] has been markedly in the direction of more light on the conduct of foreign relations. Every American President and Secretary of State has found it necessary to take the public more into their confidence even while negotiations have been in progress.

This is apart from such activities as summit and foreign ministers conferences, upon which the spotlight of publicity has focused relentlessly. The very prospect itself or scheduling of such conferences has inexorably directed the attention of the press to the preparatory negotiations preceding such conferences. Such attention brings pressure on the Executive and Congress to disclose something of what is going on behind closed doors. And it challenges the skill of numerous reporters to learn and unveil some of the secrets.

The fact that the character of certain negotiations, whether in large conferences or through diplomatic channels, has changed since the advent of the Soviet Union makes necessary a re-examination of the traditional concept of diplomatic secrecy. During summit and foreign ministers conferences with the Russians I have generally found that there were three "persons" present: the Soviet representative, the Western representative, and the representative of the world-at-large. Notes, letters, proposals, statements from the Russians were addressed as much, or more, to the representative-at-large as to the Western representative. Our own initiatives or replies constantly had to have "The Third Man" also in mind.

Before the negotiations began between the Russians and the Germans for the treaty of Brest-Litovsk which ended the First World War as far as the Russians were concerned, Trotsky said to the Petrograd Soviet: "Every word spoken by us or by them will be written down and sent by wireless to all nations who will be the judges of our negotiations." Ever since then, the Soviet delegate to an international conference speaks over the heads of the delegates across the conference table to the masses the world over.

In the conferences I attended at the summit in 1955 and later at the foreign ministers level with Molotov and Gromyko I had the impression that Messrs. Bulganin, Molotov, and Gromyko were only partly interested in convincing the Western delegates, for often their arguments were puerile. They were more concerned with convincing the millions beyond the conference table to whom their arguments were plausible.

When the Soviet Premier directs a letter to the President of the United States he is really mailing it to the people everywhere. After a series of letters back and forth between Moscow and Washington in 1958 on basic issues, the Soviets suddenly, without requesting our permission, published the whole exchange, both their communications and ours. They wanted to get their contentions before the world.

A rigid policy of secrecy on our part in negotiations with the Russians hands them the advantage of putting out their distorted version of the discussions at the time, place, and manner of their own choosing.

A prime factor militating against present-day secrecy in negotiations is the large number of participants in negotiations. Bilateral negotiations bring the least trouble. Each additional negotiating nation, however, not merely adds to but multiplies the risks to secrecy. It is one more door for the reporter to knock on, one more telephone to ring. But this one more possible channel of information multiplies the pressure on each participant to "leak" his particular position or project or objection. And at the same time the "leaker" is better protected by numbers against the chance of detection.

In handling public relations during foreign ministers conferences with the Russians I sometimes experienced more difficulty with information slipped out by one or another of our allies than with that pushed out by the Soviets. Sometimes, as when a document agreed to by all the allied participants and therefore not containing any special "line" was slipped to a reporter, it was obvious that the delegate responsible for the leak was seeking to establish credit in the bank with a powerful newspaper or news agency.

When a delegate "leaks" information to a reporter he generally passes out something it was agreed would be kept secret and he puts it out in an *ex parte* way, often not too agreeable to the United States or to the majority allied position. Consequently an American or conference statement has to be issued to clarify the point. It is an axiom of journalism, however, that second-day statements never touch the heels of first-day misstatements.

The Soviets frequently use a neat device at international conferences to infiltrate their thinking among correspondents. Instead of meeting with the press, which might counter with questions, they leak material to the reporters of the Western European communist newspapers like the *Daily Worker* of London, *L'Humanité* of Paris, and *L'Unita* of Rome, who in turn pass out the word to other correspondents.

Occasionally I have seen our diplomats regard as a deliberate "leak" and go into semi-convulsions over what was no more than a clever reporter's putting together bits of information he got here and there, from perhaps a dozen different persons—each of whom thought he was saying nothing at all—and coming up with a surprisingly accurate story. A skilled reporter can sometimes put two and two together and arrive at twenty-two, near enough to the reality of somewhere between twenty and twenty-five. Frantic security investigations of junior officers and clerical employees in State and Defense have been conducted into what were considered "leaks" but were not at all. Often, too, the basis for the supposed "leak" has come from top-level officials.

The whole Department of State was horrified one morning several years ago to see on the front page of a leading American newspaper an exclusive story quoting directly from a paper sent to Canadian Prime Minister John Diefenbaker by President Eisenhower to explain our policy toward communist China. Immediately a hue and cry was raised that someone had "leaked" the document. Fortunately, just as an investigation was about to be launched, it developed that a top officer in the Department had in all innocence given the paper to a correspondent to take home and read when the correspondent asked for an up-to-date statement of our thinking on communist China. The officer honestly forgot that the paper was invested with special importance and secrecy because it was a communication from the President to the Prime Minister of Canada.

I have long observed that the more highly classified a dispatch or paper may be, the greater are its chances of becoming public. The substance of a Top Secret dispatch might burst forth in forty-eight hours, that of a Secret paper in four days, that of a Confidential telegram in a week, that of an Official Use Only memorandum in a fortnight. And an unclassified paper might not become known at all. This is because the more highly classified matter, even though its circulation may be limited, attracts greater interest, weighs more on the minds of those involved, may call for quicker decision, and in general comports more activity, some of which seeps out into the open.

The only solution for this problem is for our own foreign affairs officers to study each type and setting of negotiations, and take it for granted that at some point a leak will occur or enough bits of information find their way through the keyhole of the closed door to make a revealing story. At that point, without allowing any more time to elapse, the State Department should reach a realistic decision to disclose something of the negotiations under way. This should be done in consultation with our allies where possible. What our officials need to realize, as I am sure most of them do, is that they require public support for our foreign policy, and they are less likely to obtain it from the American people if the first news Americans get of a given diplomatic situation—the first news makes the strongest impression—is one-sided, partly inaccurate, and misleading.

The time element should also be considered. The possibility of premature disclosure is the coefficient of the importance of the subject under negotiation times the number of participants times the length of time involved in the negotiations. After Mr. Khrushchev handed

President Kennedy a memorandum on Berlin at their Vienna conference in June 1961 it took the United States, Britain, and France all of six weeks to get their own positions in accord, to consult with the NATO allies, and to draft more or less identical replies. The press naturally carried not only complaints at this inordinate delay but also a number of speculative stories on the contents of the replies which approximated the truth.

If diplomatic notes are considered a process of negotiation, as they are, then much of the concept of secrecy in this aspect of the conduct of diplomacy has evaporated. Diplomatic notes of importance are frequently published the moment they are delivered, and sometimes even before delivery. A good portion of the blame for this malpractice rests with the Russians. Utilizing diplomatic notes for propaganda expositions, and eager to emblazon their contentions to the world public before a reaction can be prepared by the United States or other recipients, the Soviets have at times delivered long notes in Russian to our embassy in Moscow or the State Department in Washington and simultaneously or soon thereafter broadcast a text in English. When newsmen approached me and others in the State Department we had to reply that the note was still being translated from the Russian and a reaction could not be expected until the Department had a chance to study it. The United States, it must be admitted, has sometimes followed the Soviet example.*

I believe it is unrealistic for any President to expect our press, radio, and TV to come up with a voluntary code of ethics in foreign affairs and defense news handling in peacetime. Who is to determine whether the publication of a particular story will hurt the national interests? Who is to determine whether the hurt, if it exists, is greater than the hurt to what is indeed a great national interest, the freedom of the press?

Admiral Hyman G. Rickover came out in 1961 with an angry statement that a tin submarine on sale in the toy shops was a scale model of a nuclear submarine and therefore gave the Soviets invaluable information. The startled toy company replied that it had made the gadget from drawings published in press and magazines. No newspaper could be aware that the drawings and the toy were giving away

---

* EDITOR'S NOTE: The Eisenhower-Kremlin summit communications, including the matter of revelation, are discussed more comprehensively in Elmer Plischke, "Eisenhower's 'Correspondence Diplomacy' with the Kremlin—Case Study in Summit Diplomatics," *Journal of Politics*, vol. 30 (February 1968), pp. 137–59.

essential information, and I doubt that the Soviets were either until the admiral's statement alerted them. (I could thereupon picture a mad rush of employees of the Soviet Embassy to the toy shops to purchase the tin submarines. From now on the embassy must be eagerly watching the shops for the appearance of new toy airplanes, warships, and rockets. And if their Toy Shop Espionage Agent No. 63 fails to see the usual number of tin soldiers on the counter he can report impressively that we have given up men in favor of push-button warfare.)

Important news, moreover, seldom remains for long the exclusive property of one person, one newspaper, or one country. If American newspapers were to agree, which I cannot imagine, to peacetime voluntary censorship, what is to prevent a foreign correspondent from cabling the same news to his newspaper in Britain, France, Germany, or Japan? Foreign correspondents in Washington are constantly exchanging news with their American colleagues. Are the American newspapers to say nothing while the foreign correspondents carry that particular news? Also, a vital piece of news may not make its first bow to the public in the United States but in a foreign country because of a leak in that country or because a reporter has put bits of information together in that capital. Once more, is there any point in American newspapers not printing the news when it is printed abroad? If it is a case of keeping the news from the Sino-Soviets they have already seen it.

Having in mind the pre-Cuban invasion stories that stirred President Kennedy's concern, I can only suggest that if our government intends to conduct that type of activity—in this case the military training of the Cuban refugees and the making of plans to utilize them in an invasion of Cuba—then it should simply take for granted that something about it will be published in the American press. In a democracy such as ours an activity of this nature cannot go unnoticed and, sooner or later, it will be published. If the government did not want the activity to come to light it should not have conducted the activity.

Subsequent to the Cuban debacle there was much speculation that we would now engage in paramilitary training activities to utilize guerrilla fighters in communist-occupied countries such as North Vietnam in the same way that the communists utilize guerrilla fighters in free countries such as the Republic of Vietnam. This may perhaps be wise. But let us not train big batches of foreign nationals in the United States and send them in large bodies on organized missions and expect the press to remain ignorant of the operation or to keep silent when aware. The Soviets have done it by training small groups and infiltrating them clandestinely.

There is, however, one area where the press (the word "press" to me includes radio, TV, magazines, and newsreels) could exercise some restraint. This is in the number of correspondents sent to cover major international events. It is unnecessary, in fact it is ridiculous, for something like 2,000 correspondents to be accredited to a news event like the Khrushchev visit to the United States in 1959, the abortive summit in Paris in 1960, or the Kennedy-Khrushchev meeting in Vienna in 1961. In Paris Mr. Hagerty and I briefed more than six hundred correspondents jammed into one hall. It was harder for us to understand a question from the floor than to answer it.

Correspondents in such numbers tumble over one another. The competition is so great that unwarranted speculative stories are circulated and printed. The pressure on the various delegations is unbearable to try to satisfy even remotely the demands of this vast press corps. And often the newsmen, in addition to or instead of covering the news, are creating news simply through their jostling of one another. This was the case after I, as Assistant Secretary of State for Public Affairs, agreed under great pressure from the press that the State Department would arrange the transportation of nearly 300 correspondents of many nationalities to accompany Mr. Khrushchev around the United States.

It is no easy task for a host government to place an upper limit on the number of correspondents who will be accredited to a given conference or other event, and then to allocate accreditations within this limit. Most governments would prefer not to face the problem and run the risk of arousing press animosity. But the press could well assist the government in the task, particularly by cutting down on the number of reporters sent to cover an event. Certainly a smaller number of correspondents could do a better job of reporting.

In general, while secrecy may assist in the conduct of certain negotiations up to a certain point in time and be therefore desirable, it is frequently not desirable, and at times can become dangerous to our interests.

Clemenceau said that war is too important to be left to the generals. Diplomacy in the cold war has become too important to be left exclusively to professional diplomats operating in profound privacy.

"The whole idea that foreign policy should be conducted by specialists operating in a vacuum, insulated from politics and from public opinion," said J. R. Wiggins, executive editor of the *Washington Post*, "is a fanciful, nostalgic notion that is irreconcilable with the facts of modern life, with the character of our institutions and with the practical necessities of our time.

"It cannot be shown that the old-fashioned diplomats, in the past, operated with flawless efficiency and wisdom and it cannot be shown that the conduct of diplomacy under arbitrary governments, in our own time, has been uniformly effective, scientific and well-ordered.

"Even if such methods were demonstrably better, we could not follow them, for we do not provide the governmental framework for such a diplomacy and we cannot furnish it without abandoning democracy."

There can be no debate over the second of Woodrow Wilson's postulates—open convenants. Once a treaty or international agreement has been reached it should be announced. There will be exceptions, of course. One would not think of demanding the publication of secret military agreements among our allies, for instance, on how they and we would defend Western Europe against a Soviet invasion. Article 102 of the United Nations Charter provides for the registering with the Secretariat and the publication by it of every treaty and international agreement entered into by any member. By virtue of this article many thousands of treaties and agreements have been registered with the UN. A standard clause in a modern treaty is that it shall be registered with the UN.*

---

* EDITOR'S NOTE: Following World War I, treaties and agreements were published in the *League of Nations Treaty Series* (more than 200 volumes, 1920–1944), and since World War II they have been published in the *United Nations Treaty Series*. The United States has historically published its treaties and agreements. They are published in the *Treaties and Other International Acts Series (TIAS)*, *Treaties and Other International Agreements of the United States of America, 1776–1949*, 13 vols. (TIAA), and *United States Treaties and Other International Agreements (UST)*, as well as in the *Statutes at Large* prior to 1951.

Secret vs. Open Diplomacy

Hugh S. Gibson

At the end of the last war [World War I], we were told that one of the safeguards of the new order was to be open diplomacy. Secret diplomacy was to be done away with, and international affairs were to be regulated by open covenants openly arrived at.

Probably no group of phrases has led to more muddled thinking on fundamental methods.

People are not always clear in their own minds as to what secret diplomacy is, but it sounds reprehensible and they are against it.

The general assumption has grown up that the negotiations of diplomacy on international affairs ought to be conducted in the glare of pitiless publicity. There are, of course, certain reticences which are permissible for the priest, the lawyer, the doctor, or the father of a family, but governments and their negotiators should, it is held, operate under an entirely different regime.

If the Secretary of State is not forthcoming with public statements as to what he is discussing with this government or what he has said to that Ambassador, or what he has heard from one of our missions abroad, you instantly hear the cry of secret diplomacy. Secret diplomacy is one of those hobgoblins that hover around the idea of democratic control of diplomacy.

As a matter of fact, there is such a thing as secret diplomacy, and it is reprehensible. This might be defined as intergovernmental intrigue for wrongful ends, resulting in obligations for future action of which the people are kept in ignorance until they are called on to pay with their lives and fortunes. There are also secret negotiations between governments to infringe the rights of another.

Source: *The Road To Foreign Policy* (Garden City, N.Y.: Doubleday, Doran, 1944), pp. 77–89.

There is no doubt that every effort should be made to do away with this sort of thing. But we should bear in mind that this brand of diplomacy has the same relation to the real article that smash-and-grab raids have to legitimate business. We must remember that there is a broad margin between hole-and-corner intrigue and diplomatic negotiations in the glare of the floodlights. Perhaps we shall find the best results are to be had by avoiding both extremes.

If the people know the aims of their government and are kept apprised of undertakings and commitments before effective approval is given there is nothing reprehensible in carrying on the day-to-day negotiations in private—in fact, that is the only way negotiations can be carried on, not only governmental negotiations, but private business negotiations or family discussions. The less publicity there is to negotiation the greater the chance of success, but very often the advocates of open diplomacy or democratic control want to sit at the elbow of our negotiator telling him what to say, what not to say, and usually pushing him on to do stunts which have the beauty of being dramatic but don't get him any "forrader." This is nothing more or less than backseat driving, and is just about as valuable. The sound course is to choose your negotiators for their ability, tell them what they are to seek to obtain, and let them use their own discretion as to their procedure.

Perhaps the greatest proponent of open diplomacy and democratic control was President Wilson, but when he came to grips with the grim realities of international negotiation he forgot all about "pitiless publicity" and "open covenants openly arrived at," and resorted, not only to secrecy in negotiation, but in many cases to secrecy as to his objectives as well. Nobody could say that the Treaty of Versailles was openly arrived at, indeed few professional diplomats have proceeded by means that were so secret. Perhaps if we had had greater public knowledge of policy we should have had a better treaty.

Which brings us back to the point that we are wasting a great deal of energy talking about democratic control of American foreign policy. We can all advocate it subject to one condition, and that is that we have a foreign policy. Once we have formulated a plan and know what we seek to achieve, democratic control will have its chance, but while awaiting that time we should do well to spread understanding of the important difference between policy and negotiation. If the people take an interest in policy, they will insist on being informed as to the whys and wherefors, with the wholesome

125

result that the government will be obliged to explain its policies and justify them.

Most people believe in the democratic control of foreign policy, but very few of them have a clear idea of what it is. Most discussion on this subject ignores the fact that the Founding Fathers sought to establish democratic control of foreign policy by allotting to the people's elected representatives in Congress an important share in the control of foreign affairs. Many of those now deploring the lack of democratic control propose that the remedy should be found by depriving Congress of its present powers, although it is not at all clear just what form of democratic control they propose to substitute for the people's elected representatives.

Then there are those who, while believing that delegation of power to elected representatives is unsatisfactory, also believe that decisions must be taken by the whole mass of the population. For instance, in an emergency we should hold a referendum and count noses on the question of a declaration of war—this on the ground that the mass of the people will be more sober and self-controlled than Congress. How far is this belief justified by history?

This may have a satisfying sound, but we should not think of applying it even on a far smaller scale. A factory could hardly be run successfully by publishing all the details of its prices, contracts, and opportunities, so that its operations could be directed by mass meetings of the stockholders and workmen. Anybody who suggested such a course would be denounced as a crackpot. How, we would be asked, could a firm publish its confidential information for the benefit of its competitors? How could anybody be simple enough to believe that a business enterprise could be conducted by having hundreds, and perhaps thousands, of stockholders leaning over the shoulders of the general manager and the shop steward and directing them at every step?

Of course it sounds grotesque as applied to a factory, but it would be far more grotesque and dangerous if applied to the conduct of our foreign affairs. In practice this would not result in democratic control but in control by organized groups with all their attachments, antipathies, and yearnings to serve this country or to have revenge on that.

Open diplomacy comes pretty close to being a contradiction in terms.

This idea was first broached at the time, during and after the last war, when the political leaders in all countries took over the actual handling of international negotiations. Naturally, they brought their own methods to the new task. They have been at it for nearly a generation, and we have had a fairly good opportunity to see how far they have improved on the old methods.

Secret diplomacy, if we use the words in their real meaning, is nothing more than the established method of unpublicized negotiation. This method was evolved through centuries of human experience. It is predicated on systematic exploration of a subject in private by trained negotiators. Such exploration involves the exercise of resourcefulness, patience, and good will in order to arrive, perhaps after many failures, at a meeting of minds where conflicting interests are reconciled, at least in principle, under a form of agreement involving the common denominator of understanding.

The problems of diplomacy are often difficult and intricate. If they were not, they would tend to settle themselves and would not call for study by governmental representatives. It is the daily lot of the diplomat to tackle one of these problems and seek, through long and patient negotiation, to reach solutions. It is rare that he succeeds the first time of trying. More often than not he finds that the plan first envisaged cannot be accepted by the other side for reasons which emerge from the discussions. There is no clash about this, and both sides set to work to re-examine the problem in the light of what they have learned. It is the method of trial and error, and the chances are that if all concerned continue the discussions with a desire to meet each other's reasonable difficulties they will one day find an acceptable solution. It is neither showy nor speedy, yet it has a way of succeeding more often than not.

In striking contrast to this we have the method of public conferences as all too generally practiced. Here the negotiators meet in the presence of the public and numerous representatives of the press, to say nothing of microphones and newsreel cameras.* At the start, each side states its case. It would not be politic at this stage to divulge how little you could be content with. You are obliged to state your maximum requirements, in order to allow a reasonable margin for future bargaining. But, unfortunately, the other man is obliged to state his case in the same way, and thus at the outset you are entrenched upon your positions—and extreme positions at that. There is an inevitable deadlock. You are obliged to call in the press representatives and make sure that they understand that you are right and the other side wrong. You must make a speech to strengthen your position at home, and incidentally make it harder to reach agreement.

---

* EDITOR'S NOTE: As well as television and other forms of contemporary instant communications.

The representatives of your national press, being patriotic, rally round to support you. Their dispatches tend to show how sound and reasonable you are in your demands and how exorbitant are the demands of the other side. Editorial comment makes conciliation still more difficult. The press of the other party adopts a similar attitude from their own angle, and you soon find that you have to deal not only with your opposite number in the negotiation but also with a public opinion at home that has been aroused by your speeches and by the well-intentioned efforts of the press. It is often far easier to negotiate with the representative of the other nation than it is to convince the public opinion of your own country of the necessity for making some contribution to agreement. Indeed, the pressure upon any negotiator in a public duel of this sort is almost overwhelming to stand pat and fight vociferously for his original platform. Thus he becomes a hero in his own country, whereas if he makes any concession, however reasonable he may consider it and however he may have anticipated it in his own mind, he suddenly finds himself charged by the press with being spineless or having been bamboozled by the other side.

Almost anyone who has followed international conferences since the last war has seen for himself that they have almost uniformly failed to live up to our hopes and expectations. A careful study of them reveals that their failure is largely due to the fact that Pitiless Publicity and the consequent frozen position have made successful negotiations impossible.

Another thing that emerges from a careful study of international conferences is that their success is usually in direct proportion to the amount of confidential and expert spadework which has been done in advance, and to the measure of agreement that was already reached before they were convened. The most successful of all were those convened merely to adjust and ratify agreement in principle already reached.

This does not mean that we should leap to the conclusion that the conference method should be scrapped. That would be jumping from one extreme to the other. But it seems important to draw some lessons from our experience, correct our mistakes, and see if we cannot improve our existing technique.

Common sense is attracted by the apparent advantage of having negotiations conducted by a group of men gathered round a table, rather than by complicated exchange by cable. And it should be possible to get better results.

When we re-examine our earlier work, conferences seem to have suffered from two handicaps. They were conducted under a blaze of publicity. They were given impossible tasks.

If we are capable of learning from our mistakes, it should be possible to reduce and even eliminate the first.

The second calls for common-sense recognition of what conferences can do. They cannot be charged with solving fundamental problems. That is the task of governments, and these solutions must be reached by man-to-man negotiation before calling conferences. Once the general lines of agreement and the will to agree have become clear, the negotiators can be brought together to formulate the actual terms of agreement.

When two corporations seek solution to a conflict on business matters, they do not turn the problem over to their lawyers. The executives find a basis for agreement and then entrust to the lawyers the task of putting the agreement into proper form. Delegates at a conference should have somewhat the same function as the lawyers.

People at home are often impatient with our delegates at international conferences for failing to make other people go as far as we should like. They overlook one thing—that in a conference you cannot make anybody do anything. No one can make us do anything, and we labor under the same limitations in imposing our views. Many people assume that the decisions should represent the position of the most enlightened delegation, and that if only we are sufficiently advanced we should have our way. Unfortunately, things do not work out that way. The conference has to content itself with what is accepted by the most backward delegation. You can secure the adoption of only those things agreed to by everybody. The rule of unanimity is the dead hand of this sort of negotiation.*

If we can give conferences a fair chance they may prove valuable instruments, but only after we have done away with the very attributes that most appealed to many loose thinkers on the subject.

One drawback to the conference method is that it imposes upon any delegates sincerely desirous of agreement the necessity for resorting to the despised methods of secret diplomacy. They are obliged to spend a good part of their time in back-stairs negotiation in hotel rooms and to urge upon this or that delegate that he withhold any statement of his real position in order to gain time for seeking a com-

---

* EDITOR'S NOTE: In the post–World War II era the rule of unanimity has been superseded by various forms of majority decision making in some international conferences and many international organization forums. Participation proliferation, including an increasing number of microstates exercising equality of voting power, has introduced new and equally constraining and otherwise questionable practices, as noted in the last essay of Chapter 2.

mon ground. When a roomful of delegates get up in public session and express agreement on an important matter, it is usually because these same delegates have spent some time in dark corners ironing out their difficulties. The proceedings have been carefully rehearsed; the more spontaneous they appear, the more carefully they have been rehearsed. Two delegates will state divergent views; a third will intervene with a conciliatory suggestion to which the other two express perhaps seemingly reluctant, perhaps enthusiastic, agreement. Thus everybody's face is saved. But it is slow and difficult work, and amounts to achieving good by hole-and-corner methods.

The foregoing applies primarily to public conferences conducted by trained negotiators who are giving their whole time to the problem. It does not apply to the same extent to the political figures who so often come upon the scene for the announced purpose of pulling the rabbit out of the hat.

One great drawback about having intricate problems handled by political leaders is that they are busy men and cannot settle down long enough to do a thorough job. How often at Geneva, or elsewhere, have we seen a meeting called to order with the statement that we must press forward to reach a solution of this or that question because the French Foreign Minister is obliged to leave on Thursday morning. You may well ask what relation there is between these two statements. The solution need not be reached before the Minister leaves Geneva. It could be reported to him in due course by telegraph or telephone. But that is just the catch. The politician simply cannot go home with the press trumpeting the fact that he did nothing more important than sit in at the beginning of the discussion. He must have his little triumph.

And this has led to two of the worst products of open diplomacy—improvisation and the formula.

Improvisation is undoubtedly the worst possible method for settling problems in diplomacy—just as it would be in business. The mere fact that problems have been put on the agenda for treatment by the political leaders is evidence that they are difficult and call for careful, prudent handling. Such handling can be based only on study, preparation, and consultation with the people who know most about them. No amount of improvisation, however brilliant, can take the place of hard work in diplomacy any more than in the conduct of an intricate lawsuit.

So the politician puts forward some short cut to agreement, something that looks good on the surface but would not bear scrutiny and careful examination. While this shocks the professional diplomat, it is not at all shocking to the politician. He is merely applying his ordinary, everyday methods of dealing with questions as they arise. He will have his little moment of triumph, and if the solution does not work, the people will be thinking of something else by that time anyway, so why worry?

If improvisation will provide something that can be represented as a great achievement, so much the better. But, in any event, there must be something to convey the impression of progress, something to which the leader can point with pride. This has led to a whole technique of humbug—the technique of framing resolutions and reports which will hold together for the moment and can, during that period, be represented as successes. This is a delicate technique, and calls for great skill, for it is not enough to create the illusion of achievement for one country. There are various leaders present at the conference, and each one—each Prime Minister, Foreign Minister, and whatnot—must have his little triumph, must be able to point with pride, and all the rest. From this has grown up the gentle art of agreeing upon a formula. Whenever there is an obvious deadlock, some sympathetic statesman will arise and suggest a formula. If the formula can be accepted by all, there is a sigh of relief, followed by an exodus, and the conference is over.

But don't make any mistake about the nature of a formula. It is not necessarily a form of compromise on which all agree. It has, in fact, come to mean a form of words which has the outward appearance of agreement and settlement when read by the man in the street but which, either by tacit agreement among the delegates or from differences of wording in different languages, means different things to the parties.

The formula is a dangerous remedy. It does permit the delegates to get away and the conference to capture momentarily glowing headlines. Although all concerned have agreed upon a form of words for the purpose of creating an illusion of agreement, they have a tendency to forget that the words mean exactly nothing. More often than not, after reading and rereading the formula, one side comes to the conclusion that it has been promised something definite and substantial. The other side probably feels that it has got out of a tight corner and promised nothing at all. The inevitable result is acrimonious disagreement and very possibly intimations of bad faith.

The trouble with all this is that it is contrary to one of the most elementary requirements of diplomacy. A diplomatic settlement to be of value must be definite and precise, must mean exactly the same thing in the different languages in which it is drafted, and be incapable of any other interpretation.

The conference method is undoubtedly here to stay, although it is to be hoped that it will be used more discriminatingly, but there are several modifications in present procedures which would tend to secure a larger volume of agreement.

First, it is desirable that the maximum amount of preparatory work be completed by direct and private negotiation before the conference is convened, in order that its work may be narrowed down to the adjustment of minor difficulties and the drafting of the actual terms of the agreement.

Second, the conference itself should be put on a normal, workaday basis and cease to be treated as an emergency with a time limit. There is no real reason for a conference to be carried on differently from any other human activity. What we need most is the application of the laboratory method. If you are seeking a chemical formula, you do not call a meeting, choose sides, and announce to an incredulous press that everything will be tidied up before the end of the week, as Professor Snooks must return to his regular work by that time. Above all, you do not, in agreement with your scientific colleagues, and in order to meet the immediate demands of the situation, dish up a phony formula which you know any scientist with half an eye can see through. On the contrary, you assemble the members of your research staff and send them off to work in their laboratories until they notify you that they have found the answer. It may be days, or weeks, or months, or even years, but the time element is of secondary importance.

There is every reason why conferences should be conducted in the same way. The problems they have to tackle are no less intricate than those entrusted to the scientific research worker. Disarmament, for instance, is so deeply bogged in the soils of human nature that it is folly to expect a quick and simple solution. The only hope is to let men of training and resource and good will disappear into some retreat and work quietly and unhurriedly for as long as may be necessary, many years perhaps, in the hope that they will find ways and means of advancing along the road. Furthermore, conferences should, except for the purpose of stimulating public interest and announcing agreement, be held as private conversations with a minimum of speeches and publicity in order to lessen the temptation for the negotiators to cavort for the benefit of the press and public opinion. In other words, to make their first concern the solution of the problem and not ephemeral public approval for themselves.

The conference method can hardly be expected to give better results until the conference itself ceases to be regarded as a gladiatorial combat. We must get out of our heads the idea that a conference is like a football game: that we choose sides and that they continue to score until there is victory for one side or the other. That is the mentality that is expressed by the remark attributed to Will Rogers, that the United States never lost a war or won a conference. Will Rogers denied to me on several occasions with some heat that he had ever made this statement, but that is another story.

The fundamental purpose of a conference, or any other form of negotiation, is to secure agreement, not victory. In fact, victory and defeat are the negation of diplomacy. The diplomat should never forget that the problem he is working on is of only relative importance in that it is one of an unending series that must be discussed with the other party through the years, and therefore, while he must get as much as is expedient for his own country, it must be within such limits and under such terms as will obviate resentment and a sense of injustice in future negotiations. It is important to have everybody satisfied, so that they bring to the next meeting a desire for further agreement and not a yearning for revenge—the inevitable result of defeat.

This calls for a radical change in our mental attitude, for there is no doubt that the public in all countries consider international relations in terms of victory and defeat. But we may as well make up our minds that it is only when we have adopted the opposite attitude that we can hope for a larger measure of success.

If the day ever comes when a conference is conducted by these methods, while we cannot of course be sure of success, we can be sure that better machinery has been installed in order to bring that success about.

It is, of course, imperative that all international agreements, once they have been concluded, should be made of public record. For our own security and for guidance in formulating our foreign policy, it is important that we be acquainted with agreements existing among other countries. But, from a practical point of view, and disregarding the tyranny of slogans, it does not make a particle of difference whether these covenants are arrived at openly or otherwise. The method is of little importance and of no real interest to the public. The essential thing is that the covenants should amount to something when they are arrived at.

Some of the advocates of open diplomacy go so far as to maintain that the archives of the Department of State should be open to the public and that the press be at liberty to publish any documents they consider of sufficient interest. If this were done, they would probably be sorely disappointed in what they found. There would be precious little of what they would be led to expect from the thrillers of E. Phillips Oppenheim.*

Just the same, it is a method that is not to be advocated. There are certain matters regarding which any decent government must maintain reticence. There is nothing abstruse about it. It is simply a matter of common sense.

We are often told that the same standards should be applied to publicity in national affairs as in private business. There is little to disagree with in this. Even in private business there is a distinct difference between secrecy to conceal swindling and dishonest activities and reticence such as that observed by a bank in regard to the affairs of its depositors and clients.

The sort of reticence that is observed by a bank or a lawyer or a doctor is not entirely confined to business affairs, but extends to everyday life. No man is considered dishonest and secretive because he does not discuss his family affairs in the presence of strangers. A prudent man may legitimately go even further than that and not audibly proclaim such a harmless fact as his intention to purchase a farm. If he does, he perfectly well knows that his waking hours will be consumed by the importunities of salesmen, and he usually goes about this business with a certain amount of caution and reserve— in other words, secret diplomacy.

In the same way the efforts of the government to secure fair treatment for its citizens, to promote trade, to protect its interests against discrimination or injustice, need not be advertised in order to be honest.

Another important phase of this question is that a government cannot, any more than an individual, repeat information that is given under the seal of confidence. Not only is such secrecy considered legitimate, but the government would be severely condemned if it were to publish this information on the ground that there was no such thing as legitimate secrecy. The raw material upon which our Department of State operates is chiefly in the form of information gathered in all corners of the world. Much of this information is given us by other governments and by individuals, and given because they are convinced that we can be depended on to respect their con-

---

* EDITOR'S NOTE: The last essay in this chapter deals with official policy and programs for the revelation of information and documents.

fidence. A steady stream of such information pours into the Department of State, and a great deal of it is clearly labeled as having been given under an injunction not to let it become public or even to impart it to anyone outside of the government. It is given us because the people who give it realize that it will be of value to us, and that we can be depended upon not to use it in any way that will harm their interests. They are encouraged to give us this information because of a regime of reciprocity which exists between most governments under which they hope to secure equally helpful and legitimate information from us. Respect for confidence is just as important in international dealings as in private life, and if it is not observed the government suffers just as directly as the individual.

Information—sound, reliable information—is more precious than rubies. If it is good, you want more of it from the same source. So even if you lack a high sense of honor, you keep it confidential. You are kept on the straight and narrow path by the knowledge that if you betray your informant once he will lay no more eggs of golden information. And from that time on you will have to be content with the sort of information the other government is willing and ready to give to the press.

To put it in other words, the effective conduct of our foreign relations is largely dependent upon the completeness of the information upon which that conduct is based. The greater the amount of confidential information we receive, the better for the conduct of our affairs; that amount is in direct relation to the confidence felt in our discretion in the handling of such information. The minute that confidence is undermined, the flow of information stops.

The experience of the last generation should demonstrate that we should be on our guard against two dangers—secret diplomacy and open diplomacy.

No government in this country can indulge in secret diplomacy without paying the penalty when the facts become known. If it makes secret commitments, they will not necessarily be considered binding when they do become known. Any other government that accepts such commitments at face value may find that it has been swindled.

On the other hand, we should recognize the dangers of diplomacy in the market place. We should have had time to recognize the futility of trying to negotiate publicly in international conferences. We shall get farther faster by returning to the tested methods of real diplomacy, negotiating in private and making the results public.

Communication: The Weak Link

WILLIAM D. BLAIR, JR.

It is out of this combination of experiences, and the research which has been a part of them, that I have formed the belief which I offer as my thesis . . . namely, that we Americans as a people have not been very good at our communication about foreign affairs; that our performance in this field even today falls disturbingly short of the standard which our own best interests, and those of the world community, require; and that the consequences of these shortcomings have been real and costly to all of us and could become more so.

The roots of the problem are deeply buried in our history. Throughout our national lifetime, until very recently, most of us as individuals have been able to ignore international matters, and as a rule we have taken full advantage of that opportunity. There have of course been exceptional periods, exceptional moments, when a determined public opinion has exerted a compelling influence on a sometimes willing, sometimes reluctant, Government in international matters; and these exceptions have ranged in direction from what would today be called imperialism or interventionism, as in the case of the Spanish-American War, to isolationism, as exemplified by the neutrality euphoria of the 1930's. But on the whole, and within broadly accepted limits, we have tended to leave the worrying about our foreign relations to a small group of intellectuals and managers in and out of Government—a foreign policy "establishment," itself drawn from relatively small and specialized segments of the academic, business, and journalistic communities for the most part, as well as from parts of Government, and particularly the State Department's Foreign Service and certain congressional committees.

SOURCE: Alexander Graham Bell Lecture in the series, "Man's Communication With Man," Boston, Massachusetts, October 16, 1970, *Department of State Bulletin*, vol. 63 (November 9, 1970), pp. 580–86.

Within this establishment, and in the absence of an informed or concerned public, the decisionmaking process has been relatively informal, and the direction and style of our policy and even the details of its execution have tended to depend heavily on the President of the day and/or his Secretary of State. . . .

Change in U.S. Role in World Community

This contrast between an earlier day and our own suggests the principal reason, if not justification, for the historical absence of dialogue in this country about foreign affairs. This is, of course, the dramatic change in the world community since we became a part of it and particularly the drastic change in our own role in that community. It is not only the development of instantaneous global communications, supersonic transport, and nuclear weaponry which has ended forever —whether or not all of us recognize it—our persistent dream of a peaceful and prosperous isolation. Still more, it is our own transformation from a small, weak band of underdeveloped ex colonies, which but for the oceans and some skillful diplomacy could well have been the plaything and battleground of the European powers, to the heaviest single weight in the global scales—by far the largest economy, and actually or potentially the strongest military power, in the world, and thereby a nation whose very indifference to a problem in a remote corner of the earth is in fact a decision which affects millions of lives.

This transformation was gradual, and most of us were slow to recognize it; it was clear to every capital in the world by the late 1940's, if not before, but even today there are millions of Americans who do not fully understand it. In the absence of such recognition it was understandable that the man in the street would devote little attention to what seemed the rather abstract subject of international relations; and it is understandable, though in my view damaging, that this should contribute to confusion among us, and ultimately among other nations, about our purposes in the world today.

What I have suggested so far is that throughout our history until recent times, the American public as a whole has paid rather little attention to its foreign relations and that the active management of those affairs was delegated to a very small group. This condition was encouraged, if not caused by, the relatively passive role which we played in the world during most of the last two centuries. And on the whole, some serious mistakes notwithstanding, I would say that the system worked; that is, we did at least manage to preserve our independence and our chosen form of government for . . . 200 years and to increase the welfare of most though not all of our citizens at the same time. I would even go so far as to say that we have contributed, especially in modern times, perhaps a good deal more on the plus side than on the minus side to peace and progress in the community of nations. Not many nations today, large or small, can make even the first of those basic claims.

But whether my qualitative judgment is right or wrong, it seems to me clear that this historical performance has left us some damaging legacies. In addition, there are signs today of a desire on the part of the public as a whole to play a more active role in determining foreign policy, though the evidence is more mixed than appears on the surface. On both scores, we need to repair the shortcomings and extend the scope of our domestic communication about foreign policy.

Scope and Complexity of Diplomacy Today

To start with smaller matters, but some which are close to home for me, one of the damaging legacies of our foreign policy establishment is the fact that American diplomats as a group—and this is not peculiar to Americans—have not thought of themselves as communicators or attached much urgency to the need to enlist public support for their policies in order to put them into practice and maintain them. It was enough to be able to talk things over with other diplomats and other members of the foreign policy establishment, a fairly homogeneous group. I am giving away no state secrets when I say that this is one of my active daily concerns today—trying to persuade more of my colleagues throughout the State Department, and at almost all levels, to devote more time to public discussion of their problems. We have no team of professional personalities to speak for us, at meetings and on the media, and we want none. . . . While diplomacy, like other forms of negotiation, can never be wholly productive in public, a diplomat today is no different from any other public official in his need for public understanding and support if he is to be effective. Yet the habit of the past dies hard.

Equally important, we have been slow to adapt the decision-making and management processes—organized communication, if you like—in our foreign relations to the needs of the world in which we now find ourselves. In prewar days, when a Secretary of State could personally put his stamp on every instruction to the field, these processes could be simple and informal and still be effective. But since World War II both the scope and the complexity of our diplomacy have multiplied to a point at which their management requires a very high order of organization and the creative participation of large numbers of people. In this period the number of countries with which we have relations has risen from around 60 to more than 120 [now more than 160] and the number of problems has multiplied in geometric proportion. At the same time, economic and military assistance, intelligence, information, arms control, participation in international organizations, and a whole host of other specialized tools have become new or much more important elements in our diplomacy; the Department of State and its Foreign Service, at one time almost alone in the foreign policy arena, have been joined by virtually every other Cabinet department and a profusion of smaller Government agencies, to the point at which some of our larger missions abroad are staffed by hundreds of official representatives, only a small fraction of whom report to the State Department.

Informal consultation among a few diplomatic acquaintances is hopelessly inadequate to the supervision of this array, and the fact that we have done as well as we have as a nation in the postwar period is due more to a succession of strong Presidents and Secretaries of State than to the systematic organization of the resources which support them. Efforts have been and are being made, both in our embassies abroad and in Washington, to rationalize this array of agencies and foreign services, and we are making real progress; but there is clearly a good deal more to be done.

* * *

The Art of Communication

Over time, strengthening the international element in our educational curricula and our daily lives will surely help to moderate the tone and strengthen the content of our public discourse on foreign affairs, whether official or private, in the streets or on the television tube. And it will surely help us to banish what often seems to me a bitter irony: the fact that now, of all times, when the technology of communications borders on the miraculous, the art of communication so often appears to border on the forgotten. By the art of communication, of course, I mean listening to the other point of view, trying to understand it and to identify and build on the points of communion which it offers with your own.

* * *

In sum, if our communication today about our foreign affairs seems in some respects faulty, I am deeply convinced that the fault lies with the medium, not with the message. The fault lies with us as individuals, as Government agencies, as a people, who have not paid as much attention as we might have to what we have too often regarded as a secondary area of concern. As a result, many of us today are uncertain about our message to the world or have lost sight of it. . . .

Availability of Diplomatic
Information and Documents

WILLIAM M. FRANKLIN

First of all, we have to sort out our terms. "Classification" as used in this context refers to the system of marking documents as Confidential, Secret, or Top Secret, depending on their importance to the national security. "Declassification" is, of course, the reversal of the process. In general it can be said that the authority to classify or declassify a given piece of paper rests with the offices having responsibility for the policy toward the particular country, organization, or type of problem to which it relates. Historians and archivists may have a voice with respect to classification and declassification, but they do not make the decisions—at least not in State Department practice.

Not infrequently one hears the accusation that classification is nothing but a "coverup for errors by the bureaucrats." I cannot speak for other agencies, but in the State Department system this would be most unlikely. Almost all our policy officers are either political appointees or Foreign Service officers, most of whom stay in a given assignment only a few years (eight is about the maximum), after which the control over the documents that they have classified passes to other officials—perhaps of an opposing political party—who can declassify any of those documents without any reference back to the original classifiers. Documents may be kept classified far longer than scholars and reporters may consider necessary, but this is done for reasons of policy—not for the protection of persons, most of whom never thought they had made any errors anyway.

Another relationship that needs attention is that between classi-

SOURCE: "The Availability of Department of State Records," address at the University of Virginia, Charlottesville, in November 1972, *Department of State Bulletin*, vol. 68 (January 29, 1973), pp. 101–7.

fication and secrecy. The present classification system came into the United States Government only with World War II. Prior to that time documents of special sensitivity were sometimes marked as "confidential" but generally they bore no such indication at all. Does this mean that prior to World War II government documents were in principle more open to the public? On the contrary, the principle was firmly embedded that every paper prepared on official business was to be shown only to other officers on a need-to-know basis. The only papers that were properly releasable to the public were those specifically so designated by higher authority. So, ironically, it can be said that the present classification system marked in principle a step toward greater liberality in that it made thousands of unclassified documents immediately releasable to the public.

But being "unclassified" or "declassified" does not in itself make a document available to the public. Papers unclassified or declassified are still in government file rooms closed to the public.

So declassification is not enough. In order to become available to the public, official records which are unclassified or which have been declassified must be (1) published in some manner, (2) opened up for public access, or (3) released in response to requests from the public for particular documents. Each of these procedures has a history of its own in the practice of the Department of State, and from this historical perspective some useful insights may be derived.

Publication of Official Papers

The traditional and original method of releasing official papers was publication on particular topics. The practice arose in 18th-century England, where Parliament, beginning to reach for the reins of power, demanded on occasion that the government publish papers on particular subjects, particularly crises in foreign affairs which were becoming matters of increasing popular concern. When the government acceded—or when it decided on its own to release some papers—it had first to select from the files those that were to be released and then to send them to the public printer, often with portions still sensitive marked for omission. The printer would run the documents in the requisite number of copies (enough at least for parliamentary distribution) and would bind them together with "printer's wrapper"; i.e., covers of white paper. If the size of the text warranted it, he might be forced to use heavier covers, which were customarily of blue cardboard. Thus originated the eminent series of British White Papers and Blue Books which in the 19th century blazed a trail toward greater freedom of information in matters, such as foreign affairs, which had hitherto been regarded as prerogatives of the Crown, too sensitive or too complex to be shared even with Parliament, let alone the people. The time for sharing had begun.*

The young United States inherited this tradition and extended it in its own way. From the earliest days documents on foreign affairs were made available to Congress on particular subjects of interest, but the novel characteristic which developed in American practice was the annual review. To the President's annual message to Congress on the state of the Union (traditionally delivered in December) there were attached detailed reports from the various Cabinet officers—except from the Secretary of State, who customarily rendered his report not in narrative but in the form of papers illustrating American foreign policy and diplomatic relations during the year. These papers, along with the Presidential address, were printed up as a congressional document and were circulated in the Capitol. In 1861 the Department of State, for the first time, had these foreign policy documents bound in hard covers and published under the title *Papers Relating to Foreign Affairs*. Thus there began that continuing series of annual volumes which, under the newer title, *Foreign Relations of the United States*, has now reached the documents for the year 1948 [in 1979 the volumes for the mid-1950s were being processed].

It is interesting to note that the *Foreign Relations* series was started as a medium for releasing current documents of major importance. Indeed, the volume issued in 1861 contained documents of that very year, many of them on the hot and vital question of keeping the Great Powers from aiding and recognizing the Confederate States of America. Under the modern system of classification such documents could easily justify a Top Secret stamp, for they literally concerned the very existence of the United States of America and dealt with the imminent possibility of war with several European states. In those days the documents bore no stamp of classification, but it was understood that nothing of this sort was to be released without higher approval. Today this would be called "declassification"; at that time it was "clearance"—a term still used in the Historical Office of the Department. It would be my guess that the documents of 1861 were "cleared" by Secretary Seward personally, and probably also with President Lincoln, before they were published. The process has not essentially changed through all the years, although we do not gen-

---

* See Harold Temperley and Lillian M. Penson, *A Century of Diplomatic Blue Books, 1814–1914* (New York: Barnes and Noble, Inc., 1966).

erally have to go so high for clearance. The documents for each year have to be located, selected, copied, and annotated by the Historical Office. Then galley proofs are run at the Government Printing Office and copies thereof—appropriately divided up by subjects—are circulated for declassification to all the concerned policy offices in the Department of State and to all other departments, agencies, and sometimes foreign governments whose documents we are proposing to publish. Since each volume now runs well over 1,000 pages, with seven to twelve volumes per year, it is no exaggeration to say that the staff of historians working on the *Foreign Relations* series is now the Department's principal declassification team.

The release of documents through the medium of a continuing series has certain great advantages. In contrast to a haphazard releasing of individual documents, the series presents all the important documents on each subject in context. The series provides a convenient and lasting reference source for students and scholars throughout the world. The release of documents through official publication is obviously equitable; there are no favorites and no "scoops." Placed in their historical setting, the documents are often easier for the Department to declassify and release because in such context their release is less likely to be misunderstood as having some current political significance.

Some of these desirable characteristics, however, worked to the disadvantage of the series in other respects, notably in speed of publication. To the end of the 19th century the volumes were being brought out when the documents were only a year or two old. In the present century the series began to lag, and by World War I the documents published were about eight years old. The huge increase in the volume of documentation occasioned by both World Wars, plus the increasingly important role played by the United States on the world stage, worked to make the series slip back year by year, until by 1970 the documents being released were over 25 years old. This situation came to the attention of President Nixon early in 1972, and on March 8 of that year he issued instructions that the series be brought up to a 20-year line. Three additional positions have been added to the *Foreign Relations* staff, and more money has been provided for indexing and printing, but the attainment of the President's goal will depend in large measure on the speed with which busy policy officers (not historians) can be persuaded to review the documents proposed for declassification and publication.

From all this it is clear that the *Foreign Relations* series in the 20th century has no longer fulfilled its original purpose as a medium for the release of current documents. As the series slid backward in time, its place was taken on the contemporary scene by press releases and by special publications on particular subjects on which the Department felt it necessary or desirable to give out documents. The press releases were reprinted in a weekly publication entitled *Press Releases* beginning in 1929. In 1939 the title of this publication was changed to the *Department of State Bulletin*, and the scope was broadened to include not only documents, strictly speaking, but also statements, announcements, and articles which may contain information previously classified. The special documentary publications issued by the Department in the period since World War II (such as the so-called China White Paper) number several dozen, not counting the voluminous serial publications of treaties and other international acts, the digests of international law, and the multilateral publication of German documents. This is not the place to discuss any of these in detail, but it is worth noting that thousands of documents previously classified or closely held have been released in this fashion, far ahead of the *Foreign Relations* volumes.

Opening of Files to Access

The ultimate in openness is to let members of the public into the files, where they can see all the documents and copy any that interest them. If this "see for yourself" method has the advantage of high credibility, it also has the disadvantage of being a type of operation which generally can be used effectively only by graduate-level scholars and professional researchers. Documents published by the Department of State are available in all the major public and university libraries throughout the world; documents that are merely opened to access in Washington will actually reach the public only to the extent that nonofficial historians choose to reproduce or describe them in their books and articles.

One might think that opening the files (or "granting access" as we call it) would be the easiest and cheapest method of making documents available to the public, but this, too, requires some qualification. Before files can be opened, they must be declassified by decision of policy officers, and this can only be effected on the basis of some sort of examination of the documentation either paper by paper or by spot checking, or by bulk categories where these can be defined. The records thus declassified must be defined by chronology or subject; they must be brought together as much as possible and physically separated from files still classified. Finding aids (indexes) to the open records must be prepared or made accessible, and adequate accommodations for researchers must be provided, including trained personnel to service their requests.

While the publishing of documents on foreign affairs goes back to the 18th century, the opening of files to access by the public or even to eminent scholars is a comparatively recent method of making documents available. Many foreign offices still do not open their files to the public in any systematic manner, contenting themselves with letting in an occasional privileged scholar whom they regard as "reliable." This was in fact the practice followed in the 19th century by even the most democratic foreign offices, including the Department of State. And historians did not fail to complain about it. In the annual report of the American Historical Association for 1893 it was sourly noted that "historical papers in the State Department are not accessible to the historical student except as a special favor. . . ."

By today's standards it would appear that Clio's disciples had something to complain about. It was not until 1901 that Congress passed a law providing that "facilities for study and research in the Government Departments . . . shall be afforded to scientific investigators and duly qualified individuals, students, and graduates of institutions of learning . . . under such rules as the heads of the Departments . . . may prescribe."* Apparently the Department of State began thereafter to admit scholars to the files in greater numbers, but only to documents of the pre-Civil War period, and even then under the proviso that the Department would review every researcher's notes or manuscript. In 1916 some notes were withheld on papers as much as 66 years old, and as late as 1920 the Department refused a researcher's request to see files of the war years—that is, the war of 1861–65.

Not until 1921 did the Department have a regulation providing for systematic access to records, and that access was still under careful control, cases being judged on an ad hoc basis. In 1927 the Department's eminent Historical Adviser, Tyler Dennett, stated that the files were open only up to 1898 although some subjects "might be pursued down to 1906." Here was the beginning of a pattern which the Department followed for many years thereafter: (1) Records were "declassified" in bulk when they were about 30 years old, and those files were then opened to researchers. (2) There was a "restricted" period (five to ten years ahead of the "open" period) to which "bona fide" or "trustworthy" American scholars might be admitted subject

---

* 31 Stat. 1039.

to certain controls. (3) There was a "closed" period covering the most recent records. The establishment of the National Archives in 1936 did not alter this basic pattern, although it produced a sharper definition of the open period and provided much better facilities for taking care of both records and researchers.

It is no secret that in recent decades the administration of the restricted period caused increasing friction between the Department and the academic world. The determination as to which "scholars" were to be admitted provoked invidious distinctions. Those who were admitted frequently resented the censorship of their notes. After World War II a security investigation became a requirement for admission to the still-classified records of the restricted period, a requirement costly to the government and resented by most applicants for access. Accordingly, at the beginning of 1972 the Department decided to open, i.e., declassify, its records for the entire period of World War II, an action which in effect abolished the old restricted period, which at that point had included the years 1942–45. Later in 1972 the Department extended the open period to include 1946, after the last of the *Foreign Relations* volumes for 1946 had been published; and the regulations were changed to provide for just two periods, "open" and "restricted." Records of the new restricted period (1947 on) are closed to access by nonofficial researchers,* but copies of individual documents may be obtained by request, ...

Until recent years there was never any apparent relationship between the publication of the *Foreign Relations* series and the opening of files to access. This was because the series, beginning in 1861 and for all the rest of the 19th century, was publishing documents at least 50 years ahead of the period to which access was granted. In the 20th century this gap began to narrow as the publication was allowed to lag while access was rapidly advanced. Even so, the published volumes have always been far ahead of the open period of the files, and indeed they were well ahead of even the restricted period until the end of World War II. Then for a brief period some private scholars were permitted into some of the wartime records before the publication of *Foreign Relations*. This aberration was made possible by the flood of documents on the war and its origins, released through

---

* The Department's regulations provide for an exception: "Persons who previously occupied policy-making positions to which they were appointed by the President . . . may be authorized access to classified information or material which they originated, reviewed, signed, or received while in public office." EDITOR'S NOTE: Retired Foreign Service Officers who fail to achieve presidential appointment, have objected that this practice is discriminatory, and that similar access should be made available to them.

memoirs, the Pearl Harbor hearings, etc., but the usefulness of this special access was limited by the fact that these historians were not permitted to cite many of the most important classified files that they were permitted to see. In the files of the postwar period a higher proportion of important records are classified, so that no access is really possible until after the subjects have been considered and the principal papers declassified for publication in *Foreign Relations*. To say that the series is holding back access is like saying that the tugboat up front is holding back the barge.

Release of Specific Documents by Request

With the Freedom of Information Act (effective July 4, 1967) there was provided a third mechanism whereby documents might be made available to the public; namely, by special request through a designated channel. Each department and agency was required to designate an official with whom members of the public might register their requests for copies of specific documents. The act required that the documents be "identifiable" and provided that the department or agency might deny the request if the documents fell into any of nine exempted categories and that otherwise the requester must be provided with copies of what he wanted (subject to payment of a fee for research and copying). Among the nine possible exemptions the most important with respect to Department records was the one that made exemptible those "specifically required by Executive Order to be kept secret in the interest of the national defense or foreign policy." The Department, however, has not taken any general refuge in this provision. Whenever the documents requested under the act have been identifiable and have turned out to be classified, the Department has seen to it that they have been reviewed by officers authorized to declassify them and that any negative answers to requesters would be reviewed by the Office of the Legal Adviser in the Department, as well as, more recently, by the Bureau of Public Affairs. The requester may also file an appeal with the Department's Council on Classification Policy and/or with the Interagency Classification Review Committee, established by Executive Order 11652, signed by the President on March 8, 1972, which became effective on June 1, 1972.

This Executive Order contains several other provisions designed to facilitate the operation of the Freedom of Information Act. It greatly reduced the number of officers authorized to classify documents, and it set up a general declassification schedule under which many Top Secret documents will be automatically declassified after ten years,

Secret papers in eight years, Confidential ones in six years. The full effect of these measures will not be felt for some years, but obviously they will tend to reduce the number of classified documents and thus to improve the likelihood of larger returns to members of the public who ask for copies of documents.

*　*　*

In the foregoing pages I have described the three ways of making government documents available to the public: by publication, by granting access to files, and by providing copies on request. Each of these methods has characteristics of its own, and all of them are necessary to meet the varying needs of different types of persons and problems. In recent years the Department has moved to improve and expedite every one of these mechanisms, all of which admittedly need from time to time a shot of "openness." We are continuing to work to improve still further. Only in this way can there be maintained a proper balance between the immediate need of the government—in the interest of the public as a whole—for confidentiality in some matters of national security and foreign affairs and the sometimes temporarily conflicting right of the individual citizen in a democracy to know what is going on.*

---

* EDITOR'S NOTE: The process of downgrading and declassifying information and documents—involving the principle of automaticity—was liberalized in 1972 and again in 1978. These changes, together with the possibilities engendered under the Freedom of Information Act of 1967 and the introduction in the 1970s of the "twenty-year rule" for the opening of official files to public access, provide the United States with the most systematic and liberal treatment of diplomatic documentation in the world.

4

Some Dimensions of Diplomacy

. . . summit meetings and personal diplomacy—despite many pitfalls —have become almost unavoidable consequences of contemporary international politics. If summitry and personal diplomacy of leading statesmen are here to stay, their disadvantages can be avoided and their advantages can be maximized by thoughtful preparations through regular diplomatic channels and carefully selected special emissaries.

STEPHEN D. KERTESZ, *The Quest for Peace through Diplomacy*

The multilateral conference has become in our day one of the most important instruments of international co-operation. The number and variety of conferences and meetings held each year . . . is constantly increasing, while the problems with which they deal now range over virtually the entire gamut of international relations.

WALTER R. SHARP, "The Scientific Study of International Conferences"

Classical diplomacy enjoyed the aura of a rather uniform and predictable process—occasionally monarchs and foreign ministers, but more often diplomatic envoys, conferring together in closed, bilateral negotiations. Methodological uniformity in the conduct of foreign relations changed with the advent of the new diplomacy, and additional dimensions of diplomatic practice have gained widespread usage. Most of these are listed in Elmer Plischke's "The New Diplomacy" (Chapter 2), and Chapter 3 focuses on two of the more important developments—democratic and open diplomacy. Chapter 4 examines four additional elements of contemporary practice: ministerial, summit, multilateral, and crisis diplomacy.

150

"There is a general impression that the Secretary of State travels too much," writes Henry M. Wriston in his essay, "Ministerial Diplomacy—Secretary of State Abroad." He apparently shares this impression because, although he grants the need for limited ministerial participation abroad, Wriston contends that recent secretaries have been too involved in personal diplomacy compromising their ability to maintain an overall and balanced perspective of world affairs. Excessive absence from the center of government disrupts the continuity of the secretary's advice to the President and damages his relations with Congress, foreign ambassadors assigned to Washington, and his own diplomatic service. The Secretary of State, in cooperation with other foreign ministers, could initiate restraints to curtail substantially his personal involvement in the diplomatic process. Such restraints could provide him with greater opportunity to discharge his duties with "perspective and wisdom"—but developments in recent decades belie this likelihood.

According to Elmer Plischke's "Summit Diplomacy—Diplomat in Chief," the same reservations pertain to personal presidential involvement in diplomacy. This analysis discusses six distinguishable types of summitry. Plischke acknowledges the potential value of presidential diplomacy when used sparingly and selectively for the achievement of limited, clearly defined goals. But he cautions that the summit conference "is by no means a proven panacea for the international ills of the world." Presidential diplomacy may be overworked, and reliance on it needs to be restrained. Plischke warns that this potentially useful diplomatic weapon, if abused, will "lose its impact and become self-defeating"; like ministerial diplomacy, its overindulgence may have negative effects on the President's overall perspective on world affairs and distract him from other important responsibilities that deserve his personal attention.

"Multilateralism," by Inis L. Claude, Jr., provides a short, "discriminating analysis" of this dimension of the new diplomacy. While agreeing with critics that the use or misuse of multilateralism—as distinguished from traditional bilateralism—"unleashes a bull in a diplomatic china shop," he defends its usefulness in certain situations in a quasi-legislative capacity. He contends that the negotiation of international treaties and agreements, the establishment of international organizations, the regulation of processes or resources that have global significance, and the like are acts that are inherently multigovernmental rather than bilateral, and consequently require a multipartite approach. As global interdependence gains increasing acceptance, the need for multilateral deliberations and forums increases,

151

and the process of "parliamentary" interaction—which Claude calls "multiplomacy"—often prevails.

"Crisis Management," by Harlan Cleveland, offers the neophyte diplomat five basic lessons for coping with international crises and confrontations. The diplomat's objectives should be limited and clearly defined; his willingness to use force and coercive measures should be determined; he should exercise prudence in wielding the forceful and coercive measures that he prescribes for himself; he should try to rally support to his side of the conflict, and widen the community of concerned nations; and he should be wary of setting a precedent that may later injure his nation's interests. These talents, combined with a sense of conviction and decisiveness that will hold up under stress and criticism, characterize a successful crisis manager.

The authors of the essays included in this chapter have a common concern with the risks involved in the open conduct of the brands of diplomacy they discuss. They regard the inevitable publicity surrounding these diplomatic processes as a serious constraint, because the publicizing of a diplomatic encounter, be it by a Secretary of State, a President, an international conference, or a "crisis manager," tends to remove from it a certain degree of flexibility, reality, and potential effectiveness—unless publicity and propaganda are among its primary goals. Chapter 3 provides a more detailed discussion of some of the problems associated with the open conduct of diplomacy.

Ministerial Diplomacy—Secretary of State Abroad

Henry M. Wriston

There is a general impression that the Secretary of State travels too much. During three and a half years in office Mr. Dulles has gone a distance about equal to 11 times around the earth at the equator. He has visited 38 countries, several of them more than once.

Most of the comments about these relatively well-known facts tend to treat the travels of the Secretary as unique, something of a personal idiosyncrasy. Nothing could be further from the facts. It is indubitable that the Secretary likes his job, including the travel. Perhaps one should say especially the travel. Yet, despite his overpublicized totals he has not been absent as large a percentage of the time as some of his predecessors. James F. Byrnes was away from his desk about 62 percent of his year and a half in office; George C. Marshall had an "acting secretary" in his stead over 47 percent of his two-year tenure. Dean Acheson's record was close to 25 percent; Hull's was over 22 percent and Stettinius's was over 67 percent. Mr. Dulles has been represented by a substitute approximately 36 percent of his time as Secretary. It is clear from these figures that a new pattern of secretarial conduct emerged before the present incumbent took office. The development is sufficiently important to warrant an inquiry into the underlying reasons and an evaluation of the consequences.*

Until this century the Secretary was absent only when ill or vacationing. If he engaged in negotiations abroad, he resigned, as John

---

* EDITOR'S NOTE: The statistics are not comparable in all respects. In some instances the total represents chiefly long international meetings during a short term of office (as Secretary Stettinius's service at Yalta and San Francisco); in others the dominant pattern has been frequent brief trips.

SOURCE: "The Secretary of State Abroad," *Foreign Affairs*, vol. 34 (July 1956), pp. 523–40.

W. Foster did when he went to Paris to present the case of the United States in the Bering Sea controversy and as James R. Day did early in the McKinley administration to head the delegation in Paris to make peace with Spain.

The Pan American conferences were the first influence tending to a different pattern. James G. Blaine convened the first such meeting in Washington in 1889. Latin nations often sent their foreign ministers; it seemed desirable, in courtesy, for the Secretary of State to attend when the conferences were held outside this country. Nevertheless, it was not until 1906 that a Secretary of State did so. Elihu Root delivered an address to the third conference in Rio, but did not participate in negotiations. The conference in Montevideo in 1933 was, according to Cordell Hull's "Memoirs," "the first time that an American Secretary of State had ever headed a delegation to a Pan American Conference," and he was active in negotiations; at Rio in December 1936 Hull proposed his "Eight Pillars of Peace." He also took a leading role at Lima in 1938 and at Havana in 1940.

The Pan American conferences also stimulated "good will" trips. Secretary Root initiated this practice as well. To visit the American Republics he left the Department at the end of June and did not return until October 1906. Philander C. Knox made a "good will" tour of the Caribbean. Charles E. Hughes attended the centennial celebration of Brazilian independence, and Bainbridge Colby went to Brazil and Uruguay in December 1920.

War meetings were the second type of conference to draw Secretaries of State abroad. Robert Lansing went with President Wilson to Paris but did not resign as Secretary despite the length of his stay. Secretaries Hull, Stettinius and Byrnes all accompanied the President abroad. Secretary Hull also attended the Conference of Foreign Ministers in Moscow in 1943, and Mr. Byrnes was in Paris for a meeting of foreign ministers when the famous Wallace speech was delivered.

Wilson had ushered in an era of personal diplomacy. The pattern was suspended during the Harding and Coolidge administrations, but there was a partial return by President Hoover. On the initiative of Secretary Stimson, Prime Minister Ramsay MacDonald came to confer with President Hoover on the limitation of naval armaments. This was, perhaps, the first peacetime negotiation between heads of state in which a President participated. The practice is now so fully accepted as normal that there was impatience, especially abroad, with the obvious reluctance of President Eisenhower to meet "at the summit," and even more at the strict limitations which he set upon the subject matter and the time he was willing to devote to the meeting.

Mr. Stimson attended the London Conference on Naval Limitation in 1930, and returned to Europe the following year to explore the possibilities of a reduction of land armaments, visiting Rome, Paris, Berlin and London. At a subsequent conference in which Hugh Gibson was head of the delegation, Secretary Stimson went in person to stimulate action when matters did not progress to his satisfaction. Cordell Hull went to the London Economic Conference as "head" of our delegation, but found Assistant Secretary Moley in easier and more frequent communication with the President. Mr. Roosevelt's habit of bypassing the heads of departments kept Hull from going abroad with him upon some occasions, the most conspicuous instance being the second Quebec Conference, in 1944, when the President was accompanied by Henry Morgenthau, Secretary of the Treasury. Nevertheless, by the time Hull resigned late in 1944, the pattern of Secretarial diplomacy was fairly well set.

Four other factors considerably broadened early precedents. The liquidation of peace conference business after the First World War was left in the hands of a Council of Ambassadors; by contrast, in 1945 matters were referred to a Council of Foreign Ministers. It was hoped that this would involve fewer delays, since it is not desirable for any nation to have its foreign minister absent for long periods at a time, whereas ambassadors live abroad and there is less pressure to act expeditiously. It was hoped, also, that negotiations might prove more flexible, since foreign ministers have wider discretion than ambassadors.

The establishment of the United Nations at San Francisco in 1945 was a second factor. The idea had long been discussed; a major effort was necessary to crystallize it into an institution. The President lent the prestige of his presence and the Secretary of State headed the American delegation. The foreign ministers of most of the founding nations were there. From this precedent arose the practice of having the chief diplomatic officer of each great nation attend some of the sessions of the General Assembly each year. While they are usually held in New York, they take the Secretary away from his desk; when they are held abroad, his absence is that much longer.

A third factor subsequently added other occasions for absence. For the first time the United States entered upon peacetime alliances. NATO holds a vital place in the diplomatic as well as the military structure of the West. The Secretary of State is a member of its Council and obligated to attend. SEATO, in like manner, requires his personal attention. Multi-national negotiations, which the sessions arising from these alliances typify, are a temptation to make the Secretary the negotiator. Norman H. Davis, as Special Ambassador in the Hoover administration and as our first Ambassador-at-Large in the Roosevelt administration, performed the function of negotiator in multilateral meetings very acceptably. Nevertheless, the practice of diplomacy by conference has united with increasing speed and comfort of air travel to induce more and more participation by the Secretary.

Soviet tactics supplied still other occasions for Secretarial negotiation. Ambassadors from the Soviets have not had wide discretion; they seem to have been treated, for the most part, as diplomatic errand boys. There has been an almost equal tendency for the top officials of the Kremlin to see foreign ambassadors only sparingly; even when they were admitted, there was marked reluctance to discuss important matters. The Soviet rulers prefer to deal directly with the President, bypassing even the Secretary of State and their own Foreign Minister. World public opinion clearly demands every sacrifice to mitigate tensions. This was dramatized by the demand for a conference "at the summit" and by Churchill's obvious distress that it was so long deferred. Finally, the President yielded, but attached stringent conditions governing length of time, procedures and topics, and made plain that he would refuse to engage in negotiations personally.

The Secretary of State cannot be so firm in setting limits of that sort. This subjects him to the Soviet habit of protracting "negotiations" interminably, while making repeated propaganda speeches. Such tactics are tolerated because there is always a chance that the forms of patience and the reality of persistence will produce a desirable result. One instance was the sudden Soviet reversal from obstructing an Austrian peace treaty to haste in signing one. The unexpected revision of position on the "package deal" regarding enlarged membership in the United Nations was another. A series of such episodes during the cold war could be mentioned; they explain why patience hopefully waits its reward. Apparently the Soviet Foreign Minister has no such exalted status in the policy-determining hierarchy that his frequent and long absences are as inconvenient as those of the Secretary of State.

Such are a few of the principal reasons for the extraordinary percentage of the time recent Secretaries of State have been away from Washington. Before assessing the benefits and disadvantages it is essential to emphasize that peripatetic diplomacy on the part of foreign ministers is not unique with the United States.

Since the phenomenon is not confined to the United States, much less to the present Secretary, there must be a more fundamental reason than any so far mentioned. The underlying cause is to be found in the drastic change in the political structure of the current world, and an even more profound change in the political climate. In the nineteenth century there were many fewer nations, and their order of precedence in international matters was reasonably well established.

The United States was not one of the Great Powers. That we did not so regard ourselves was strikingly symbolized by the fact that, though the Constitution spoke of "ambassadors," Congress did not authorize that grade until 1893. When we started to change our legations to embassies, only four were selected, London, Paris, Berlin, St. Petersburg—all capitals of recognized Great Powers. Within the memory of men still active in British public life, Britain had only eight diplomats of ambassadorial rank. That supplies us with a rough estimate of the number of "Great Powers" which made world policy. Britain, for example, still had a vast empire; the dominions had no ministers of external affairs. All that is now changed. . . .

The political climate has altered even more. It used to be no disgrace to be one of the lesser Powers. The United States could have sent ambassadors earlier; we did not choose to. Until last year [1955] Switzerland sent ministers, and was content. But now every nation wants to be treated as a first-class Power and send and receive ambassadors. This is a symptom of acute sensitiveness about status; states are insisting upon equality so far as dignity is concerned. True, the "Great Powers," arbitrarily defined, have a permanent seat and a veto in the Security Council of the United Nations. But the leadership of the Great Powers is no longer meekly accepted. There is a vigorous assertiveness on the part of the smallest and weakest which must be handled with great sensitiveness and consideration. Each has one vote in the United Nations Assembly; more important, voices never heard, or long muted, now speak—sometimes in strident tones—in that world forum.

These circumstances have led to a fundamental decentralization of diplomacy, and the habit of making visits is firmly engrafted upon current practice. The peregrinations of Khrushchev and Bulganin are well known and conspicuous. A colleague of the Canadian Minister of External Affairs spoke of him, kindly, as "ubiquitous." It is said that during his first two years as Secretary of State, Mr. Dulles met Mr. Eden, then Foreign Secretary, no less than 17 times. During his brief tenure at the Foreign Office, Mr. Harold Macmillan was abroad much of the time. While our Secretary of State was at the SEATO meetings, it transpired that the percentage of time spent away from

London by Mr. Selwyn Lloyd, the . . . Foreign Secretary, was almost identical to the absentee percentage of Mr. Dulles.

Many high-ranking foreign officials come to the United States; a casual inspection of the guest book at the Council on Foreign Relations shows visits from a large number of prime ministers and foreign ministers in a single year.* It may be thought that this is not surprising since the United States is so dominant a power in world affairs. New Delhi, on the other hand, is the capital of a nation newly independent, with no great military or economic strength though an important strategic position. Yet in the course of less than two years it has been visited by heads of state or foreign ministers of 19 nations, including all that have any claim to be called Great Powers. And the Secretary-General of the United Nations also went to India. No further evidence need be adduced to show how gross is the error in supposing that travel is characteristic of the American Secretary of State alone. The practice of concentrating an extraordinary amount of negotiation in the hands of the foreign minister is endemic.

There are some favorable consequences of this acquired habit. When it succeeds there are unquestioned economies of time and effort. The fewer minds a policy formulation passes through on the way toward action, the less chance there is of distortion, misunderstanding and consequent confusion. Historically, peacetime alliances have been held together more by external pressure than by bonds of common interest. Whenever the immediate threat is relieved, or even appears to be, the difficulties of concerted action increase. These circumstances accentuate the advantages of high-level contact. The fabrication of concerted policy proceeds more expeditiously (a relative term, in diplomacy) when meetings are at the highest practicable level. Former Secretary James F. Byrnes remarked that "dividends from personal contacts between leaders flow in long after" the conference ends. After his trip to Asia in March, Mr. Dulles spoke of the importance of talking "intimately with the leaders of each of these ten countries" and asserted that "talking face to face is the best way yet invented for enabling men to understand each other." The same theme appeared in the Anglo-Soviet communiqué as Khrushchev and Bulganin left London: "one of the important factors in strengthening international confidence consists in personal contacts between leading statesmen, which have produced positive results." This point of view

---

* EDITOR'S NOTE: Since 1968, the Office of the Historian, Department of State, has published an annually updated listing of visits to the United States by foreign chiefs of state and heads of government. See *Lists of Visits of Foreign Chiefs of State and Heads of Government to the United States, 1789—*.

has been universally accepted; instances of its expression could be multiplied indefinitely.

Sometimes, however, there are what used to be known in business as "Irish dividends"—deficits. High-level contacts may accentuate difficulties arising not so much from substantial difference in national interest as from personal vanities, irritability and a whole host of like negative factors. Those who have attended such meetings know there are personal frictions as well as personal friendships. The issues are national, not personal; the tendency to personalize them obscures to some degree their national character. It makes a change from one Secretary to another more serious than it ought to be in the light of the continuing nature of the national interest and the broadly non-partisan character of foreign policy. To focus the spotlight on one individual rather than upon the State Department and the Foreign Service as a continuing organization tends to make the political standing or the ambition of the Secretary assume a larger share of public attention than is wise. Personal idiosyncrasies should play as small a role in the pursuit of national policy as possible. At best it will not be inconsiderable, but to make policy and negotiation appear to be a one-man affair tends to dislocate public opinion.

Among the basic reasons for a professional foreign service and for great emphasis upon the somewhat archaic ritualism of international communication is precisely the need to dissociate the public interest from personal qualities, so far as is practical. The resort to personal diplomacy in our time has produced many instances where the clash of personalities retarded the accommodation of international issues.

There are certain characteristics of the American Government, moreover, which make protracted absence by the Secretary disadvantageous—even if the total is composed of brief, frequent dashes to and from the corners of the earth.

In the first place, the Secretary of State is the principal adviser to the President on foreign affairs. Many issues, however, do not readily yield to simple classification as "foreign" or "domestic"; indeed, as time goes on the distinction becomes ever more difficult to maintain. For these and other reasons there has always been competition for influence among the President's advisers, official and personal. Inevitably that rivalry has been intensified since the United States became a World Power with many complex interests everywhere.

* * *

The vast multiplication of agencies during the war [World War II], many of them dealing with situations abroad, also multiplied the occasions in which the President was influenced in vital matters of foreign policy by advisers other than the Secretary of State, who said his work was "bedeviled" by them. The continuation of such separate agencies since the war has perpetuated dangers of confusion in giving advice to the President. Such diffusion of powers and responsibilities makes it the more essential for the Secretary to remain at home and maintain constant contact with the members of the Cabinet and with every agency by which he can keep in touch with the views of others and take them into account in advising the President. One new development emphasizes this point. The National Security Council has been made the principal forum for the discussion and determination of basic policy. It now meets regularly and frequently, with the President himself in the chair. When the Secretary of State is absent no substitute can bring to these critical meetings the weight and authority that go with his office.

* * *

Clearly, when the Secretary is absent for very considerable periods all the various competing influences have much freer play. Secretary Acheson seems to have been aware of this. He revived the post of ambassador-at-large, which had lapsed after the retirement of Norman Davis; when Philip Jessup was appointed it was stated that he would represent the President and Secretary of State in United Nations meetings and in other multilateral negotiations such as the Council of Foreign Ministers. The principal reason for reviving the post was to enable the Secretary of State to stay close by the President and serve more continuously as his adviser on foreign affairs than had some of his predecessors. Not all these hopes were fulfilled, for foreign ministers of other nations were reluctant to accept any substitute for the Secretary. Nevertheless, the appointment may well account for the fact that Mr. Acheson's percentage of absences was lower than the postwar norm. His influence with the President in matters of foreign policy suffered no such challenge or diminution as had been evident with some of his predecessors.

When the Secretary is away the Under Secretary cannot exercise this central function of advice to the President with the authority of the Secretary himself. This is the more true since, in contrast with early precedents, the Secretary takes with him a very large section of the high-level officers of the Department. In the meeting of Foreign Ministers at Geneva last fall, the following were in attendance in addition to the Secretary: The Counsellor of the Department, the Assistant Secretary for Policy Planning, the Assistant Secretary for European Affairs, the Assistant Secretary for Public Information, the chief legal officer, the chief cultural officer, as well as the President's Special Assistant on Disarmament Problems. Of course, each of these officers took some of his chief aides. One ambassador was in attendance through the entire meeting, another part of the time. This serious drain on the Department is now virtually standard practice.

Several results flow from such a departmental exodus. The Acting Secretary is in the position of a substitute quarterback with a third string team to direct. Further, the "ordinary" work of each absent officer's section of the Department is to some extent hampered or crippled; taken as a whole this amounts to a serious dislocation of departmental work. Moreover, advice to the President, under these circumstances, will inevitably hew closer to precedent; it will certainly lack the imaginative initiation of new tactical approaches which is often vital to success.

After his status as adviser to the President, the second principal function of the Secretary is to keep under continuous overall review every phase of our worldwide responsibilities and opportunities. In the present state of world affairs this alone is a back breaking task. Over-concentration upon one area seriously impairs the balance; and when so many principal officers are also over-concentrating upon the same phase, the effect in producing imbalance is multiplied.

Indeed, it is fair to say that the greater the Secretary's capacity as a negotiator, the more serious is the distraction from his broader task. For negotiation is not just a gift; it requires intense preparation and absorption in the immediate matter, mastery of details as well as broad outlines. This can be acquired only by neglecting, for the time being, other phases of our foreign relations, all of which are constantly changing in perspective. Inevitably he loses touch with things done in his absence and may miss the significance of events in other areas. But for one such absence, it seems inconceivable that identical notes would have been sent to Greece and Turkey last September after Turkish riots in Istanbul and Izmir had done so much violence to Greek sensibilities. Under less tense circumstances, the haste and consequent inadvertence which occasioned such an error might not have had damaging results. In the delicate balance of forces presently operative in that area, however, any dislocation of relationship produces serious consequences. The repercussions of that error have not yet been fully realized. In somewhat the same category is the mysterious Goa statement; any benefit to our relations with Portugal was greatly outweighed by its disastrous effect in India.

So swift is the movement of events that even brief absences can seriously dislocate policy formation. The crisis over Cyprus reached

161

an acute stage with the exile of Archbishop Makarios, the orientation of Jordan was put in doubt with the dismissal of General Glubb, the conference of Colonel Nasser with the heads of Syria and Saudi Arabia still further heightened tension between Israel and the Arab nations—all while the Secretary of State and the British and French Foreign Ministers were absent in other parts of Asia. Essential and urgent political and military joint planning had to take place without them. So far as the United States was concerned it had to go forward in the absence, also, of the Assistant Secretaries of State in charge of policy planning and of the interests of this country in that explosive area. The result was not only delay in reaching conclusions until their return; it required that joint policy be designed while the principal architects were elsewhere.

A third disadvantage of absence from Washington is its effect upon our own ambassadors abroad. They are responsible for keeping the Secretary informed. One remarked that he had learned to time his most important dispatches to catch the Secretary (and his area Assistant Secretary) in Washington. Another used baseball terms to give vent to his feelings: I feel I am in there pitching with no one catching.

Sometimes it seems to be forgotten that while it is easy to fly the Secretary to a foreign country, it is just as easy to fly an ambassador back to Washington for consultation and instructions. When our foreign relations were relatively simple their conduct was decentralized. Now that they are manifold and complex they tend to be more and more concentrated in one man. This is inherently wrong because it impairs the Secretary's opportunity for balanced review and supervision; it fails to take advantage of better means of communication.

When the post of ambassador-at-large was discontinued, it was said to be in consequence of a policy decision to rely more on regular ambassadors, even in special situations, and to use fewer special ambassadors. Events have shown that the policy was not deeply imbedded. Not only has the Secretary often gone abroad, but the Under Secretary, the Deputy Under Secretary and several Assistant Secretaries have also traveled a good deal; and there have been a number of special envoys with the rank of ambassador.

It might be possible so to manage visits of the Secretary as to increase the prestige of ambassadors. That this has not been the usual result is evidenced by their continued unhappiness at being temporarily superseded as the President's personal representative. There is no novelty in this feeling. Regular ambassadors have always resented "intrusion" into the area for which they have responsibility. The bitterness of Charles Francis Adams during the Civil War is classic. Modern diplomats share his feeling that special visits make the ambassador appear inadequate and reduce his prestige. It has an effect, too, upon the foreign offices with which we deal; some in critical areas have shown a marked tendency to hold out rather than conclude an arrangement with the ambassador, in the hope (too often fulfilled) that someone will come out from Washington bringing larger concessions. Instances of this tactic are not difficult to find.

Moreover, one trip breeds another. This has been particularly true in the case of Secretary Dulles. In a press conference on February 28 of this year he spoke of the imminence of a trip "to South Asia and the Far East that will take me to ten countries, *two of which I have never visited before.*" This statement highlights one very significant difference between the travels of the present Secretary and the journeys of his predecessors. Mr. Dulles has visited more United States missions abroad than any other Secretary, probably more than all his predecessors added together. He seems to feel some sort of obligation to "touch base" at all of them during his tenure of office. The airplane has become more than a convenience; it is a temptation

Despite the speed of modern travel, each individual call is very brief. So far as the nation visited is concerned, there is hardly sufficient time for important diplomatic exchanges. It is doubtful that such stopovers reflect enough thoughtful consideration to be considered properly even as courtesy calls; their pace is quite out of keeping with the ceremonial tempo of Asian hospitality, for example. The timing and length of stay are often very sensitive matters which a hurried schedule cannot fully take into account; a shorter stay in New Delhi than in Karachi is a case in point. These hasty stops contrast sharply with the conduct of the representatives of the Soviet. Khrushchev and Bulganin took two weeks to see India; they traveled widely, they not only saw officials but gave attention to the intellectuals and, even more, assiduously cultivated people in the mass. They spoke innumerable times and always in appreciative terms regarding the culture and attainments of the Indian nation. They did not give the appearance of wanting anything but friendship; they asked no guarantees and no alliances.

There is room for good-will visits and for sending special embassies to participate in national celebrations and ceremonies. Nevertheless, the growing habit of reducing the resident ambassador to a social symbol and transmitter of communications denigrates his legal status as the personal representative of the head of the state and

163

makes it needlessly difficult for him to fulfill his important and wide-ranging duties.

Frequent and protracted absences of the Secretary of State from the Department limit his contact with the ambassadors of other nations accredited to this Government. Of course, much of the business with the Department is carried on by embassy and departmental offices; not even every occasion for an ambassador to visit the Department requires the presence of the Secretary. In some instances, however, it is important. When, late last year, the ambassadors of Egypt and Israel were "summoned" to the Department, the purpose was to give a stern warning and dramatize the interest of the United States in the preservation of peace in an explosive area. When they were met by an Assistant Secretary, no amount of skill on his part could substitute for the authority and prestige of the Secretary himself. Certain purposes can never be served by a deputy; when such tasks are committed to others the effect is to treat foreign ambassadors as a good deal less than the personal representatives of the heads of their states.

Even more serious is the break in essential contacts with the Congress. There is an Assistant Secretary for Congressional Relations; he performs many useful functions. But there are other relationships, in a bipartisan policy, which the Secretary himself must establish and maintain. The tension between the Executive and Legislative branches is historic. Washington presided over the Constitutional Convention, and was extremely cautious in setting precedents; yet he sought to attend the Senate to discuss a proposed Indian treaty—to get its "advice" as a prelude to its "consent." He was rudely treated; when a second visit failed he never returned, nor has any President since. This breach has made the Senate, if anything, even more sensitive to its prerogative in foreign affairs. The House, as early as Jay's Treaty, tried to use the power of the purse to gain an influence upon foreign policy, and was rebuffed by a slender margin. Ever since the effort has been renewed from time to time and in diverse ways.

Members of both houses want to be briefed by the Secretary. In his three years in office, Mr. Dulles met with committees or subcommittees of Congress 120 times. It is, perhaps, significant that there were 70 such meetings in his first ten months as Secretary, and only 50 in the more than two years since.

Moreover, numbers of appearances do not fully compensate for absence at strategic times. Last November, for example, the Subcommittee on Foreign Economic Policy of the Joint Committee on the

Economic Report held six days of hearings. The statement of the chairman in opening the hearings contains the following words:

> I need not repeat how important we feel these hearings are to the strengthening of our foreign economic policy. It was for this reason, hoping for a strong policy statement at the highest level, that we invited the Secretary of State to appear to deliver an opening address. We are all aware that he is away. . . . We suggested that the new Deputy Under Secretary for Economic Affairs might come. But the Department felt that Mr. Prochnow is too new in his job to be familiar with the entire range of matters which might come up.
>
> We suggest alternatively the name of Mr. Thruston B. Morton, Assistant Secretary, who is very well known and respected here on the Hill. He is in Geneva, too.
>
> . . . Senator Flanders aided us by requesting the appearance of Mr. Herbert Hoover, Jr., the Under Secretary. Mr. Hoover was unable to come.

Such passages are, to put it mildly, unfortunate.

In any event, formal appearances are not enough; there is need for personal and social contact as well, a process that requires time and fails when it is hurried. The maintenance of a reasonable degree of bipartisanship makes frequent and free communication with influential Senators and Representatives absolutely vital. Fruitful contacts for this purpose cannot occur in either public or "closed" sessions of committees; they can be effective only when nothing has to be done for effect. This needs private conversation with no object save enlightenment, which should be mutual. A Secretary can profit by what he hears as well as win support by what he says. It is no accident that the period during which successive Secretaries have been away so much has been one of great difficulty in maintaining this contact. The effort to do so, in addition to all other things which demand his personal attention, adds to an already crushing load. Of course, even with the Secretary in Washington, relations may become strained. Mr. Acheson as Assistant Secretary was popular with the Congress; after he became Secretary his relations with it deteriorated.

Absentee Secretaries cannot give the help essential to departmental officers in dealing with the Bureau of the Budget [now the Office of Management and Budget] and appropriations committees of the Congress. Historically, the Department of State is starved. By ill-luck, when it became a vital instrument, at the time of both world wars, neither President Wilson nor President Roosevelt gave it strong support; both were too much inclined to personal diplomacy to appreciate the importance of the continuous, professional organization.

There is, therefore, a desperate need for the Secretary to pull a laboring oar, as do the heads of other departments who are seldom absent. The Secretary cannot make the departmental budget, but he can fight for decent salaries and proper allowances, for adequate manpower, for a building appropriate to the task and efficient in operation. No Deputy Under Secretary, however able, can substitute for the personal interest, attention and effort of the Secretary himself. There is a direct relationship between the fiscally adverse position of the Department and Foreign Service and the long absences of recent Secretaries. So tenuous, indeed, had become the relation of the Secretary to the operations of the Department since the war that it was even suggested that his office should be moved back to the old State Department building—bringing him into closer contact with the President, but separating him even more from his own organization.

Any separation from his own department is very serious indeed. There are significant energies and valuable talents in the professional staff of the Department of State. Sometimes they seem to be buried there. Secretaries of State have been known to go outside the Department for advice and assistance, just because they did not know where to find them in the Department, or, in any event, how to get free, informal access to them. It has always been difficult for such staff talents to be fully exploited by the Secretary, because the thoughts and works of his staff come to him through so many bureaucratic filters that sometimes the substance is all but gone. Nevertheless, some Secretaries have been able to identify able officers and bring them and their ideas to the surface. It cannot be done in absentia.

Finally, the itinerant Secretary does not, in practice, improve flexibility in negotiation. It may be true, indeed, that making the Secretary the principal negotiator actually impairs flexibility. An ambassador can alter his position more readily; it is a hoary device to put forward a position, under instructions, "on his own responsibility," and when that position proves untenable he may have "new instructions." Ambassadors, moreover, can work outside the glare of publicity. They can work in secrecy, which always makes for more flexible negotiation. A prime example was the settlement of the thorny Trieste problem by agreement in October 1954, after eight months of confidential diplomatic interchange. It should remind us that the business of advancing the interests of the United States can sometimes be accomplished in quiet, in confidence—even in "secret," though that has become an odious word. The Secretary, on the contrary, moves abroad in a blinding glare of publicity. It is "open diplomacy" with a vengeance. In the conference of foreign ministers at Geneva last fall,

The New York Times alone had five topflight correspondents on hand. Other papers made similar efforts. The "briefing" after each session, the calculated leaks by different delegations and the assiduity of seasoned news gatherers made nearly every word spoken in the conference room publicly available. Under such circumstances, every slight alteration of position is a "defeat," any lack of tangible progress is a "failure." If there is no "hard news" the public reads a dispatch saying the Secretary looked cheerful, accompanied by extended speculation as to the sources of his inexplicable optimism; or he looked gloomy, with equal ruminations about possible causes—very soft news indeed.

Over-dramatizing negotiation creates an expectation of tangible results. One of Secretary Hull's wisest remarks was, "There are no real triumphs in diplomacy." Ambassador [Livingston T.] Merchant, while Assistant Secretary, enlarged upon this theme. "Diplomatic victory," he said, "is something of a contradiction in terms, since a successful diplomatic effort usually involves an accommodation of interests with other countries, and its fruits may be dissipated by the claim that one country or another has achieved a 'victory.'" International issues of such magnitude as to draw the Secretary into negotiation are complex, and have long, stubborn histories. Rapid "progress" is likely to be a superficial evasion of reality. Often the most important result of a negotiation is clarification, an improved estimate of the situation. What appears in short perspective as a "failure" may well prove a step toward a better approach.

Putting the spotlight upon every step in a long process, moreover, tends to overstress the "initiative." The initiative is valuable, but not always essential. In football many a team with the most first downs and yards gained has nevertheless lost the game. There are times in negotiation when it is desirable to adopt tactics equivalent to a punt in football. Letting the other side carry the ball—that is, assume the initiative—may be a profitable maneuver. It becomes almost impossible when immediately there are loud cries of "failure" and "defeat."

Negotiation in the spotlight by the Secretary inevitably invites propaganda by the Soviets. It is almost impossible not to respond with counterpropaganda. It seems an anomaly to banish the U.S.I.A. [now the International Communication Agency (ICA)] from the Department of State because its function is propaganda, and then put the Secretary in a position where he is forced to make propaganda. Yet that is one result of current practices.

No one who has followed events closely since the outbreak of the First World War can expect to eliminate the attendance of the Secretary of State at all international conferences. The practice is not unique with this nation, and cannot be discontinued unilaterally. Some relief might, however, be achieved by joint action. At one of their frequent meetings the foreign ministers could talk over the dilemma in which they all find themselves and set informal limitations upon excessive travel. For example, they might agree that all foreign ministers would attend the early weeks of each United Nations Assembly. This would facilitate mutual acquaintance and provide opportunity for private and personal discussions of a very wide range of common concerns. Secretary Hull used the Pan American conferences to develop such personal contacts with the Latin American foreign ministers, and Secretary Marshall followed much the same practice when attending the United Nations Assembly.

It is particularly important that our Secretary of State take the initiative in such a curtailment, for absenteeism has gone further in the United States than in any other Great Power. Moreover, it is less to our interest to perpetuate it upon the present scale than to the interest of other nations. The practice can and should be curbed, in the interest of more continuity in advice to the President, a better chance for the Secretary to maintain overall perspective, a more reasonable share in government cost for the department of the government which must "wage peace," better contacts with Congress in maintaining bipartisanship, more fruitful relations with ambassadors accredited to the United States and better relations between the Department and members of our own Foreign Service scattered about the world.

The vital requisites for the effective discharge of the duties of the Secretary of State are perspective and wisdom. Those qualities find their most effective employment when there is at least a modicum of leisure for quiet reflection. Such qualities are not always accompanied by the rugged constitution and physical endurance required for perpetual motion. There should be such review and reform as to make it possible for men of normal strength hereafter to carry the load.

Summit Diplomacy—Diplomat in Chief

Elmer Plischke

In centuries past reigning monarchs managed personally and directly both their internal and external public affairs. As the modern state system emerged, however, and especially with the growth of democratic government, chiefs of state came to play a decreasing immediate role in foreign relations, and they relied more and more upon their heads of government and cabinet ministers, and eventually also upon their professional diplomats. Although diplomacy at the summit declined in certain respects, it did not disappear entirely, and since the outbreak of World War II it has experienced considerable resurgence. It is a misreading of history, therefore, to conclude that it is a new phenomenon. Contemporary developments, rather, evidence an identification by a new title, increased usage, the refinement of new forms, and popularization in the news media and public consciousness.

The founders of the American Republic could scarcely have envisioned the global diplomatic role that has come to be played by the President. His involvement in personal diplomacy at the summit—as Diplomat in Chief—is one of the more significant if not auspicious developments in the conduct of contemporary American foreign relations.

History recounts the personal diplomatic exploits of emperors, kings, princes, and churchmen, as well as twentieth-century dictators, premiers, and presidents. So far as the United States is concerned, since the days of George Washington, American Presidents have proclaimed American foreign policy, written letters and telegrams to foreign leaders or talked with them on the telephone, sent personal emissaries to consult with them, received them in official visits to

Source: "Summit Diplomacy: Its Uses and Limitations," *Virginia Quarterly Review*, vol. 48 (Summer 1972), pp. 321–44.

Washington, visited them abroad, and met with them in a series of meetings and conferences.

For varying reasons—ranging from voluntary concentration on internal pressures and issues to uncontrollable emergence of foreign-relations problems and crises, and from the particular persuasions and methods of operation of individual presidential incumbents to the insistence by other leaders on dealing at the highest level of political power and responsibility—some Presidents have remained relatively immune, while others have succumbed to the lure of the summit. The names of those who remained aloof rarely appear in the diplomatic chronicles. Other Presidents are remembered for an occasional or a few memorable foreign-policy pronouncements or international actions. A number have engaged in personal diplomacy of some consequence—such as Washington, Jefferson, Polk, Cleveland, Truman, Eisenhower, and subsequent Presidents. A few have pursued active if not decisive summit careers, at times virtually becoming their own Secretaries of State. Among these, in the present century, are Theodore Roosevelt, Woodrow Wilson, and Franklin D. Roosevelt.

While "diplomacy" is variously interpreted, as a matter of both intellectual conceptualization and pragmatic state action, it may be defined succinctly as the political process by which political entities (principally national states) conduct official relations with one another in the international environment. Put another way, diplomacy is equatable with the conduct of foreign relations, as distinguished from the substance of foreign policy. In this guise it embraces the making and implementation (but not the essence) of foreign policy, both centrally and in the field.

Diplomacy at the "summit," as Prime Minister Winston Churchill characterized it in a foreign-policy address before the House of Commons in 1953, is diplomacy at the "highest level." The word "summit," therefore, identifies the level at which the diplomatic function is exercised, and does not necessarily connote an entirely new form of interstate action. Simply stated, it is diplomacy engaged in by political principals above the cabinet or ministerial rank, including the participation of chiefs of state, heads of government, a few others who qualify by virtue of their official positions (such as presidents-elect, crown princes, and the ranking officers of international organizations), and certain agents of heads of government who genuinely represent them at their level.

Although the expression "summit diplomacy" only came to be

used journalistically in the 1950s, as a form of state practice it is as old as history itself. When adopted as an appellation by the news media, it was restricted largely to top-level East-West international conferencing, but its scope has gradually been broadened to include less formal meetings, official visits, and communications among political leaders. Actually, it is broader still, encompassing the following distinguishable elements: (1) presidential foreign policy-making and enunciation, (2) personal presidential communications, (3) presidential personal representatives or special agents, (4) visits of world leaders to the United States, (5) presidential visits and tours abroad, and (6) summit meetings and conferences.*

Each of these forms of diplomacy at the summit has its uses and limitations. In the second half of the twentieth century, no President can completely escape their attractions. Nevertheless, because of differing perspectives and temperaments, as well as the exigencies of the times, Presidents differ materially in how they employ them. While the modes of summit diplomacy may serve fruitful purposes and personalization may prove to be gratifying, Presidents need to exercise restraint to avoid what Dean Rusk has called the temptations flowing from the chemistry of the office which seem inexorably to entice them to the summit.

No President since the founding of the Republic has been able to avoid personal participation in foreign policy-making. The issue is not presidential involvement per se, but rather the nature and degree of his role. President Truman's pithy observation that "the President makes foreign policy," while indisputable though simplistic, is not, remarked Dean Rusk before he became Secretary of State, the whole story, "but it will serve well enough if you want to say it all in five words." The Constitution is mute on foreign policy-making authority, but since the days of Washington, history records, the President has served as "Foreign-Policy-Maker-in-Chief," assuming initiative and governmental leadership in formulating and promulgating the basic principles and guidelines that govern external relations.

United States diplomatic history reveals some forty-five to fifty major foreign-relations developments identified with sixteen specific Presidents. Of these, only six antedate the present century, including

---

* EDITOR'S NOTE: For a more comprehensive, though earlier, analysis of the principal aspects of the subject, see Elmer Plischke, *Summit Diplomacy: Personal Diplomacy of the President of the United States* (College Park: Bureau of Governmental Research, University of Maryland, 1958; reprinted Westport, Conn.: Greenwood, 1974).

Washington (remembered for abstentionism—both neutrality and iso-lationism), Jefferson ("no entangling alliances," the Louisiana Pur-chase, and freedom of the seas), Monroe (the Monroe Doctrine), Polk (expansionism or "manifest destiny"), Cleveland (arbitration of the British Guiana-Venezuela boundary dispute), and McKinley (annexa-tion of the Philippines, which introduced the United States into eastern Asian affairs).

On the other hand, every President since 1900, except for Hard-ing and Coolidge, has made significant foreign-policy contributions. Examples prior to World War II include Theodore Roosevelt's Panama Canal policy and his corollary to the Monroe Doctrine, Taft's "dol-lar diplomacy," Wilson's Fourteen Points, self-determination, glo-balization of the Monroe Doctrine, and the League of Nations, and Hoover's non-recognition policy. Franklin D. Roosevelt is remem-bered, among other things, for the Four Freedoms, the Atlantic Charter, and the United Nations. More recently, of possible historical import are Truman's Point Four, the Truman Doctrine, and the Korean police action, Eisenhower's atoms for peace and open-skies inspection policies, Kennedy's Alliance for Progress and the nuclear test ban, Johnson's nuclear non-proliferation treaty and the Viet-namese venture, and the Nixon Doctrine.

It is interesting to contemplate why certain other major foreign-policy developments are not historically associated with particular Presidents, such as the annexation of Texas and Hawaii, affiliation with certain important international organizations, containment, or the consummation of such multipartite collective defense arrange-ments as the Rio Inter-American Reciprocal Assistance Pact and the North Atlantic Treaty. A few comparable policy developments live in history identified with Secretaries of State, illustrated by James G. Blaine's inter-Americanism launched at the Washington conference of 1889, the Hay Open Door policy, Secretary Hull's trade agree-ments program, and, since World War II, the Marshall Plan.* By way of comparison, it is worthy of note that no foreign policies or actions of similar historicity are associated with the Congress, with either of its chambers, or with any of its individual members.

Presidents have exercised varying capacities in conceptualizing and framing the policy remembered historically in association with their names. Rarely has such policy been conceived initially and solely in the mind of the Chief Executive. Most frequently the President ex-

---

* EDITOR'S NOTE: For a more detailed examination of the secretary of state's role in American diplomacy, see the preceding essay, "Ministerial Diplomacy—Secretary of State Abroad."

ercises the central and decisional capacity in its resolution and, by accepting it as his policy, he renders it the policy of the nation. In doing so, he usually propounds it personally—in a message to Congress, an executive proclamation, an exchange of communications with foreign governments, a presidential directive, or even a farewell address. Often it is the enunciatory action which emblazons his brand upon it, whether or not he originally conceived or refined it. The greater the extent to which the President personally becomes involved in its devisement, or has it framed under his immediate direction, and the greater the degree to which he personally proclaims it publicly and solicits public support for it, the more is such foreign policy imbued with the aura of the summit.

In summary, enduring, long-range, and significant United States foreign policy (distinguished from procedural, tactical, and subsidiary policy) tends to be presidential policy—perhaps in origin, sometimes in form, occasionally in language, and most often in impulsion and dissemination. The international leadership if not the quality of statesmanship of a President, by and large, is equated historically with the proficiency of his administration and his personal leadership in foreign policy-making.

Each President's individual policy contribution is likely to be influenced by his personal qualities and attributes. Equally influential are the demands placed upon him by the international events of his era. His compulsion to action as a foreign policy-maker is determined, to some degree, by the need he perceives for policy, his fundamental disposition to act, and the policies and likely reactions of other nations. Presidential initiation of new policy occurs most naturally, therefore, when optimum internal and external motivation exists —that is, when the President wears the cloak of chief foreign policy-maker with equanimity and relish, when he is inherently stimulated to recognize the international need and the course of essential national response, and when he is impelled to do so by the flow of history.

At the peak of his remarkable interchange of communications with the leaders of the Kremlin, discussed more fully later, President Eisenhower wrote: "For several centuries personal correspondence between Heads of Government and Heads of State has been an extremely valuable channel of communication when the normal diplomatic channels seemed unable to carry the full burden." When President Washington sent a personal message to the Sultan of Morocco on December

1, 1789, only seven months after the birth of the new Republic, he scarcely could have realized the important diplomatic precedent this letter to a foreign dignitary was setting, or the degree to which his successors would be communicating personally with the ranking leaders of the world.

The transmittal of such communications—at the President's level and bearing his signature—in the conduct of United States foreign affairs has become well-established practice. Ceremonial, congratulatory, and condolence communications, the customary responsibility of the Chief Executive, though often pro forma, have proliferated with the expansion of the family of nations. Some messages are mediatory in nature, the President assuming the mantle of peacemaker, as was the case with Theodore Roosevelt during the Russo-Japanese War and the Moroccan crisis after the turn of the century, with Woodrow Wilson during World War I, and with Franklin Roosevelt in relation to the Sudetenland and Danzig crises in the 1930s.

It is difficult to categorize the nature or purpose of the remaining mass of summit communications, largely because their subjects range across the spectrum of foreign relations. The following merely illustrate some of the better known, recent experiences. An exchange may be exceptional in both importance and infrequency, as in the case of the Cuban missile crisis of 1962. Of the five "eyeball-to-eyeball" summit notes, three were incoming from Premier Khrushchev and two were outgoing from President Kennedy. They constituted the central diplomatic vehicle for defusing the crisis. While the need for rapid accommodation was imperative, and other diplomatic techniques were employed as well, this process of personal communication between the leaders of the East and West risked foreclosing all appeal to higher authority.

Other exchanges are more numerous, exemplified by President Eisenhower's correspondence diplomacy with the Kremlin from September, 1955, to 1960. This series of seventy-two communications was remarkable in a number of ways. Initiated and maintained by the Soviet leaders, the President appears to have been an unhappy respondent, and yet he failed to lower the exchange to either the ministerial or the traditional diplomatic level. The principal subject of discourse was disarmament, an intricate negotiatory problem dealt with in considerable detail, even though parallel United Nations-sponsored deliberations were in progress. Some of these communications were lengthy, detailed, and complex, and might more appropriately have been left to the professionals. They aggregated over 100,000 words, and the longest message, with its annex, runs to twenty-two pages in print. Most important, because they were immediately published—and were closely observed throughout the world—they came to be used for propaganda purposes rather than serious discussion and bargaining, and consequently they degenerated into a strange example of diplomacy by speechifying.*

The most prolific summit correspondence at the presidential level was that of Franklin Roosevelt with the British, Chinese, and Soviet leaders during World War II. More than 2,500 summit messages coursed between Washington, London, Moscow, and Chungking, many of which were personalized as well as personal. Language was courteous despite the wartime pressures, even when the leaders disagreed on important policy matters, and the style often was succinct if not cryptic, sometimes making a major point in a single sentence or two. They were devoid of polemics, remarkably direct and forthright, and frequently not only confidential but in utmost confidence. The bulk of these exchanges were concerned with co-operation in waging and winning the war against the Axis, postwar territorial issues, and preparations for the wartime summit conferences. Not only was this a prolific exchange, but each of the wartime leaders seemed to welcome personal participation in communicating expeditiously at his level.

To be effective in such summit communications (and this applies to telephonic exchanges as well), the participants must be sincere and convince their correspondents that they are personally trustworthy and earnestly desire to exchange views and positions purposefully. In short, they, as well as what they have to convey, must be credible, and for this reason usually will conduct the exchanges in quiet. To be fruitful summit interchange cannot degenerate into a "talking war," and such propaganda value or internal political advantage as may accrue should be a byproduct rather than a primary objective.

While substantial criticism is directed at presidential "meddling" in diplomacy by means of personal summit communications, the current trend of presidential involvement—sometimes approximating "pen pal" relationships—is not likely to be reversed. Because presidential action, at times, is in response to the messages of other world leaders, the President is not entirely a free agent. Essentially, however, the extent to which he engages in summit communications re-

* EDITOR's NOTE: See Elmer Plischke, "Eisenhower's 'Correspondence Diplomacy' With the Kremlin—Case Study in Summit Diplomatics," *Journal of Politics*, vol. 30 (February 1968), pp. 137–59.

flects the degree to which he is disposed to become his own ambassador.

On occasion, but with increasing and perhaps surprising frequency, the President appoints special diplomatic representatives to supplement regular emissaries—in order to keep himself informed, negotiate in his behalf, and extend his personal influence and service abroad. This practice, while often questioned, especially by professional diplomatists, and even jokingly referred to as "Rover Boy diplomacy," nevertheless has become a time-honored and broadly employed form of diplomacy at the summit.

Presidents who assume active leadership in foreign affairs have been especially prone to employ such personal emissaries. At the outset, appointments were sufficiently uncommon to be readily identifiable in the chronicles of diplomacy, but in recent decades they have come to be so freely engaged that more than two dozen may be dispatched in a single year, and in all probability the total number to date, while not tabulated, amounts to several thousand.

The presidential agent, initially, was commissioned by the Chief Executive only on a special occasion for a particular purpose, although sometimes for extended periods. More recently, usage has been extended to cover virtually any matter of diplomatic assignment which the President wishes to handle outside conventional channels—whether it be information gathering, conveying of official positions and policy, special resident representation, trouble shooting, mediation, negotiating, or conference participation. Dr. E. Wilder Spaulding, on retiring from the Department of State after approximately thirty years, assessed the diplomatic appointments of this country and commented rather bitterly: "It has been too easy for the White House to appoint a whole bevy of second-rate chiefs of mission and fill the near-vacuum later . . . with special agents."

The presidential personal representative may be defined as one who is sent abroad in a diplomatic capacity by the President without senatorial confirmation and at times even without consulting the Department of State. Usually such an emissary's authority, duties, and compensation are determined by the President alone. The appointee is responsible to the Chief Executive directly and personally, and generally he reports immediately to the White House.

As thus defined, presidential agents may be classified according to the position they occupy prior to appointment, the nature of the tasks assigned, and the extent to which they actually represent the President in an intimate and personal way. According to one classification, there are those who otherwise occupy no regular official positions in the Government, such as President Wilson's Colonel Edward M. House and President Roosevelt's Harry Hopkins during World War II. On the other hand, there are those who, although having regular official positions, are sent on particular diplomatic missions by the Chief Executive.

It appears, however, that the nature of the assignment is a more meaningful index to the significance of appointment than is the source from which the appointee comes. Based on the nature of their functions special representatives may be categorized as follows: the ceremonial emissary representing the President at an important foreign function, such as a coronation, wedding, funeral, or commemorative celebration; the conference commissioner or delegate, of which there have been many throughout United States history; the intimate type, represented by Colonel House and Harry Hopkins; the "trouble-shooting" or special negotiating type, illustrated by the George Marshall mission to China and Harold Stassen's arms limitation negotiations; the extraordinary resident mission, such as Myron Taylor's World War II assignment to the Vatican; and the roving type, exemplified by W. Averell Harriman on a number of occasions.*

One of the most serious risks in the utilization of such special agents is the ease with which the President can resort to using them. The facility with which they can be appointed—rapidly, quietly, and without Senate debate—and the success with which they often perform their tasks, tends to habitualize the practice. Frequent usage, it is claimed with some justification, demoralizes the Department of State and the career diplomatic service. Nevertheless, so long as Presidents assume personal direction over foreign relations, they will doubtless continue to appoint as special representatives individuals who are able to cut through bureaucratic red tape and the inhibiting protocol and restraints of ordinary diplomatic practice, who are believed to be able to assist Presidents more effectively or expeditiously than others with the tasks at hand, who are comfortable speaking with the immediate authority of the White House, and in whom Presidents repose special confidence.

In an age of Madison Avenue public relations, mass communications, and mercurial travel, it is not surprising to see government leaders

---

* EDITOR'S NOTE: Subsequently, Henry A. Kissinger, as special assistant to the president and as secretary of state, served in several of these capacities—as personal advisor, special envoy, trouble-shooter, and roving emissary engaged in shuttle diplomacy.

crisscrossing the globe to consult one another and to meet and address their peoples as they ply their statecraft. Stimulated by the growth and increasing interdependence of the community of nations, the effects on international affairs of giant strides in scientific technology, the intensity of conflict over national interests, and the polarization of power relationships, diplomacy has lent itself to increasing face-to-face relations at the summit.

In January, 1957, President Eisenhower indicated that he was "always obliged" when foreign dignitaries visited him, because his "peculiar constitutional position," as both chief of state and head of government, made it difficult for him, in going abroad, to be absent from the United States for any length of time. He added that foreign officials, appreciating this, happily were willing to come to Washington without expecting that, as a matter of courtesy, he would need to return the visit.

The earliest summit visit to the United States, in 1805, grew out of the problems American maritime interests were having with the Barbary states in the Mediterranean. The President dispatched Commodore John Rodgers, in command of a squadron of vessels, to negotiate with the Bey of Tunis, and when it was decided to continue discussions in the United States, the African leader appointed the Bashaw of Tunis as his emissary to this country. The latter visited a number of cities as the guest of the American government, remaining into the following year, and a settlement of outstanding claims resulted in 1807.

Since that time several hundred foreign chiefs of state, heads of government, and other leading dignitaries have come to the United States on official and unofficial summit visits. The increased tempo in recent decades of pilgrimages to Washington by kings and presidents, premiers and princes, presidents-elect, vice presidents, and ranking officials of international organizations has been occasioned, in part, by the leading position of the United States in world affairs, and was rendered possible by the mid-twentieth century revolution in mobility. Ambassador Angier Biddle Duke, President Kennedy's Chief of Protocol, asserted that in the early 1960's the prestige of the United States polarized the leadership of more than half the countries of the world in the form of visits to Washington in the span of but a few years, and he added half seriously that, to prove its sovereignty, an emergent nation's leader "must run up the new flag, take the oath of office, and visit with" the President of the United States.

To date [1972] there have been approximately six hundred summit visits to the United States, of which only twenty-three took place prior to Franklin Roosevelt's inauguration. Roughly three-fourths have occurred since President Truman left office in 1953, averaging fifteen to twenty per year but reaching a peak of forty-five in 1970. Recent figures are somewhat inflated by the large number of simultaneous visits occurring on a special occasion, as at the time of the funerals of Presidents Kennedy and Eisenhower and the White House dinner given for approximately thirty state guests by President Nixon on October 24, 1970, to commemorate the twenty-fifth anniversary of the United Nations.

When a foreign political leader comes to the United States on a summit visit, the manner of his reception and treatment are determined primarily by his official and personal rank, the purpose of his visit, and the nature of the invitation. Until the time of President Truman, each visitor's reception and schedule were separately devised, although certain practices became accepted guides for subsequent preparations. It was not until the 1950's, however, that the White House and Department of State crystallized protocol and formalized procedures for such visits. Several types of summit visits have been delineated—the formal and largely ceremonial state visits for chiefs of state, the official visits of heads of government, informal and "working" visits, and private visits for personal reasons, such as acquiring medical treatment. Potentially the most important are those involving heads of government who come primarily to confer on significant matters of public policy.

Having become so commonplace, their frequency raises questions of time and cost in relation to value. Each visit takes hours of the limited time of the President and other top-level members of the government, and it also requires thousands of man-hours on the part of a host of others concerned with its planning and management. Moreover, as the quantity of summit visits has increased, there has been some danger that they become so routine that government leaders and the people tire of them. Techniques are devised, therefore, to give each visit, or at least the most formal and important, some air of individuality, which taxes the ingenuity of the planners because innovations must be appealing and yet avoid demeaning the dignity of the guest.

A public, ceremonious, official reception in Washington for a foreign leader may enhance his prestige internationally as well as in his homeland, which may be of consequence both to the United States and to his country. On the other hand, the failure or refusal to proffer an invitation similarly may affect the foreign relations of the two countries. Injured pride, and conceivably even alleged affront to national honor, may result from a failure to invite a particular foreign dignitary, or from inviting him less frequently than others, or from extending an invitation at what is regarded as the wrong time.

It is difficult to assess accurately the importance of most summit visits, except with considerable hindsight. This results from inability to perceive and evaluate direct benefits resulting from them, while indirect and subsidiary consequences often are less apparent or may seem to be unimportant. Nevertheless, foreign relations may be shaped—or at least colored by the manner in which state guests are received and treated. Undoubtedly the impression most meaningful to many of these summit visitors is the American way of life, the panoply of which is easily visible to them. The state guest may tour the country, but, even if he remains in Washington, he is able to see variegated Americana flowing past his very door, all of which may produce a lasting and visible impression of incalculable effect. Most important, however, may be his policy discussions with the President. Nevertheless, even if the results are intangible, consisting simply of augmented good will, the visit may be worthwhile, for the same results generally are unachievable at lower diplomatic levels.*

The smoke of war had barely subsided when, late in 1918, President Wilson went to a shell-shocked but expectant Europe to participate in the World War I peace negotiations. Although he was to endure months of delay and disappointment, and eventual repudiation at home, he was acclaimed enthusiastically by the peoples of Europe. They lionized him as the herald of the principles for which the Allies had battled and suffered so much. Only superlatives can describe his reception in Paris, London, Rome, and Brussels. Never had a President of the United States been received so widely with such laudatory public approbation in foreign lands, and rarely had any foreign political leader been so closely grasped to the hearts of so many people.

Four decades later, in December, 1959, President Eisenhower set forth on his eleven-nation "Quest for Peace" mission—a remarkable grand tour of portions of Asia, Europe, and the Middle East, on which he traveled 22,000 miles in nineteen days, and was "viewed" by more than five million people. He addressed three parliaments, participated in a series of commemorative celebrations, and jointly issued eleven communiqués. He consulted with the leaders of ten countries and the

---

* EDITOR'S NOTE: For additional commentary, see Elmer Plischke, "Recent State Visits to the United States—A Technique of Summit Diplomacy," *World Affairs Quarterly*, vol. 29 (October 1958), pp. 223–55.

Vatican, and in Paris he met with Prime Minister Harold Macmillan, Chancellor Konrad Adenauer, and President Charles de Gaulle in a Western heads of government conference.

In certain respects, however, few foreign visits of a world leader equal that of President Kennedy when he spent three days in Germany in June, 1963. Undertaken to discuss policy matters of grave concern to both Bonn and Washington, the visit was converted by the populace into an impressive German-American demonstration. Though replete with the customary ceremonies, receptions, motorcades, major and minor addresses, glowing toasts, and massive throngs of people, the youthful and eloquent American President electrified the entire land. He displayed the rare gift of saying the right thing in the right way, with the right nuances, so that his empathy with the German people appeared to be consummate. Yet the climax was not reached until he addressed 400,000 Berliners in the city square where, to a thunderous ovation, he proclaimed: "as a free man, I take pride in the words: *Ich bin ein Berliner.*"

Such vignettes characterize one of the striking changes in the new diplomacy. Early American tradition established that the President should not leave the territory of the United States during his incumbency.* Theodore Roosevelt was the first to break with precedent by visiting Panama in November, 1906, to inspect progress being made in constructing the canal. William Howard Taft, as President-elect, also went to Panama early in 1909, and later the same year, as President, he introduced the diplomatic practice of meeting with the Mexican President.

Wilson was the first United States President to be formally received in official visits to foreign capitals and to negotiate personally at an international conference. He visited four countries, which converted the venture into the first presidential "tour," a staple of presidential diplomacy by the mid-twentieth century. Warren G. Harding and Herbert Hoover went abroad as Presidents-elect, Harding going to Panama in November, 1920, on an informal visit, and Hoover introducing the good-will tour by visiting ten Latin American countries late in 1928. On his return from Alaska in July, 1923, President Harding also passed through Vancouver where he delivered an address, which launched a series of presidential visits to Canadian territory. Calvin Coolidge was welcomed by Havana in 1928 when he arrived personally to open the sixth Inter-American Conference.

---

* EDITOR'S NOTE: For commentary on the legality and political development of presidential travel abroad, see Elmer Plischke, "The President's Right to Go Abroad," *ORBIS*, vol. 15 (Fall 1971), pp. 755–83.

To the time of Franklin Roosevelt, only five Presidents had set foot on foreign soil, and yet, except for the formal state visit, they had introduced the principal types of presidential foreign visits. Except for Hoover, all Presidents since World War I have been to foreign territory during their tenure in the White House. Yet it was not until the administration of Roosevelt that this form of summit diplomacy became a normal presidential activity. He went abroad thirteen times. Half of his foreign journeys were to single countries, and three of the earlier trips entailed vacations with passage through or short stopovers in foreign lands. He traveled widely for intensive negotiation and consultation purposes and he introduced both the regularized exchange of United States summit visits with Canada and Mexico and the short summit conference with allies. After Pearl Harbor, except for a single border exchange with the Mexican President in 1943, all his trips abroad were devoted to serious matters of wartime policy and strategy.

Much less prone to venture abroad, in part because for nearly four years he served without a Vice President, Truman made only four trips to foreign territory, but was received in the first presidential state visit when he journeyed to Mexico City in 1947, and he attended the last of the wartime summit conferences at Potsdam. President Eisenhower, on the other hand, utilized the foreign visit extensively. In addition to his trip to Korea as President-elect, he went abroad sixteen times, including extensive good-will tours, the East-West Geneva Summit Conference of 1955, and the aborted four-power conclave at Paris in 1960.

President Kennedy might have maintained or even increased this tempo, for he went abroad eight times in less than three years. He journeyed to thirteen countries, was received in state visits in Canada, France, and Mexico, undertook four tours, and engaged in four summit meetings. When Lyndon Johnson succeeded to the presidency, except for a ceremonial meeting with the Canadian Prime Minister in Vancouver in 1964, he refrained from going abroad for more than two years, largely because he was without a Vice President. In 1966, however, he launched a series of trips—to meet with Vietnamese leaders in Honolulu, to visit Canada and Mexico, to attend the funerals of Chancellor Adenauer and Australian Prime Minister Holt, to tour seven Asian lands and attend the Manila summit conference, and to join in a meeting of the Presidents of the Central American Republics in 1968. President Nixon has gone abroad eleven times in less than four years—to attend the funeral of President de Gaulle, to participate in a NATO Council session, to undertake a globe-girdling tour, and to confer with Communist leaders in Rumania, Yugoslavia, Peking, and Moscow.*

Thus, presidential visits to foreign lands have become a traditional feature of summit diplomacy. To 1972, Presidents went abroad on sixty-eight trips, visiting fifty foreign countries and the Vatican. These vary from the short visit to make a single speech, spend a few moments consulting with government leaders while en route, await the refueling of a plane, sign a negotiated agreement, or engage in some official or private ceremony, on the one hand, and to gala state visits, extensive consultations regarding serious issues of foreign policy, and major negotiating conferences, on the other hand. They fall into the following principal categories: international conferences and informal meetings, formal state visits, official informal and "working" visits, presidential tours, ceremonial visits, "state pauses," and vacations. The groupings are not always clear-cut nor are they mutually exclusive, because many foreign ventures include more than one visit, and individual trips often fall into more than a single category.

President Eisenhower said that he would go anywhere, at any time, to meet with any government in the cause of peace, and his successors in the White House have echoed this determination. It is good to have leaders who are dedicated to serve personally the cause of peace, but many presidential visits have insubstantial relevance to critical issues of peace, and frequently other forms of diplomacy may be more effectively attuned to achieve their purposes.

Nevertheless, the President cannot afford to default on the obligation to do all that is essential, and the magnetic attraction to the summit persists. The President functions in a competitive milieu, in which other peripatetic salesmen of statecraft seek to influence the policies, politics, and images of important segments of the world by their foreign trips. In his quest to satisfy the hopes and expectations of the people who look to him for leadership, therefore, he will be impelled to continue his foreign odysseys.

The type of summit diplomacy that receives the greatest amount of popular, journalistic, and, at times, official attention is the summit conference. The practice of chiefs of state and heads of government to confer with one or more summit leaders is by no means new. In earlier centuries they met to air grievances, strengthen positions, resolve

---

* EDITOR'S NOTE: President Nixon undertook sixteen foreign trips (1969–1975) and President Gerald Ford followed with four such trips—for a total of twenty in eight years.

conflicts, cement alliances, promote mutual objectives, or join their sovereign families in wedlock. Prior to the era of classical diplomacy, the conference or consultation at the highest level was accepted as the normal process for conducting much of the major business of reigning monarchs and leaders of the Church.

In a lecture presented at the University of New Hampshire in 1958, former Secretary of State Dean Acheson claimed that there are fashions in most societal relations, so that, while mankind has experienced ways of behavior respecting the horrors of warfare, there also are countervailing fashions in remedies to avert holocaust—including, especially in recent years, the meeting at the summit. Although high-level conferencing became more common than ever during and after World War II, it is in fact a recurring fashion. Through the years, as the state system developed and diplomacy became the principal peaceful medium of interstate relations, ordinary diplomatic channels, relying on resident and occasional special emissaries, generally supplanted the earlier system of direct, personal contact among sovereigns and heads of government.

At times state leaders have reverted, nevertheless, to face-to-face consultation. Presidential involvement in summit conferencing began with Theodore Roosevelt's indirect participation in the Portsmouth Conference during the Russo-Japanese War in 1905. Since that time, every President has become involved personally in conferences and meetings in some capacity.* In the three and a half decades following the inaugural of Franklin Roosevelt, the President joined other world leaders in more than one hundred summit gatherings, currently averaging approximately four a year. In many ways the classic though exceptional example was Wilson's attendance at the Paris Peace Conference in 1919. Extensive presidential conferencing emerged, however, only when the United States acquired the status of a leading world power during World War II. Franklin Roosevelt became an enthusiastic exponent, engaging in twenty summit-level gatherings in less than five years—many of which constituted what later were called "military staff meetings at the highest levels." On the other hand, President Truman, aside from exercising a ceremonial function at several international gatherings at which major diplomatic instruments were signed, became involved in only four summit meetings, including the Potsdam Conference, which concluded the World War II series of Big Two and Big Three conclaves.

---

* EDITOR'S NOTE: For an analysis of presidential conference diplomacy, see Elmer Plischke, "International Conferencing and the Summit: Macro-Analysis of Presidential Participation," *ORBIS*, vol. 14 (Fall 1970), pp. 673–713.

President Eisenhower engaged extensively in summit conferencing. He varied the form of his participation, played less of a ceremonial role, and displayed the courage of venturing to two formal East-West four-power conferences with Kremlin leaders, an experiment not repeated by his successors, who nevertheless maintained a high level of involvement. Except for inter-American summit gatherings and the seven-nation Manila Conference of 1966, Presidents Kennedy and Johnson adopted the practice of relying on the more personal and less formal styles of summit conferencing. President Nixon is following suit, and barring a significant change in the international posture of the United States, this trend is likely to continue.

* * *

The President meets more freely on an individual basis with the leader of a single country than in a multilateral conclave. Approximately three-fourths of his meetings are bilateral. Many of these sessions are associated with visits of foreign leaders to the United States or with presidential tours abroad. At times the elements of the summit visit predominate although serious discussion becomes an important accompaniment of ceremonial formalities. Usually the overriding purpose is to provide an opportunity for summit-level conferral and exchanges of views.

Of the multipartite gatherings, the better remembered, aside from the Paris Peace Conference of 1919, include the Big Three World War II conclaves at Cairo, Tehran, Yalta, and Potsdam, the Western four-power gatherings with the leaders of Britain, France, and West Germany since 1945, and the East-West four-power conferences. In addition, the President has joined in multilateral conferences in a negotiatory capacity at the North Atlantic Treaty Organization sessions in 1957 and 1969, the seven-nation Manila Conference of 1966, and several inter-American gatherings. From time to time, he also may attend multilateral international meetings purely in a formal capacity, principally to welcome the negotiators if they convene in the United States, to deliver an address at the commencement or termination of deliberations, or to witness the signing of an important document.

Official publications and the press variously describe the presidential function in summit conferencing as discussions, conversations, conferring, exchanges of views, or just plain "talks"—all of which denote face-to-face oral communication, the principal quality and advantage of this form of summit diplomacy. It affords an opportunity for planned presidential presentation of policy positions and views, listening to the interests of other summit leaders, gaining acceptance of such explications, and, perhaps, attempting to achieve an adjustment of interests. Understandings, both informal and formal, may be reached, but rarely is the President subjected to the tortuous hammering out of the text of an important treaty or agreement.

Such summit conferencing has become an accepted and vital part of the diplomatic practice of the United States. Contemporary international relations, often requiring rapid and significant accommodation, appear to justify negotiation at the highest level as an occasional supplement to the conduct of foreign affairs through other forms of diplomacy. Much may be accomplished if the summit gathering is judiciously planned and wisely employed. In view of the protracted Wilsonian negotiations at Paris—extending over six months—and certain other disappointing and unproductive experiences at summit conferences, it may reasonably be expected that presidential participation in a formal negotiating capacity concerning extensive, complex, and sensitive problems, or in highly advertised meetings with avowed adversaries, is likely to be exceptional. Summit gatherings are bound to be resorted to more freely among friendly powers, but even in competitive relations they can bear significant fruit if they are sagaciously handled and the participants are sincere in mutually seeking to adjust their differences and achieve better understanding and acceptable solutions to critical issues.

On balance, the summit gathering is by no means a proven panacea for the international ills of the world. The urge simply to "take it to the summit" needs to be restrained, and the boast that the President "can handle" another particular summit leader, or "stand up to him," must be curbed. These are exaggerated, illusory nostrums. On the other hand, history has not disproven that the summit gathering may serve as a useful forum in which to ameliorate or resolve some international problems, and, in those cases in which circumstances and attitudes are right, they will continue to be productive. Nevertheless, presidential conferencing needs to be employed sparingly, lest it lose its impact and become self-defeating.

The functioning of the President as Diplomat-in-Chief, to conclude, although widespread, time-tested, and above all newsworthy, is far from being a magic cure-all for international malady. At best, diplomacy at the summit is only one of several alternative medicaments, to be used frugally and for limited, well-chosen purposes. It should not be regarded as an instant elixir for the assuagement of crises or a subliminal narcotic to dissimulate relief from the realities of inter-governmental ailments. Much of the diplomatic diagnosis, prescription, and pharmaceutics must be left to others—the professionals. Painstaking quiet diplomacy—without fanfare, overshadowing personalities, or open dialogue—normally affords the soundest international therapy.

On the other hand, summit diplomacy in its various guises may serve beneficial purposes. If prudently managed, and if summit leaders are prepared to learn, to listen, to reason, and to seek better understanding, and they not only wish to improve the international atmosphere but also are prepared to do something about it, diplomacy at their level may facilitate improvement of relations among nations. The effectiveness of human institutions and processes, including diplomacy at the highest level, is determined by the willingness participants devote to having it succeed, not to vindicate the process or enhance the image of the leaders, but to achieve their objectives. Under the right conditions, in short, presidential diplomacy is capable of providing some though only limited curative results, and caution must be exercised lest it is mistakenly besought simply as a hallucinatory opiate yearned for to induce imagined euphoria.

Multilateralism

INIS L. CLAUDE, JR.

"Multilateral diplomacy," like many other terms current in the literature of international relations, tends to serve less as a topic for careful study than as a symbol, evoking generalized reactions of approval
or disapproval, confidence or anxiety. In the mind of the public, the
mention of those two words today calls up a picture of a big, noisy
international conference, complete with committees and chairmen,
agenda and rules of procedure, debates and votes, rostrum and gal-
lery, earphones for simultaneous translation and microphones and
cameras for world-wide transmission of the proceedings.

This image of multilateral diplomacy does not affect all men alike,
nor have reactions to it remained fixed during the last generation. The
Wilsonian vision of a world forum in which the conscience of mankind could be mobilized to promote international justice, decency, and
peace has been largely displaced by the reaction typified by Sir Harold
Nicolson when he alleges that public international conferences "tend
to promote rather than allay suspicion, and to create those very states
of uncertainty which it is the purpose of good diplomatic method to
prevent." Multilateral diplomacy has come to suggest propaganda and
insult, not the wholesome ventilation of differences among nations.
On the basis of recent experience, we are inclined to make multilateral
diplomacy the symbol of a vituperative, publicity-ridden assembly
which provides the worst possible setting for the bargaining, the
maneuvering, and the compromising which we associate with effective
diplomacy.

The sober recognition of the demerits of what passes as multilateral diplomacy poses the temptation to fasten an uncritical and

SOURCE: Inis L. Claude, Jr. "Multilateralism—Diplomatic and Otherwise," *International Organization*, vol. 12 (Winter 1958), pp. 43–52.

wistful gaze upon the more intimate, closed diplomacy of an earlier day. There is a danger that the old diplomacy may become invested with an idealized glow, stemming from a nostalgia which is forgetful of the fact that the old system produced failures giving adequate motivation for reasonable men to undertake the development of more satisfactory ways of conducting relations among states. If we are dealing in images, we would do well to recognize that mixed emotions ought to be engendered by both the assembly hall of "multilateral diplomacy" and the green-baize table of traditional diplomacy.

However, the urgent need is to develop a discriminating analysis of the functional significance of multilateral techniques in international relations which can counter the massive reactions of approval or disapproval which the term "multilateral diplomacy" tends to engender. What *is* multilateral diplomacy? Is it simply diplomacy, with a larger cast of characters, with the organization and techniques which are necessitated by the larger cast, and with the lack of privacy which is inevitable in such a situation? I think not. I suspect that the beginning of wisdom in this matter is the recognition of the fallacy in the proposition that multilateral diplomacy is merely diplomacy on a large scale and with the door open.

The truth is that the term, multilateral diplomacy, is commonly used to connote a wide variety of activities, which are more consistently multilateral than diplomatic in character. The techniques of multilateralism are sometimes turned to the problem of achieving the settlement of specific disputes, or the diminution of tensions in particular situations; in such cases, multilateral diplomacy is a term of literal description. But multilateralism is also applied to such matters as mobilizing the collective condemnation of a state whose behavior is alleged to fall below acceptable international standards, organizing a general colloquium on the problems of the global situation and on national policies for dealing with those problems, drafting conventions of the sort which have come to be known as "international legislation," and formulating arrangements for the establishment of international organizations and the initiation of international programs. Activities of this type are perhaps better understood if they are not labeled "diplomatic." Of course, every student of international relations is free to invest the term, "diplomacy," with whatever meaning or meanings he wishes; I have no license to establish the "true" definition of diplomacy. But the point is that no valid generalization can be made concerning the appropriateness or usefulness of multilateralism in diplomacy if the latter term is taken to include too broad a range of interstate relationships. I propose to set out with the assumption that the diplomatic process is most clearly in operation when states are negotiating with each other to achieve peaceful settlement of a dispute or agreement on a matter of mutual concern, and when such negotiations have the fundamental quality of a *bargaining* session, involving the necessity of reciprocal concession to produce an agreed result. Admittedly, this formula does not serve as a basis for making absolute distinctions between what is diplomatic in character and what is not. It may, however, contribute to the possibility of reaching a proper evaluation of what is called multilateral diplomacy, by facilitating an analysis which distinguishes the more diplomatic from the less diplomatic functions of multilateralism.

Critics of multilateral diplomacy tend in fact to adopt, consciously or not, a definition of the diplomatic process not unlike the one suggested above. Most of the standard criticisms of multilateral diplomacy are applicable primarily if not exclusively to cases in which the problem is that of obtaining the peaceful settlement of a dispute. States A and B are locked in a quarrel; a mutually acceptable compromise must be found; a bargain must be struck. Here, clearly, is a situation in which a big, well-publicized international conference may do more harm than good; open debate may produce rigidity, arouse passion, and inhibit concession. The attractiveness of quiet consultation and private bargaining is very great in such a situation.

This is not to say that multilateralism has no proper or useful role in cases of this kind. But the question is, *what* role does it have? And the fact is that this question has too often been wrongly answered. It seems to me that an international assembly has two major functions which can properly and usefully be exercised in disputes between states: (1) it can and should express the determination that disputes must be settled without recourse to violence; (2) it can and should make available to the disputants a suitable assortment of instruments for facilitating peaceful settlement. Pressure to settle and assistance in settlement: these are the vital contributions of multilateralism to diplomacy.

The first point expresses the basic justification for multilateral intervention. There are no longer any private disputes in the international sphere; a conflict between two states is everybody's business, because everybody's welfare, everybody's civilization, everybody's survival is involved in the maintenance of the peace of the world. This point was made in [Article 3 of] the Convention for the Pacific Settlement of International Disputes formulated at the Hague Conference of 1899, with its recognition of the friendly right of any state to remind disputants of the urgency of achieving pacific settlement, and it cannot be made too often. Collective pressure upon quarreling states to recognize and respect their responsibility for preserving the peace is of the utmost importance.

The second point has both positive and negative implications. Positively, it reflects the unchallengeable fact that facilities, procedures, and personnel provided by an international agency may supply the indispensable ingredient of diplomatic success. Such devices as the rapporteur of the League era or the independent mediator of the UN period, the commission of inquiry and conciliation, and the international team, military or nonmilitary, for observation and supervision of truce agreements have proved their value in the promotion of pacific settlement, and they have higher potentialities which can be realized if care and skill are invested in their future development. Negatively, the point suggests that a multilateral assembly should not itself undertake to serve as an agency of conciliation. This is the critical mistake, so often made, which accounts in large measure for the low repute into which multilateral diplomacy has fallen. Such a body as the General Assembly of the UN can serve diplomacy well as the creator and sponsor of specialized bodies and intimate procedures for mediation, but if the nations undertake to use it as a peace conference, they are likely to make it resemble a battlefield.

It is a fact of life that states are disinclined to confine international assemblies to the role of insisting upon and providing facilities for peaceful settlement. States involved in disputes normally succumb to the temptation to use multilateral forums for the purpose of enlisting support for their positions. Thus, we frequently find the General Assembly serving as a forum in which disputants struggle to achieve the mobilization of multilateral disapproval of each other's policies and actions. I do not deny that there are occasions when collective condemnation of a party to a dispute is morally and legally justified, nor that there are times when such condemnation may constitute or lead to effective action in restraint of antisocial international behavior. But the resort to collective pressure of this sort can seldom serve as a useful preliminary to diplomatic negotiation. Collective insistence upon the avoidance or cessation of military action may be essential to preserve the possibility of peaceful settlement, but multilateral endorsement of the case of one party to a dispute as against the other is likely in most instances to inhibit rather than to facilitate conciliatory processes, and thus should be characterized as an *alternative* to diplomatic negotiation. Resort to this alternative should be controlled by a fine sense of discrimination—a sense which statesmen embroiled in a dispute are unlikely to exhibit. The invocation by a government of multilateral curses upon its opponent is not so much the exercise of multilateral diplomacy as an indication of refusal to engage in diplomacy of any sort. In ideal, the world forum should encourage and facilitate diplomatic negotiation; in practice, it all too often provides an opportunity for the evasion of diplomatic negotiation.

The remedy for this situation is probably not to be found in any alteration of the legal and mechanical structures of multilateralism. The task of maximizing the contribution of multilateralism to the success of diplomacy is essentially that of ensuring that the world forum will be dominated and directed by statesmen who are concerned to use it for the purpose of upholding the world's interest in the achievement of peaceful settlement, rather than by disputants who are concerned to use it for the purpose of promoting political triumph over their rivals. This objective can be realized only if the great majority of states develop and maintain a vigorous political determination to realize it. If such determination is lacking, disputants will be quick to exploit international machinery for purposes which have little in common with multilateral diplomacy, as I conceive it.

A major aspect of contemporary multilateralism is the general forum on the state of the world and the policies of the nations which is best exemplified by the so-called "general debate" at the annual sessions of the UN General Assembly. It must be emphasized that it may be dangerously misleading to characterize this kind of performance as multilateral diplomacy, for such a characterization invites the application of wholly inappropriate standards of evaluation. This is multilateral, but not multilateral diplomacy. It is not a substitute for diplomacy, its functions are not those of diplomacy, and it ought not to be judged by the criteria of diplomatic achievement. I suspect that Lester Pearson was on the right track when he described this role of the UN as "essentially parliamentary." This characterization is safe for public consumption only if one makes it clear that he is not talking in terms of the unsophisticated notion that parliaments are simply places where laws are made. The general international debate is parliamentary, not, of course, in the legislative sense, but in the sense that a major part of its value, to quote Pearson, "lies precisely in the ability to mobilize and focus opinions, to encourage the formulation, expression, and dramatic confrontation, of major viewpoints."

While the general debate is not, I suggest, a diplomatic enterprise, it may have great influence upon the quality of diplomacy. For it is the function of this brand of multilateral activity to help establish the context within which diplomacy is to operate. At its best, the general debate is an exercise which Abraham Feller aptly described as "the world . . . looking at its problems in the round." It involves the laying out, for all to see, of the problems which lie between humanity and the goal of a decent, orderly, secure world—the problems with which realistic foreign policy must be concerned. It is a collective introduction of the responsible or irresponsible leaders of governments to the facts of international life—to the ambitions and anxieties, the demands and expectations, the passions and sensitivities, which they can ignore only at their peril, and mankind's peril. It is an exposé of the world's dangers and the world's opportunities. The debate affords vital information about the prospects for a foreign policy, the nature of competing foreign policies, the extent and intensity of opposition, the degree of tolerance or acquiescence, the breadth and depth of the support which may be anticipated. Finally, the collective consultation of the nations provides an opportunity for the crystallization of whatever standards of international behavior the world may be capable of agreeing upon at any given time. These are useful, if not, indeed, indispensable, functions for a world which can no longer afford the tragic mistakes which may result from blind, ignorant, or obtuse diplomacy.

Up to this point, I have suggested that the proper role of multilateral institutions in relation to diplomacy is to dramatize the insistent requirement of the international community that disputes be settled by diplomatic rather than military methods, to provide instruments and procedures for promoting the achievement of diplomatic agreement, and to formulate the broad outlines of the political setting within which the diplomatic process must function.

Now I turn to an area of activity which involves, and ought to involve, the operation of multilateralism as a central and not a peripheral factor: the formulation of what might be called legislative and constitutional treaties. In one sense, this is perhaps the most precisely "diplomatic" of the functional areas of multilateralism; the negotiation of treaties is, after all, a classic instance of diplomatic function. But in another sense, it is far removed from traditional concepts of the diplomatic process. Diplomacy is a term heavily weighted with such ideas as giving a *quid* and getting a *quo*, striking a bargain, arranging mutual concessions so as to satisfy both sides in a two-sided situation—and I have taken these ideas to be central to the meaning of diplomacy as the term is used in this article. It is arguable that what we have in the formulation of multilateral treaties is a quasi-legislative, rather than an expanded diplomatic, process. In stating this, I have reference not specifically to the legal quality of the anticipated result of the negotiation, but to the political quality of the negotiating process itself. With regard to what goes on in the multilateral negotiation of a convention, the analogy of a collective bargaining effort to agree upon a contract is less apt than the analogy of congressional maneuvering to synthesize numerous interests and viewpoints in a project for a governmental program or a public policy. The process of reaching multilateral agreement on a human rights treaty, or an international code for the regulation of air traffic, or a convention on copyrights, or the constitution of a new specialized agency is an exercise in accommodation calling for attitudes and skills which have long been associated more closely with the legislative than the diplomatic process. This is not to deny that dualities—tugs of war between two interested parties—arise in both types of negotiation, or that political compromise is an essential component of both processes. The differences are neither easily definable nor absolute in character, but I think there is a difference in kind which the working diplomat and the working congressional politician would be among the first to recognize. The shift from diplomacy to *multiplomacy*, if I may take a chance on incurring the wrath and contempt of the etymologists, is one which involves basic challenges to the traditional procedures of international negotiation.

One thing is clear: the standard criticisms of multilateral diplomacy are not generally pertinent to this zone of activity. The case against premature and excessive publicity applies most explicitly to a situation in which two states are in conflict over an issue. The ill-judged use or the politically motivated abuse of multilateralism in such a situation may so inhibit concession and counter-concession as to jam up the diplomatic works. But in the case of a quasi-legislative international endeavor, the general exposure of differences of view and the open exploration of possible points of agreement would seem to be not a dangerous but an essential procedure. This does not mean that private consultations can be dispensed with; it does mean that public confrontations must be regarded as an integral part of the process. The delicate bargaining of diplomacy cannot be carried out in the wide open spaces of the multilateral arena; the hammering together of international public policy, as expressed in institutions and programs, cannot be carried out *except* in the wide open spaces of that arena. The multilateral arena obviously provides no guarantee that the latter process can be successfully carried forward, as any observer of human rights discussions in the UN must be aware. Nevertheless, it does provide the appropriate setting for the exploration of the possibilities of general agreement on issues of international public policy.

* * *

There are serious difficulties involved in reaching agreement on significant matters when negotiations are conducted on the scale of unlimited multilateralism. Hence, there is a persistent tendency to try to escape this hard reality by setting up artificially restrictive boundaries of multilateralism. For better or worse, this effort is seldom successful today. The great powers met at Dumbarton Oaks to formulate the UN Charter; the San Francisco Conference turned into an exercise in multilateral negotiation, not a ceremony of acceptance by multilateral acclamation. The UN has created two bodies of carefully balanced and limited multilateral membership, the Trusteeship Council and the Committee on Information from Non-Self-Governing Territories, for dealing with colonial matters; these matters tend in practice to be pulled into the unlimited multilateralism of the General Assembly. After abortive efforts to negotiate with the Soviet Union on the creation of an International Atomic Energy Agency, the United States attempted to confine the preparation of the charter of that agency to a hand-picked group of states, a highly selective multilateral commission excluding what Americans might regard as "troublesome elements"; this scheme was resisted and frustrated in the General Assembly. The western powers summoned Egypt in 1956 to bring its Suez policy before a conference whose multilateral dimensions were determined by themselves; Egypt refused to buy their brand of multilateralism. One can only conclude that the difficulties of all-out multilateralism must be faced, not evaded.

It would be unrealistic to allow preoccupation with the problems of this sort of multilateral activity to blot out the significant progress which has been made in the development of the structures, the techniques, and the political habits which are essential to the effective conduct of large-scale international consultation and negotiation. The first half of the twentieth century has been a period of remarkable inventiveness in the sphere of international organization. The nations have acquired a great variety of new equipment, ranging from the institution of an international secretariat to the system of simultaneous translation and from rules of international parliamentary procedure to the ability to absorb undiplomatic language in international debate. National legislative bodies might well be envious of the elaborate mechanisms which have been developed in certain international organizations to assist delegates in producing intelligently formulated drafts for multilateral acceptance. For instance, the process used by the International Labor Organization for the preparation of conventions or recommendations involves staff research studies of the problems under consideration, collection and dissemination of comments by governments, preparatory technical conferences when appropriate, and a "double discussion" procedure requiring consideration of drafts at two successive annual sessions of the International Labor Conference. Somewhat similarly, such agencies as the International Civil Aviation Organization and the World Health Organization routinely utilize the services of expert bodies in the preparation of technical regulations and standards which are to become a part of the growing body of international administrative law. Owing in large measure to such developments as these, the big international conference has become a feasible thing, a normal thing, and a more and more effective instrument for handling some of the business of international relations.

Nevertheless, it remains true that there are difficulties and frustrations to be encountered in the multilateral conference chamber. There is a limit to what can be accomplished there. How can these problems be overcome? How can this limit be transcended?

One of the favorite answers of our time is the proposition that this quasi-legislative process should be allowed to produce a legislative result; let the majority not only out-vote the minority, but bind the minority in so doing. The multilateral conference ought to be transformed, in limited degree at least, into an international legislature. This suggestion seems to me to raise more problems than it solves. Although some international agencies have in fact acquired certain very modest installments of legislative capacity, I do not think that we stand on the threshold of a global legislature. Moreover, I think that this suggestion reflects an exaggerated view both of the fitness of the units of international society to be legislated *for*, and of the practicability and appropriateness of the legislative method for the ordering of relations among the constituent units of any pluralistic society. The experience of a national community such as the United States indicates that the necessity of negotiating agreement among the significant units of a society is never eliminated by the development of a theoretical capacity to impose legislative enactments upon them. The politics of accommodation is here to stay, at all levels of human society.

I suspect that the most fruitful approach to the development of a global order is not to nourish the vision of a world in which "law" has supplanted "politics," but rather to seek means for the improvement of the international political process. We suffer from a qualitative deficiency, not a quantitative excess, of politics in international relations. Politics, conceived as a matter of arranging consent, is an essential function in the ordering of any social grouping. Internationalists would do well to devote less time to bemoaning the necessity of promoting agreement and voluntary cooperation among states and more to the imaginative consideration of ways and means for meeting that necessity.

I would suggest that the most pressing requirement for the improvement of the multilateral conference as an instrument for conducting international business is the development of internationally oriented leadership. The quasi-legislative process ought to operate under quasi-executive leadership. The agencies of international organization are still too nearly exclusively the domain of national statesmanship, too dependent upon the initiative of men who, by the nature of their positions, tend to be fundamentally spokesmen for a narrow national interest and viewpoint. Given the meaningfulness of the national state as the basic unit of today's world, it is necessary and proper that state-oriented men should *dispose*; given the reality of the ties of interdependence which unite the nations in a common destiny, it is necessary and proper that world-oriented men should *propose*.

We have made some progress in the development of openings for international statesmanship, particularly in the office of the Secretary-General in the League and the UN and the corresponding position in the specialized agencies, and, most recently, in the North Atlantic Organization. The position of the independent commissioner, originated in the High Authority of the European Coal and Steel Community and imitated in the structural designs for Euratom and Euro-market, provides a major opportunity for the emergence of leadership on a higher level than that of national interest. Similarly, the device of the permanent chairman, as it applies to the Councils of the Food and Agriculture Organization and the International Civil Aviation Organization, offers significant possibilities for development.

In practice, a few outstanding individuals have undertaken imaginatively and adventurously to develop the potentialities of those offices. The list of international officials who have undertaken to push beyond the limits of administrative functions to make creative contributions to world order must certainly include such names as Albert Thomas, Trygve Lie, Dag Hammarskjold, Brock Chisholm, David Morse, and Jean Monnet. Opportunities for statesmanlike service to the global community have come to, and been grasped by, such men as Count Bernadotte, Ralph Bunche, Frank Graham, and General E. L. M. Burns. Nor should it be assumed that the pioneering development of international leadership has been restricted to secretariat officials and other formally "internationalized" individuals. The League period provided occasional examples of national statesmen, most frequently representing small states, who found it possible to give loyal service to the interests of their nations and yet to transcend their national status in becoming spokesmen for an international point of view; Nansen was not less "Nansen of Norway" in becoming Nansen of the World. The names of Paul-Henri Spaak and Lester B. Pearson come to mind when one surveys the decade after World War II for evidence of the continuing development of international statesmanship among governmental leaders. Significant beginnings have been made in exploiting the possibilities of the two functions which I would regard as the major tasks of international leadership: the provision of disinterested mediatorial assistance to participants in disputes, and the provision of independent initiative, reflecting concern for the general welfare of mankind, in the formulation and execution of international programs and policies. Moreover, this sort of leadership has on occasion been welcomed, honored, and even requested by national statesmen, individually and collectively.

However, the role of the spokesman for the international interest is still too marginal, too exceptional, too poorly defined, too grudgingly accepted. The prospects for the increasing usefulness of multilateral institutions are tied up with the possibility of giving ever larger scope to international statesmanship.

In summary, the usefulness of the modern multilateral technique varies with the uses to which it is put. The injection of multilateralism directly into the contention between quarreling states is a risky business, subject to serious abuse. It is likely to create impediments to successful negotiation unless it is controlled with a careful regard for the delicacy of conciliatory possibilities which is all too rarely dominant in international political assemblies. In this sense, the critic of multilateral diplomacy is justified in deploring the trend toward the big, wide-open international debate.

But the management of international affairs involves a broad range of activities to which the principle of multilateralism is entirely appropriate and, in fact, increasingly indispensable. It is important that the world should learn to avoid the misuse of multilateralism which unleashes a bull in the diplomatic china shop. It is equally important that the world should continue the encouraging progress that it has made in developing multilateral contributions to the accomplishment of tasks that are vital to all who live in the age of interdependence.

Crisis Management

Harlan Cleveland

To judge from the daily news, the management of American foreign policy is the art of throwing ourselves into one crisis after another. By shifting the spotlight from one trouble spot to the next, the impression is created that the United States Government deals exclusively in short-range reactions to external emergencies.

Most of the people engaged in the management of American foreign policy, most of the time, are not working on the headline crises, but on other subjects. A round of tariff negotiations, a student exchange program, the use of surplus food for economic growth, the tedious but important process of getting to know hundreds of leading personalities in more than a hundred foreign countries, the analysis of bits and pieces of intelligence from all over the world, the selection and instruction of government delegates to 500 conferences a year— these and many, many other necessary works are also "American foreign policy."

Yet in the upper reaches of our Government, and particularly at the level of the President and his nearest echelon of advisers, the newspaper version of relative priorities is not, after all, so far from the facts. The President, the Secretaries of State and Defense, the Director of Central Intelligence and several dozen other men do spend a very large part of their time working on the crises of the moment. (This does not, paradoxically, mean that long-range policy is neglected; for it is often at moments of crisis that the most basic long-range decisions about foreign policy are made.)

The highest officials of our Government spend their time on crisis management because there is no other way for responsible men to take the responsibility for crucial decisions. For the problem of

SOURCE: "Crisis Diplomacy," *Foreign Affairs*, vol. 41 (July 1963), pp. 638–49.

decision-making in our complicated world is not how to get the problem simple enough so that we can all understand it; the problem is to get our thinking about the problem as complex as humanly possible—and thus approach (we can never match) the complexity of the real world around us. And only the highest officials are in a position thus to maximize the complexities.

Albert Einstein is supposed to have said that every proposition should be as simple as possible—but not one bit simpler. The decision-maker in any large-scale enterprise—and *a fortiori* the maker of decisions in international affairs—has to immerse himself *personally* in the full complexity of the problem at hand. "Completed staff work" is the last thing he wants, or should want, from his advisers. For if he is to make a responsible decision, he must himself measure the options and filter the imagined consequences of each through his most dependable computer, which is his own brain.

By the same token, "contingency planning" must normally deal with many contingencies which do not, as things work out, come to pass. Last fall, countless man-hours went into contingency planning for the crises elsewhere which were thought to be the Soviets' possible reaction to a quarantine of Cuba. Yet contingency planning is never wasted—for it develops the analytical skills of the contingency planners and thus puts the Government in a more "ready" position.

The most usable end-product of planning is not a paper, but a person thoroughly immersed in the subject—a person whose mind is trained to act, having taken everything into account, on the spur of the moment. And that is why the ultimate decision-maker must himself participate in the planning exercise. A busy boxer, training for the bout of his life, cannot afford to let his sparring-partners do all his daily calisthenics for him.

The management of a foreign-policy crisis, then, is an exciting, demanding form of organized thinking, in which the maximum degree of complexity must be sifted through the minds of those few men in a position to take the ultimate responsibility for action. And as Josiah Royce said: "Thinking is like loving and dying; each of us must do it for himself."

Is there a pattern to so personal a process? At least five lessons about crisis management seem to emerge with some clarity from the talk-filled rooms where the makers of policy foregather and our destiny is shaped.

Lesson No. I: Keep Your Objectives Limited. Somewhere in his writings Emerson advises young people to be very careful in deciding what they most want out of life—for they are likely to get it. A similar, but qualified, principle applies to American foreign policy: select your objective carefully, for *if it is limited enough* you are quite likely to achieve it. International politics, like local or national politics, is the art of the possible, but in international politics the price of overreaching the possible could be nuclear extinction.

In the Cuba missile crisis, the President decided that since an adverse shift in the world power balance was in the making, our basic security interests required the removal of "offensive weapons" from Cuba. That term might be subject to varying interpretations having to do with both weaponry and purpose; but clearly it covered the I.R.B.M.s and M.R.B.M.s, the I.L.-28 medium-range bombers and nuclear warheads for these and any other weapons. For this over-riding but still limited goal the President was prepared to commit U.S. power and prestige to the hilt.

Critics now say that the objective should have been broader, that the outright elimination of both the Soviet presence and Castro-Communism from Cuba should have been the objective. . . . But the judgment of the moment, confirmed by the eloquent silence of those critics at the time, was that the missiles and bombers were the only threat so great as to require the immediate counter-threat of force to remove them. The Soviet troops are a dangerous nuisance, and we should and will continue our efforts to get them out. But they do not represent—as the missiles did—a fundamental change in the balance of world power. Castro, too, is a serious problem, but relief from the embarrassment of his presence in the Caribbean is not to be measured in megadeaths throughout the Northern Hemisphere. In the Cuba missile crisis, then, a limited objective was attained brilliantly—partly, at least, because it was specific, limited and attainable.

In the [Democratic Republic of the] Congo [now Zaire], too, the Administration's objective was a limited one. In 1960 President Eisenhower decided to back a United Nations peace force for the Congo, instead of responding to the new Congolese Government's urgent appeal for our direct intervention. Neither then nor since has the United States Government undertaken to prevent internal trouble in the Congo except to the extent that such trouble invited foreign intervention and therefore threatened (in U.N. Charter language) the Congo's "territorial integrity and political independence." Foreign intervention in fact took place—including the returning Belgian paratroops and a large-scale attempt by the Soviet Union to establish its military presence in the Congo; and foreign funds and leadership were plainly evident in both the Communist-backed sedition of the Stanleyville régime and the secession based on copper revenues in South Katanga. But our concern with the Congo's internal troubles has been carefully limited to the original objectives by both the Eisenhower and the Kennedy Administrations.

* * *

In all these examples our objectives are limited, not by some absolute yardstick, but by a relative standard which matches them with our vital interests. Since our "must" list cannot include everything we would like to see happen in a turbulent world, the first task of crisis diplomacy is to decide what immediate aims are really worth the impressive resources we can deploy to achieve them.

Lesson No. 2: Decide How Far You Would Go. Having limited his aims to match the vital interests of the United States, an American President facing a foreign-policy crisis must make another decision: how far down the road to the use of force he would, realistically, be willing to travel if things go from bad to worse. This is partly a judgment about his allies: who will be with him in the first instance— and in the last? But in the ultimate clutch would he—honestly now —order United States armed forces into action to support the policy, and if so, on what scale?

Some version of these questions must also be asked by decision-makers elsewhere, including those in the Kremlin. But in a democratic society so powerful that it must lead, not follow, the early facing of these questions is of the essence. For on matters of life and death, a democracy cannot bluff. It has to mean business.

A democratic government can—for a little while at least—cloak its tactics in official secrecy. But it does well to assume that its ultimate intentions are bound to show. Many people are looking on; many are asking questions; there is too much tradition and habit and impulse toward openness for a democracy to keep a very big secret for very long. And while this adds to the frustrations of doing business in world affairs, it is, in the end, not a price but a blessing of the system.

In the crisis over Soviet missile bases in Cuba, it was plain as day that the United States would, if need be, eliminate them by force —and alone if necessary. It was this very clarity of resolve which made our quarantine action, that relatively restrained first response, so extraordinarily effective. The Soviets had to crank into their calculations, not just the effect of a naval quarantine, but their own willingness to escalate to hostilities that might lead to nuclear war as the price of keeping their missiles on an island off Florida. Looked at this way, it simply did not seem worthwhile, and they took the missiles and bombers out.

In the Congo, it was clear from the outset that if the Soviets threatened to introduce a military presence in central Africa, we would have to reply in kind. Yet this was one of the last things we wanted to have happen—which mainly accounts for our consistent support for the alternative afforded by the United Nations.

Perhaps it will illuminate the central importance of deciding about the ultimate use of force if we note some cases closer to the other end of the crisis spectrum.

* * *

At the extreme end of the spectrum, there is the case of Goa. The future of this Portuguese enclave in India should have been negotiated—as had already been done with the similar French and British enclaves. The Goans themselves might well have been asked what they thought about their future, but neither side was prepared to ask them. Our Government and other governments worked hard behind the scenes to get talks started and to prevent the use of force in Goa. But the Indians did not want to wait any longer, and the Portuguese did not want to talk.

When the crunch came, the United States like other governments had to face up honestly to whether it was prepared to defend Goa from the Indians, and had to concede that this would not be a prudent and sensible use of its armed forces. As an exercise in random opinion-sampling, I have asked hundreds of Americans since then whether they would have wanted to put the Marines into Goa, or even go there themselves to fight. I have yet to find a volunteer.

Since nobody was prepared to stop the Indians by force, there was no possibility of the United Nations "doing something" about Goa. We and others publicly complained, with irrefutable logic, that India's use of military force to accomplish the takeover was in flat violation of her commitments under the Charter. But we and other military powers are the Charter's teeth; in cases where we are not prepared to bite, the U.N.'s only recourse is moral suasion—and the Indians knew it.

Lesson No. 3: Creep Up Carefully on the Use of Force. The "next step" in a foreign crisis depends, then, on what limits are set to the objectives sought, and how far we are willing to go to achieve them. But even if the responsible executive decides he is willing to risk nuclear war for an objective of vital concern, it behooves him to select first the gentlest form of force that has a good chance of being effective.

The purpose of the use of force is not to kill people we fear, nor is it to provide a release for the frustrations of the user. It is to accomplish the limited objective sought in the particular case, with the least risk of escalation to more damaging forms of force.

Thus in the Cuba crisis, the advantage of a naval quarantine over an air strike was that it put the option of starting violent action up to the Soviets, and gave them 48 hours (the time it would take the nearest Soviet freighter to reach the quarantine line) to think it over. Now, with hindsight wisdom, we know that decision was right. Latent power worked so well that power in being was never engaged at all.

Responsible political leaders will always start the use of force at the cautious end of the spectrum of possibilities, for force is a one-way moving staircase: it is easy to escalate, very hard to de-escalate. Much theoretical argument and many books on thermonuclear war have partly obscured the very wide range of lesser ways to apply force. Yet it is precisely in the controlled, political use of force that we have useful current experience. We know that once the decision is made to go much further if necessary, many moves short of war are both possible and effective. We can move military equipment around to dramatize our resolve—as in positioning tanks in Friedrichstrasse in Berlin or moving the Seventh Fleet into the Formosa Strait. We can shift ground forces into positions of readiness for quick action—as in the placement of American troops on the Thai border during last year's Laos crisis. We can inject a military force into a trouble spot to keep the lid from blowing off, and then encourage the U.N. to take a hand—as President Eisenhower did in 1958 by landing Marines in Lebanon. We can help finance and provide logistic support to a U.N. peace force, as we have done for six and a half years in the Middle East and for three years in the Congo. In the hands of rational men, the escalator to nuclear war is very long, with many steps and the opportunity for much talk along the way.

The use of force in a dangerous world demands adherence to a doctrine of restraint—the cool, calm and collected manipulation of power for collective security—and the sophisticated mixture of diplomacy with that power. For until the ultimate thermonuclear button is pressed, and mutual destruction evolves from mutual desperation, force is just another manner of speaking—with a rather expensive vocabulary. But if force is to be a persuasive form of discourse, its modulations must carry not only the latent threat of more force but equally the assurance that it is under the personal control of responsible men.

Lesson No. 4: Widen the Community of the Concerned. The unilateral use of power is becoming as old-fashioned as horse cavalry. Even when the decision to employ power is essentially our own, we find it highly desirable to widen the community of the concerned—to obtain sanction for the necessary "next step" from the broadest practicable segment of the international community.

It was President Truman who made the first decision to stand against aggression in Korea, and it was ultimately American power which enabled the South Koreans to throw it back. But on the day of the President's decision the United States Government went into the U.N. Security Council and transformed our own resolve into a system of collective security. Acting under commission as executive agent of the United Nations, we later welcomed the participation of 14 other nations in the defense of Korea.

* * *

In the Cuba crisis, the decision to apply American power was enveloped from the very outset in a plan for widening the communities of the concerned. In the hours before President Kennedy unveiled the Cuba scenario in his television speech of October 22, dozens of allies were made privy to our plan of action. While the President was speaking, a formal request for an emergency meeting of the Security Council was delivered to its president. The next morning Secretary Rusk presented to the Organization of American States in emergency meeting a proposal for collective action; and that afternoon the Rio Pact nations decided on a quarantine of Cuba and continued aerial surveillance as minimum first steps. The same afternoon, Ambassador Adlai Stevenson opened in the Security Council the case for the United States. And not until that evening, October 23, did President Kennedy, acting under the Rio Pact, proclaim the quarantine.

In the days that followed, the United Nations went to work in three different ways. It served as the forum in which we could demonstrate the credibility of our evidence about the Soviet missile sites, and explain to the world why we and our Latin American allies had to act on this evidence. Then the U.N., through the Secretary-General, served as a middleman in crucial parts of the dialogue between President Kennedy and Chairman Khrushchev which led to a peaceful solution. It was an appeal from U Thant which Chairman Khrushchev was answering when he said that his ships would not challenge the quarantine line. Finally, the U.N. was ready, at our suggestion, to provide inspectors to examine missile sites in Cuba, to make sure the missiles were gone.

Castro, as we know, would not allow U.N. inspectors into his island. But while we would have preferred to have him accept onsite inspection, his refusal to cooperate with the United Nations had useful side-effects. For Castro thus branded himself an outlaw, and convinced practically all the vocal bystanders that this was not a case of little Cuba versus the big United States; this was intransigent Cuba thumbing its nose at the world community.

The object of our policy was to get rid of those missiles and bombers, peacefully if possible. There is no doubt that debates and operations in the Organization of American States and the United Nations had much to do with the fact that most of the world came to agree with this aim, and thus helped to achieve it.

To merge our efforts with the efforts of others does not, of course, subtract anything from our "national sovereignty," nor does it inhibit something called our "freedom of action." Notions like these are a hangover from the now-obsolete assumption that, acting alone, we are sovereign and free. In these days of interdependence, a stronger case can be made for the contrary proposition: that in each crisis we are born naked—and free to use our power in concert with whatever group of nations is most relevant to the task at hand. That this is true of little countries hardly needs to be argued; it is, indeed, why most small countries are so partial to the United Nations. That it is becoming true of all countries, even the most powerful, is one of the lessons of each foreign-policy crisis in our time. The matrix of alliances and international organizations, more even than the power of individual nations, is the hallmark of modern international relations.

Lesson No. 5: The Law You Make May Be Your Own. In the ebb and flow of crisis diplomacy, those who watch the "Operational Immediate" cables and write the contingency papers are very much involved with international law, and with its unanswered questions. Laymen as well as lawyers can readily perceive how principles that are valid in one area may be silly in another, how improvised instruments tend to harden into permanent institutions, how scientific invention and technological innovation outrace man's thinking about law, how old doctrine grows obsolete and gets altered in practice. If we are to add one more "lesson from flaps we have known" it would be this: Watch carefully the precedents you set. You will have to live with the institutions you create. The law you make may be your own.

Consider what is happening to the doctrine of non-intervention in the internal affairs of other nations. The facts of modern international relations are clear: nations are deeply involved in each other's internal affairs, through aid programs and military training and fellowships for students and leaders; through the beneficent dispatch of culture and the acrimonious exchange of propaganda; through a thousand pluralistic channels ranging from trade unions to the Children's Fund. When the question comes up, we tell ourselves that this is all right as long as the government of the receiving country asks the foreigner to come and allows him to stay. But our generation has also witnessed too many perversions of this practice—who can forget the "request" from the Kadar government for the Russian tanks that crushed the freedom fighters in Hungary?—to be sure that it is the last word in law for an era of deep mutual involvement in each other's internal affairs.

Consider, further, the mutations in air and space law. The law used to be simple: you cannot fly through my air space unless I say you can. But what if I fly over your nation in *outer* space, above the "air"? Judging from Soviet and American practice, and from a U.S. resolution unanimously passed by the U.N. General Assembly in 1961, the doctrine of air space runs out of gas somewhere in the upper stratosphere.

How is civilized man to set standards on intervention or surveillance or on a host of other matters which differentiate the world community from a jungle? In our world, the standards are being set and international law being written more and more by the actions and reactions of international organizations. Every action in every crisis has implications for the United Nations peace system; it can be strengthened—or weakened—by the manner in which it is put to work in each crisis. So this consideration, too, must pass through the mind of the decision-maker.

Most citizens would be surprised how often, when the world thinks we in Washington are working on the next day's tactics, we are instead discussing the long-run growth of law and institutions, the issues suddenly illumined in the dead of night by the blinding light of a Cuba, a Laos or a Congo.

When we put all these lessons together, perhaps we have nothing more than another, more up-to-date, way of thinking about political leadership in its most complex form. We have said that the decision-maker in times of crisis must keep his objectives in line with his nation's vital interests, must decide how far he would go in the clutch, must use force gently while widening the community of the concerned, and must set only those precedents he would be willing to live with later.

If the known factors and the rational considerations indicate a clear preference for one policy alternative over any other, then decision-making is easy—and responsible criticism correspondingly more difficult. That is why such decisions seldom reach the Secretary of State or the President. It is when a rational weighing of measurable factors still leaves two or more reasonable options that the man who makes the ultimate decision must somehow stuff the whole problem into his own head, and add those priceless ingredients—personal judgment, sense of direction, feel for the total political environment in which the decision is made.

The fact that the most important decisions are often close decisions, that the personal judgment of political leaders is so deeply involved, makes them peculiarly easy to criticize. But the responsible critic of foreign-policy decisions must also wrap his mind around the full complexity of the problem. He too must think in terms of limited objectives; he too must decide when and where he would use force, how he would deal with allies and neutrals, what laws and institutions he is prepared to make—or break. If the critic is not willing to propose an alternative policy that meets these tests of relevance, then he is not criticizing American foreign policy but merely scratching an itch of his own.

At the moment of action the man who has to take the personal responsibility for the final decision, and face the political crossfire it may produce, is alone with his own understanding, his own moral gyroscope and his own fund of courage. It takes no courage to bluster; it takes some to stand up to a mortal threat that plainly has to be faced. But what takes the most gumption is to persevere in a decision that takes months or years to prove itself. There were moments during the chronic Congo crisis when the brickbats were very thick in Washington; but the President stuck to his position, simply because the alternative of great-power confrontation in the middle of Africa seemed even more unattractive than the swelling noise level on his Congo policy.

The capacity to go on working with brickbats whizzing past the ears is, of course, the first qualification for public leadership in an open society. But the saving grace in the management of foreign-policy crises is this: dyspeptic criticism of a policy that turns out to be successful has a remarkably short half-life.

5

Envoys Ordinary and Extraordinary

*The choice of a prince's ministers is a matter of no little importance;
They are either good or not according to the prudence of the prince.
The first impression that one gets of a ruler and of his brains is from
seeing the men that he has about him. When they are competent and
faithful one can always consider him wise, as he has been able to
recognize their ability and keep them faithful. But when they are the
reverse, one can always form an unfavorable opinion of him, because
the first mistake that he makes is in making this choice.*

NICCOLÒ MACHIAVELLI, *The Prince*

*Nations, it has frequently been observed, are judged by their repre-
sentatives abroad. For this if for no other reasons governments should
take special pains in selecting their envoys.*

CHARLES W. THAYER, *Diplomat*

Earlier chapters surveyed various aspects of the art of modern diplomacy; chapter 5 turns to an examination of the men and women of
the diplomatic community, their essential qualities, their historic profiles, and their status and potential.

In the two opening essays Thomas A. Bailey, an eminent American diplomatic historian, characterizes the consummate diplomat. His
first treatise, "Qualities of American Diplomats," reads like a modern
companion to Baldassare Castiglione's *Book of the Courtier*. The
personal qualities of Bailey's ideal diplomat, like Castiglione's model
courtier, include intelligence, temperance, imagination, loyalty, foresight, objectivity, strength, dignity, and more—in short, nearly all
virtues and assets attainable by man. If Bailey's first effort is reminiscent of Castiglione, his "Advice for Diplomats" resembles Niccolo

Machiavelli's *The Prince*. Bailey prescribes a series of fundamental and pragmatic maxims that are essential for the successful diplomat. An image of the perfect diplomatist—at least by Bailey's standards—emerges from the combination of personal qualities and guidelines for action presented in these essays.

Such paragons of the diplomatic art rarely emerge in the real world, however. Nevertheless, according to Elmer Plischke, American diplomats often deserve more credit than their critics are willing to concede. In "Profile of United States Diplomats: Bicentennial Review and Future Projection," he shows trends in the typical diplomat's age, nature of appointment, number of assignments, duration of mission, earlier and subsequent careers, and similar topics. Plischke demonstrates that the popular perception of the diplomat as a "rich, punctilious Beau Brummel" and other equally derogatory characterizations are most often "misty preconceptions" founded on unsubstantiated conjecture or isolated illustration.

Even so, there is always room to improve the effectiveness of the modern diplomat and, according to J. Robert Schaetzel, to keep him from degenerating into a "passive, acquiescent clerk." Although recognition of the need for improvement is widespread, prescriptions for meeting it differ markedly. "Role of the Ambassador: Existing Status and Proposal for Improvement," by Foy D. Kohler, argues for retaining the traditional capacity of the ambassador but invigorating his charge and strengthening his posture. On the other hand, in "Modernizing the Role of the Ambassador," Schaetzel suggests that the traditional mission of the diplomat has been rendered obsolete by the New Diplomacy. Rather than empowering an ambassador—whom he calls "an endangered species" and an "anachronism" —to execute an obsolete task, he calls for a redefinition of the ambassadorial function. The diplomat should surrender the realm of strategic management of foreign affairs to Washington, he says, and concern himself largely with matters of tactical importance that can best be dealt with in the field. These authors—both retired professionals—concede that revamping the diplomatic corps and increasing its effectiveness are difficult tasks because of the inertia of tradition affecting the career service, but they also agree that change and improvement are imperative if the modern ambassador is to have a commanding function in the new diplomacy.

Qualities of American Diplomats

THOMAS A. BAILEY

Diplomats are often caricatured as frock-coated bunglers whose chief occupation is to get us into wars, or at least to stir up more trouble than they settle. They are also supposed to have thick heads, further thickened by alcohol. Zealous members of the Woman's Christian Temperance Union have long insisted that America's so-called diplomatic defeats at Yalta in 1945 were due to the devastating effects of Stalin's secret weapon—vodka.

What in fact should be the qualifications of the ideal American ambassador?

Without being a stuffed shirt, he must first of all have presence and dignity. He must in his person convey something of the grandeur of the country he represents, as Commodore Perry succeeded in doing in Japan in the 1850's. If he cannot command respect, he is not likely to receive respect. He must be courteous, gracious, tactful, tolerant. He must have simple good manners and not emulate John Randolph, who, when presented to the Russian Czar in 1830, allegedly blurted out, "Howaya Emperor? And how's the madam?"

A diplomat must possess the necessary social graces and entertain appropriately, although Mrs. Perle Mesta in Luxembourg, with superabundant private means, recently left the impression that this was all she was doing. The ambassador abroad is the eyes, ears, mouth, and even nose of his government in Washington. The more he can get around, the more information he can pick up, especially after the fourth round of cocktails. As Secretary of State Robert Lansing once remarked, the individual whom you see in your office the day after a successful social affair is likely to be more accommodating than one whom you have never met socially.

SOURCE: "A Hall of Fame for American Diplomats," *Virginia Quarterly Review*, vol. 36 (Summer 1960), pp. 390–404.

Above all, the diplomat must avoid bad taste. He should on all occasions dress appropriately, and never appear at his office, as one of our representatives in the Caribbean once did, clad in a bare red undershirt. He must not ruin valuable Persian rugs by spitting tobacco juice on them, as at least one of our less polished envoys once did. If he drinks, he must hold his liquor like a gentleman. (Unfortunately the record reveals embarrassing departures from this rule, notably when one of our ministers in Germany was so drunk that he could not be officially presented to the Emperor.) Whatever the provocation, he must not become involved in fist fights, as did our Minister to Russia (Cassius M. Clay) in the 1860's, nor in café brawls, as did our Minister to Bulgaria (George H. Earle) in 1941. His relations with the opposite sex must be conventional or, if not, exceptionally discreet. General Daniel E. Sickles, who had lost a leg at Gettysburg, not only did his best to provoke war as Minister to Spain in the 1870's, but created a scandal by becoming the paramour of the adulterous ex-Queen Isabella, then exiled in Paris.

The ambassador must be highly resourceful and intelligent. It is gratifying to note how many, including John Quincy Adams, John Hay, and Dwight W. Morrow, could wear the key of Phi Beta Kappa. He must be literate and usually is, although Romulus M. Saunders in Spain in the 1840's, according to the Secretary of State, "sometimes murders" the English language. He should be articulate and able to represent the nation properly at the unveiling of monuments and other ceremonial occasions. If he has a flair for oratory, he should hold himself in leash; if he must make speeches, he would do well to confine himself to platitudes about home, mother, and the flag. In the 1890's Ambassador Thomas F. Bayard in London delivered several addresses that were so pro-British as to infuriate the Irish-Americans at home and elicit a vote of censure from the House of Representatives. Above all, the envoy must avoid important new pronouncements on policy, unless specifically instructed to do otherwise. Policy should be made in Washington and implemented by the man in the field.

The diplomat must not only be gifted with keen intelligence but must be broadly informed. If he is to observe as well as see, he cannot know too much about too many different areas of human activity—government, politics, economics, psychology. A comprehensive historical background, including that of the United States and that of the country to which he is accredited, is especially desirable, and in this respect historians like George Bancroft in Prussia and Andrew D. White in Germany had an advantage over their predecessors. Less fortunate was Minister Denby in China in the 1890's; he believed that the Cossacks came from Corsica.

The envoy must not only have the capacity to learn quickly and adjust himself mentally to new situations, but he must possess an uncommon amount of common sense. Canny old Benjamin Franklin, the compiler of Poor Richard's sayings, was wise enough in the ways of men to do a superlative job as American commissioner and minister in Paris during the anxious years of the American War of Independence.

Common sense should be combined with creative imagination and with foresight—the capacity to foresee, as a good chess player must, more than one move ahead. Associated with this quality is perceptiveness, sometimes called "political sense." A cynic once remarked that fortunately many diplomats have long noses because they cannot see beyond the ends of them. Ambassador to Russia Joseph E. Davies, whose "Mission to Moscow" became one of the most insidious weapons of Soviet propaganda in World War II, was badly taken in by the purge trials of the 1930's, even though he was a lawyer by profession.

Ranking high also among the attributes of the superior diplomat is reportorial skill. It would in fact be difficult to name a single qualification for a first-class foreign correspondent that one would not also seek in a first-class foreign envoy. The ambassador, who has long been regarded as a kind of licensed spy, must report the information, plus recommendations, on which his government in Washington can base its policy. The dispatches of Andrew D. White from Berlin in the 1890's were models of penetrating reporting; those of Thomas F. Bayard in London, who had been Secretary of State and who should have known better, consisted largely of pasted-up clippings from British journals. The foreign service has no place for the lazy man or the windy man.

Finally, the diplomat must be an objective reporter. He should tell the truth as he sees it, however unpopular, and even though the way to promotion and pay may lie in sending home rose-colored accounts designed to please his superiors. His assessment may later prove to be erroneous but it must be honest. One of the many unfortunate effects of McCarthyism was to put pressure on the man in the field not to report probable Communist successes lest he later be denounced, demoted, dismissed, and disgraced.

General Charles G. Dawes, with his underslung pipe and picturesque profanity, was sent to the Court of St. James' in the Hoover era, and he reported with some bitterness that "American diplomacy is easy on the brain but hell on the feet." Henry P. Fletcher, ex-ambassador to Italy, counter-quipped, "It depends on which you use."

Both men were stressing an important truth. The diplomatic service is no place for weaklings: it demands good health, physical and nervous. Despite the illusion of glamor, it can be, and often is, grueling work. Standing at the head of a reception line for hours with a frozen smile, attending countless functions, trying to be pleasant at all times to all men—this takes a heavy toll. One also needs a cast-iron digestion to accommodate strange foods—including stewed cat—that may be served. Many a man has regretted that he had only one stomach to give to his country.

Physical courage is also a prime requisite. One must face strange diseases in the tropics, pneumonia in Bolivia and Russia (many men succumbed in pre-penicillin days), and physical injury at the hands of plotters and mobs. Ambassador Robert M. McClintock in Lebanon in 1958 had several close calls from bullets and bombs, while in 1924 Major Robert W. Imbrie, American Vice-Consul in Persia, was beaten to death by a mob of religious fanatics. On the walls of the State Department hangs a plaque commemorating the sixty or so diplomats in our history who were killed while serving on foreign soil.

In the good old horse-and-buggy days, campaign contributors often requested foreign posts for rather irrelevant reasons, including cultural opportunities for wives or daughters, or a more salubrious climate for their own rheumatism or other ailments. President Lincoln is supposed to have told a Congressman who was seeking a foreign post for one of his constituents, "There are nine candidates for the place ahead of you, and every one of them is sicker than yours." One may doubt if the best interests of the United States were being served when John Randolph, then dying of tuberculosis, was sent to chill St. Petersburg in 1830.

The American representative must be a man or woman of the highest integrity. An ambassador has long since been cynically defined as "an honest man, sent to lie abroad for the good of the country." This ancient concept does not square with the American tradition, although there have been painful exceptions. "Tell the truth," replied Sir Henry Wotton when asked by a young diplomatist how best to confuse his adversaries. American diplomacy, which has often been described as of the shirt-sleeves or house-top variety, has generally avoided the devious. Men of transparent integrity, like Charles Francis Adams in

London during the Civil War, have helped their cause by speaking out with vigor and candor.

If integrity is such a prime requisite, we serve the short-range interests of the party rather than the long-range interests of the country by sending abroad men of shady character. President Lincoln bundled Secretary of War Simon Cameron off to St. Petersburg in 1862, when embarrassing scandals began to erupt in the War Department. In 1943 President Franklin Roosevelt, seeking a refuge for the Tammany boss Edward J. Flynn, appointed him minister to Australia, then threatened by Japanese invasion. The resulting public uproar forced a withdrawal of the nomination.

Certain qualities of temperament are essential. The diplomat must be patient, able to stand the boredom of routine with equanimity, as Townsend Harris did in the 1850's in his lonely Japanese outpost. He must be inoffensively persistent, as Robert R. Livingston was in Paris in 1803 while pressing for the acquisition of Louisiana. (One French official offered to give him a certificate as the most importunate diplomat he had ever met.) He must display humility and evenness of temper, as Albert Gallatin conspicuously did during the Ghent negotiations of 1814. The diplomatic service has no place for hotheads like the French expatriate Pierre Soulé, American minister to Spain in the 1850's. He wounded the French ambassador in a duel, handed down an unauthorized ultimatum, and tried to pick a war with Spain over the *Black Warrior* affair. One critic observed that he was more of a matador than an ambassador.

The diplomat must be non-partisan in representing the interests of his country, even though he be a party man at home. The outspoken George Harvey, in his Pilgrims' Club speech in England in 1921, delivered a violent harangue in which he presented the Republican case against the League of Nations. Although he spoke with President Harding's private blessing, he evoked a bitter outcry from the Democrats, whose taxes were helping to pay his salary.

The envoy must be dedicated to his job, and not regard it merely as a plum for political service or for a lush campaign contribution. He must also be devoted to the interests of his own country, and if he is, he will not lose the respect of foreigners. Many a man has fallen into the pit, as was true of Walter Hines Page in England during World War I, of currying favor with his hosts by embracing their viewpoint too wholeheartedly. Page's dispatches home became so pro-British that in effect the British had two ambassadors to the United

States: one in Washington on their payroll, and one in London on ours. The ideal ambassador should not be too popular, unless, like Franklin in France, he can keep his head. Nor should he be unpopular; he should try to steer a safe middle course.

He must also be discreet: the diplomatic service needs no blabbermouths. Frederick Van Dyne—brave man indeed—opined in 1909 that one reason why so few women have risen in the service is their notorious inability to keep a secret. And when the diplomat says something, he must avoid statements that are twistable. The brilliant Ambassador George F. Kennan, provoked beyond endurance, let slip a remark in 1952 about the internment-camp isolation of Western diplomats in Moscow. The Kremlin was quick to seize upon this indiscretion as a pretext for demanding his recall.

The diplomat must be a loyal subordinate, willing to take orders and execute them promptly in the chain of command. John Jay deliberately violated his instructions in Paris and entered upon separate negotiations with the British in 1782. The result in this case turned out to be happy, but complete chaos would result if each envoy were a law unto himself.

The ideal ambassador must be flexible and adaptable, as Anson Burlingame was in Peking in the 1860's. He must be willing, if necessary, to wear knee breeches and walk backward in leaving the presence of royalty. No amount of nonconformity or rebellion, as John Adams noted, will chance ancient customs abroad. He must be willing to yield a little while taking perhaps a little more; and he must be sparing in his use of the flat negative. As the old saying goes, "When a diplomat says 'yes' he means 'perhaps'; when he says 'perhaps' he means 'no'; when he says 'no' he is no diplomat." This observation had more validity before the ungentlemanly Bolsheviks appeared on the scene with short and ugly words and emphatic noes.

No one should enter the diplomatic service who does not like mankind in general and his potential hosts in particular. Handsome, kindly Myron T. Herrick, an able politician, banker, and organizer, distinguished himself in Paris from 1912 to 1914 and again from 1921 to 1929. Such were his qualities of heart and mind, particularly as revealed during the hectic invasion summer of 1914, that the French conferred upon him the Grand Cross of the Legion of Honor and conveyed his remains to America in a French warship after he had died at his post.

Experience must take a high place among the desired qualifications, although no one wants a life-tenure snobocracy. In the morning years of the republic, when we dispatched ill-trained militiamen to the fighting front, we tapped able but inexperienced men like John Adams and John Jay for the diplomatic front. The system worked surprisingly well, partly because men who have achieved distinction in a profession often have the capacity to adjust themselves to diplomacy. The good lawyer in fact can rather quickly acquire the essentials of international law, without which he is definitely handicapped.

But the militia days are gone and the complexities of international life are such that there is little place for the well-meaning amateur, however gifted. We must discard the naïve notion that diplomacy is the only profession that requires neither preparation nor experience. American diplomacy has now become deeply entangled with power politics, and this largely explains why we train selected career diplomats at the National War College. Significantly, the roster of American ambassadors to Moscow since 1942 includes two admirals (Standley, Kirk) and one general (Smith). The chief of mission often finds himself the co-ordinator of a complex organization involving economic aid, military aid, propaganda efforts, and other activities, all of which call for both business experience and administrative skill. In such a capacity, and with the aid of the permanent career staff, an able politician-businessman, like Chester Bowles in India, has often acquitted himself creditably.

Knowledge of the relevant foreign languages is likewise eminently desirable. If a Turkish ambassador were to come to Washington knowing no English, we can imagine how seriously handicapped he would be in attempting to sample newspaper opinion, secure the views of the American in the street, discharge his social obligations, and communicate orally with the Secretary of State. Similar difficulties would beset the American Ambassador in Ankara if he knew no Turkish. Linguistic gifts in themselves are no guarantee of diplomatic competence, but if the envoy has the other essential qualifications he can add immeasurably to his effectiveness by communicating with his hosts in their own tongue.

Prestige can also be helpful. Robert Todd Lincoln, the somewhat disappointing son of the Great Emancipator, went to the Court of St. James's in 1889, and there found his influence greater because of the name he bore. A distinguished general, like the late George C. Marshall in China after World War II, normally finds his path made smoother, especially if he is known, as was true in this case, to have the ear of the President.

Finally, the top-ranking American ambassador should have money —made, married, or inherited. One of the supreme paradoxes of our vaunted democracy is that in the upper diplomatic reaches, thanks to a penny-pinching Congress, we are a plutocracy. The outlay for entertainment at a half dozen or so of our key embassies—notably London, Paris, and Rome—is such that only a wealthy man can provide the additional forty to seventy thousand dollars a year. For such posts the first question is not: Does he have the attributes herein outlined? It is: Does he have money? The list of ambassadors to London since the late 1920's reads like a millionaires' club: the Daweses, the Mellons, the Binghams, the Kennedys, the Harrimans, the Aldrichs, the Whitneys. Many a man of the highest capabilities has been compelled to decline the honor of bankrupting himself in the service of his rich but parsimonious country.

Before unveiling my nominees for a Hall of Fame, I must first of all explain why certain names will not appear.

A man of exceptional ability, like the famed lawyer Joseph H. Choate in London (1899–1905), may have the ill fortune to be serving at a time when routine is the order of the day. On the other hand, Robert R. Livingston happened to be minister to France in 1803 when Napoleon, for reasons purely realistic, decided to dump all of Louisiana into the lap of the United States. This lucky windfall has enshrined Livingston in our textbooks, while Choate is embalmed in the archives of the Department of State.

We shall also have to keep in mind whether we are considering the B.C. or the post-B.C. era—before the cable or after the cable. Livingston, in violation of his specific instructions, could take it upon himself to sign the Louisiana purchase treaties because the bargain was too overwhelming and time was too short. "Thim was th' days," remarked the droll Mr. Dooley, "whin ye'd have a good time as an ambassadure." But the wire and then the wireless wrought a vast change. When ex-Secretary of State Richard Olney declined the ambassadorship to Britain in his seventy-eighth year, he supposedly declared, "An Ambassador is nobody these days: he sits at the other end of a cable and does what he is told." The grain of truth in this complaint has sprouted into the myth that today the envoy is nothing but a white-spatted puppet dancing to the strings pulled in Washington. The fact is that there is still no substitute for a personable and perceptive diplomat on the ground, particularly one who has a delicate sense of timing.

An additional cause of confusion is the reflected glamor of distinction in another high office or field of endeavor. John Marshall was a distinguished Chief Justice, but hardly a distinguished envoy to France in 1797–1798. John Quincy Adams was an eminent Secretary of State, but less eminent earlier as a diplomat abroad. During the nineteenth century, in the absence of Fulbright grants, the authorities in Washington would rather frequently send abroad literary luminaries—"damn literary fellers" Simon Cameron dubbed them. Washington Irving served as minister to Spain and James Russell Lowell as minister to Britain; Nathaniel Hawthorne, Bret Harte, and William D. Howells all occupied consular posts. John Hay, himself a minor literary figure, ultimately achieved a global reputation as Secretary of State, but his earlier career as ambassador in London was unspectacular.

Another source of misunderstanding lies in the behind-the-scenes nature of diplomacy. The most successful diplomat, like the most successful secret-service agent, usually works the most quietly, as Townsend Harris did in Japan. The headline hog—like theatrical Pierre Soulé in Spain in the 1850's—has no place in the foreign service. If he crows over his triumphs, his diplomatic adversaries will be doubly vigilant to prevent further loss of face. The highly skilled negotiator achieves many of his successes without either his opponents or the mass of his contemporary countrymen knowing they are successes.

The career diplomat, who knows the value of prudence, is at a disadvantage in attaining fame. Men like Henry White and Joseph C. Grew, both of whom served for many years at varied posts, were the victims of day-to-day routine and professional discretion. On the other hand, politicians like the noisy George Harvey at the Court of St. James's in the 1920's, need have little concern for their diplomatic career. It presumably will last no longer than the incumbent administration, which in turn is at the mercy of both the ballot and the bullet.

With the foregoing qualifications in mind, I herewith propose six names as the nucleus of an American Diplomatic Hall of Fame.

First chronologically, and still towering above all others, stands Benjamin Franklin, the canny and urbane Jack-of-all-trades. His spectacular experiments with electricity, to say nothing of his other notable achievements, had already marked him as one of the giants of the age. Dedicating the tag end of a busy life to his country, he played a vital rôle in securing the crucially important French Alliance of 1778 and the Peace Treaty of 1783. He had virtually all of the major qualifications herein set forth, including a quaint knowledge of French and more than a decade of diplomatic experience as a colonial agent.

His fur-cap showmanship caught the fancy of the French, and further established him as our first great public-relations expert. His wife had died—and a socially conscious wife can be a valuable asset—but this presumed handicap merely increased his mobility and popularity among the French ladies. His intellect was still razor sharp; his tact was Chesterfieldian; his writing skill superb. His only major weakness was a diminution of energy resulting from gout, bladder stone, and other infirmities of old age. But an ailing Franklin in his seventies had enough left to qualify him easily for our first place.

Albert Gallatin, though Swiss born and speaking with a foreign accent, ranks as a statesman in the same bracket with Jefferson, Hamilton, John Adams, and John Quincy Adams. For sheer nobility of character he had few equals and no superiors among his contemporaries. His greatest diplomatic achievement came at the peace table of Ghent, where he held together the quarreling American quintet long enough to extract an unexpectedly favorable treaty from the British negotiators at the end of the War of 1812. Highly intelligent and literate, moderate and conciliatory, patient and persistent, yet withal tactful, he continued to serve his adopted country admirably both in Paris and in London. His only real handicap was an unfounded suspicion among his countrymen that he had never become truly Americanized.

Charles Francis Adams—a son of John Quincy Adams, and a grandson of John Adams—was born with diplomacy in his blood. While a boy with his father in St. Petersburg, he had mastered French so well as to prefer it to English. Ultimately graduating from Harvard (Phi Beta Kappa honors), he became a prominent lawyer and politician, and in 1861 was sent by President Lincoln to London. Armed with a famous name, an English-like reserve, and a knowledge of British character growing out of two rugged years in an English boarding school, he raised the prestige of American diplomacy not only in England but also on the Continent. Through four desperate years of the Civil War he labored valiantly and successfully to stave off the British intervention which would have guaranteed the success of the Confederacy. In handling a series of harrowing crises, his foot never slipped. He commanded respect by his outstanding ability, his balance of mind (in which he excelled both his father and grandfather), his logic, his moderation, his reasonableness, his evenness of temper, his persistence, his directness, his sincerity, and his transparent integrity. While valiantly upholding the intrests of his own country, he won the admiration of his hosts. In 1868, when his name was mentioned during a debate in the House of Commons, the assemblage broke into cheers.

Townsend Harris, a largely self-educated New York merchant who helped found the College of the City of New York, served as consul general and then minister in Japan from 1855 to 1862. A bachelor and formerly an intemperate drinker, he became a total abstainer, and despite bad food, rats, cockroaches, cholera, and lonesomeness—he once did not see an American ship for fourteen months—he finally won the confidence of the Shogun's régime by his frankness, tact, patience, persistence, and forbearance. His great achievement was concluding the epochal commercial treaty of 1858 with Japan during an era of nerve-racking domestic turmoil. The remarkable influence that he exercised on the Japanese government stemmed in part from his determination, unlike that of some of his Western colleagues, not to take undue advantage of Japan's weakness.

Anson Burlingame, a prominent Massachusetts Congressman, lawyer, orator, and politician, was sent to Peking in 1861 as a reward for having helped elect Lincoln president. Magnetic, urbane, candid, tolerant, and devoted to the cause of the underdog, he developed a strong admiration for the Chinese. Such were his qualities of personality that, although a novice, he almost immediately assumed leadership of the diplomatic corps in Peking during a period of acute East-West tension. Although best known for the Treaty of 1868 regulating Chinese immigration, he probably staved off the partition of China by the European powers, or at least a serious encroachment on her sovereignty. When he was about to resign, the Peking government appointed him head of a special diplomatic mission of Chinese to the principal Western powers, even though he spoke no Chinese. This compliment was not only unique but eloquent testimony to the impression he had made by his fairness, sympathy, and absence of race prejudice.

Dwight W. Morrow is a prime example of how a gifted amateur may become a professional almost overnight. A graduate of Amherst with Phi Beta Kappa distinction, he enjoyed a remarkable career as a lawyer, a House of Morgan banker, a politician, a humanitarian, and an organizer. (He received the Distinguished Service Medal for work in organizing Allied transport in World War I.) One of his great gifts was an uncanny knack of finding the common ground on which differences could be resolved. Appointed Ambassador to Mexico in 1927 by his former Amherst classmate President Coolidge, he stepped into a seemingly hopeless imbroglio over oil and agrarian rights. "I know what I can do for the Mexicans," he remarked. "I can *like* them." Small wonder that the masses greeted him on his travels with enthusiastic cries of approval. Morrow's intelligence, tact, sympathetic understanding, and a capacity to inspire trust wrought a diplomatic miracle in an incredibly short time.

Other names are no doubt deserving of a place in our Hall of Fame. Some critics will miss John Quincy Adams, who may properly be reserved for high rank among the great Secretaries of State. But the immortal six here listed may serve as a beginning. Though mostly amateurs at the outset, they were all diplomats in the finest tradition and worthy of grateful remembrance by their debtors—the American people.

Advice for Diplomats

Thomas A. Bailey

"You are in a sense soldiers in the front-line trenches of our foreign policy. Nowadays anything of any importance that happens anywhere in the world is of importance to the United States."
SECRETARY OF STATE DULLES, from customary speech to
foreign service officers while on his trips.

Prologue

An American envoy to a foreign country stands in much the same relationship to the Department of State as the foreign correspondent does to his newspaper. The journalist digs up the facts upon which the editors at home in part base their editorial policy; the ambassador digs up the facts upon which the officials in Washington in part base their foreign policy.

It would be difficult to name a single qualification that an ideal foreign correspondent should possess that an ideal ambassador should not also possess. Both men should have training, experience, tact, the social graces, and the ability to report discriminatingly and objectively in precise and concise English. Both should have an intimate knowledge of the host country—its language, history, economy, social structure, and aspirations. Both should be men of vigorous and attractive personalities who circulate in all strata of society, who genuinely like the people (within limits), and who in turn are liked by them (within limits).

Such men are not easy to find or to persuade to enter upon this

SOURCE: "Advice for the Diplomat," *The Art of Diplomacy: The American Experience* (New York: Appleton-Century-Crofts, 1968), chapter 5.

kind of demanding public service, whether in the fields of diplomacy or journalism.

The Ambassador Should Brief Himself Adequately. If the American envoy is to be the interpreter of the host country to the Secretary of State, he must discover all he reasonably can about it. He should steep himself in its traditions and history, primarily because such knowledge will help him to comprehend and interpret current trends. More than that, his hosts will be flattered by evidences of such interest and understanding, and the success of his mission will be furthered.

Several special sources are usually available. The ambassador should keep closely in touch with the abler foreign correspondents in the capital, for they are often better informed than the foreign service officers themselves. He should cultivate friendly relations with his colleagues of the diplomatic corps; Ambassador Grew in Japan in the 1930's at times got better information from the British envoy than he did from Washington. Finally, the ambassador should study the back files of instructions and dispatches in the embassy, so as to discover the thrust of policy prior to his coming.

George F. Kennan, stationed in Moscow during the 1930's as a subordinate, spent considerable time reading the dispatches written by American ministers in the nineteenth century. He was to some extent comforted to find that there was little basically new about the Bolsheviks. Minister Neill S. Brown in the 1850's had been complaining about Russian secretiveness, dilatoriness, evasiveness, suspicion, and other traits—the selfsame traits that Americans were still complaining about in the 1930's.

The American ambassador should also be well informed about American history, for he is, in addition to other duties, an interpreter of his country to the host nation. He can hardly interpret it faithfully unless he knows it well, and this is one of the reasons why American history should form a substantial part of the liberal arts background expected of every candidate for the foreign service.

Employ Reliable Interpreters. If the American envoy is unable to speak directly to foreign officials in their own tongue, he should make every effort to secure the ablest and most trustworthy interpreters. Communicating ideas is difficult enough even when all parties to a negotiation are thoroughly familiar with the same language. At the Yalta Conference, Roosevelt and Churchill had to speak to Stalin through an interpreter, and Roosevelt made use of the able and reliable Charles E. Bohlen, subsequently American Ambassador to the Soviet Union. Even so, some of the misunderstanding about what was supposedly agreed on at Yalta probably arose in part from faulty communication.

When Secretary Dulles flew to Formosa to confer with General-issimo Chiang Kai-shek, the Madame insisted on being present and serving as interpreter. "The trouble was," Andrew H. Berding reported, "that the lovely Oriental was not content to be merely an interpreter; she was constantly injecting her own opinions, and one could never be sure that she was transmitting the Generalissimo's thought to the Secretary, or the Secretary's to the Generalissimo, without adding her own coloration and embroidery."

The same caution about securing trustworthy interpreters applies also to translators. In the 1830's the quarrel with France over some unpaid damages worsened when the State Department was irked because the French used the word *prétendu* in connection with the American claims. The French foreign minister was forced to write a formal note solemnly explaining that the offensive word did not mean "pretended" but rather "so-called."

Precise and Objective Reporting Is Essential. A primary duty of the ambassador is to send home to Washington detailed descriptions and analyses of what is going on in the host country in reports (dispatches) that are prompt, clear, candid, succinct, interesting, comprehensive, and accurate. In theory, he is not supposed to make policy but to provide the facts upon which the officials in Washington, looking at the world spectrum, can formulate policy. But he can interpret the facts and make recommendations based on those facts. Indeed, he is generally encouraged to do so. He can also help orient policy by handpicking facts which he regards as important, or misrepresenting the facts in such a way as to mislead the policy-makers in Washington.

The ambassador is in such a critical position that he should be in the highest degree objective and truthful. If his earlier assessments prove incorrect, he should make haste to confess his error (which few men want to do) and put things back on the track. He should not report just "happy thoughts" or observations that he feels will conform to the "party line" then being pursued by Washington, with a consequent boost in his promotion and pay.

Before Senator McCarthy's anti-Communist "crusade" in the 1950's, certain foreign service officers, particularly in the Far East, had sent home reports about the gains or prospective gains of Communism. These dispatches were later interpreted to be, not factual reporting, but evidences of sympathy for the Communists. The veteran ambassador, W. Averell Harriman, testified in 1963, "I have seen men's careers set back and in fact busted because they held the right views at the wrong time, or for reporting accurately facts which were not popular at the time, or at some later time."

Such pressures to report a "party line" are in the highest degree dangerous. The policy-makers in Washington have difficulty enough when they operate on the basis of an objective gathering of the essential facts.

Prolixity Is the Foe of Clarity. The ambassador, no matter how small the country where he is stationed, is disposed to assign an exaggerated importance to his post. He is also tempted to prove his worth by drafting over-long dispatches.

Today, more than ever, brevity is a virtue which carries with it some assurance that one's reports will be read. By the mid-1960's the volume of "telegraphic traffic" between Washington and the embassies abroad was more than 400,000 words a day, or one large-sized printed book. This, of course, was in addition to the much vaster volume of nontelegraphic reportage. As Senator Henry M. Jackson's subcommittee concluded in 1965, "The resulting flood of information swamps Washington's absorptive capacities."

A constant complaint of the men in the field is that their dispatches are not read, or if read, ignored. The reaction is not surprising when we remember that the State Department is virtually drowned in words.

The frustration that flows from being ignored has prompted many envoys to go outside regular channels to get their messages through to high places. President Franklin Roosevelt encouraged some of his ambassadors to communicate with him directly through private letters or secret codes. Some write or have written directly to congressmen. But all these irregular approaches must be used with extreme caution and in the knowledge that they tend to throw the delicate diplomatic machinery out of gear.

The Ambassador Should Obey Instructions. Just as a general must loyally carry out the orders of his Commander-in-Chief, so must the warrior-diplomat carry out the orders of his superiors if overall strategy is to succeed. Otherwise chaos would prevail, whether on the military battlefield or the diplomatic battlefield.

The diplomat, like the general, may remonstrate and give his reasons for disagreement, often based on inadequate or localized information. But when overruled, he must carry out his instructions, both in letter and in spirit, without indicating dissent through facial expression, gesture, or voice. He must even defend his government's position loyally, even though disagreeing with it. If he finds he cannot do so, he should request a transfer or resign. Ambassador Arthur B. Lane, stationed in Warsaw from 1945 to 1947, not only resigned but published a book in 1948. It sharply criticized the failure of the State Department to take a stronger stand against the Soviet absorption of Poland, contrary to Stalin's pledges at Yalta and Potsdam.

The classic case involves Walter Hines Page, Wilson's Ambassador to the Court of St. James. Pro-British, a noncareer man, and a journalist (hence an undisciplined soldier), he shamelessly sabotaged his instructions.[1] Disapproving of a strong protest from Washington against British blockade practices, he took it to the Foreign Secretary Grey (as instructed) and avowed his disapproval of it (not as instructed). He then proceeded to collaborate with Grey in framing a reply. This type of sabotage was in fact a species of treason.

There are occasions when a circumstance occurs or when an atmosphere develops which seems to warrant a departure from orders. Minister Charles Francis Adams in London during the Civil War toned down some of Secretary Seward's more bellicose instructions, and Ambassador Josephus Daniels in Mexico in the 1930's on occasion declined to act as requested. In both of these cases the envoys escaped unscathed, but such free-wheeling is risky. If Washington disapproves, the headstrong subordinate may be recalled.

Above all, the ambassador must take orders from his superiors in the State Department and White House, and not from the Chairman of the Senate Foreign Relations Committee or some other member of Congress. The minister-historian John L. Motley, stationed in London (1869–1870), followed the policy line of the Chairman of the Foreign Relations Committee, Charles Sumner, rather than that of the Secretary of State, Hamilton Fish. President Grant, an ex-military man, resented this flagrant insubordination and finally sacked Motley.

Almost as indefensible as defying instructions is giving assurances for which there is no authorization. Andrew D. White, the

[1] Critics complained that from 1914 to 1918 the British had two ambassadors: one in Washington, on their payroll, and one in London, on ours. Page's pro-British bias has often been forgiven because the war in which he sought to involve us became ours in 1917. It also became a righteous war for democracy which many Americans believed we should have entered much sooner.

able American Ambassador in Berlin, stumbled badly in 1898 when he encouraged the Germans to believe that Washington would not object to their having at least a foothold in the Philippines. These encouraging words were not only unauthorized but they ran counter to the policy being pursued in Washington. Ambassador White, though an immensely competent man, had his knuckles sharply rapped by the Secretary of State.

Refer Important Proposals Home. Just as the envoy should not act contrary to instructions in a positive way, he must not take negative action on the assumption that Washington will agree with him. For all he knows, basic policy has changed at home, or is changing.

In 1823 British Foreign Secretary Canning approached our Minister in London, Richard Rush, with a startling proposal. It was in effect that the two nations should form an alliance to prevent the European powers from restoring the revolted Spanish colonies to their former overlords. Rush had no instructions to cover this flattering proposition, so he quite properly referred it to Washington. The result was the independently declared Monroe Doctrine.

In 1845 the American Secretary of State suggested to the British Minister in Washington, Richard Pakenham, that the explosive Oregon boundary dispute be compromised along the line of the 49th parallel—the present frontier. Since London had already spurned a similar proposal three times, Pakenham evidently felt safe in rejecting it out of hand without referring it home. On this issue hung peace or war, and he presumed too much. British policy was shifting, and by this time London was more receptive to the proposed compromise line, which was agreed upon some months later.

Develop an Empathy for the Host Nation. No ambassador should ever be sent to a country whose people he dislikes. The American press reported that Ambassador Chester Bowles in India won the sympathies of the Indian people in the 1950's by his "you're as good as we are" approach. He even rode a bicycle through the streets of New Delhi and sent several of his children to Indian schools.

When the Salerno floods in Italy left a hundred or so dead and thousands homeless in 1954, Ambassadress Clare Boothe Luce arranged for United States army trucks to transport food and supplies. More than that, she spent two days in the wet and mud comforting the victims. This is clearly the kind of foreign aid that can pay rich dividends in good will and throw Communist propagandists on the defensive.

Empathy is helpful, but the ambassador must never let his attachment to a foreign people cause him to forget that he is there to promote the interests of his own country. In many cases sympathy is to the advantage of both nations, but in some spectacular instances it has been overdone. This was painfully true when in 1794 James Monroe, as American Minister to France, too enthusiastically identified himself in public—fraternal kiss and all—with the cause of the French revolutionists.

The envoy is not engaged in a popularity contest: he should be neither too popular nor too unpopular. He should steer a correct middle course and seek to command respect rather than adulation.

Cultivate Friends but not Intimates. The ambassador should develop honest friendships with most persons but "entangling alliances with none," in Jefferson's phrase. If he becomes too friendly with certain factions, he may incur the hostility of their opponents and at the same time strain, if not undermine, his objectivity.

After Hitler overran France in 1940, the Roosevelt administration attempted to maintain correct relations with the unpopular Vichy regime, tool of the Nazi conqueror, despite vehement criticism from so-called liberal elements in America. By nursing such contacts, notably with the Vichyite Admiral Darlan, we were in a stronger position to induce the French to cooperate in the Anglo-American assault on French North Africa in 1942. Without such collaboration the American casualties would certainly have been much heavier, and the invasion attempt might even have failed.

As a rule, an envoy should avoid seeing too much of the opposition leaders. Joseph P. Kennedy, father of John F. Kennedy and himself the politically appointed Ambassador in London in the late 1930's, made this error. Dedicated to isolation and appeasement, he hobnobbed too freely with the isolationist Cliveden set. Loud-mouthed and indiscreet, he was also outspokenly disloyal to his chief, President Roosevelt.

The rule of nonfraternization is also relevant to the highest levels. In 1966 President Johnson flew out to Honolulu, where he met and put his arm around the militaristic Premier Ky of South Vietnam, at a time when Ky's foothold was extremely shaky. This public affirmation that the Vietnamese quasi-dictator was "his boy" aroused the "Yankee Go Home" agitators in South Vietnam. Ensuing riots, whether triggered by the Honolulu meeting or not, almost brought the Ky regime down in ruins. President Johnson would have been on sounder ground if he had also invited to Honolulu other leaders of

Asia and the far Pacific who were making token contributions to the war effort.

The Ambassador Should Maintain Mobility. The American envoy should not remain exclusively in the capital city, pleasant though living there may be, but try to visit as much of the hinterland as feasible ("diplomacy by jeep"). Paris is not France, and to form conclusions about the entire country after viewing only the metropolis can be dangerous. One of the handicaps from which American diplomats in the Soviet Union have suffered has been the severe limiting of their movements to restricted areas. The Washington government, having tried other forms of suasion, has been forced to retaliate with similar but seemingly childish restrictions on Russian representatives.

Social mobility should parallel physical mobility. The diplomatist ought to familiarize himself with the various strata of society, not just the upper crust among whom he most naturally moves. In the Russia of 1917 few, if any, of the American officials established contact with members of the lower classes, and this oversight does much to explain their singular blindness to what was about to erupt in that war-ravaged country. On October 4, 1917, Ambassador Francis (the grain merchant) cabled: "My sympathy with Russia deep, sincere and my conviction strong that the country will survive ordeal and be safe for democracy if we and other Allies are patient and helpful."

Hardly a month had passed before the Bolsheviks seized control. The rest is history—unpleasant history for most Americans.

The Ambassador Should Avoid "Localitis." The disease of "localitis" is easy to contract. A conscientious foreign service officer is apt to feel that his embassy is the navel of the universe, whether located in Mogadiscio (Somalia) or Ouagadougou (Upper Volta) or Tegucigalpa (Honduras).

"Localitis" flourishes in all climes. It is one more reason why the ambassador should be summoned home at relatively frequent intervals for a fresh briefing, and why he should endeavor to keep himself informed by studying trends in other countries as well as in his own.

One of the worst cases of "localitis" attacked General Douglas MacArthur. Best known as a strong-willed military hero, he occupied several quasi-diplomatic posts after 1945, including that of "Yankee Mikado" of Japan. Finally dismissed from his Far Eastern commands in 1951 by President Truman, he returned to the United States, which he had not visited for fourteen years. The nation that he then saw was not the same one that he thought he had been serving.

During the Korean War, General MacArthur found himself in a galling position. Placed in command of the United Nations forces, and understandably jealous of his reputation as an ever-conquering general, he became intolerably headstrong. He tried to shift the major emphasis from the line-holding European theater to the blood-letting Asiatic theater, despite the fact that Red Russia, not Red China, was the most formidable potential adversary. A famous Herblock cartoon of the era had Secretary of State Marshall saying to the General that the officials in Washington were using a round globe and not the square one, with Asia on top, that MacArthur was consulting.

The Diplomatist is a Warrior for Peace. The diplomatic establishment, not the military establishment, is the first line of defense. This fact of life is something that Congress often overlooks when it appropriates tens of billions of dollars for military hardware and tens of millions of dollars for the foreign service, normally in about the ratio of 50 to 1.

One of the most enduring myths is that white-spatted diplomats cause wars. Hence, if we could only get rid of the "cooky pushers," there would be no wars or, at any rate, fewer wars.

Inept diplomacy has no doubt often contributed to the coming of armed conflict. This was conspicuously true when President Jefferson, in the years prior to the War of 1812, overplayed his hand and tried desperately to wring unacceptable concessions on impressment from the British. But in general the explosives are already present when they explode in the hands of the diplomats, sometimes by spontaneous combustion.

Diplomatists are keenly aware that the outbreak of war means that their mission has failed, and that they have to go home. For this reason the Department of State has often been called the "Department of Peace." One of the ablest diplomat-warriors in our history was Minister Charles Francis Adams, in his lonely outpost in an unfriendly London during the Civil War. By nerve-wracking diplomacy he helped to dissuade Britain from intervening, at a time when such intervention probably would have widened the conflict into a world war. In such an eventuality the Confederates almost certainly would have won their independence.

231

It is better that the diplomats should get ulcers than that the soldiers get bullets.

Public Loquacity is Poor Policy. Traditionally the State Department has discouraged ambassadors from making too many public speeches. If they must speak, as on ceremonial occasions, they would do well to confine themselves to pious platitudes and harmless generalities. Above all, they should avoid detailed discussion of current political issues, unless specifically instructed to do so. The danger is ever present that some innocuous remark will be misunderstood.

If the American envoy speaks the language of the host country fluently, he can often build up good will by speechmaking. This was conspicuously true of General Horace Porter, who served as Ambassador to France from 1897 to 1905.

In England, where there is no real problem with a foreign language, American envoys are sorely tempted to let themselves go. Joseph H. Choate, one of the most eloquent ornaments of the American bar, became "a British lecturer at large" at the turn of the century. In 1921 Ambassador George Harvey, a political appointee of Republican President Harding, delivered a violent harangue in which he presented the Republican case against the League of Nations. Although he spoke with President Harding's private blessing, he provoked a bitter outcry from Wilsonian Democrats, who were also Americans and who were helping to pay his salary. Not content with this brutal frankness, Harvey stirred up more animals when he indiscreetly tackled a less political subject: "Women's Souls." He facetiously but tactlessly tried to prove that they had none.

A Diplomat Should Avoid Criticism in Public. The ambassador should not publicly criticize any nation, whether it be his own or the host country or neighboring countries. Nor should he create antagonism by overpraising his own nation. He should also remember that his largest audience is probably at home, and for this reason he should not condemn elements within his own constituency.

James H. R. Cromwell, a millionaire playboy-politician, is a case in point. A heavy campaign contributor to Democratic coffers, he received an appointment in 1940 as Minister to Canada, which was then at war with Hitler. He stepped badly out of line when, as a neutral envoy in a belligerent country, he openly took sides by condemning Nazi Germany. He also condemned those isolationist groups in the United States that were not anti-Hitler. He thus violated two rules of the diplomatic game, first by publicly discussing relations between foreign nations, and second, by publicly criticizing his own country.[2] Shortly thereafter his resignation was accepted.

As a corollary proposition, the envoy should not wash dirty linen in public or "turn state's evidence" after leaving the service. In 1919, William C. Bullitt, a minor official on the American Peace Commission in Paris, resigned resoundingly when he found that the Treaty of Versailles did not measure up to the promised Fourteen Points. Then, when President Wilson was breaking himself down on a speaking tour for the Treaty, Bullitt appeared as a willing witness before the Senate Foreign Relations Committee, there to present damaging testimony from a private conversation with Secretary Lansing.[3]

In a number of instances conscientious men have convinced themselves that the national interest is so greatly jeopardized that conventional ethics must be compromised.

Meddling Leads to Muddling. The ambassador should confine his meddling, if meddle he must, to his own bailiwick—that is, foreign affairs. The French Minister Adet secretly and openly pulled wires in 1796 for the election of the allegedly pro-French Jefferson over the allegedly anti-French John Adams. He did not succeed, but his scheming had the unfortunate effect of stirring up much ill will and the fortunate effect of partially inspiring Washington's Farewell Address.

This type of interference is still used and abused to some extent. Sometimes foreign ambassadors in Washington, failing to win their point with the State Department, make contact with congressmen and try to prevail through the back doors.

Public lobbying is even more offensive. In 1945 the United States Ambassador in Argentina, Spruille Braden, vigorously opposed the rise of dictator Perón. Brought home to become Assistant Secretary of State, Braden was thought to be continuing his campaign when the State Department issued a Blue Book condemning Perón as a pro-Nazi. The Perónistas, then involved in a presidential

---

[2] In 1947 ex-Prime Minister Churchill wittily declared that "when I am abroad I always make it a rule never to criticize or attack the Government of my own country. I make up for lost time when I come home." Kay Halle, ed., *Irrepressible Churchill* (1966), p. 276.

[3] Premier Clemenceau of France was wounded by an assassin during the Peace Conference. He was reported as remarking wryly, "I got my bullet at the Conference, but Lansing got his afterward." Bullitt later pooled his anti-Wilson prejudices with those of Sigmund Freud in a highly questionable psychoanalytical explanation of Wilson's failures, with emphasis on reactions to father-domination.

election, raised the cry "Perón or Braden!" and swept to victory, no doubt aided by Yankee officiousness.

Sir Lionel Sackville-West, the British Minister in Washington, naively thrust a hand into American politics in 1888, when he penned a private letter indicating that a vote for President Cleveland was a vote for England. The blundering Briton not only violated the rule against meddling in local politics, but, worse still, he had been caught.

In sum, if one must meddle, meddle secretly, anonymously, and effectively. The British statesman Lord Palmerston once remarked that the ambassador might break all the commandments in the Decalogue except the Eleventh: "Thou shalt not be found out."

Never Lie for Your Country. Silence is golden but lies are leaden, and the diplomat is under no obligation to tell everything he knows. He can always duck the issue or change the subject. But if he makes a presumed statement of fact, it should be the truth, even though a qualified or partial truth. The common expression, "You're a diplomat, all right," usually means "You haven't told the entire story."

European diplomacy was traditionally more or less synonymous with duplicity: to lie and deny were among the envoy's first duties. He was not only a licensed spy but a licensed liar. Sir Henry Wotton, the English Ambassador to Venice, coined a famous pun in 1604 that has been polished to read: "An ambassador is an honest man, sent to lie abroad for the good of his country." The French King Louis XI instructed his envoys to fight fire with fire: "If they lie to you, lie still more to them." "Accredited mendacity" became so much the norm that Count Cavour, the nineteenth-century Italian statesman, reported, "I have discovered the art of deceiving diplomats. I speak the truth and they never believe me."

If a banker scores a financial *coup* in a crooked deal, he forfeits the confidence of the business community. If a diplomat scores a brilliant initial success by lying, he immediately impairs his future usefulness. His statements will thereafter be suspect all over the globe, his adversaries will be put on their guard, and he will not be believed even when telling the truth. The Russian Ambassador in Washington, Count Cassini, arrived there in 1898, fresh from diplomatic triumphs in China. He was notorious for his denial of the Cassini Convention, which he had negotiated while in Peking, and thereafter his every word was regarded with suspicion. Lying not only reveals that the diplomat is too lacking in skill to achieve his end by above-board means, but it arouses aggravation, a desire for vengeance, and even hatred.

Lying by the President or the Secretary of State—"lying in State"—may at times be defensible in the national interest. But these officials are operating on a different level from that of the career man in the field, who is looking forward to a lifetime in the service. As Socrates remarked, "The rulers of the State are the only ones who should have the privilege of lying, either at home or abroad; they may be allowed to lie for the good of the State."[4]

The Soviet rulers have notoriously followed the rule of Socrates, notably when they assured President Kennedy in 1962 that they were only supplying defensive weapons for Cuba at a time when they were sneaking in intermediate range missiles. But they were caught red handed, thus violating Palmerston's Eleventh Commandment.

Have No Traffic with Spies. The ambassador has often been termed an "honorable spy," and that he normally is. One of his prime duties is to cast his eyes around the host country and report to Washington. The American attachés—military, naval, and air—also have this responsibility, and it is reciprocally tolerated by both nations, provided that it does not overstep the conventional bounds.

All great powers, and many of the smaller ones, engage in spying, which is sometimes called the second oldest profession. They must do so to insure their own security in this insecure world. But the American ambassador must remain aloof from cloak-and-dagger operations, or he will fatally compromise his position. His face is too well known to escape detection, and he risks too much when he has to rely on traitors, some of them double agents, who are for sale to the highest paymaster. The "dirty work" of spying is left, at least supposedly, to the Central Intelligence Agency.

Soviet embassies, usually overstaffed out of all proportion to legitimate business, are notorious espionage centers. This is one of the reasons why many nations, as was true of the United States, have been slow to extend official recognition to the Soviet Union. In 1964 Moscow and Washington negotiated a treaty which would mutually facilitate the establishment of consulates. J. Edgar Hoover, head of the Federal Bureau of Investigation, badly hurt chances of ratification when he testified before a House subcommittee that the

---

[4] The rule about envoys not lying obviously has less applicability in wartime situations. Robert Murphy, acting under instructions, lied to the French about the size of the American force invading North Africa in 1942, and neglected to mention the British components. In 1962 President Kennedy instructed Press Secretary Pierre Salinger to deny that the United States was preparing for an invasion of Cuba at the time of the Cuban missile crisis.

proposed pact would add to Soviet facilities for espionage and hence make more difficult the task of combating Communist subversion in America. He was no doubt correct, and the Senate had to weigh this disagreeable fact against the undoubted advantages that consular services in the Soviet Union would confer on the United States. The pact was narrowly approved in 1967.

Secrecy Must Be Safeguarded. A primary duty of the ambassador is to protect security. He must keep code books and all top-secret papers under lock and key when not in the hands of the most trusted employees. With professional spies and enterprising reporters everywhere under foot, this is no easy task.

In 1854 the American ministers to Britain, France, and Spain, acting under instructions, met secretly at Ostend, Belgium, to devise recommendations to the Secretary of State for the acquisition of Cuba. Their top-secret recommendation—seizure, if purchase was not possible—leaked out and made the land-grabbing Yankees the laughing stock of the civilized world. Redfaced, the administration in Washington was forced to repudiate the proposals of its diplomatic agents.

The ambassador, though a private citizen, is a public official, and in a sense can have no private life. Two of the most sensational incidents involving foreign envoys in Washington—the Englishman Sackville-West in 1888 and the Spaniard de Lôme in 1898[5]—grew out of revelations that leaked out through private letters. Frederick Van Dyne, in a book on the foreign service published in 1909, concluded—brave man indeed—that one reason why so few women have risen in the service is their notorious inability to keep a secret.

If discretion was advisable in the nineteenth century, it is imperative today. Science has provided too many sensitive "bugging devices" and other eavesdropping instruments for picking up at long range the most confidential conversations. Moreover, there is the problem of leaky allies, of whom we now have some forty. There is pith in the Irish proverb, "It's no secret that's known to three."

---

[5] Minister Sackville-West wrote a letter advising an American voter to vote Democratic in the upcoming election; Minister de Lôme criticized President McKinley's weakness and lack of good faith.

Profile of United States Diplomats: Bicentennial Review and Future Projection

Elmer Plischke

The national bicentennial affords an opportunity to reflect upon the past, including two centuries of American diplomatic experience. One important aspect of such review centers upon the diplomatic emissary who, although he plays a major role in the conduct of foreign relations, is frequently misunderstood or misjudged. This is understandable—in view of the large number of individuals who have labored in the diplomatic vineyard under changing conditions, and because they collectively represent a broad spectrum of personal backgrounds, qualities, assignments, achievements, and fame or notoriety. The elemental notion—that traditionally the American diplomat is a middle-aged male, hails from the Northeastern seaboard states, serves a relatively short tenure as envoy to a foreign government, is sometimes reappointed to a succeeding assignment in another country, and then passes from the diplomatic scene—while generally accurate, is subject to many exceptions.

At the same time, differing images of the diplomat, unscientifically contrived, have come to be held by various groups, such as political leaders, journalists, and scholars; by the practitioners themselves; and by the man in the street. Depending on the perspective of the perceiver, and focusing largely on personal qualities, functions, and

---

NOTE: Except as otherwise noted, the statistics contained in this survey cover the period from 1778 to March 30, 1973, as summarized from the author's *United States Diplomats and Their Missions: A Profile of American Diplomatic Emissaries since 1778* (Washington, D.C.: American Enterprise Institute, 1975). Statistics were compiled from information contained in Richardson Dougall and Mary Patricia Chapman, *United States Chiefs of Mission, 1778–1973* (Washington, D.C.: Historical Office, Department of State, 1973).

SOURCE: "United States Diplomats Since 1778: Bicentennial Review and Future Projection," *World Affairs*, vol. 138 (Winter 1975/1976), pp. 205–18.

impact, impressions vary from regarding diplomats as the agents of competitive national self-interest who engage in chicanery and deception to paragons of virtue and value, and from viewing them as members of a loyal, dedicated, hard-working elite to an effete, artificial brigade of rich, punctilious Beau Brummels, or what Hugh S. Gibson referred to as idle playboys and "cookie-pushers." Such notions are often founded on misty preconceptions, isolated circumstances, personal bias, or nebulous imagery, rather than on explicit and comprehensive analysis. Cumulative measurable evidence over the past two centuries, however, evokes quite different, but far more precise and meaningful, adjudgments.

Since the American Revolution, approximately 1,900 diplomats have been designated to some 3,000 senior assignments. From 1778 to 1973 these included 2,497 appointments as chiefs of mission to foreign governments, 364 to ranking positions in the Department of State (including Secretaries, Under Secretaries, Assistant Secretaries, and officials of comparable rank), 55 as chiefs of mission to international organizations, and ten as ambassadors at large. Of the nearly 2,500 appointments as envoys to foreign capitals, only nine of every ten served in their missions, whereas 227 diplomatic appointments (9.1 percent) failed to be consummated fully.

In the past, seven of every ten American diplomats have been in their 40s and 50s on initial appointment. One in three has been named to multiple assignments—including both sequential and simultaneous. More than 50 percent have remained in their missions less than three years; of these nearly one in every five endured for less than twelve months. Overall, more than half hailed from the Northeastern seaboard and, since the outbreak of World War II, one of every two has come from only six of the 50 states and the District of Columbia. During the past two centuries 16 percent have previously served in Congress, but since 1920 this ratio has declined to approximate merely one in every 50. Only one of every 125 American diplomats has been a woman, although since 1930 this ratio has increased to roughly one in 80 assignments.

Subsequent to the introduction of the careerist designation early in the 20th century, only one of every two diplomatic appointees has belonged to this category, but since 1950 more than 65 percent of all American envoys accredited to foreign governments have been careerists. Based on past practice, very few emissaries have their missions terminated on the request or demand of the host government; more than one of every 25 have died in active service. In the future some two-thirds of all emissaries will be accredited to the governments of

Mideastern, African, and Asian countries, while only one of three will be sent to European and Western Hemisphere capitals. Although, in earlier history, diplomatic service often served as a steppingstone to the secretaryship of state and even the presidency or vice presidency, this probability has largely evanesced.

Growth of American Diplomatic Community

Prior to 1789 American envoys were appointed and commissioned by the Continental Congress. These included Benjamin Franklin who was sent to France (and commissioned also to Sweden—one of the early simultaneous multiple assignments), John Adams who was accredited to the Netherlands and Great Britain, Francis Dana who was dispatched to Russia, John Jay who represented the emergent Republic in Spain, and Thomas Jefferson who succeeded Franklin in Paris. Dana and Jay, although they remained at their posts for several years, were not formally received.

After the formation of the Federal Union, as the United States was emerging into the diplomatic arena in the late 18th century, the President appointed a handful of officers to conduct the foreign affairs of the new Republic—a Secretary of State and a small team of emissaries, possessing somewhat inferior ranks and titles, accredited to seven of the leading European powers. The President, the Secretary, and the envoys were well known to one another. This diplomatic community was expanded in a series of recognizable waves—peaking in 1823–1838, the two decades following the War with Mexico, the early 20th century, and especially the period since World War II. United States diplomatic representation tripled to 22 countries by the late 1830s, and increased to 37 by 1870, 42 by 1900, and 56 by 1922. By far the most extensive independence boom occurred after World War II when in little more than a quarter century some 75 new states were added to the American diplomatic community, primarily in the Arab world, Africa, Asia, and the Pacific. As a result, the United States more than doubled its diplomatic representation to nearly 140 by 1974.

To March 30, 1973, the United States had established diplomatic relations with 141 countries but, for various reasons, discontinued sending emissaries to nine of them—Albania, Estonia, Hawaii, Latvia, Lithuania, Montenegro, Texas, the Two Sicilies, and Vatican City (Papal States). Relations also had been discontinued with Korea from 1905 to 1949. Assuming the revival of normal diplomatic relations in those cases where they are temporarily severed or suspended, and adding the recent commencement of relations with the Bahamas, East Germany, Granada, and Guinnea-Bissau, and the special arrangement with the Peoples Republic of China, currently the diplomatic community of the United States embraces 137 countries.

In addition, the President commissions some 20 Deputy Secretaries, Under Secretaries, Assistant Secretaries, and other ranking departmental officers to assist the Secretary, and he appoints one or more ambassadors at large and a corps of chiefs of mission to ten international organizations—approximating an aggregate of 170 top-level officers concerned directly with American diplomacy. Adding replacements and reassignments, the total may average more than 200 presidential appointments every four years. Quantitatively, in the 1970s ranking diplomatic appointments, therefore, amount to nearly 25 times the number commissioned in the late 18th and early 19th centuries. The task of selection, accreditation, and appointment has become more demanding, and the opportunity of the expectant diplomat is enhanced, but the degree of acquaintance, personal friendship, and intimacy among the participants may suffer appreciably.

Since 1778 roughly 88 percent of all top-level diplomatic appointments have been to the field, predominantly as emissaries to foreign governments, and, cumulatively, only 12 percent have been to ranking departmental offices. The probabilities of the contemporary appointee in terms of major categories of assignment remains relatively unchanged. At present, he has less than a 12 percent chance of serving at the upper levels of the Department of State, approximately an 81 percent certainty of designation as chief of mission to some foreign government, and only a minor possibility (7 percent) of accreditation to an international organization or commissioning as ambassador at large. Although this general distribution is not apt to change extensively, the number of missions to both foreign capitals and international organizations could increase by as much as 15 to 20 percent in the next decade or two, an outcome which would simply reinforce the obvious—that future top-level diplomatic appointment opportunity lies predominantly in the field.

Geographic Change of Diplomatic Arena

Whereas, prior to 1840 American emissaries were assigned solely to some 20 European and Latin American countries, the diplomatic community not only has expanded numerically but also has changed in basic geographic composition. The earliest non-European and non-Western Hemisphere countries to be added were Turkey (1831), China (1844), Egypt (1849), Hawaii (1853–1898), Japan (1859), Liberia (1864), Thailand/Siam (1882), Iran/Persia (1883), and Korea (1883–1905). Early in the 20th century, prior to World War I, Morocco (1906) and Ethiopia (1909) were added. By this time, nevertheless, 40 of the 49 countries with which the United States exchanged diplomats were in Europe and Latin America. The large increases in other regions occurred after 1940, and current American diplomatic representation (not excluding states with which relations are temporarily suspended) may be summarized as follows: Sub-Saharan Africa—37, Europe—28, Western Hemisphere—27, Asia and the Pacific—25, and the Middle East—20.

In terms of areal possibilities, therefore, the late 20th century diplomat has only a 20 percent opportunity of being assigned to either a European or Western Hemisphere government, and chances are nearly as great that he will be sent to one of the Asian and Western Pacific countries, somewhat less probable that he will go to the Mideast, and considerably greater that he will be destined for sub-Saharan Africa. If the United States should add two dozen more countries to its diplomatic roster—largely in Africa, Asia, and the Pacific—by the beginning of the 21st century an average of less than two of every ten American diplomats will be commissioned, respectively, to Europe and Latin America, whereas one will be accredited to the Mideast, more than two to Asia and the Pacific, and nearly three of every ten will serve in Africa south of the Sahara.

This basic geographic ratio of assignments is unlikely to change materially for some time. Consequently, the fact that 60 to 70 percent of all American emissaries accredited to foreign governments (as compared with only 20 percent prior to World War II) will be accredited to the Mideast, Africa, and Asia is bound to affect future diplomatic recruitment. It also will mean that competition for designation to what have sometimes been regarded as preferred European and Latin American posts is likely to intensify. The emergent careerist who covets ambassadorial appointment will need to plan his professional development, therefore, to take account of these changes in the representational pattern of the United States.

Multiple Diplomatic Assignments

During the two centuries since the 1770s, almost one of every three American diplomats has been accorded multiple top-level diplomatic assignments, the preponderant majority of which (approximately 85 percent) have been and are likely to continue to be sequential rather than simultaneous. According to past experience, more than half of the reappointees will be given two assignments, while one of every five may aspire to three, and one in every four may be designated to four or more such posts.

Prior to 1973 some 98 United States emissaries were given as many as five or more diplomatic appointments. Only 18 of these (18.4 percent) served during the period of more than a century and a quarter prior to the outbreak of World War I, suggesting that the high level of reappointment is on the increase. Of this dozen and a half, three— John Quincy Adams and James Monroe (each of whom also became Secretary of State and was later elected to the presidency) and Christopher Hughes, Jr. (accredited to Sweden, Norway, and the Netherlands from 1819 to 1845)—were appointed in the early history of the Republic. The rest held their appointments between 1870 and World War I.

Since 1915 more than four-fifths (81.3 percent) of such reappointees have been careerists—including, by way of illustration, Charles E. Bohlen, Ellis O. Briggs, Selden Chapin, Hugh Gibson, Loy W. Henderson, H. Freeman Matthews, Livingston T. Merchant, Robert D. Murphy, and Charles W. Yost—all names well known in the annals of diplomacy. Representative of the noncareerists with five or more appointments are David K. E. Bruce and Ellsworth Bunker (each serving approximately 15 years as of March 1973), Lincoln MacVeagh (more than 20 years), and Laurits S. Swenson (nearly 25 years). Fourteen noncareerists appointed to the highest number of reappointments as chiefs of mission and in ranking Department of State offices since 1915 served for the remarkable combined total of approximately 190 years—averaging more than 13 years each.

Simultaneous multiple appointments serve a variety of useful purposes, but they tend to be exceptional and may very well decline if not disappear in American practice except for emergency situations and for the temporary handling of representation to some of the smaller, newer countries as they emerge into the diplomatic arena. Aside from the early multiple commissioning of emissaries like Benjamin Franklin and John Adams, only approximately 80 American diplomats (5 percent) have been named to simultaneous missions. In the past roughly 70 percent of these appointments have been to two conjoint assignments, and only in 32 cases have they been to three or more posts. The preponderant majority have involved simultaneous designation to the Central American Republics from the 1820s until late in the 19th century, the Balkan countries (Bulgaria, Greece, Montenegro, Romania, Serbia, and Yugoslavia, in varying combinations) prior to World War I, the Baltic states between the two World Wars, groups of governments in exile in London, Ottawa, and Cairo during World War II (largely careerists Ray Atherton, Alexander C. Kirk, and Rudolf E. Schoenfeldt, and noncareerists Anthony J. Drexel Biddle and Lincoln MacVeagh). Since World War II, various combinations of Middle Eastern, African, and South Asian countries have been involved.

Whereas, overall, only four of every ten multiple appointees were careerists, since World War I approximately two of every three have been career officers. If this later ratio continues—and the logic and pressures favoring a high degree of reappointment of careerists is not apt to change—Foreign Service Officers who gain admission to this inner circle of ranking emissaries in the field and senior departmental officers enjoy a substantial expectancy of reappointment. The current ratio, however, could be affected by lengthening the average period of mission tenure, by increasing the number of potential career appointees, by raising or lowering the retirement age of careerists, or by altering the existing balance between careerists and noncareerists.

Nonconsummation of Diplomatic Appointments

If experience since 1778 were a reliable guide to the future, nearly one in every ten nominations for appointment as chiefs of mission to foreign governments would fail to be consummated (227 of 2,497). However, since 1910 this ratio has declined to less than one of every 25, so that the contemporary diplomatic nominee enjoys far greater certainty of appointment than was the case with earlier candidates. Nevertheless, employing the yardstick of the past, approximately one-third of the nonconsummations of appointment will be due to Senate inaction or rejection of the nomination, more than one of every five (22 percent) will be due to appointment declination by the nominee, and one of every 20, though confirmed, will die before his commissioning and reception are fully effectuated. Among other reasons ascribed by the Department of State for nonconsummation are that the appointee failed to proceed to his post (21 percent), to present his credentials (8 percent), or to serve under his appointment (8 percent) —none of which clarify the actual reasons for nonconsummation. Only three appointees failed to serve because they were held to be *persona non grata*—Anthony M. Keiley (Italy and Austria), former Senator Henry W. Blair (China), and James W. Gerard (Mexico).

Diplomatic Ranks and Titles

The effects of the Congresses of Vienna (1815) and Aix-la-Chapelle (1818) on stabilizing the titles and ranks of diplomats and the fact that no resident American diplomats were designated as ambassadors until late in the 19th century are well known. Less familiar is the development of American usage respecting ranks and titles. The highest rank employed by Washington for a century and a quarter was that of envoy extraordinary/minister plenipotentiary, which came to be generally ascribed to American emissaries to Europe, but the designations of early envoys to Latin America were less consistent, ranging from envoy extraordinary (Mexico throughout the 19th century) and minister resident to chargé d'affaires. Major upgrading of diplomatic ranks occurred in the 1850s, when a number of envoys to Europe and Latin America were elevated to the level of minister resident, and in the 1880s and 1890s, when emissaries to approximately two dozen countries were raised to the rank of envoy extraordinary/minister plenipotentiary, so that by the mid-1890s some 85 percent of United States diplomats possessed this rank.

The most notable advancement began in 1893 with the immediate upgrading of American emissaries in France, Germany, Italy, and the United Kingdom to the rank of ambassador extraordinary and plenipotentiary. In 1898 similar advancements followed for emissaries in Mexico and Russia. Diplomats in other countries were upgraded by President Wilson, but the most sweeping change was instituted by President Franklin D. Roosevelt who raised the ranks of United States emissaries to all of Latin America, most European countries aligned with the wartime United Nations or occupied by the Axis powers, and certain other states, including Canada and China. Since World War II existing legations and new missions were gradually elevated to embassy status. Among the last to be changed were the American diplomatic establishments in Romania (1964), Bulgaria and Hungary (1967), and Yemen (1972).

To summarize, from 1778 to 1973 in the aggregate American diplomats held the following titles: Ambassador Extraordinary and Plenipotentiary—1,011 (40.5%), Envoy Extraordinary/Minister Plenipotentiary—901 (36.1%), Minister Resident—300 (12.0%), Chargé d'affaires—189 (7.6%), Minister Plenipotentiary—36 (1.4%), Commissioner—17 (0.7%), and Agent, Diplomatic Agent, and others—43 (1.7%). Although it took nearly 80 years, currently all regular resident United States missions are at the ambassadorial level. Consequently, contemporary and future United States diplomats, even when accredited to minor countries or ministates in remote corners of the globe, no longer need to suffer the stigma of secondary diplomatic status.

Most chiefs of mission to international organizations also are commissioned as ambassadors. A few, assigned to United Nations specialized agencies, still hold the rank of minister, but in the years ahead these may also be elevated to the ambassadorial level. A major exception to the current norm is the ambassador at large. This lofty title is relatively new and sparsely used, and, although at present it does not signify an added super grade internationally, if it is employed freely by the White House in the future and also is adopted by other countries, it could come to denominate such a superior diplomatic rank.

Geographic Origins of Diplomats

More than half of the diplomats of the United States have hailed from the Atlantic seaboard states, ranging from Maine to Virginia. Since 1940, however, one of every two chiefs of mission has come from six states—California, Connecticut, Illinois, Maryland, New York, and Pennsylvania, plus the District of Columbia—and the pattern is roughly identical for careerists. New York has been the acknowledged state of residence (on appointment) of the largest number of American emissaries—approximately 15 percent—but in the 1960s the quota selected from the District of Columbia rose to virtually equal that of New York. On the other hand, as of 1973 no emissaries had been recruited from three states (Alaska, Hawaii, and Idaho), only one heralded from North Dakota over a period of nearly 85 years, and ten or less had come from each of half a dozen states (Montana, Nevada, New Mexico, Oklahoma, South Dakota, and Wyoming). Only relatively small numbers have been chosen from 14 of the West-South-Central, Mountain, and Pacific states. Population size of states is only partially relatable to the geographic origin of diplomats. The same may be said of the consequences of the Civil War. In the 20th century the geographic origin and background of appointing presidents bear no discernible relationship to the territorial origin of American diplomats.

Because American practice evidences little consciousness of areal distribution and proportional representation in the selection process, it appears that this factor need not seriously concern future diplomats. Yet, in view of the political sensitivities of members of Congress, it is not beyond the realm of possibility that some effort may be launched—overtly or discreetly by pressures behind the scenes—to redress blatant discrepancies in order to achieve a greater geographic spread of appointments, at least so far as noncareerists are concerned. Nevertheless, the geographic origin of ranking diplomats has limited, if any, logical relevancy to the measure of their service, and certainly an arbitrary program of proportional distribution—even on a modified basis—could be detrimental to the quality and flexibility of United States diplomatic practice.

Age of Diplomats

It is no surprise that historically more than seven of every ten American diplomats have been in middle age at the time of their appointment—35.1 percent in their 40s and 36.2 percent in their 50s—with the largest numbers ranging between the ages of 47 and 53, although some have been as young as their 20s when first commissioned, e.g., Charles Denby (China in 1885) and E. Rumsey Wing (Ecuador in 1869), both of whom were in the mid-20s, and John Quincy Adams, who was sent to the Netherlands when he was but a few years older. Such appointments are rare, however; only five were made in the 20th century, and none has been made since the 1920s. Moreover, even though a few youthful diplomats may still be accredited in their 30s to serve in interim assignments, as American mission staffs increase in size this practice may disappear except in extraordinary circumstances.

During the post-World War II expansion of the American diplomatic family, careerists were generally designated to ranking diplomatic positions while in their 50s—often the lower 50s—and the 1960s provided some trend toward earlier appointment, with a few diplomats selected in their 40s. On the other hand, most of the diplomats who were in their 60s when first appointed, and certainly those in their 70s—such as Herman B. Baruch, Josephus Daniels, Andrew W. Mellon, Douglas Maxwell Moffat, and Alphonso Taft—have been noncareerists. Careerists remain in their diplomatic careers only until they reach the mandatory retirement age of 60—or, in special circumstances, until the age of 65—but it is unusual for them to continue longer, as was the case with Norman Armour, Jefferson Caffery, and Loy W. Henderson. Some noncareerists, on the other hand, endure into their late 60s, with a number surviving into the 70s and even the 80s—e.g., Thomas Sumter (appointed at 75 and served in Portugal for about a decade). The younger diplomats, both careerists and noncareerists, obviously have a greater opportunity than do their older colleagues for sequential multiple appointments, but such reappointment is not guaranteed, even for careerists. Nevertheless, some noncareerists are reappointed at an advanced age, in exceptional cases as late as their upper 70s and early 80s—e.g., Ellsworth Bunker (appointed at 57 and reappointed to his seventh mission in 1973 when he was over 80).

246

No significant trend is discernible in these developments, and existing averages and ratios are not likely to change unless the law should be modified respecting the maximum careerist retirement age, the ratio of careerists to noncareerists should be altered materially, or a particular presidential administration should develop a preference for either younger or older diplomats. Consequently, it is possible that some careerists will leave active service disgruntled that they could not continue at the highest level of diplomacy for longer periods—or, perhaps, not even achieve it—while their continuance probably would be opposed by younger career officers who are standing by vying to achieve ambassadorial status.

Duration of Diplomatic Missions

The age and reappointment factors impinge directly upon the duration of diplomatic missions which, in isolated cases, have varied from only a few days to more than 20 years. Statistics indicate that the average length of service of United States envoys in individual missions—determined by computing the ratio between the total number of American diplomats who served in each foreign country and the length of time the United States has maintained diplomatic relations with it, as grouped by major geographic areas—runs from 2.7 to 3.4 years. Over a span of nearly two centuries the arithmetic mean—counting all countries, including those with which diplomatic relations had just commenced—amounts to 3.1 years.

If the time gap between departing and replacement emissaries is calibrated into the equation, the assignment tenure average is lower, and if other interruptions in representational continuity—such as the temporary suspension of diplomatic relations—is taken into account, concrete assessments are lower still. Discounting those emissaries still fulfilling their mission as of March 30, 1973, since 1778 only 26 percent of American diplomats served in their missions for four years or longer, and less than 19 percent continued for periods of three to less than four years. On the other hand, 55 percent endured for less than three years, of which approximately one of every five appointees remained less than a year.

Twenty-four American chiefs of mission have achieved the record of persevering in a single mission for ten years or longer. The lengthiest tenure was achieved by career officer Edwin V. Morgan who survived as Ambassador to Brazil for more than 21 years (1912–1933). George P. Marsh might have exceeded his 21 years as Envoy Extraordinary/Minister Plenipotentiary to Italy (1861–1882) had he

247

not died in office. Half a dozen others continued in their mission for 12 to 14 years. Nearly three-fourths of these 24 long-tenured envoys were appointed prior to World War I and none was designated in the 1940s and 1950s, but Foreign Service Officer Walworth Barbour, accredited to Israel in 1961, remained for nearly 12 years.

In summary, statistics indicate that, on the average, American diplomatic missions approximate three years or less, with turnover least frequent in the countries of Europe and most rapid in sub-Saharan Africa. Because of the short experiential time span involved, the recent situation in Africa may be unique, and the future turnover rate for this area will probably conform with the overall norm. There appears, therefore, to be little demonstrable interrelation between the duration of missions and their geographic distribution, and much the same may be said respecting historical timing, except for an apparent tendency to reduce the quantity and frequency of prolonged missions.

Doubtless this is attributable in some measure to the increasing number of careerists seeking appointment as chiefs of mission and the continuance of some for relatively limited periods—sometimes for a few months to top off individual careers, but more frequently as the by-product of chain reaction appointments. Augmenting the level of careerism, therefore, does not necessarily portend extending mission tenure averages. As a matter of fact, careerists account for 80 percent of the shortest appointments (six months or less) since World War I, which may evidence, in part, the relationship of limited tenure to turnover chain reaction among careerists.

Women Diplomats

Prior to the Franklin D. Roosevelt administration no women were designated as American chiefs of mission, and, beginning with Ruth Bryan Owen's appointment to Denmark, in 40 years (to March 1973) only 15 were named to 19 ranking diplomatic missions. President Truman commissioned the first full-fledged woman Ambassador (Eugenie Anderson, to Denmark in 1949). President Eisenhower named the first careerist woman mission chief (Frances E. Willis, to Switzerland in 1953), and he also accredited the first woman ambassador to a major foreign power (Clare Boothe Luce, to Italy in 1953). In the 1960s women chiefs of mission were sent to such non-European countries as Barbados, Nepal, and Ceylon (Sri Lanka), and in the early 1970s to Gambia and Ghana. Presidents Johnson and Nixon also commenced designating women diplomats as United States representatives to major international organizations (Betty Crites Dillon, to the International Civil Aviation Organization in 1971) as well as to high office in the Department of State (Barbara Watson, as Administrator of the Bureau of Security and Consular Affairs in 1968, and Carol C. Laise, as Assistant Secretary for Public Affairs in 1973).

Nevertheless, the number of women appointed to ranking diplomatic posts remains minuscule, amounting to only 0.7 percent overall, and merely 1.3 percent since 1930. There is some evidence of a trend, however, to increase the number of women diplomats and to expand the types of positions to which they are commissioned and the range of countries to which they are sent. In the past the restriction on the number of women appointed as ranking diplomats has reflected, but only to a degree, the status of their recruitment by the career service, but in recent decades this has been in the process of liberalization. Although the modification of attitudes both in the United States and abroad has been slow, changes are under way and certain recent emergent pressures are bound to compel the designation of more women to senior diplomatic posts in the future.

Former Members of Congress as Diplomats

American diplomats have been drawn from a broad spectrum of backgrounds and professions—statesmen, politicians, bureaucrats, lawyers, businessmen, financiers, historians, educators, men of letters, publishers and journalists, a few missionaries, and others—and political patronage influenced the selection of a good many nominees. Some of these diplomatic appointees—at one time amounting to a substantial proportion—who benefited from the spoils system were former members of Congress. As a matter of fact, to 1973 nearly 300 American diplomats (about 16 percent of all appointees) had previously been elected to Congress. To 1870 the quantity of diplomats who possessed previous congressional experience ranged from 25 to as high as 70 percent per decade. However, since 1920 this ratio has dropped to only five to twelve individuals (amounting to less than 1.0 to 3.3 percent of the total number of diplomatic appointees per decade—averaging only 2.13 percent during more than half a century). Prior congressional service, consequently, has become a negligible prelude to diplomatic appointment and, while the practice has not entirely disappeared, the number of such appointees has become minute.

Of the 294 congressmen/diplomats, 66 specifically resigned their legislative seats to accept diplomatic assignments, 22 were appointed directly as Secretaries of State (plus one as Secretary of Foreign Affairs and two as Secretary ad interim), whereas 262 were named chiefs of mission in the field. More than one of every five was accorded multiple missions, such as John Quincy Adams, Chester Bowles, and Henry Cabot Lodge. Nine gained their legislative experience in the Continental Congress, 55 served in the Senate as compared with 184 in the House of Representatives, and 46 were elected to both chambers. Some 142 were Democrats, 89 were Republicans, and the remainder included 33 Whigs, 7 Federalists, and members of other lesser political parties.

Diplomatic Careerists

Although vestiges of the spoils system remain, they have been substantially offset by the institution of diplomatic careerism. Following the introduction of the careerist designation, beginning during the World War I period, careerists have been the recipients of approximately 55 percent of American appointments to diplomatic missions abroad and as ranking members of the Department of State. This overall quota has been influenced somewhat by the relatively large number of noncareerists appointed to the limited number of top-level positions in the Department—approximating 70 percent since 1778, but declining to 60 percent since 1920, and to 50 percent during the 1920s and 1950s. On the other hand, the obverse pertains to American chiefs of mission accredited to foreign governments since 1920, of which some 60 percent have been careerists, and this average has risen to more than 65 percent since 1950.

In other words, the proportion of careerists has been gaining at the upper levels, both within the Department of State and in the field. Especially high has been the quantity of careerists accredited to the East European communist countries (approximately 85 percent since World War II), and to the Mideast, Africa, Asia, and the Pacific (in each case ranging between 73 and 78 percent). While the general averages for Europe and Latin America remain somewhat lower, the era of large-scale sanctuaries for political rewardees and other noncareerists has diminished markedly; whereas, conversely, extensive preserves for careerists appear to have become entrenched in American diplomatic practice.

In general, the upward ascent of the ratio of careerist appointees seems to be leveling off at between 65 and 75 percent. This proportion may fluctuate somewhat from time to time and place to place but, given the American tradition and political system, the level of careerism is unlikely to achieve total universality. Certain categories of diplomatic officials—such as some of the senior departmental appointees, ambassadors at large, and even particular chiefs of mission—may continue to be recruited from outside the career service. Every President is persuaded to exercise his prerogative of designating his ambassadors to the point of transcending the Foreign Service to some degree. Nevertheless, perhaps portending a significant change, statistics reveal that Presidents Eisenhower, Kennedy, and Nixon—each representing a political change in the White House—established an increasing trend of retaining careerists appointed by predecessors, designating more careerists than noncareerists as their initial appointees, and naming more careerists than noncareerists to new countries with which diplomatic exchanges were commenced.

Account also needs to be taken of the fact that a nucleus of noncareerists evolve into genuine professional diplomats—represented in recent decades by George W. Ball, David K. E. Bruce, Ellsworth Bunker, W. Averell Harriman, Alan G. Kirk, Lincoln MacVeagh, George C. McGhee, Laurence A. Steinhardt, and others. They, together with the Foreign Service Officers, provide a substantial preponderancy of senior American diplomats In view of the level of careerism already achieved, it seems logical to suggest that the problem with the appointment of noncareerists is no longer a matter of basic principle—as it once was— but rather a question of judgment respecting the specific individuals selected, whether noncareerists or careerists.

Termination of Diplomatic Missions

Diplomatic missions to foreign governments and international organizations, naturally, are terminated on the determination of the White House and the Department of State. Such action is normally initiated formally by the sending government, often at the behest of the diplomat himself. The reasons technically ascribed in most cases—such as recall presentation (20 percent), relinquishing charge of the mission (4 percent), supersession of the appointee (2 percent), and leaving the post or the country of assignment (65 percent)—fail to reveal the real causes of mission termination. The latter consist rather of the wishes of an incoming President to name his own ambassadors (sometimes by shifting individual emissaries to new assignments), the desire of the White House or the Department of State to accredit a different individual to a particular country for specific reasons, the request of the noncareerist to leave the diplomatic service, the compulsory retirement of the careerist, the desire of an envoy to change his post, and the like. More than 93 percent of American diplomatic missions in the field since 1778 have been terminated for such quite normal reasons.

Only in a small number of cases, on the other hand, is there coalescence of formally acknowledged and genuine reasons for diplomatic mission termination. These include recall of the emissary on the request of the host government or dismissal by it (0.7 percent), temporary interruption or severance of diplomatic relations (1.3 percent), military occupation in time of war or change in the legal status of the country to which the envoy is accredited (1.1 percent), and the death or assassination of the emissary (3.6 percent). The probability that the individual diplomat is apt to have his mission expire for any of these reasons is not very great, although if careerists increase in quantity and are given multiple appointments until they reach retirement age, or noncareerists are appointed or reappointed at an advanced age, the ratio of those who die in service may increase, but this would be no more abnormal than it is for other professions.

Presidential and Vice Presidential Aspirations of Diplomats

On leaving their appointments, in the past American diplomats often returned to their former professions, and others passed gracefully into retirement. With the increase in the number of careerists who are required to retire by the time they reach 65 or earlier, however, a higher percentage may proceed from active service directly into retirement, although some Foreign Service Officers have been moving into a second career.

Some American diplomats not only have prior congressional experience, but also harbor presidential and vice presidential ambitions. Overall, during nearly two centuries 15 of 64 individuals—approximately one of every four—who served as President and Vice President also received diplomatic appointments, either as Secretary of State, as chief of mission abroad, or both. Since 1778 nearly 50 such diplomatic appointees subsequently stood for election (in the Electoral College) to the highest executive offices in the United States.

During the first century the relationship between diplomatic office, including the secretaryship of state and candidacy for the presidency and vice presidency, was particularly evident. To the time of the Civil War, nearly 60 percent of those who were elected President and Vice President had previous diplomatic experience, and prior to 1870 approximately two-thirds of those who stood for election to these offices but were defeated in the Electoral College had also been nominated for some diplomatic appointment. Aside from those who also became Secretaries of State, they are represented by such political figures as Charles Francis Adams and Rufus King, journalist Horace Greeley, and General George B. McClellan. In more recent times they include Adlai E. Stevenson and Henry Cabot Lodge. While this relationship between diplomatic appointment and presidential aspiration, therefore, has not disappeared entirely, the ratio has declined so substantially during the past century that it has become unique, and the professionalization of the diplomatic corps has doubtless contributed significantly to this change.

Role of the Ambassador: Existing Status and Proposal for Improvement

Foy D. Kohler

The Basic Principle

As is attested by his commission and letters of credence, the Ambassador is the direct representative of the President, as Chief of State and Head of Government of the United States, to the Chief of State (and Head of Government) of the country of his residence. He is thus the President's counterpart, responsible for the full panoply of interests and activities of the United States within his area of jurisdiction. This status has not only been traditionally recognized and accepted, but was wisely reflected in the Rogers Act of 1924 and the Foreign Service Act of 1946, which established not a foreign service of the Department of State but *The Foreign Service of the United States.* This is not to say that every Foreign Service Officer can expect to rise to the rank of Ambassador or that qualified persons from outside the Government should be excluded from appointment as Chiefs of Mission, but it does mean that every Foreign Service Officer is expected to consider himself as being in the service of the nation as a whole and to prepare and conduct himself accordingly.

The implementation of the concept presented no problem, other than occasional skirmishes with the Departments of Commerce and Agriculture, so long as the activity of American Missions abroad was largely limited to the traditional functions of representation, negotiation, reporting, assistance to citizens and promotion of trade.

However, with the emergence of the United States as a "super-

Source: "The Role of the Ambassador," Commission on the Organization of the Government for the Conduct of Foreign Policy (Robert D. Murphy Commission), *Appendices: Commission on the Organization of the Government for the Conduct of Foreign Policy* (Washington, D.C.: Government Printing Office, 1976), vol. 6, Appendix Q, pp. 319–24.

power" on the world scene during and after World War II, new instruments of foreign policy were developed and new agencies were established to operate them, both at home and overseas—propaganda, intelligence, cultural relations, military and economic aid, and disarmament. At the same time, the explosion of American interests on a global scale soon impinged on the functions of practically all Departments and agencies of the Federal Government as the boundary between foreign and domestic policies became blurred, and these organizations began to seek representation of what they considered to be their legitimate (if specialized) interests abroad.

Washington: I leave aside the consequent and repeated efforts to bring under control of the President and the Secretary of State the formulation and conduct of the nation's foreign policy in the capital, other than to express my conviction that agencies dealing exclusively and overtly with foreign policy operations should be integrated into and administered uniformly by the Department of State, and that the foreign activities of other agencies should be closely coordinated by State. But whatever bureaucratic structures, pressures and conflicts may be tolerated in Washington, the United States Government must speak with one voice and act as one person—the person of the President as represented by the Ambassador in foreign lands.

Overseas: With the mushrooming of separate overseas services after World War II, confusion arose abroad as well as at home. Here, too, efforts were made to restore order by a series of Presidential pronouncements, executive orders and letters affirming the primacy of the Ambassador over all elements (except military theater commands)* and by the administrative introduction of the "country team" concept. These were perhaps useful devices for the times. However, they fell short of a clearcut confirmation of the authority of the Ambassador commensurate with his responsibilities as established by law and long-standing practice. They also deviated from the basic principle by implicitly, or in some cases explicitly, treating the Ambassador as the representative, not of the President, but of the Department of State (the senior Department) and thus tended to transfer some interagency conflicts from Washington to the field. Moreover, implementation in general left much to be desired. Secretary of State Dulles, for example, resisted integration of operating services and would have limited the Department of State to formulation of foreign policy and a measure of coordination and supervision. The Foreign Service, crippled by a long period of non-recruitment and limited participation in wartime operations, was unable to provide a sufficient number of officers with

---

* EDITOR'S NOTE: See Appendix C for examples of these documents.

executive experience and other qualifications to "take charge" of the new instruments of foreign policy. Indeed, many old-line Foreign Service Officers publicly pined for a return to the good old days of traditional diplomacy and wished that the war and cold-war engendered excrescences would simply fade away. Despite these negative factors, however, there were many brilliant performances, both by career and by non-career Chiefs of Mission, in integrating and directing purposefully the activities of all elements at their posts. Many of these, reflecting a viewpoint which I shared, refused to use the term "country team."

The basic concept was succinctly set forth by Ambassador Graham Martin in his article "Organizational Imperatives" in the *Annals* of the American Academy of Political and Social Science (November, 1968):

> The ambassador, as the personal representative of the President of the United States, must assume responsibility, in the President's name, for everything that the United States government does in the country to which he is accredited. To discharge that responsibility effectively, he must also assume command in the President's name, of all activities of all United States personnel in the country. No ambassador worthy of being given such authority in the first place is likely to abuse it. If he does, the remedy is not to overrule him constantly, but to dismiss him.

Implementation of the Principle

The extent to which our overseas missions can be expected to operate efficiently and effectively depends primarily on two factors:

1. The attitudes and method of operation of the President and the Secretary of State;

2. The quality of our Ambassadors and their supporting personnel.

Washington Aspects. *Identification with the President:* The President's "special trust and confidence" in his Ambassadors must be more than the words on their commissions. It is essential to the Ambassador's status and performance that he know the President, and that he be known in the country of his residence to have a personal relationship with him (as well as, of course, with the Secretary of State). With the proliferation of Missions to the emergent nations (in ex-colonial areas previously not even warranting a Consulate) and to multilateral organizations, bringing the Ambassadorial total to 137, some problems arise which cannot be solved by the traditional personally autographed photograph. The President should see and should want to see individually his Ambassadors heading all Class I (23) and most Class II (33) Missions before they go to their posts and when they return to Washington on consultation and Leave. Ambassadors heading lesser posts (Classes III & IV-81) could be seen in small groups, perhaps at regular weekly meetings held for this purpose. All meetings, whether individual or group, should be on the official calendar, be referred to in daily White House press briefings, and be publicized by USIA [now the International Communication Agency] media. Consideration should also be given to holding the regular regional Ambassadorial Conferences, not in the field as at present, but in Washington, with the President addressing the group and participating in some of the discussions, and with the Secretary of State and other top-level officials from State and other Departments and agencies in attendance.

The Problem of Change in Administrations: Changes in the national Administration present a particular problem, especially when they involve a turnover in Party. The new Administration is likely to be unaware of the far-flung human resources at its command in the Foreign Service, unconvinced of (if not actually suspicious about) the non-partisan nature of this personnel, and unacquainted with most of its members. Naturally, the first concern of the new President is the selection of his immediate White House staff, then of the top-level personnel in his Cabinet and major Government agencies. Emerging from a domestic political campaign, he is likely to give less attention than they deserve (and probably less than he later wishes he had given) to Ambassadorial appointments, leaving these largely to his new Secretary of State and his domestically-oriented appointments aides (whose interest is mainly political patronage). Thus, the typical picture after a change of Administration is a surge of political appointments, considerable uncertainty in the career ranks, and some resultant marking of time in the development and carrying out of foreign policy. By midterm, the tide begins to turn; the political appointees abroad and in the immediate entourage of the new Secretary of State begin to disappear and be replaced by professionals as the new leaders begin to know them.

It would surely be in the national interest to improve this process. The senior Foreign Service Officer in the Department or a distinguished career Ambassador specially recalled from his post and/or the Director General of the Foreign Service should be placed at the direct disposition of the Secretary and the White House during the transition period to advise and assist in the Presidential appointments decisions to posts in the Department and at diplomatic missions. Such an officer (or officers) should be able to define any special criteria affecting selections for specific posts being considered; should be armed with the records and ratings of senior Foreign Service Officers and prepared to make specific recommendations for appointments from the Foreign Service; and should provide professional evaluation of the qualifications of proposed appointees from outside.

Informing the Ambassador: The Ambassador must be kept informed of all Government decisions and activities affecting the relationship between the United States and the country to which he is accredited. There has, of course, been a revolution in communications and transportation which has enabled (and tempted) top-level government officials, from the President down, to engage more actively in foreign travel and even to communicate directly with their counterparts in foreign countries—ranging from Presidential use of the "hot line" in crisis situations, to personal correspondence, to telephone conversations, to attendance at meetings of OECD [Organization for Economic Cooperation and Development] Finance Ministers or NATO Defense Ministers. This technological revolution has certainly quickened the pace and changed some of the methods of diplomacy, but it does not change the underlying importance of the bilateral relationships between individual countries in a world of sovereign nation states. Indeed, the state of these bilateral relationships may well have a decisive influence on the results of multilateral diplomacy.

Since most American officials are inexperienced in international affairs, an Executive Order should be issued making it clear throughout the Government that records must be kept of any contacts or conversations with officials of foreign governments and that these records must be provided to the Secretary of State and to the American Ambassador in the country involved. Any official contact of high-level United States Government officials visiting foreign countries should be made only after adequate consultation with the Ambassador and the appropriate member of the Embassy staff should be present to keep records of any conversations. Unless the Ambassador and his supporting element in the State Department are the repository of the totality of information bearing on relationships between the United States and the country in question, there will nowhere be any complete record of the relationship and the conduct of foreign affairs will be fragmented, with the risk of becoming counter-productive if not actually contradictory.

The same rule should apply to the members of the Congress and they should, of course, be kept aware of the importance of the considerations involved. I would observe parenthetically, however, that, within my experience, Congressmen have usually been more cautious and careful in their foreign contacts than Administration officials, relying on State Department support and advice in their travels abroad and preparing reports after their return.

Washington Liaison: In fulfillment of his role as the representative of the President (and thus of the entire Administration), the Ambassador, on his part, should keep in touch not only with the Secretary and Department of State but also with other interested Departments and agencies. Thus, it is important that, before he leaves for his post and whenever he returns to Washington, he call on other Cabinet members and key officials with substantial interest in the country to which he is accredited and/or having personnel assigned to his staff. In order to facilitate continuing liaison, he should be accompanied on such visits by appropriate members of his supporting "country desk" staff in the Department of State.

Foreign Ambassadors in Washington: Problems sometimes arise with respect to contacts with foreign Ambassadors accredited to the United States. Just as the American Ambassador in the foreign capital should be purposefully used to promote American interests and achieve American objectives abroad, so foreign governments consider their Ambassadors in Washington are in a preferred position to serve their purposes vis-a-vis the United States. The general rule is, and should be, that the Ambassador's business should be conducted primarily with the Ministry of Foreign Affairs (State Department) and that the Ministry (State Department) should arrange and facilitate, or at least be aware of, his contacts with other agencies. In relatively undisciplined societies such as ours, however, there is a tendency for other government officials to be intrigued by the idea of "playing diplomat" on their own. The White House staff, in particular, is frequently less than prudent in letting itself be drawn into conversations and negotiations with foreign diplomats in Washington on matters which should be handled by the State Department or by the United States Ambassador abroad.

The President is obligated to receive the credentials of all foreign Ambassadors when they arrive in Washington and normally tries to entertain the Diplomatic Corps at least once a year. He also sees the foreign Ambassadors accompanying distinguished visitors from their home countries. Contacts, whether by the President or by his National Security Adviser or other members of the White House, do involve a number of risks. For one thing, foreign governments sometimes try to use the White House channel to end-run around the American Ambassador in their own capitals and to reverse or modify unfavorable decisions which may have been communicated to them by the Ambassador on the spot. For another, it is manifestly impossible (as well as undesirable) for the White House to be adequately informed of the myriads of problems between the United States and other countries, or to deal effectively with specific issues outside the context of an ongoing broad relationship. Furthermore, as a physical matter, the President and his staff cannot maintain contact with more than a handful of the 130-odd Ambassadors in Washington and the net result is the creation of resentment and frictions among those who are unable to obtain such "favored status."

* * *

Overseas Aspects

Department Support: The Ambassador must have strong rear echelon support in the State Department. His back-up at home should be raised from its present level and strengthened to provide a sort of duplicate of the mission abroad, able to maintain liaison and get action from all interested agencies in Washington, and to provide quick replies to the Ambassador's communications. It is impossible to conduct United States foreign policy effectively if what are now called "country desk" elements in the State Department are denied access to important communicatons to and from the field and with foreign representatives in Washington, as is the case today. Important personnel resources are thus condemned to under-employment, while overworked senior officers are deprived of invaluable assistance and advice. It appears that the justification for such restrictions in the distribution of essential information has been due to top-level obsession with "leaks." As is well-known (to borrow a Soviet expression), most Washington leaks come from the top, anyway. The way to prevent leaks at lower levels is to create a feeling of responsibility, trust and participation. Indeed, the cutting off of operating levels from essential information could constitute a provocation to disgruntled personnel to take liberties with such information if and when they do happen to come by it.

Communication : The Ambassador will normally use the State Department channels of communications. He must, however, have access to and authority over other channels of communications from the Embassy operated by Defense and CIA. He must be kept regularly informed of all important substantive matters reported through these channels and be provided, at his request, with all reports or other communications sent through them.

Contacts: The Ambassador must control access by all members of his Embassy to officials of the government to which he is accredited. No element of the Embassy can be authorized to establish or maintain official contacts without the Ambassador's knowledge and approval. This is not to say that contacts should be restricted to or handled by the Ambassador himself. On the contrary, a good Ambassador will delegate responsibility broadly (his ability to do so should be a principal criterion in his selection), and not only authorize but actively encourage the development of working and social relationships at all levels and by all elements of the Embassy.

Personnel Control: If the Ambassador is to exercise effective authority over personnel in the service and on the payroll of other Departments and agencies than State, it must be made clear to them in Washington that his evaluation of their performance will have an important bearing on their future progress in their own services. The present informal and frequently *pro forma* rating procedures should be replaced by a systematic, uniform, accepted system of Ambassadorial performance reports on the senior personnel of all Departments and agencies comparable to those submitted on senior Foreign Service Officers.

A Unified Mission: An effective Ambassador will encourage all elements of the Mission to consider their specialized activities as contributing to the accomplishment of the overall objectives of the United States in the country of their assignment. Indeed, with a proper understanding of the common mission of all elements useful intramural cooperation in exchange of information and other forms of mutual aid can be developed, enhancing the overall performance of the Mission.

* * *

Modernizing the Role of the Ambassador

J. ROBERT SCHAETZEL

The presumptive conclusion is that if the ambassador is not obsolete, he certainly is obsolescent. The more charitable notion of "an endangered species" insinuates that the ambassador, roaming his exotic habitat, is worth preserving, perhaps as an anthropological specimen. In any event the question is timely, for the ambassador, wrapped in the yellowed trappings of diplomacy, is in the way of becoming one of the modern world's anachronisms.

Assumptions

This appraisal of the present and possible future role of the ambassador focuses on Western Europe where my experience lies, but implicitly includes such other industrialized countries as Canada, Japan, and the multilateral Atlantic organizations. I also submit that these remain the areas of fundamental interest to the United States. There are two errors of analysis—to attempt to force all foreign relations into the same matrix or, on the other extreme, to draw sharp distinctions between American foreign relations with the industrialized democracies, the communist world, the rich and the poor, developing nations and, finally, that new element, the multilateral organization. While the differences among these groups are extensive, nonetheless many of the observations to be made about the ambassadorial role in Western Europe and with respect to the multilateral organizations have applications to the role of chiefs of mission elsewhere in the world.

SOURCE: "Is the Ambassador an Endangered Species, or Merely Obsolete?" Commission on the Organization of the Government for the Conduct of Foreign Policy (Robert D. Murphy Commission), *Appendices: Commission on the Organization of the Government for the Conduct of Foreign Policy* (Washington, D.C.: Government Printing Office, 1976), vol. 6, Appendix Q, pp. 325–33.

As a caveat and to clarify this analysis, a few remarks should be made about the developing countries. These are more suppositions and questions than assertions. These countries, containing the bulk of the world's population and most of its poverty, struggle with basic internal problems of political and economic development. Even in the expansive, self-confident days of American foreign policy under Presidents Truman and Kennedy the specific problems of these countries rarely caught and held Washington's attention. This lack of political attention and the peculiarly local nature of the problems open a special role for the American ambassador. The right man, with a feel for the people and its regime, with energy and a small competent staff, can play a remarkable and constructive role. It is a role for a trained, experienced, sympathetic official who sees the job as the culmination of a career dedicated to the improvement of man's lot. This definition excludes the career officer who views the assignment as a necessary purgatory, or the political appointee who contributed so little his reward was Africa, Central America, or nothing.

The first general assumption is the phenomenon of a constricted, interrelated world, summed up by the word "interdependence." Interdependence, which subsumes the overwhelming importance of economic factors, means that international relations have become inseparable from domestic policies and programs. Of the many implications of this fundamentally altered basic situation, one is the change it imposes on diplomacy. From the Renaissance, when modern diplomacy was born, to the Age of Enlightenment and the 19th century intrigues of Metternich and Talleyrand, diplomacy was the exclusive province of the sovereign, accepted as such by the public. This remoteness of foreign affairs from the daily life of the citizen is a thing of the past.

A second assumption is the . . . change in the order of priorities among the several elements that make up international relations. While many of the familiar factors remain significant—political, defense, cultural—economic issues have come to dominate. This fact imposes a further set of priorities: the vital role of Western Europe and Japan, which with the United States will determine whether the world's economic and financial system works or fails. This is no classic problem in bilateral foreign relations, but a question of "system," of viable international organization.

A third assumption is that the decline in the status and authority of the State Department is irreversible. As Secretary Rogers's peculiar regime illuminated this trend, Secretary Kissinger's personal, fortissimo, performance temporarily obscures the Department's altered status, but does not change it. This decline only partially results from the supremacy of domestic economic and social factors. It is substantially due to the inevitable absorption by the office of the President of the tasks of intragovernmental coordination. With most domestic economic decisions profoundly affecting foreign policy and, conversely, the pursuit of foreign policy objectives requiring domestic economic adjustments or sacrifices, unless the State Department is to become a super-agency or an adjunct of the President's personal office, matters of such vital national concern must be managed at a level above that of the governmental departments. All of the major industrial nations experience similar decline in the prestige and authority of their foreign offices, and for the same reasons.

These are the forces that hasten the obsolescence of traditional diplomacy and its symbolic figurehead, the ambassador.

The Impact of Technological Change

Within a generation science and technology have had a revolutionary impact in traditional diplomacy. Electronic communication has eliminated distance. The jet aircraft has brought every capital within 24 hours of Washington. Thus the earlier isolation of the foreign mission in space and time, which enhanced the independence of the ambassador and extended his latitude for personal action, has been erased by modern technology.

The emergence of the pervasive media, visual and printed, has further circumscribed the ambassador's independence. Until the recent past governments and foreign offices had a considerable capacity to control the coverage of international affairs. In America, an isolationist tradition, a domestic press ready to accept the official dogma with respect to foreign developments, changed at the end of World War II. The media became a major factor in the conduct of international affairs. What an ambassador says or does, or is reported to have done, can become instantly known, and embarrassing, to his government. And as the media limits dramatically the area of maneuver of the Executive, so this reporting curtails further the latitude earlier enjoyed by the ambassador.

The foregoing factors interact with the maturing of the principle of non-discrimination as a tenet of contemporary international practice. The Hull trade agreements program, with its most-favored-nation principle, cemented non-discrimination into American foreign policy. Discrimination was to become the unusual instrument of diplomacy, indeed a weapon. Hence, any action that favored or punished one country would, thanks to the combination of modern technology and the media, become quickly and generally known. It was no longer possible, on the basis of general instructions, for an ambassador to offer or deny economic benefits within the exclusive framework of a bilateral relationship. In short, every bilateral action now must be weighed to assess its international reverberations. This analysis and the conclusions to be drawn from it can only be done in Washington.

Multilateral Diplomacy*

The development of multilateral diplomacy has been as striking as the foregoing, and has had equally dramatic effect on the conduct of American foreign relations. "Multilateral" covers a variety of international institutions, some of which we belong to, others of which we do not. The distinction is important. The organizations of which we are members—the United Nations, the OAS, the OECD, the new International Energy Agency—have the general pattern of a headquarters, resident American missions and periodic conferences involving delegations dispatched from Washington for limited periods. For organizations in which we are not members, for instance the European Community, the American role is different. It is similar to that of the traditional diplomatic mission, accredited to the organization in question with the duties of reporting, representation and negotiation.

The common denominator is a sharp change away from bilateral, nation-to-nation diplomacy. The areas of work tend to be specialized. It is the era of the expert, the technician who flies out from the capital for the periodic meeting and who is serviced by permanent, technical international staffs. All foreign offices have found it increasingly difficult to supervise effectively this technical work—in air safety, water pollution, allocation of broadcast frequencies; the experts and the detailed instructions originate in the competent substantive departments and agencies. For the State Department officers responsible for overseeing this work, the greater their immersion in the technical fields the less they seem a part of the general work of the State Department. Thus, insofar as the Department is the protector of the embassies' interests, this association of the Department's specialists with the functional agencies alienates still further the ambassador and his staff.

As the incessant international conferences move away from the several headquarters such as New York or Geneva and descend on one or another foreign capital, an ambassador suddenly finds his em-

---

* EDITOR's NOTE: See Chapter 4 for more commentary on multilateral diplomacy.

bassy crawling with experts from the Federal Aviation Administration or the National Science Foundation. He and his staff are reduced to performing service functions—administrative support, communications to and from Washington.

Another variant of multilateral diplomacy is the protracted international conference with a defined task and presumed terminal date. This device has proliferated and the meetings can end up anywhere —Helsinki, Vienna, Geneva, Paris. A similar administrative load is imposed on the ambassador and his staff, although with unpleasant variations. The agenda of some of these conferences may be at the center of political relations as distinct from the predominantly technical work referred to above. Whether the issue is Vietnam or conventional arms control, the ambassador has less excuse for unfamiliarity with the subject and the results will frequently affect his normal responsibilities. At best he will be a supernumerary and his primary obligation that of discreet host.

Thus, multilateral diplomacy accelerates the diminishing role of the resident ambassador. The national state remains a pawn on the board, but the game is elsewhere, played out by different pieces.

Why the Sense of Obsolescence?

The changes and innovations outlined set the framework which diminishes, inevitably, the role of the ambassador. But other, more specific developments and actions have depreciated the currency.

Like all institutions, diplomacy moves under its own inertial force. Practices once pertinent, but now irrelevant, are thoughtlessly or stubbornly continued. The most obvious is the timeless charade of formal social activity which has become synonymous with diplomacy and occupies much of the ambassador's life—the incestuous receptions and dinners within the confines of the diplomatic community. It is a subculture established by tradition and carried on by traditionalists. The more irrelevant the social practice, the more frantic the pace. The indulgent public amusement of "Call Me Madam" seems lacking today.*

America's peculiar process of appointing ambassadors has contributed to the sense of their obsolescence. Happily enough, no other country follows our practice of using diplomatic posts, especially in Europe, as a reward for political service or contribution or as a means of dealing with an embarrassing domestic political problem. This may

---

* EDITOR's NOTE: "Call Me Madam" was a successful musical satire on Perle Mesta, appointed Minister to Luxembourg in 1949.

be a remnant of Jacksonian cynicism, of the conviction that public service is the only profession for which neither experience nor training is required. Some of the men and women imposed as American ambassadors on helpless foreign governments lead only to the conclusion that our Presidents have not regarded these appointments as serious. Statistics frequently employed to prove that career officers hold all but 20, 25 or 30 percent of the ambassadorial posts only demonstrate again how statistics can lie. In a disproportionate number of cases the political appointee has been named to the most important, certainly the most comfortable, foreign post. Whatever his innocence of foreign affairs, the big contributor or the evicted cabinet officer knows that the good life does not lie south of the Sahara.

It is impossible to take seriously positions the President treats frivolously. Over the years our chief executives have unambiguously proven that rather than assignments for placing abroad the President's alter ego, London, Paris and Rome are regarded as overseas fringe parking areas where awkward political problems can be temporarily stored. Indifference to adverse foreign reactions adds arrogance to this peculiar practice.

In this make-believe world one illusion is carefully nurtured: the ambassador as the personal representative of the President. The notion assuages the egos of career and non-career ambassadors and is furthered by their staffs whose personal dreams require that they share the luster that surrounds this fable. Normally no more than an oddity, translated into reality the illusion can become embarrassing. For instance, Graham Martin, when ambassador to Thailand, exercised the prerogative, insisting that as personal representative of the President he outranked the visiting Vice President, to Hubert Humphrey's astonishment and subsequent irritation. Episodes such as this disclose a diplomatic netherworld and contribute to the feeling that diplomacy as presently conducted is entirely obsolete.

Personal diplomacy, whether by the head of state or foreign secretary, was not an invention of President Nixon or Dr. Kissinger. But they dramatized a practice that had attracted and seduced predecessors and politicians holding similar positions abroad. There is no reason to believe that the glamor of the state visit or the excitement of personal diplomacy will diminish. Politicians have convinced themselves that the practice enhances their domestic position; it certainly provides a momentary escape from realities at home. As with the diplomatic life in each capital, the state visit begets return visits. The increased tempo of these visits requires that they be described as "serious" and "working," designed to produce or seem to produce concrete results as contrasted with the formal, ceremonial excursion, without substantive pretension. Inevitably, the new genre must be intimate as well. This means the pruning of aides in attendance. More often than not, and at American initiative, the Presidential head of government tête-à-têtes or even those of visiting foreign ministers exclude the American ambassador. One result is the parallel exclusion of the ambassador of the other side. The result is devastating. Neither the American ambassador nor his foreign counterpart in Washington nor their respective staffs will have more than the most rudimentary or superficial account of the substance or the atmosphere of the discussions. No matter what the ability of the American representative or his personal status with the host government, his effectveness cannot withstand this signal of a lack of confidence by his master. The cult of intimacy, secrecy and exclusion underscores the degree to which the ambassador has become irrelevant, particularly where serious matters are discussed. If the ambassadorial position were considered important and regulated as a consequential, continuing channel of communication, then both the President and the Secretary of State would deem it in their interest to impress upon the principal members of the other government that the ambassador was an esteemed, trusted colleague and obviously an indispensable part of the United States foreign policy machinery.

The aura of ambassadorial irrelevance is furthered by the intensified contacts between specialized ministers—especially finance and defense, but the fraternal relationship is spreading rapidly to officials in other functional fields. The generally technical nature of the business and the personal relationship developing out of attendance at international conferences and meetings, furthered by the handy telephone and airplane, lead to the present regime of personal contact. The American Secretary of Defense, meeting his counterpart at the NATO Nuclear Planning Group or at some military exercise, will generally have a closer personal relationship with these colleagues than with any American ambassador Once again, the chief of mission is assigned the role of resort hostess for his cabinet visitor, offering his table for the working luncheon and opera seats in the evening.

The fact of mounting irrelevance is driven home by the ambassador's remoteness from most consequential international negotiations. Only if the matter is utterly trivial and local in nature will the task be given to the local chief of mission, and then only under close instructions and with the physical support of Washington experts. But for the serious matters, where the side effects may be considerable, the rule is to dispatch negotiators from the capital. The ambassador, at best a silent observer, may be humored by polite inquiries, but he will not be a serious part of the delegation. Under Kissinger the practice has been refined to the point that on occasion the ambassador has been unaware of the Secretary's presence in the nation.

In a word, the ambassador is out of the serious play. He is rarely viewed as the best channel of communication with the head of government, he is not charged with the critical negotiating tasks, he is subordinated to visiting Washington officials and negotiating experts (visitors would be amazed if he had the temerity to offer substantive views), and—to make the message unmistakably clear—his expected duties are those of the hosteler.

It should be evident by now that the Ambassador is not a policy officer. He is remote from the Byzantine process which evolves the broad structure of American foreign policy, policy that will encompass his domain and control his actions. Even with respect to bilateral policy his recommendations will be only part of the raw material that will finally emerge as governmental policy. If he happens to be assigned to a country which Washington has ignored or where there is some unease due to changed local situations, then, without alternative, the views of the ambassador may be sought; he may even be brought home for consultation. But the pattern is clear. The ambassador is no more than one of the many sources of data that pour into the Washington policy computer.

* * *

Can the Ambassador's Role Be Redefined and Redesigned so as to Be Useful in Today's World?

Obviously, the ambassador, his functions and possible re-tooling make sense only as part of the general scheme of American foreign relations. For instance, if, by decision or indolence, it is decided to perpetuate the present organization and method of conduct of American foreign affairs, there is neither incentive nor need to agonize over the role of the ambassador. On the assumption, however, that substantial change in the basic structure and practice should and will be made, it should be clear from what has been said earlier in this paper that the kinds of ambassadors we appoint and their functions must change radically.

As far as the bilateral ambassador is concerned, again in the context of the advanced industrialized countries, his responsibilities should lie primarily in the analytical realm. His goal should be to know better and more intimately than any other American official the dynamics, the problems and the potentialities of the country to which he is assigned. This means the systematic development of personal contacts with the elite, those who shape opinion. "Elite," incidentally, while including ministers and their satellites in the capital, encompasses certainly those who have or may in the future have authentic influence. This description includes those out of power and, for instance in France and Italy, members of the Communist parties and Communist-dominated trade unions.

Concentration on incisive, detailed analysis and the human contacts to supplement this analysis would provide the basic material for the other significant tasks of the "new" ambassador: familiarity with the points of pressure where American policies or interests can be advanced; knowledge of the local scene so authoritative that the ambassador becomes an inevitable and indispensable part of any American negotiations which involve his country.

From these personal qualities and responsibilities flows the obligation to administer and lead an embassy of which the purpose is an extension of his own role. Rather than the present practice with the ambassador pursuing his own substantively inconsequential social business or such specific tasks as the Department and his own staff think he can perform under instruction and without endangering the Republic, the future ambassador should be in fact the senior responsible officer and the intellectual leader of his mission. This implies administrative direction of the embassy.

If this is the evolution of the job, then what is the function of the deputy chief of mission? In the past, the methodical elaboration and expansion of the role of the DCM has been partly cynical, anticipating the appointment as chief of mission the naive politician, party benefactor or career officer coasting toward retirement. More creditably, the deputy has come to be the administrator and manager of the embassy, the engineer of a ship where each section has its established and defined tasks. His concern is more to see that these tasks are accomplished than to determine whether they are worth doing or even done intelligently. In many situations, where his chief is a political appointee, the deputy may serve as chargé for a good part of the time —to the common relief of his staff and the host country. He will also have the delicate and frequently difficult job of nurturing the illusion that the ambassador is authentically in charge and understands what his embassy is doing. No one should deprecate the challenge of this assignment or fail to give credit for the admirable way in which the function is generally performed.

But under the revisionist theories advanced here the DCM's role changes. It may become even more difficult. The more the ambassador is the actual leader and administrator of the embassy, the more he reduces the heretofore central position of the deputy. Indeed, the DCM would enjoy all the frustrations that are the curse of any deputy. His primary function would be to fill in when the ambassador is away or to perform specific tasks assigned to him by his chief of mission. He would no longer be the chief executive officer of the embassy. Because of the peculiarities of the present arrangement, the myth exists that the DCM will possess those administrative skills the ambassador lacks. If future ambassadors have the intrinsic qualities premised here, they will have as much administrative ability as any deputy. In point of fact, authentic administrative talent is one of the rarest human attributes, and one should have a low level of expectation that men such as General George Marshall will appear frequently on the scene as ambassadors, deputies, or secretaries of state.

The qualifications to be sought in the ambassador would appear to be these: First, one assumes extensive and intensive experience in foreign affairs. Generally this competence will have been acquired in the career service, but it may also be the result of work outside of government—in academia, foundations, business, or law. The postulate is that foreign affairs is a serious, valid, responsible field of human endeavor like medicine, law, or plumbing. The notion is rejected that a successful housing contractor can pick up this expertise in on-the-job training once he arrives at his post.

Second, in addition to a general knowledge of foreign affairs the future ambassador will have to be well grounded in international economics. It should be emphasized that there is no necessary correlation between business experience and the kinds of economic knowledge which will be a prerequisite to the modern ambassador's effective performance.

Third, he must also know and have a feel for the way the American government works—the mechanics of the State Department, the interdepartmental relationships and pressures, the White House and, perhaps of greatest importance, the workings of the Congress. And this least static of all fields will require constant up-dating, necessitating frequent visits to Washington, contacts with each point of political power and, again, especially with the Congress.

Fourth, another essential area of knowledge is the multilateral system. He must know what it is, how it is supposed to operate, how it actually works, why it is important, what American policy is toward the system; and, specifically, he must appreciate how bilateral relations fit into this system. Granted this is like insisting that a Catholic priest know and sympathize with an evolving ecumenical congress. In Europe, for example, the bilateral ambassador must recognize that in certain areas, frequently the most critical, he must work for the subordination of the national and bilateral interests within the multilateral system. He may find even more difficult the need to accommodate himself to the superior substantive knowledge of the multilateral ambassador and accept the latter's judgment on tactics.

The bilateral ambassador is part of a complex, dynamic process of change in which the multilateral system grows in importance at the expense of the nation state and, coincidentally, of that notable symbol of national sovereignty, the ambassador. Furthermore, this icon of sovereignty must henceforth see himself as one part of a field operation, of a team, with others directing the play.

Fifth, this prescription assumes that the ambassador will possess the qualities definitively enumerated by Harold Nicolson, especially the diplomatic temperament. At heart, this is the capacity to understand the other man's point of view, his goals, interests, problems and frustrations without losing sight of American interests and policies. It is the command of this material, conveyed persuasively to Washington, that establishes the limits and opportunities of American policy. As economic and social factors increase in importance, the ambassador must extend the range of his interest well beyond the fusty embassy-foreign office connection to the whole field of governmental ministries and programs.

The foregoing might seem to ignore the classical diplomatic problems. In fact, any ambassador must be equipped to cope with an internal political upheaval, war, the evacuation of American citizens, etc. While the likelihood may be remote, he and his staff must be prepared to meet such crises.

*　*　*

There are certain things the future ambassador should *not* be and should *not* do. He is not America's public relations officer, roaming the foreign countryside selling himself and the United States. Large, complicated and dynamic foreign societies are highly resistant to PR campaigns. Indeed, intensive polls of European opinion about the United States show an extraordinary propensity of the European to ignore the persistent urgings of his own government and national media as to what his attitude should be toward the United States. After years of Gaullism and its open animus toward many things American, the Frenchman stubbornly clung to his own, peculiarly friendly regard for the United States. The public relations gambit is an easy escape for the non-career ambassador, for as a businessman or politician it is a familiar way of life. It can consume all the energy of the most insatiable ambassador. It is an activity to which the resources of the embassy can be easily rallied. If one concludes that the objective of foreign policy is good relations, then the techniques of the advertising agency become the new tools of diplomacy. Good relations may be abstractly desirable but as a practical matter irrelevant. We should have learned this, if nothing more, from a decade of General de Gaulle. If the ambassador should perform the tasks outlined here, the public relations function is distinctly secondary. In this new role of ambassador he may establish the image of a serious, competent and responsible representative of the United States and coincidentally grace the profession and his country. At the same time he will in all probability frustrate and irritate the garden clubs and diplomatic community by his unavailability for the spring tours and national days.

It must be accepted that under the best of circumstances the ambassador will be only peripherally involved in the design and direction of American foreign policy. On the other hand, he should be given a significant role with respect to tactics, an element critical to the effectiveness of foreign relations. In recent years the leash has been short and the ambassador on a choke collar. It has become habitual for Washington to issue instructions to an ambassador in the same painstaking detail normally used in parental guidance of very young and potentially wayward children. It is essentially absurd to believe that the blueprint for tactics can be intelligently formulated in some Washington darkroom. The management of American interests with the foreign government is the one area where the knowledgeable and experienced embassy should have primacy. Contrariwise, precise, inflexible Washington instructions, written by officers and committees whose attention is riveted on interdepartmental competition and the effect of any action on the array of Congressional pressures and interest groups will invariably subordinate the chances of actually achieving the American objective to the making of a domestic record.

Within the broad framework of responsibility for tactics the ambassador must regain control of visiting delegations. Today, as hosteler, he is subject to laws which insist that he accept all those who seek bed and board. He must be able to object to a proposed delegation and indicate why its dispatch or its composition or its timing may be adverse to American interests and even contrary to the purpose of the enterprise. Obviously, in certain circumstances there may be overriding reasons, known only to Washington, dictating the visit despite the valid objections of the ambassador.

There are related dangers in this absent-minded conversion of the ambassador into a passive, acquiescent clerk. As America becomes more inward-oriented, quasi-isolationist, the inclination to solve or ease domestic tensions by exporting them can take on epidemic proportions. It is routine in the trade field to attack foreign behavior and practices in order to curry domestic favor, to show stoutheartedness and American bravado. Those few who are honest enough to admit the excess of the American charge or the likely outcome of harmed relations insist that this is the price to be paid to placate domestic forces. Any democracy will demand some of this. The risk is real that the anti-internationalist trend in the United States will encourage even greater use of this nasty practice. The ambassador should be one brake on the excesses of this habit.

Earlier reference was made to the puffery of the ambassador as the "personal representative of the President." This is, today, quite clearly a conceit. The demands on the President's time are such, his taste for personal diplomacy so highly cultivated, that any reversal of this situation to the relationship between Renaissance prince and royal agent is entirely improbable. Should a well placed and feisty ambassador decide to appeal over the head of the Secretary of State to the President he would do so at considerable peril. Only a Franklin D. Roosevelt, with a Florentine taste for intrigue and contrived confusion, would decide to embarrass his senior and resident foreign affairs adviser. It would have to be the most arrogant or obtuse ambassador who would wish to alienate the man who controls and supervises his daily life.

One argument for perpetuating the myth is to enhance the ability of the ambassador to control those officers on his staff who are employees of one or another domestic agencies and to strengthen his hand against invasions of Washington delegations. This is not a particularly persuasive argument. Short of sustaining illusion, there would seem to be other means of achieving these worthy objectives. The President and the Secretary of State can lay down and enforce the rule: the ambassador on the ground has full authority. If the chief of mission is experienced and competent, exercises his command intelligently and is supported by the President and Secretary, the shaky crutch of "personal representative" could be gently discarded.

Conclusions

A subordinate but recurrent theme in this dirge is the casual manner in which the Congress accepts and even abets a system within which the ambassador has become an expensive anachronism. At a time when the nation questions all government, looks hopefully for both honesty and competence in its elected and appointed officials, the Senate could assist greatly in the responsible conduct of foreign relations (and its own image) by indicating its intention to infuse the words "advise and consent" with meaning and that in the future the Committee will confirm only fully qualified nominations. As I have proposed elsewhere, the Foreign Relations Committee could borrow from the procedures developed by the American Bar Association to review, informally, proposed nominations to the judiciary. The Foreign Relations Committee could establish a senior, nonpartisan panel of private experts to review presidential nominations prior to formal consideration by the Committee. The panel would be expected to advise the Committee whether the candidates met minimum qualifications for confirmation. The first act of such a panel would be to develop in cooperation with the Committee the criteria to be used subsequently in judging the nominations. When the Committee under Senator Fulbright made a timid and more limited effort toward this objective it encountered Administration resistance and the reform movement collapsed. It would be nice if the Senate were to take seriously its Constitutional duties. But it seems unlikely that anything of the sort suggested here will be initiated by the Congress in the absence of interest and support of the Executive Branch.

An objective appraisal of world trends and present American instincts and practices leads to the conclusion that the ambassador of the future will play a more limited role than the pompous illusion of the President's alter ego abroad, or the inflated image of a policy-maker working in tight partnership with the Secretary of State. If the new ambassador is to be useful he must be a modern, highly professional man, knowledgeable in economics, expert at his business, particularly with respect to the country or organization to which he is accredited. This implies a considerable time in place. From this base he should become a major source of information and insight and, thus, an important part, but only a part, of the policy-making process. His impact on policy will derive from his mastery of his profession and sure knowledge of his specific assignment, not from his title or social graces.

A reconstructed embassy, with different, more limited and specialized functions, and a renovated, modernized ambassador will be exceedingly difficult goals to achieve. All of this change goes against tradition and the momentum of the service. It would cause reexamination of shabby domestic political mores to determine whether the interests of the country are actually served by a process of appointment which puts knowledge and competence at the bottom of the list of qualifications. Such a revolution must work against a massive, silent conspiracy among all diplomatic establishments, whose self-interest it is to perpetuate and enjoy their baronial, genteel obsolescence. The best that might be hoped for would be to set a new direction. Even this modest goal has not the slightest chance of success in the absence of conviction on the part of the President and the Secretary of State, supported by the Senate, that American foreign relations demands a new orientation and approach.

6

Professionals and Amateurs

*Diplomacy is not a thing that can be fully mastered by any system
of training, and proficiency can be secured only after long experience.*
HUGH S. GIBSON, *The Road to Foreign Policy*

*The professional diplomatist is, after all, only a species of physician.
He has, like all physicians, a shabby and irritating group of patients:
violent, headstrong, frivolous, unreasonable. He will go on treating
them as long as he is permitted to, saving them from such of their
follies as he can, patching up the damages done by those follies
from which he could not save them. He will do this because it is
his professional nature to do it, and because he probably loves these
shabby patients in his heart even while he despairs of them.*
GEORGE F. KENNAN, "History and Diplomacy As Viewed
by a Diplomatist"

Preceding chapters have examined several dichotomies in diplomatic
practice, such as the old diplomacy versus the new diplomacy, secrecy
versus openness, diplomacy versus propaganda, conventional bipartite
versus multipartite forums and relations, and diplomacy at the traditional versus the ministerial and summit levels. Chapter 6 explores
another such dichotomy in diplomatic thought and statecraft—professionals versus amateurs, or careerists versus noncareerists.

The first two essays deal specifically with the United States
Foreign Service or the career professionals, on which a flood of de-
scriptive and analytical literature has been produced in recent decades.
In "Foreign Service as a Career," William Barnes and John Heath
Morgan discuss the basic role of the Foreign Service, the requisite

qualities of the career officer, and the variety in the life and work of the careerist. George F. Kennan adopts a more critical approach in his essay, "Foreign Service—Past and Future." He assesses the development of the career Foreign Service within the political system. He concludes that the Foreign Service's emphasis on bureaucratic over-organization and depersonalization, rather than on individual competency and initiative, are "the marks not of the Foreign Service alone but of the very environment in which it exists; and the young person seeking the road to self-fulfillment will not be likely to escape them by avoiding the Foreign Service career."

In the next essay, "Why Not Give Diplomacy Back to the Diplomats?" Ellis O. Briggs criticizes the expansion and overstaffing of U.S. diplomatic missions and the proliferation of overseas activities administered by a variety of "peripheral performers" who unnecessarily complicate diplomacy's tasks. Diplomats, he argues, should not be expected to "transform institutions" in foreign lands, but should concern themselves with their proper traditional responsibility of influencing the policies of other governments.

The chapter continues with four essays comparing the essence and virtues of professionals with the virtues of amateurs—whom Kennan has referred to as dilettantes—in the diplomatic service. Elmer Plischke's "Career Status of United States Diplomats" forearms the reader for the debate by analyzing the American diplomatic corps, providing statistical breakdowns on the worldwide distribution of careerists and noncareerists based on types of missions, historical trends in the ratios of careerists to noncareerists, and similar factors. In "Ambassadors: Professionals or Amateurs?," Clare Boothe Luce, herself a noncareerist envoy to an important European capital, makes several observations on the value of "amateurs," or non-Foreign Service ambassadors, in the American diplomatic corps. In an essay that is reminiscent of the commentary on summit diplomacy contained in Chapter 4, she reminds the reader that the President, by constitutional mandate, is the number one amateur in American diplomacy. She contends that ambassadorial appointments should be made on the basis of "the best qualified" persons, and not simply on the basis of their membership in the Foreign Service. This view is also held by many others, including Lincoln Gordon who, in "Careerists vs. Noncareerists," asserts that he does not believe the interests of the United States would be best served by reserving all ambassadorial appointments to members of the Foreign Service. Among the noncareerists, however, he distinguishes between "purely political appointments," which he deplores, and what he calls "semiprofessional noncareerists."

The task, he concludes, is to find "the most competent people for the jobs" and, in the case of equal competence, he recommends giving preference to the careerists.

In the final essay of this chapter, career Foreign Service Officer Charles W. Thayer espouses the "Case for Professional Diplomats." He insists that the better qualified person is likely to be found in the Foreign Service in the overwhelming majority of instances. He admits that there have been "rare occasions" when a noncareerist has become an able ambassador, but suggests that there has been an inordinate number of failures of noncareerists in American diplomacy. Like most commentaries of this issue, Thayer's essay rails against the use of diplomatic missions as payoffs for political debts and maintains that the American diplomatic corps will be served best by those who have made a career of diplomacy.

Foreign Service as a Career

WILLIAM BARNES AND JOHN HEATH MORGAN

The Role of the Modern Foreign Service

Foreign policy may be defined as the course of action planned by a government to guide its relations with foreign countries. Under the Constitution the President has primary responsibility for formulating and directing our foreign policy, subject to the powers reserved to the Congress in this field. The Secretary of State is the chief adviser to the President on foreign policy and the executive agent of the President in carrying out that policy. The Department of State and the Foreign Service are the staff on which the Secretary relies for the information and counsel essential to his task of advising the President and executing his policy.

The original institutional separateness of the Department and the Foreign Service has now largely disappeared following the completion in 1957 of the amalgamation of the foreign affairs personnel of the Department and the Foreign Service in a single new service, all whose members are obligated to serve both at home and abroad. These members of the new Foreign Service, whether stationed in the Department or abroad, are all engaged in the day-to-day conduct of foreign policy.

The tasks of the Foreign Service have multiplied in number and broadened in scope as the international outlook of the United States has changed from one of early aloofness to one of deep involvement in complex political, economic, military, and cultural relations with all the world. During the 185 years of its existence the handful of amateurs originally comprising the Foreign Service has grown to a

SOURCE: *The Foreign Service of the United States* (Washington, D.C.: Government Printing Office, 1961), pp. 300–1, 323–30.

professional corps of several thousand persons of widely diversified and specialized skills. Today the Foreign Service is required to play a part in both the conduct and the formulation of foreign policy, to observe, report, interpret, and advise concerning all developments in foreign countries which may have a bearing on our foreign policy, and to provide guidance for the extensive and comprehensive programs, frequently involving other agencies, which may be required to give effect to our foreign policy.

To deal adequately with these tasks requires not merely a corps of officers trained in the traditional diplomatic and consular functions but also large numbers of officers skilled in such fields as international finance, foreign trade, labor relations, science, geography, personnel administration, budgetary and fiscal work, and business management. The new Foreign Service, therefore, offers challenging careers not only to those primarily interested in political science and international relations but also to those interested in general public administration and to those skilled in many specialties. One of the principal purposes of the amalgamation of the Departmental and Foreign Services was to provide the organizational framework and career status essential for the incorporation of such administrative and specialist personnel in the Foreign Service in adequate numbers. The recruitment and development of such personnel remains a primary concern of the administration of the Foreign Service.

* * *

The Foreign Service as a Career

Today more young people are attracted by the idea of a Foreign Service career than at any previous time. This attraction is due to recognition both of the importance and interest of the work of the Foreign Service and of the fact that the Service as now established appears to constitute a stable profession of high prestige and adequate remuneration with good prospects for personal development and advancement.

Among these young people are persons of widely varying types, many of whom possess specific qualifications which would be of value in a Foreign Service career. Every potential candidate should take into account the fact, however, that the Foreign Service career calls for a balance of capacities and attitudes difficult to achieve and which may not be compatible with his own interests or bent of mind. In the latter case the candidate should consider whether some other career might not offer greater personal satisfaction and usefulness.

Among the various types attracted to the Service, one of the more usual is the scholarly young student of international affairs whose choice lies between an academic and a Foreign Service career. Such a candidate will make an excellent officer if he is able to meet and accept not merely the requirements for a broad knowledge of international affairs but also the perhaps more difficult personal requirements.

The Foreign Service officer's tasks, for example, require wide association with people. He must know and be on friendly terms with many people in diverse walks of life in order to obtain the views and information necessary for his work as an observer and reporter. He must therefore like to know people, to meet new people, and to extend his acquaintanceship at his post as far as possible. When he goes to a new post he must be ready and willing to begin all over again, without loss of zest, the process of acquiring numerous, knowledgeable, and reliable contacts. The candidate whose temperament and inclinations are not in this direction may not find the Foreign Service a sympathetic career.

Just as the scholar is attracted by the intellectual content of the Foreign Service officer's work, so the socially inclined young person is often attracted by the social and ceremonial aspects of Foreign Service life. Social talents are useful in the Foreign Service career, but, unless the socially minded officer can utilize the social activities of the Foreign Service to obtain results valuable for the furtherance of his work, he may not be more successful than the introspective scholar.

Still a third type, the missionary minded, appears also to be attracted by the idea of a Foreign Service career. Some young men whose early inclinations have turned toward religion but who have not been quite sure enough of their religious vocation to enter the ministry are inclined to think of the Foreign Service as a substitute in which they could realize their desire to benefit mankind. These persons also are unlikely to be successful unless they can bring their desires into practical focus within the range of the mission of the Foreign Service, which is primarily to promote the interests and policy of the United States.

Since the mission of the Foreign Service is, moreover, not merely to observe and report but to execute American foreign policy, the successful Foreign Service officer must be not merely everyone's friend but also the vigorous expounder, the determined defender, and the patient, prudent, and persistent negotiator of our foreign policy.

The Foreign Service aspirant who is prepared to meet all these requirements must further reckon with the fact that the Foreign Service has its share of hardships, discomforts, and hazards. Among these are the hazards to health present at many posts, the difficulties of educating children, and the financial burdens and other problems involved in transferring from one post to another every 3 or 4 years. Approximately one-third of all Foreign Service posts are classified as "hardship posts" because of extraordinarily difficult or notably unhealthful living conditions. At times officers may be assigned to posts where, because of war or disturbed political conditions, their families cannot accompany them. A Foreign Service officer and his family must accept these and other conditions of official life abroad and adjust to them as best they can.

*   *   *

Diversity of Life and Work. The diversity of environments and conditions of life in the Foreign Service present a constant stimulus and challenge. Foreign Service officers live and work in all the major cultural areas of the world—the British Commonwealth, Latin America, Western Europe, Eastern Europe, the Near East, Africa, South Asia, and the Far East. Wide differences exist in their material environment—including such factors as climate, health, and living conditions—which may be epitomized by the contrasts between life in London and Paris and life in a tropical Africa post. The cultural environment in each area also presents major contrasts in language, customs, religion, and psychological attitudes. For example an officer at a post in Canada lives and works in an environment not markedly different from that of the United States; on the other hand, an officer in Kabul, Afghanistan, must operate in a cultural setting that is almost entirely outside American experience.

The diversity of conditions under which a Foreign Service officer lives is paralleled by the infinite variety of his daily work. In the course of their duties individual officers may write a report on the local market for American office equipment; read the President's Thanksgiving Day Proclamation to a gathering of American residents; register the birth of an American baby; locate the lost relatives of Americans; intercede with the local authorities on behalf of an American tourist who has been robbed; arrange for the burial of a deceased American and the settlement of his estate; exercise good offices in settling a wage dispute between the master of an American vessel and his crew; pass on the applications of immigrants for visas to enter the United States; issue passports to American citizens; cooperate with the public affairs officer in recommending travel grants for foreign students to visit the United States; assist in drawing up a post operating budget; deal with office personnel and staffing problems or questions of post operation and maintenance of Government property and equipment; participate in the negotiation of a commercial treaty; and prepare reports on local political and economic developments. The wide range of Foreign Service work, embracing as it does almost every field of human activity, provides an interest and intellectual stimulus which can be matched in few occupations.

Opportunities for Specialization. Many candidates for the Foreign Service think of the Service as offering a career specifically in the field of international political relations. Actually the complex and difficult process of formulating and executing our foreign policy calls for a wide range of specialized skills and knowledge outside the general political field. Operation of the vast and intricate machinery required to administer the Foreign Service demands a high degree of management ability and executive competence. There is thus room in the Foreign Service not only for specialists in political affairs but also for skilled technicians in a diversity of subjects within the broad fields of economics and administration.

Officers are given the opportunity, through assignments and training, to develop special competence in various lines of work for which their previous experience may fit them or for which they may have an inclination. Experts are needed in such fields as international finance and trade, commercial promotion, petroleum, minerals, aviation, shipping, telecommunications, labor affairs, international organizations, and administration—including fiscal, budget, personnel, and property management work. In addition to these functional specialties, officers may become experts on different areas of the world through special courses of study in their languages, history, and culture, combined with assignments in the area of specialization. While encouraging and assisting officers to develop specialized skills, the Department guards against overspecialization by occasionally rotating specialist officers to other duties that will broaden their perspectives and help prepare them for positions of higher responsibility outside their individual specialties.

Human Relationships. One of the most attractive aspects of the Foreign Service is the opportunity it affords an officer to establish personal associations and friendships with fellow workers—Americans and foreigners—in every walk of life. The Service itself has a strong *esprit de corps*, and there is a general feeling of fellowship and *camaraderie* among its members. Friendships formed by officers within the Service tend to be durable and rewarding. An officer also derives much pleasure and profit from the personal relationships he establishes in the exercise of his duties. His value to our Government is determined in large measure by the success which attends his efforts to cultivate and gain the confidence of local government officials, local political leaders, leading businessmen, educators, and professional men, religious and cultural leaders, representatives of the press, and leaders of labor organizations. The development of a wide circle of personal contacts brings its own reward in terms of stimulating human relationships and comprehension of the political, economic, and social forces at work in the country.

For the young man or woman who seeks interesting and challenging work providing broad and varied experience, the advantages and opportunities of a career in the Foreign Service far outweigh the hardships and handicaps. To work in a field vital to the welfare of one's country, to represent that country before other governments, to live among the peoples of other countries, and to learn and understand the diverse histories, cultures, languages, and institutions of many stimulating aspects of a career that offers high rewards in terms of self-fulfillment and personal satisfaction.

Foreign Service—Past and Future

GEORGE F. KENNAN

The idea that the United States of America ought to have a professional service for the performance of diplomatic and consular functions abroad had its origins in the final years of the last century. By 1914 it had already found recognition in the creation of separate career services for these two main branches of activity. Its fruition was reached in the mid-twenties with the passage of the Rogers Act, which combined the two existing services into a single "Foreign Service of the United States." High hopes prevailed at the outset for the future of the new combined service. No one doubted that a corner had been passed. The United States Government, it was assumed, would now proceed to develop in permanence a good professional arm to assist in the work of representation of this country abroad and to act as the main source of information and advice for American statesmen and envoys who were themselves not likely to be professionals. In the ensuing years a number of trustful young men, among them this writer, took the prescribed examinations and entered the new Foreign Service, confident that the country had made up its mind about the virtues of career diplomacy; that it wanted a real professional service; that the basic principles underlying the Rogers Act had been permanently accepted; and that one could rely on the uniformity and stability of the conditions in which, from then on, the competition for advancement and recognition would proceed.

These hopes and expectations, as experience was to prove, were largely unfounded. Those who nurtured them had failed to take account of the unsuitability of the American governmental system for the promulgation of any sustained administrative program (partic-

SOURCE: "The Future of Our Professional Diplomacy," *Foreign Affairs*, vol. 33 (July 1955), pp. 566–69, 584–86.

ularly one calling for the annual appropriation of sizable sums of money) that was not supported at all times by the enthusiasm of some interested domestic pressure group. But beyond that it gradually became apparent that the rationale of the Rogers Act was poorly understood outside the small circle of its authors and the members of the Foreign Service itself. Neither the public at large, nor the press, nor the leaders of succeeding administrations, nor the majority of the members of succeeding Congresses had any very clear idea of what was involved in the experiment or cared very much whether the Foreign Service, as envisaged in the Rogers Act, prospered or languished.

Since the development of a good professional service is a long-term operation, where the normal time-lag between decision and result in major matters is measured in decades rather than in years, this lack of comprehension and of sustained interest was gradually to prove fatal to the experiment. One by one, the principles on which it was intended that the new Service should operate were neglected, distorted or abandoned. I shall not attempt to recount the involved and painful stages by which this decline took place. The immediate causes were numerous and varied. The constantly recurring failure of senior government officials to understand why the Foreign Service should be treated any differently from the Civil Service as a whole; the endless jealousies aroused by what seemed to many the glamourous and privileged nature of the Foreign Service function; the tendency of other government departments, more powerfully supported in Congress than was the State Department, to set up competing foreign services; Mr. Roosevelt's dislike of the Service and unconcern for its future; the complete suspension of admissions for periods of years on end, a procedure which starved the Service at the bottom and sharply disbalanced its age structure; the failure to clarify the relationship of the Service to the war effort in 1941–1945; the proliferation of parallel and rival organizations during and after the war; the latter-day illusion that "management" is something wholly divorced from function, and the consequent burdening of the Service with a succession of administrative heads who had no experience or understanding of the diplomatic profession; the repeated and extensive "lateral" infusions of new personnel at intermediate levels; the growing tendency of able older officers to seek more promising fields for self-expression; and last but not least the operation of the postwar security programs, bringing humiliation, bewilderment and the deepest sort of discouragement to hundreds of officers—all these factors played a part. But all of them, it will be noted, were embraced in the major causes mentioned above: the unsuitability of the American governmental system for a prolonged administrative effort of this sort, and lack of comprehension for the nature and exigencies of the diplomatic function on the part of a great continental society not accustomed to regard prospering foreign relations as important.

The result of all this was that by 1953 the old Foreign Service was weakened beyond real hope of recovery. The present Administration inherited not a going professional service but an administrative ruin, packed with people who had never undergone the normal entrance requirements, hemmed in and suffocated by competing services, demoralized by anonymous security agents in whose judgment and disinterestedness its members had little confidence, a helpless object of disparagement and defamation at the hands of outside critics. This was the tragic ending of an experiment launched, with high hopes and with none but the most innocent and worthy intent, three decades earlier. As of the year 1953, it was no exaggeration to say that the experiment of professional diplomacy, as undertaken by the United States in 1925, had failed.

Members and friends of the Foreign Service watched with deepest interest to see what the new Administration would do about the state of America's professional diplomacy. While what was left of the Foreign Service remained—as it always had been—genuinely nonpartisan in spirit, older officers could not but remember that the Rogers Act was the product of a Republican Administration and that most of the vicissitudes that had befallen the Service (though not all) had occurred during the subsequent period of Democratic ascendancy. There was, accordingly, a natural curiosity as to whether a new Republican Administration would not again show appreciation and concern for the principles on which the Service had originally been established, awareness of the reasons for its decline, and a desire to make a new start, this time perhaps on broader and more hopeful foundations, at the creation of a creditable and efficient diplomatic arm.

The first steps of the new Administration, consisting of a further tightening of the screw of the security controls (which most officers felt had already been tightened far beyond the requirements of any demonstrable national interest), were not encouraging. But there was still the hope that all this represented only the last phase of a governmental response to a wave of popular emotionalism—a final application of the lash, designed to disarm suspicion that the Administration would be "soft" in security matters and in this way to win Congressional confidence for a new program that would in itself be sound. And while the Service as a whole would long remain saddened and troubled by the memory of what had been done to individual officers in the name of "security," there was readiness in most quarters to accept even this final salt in the wound if the result were to be the laying of a new foundation for healthy service. When, therefore, the Secretary of State announced in the early spring of 1954 that he had appointed a committee of distinguished persons, headed by Dr. Henry M. Wriston, President of Brown University, to examine into the state of the Foreign Service and to advise him as to what should be done about it, this action was greeted with deep and hopeful satisfaction by all those who had the interests of the Service at heart.

*   *   *

A year and a half ago, just before the Wriston Committee undertook its work, the writer was asked by a student editor to comment for the benefit of his readers on the merits of the Foreign Service as a career for young men leaving college. He replied that as things stood at that sad moment, he could not encourage any young man to enter the Service at the bottom by examination and to start up the ladder in the normal manner. He pointed out that the Administration was about to undertake a study of the whole problem and voiced the hope that this study would lead to measures which would again make the Service a promising and satisfying career. He urged the student-readers to await the results of this study before making any final judgment.

Today, the study is complete; the results are in large part at hand. What is there now to be said about the prospects of the Foreign Service as a career?

Democracy, as Cambon observed, will always have diplomacy. There will always be a group of civilian officials of this Government charged with the representation of the country's interests abroad. However the service of these officials may be administered, the work and the life will remain in many ways stimulating and interesting, particularly for the officer who wishes to make it so. It will always carry with it the excitements, the rewards, the challenges, often the hardships, of foreign residence. However the Government may try to reduce these advantages through the anxious paternalism with which it now surrounds its officers, something of them will always remain for the officer who has enough intellectual curiosity to turn his back on the American colony cocktail parties and to learn something of the life around him.

Beyond that, the life of the Foreign Service officer will continue to be enriched by his association with other Americans in the same work. As in so many other American institutions, the deficiencies of administrative structure will in part be corrected by the virtues of the national temperament. Whatever the selection system, intelligent and talented people will, by the law of averages, find their way into the Service, to enrich others with their insights and to inspire others with the example of their own growth. Whatever the Government's views on specialists as opposed to generalists, there will always be magic moments when minds previously confined within the walls of a narrow special interest are suddenly awakened by the Foreign Service experience to a realization of the unity of all knowledge. However ill-designed the security system and whatever premiums it may place on timidity and a cramped suspiciousness of outlook, friendships and loyalties will develop; men will find satisfaction in the appreciation of their colleagues for work that goes unnoted or unappreciated at home; there will be times when men will be privileged to stand by each other in danger and adversity and thus to taste one of the richest forms of human experience. Everywhere, even within the ranks of the security officers themselves, the golden mean of American characteristics will not fail to break through: men will learn by doing; experience will breed understanding and maturity; the instinct for common decency and fairness, instilled by a thousand earnest American mothers and on a thousand sand-lot baseball fields, will rise to assert itself and to do battle, wherever it can, with whatever is stupid or unjust in the system. Finally, and perhaps most important of all, the work of the Foreign Service will always have, in the eyes of those who perform it, that ultimate dignity that comes from the fact that it is the work of a great government, on whose performance rests the fate of a great people, indeed, in many respects, of the world at large—a dignity which means that whatever the Foreign Service officer may be occupied with in his official work, it will never be meaningless, never wholly trivial.

These things will go far to redeem the Foreign Service of the future, as they have redeemed that of the past. They will redeem it both as a subjective experience for those who live and work in it and as an instrument for the transaction of the Government's foreign business. And in many respects the changes introduced by the implementation of the new program will represent improvements over the state in which the Service has found itself in recent years.

Conditions will of course continue to exist which most older officers will be unable to view otherwise than as burdens on the development of an efficient and well-adjusted organization. In particular, no outsider can yet give to the young man entering the Service the assurance that the treatment he may receive at the hands of the security authorities will necessarily bear any relationship to the devotion and talent he may have given to his substantive work, and that it may not work tragic and undeserved hardship upon him. But in this, as in other respects, the future Foreign Service will be only in tune with an age committed to bigness, to over-organization, to depersonalization, to the collective rather than individual relationship. Skepticism of the value of individual excellence and reluctance to allow any of the weight of society to come to rest on the insights and intuition of the individual spirit will be the marks not of the Foreign Service alone but of the very environment in which it exists; and the young person seeking the road to self-fulfillment will not be likely to escape them by avoiding the Foreign Service career.

Why Not Give Diplomacy
Back to the Diplomats?

Ellis O. Briggs

No one dealing with the operational aspects of foreign affairs can be unaware of the problem of personnel proliferation—the dismal and frustrating drag on performance resulting from too many people. . . .

The American Foreign Service, at upwards of thirty-six hundred commissioned officers, is already at least one thousand men and women too large. At every Embassy with which the writer is familiar—as Ambassador to seven countries on three continents, plus continuing study of our operations abroad—the business of the United States could have been transacted more effectively by one half, or less, of the personnel assigned to each mission.

Outside the Foreign Service, overstaffing abroad by other agencies is even more serious. These Peripheral Performers—the dispensers of foreign aid, of development, of prescriptions for "emerging societies," of magic and martial music, of propaganda, and of the Crusading Spirit—are all more proliferated than the diplomats, and their ranks are in correspondingly greater need of fumigation and retrenchment. (Former President Johnson's 1968 reduction-in-force program, albeit in the right direction, turned out to be mostly hocus-pocus: the reductions were minimal, and the repatriates remained on the payroll.)

Just as during the so-called missile crisis in Washington in 1962, only a handful of persons were involved in decisions, so in even the most important of Embassies, confronting the gravest of situations, the Ambassador needs few aides to assist him. An Ambassador is supported by his Deputy, a seasoned and senior official, and between

Source: "Why Not Give Diplomacy Back to the Diplomats?" *Foreign Service Journal*, vol. 46 (March 1969), pp. 48–49, 68.

them they do what requires to be done with the Chief of State, the Prime Minister, or the members of the Cabinet of the country to which the Ambassador is accredited. In addition the Ambassador may be advised by the Political Counselor (or by the Counselor for Economic Affairs, depending on the subject matter) and perhaps by one or two subordinate Embassy officers who possess special training or experience in the area in question. Including secretaries, stenographers and clerks, an Ambassador uses a maximum of ten people to confront a critical or emergency situation; less, of course, for normal operations.

The rest of the Embassy cast contribute little except confusion, delay, cross-purposes and unread "position papers." In short, there is not enough substantive, useful, challenging or interesting work for an American Embassy of hundreds upon hundreds of people. The consequent feather-bedding is as unprofitable to the taxpayers as it is stultifying to the individuals concerned.

The presence of these gigantic staffs in foreign capitals has an ill effect in another direction. It is a source of derision and disrespect on the part of the very foreigners whose good will the United States is theoretically cultivating. They manifest their attitude by destroying with monotonous and humiliating regularity such well-meaning tokens of the conspicuous American establishment as libraries and cultural centers, and even by attacking the Embassy premises. No other country in the world maintains outside its borders a fraction of the personnel camped in successive "Little Americas," where teeming administrators seek to reproduce the suburban way of life, but often merely succeed in reducing the natives to popeyed resentment. . . .

In searching for reasons why these truths, which are self-evident to so many professional practitioners, seem to have escaped successive administrations since World War II, it is clear that what is lacking is agreement as to the nature of foreign affairs, and above that, an understanding of the purpose of diplomacy.

The object of diplomacy is to influence the *policy* of another country, in ways favorable to the first country. It is as uncomplicated as that. That is the same object diplomacy has sought since cavemen inhabited adjacent cliffs, and pastoral societies coveted contiguous grazing areas. It is the same purpose that diplomacy will always have; the label "modern diplomacy" is therefore a misnomer, denigrating to the past and unhelpful to the future.

This definition of diplomacy as inseparable from *policy*, can be expanded to render it more specific. Take the statement: "the object of American diplomacy is to influence in ways favorable to the United States the policy of governments important to the United States." Such a declaration is both accurate and intelligible. It encourages the establishment of the priorities essential to the orderly transaction of business, without which American resources are in danger of being frittered away. It implies that the demands of Abidjan, Tegucigalpa and Reykjavik, although not necessarily unworthy, may nevertheless be less important to the American people than the problems emanating from Moscow, Rio de Janeiro or Tokyo.

Within this true definition of diplomacy, the foreign business of the United States is not ideological warfare, nor evangelism, nor huffing and puffing to accelerate alien development, nor the preservation of a balance of power or any rigid *status quo*. The business of American diplomacy is the promotion of the national interests of the United States, and the protection of those interests, in a changing and turbulent world, from whatever menace that is capable of producing an intolerable explosion.

Diplomacy as influencing the *policy* of other governments is hardly the definition that has prevailed in recent Potomac councils. For instance, the young soothsayers of the Foreign Service Association, writing in collaboration with assorted Peripheral Performers (who perhaps cannot be expected to advocate measures tending to thin their ranks or curb their activities), appear to view diplomacy, and especially what they characterize as "modern diplomacy," as something far more gaudy and uninhibited than influencing policy. Not content with that, they desire to *transform institutions*.

Now *transforming institutions* is a different proposition altogether from *influencing policy*, and it is at that point that the paths of diplomats and reformers most frequently diverge. Influencing policy involves discipline, analysis, understanding of facts and possibilities, and comprehension of their bearing on the national interests, seen in realistic perspective. It involves attention to detail, and patience, and "the application of intelligence and tact to the conduct of official relations."

Transforming institutions, in contrast, would seek for diplomacy —"modern diplomacy," to be sure—a worldwide hunting license of infinite scope and unlimited validity, encouraging the participants to thrash about in hemisphere briar patches, brandishing megaphones and bazookas.

Under that definition of diplomacy, a case can of course be made for the retention of almost limitless performers, all allegedly assisting the hunters; for an army of beaters, making the forests echo and startling the game from habitat to Helsinki; for guides tying goats to *ceiba* trees, scattering cracked corn on the ponds, and locating saltlicks; for researchers and biologists to plot the flyways and locate the spawning areas; and even for missionaries to explain to the penguins that they would really be happier if they laid their eggs along the Amazon River, where the water is comfortably warm, instead of along the shores of McMurdo Sound, where the water is uncommonly cold.

Under that definition of diplomacy, there is no end to the legions that can be recruited. Battalions of imagemakers, flashing their mirrors; gaggles of wreakers-of-good, waving lofty intentions; regiments of attaches, measuring culverts and bridges; prides of welfare workers, one foot on the accelerator and one eye on the cookie jar.

That, in fact, is precisely what has been happening.

It is beyond the scope of this paper to trace how this came about, gradually, in the wake of World War II, sometimes over the protests of an ineffectual State Department, sometimes with its blessings. But come about it did, with results that now confront us.

The American Government has been in the transforming institutions business for nearly a quarter century. To show for it, the United States has a balance of payments problem, and microscopic return on an incalculable investment.

It is time for the American people to dedicate themselves not to "modern diplomacy" but to *effective* diplomacy, with less free-loading of international freight, and no free-wheeling by crusaders.

That does not mean abandoning compassion as a legitimate ingredient in the foreign affairs equation. It does imply that a decent regard for self-interest ought no longer to be considered discreditable, and that a *quid pro quo* in the diplomatic marketplace should once again have value.

That does not mean the extermination of the Peripheral Performers, whose operations, nevertheless, should henceforth be understood as *adjuncts* of diplomacy, and no longer as controlling components. Projects to foster cultural osmosis, public relations planning (labeled propaganda when someone else does it), aid of one sort or another to selected developing lands, military assistance, credits, sharing of scientific knowledge and the paraphernalia of technology— each of those things, in given circumstances to be decided upon one country at a time—can sometimes provide fruitful though usually limited assistance in the functioning of diplomacy and in the conduct of international relations.

Thus, while peripheral activities should not all be abandoned, past experience with them, their cost and their limitations, ought to be brought into focus. And future operations should be both closely scrutinized and sharply patrolled by the Department of State. Moreover, most of the personnel concerned are not diplomats, and those who are not should be detached from the diplomatic establishment.

* * *

There is no area of the federal government that has been the object of more solicitude on the part of uninformed kibitzers and aggressive reformers than the American Foreign Service. Most of them have operated under the banner of "modern diplomacy," discredited though that emblem may be as a result of costly, futile and interminable experiments. It may be that in the nature of his work, a diplomat finds himself unable to cultivate the kind of grassroots constituency that supports other government operations. He can boast of no lobby comparable to those beating drums for the Departments of Defense or Agriculture, for example. That does not mean that the Foreign Service must cultivate a supple spine, or that diplomats should hesitate to stand up and be counted. In fact if they do not stand up, they are likely to be counted out, and at no distant date in the future.

It is high time that diplomats do speak up, for improvements generated from within testify to the vitality of the organization, and moreover among the assets possessed by professionalism is an aroused awareness on the part of the American people of the importance of foreign affairs, properly conducted. That awareness should include simultaneous acceptance of the proposition that if an American householder has a broken-down furnace, he does not call in an astrologer, a paperhanger, or a professor-who-says-he-knows-all-the-answers. Nor does the home owner invite to his cellar a traveling circus. He summons a plumber who knows about furnaces.

It is perhaps reassuring to the general public that diplomats and plumbers have that much in common. At any rate, having tried without success practically everything else since World War II ended, it might be a good idea to try giving diplomacy back to the diplomats. There would be a saving in fuel oil, and they might even repair the furnace.

Career Status of United States Diplomats

ELMER PLISCHKE

The literature on American diplomacy has debated and often criticized presidential appointment of noncareer outsiders, the professional competence of United States diplomats, and their career status. It has been disputed whether diplomacy is an art or a science—whether the artful negotiator is more essential than the systematic policy maker and implementer. The presumption is that if diplomacy is primarily an art, it can best be practiced by carefully selected and trained members of an efficient career service. Although American diplomacy may be regarded as having been emancipated from earlier confinement as the preserve of the wealthy, some still deem it to be excessively the stepchild of the spoils system—or, at least, as being insufficiently professionalized.

E. Wilder Spaulding, writing after a lifetime of concern with American diplomatic practice, concludes that it may be easier to evolve a formula for the "ideal ambassador" than it is to recruit him. It may appear to be relatively simple to assess the success of a particular appointee at the conclusion of his service, but it is far more difficult in most cases to foresee accomplishment or failure—or even ability or latent inadequacy—at the time of appointment. Little comfort may be found in the illusory proposition that the only solution is the invariable appointment of the right man to the right assignment at the right time. These—the man, the post, and the moment—together with other identifiable variables and imponderables in the appointing equation render the process both uncertain and difficult.

SOURCE: "Career Status of Diplomats," *United States Diplomats and Their Missions: A Profile of American Diplomatic Emissaries Since 1778* (Washington, D.C.: American Enterprise Institute, 1975), pp. 97–105.

Given the need to designate an average of some thirty to forty diplomats each year and to accredit them to disparate countries, and having in mind not only the problems of the availability of qualified candidates at the moment of need[1] and their acceptability to particular governments, but also existing political relations and unforeseeable probabilities, it would take consummate genius and inordinate luck to achieve such a goal.

In retrospect, the United States is fortunate to have been blessed with so many able diplomats, some of whom may have emerged despite, rather than because of, the prevailing system. At the same time, it cannot be gainsaid that more unfortunate appointments were made than should have been the case. Those charged with recruiting and developing able diplomatic careerists and with appointing equally competent noncareerists to high positions in the Department of State and as chiefs of diplomatic mission bear a heavy burden of responsibility.

This analysis is less concerned, however, with devising a formula for dealing with such issues, or with passing judgment on either the system or specific individuals, than it is with reviewing the career status of American diplomats. In doing so, several fundamental distinguishing designations need to be clarified. The first of these—the "career diplomat"—generally reflects the status of an individual as a member of a formal career service, which, at present, means a Foreign Service Officer. They enter the Foreign Service with the intention of making diplomacy their profession and, rising through the ranks, they may ultimately be appointed as chiefs of mission to foreign governments or to other top-level posts. In principle, this appears to be straightforward and uncomplicated. Prior to 1946, however, FSOs were required to resign from the career service when they accepted appointment as an ambassador or minister, and technically they ceased being career diplomats.[2] To allow for this and to provide a rule of thumb for designating career diplomats, the Department of State has determined that the appellation "career diplomat" be accorded to all those who were members of the Foreign Service when appointed chief of mission and to certain others who qualified for the designation at the time of the enactment of the law (15 Febru-

---

[1] It must be remembered that the transfer of a career diplomat from one foreign capital to another is likely to produce a chain reaction of reassignments.

[2] Since the enactment of the Foreign Service Act of 1946 this requirement has been rescinded, so that FSOs appointed as chiefs of mission now retain their status in the career service.

ary 1915) which restructured the Diplomatic and Consular Services.[3] In this survey, consequently, three categories of designation are used, namely, the pre-1915 appointees, the careerists, and the post-1915 noncareerists. . . .

A second distinction to bear in mind is that of the "professional diplomat." Defined in one sense, all diplomatic careerists are professionals, but if the latter concept is limited solely to careerists, then the United States had no professional diplomats prior to 1915, which cannot be maintained. Even if all careerists are deemed to be professionals, there are a good many others who, in terms of length of service or accomplishment, must equally be regarded as professional diplomats.

This applies to certain chiefs of mission in the pre-1915 period, some of whom served for extended periods in a variety of missions, as already noted. Some of these—such as Benjamin Franklin, John Quincy Adams, James Monroe, James Buchanan, and Richard Rush in our early history, Charles Francis Adams and John Bigelow in the 1860s, and Joseph H. Choate, Arthur S. Hardy, David Jayne Hill, and William W. Rockhill at the turn of the century—because of the nature of their service and achievement occupy a status in American history as professional diplomats well above that of a contemporary FSO who may cap his career with a few years as a chief of mission, even though he is designated a career diplomat. Equally significant is the post-1915 appointee who may enjoy an extensive record of service at the highest levels but, because he is not an FSO, is regarded as a noncareerist. Illustrations, again to mention but a few, include George W. Ball, Anthony J. Drexel Biddle, David K. E. Bruce, Ellsworth Bunker, W. Averell Harriman, Henry Cabot Lodge, George C. McGhee, and Laurence A. Steinhardt.[4]

While the career/noncareer distinction is necessary and important, its limitations as compared with the differentiation between the professional and the amateur—a category which some brand as dilet-

---

[3] Such others include those who, serving in 1915, had at least ten years of continuous diplomatic service, or, if appointed later, had at least five years experience in the Foreign Service or the earlier Diplomatic and Consular Services prior to appointment. The career designation has also been assigned to those few individuals who had served as diplomatic secretaries, who had then been commissioned before 1915 as chiefs of mission or as presidential appointees in the Department of State, who were not serving as chiefs of mission in February 1915, but who were subsequently appointed or reappointed to head diplomatic missions.

[4] Among a great many others who might be included are Spruille Braden, Wilbur J. Carr, William R. Castle, Angier Biddle Duke, Henry F. Grady, Stanton Griffis, Lloyd C. Griscom, Robert C. Hill, Alan G. Kirk, and Lincoln MacVeagh.

tantism—are obvious. The point is, simply, that some careerists are professionals only in a limited and formal sense, and not all non-careerists are dilettantes—again except in the sense that they may not be long-lived Foreign Service Officers; in reality, they may be first-rate professionals.

The concept of professional diplomat, as related to service as chiefs of mission and at high levels in the Department of State, might usefully be defined arbitrarily as being based on a minimum number of years of service in such assignments, or on a minimum number of such assignments, or on a combination of these factors. However, to identify the genuine professionals among both the careerists and non-careerists, other criteria would be needed. These might include reputable experience, acknowledged negotiatory achievements, management ability, facility at functioning at the highest political or other professional levels and the like, but it is not the purpose of this analysis to define or attempt to apply such criteria. Moreover, even if they were to be established and applied, the categorization of careerist professionals and nonprofessionals, and noncareerist professionals and nonprofessionals could create greater complexity and confusion. Suffice it to say that there have been and are diplomatic professionals—or professional diplomats—who are not careerists, and that the limitations of the concept of careerism must be acknowledged.

. . . Of the 2,926 [American diplomatic] appointments made [since 1778], 1,202—or 41 percent—predated 1915, and since then 935 (32 percent) of the total number of appointments were of careerists, with the remaining 789 (27 percent) being accorded to noncareerists.

In keeping with this differentiation, an aggregate of some 1,991 of 2,926 (68 percent) are technically regarded as noncareerist American diplomats. More significantly, however, of the 1,724 appointments since 1915, more than half (54 percent) have been careerists. This means, on the one hand, that, even if post-1915 professional noncareerists are added to this number, the extent to which nonprofessional noncareerists are appointed is still high—to some analysts, even excessive. Nevertheless, evidencing an important trend, the ratio of careerists appointed to high level diplomatic positions since 1940 has increased, overall, to nearly 60 percent.

In view of the number of appointments made to the secretaryship of state and the other senior department officers prior to 1915, and the very nature of these positions, it is not surprising that, in the aggregate, only 30 percent of these appointments have gone to careerists. Of greater consequence, however, are the facts that since 1920 the number of careerists has amounted to nearly 40 percent of these departmental appointees, and that during this half century the number of careerists approximated half the appointees during two decades, the 1920s and 1950s.

Since 1920 the record with respect to chiefs of mission to foreign governments is far more favorable to careerism in that 799 of 1,315 (61 percent) have been careerists. In the 1940s the ratio of careerists reached 64 percent and since 1950 it has approximated or exceeded 65 percent each decade, so that together with the professional noncareerists, they currently account for more than two-thirds of American resident chiefs of mission.

Aside from such general statistics, a number of detailed developments are material to understanding the nature of, and trends regarding, the career status of American chiefs of mission. For example, one of the criticisms of ranking United States diplomats is that presidential appointments to the principal capitals of the world represent an undemocratic stronghold of exclusiveness and wealth in government service. The widespread belief that certain diplomatic posts are the guaranteed preserve of noncareerists is valid, but only to a very limited extent. True, no careerist has been appointed to the United Kingdom, and since 1915 only six of thirty-one appointees to France and Germany have been FSOs. Yet, noncareerist professionals like David K. E. Bruce, William C. Bullitt, George C. McGhee, and Henry Cabot Lodge have held such appointments. Other posts favored with an exceptionally high proportion of noncareerist appointees include Ireland (with only one of fourteen appointees chosen from the career ranks), Australia, Denmark, India, the Philippines, and Spain—to each of which two-thirds or more have been noncareerists. Belgium, Luxembourg, the Netherlands, Norway, and Japan have also been favored somewhat for noncareerist appointments.

After diplomatic relations were revived with the Soviet Union in 1933, the United States appointed seven noncareerists over a period of nearly two decades, but has named only careerists since 1952. Moreover, three of the noncareerists were former military officers—Admirals William H. Standley and Alan G. Kirk and General Walter Bedell Smith—and three others—William C. Bullitt, Laurence A. Steinhardt, and W. Averell Harriman—may be ranked among the acknowledged professionals. Nearly two-thirds of American chiefs of mission to the Eastern European Communist countries have been careerists. While in the case of Poland the number of noncareerists approximated that of careerists after 1915, since World War II only five of thirty-four (15 percent) appointees to these six countries have been noncareerists.[5] Thus, the President tends overwhelmingly to accredit careerists and other professionals to the Communist countries of Eastern Europe.

The United States has also appointed more careerists than noncareerists as its chiefs of mission to countries in the Western Hemisphere. Only in the case of four of the twenty Latin American countries has the number of noncareerists exceeded the careerists, and then only by one or two appointees per country;[6] moreover, half of the emissaries accredited to Canada since relations were established in 1927 have also been careerists. An unusually high proportion of careerists has been assigned to such countries as Haiti and Uruguay, and the number also has been substantial (two-thirds or more) in the case of Brazil and the Dominican Republic. The largest numbers of noncareerist appointments in the Western Hemisphere have been to two new countries—Jamaica, and Trinidad and Tobago, and they are likely to change. The notion, therefore, that such posts as Buenos Aires, Mexico City, Rio de Janeiro, and Ottawa are the sanctuary of noncareerists cannot be sustained. Even including Canada—where the ratio of careerists remains approximately 50 percent—careerists have increased each decade since 1940, rising from some 55 percent to nearly 70 percent.

The degree to which American diplomatic appointments to the Middle East, to sub-Saharan Africa, and to the newer countries of Asia have been assigned to careerists since 1915 should also please the proponents of diplomatic careerism. In the Middle East the percentage of noncareerists is highest for the three countries with which the United States has maintained the longest records of diplomatic relations—Egypt, Iran, and Turkey—and yet in only one of twenty Middle Eastern countries has the number of noncareerists equaled that of the careerists. Not a single noncareerist has been appointed to eleven of these countries, and even in the case of Saudi Arabia and Syria, with whom relations were commenced as early as 1939 and 1942 respectively, only one or two appointments have involved noncareerists. This area, therefore, has clearly become the domain of career American diplomats.

United States chiefs of mission accredited to the new countries

---

[5] Bulgaria, Czechoslovakia, Hungary, Poland, Romania, and Yugoslavia. The United States has sent no resident emissaries to Albania since World War II. Among the five noncareerists were Eugenie Anderson, appointed to Bulgaria in 1962, Stanton Griffis, who served as ambassador to four countries, and Leonard C. Meeker, who had previously been legal adviser in the Department of State for more than four years.

[6] These include Chile, Cuba, Mexico, and Paraguay.

of sub-Saharan Africa also have largely been careerists. No noncareerists were sent to thirteen of thirty-three of these countries[7] and, as of 1973, only thirty of 138 (22 percent) appointees to these countries were noncareerists. Career diplomats sent to Ethiopia, with which diplomatic exchanges began in 1909, and South Africa, with which relations were commenced in 1930, also outnumbered noncareerists by two to one. Of all the thirty-six sub-Saharan African countries, the United States has named fewer careerists than noncareerists only to Liberia. Even in this case, however, since 1950 the majority have been Foreign Service Officers. Should this trend continue, and the cumulative quota to 1973 amounted to 73 percent, American representation—as in the Middle East—will be predominantly careerist.

Aside from the countries of Asia and the Western Pacific already mentioned, the United States has generally accredited only a slightly larger number of careerists than noncareerists to such older diplomatic partners as China, New Zealand, and Thailand. However, careerists have been overwhelmingly appointed to Afghanistan, Burma, the Khmer Republic, Korea, Laos, and Malaysia, and, overall, less than one fourth (23 percent) of more than 100 chiefs of mission accredited to seventeen Asian countries since World War II have been noncareerists. It may be concluded, therefore, that except for a few specific countries, the trend outside of Europe is clearly to appoint careerists as United States chiefs of mission and, for some groups of states, the appointment of noncareerists has become so infrequent as to be exceptional.

It has been said that, because of the politics involved in making diplomatic appointments, normally a new President is initially likely to recruit a higher percentage of noncareerists and subsequently, as posts are vacated and replacements are named, he turns more and more to the careerists. As a matter of fact, however, while there was some validity to this impression, the situation has been changing markedly since World War II. When Franklin D. Roosevelt became President, he named twice as many noncareerists as careerists (twenty-nine to fifteen) to be his initial diplomatic replacements, but he also retained more than a dozen careerists who had been appointed by his predecessor, so that the two groups were equal in number, and as diplomatic relations were launched with new countries, he also named approximately as many careerists as noncareerists.

Presidents Eisenhower, Kennedy, and Nixon—each of whom rep-

---

[7] Excluding Ethiopia, Liberia, and South Africa.

resented a political change in the White House, at which time the replacement of diplomats is apt to be greatest—named increasing numbers of careerists as their initial appointments. President Eisenhower continued nearly two dozen of President Truman's careerist appointees in their posts,[8] designated more newly appointed careerists than noncareerists,[9] and accredited more than twenty careerists and only one noncareerist to new countries as his initial appointees. President Kennedy retained more than twenty Eisenhower careerists in their posts when he took over, appointed more than forty-five careerists and approximately thirty noncareerists as his initial appointees, and also named more careerists than noncareerists to new countries as diplomatic relations were inaugurated. President Nixon favored careerism even more, continuing some two dozen of his predecessor's careerist appointees in their assignments, designating more than fifty careerists and approximately thirty noncareerists as his initial appointees, and also naming more careerists than noncareerists to new countries. These three Presidents have established a decided precedent, and taken together they appointed or continued at their posts more than twice as many careerists as noncareerists when they commenced their administrations.

As of 1948 there were some two dozen chiefs of mission holding ambassadorial and ministerial posts who had risen within the ranks of the career service. On the average about half of all diplomats were careerists during the Truman administration and, while the same was true early in the Eisenhower administration, the ratio increased to two-thirds careerists by the time he left office. In the mid-1960s the figure had risen to approximately 75 percent careerists, and it dropped to roughly 70 percent in 1970 and to 66 percent by 1974.

As a consequence, while fluctuations have occurred in the ratio of careerists, the trend since World War II has clearly been in favor of increasing the quantity of career diplomats, varying from two-thirds to three-fourths. The issue of careerism versus noncareerism appears to be of diminishing importance, and as more and more careerists gain initial appointment as chiefs of mission and are available for transfer from one ambassadorial post to another, future Presidents are likely to be even more prone to retain or reassign them. Moreover, with the complementary designation and reappointment of noncareerist professionals, the current status of, and future prospects for, the professionalization of United States diplomatic representation have become gratifyingly salutary.

---

[8] By this is meant that the incoming President retained an incumbent diplomat for at least fifteen months without change.

[9] This refers to appointments made within fifteen months of inauguration.

Ambassadors: Professionals or Amateurs?

CLARE BOOTHE LUCE

A public controversy has arisen concerning the conduct of our foreign affairs, namely whether amateurs or professionals should be appointed to head our embassies abroad. If we are to examine the issue seriously, we must agree not to prejudge it by using the terms "professional" or "amateur" in any deprecatory or pejorative sense, such as equating them with "cookie-pushing" and "pin-striped pants" on the one hand or "bungling" and "political payoffs" on the other. Amateurs are frequently called upon to wear pin-striped pants and professionals have been known to bungle; and in the intramural politics of the State Department, no less than "on the Hill," there have also been "political payoffs." If the issue is valid, we must discuss the merits of the amateur ambassador as opposed to the merits of the professional.

Certainly it will readily be agreed that a man who has made the practice of diplomacy his life work, his only career, can be called a "professional." We can also agree that the term "amateur" may then be used to designate a man who has come into diplomacy from any other walk of life, and who does not intend to pursue it as his profession or career. We may further agree that an "amateur," that is to say a non-career man, who has worked closely with professionals over a period of years—who has, for example, served in the State Department, the non-career missions attached to our embassies, or other branches of government where he has acquired a wide and practical knowledge of foreign affairs—might fairly be classed as a semi-professional, or in the language in which the professionals themselves classify him, as a "foreign expert." Defined in these terms, the issue of "amateur versus professional" is a relatively new one, for the

SOURCE: "The Ambassadorial Issue: Professionals or Amateurs?" *Foreign Affairs*, vol. 36 (October 1957), pp. 105–21.

reason that a realistic choice between the professional and the amateur ambassador has existed only in recent times.

Envoys of the United States of ambassadorial rank were not sent abroad until the year 1893. At that time America began to be recognized, and recognized itself, as a world Power. The Foreign Service, as an organized, united, systematically staffed profession, providing the framework of a corps of highly trained career diplomats, first came into being with the Rogers Act of 1924. Submerged and disrupted by World War II, it was reformed as an élite corps again by the Foreign Service Act of 1946, when the rank of "career minister" was created. The rank of "career ambassador" was established only in 1955, and both ranks require Presidential appointment and confirmation by the Senate.[1]

The Foreign Service today claims to have available from the ranks of its "hard core" regular officers enough career men to fill the top jobs in all our embassies abroad. It is this fact which seems to give the issue validity today.

Plainly, when the ambassadorial question is raised solely in terms of a categorical choice between "amateur" and "professional," the issue seems to settle itself: the skilled practitioner of the art of diplomacy is clearly to be preferred to the novice; the diplomatic "generalist," or "trained political specialist with a knowledge of everything," to the untrained neophyte. When we further consider that the very survival of our nation, in this age of the hydrogen bomb and atomic weapons, depends on the success of our multitudinous, world-wide diplomatic undertakings, can any other answer be reasonable or prudent? Is it not, therefore, desirable—indeed vital—that our professionals, who are now fortunately available, should be put in charge of all our embassies, especially in sensitive areas where the lack of diplomatic skill, not to mention a "blooper," might endanger the success of our policies, perhaps the security of the United States itself?

---

[1] The Foreign Service has been engaged in a 30-year struggle for the achievement of two objectives: the maintenance of the Foreign Service Officer corps as an élite body of diplomatists, with an identity separate from other branches of the State Department and other U.S. agencies overseas; and second, the acceptance of the principle that the chief coördinator, at a country level, of all U.S. representational activities overseas should be an officer of this corps. The vast multiplication of American agencies overseas has made coördination necessary, and today this function rests squarely with the ambassador. Apart from his position of seniority, as the President's personal representative, he has a special coördinating charter in the form of Executive Order 10575 of November 6, 1954. EDITOR'S NOTE: Also see Appendix C below.

With these definitions, and with these dangers well in mind, let us leave the field of argument to survey the field of facts.

How many professional U.S. ambassadors are there in our missions abroad today, and how many non-professionals? In what important posts, and in what sensitive areas of the world, are they stationed?

The first pertinent fact is that today two-thirds of all our ambassadors abroad are professionals. As of this writing, 54 of 76 United States diplomatic missions spread about the world are headed by career men.

The second pertinent fact is that they are in command of almost all of those areas considered by the State Department to be sensitive or crucial: the revolutionary areas and the areas which threaten us with aggression or are themselves imminently threatened by the Soviet Union or other Powers. . . . Every one of our ambassadors to the Iron Curtain countries is a "pro." In the 33 top posts in Africa, the Near, Middle and Far East, and the Pacific, the professionals outnumber the amateurs by 28 to 5. . . . Of the 21 countries in the American hemisphere, the "pros" occupy 14 posts. . . .

Let us now consider the whereabouts of the remaining 22 diplomats, whom we have agreed to classify either as amateurs, or foreign affairs experts—in either case, as non-career men. . . . Of all these 22 posts which are today occupied by amateurs, only six are classified, in the language of the Foreign Service itself, as major diplomatic posts. . . .

* * *

Here it may not be beside the point to comment briefly on the question of the part "speaking a foreign language" plays in the qualifications for an ambassador. The lingua franca of diplomacy throughout the Middle Ages and well into the seventeenth century was Latin. French became the accepted language of organized diplomacy in the eighteenth and nineteenth centuries. French power under Louis XIV and XV was great on the continent of Europe, and Cardinal Richelieu had set the mold of diplomacy for an era that ended with the Napoleonic expansions and conquests. Consequently, expediency and prudence dictated to the other chanceries of Europe that all their professional diplomats would be well advised to learn to speak French like Frenchmen. Moreover, until the middle of the eighteenth century, most Englishmen, as well as Europeans, of the cultured and ruling classes were bilingual in French. But most importantly, a lingua franca is a diplomatic necessity. Accordingly French, a language of precision and courtesy, offered the necessary neutral ground of a "dominant language" in which the diplomats of all other nations could converse with one another. Today, the use of French as the language of diplomacy is a dying tradition.

As the result of the long ascendancy of the English-speaking nations, English has already become the lingua franca in vast areas of the world. It is the favored "second language" in the chanceries of most great capitals, especially in the Orient. It is the "common tongue" in India, and among many Middle East rulers.

The practical use of a second language to an ambassador is limited by the fact that no wise diplomat (of any country) will try himself to conduct any delicate diplomatic negotiation in a tongue in which he is not bilingual. A reasonable knowledge of the language of the country to which he is posted is unquestionably an asset to an ambassador in his diplomatic and social contacts. In democratic countries, it is especially helpful with the people of that country, who are always flattered by the diplomat's attempts, however awkward, to use it. But a diplomat who is not completely fluent, indeed bilingual, will transact, at the peril of his nation, the real business of his nation in a language which is foreign to him. . . .

In conclusion, one has only to reflect that if a top diplomat's knowledge of another diplomat's language were *essential* to the successful conduct of our foreign affairs, no conferences or meetings between prime ministers of various countries would be possible, certainly no "summit meetings." And the United Nations would be forced to close its doors. What *is* essential is that every American Embassy should have in residence an American officer cleared for security who is bilingual, in order to translate accurately any important negotiations between his ambassador or minister and the officials of the country. It is *this* deficiency of professionals who are linguistic experts in our embassies and not the ambassador's *personal* inability to speak the local tongue which has often created embarrassments, difficulties, even dangers for us in the conduct of our diplomacy. It is the task of the State Department to supply these bilingual experts wherever they are needed, just as it is the responsibility of the Congress to appropriate the sums needed for their training.

Certainly this review of the facts concerning the numbers, and whereabouts, of our amateur versus our professional ambassadors should remove any sense of public alarm or urgency which may today surround the issue. Two-thirds of our ambassadors are already professionals, and many of the remaining amateurs can be classified as semi-professionals and foreign experts.

These facts, however, do not invalidate the real issue—namely, *in principle* should United States Missions abroad be headed by professionals or amateurs? Is there any room for amateurs, even for those who have, in the course of time, become "experts" in American diplomacy? We cannot answer this question without widening the focus of our argument, by asking what room the American system, and the American Constitution itself, make for the "amateur diplomat."

The room that the Constitution itself provides is the President's room in the White House, and the Secretary's room in the Department of State.[2] The Constitution designates the President as our no. 1 American diplomat. Throughout our history all our top diplomats have embarked on their great appointed task of formulating and carrying out our foreign policy as "amateurs." The Constitution also permits our no. 1 diplomat, the President, personally to pick our no. 2 diplomat, that is his Secretary of State, from any walk of American life he chooses. The President is similarly empowered to appoint, with the advice and consent of the Senate, all our diplomats to foreign countries who are then sent abroad as the President's *personal* envoys.

Any comprehensive list of the Presidentially appointed amateurs who have been sent throughout our history to negotiate for the United States abroad, and who have done so with distinction, would be far too long to include here. One can only mention the names of a few amateur envoys of the past: Benjamin Franklin, Thomas Jefferson, Gouverneur Morris, John Jay, James Monroe, John Quincy Adams, Albert Gallatin, Washington Irving, John Hay, James Russell Lowell, Joseph Choate, Jacob Gould Schurman, Myron T. Herrick, Richard Washburn Child, Lewis W. Douglas, Admiral William Harrison Standley and General George Marshall—all names first associated in the public mind with achievements outside the field of diplomacy.

Nor can we limit the room made by the Constitution for non-professional diplomacy to the President, the Secretary of State or the President's personal envoys. Every United States Senator and Congressman functions at one time or other—and these days with increasing frequency—in the field of foreign affairs. Legislators who set about, by voice or vote, to support, amend, cripple or destroy the foreign policy of any given administration are profoundly affecting

---

[2] The statutory basis for this responsibility lies in the Act of Congress, July 27, 1789.

the conduct of our relations with foreign countries. They are, in the true sense of the word, foreign policy-makers. One has only to consider the impact abroad of certain resolutions . . ., immigration and tariff bills, and the vast complex of foreign affairs legislation and appropriations, to realize that in the final analysis our amateurs in the Congress have more influence on the foreign affairs of the United States, and wield more "diplomatic" power, than all the practitioners of "organized diplomacy" put together. In our constitutional democracy, the members of the Congress, amateurs all, are empowered to play a decisive part in the nation's diplomacy. As a result of the increased speed of communications, and the necessities of American foreign policy, many of them have now become familiar figures in our embassies and in foreign chanceries.

Senator Fulbright, author of the Fulbright Exchange Program, which is considered by all American professionals as one of the State Department's most successful undertakings, is frequently hailed as a "real diplomat" as well as statesman on his frequent trips abroad to investigate the workings of the program. I recall a speech made to him in my presence by an Italian official. "Few American Ambassadors," he said, "have ever done more to cement good relations between the United States and other nations than the Senator from Arkansas." Senator Mansfield, of the Senate Foreign Relations Committee, is another amateur laboring in the substantive field of foreign affairs whose appearance in any American Embassy around the world is hailed by the "pros" as a professional opportunity to listen as well as to talk. Not infrequently, Senators and Representatives "junketing abroad" are "briefed" by our Embassy before they call on local leaders in order that they may "drive home" some point the Embassy itself has not succeeded in putting across; and some of them have succeeded admirably in their diplomatic rôles.

We must also take into account the amateur diplomacy practised by the million or more Americans who visit, live or work in foreign lands: the American businessmen, creating better and more abundant commercial relations; the scholars, artists, lecturers, students, creating wider and deeper cultural relations; the agricultural experts, scientists, engineers and technicians, spreading American "know-how;" the news bureau men, constantly reporting to the home front on conditions abroad; the medical and religious missionaries, creating good health and good will among men; the hordes of American tourists who leave behind them a realistic impression of the American character; the organized groups of American labor men, spreading knowledge about the uses and practices of free trade unionism to the working men of other lands; the editors' groups, learning about foreign attitudes, explaining America's as they go; the members of our armed services, bringing the actual sense of America's solidarity with the countries where they are posted. All of these are "amateurs" (and I have listed only the most notable groupings) who are consciously or unconsciously assuming some of the tasks of modern diplomacy.[3]

More than 30,000 civilians are working for the United States Government abroad. Less than one percent of them are officers of the Foreign Service corps. Even at the level of organized diplomacy, the amateurs vastly outnumber the professionals. About 20,000 of these men and women, who do not consider diplomacy their life work, are nevertheless engaged overseas in the conscious and full-time pursuit of our diplomatic objectives. These amateurs in organized diplomacy are to be found in great numbers in the missions outside the regular Foreign Service establishment, and among the attachés of other government departments—Treasury, Agriculture, Commerce, Defense, Atomic Energy Commission, and so on. Thousands of them, for example, are in the I.C.A. (economic), the C.I.A. (intelligence), and the U.S.I.S. (information).* It will not do to dismiss all the members of these missions from the argument as being "specialists" and "technicians." Their presence in organized diplomacy is germane to the professional-versus-amateur argument, since no American Embassy today could carry out its complex and voluminous instructions, negotiations, programs or even representational functions without their know-how and assistance.

But that is not all: even in the Service itself amateurs are now plentifully present. As a result of the "Wristonization" program of 1954, there has been a great influx of non-professionals into the ranks of the Service in all classes.

It seems that, under the American system, at least in the cold war world, there is not only some room for amateurs in diplomacy, there is very great room indeed. Initially provided by the Constitution, and sustained by the American tradition, amateur diplomacy

---

[3] One fact is certain, regardless of how favorable or unfavorable the impression of America that is left behind by these amateurs; they do leave a favorable dollar balance in all the countries they travel through. These dollars, estimated in billions, achieve one very definite objective of U.S. foreign policy: they raise living standards in foreign countries.

* EDITOR'S NOTE: The International Cooperation Administration (ICA) was superseded by the Agency for International Development (AID), and the United States Information Service (USIS) was supplanted by the United States Information Agency (USIA), and later by the International Communication Agency (ICA).

is the American method, not only in the actual machinery, but in the theory which puts the machinery into motion. Indeed, it is impossible to see how our democracy could conduct its foreign policy without the organized and unorganized assistance of amateurs.

> The mid-20th century American ambassador has to enact many roles on a very broad stage and in relation to a cast of great number and variety, whereas, until shortly before World War II, the ambassador's contacts were largely confined to a relatively small circle composed of high officials of the host government and his opposites of the diplomatic corps.
> In today's vastly enlarged diplomatic field, the ambassador must be a man with many and diversified interests and with the mental capacity to absorb the substance of various branches of knowledge. No longer can the diplomat confine his attention to politics and policies—important though they are. As executor of his country's comprehensive foreign policy, the American ambassador may be concerned with any or all aspects of human activity. His interests and his responsibilities range through politics, economics, commerce, industry, agriculture, finance, labor, standards of living, transport and communications, social welfare, education, science, art, religion—in fact all aspects of life in the country of his assignment. Not one can be neglected by today's ambassador, whose mission is to carry out a foreign policy based on the interdependence of nations and dedicated to removing the causes of war from the world.[4]

Where does the conclusion that amateur diplomacy is the American method leave the ambassadorial question? Closed? Not at all. It simply puts it into its proper perspective. It consequently permits us to raise the ambassadorial issue in realistic terms; namely, who should represent America abroad: the professional, the amateur, or the *best qualified man who can be found?* Obviously, the latter. And just as obviously, the reasonable presumption must be that the professional is most likely to be that man.

Certainly, *all other qualifications being equal*, in simple justice, the career man should be given preference over an amateur when an ambassadorial assignment is being made. He has spent his life in the Service, always a life of discipline and hard work, often of

---

[4] "The American Ambassador Today," Department of State Publication No. 6420.

sacrifice and danger. If he has risen on merit close to the top of his profession he is entitled to reap its proper rewards, the prestige, the position, the power and the pay of an ambassador. Similarly, all posts, in all areas, should be as open to him as they are to an amateur.

It is natural and proper enough that the Foreign Service resents that this is not the case today. Of our 76 ambassadorial posts, career men today occupy *all* of the "hardship posts," while the non-career diplomats hold many of the easy, and *all* of the "plush," ones. That is to say, wherever you find a post where living and working conditions are inadequate and uncomfortable, where disease is rife or danger imminent, where strange customs and alien ways are practised, where it is too hot or too cold, too damp or too dry for the average American, there you will find not the amateur but the career man.

Life for an ambassador in a satellite country, and in many of the countries of Africa, the Middle East and Asia, can be worse than hard: it can be grim, ugly and depressing. Medical, hospital, educational and recreational facilities for American children range from poor to nonexistent. Social life is dreary beyond belief. American diplomats and their families in some parts of these areas can seldom enjoy, in their leisure hours, the normal pleasures of an American— restaurants, movies, sports, or even visits to or from friends. Worst of all, vast distances, as well as dangers, give them the feeling of isolation from their fellow countrymen, and from America itself.

To be sure, in point of expenditure of energy, effort and work, the European posts are no easier than they are, say, behind the Iron Curtain. Indeed, in the big European posts an ambassador's day is one of endless effort, sometimes to the point of exhaustion. But the honor, in the eyes of his countrymen, is greater. And life can be pleasant, stimulating, rewarding in Europe, especially for an ambassador's family. Where ambassadorships are concerned, we must admit that the professional often gets the skimmed milk of diplomacy, and behind the Iron Curtain the sour mash, while the non-career ambassador gets the cream.

All this strikes the men of the Foreign Service, and not without reason, as unjust. And the sense of injustice is in no way alleviated when they are told, true though it generally is, that they "couldn't afford the big European posts anyway." Rome, London, Paris, for example, are posts around which a dollar curtain has long been drawn. They can be assumed for any reasonable length of time only by men with private fortunes.[5]

---

[5] To this point I can speak from experience. In Rome I spent, over and beyond my salary and representational allowance, some $30,000 a year. This expenditure

It seems to every career officer, as it must seem to any thoughtful citizen, that whatever other factors should be, or are, taken into account by the President in the choice of an American ambassador for any given post, money should not be one of them. When the mere possession of private wealth becomes a major qualification for an American diplomat, the Foreign Service has the right to feel "sore," and the American people ought to feel ashamed. The post of ambassador should not be an honor that can be put on an auction block. Nevertheless, the President today faces the necessity of picking only very rich men for certain posts. The way to remedy this situation is for the Congress to appropriate adequate funds to the posts themselves, for their representational maintenance.

We have agreed that wherever an amateur is not *better qualified* than a professional for a top diplomatic job, the job should go to the professional. We have also agreed that the mere possession of money should in no way constitute a qualification. Obviously, neither should it constitute a disqualification.

We come now to the basic question: Are there any criteria equally acceptable to professional and amateur which we can use in determining the "better qualified man"?

What criteria does the Foreign Service itself set in rating its officers for promotion? A large part of the answer can be found in studying the Foreign Service "efficiency report." This is a form which is periodically filled out on a Foreign Service Officer by his immediate superior.[6] The accumulated efficiency reports made on an officer as he comes through the ranks from the lowest class, 8, to class 1 (at which point he becomes eligible for promotion to minister or chief of mission) are the basis on which the Selection Board which sits annually in Washington considers him for promotion. On this form there are listed eight "qualities:" character, ability, conduct, quality of work, industry, experieice, dependability and general usefulness.

Thirty additional "factors" are also listed: general knowledge

---

was on efforts, entertainments, etc., that were closely connected with my ambassadorial functions. The financial drain of a "big post" on the minister counselor is relatively as great. Within recent weeks, the minister counselors in the American Embassies in London and France have asked to be transferred to other countries because their salaries would not cover the expenditures the duties of the posts required.

[6] It is reviewed by *his* superior, and can also be reviewed by the ambassador, at his discretion, where the ambassador himself is not already the rating or reviewing officer.

of the Foreign Service; understanding of political and economic factors; of information programs and techniques (in the country in which he serves); knowledge of administrative practices and consular duties; effectiveness in applying laws and regulations correctly; thoroughness and accuracy of work and observation; effectiveness of written and of oral expression; negotiating ability; judgment; skill in dealing with the public; effectiveness as a supervisor; managerial effectiveness; ability in the field of intelligence; ability to get along with others; tactfulness; initiative; resourcefulness; decisiveness; forcefulness; adaptability; coöperativeness; patience; cost consciousness; security consciousness; good manners and politeness; and sense of humor.

The Foreign Service superior rates his subordinate officer on a basis of one to six on each of these 38 "qualities" and "factors."[7] These are further analyzed by the rating officer in brief comments appended to the report. A perfect score would be 228 points, assuming of course that all the factors listed were relevant to his particular embassy task.

In actual practice, if an officer consistently maintains a score of five on each relevant point, he is well headed for continual promotion—always assuming that he doesn't hit a snag in the form of a superior who takes a personal dislike to him. (The professional deformation of the career officer, "not getting his neck out," is often acquired after he reads his first efficiency report.) On the other hand, the career officer who is able or lucky enough to make the right friends in the Department can always survive a poor efficiency report made out by a prejudiced rating officer. The Foreign Service is, after all, a human institution. Making the right friends, influencing the right people and "playing politics" are not confined to the non-career world.

This efficiency report is relevant to our inquiry because it offers interesting proof that the main qualifications for a good ambassador are the same as they are for a good anything: they are human qualities.

We have only to review the above list of the human qualities desirable in a professional to see that these same qualities are equally valued in the non-professional. They are possessed in a greater or lesser degree by any man who has risen to eminence in public life, or who has made a notable success in any enterprise or profession

---

[7] His degree of fluency in foreign languages is taken into account as an asset, but is not rated.

which calls for continuous teamwork, and wide and fruitful contacts with his fellow citizens.

Nevertheless, there can be little question that the non-career man would get a pretty low mark on "general knowledge of the service," "consular duties" and "administrative practices" and "effectiveness in applying laws and regulations correctly." It is not enough to say that he would soon learn them (as he probably would), or that his minister counselor and his staff of professionals are there to see that his personal deficiency in these technical respects should not embarrass him. We have agreed that in justice to the professional, the non-career man must be *the better man*, he must offer other virtues or qualifications which will clearly outweigh his professional deficiencies.

What qualifications over and beyond those required of the professional can the amateur ambassador bring to his job?

Now a curious fact emerges from a study of the efficiency report: the great intangible assets that throughout the long history of foreign affairs in all countries have rendered envoys most effective in the art of diplomacy are not listed here. They are: prestige and esteem in the eyes of the diplomat's own countrymen, a proven interest in public affairs, a knowledge of political and economic realities at home and abroad and friendly contacts with leaders on the domestic scene.[8]

When a man has acquired great prestige at home through his own successful and popularly esteemed efforts as scholar, banker, industrialist, statesman, publicist, businessman, public servant or humanitarian; when he has, over the years, demonstrated a lively and constructive interest in public affairs; when he has wide and varied contacts with other leaders on the American scene, and if in addition he enjoys the prestige that flows from a mutually valued personal friendship with the President or Secretary of State, such a man can certainly be called "a man of proven distinction," a Somebody with a capital S.

The prestige of a Somebody will give him the power to influence public opinion at home, to approach "key figures" without diffidence and make suggestions to them without impertinence. He will be a

---

[8] In the words of a recent article by Walter Lippmann, "An appointment outside the career service . . . has to be justified by the special quality and the proved distinction of the candidate . . . [he should be] a man of demonstrable ability in public life." Harold Nicolson, in "The Evolution of the Diplomatic Method," writes that "the Greek cities were constantly sending and receiving ambassadors of a temporary, or *ad hoc* character." These ambassadors "were chosen for their known respectability, and reputed wisdom."

man who can "get things done" and "put things across" at home. And he will always get a warm welcome from the diplomats of the country to which he goes, who will view his appointment both as an honor to them and an opportunity to transact mutual business fruitfully and rapidly. And when such an ambassador arrives to take up his post, there is general rejoicing on the part of the professionals on his staff. After all that has been said, this is not as strange as it seems: the Foreign Service is a service dedicated, above all else, to the furthering of our country's objectives abroad.

As the constitutional right to appoint envoys rests squarely with the President, so, also, the prime responsibility for finding "the better qualified man" lies with him.

We have seen that two-thirds of President Eisenhower's appointments have been career men. . . .

Nevertheless, a few appointments to lesser posts have evoked heated charges of "political payoffs."[9] This charge is not a new one in American history. It has been made not only against certain of President Eisenhower's choices, but in the past, against some of Mr. Truman's, Mr. Roosevelt's, and against many previous presidential appointments. What is a "political payoff," and how can the appointment of "political payoffs" be prevented?

Certainly there is a large measure of public agreement on what constitutes a "political payoff." In American political practice, the personal political convictions of an appointee; the size of his private fortune; the campaign contributions he has made in the past to the party of his choice; the private services he has rendered the party; his personal relation to key figures in government (such as his blood relationship, friendship or business association with them)—all are considered to be circumstances which *as such* neither qualify nor unqualify him as a candidate for any high office. But when these same circumstances are presented as being *qualities* or *virtues* of the candidate's person; especially when they seem to be his *only* qualifications for the job to which he aspires, it can be assumed—and the assumption is generally a valid one—that the appointee is a "political payoff."

In view of the President's constitutional right to appoint whom

---

[9] The term "political appointment" has no meaning in the ambassadorial context, except the derogatory one the speaker may intend to give it, since *all* appointments made by our top politician, the President, including those of career envoys, are by definition political appointments.

he pleases, his appointments cannot be prevented. But, fortunately, the Constitution itself provides a recourse against the assumption of office by such men: the Senate has the power to *disqualify* them. It has the right to refuse to confirm their appointments.

In passing, let me say that although it is conceivable that legislation could be drawn to prevent their designation, in the first instance, by the President, it would be very difficult indeed to draw such legislation in view of the many reasons listed above why they are, in political practice, "paid off." Often the least of these is "the size of the campaign contribution." A "crony" of somebody high in government always has an inside track over the campaign contributor. Moreover, if the Senate fulfills its duty—which is to refuse confirmation of unfitted candidates—such legislation is obviously unnecessary.

Not only in recent years, but also in the past, the Senate Foreign Relations Committee has failed in this, and even while "leaking" opinions from its secret hearings about the unfitness of some ambassadorial candidate, has proceeded forthwith to confirm him. It is this fact which makes subsequent charges of "political payoffs" both specious and hypocritical.

Such failures on the part of the Senate Foreign Relations Committee tend to prove that too many of the Senate's members— Opposition no less Administration—still regard ambassadorships as a part of the political spoils system; and that the chief motive underlying their charges of "payoff" is the desire to embarrass the President and the party in power in order to score a party advantage in future campaigns. This suspicion is especially justified when—as is the case today—the Opposition controls the Senate Foreign Relations Committee, and with it the power to refuse confirmation to an Administration candidate.

The Senate would do well to remind itself that the public today ardently believes that whatever room there may be for amateurs in modern American diplomacy, there is no room for the kind of amateur who was once graphically described by a Congressional friend of mine as "an unknown public nonentity." When the Senate confirms a man who, in the considered judgments of a substantial number of the Committee, is not qualified to represent America abroad, it is doing an unpatriotic act. An ambassador's prestige, when he arrives in a foreign country, is America's prestige. And obviously, when members of the Senate Committee set about to damage the reputation of a qualified man in order to secure some slight party advantage, the action is unpatriotic.

The responsibility for preserving and increasing American prestige abroad, as it is reflected in the calibre of our "Ambassadors Extraordinary and Plenipotentiary," is the dual responsibility of the President and the Senate. As concerns the rôle of the President in this connection, I might quote the words of Mr. James Reston in *The New York Times* of August 7 [1957]. "The issue is not," he wrote, "whether the Eisenhower Administration is being more political in its ambassadorial appointments than the Democrats, or whether these jobs should be given to the top-career men in the Foreign Service, but whether the appointments have met the President's principle of appointing the best man available, regardless of party, wealth or foreign service record."*

As concerns the Senate, I might quote Senator Hubert Humphrey, who led an important and illuminating debate on this subject in the Upper House on August 15: "Let us have a little more public discussion of nominations when they come to the committee. I think all of us have been slightly derelict."

In conclusion, let us remind ourselves again that, while there admittedly have been some lapses on this score, on the whole both the President and the Senate have recognized their responsibility. On the record, as we have shown, they have not done too badly by American diplomacy. Under the "amateur" guidance of 34 Presidents and their Secretaries of State and ambassadors, and in spite of the "unwarranted diplomatic interventions" of 85 Congresses, the "uninformed" advice of an uncontrolled press, and the pressures of hundreds of millions of "undisciplined Americans" on our foreign affairs, the United States has nevertheless reached the peak of world leadership.

It is the wisdom of the Foreign Service itself to understand that whatever else diplomacy is, or is not, it is a pragmatic art. "By their fruits ye shall know them." In its 181 years of diplomatic life, America has not yet made "the irrevocable diplomatic error."

---

* EDITOR'S NOTE: To assist the executive in the selection of noncareerists as ambassadors, under the Federal Advisory Committee Act (5 U.S.C. App. I) on February 5, 1977, the President issued Executive Order 11970 providing for the creation of a Presidential Advisory Board of Ambassadorial Appointments to make confidential recommendations on prospective nominees.

Careerists vs. Noncareerists

LINCOLN GORDON

As a representative of the group of noncareer Ambassadors, it is with some diffidence that I comment on this topic. Like others who have testified to your committee, I believe in a strong career service. Such a service can attract and hold good men only if they have a legitimate expectation of coming to serve as chiefs of mission or Assistant Secretaries of State. With over 100 [now over 140] posts abroad, I would normally expect well over half of them to be headed by career officers.

I am not persuaded, however, that the interests of the United States would be served by reserving all of these posts to career officers. The exigencies of our oversea operations in today's world—and for the foreseeable future—sometimes require experience and qualifications which occur only rarely among career officers. I have noted the distinction made by some of your witnesses between purely political appointments, based merely on contribution to political party finances, and semiprofessional appointments of men or women with broad experience in public service as well as in civilian life. Like the other witnesses, I am opposed to the former type of appointment, but see great merit in the latter. Taking at random the names of a baker's dozen of men out of personal acquaintance among present or recent Ambassadors, I would offer for your consideration Ambassadors John Badeau, Chester Bowles, David Bruce, Ellsworth Bunker, Charles Cole, James Conant, John Ferguson, Kenneth Galbraith, Averell Harriman, Walter Howe, Henry Labouisse, George McGhee, and Edwin

SOURCE: Memorandum on "Organization and Coordination of Foreign Policy and Oversea Operations," U.S. Senate, Committee on Government Operations, Subcommittee on National Security Staffing and Operations, *Administration of National Security*, Hearings, Part 5, December 11, 1963 (Washington, D.C.: Government Printing Office, 1964), pp. 373–74.

Reischauer as examples of this semiprofessional category. To these male names I would add those of Mrs. [Helen Eugenie] Anderson and Mrs. [Clare Boothe] Luce. All of them have served with distinction, and very much to the positive interest of the U.S. Government.

Even if we were recruiting into the Foreign Service the very best young men and women available, occasions would often arise when the particular needs of an Embassy in one or another country would suggest appointing to it someone with specialized background and skills not available within the Service. As a university professor with a fair range of experience in observing career choices by exceptionally able young persons, however, I must state candidly that while the Service is getting some very good ones, it is by no means always getting the best. Anyone familiar with the career choices of college seniors or postgraduates at the better universities, observing the choices among the classic professions, business, academic life, and the public service is aware of this fact. One reason for this difficulty is the simple bread-and-butter fact that the pay scales at the higher levels of Government service are no longer competitive with those of other occupations attractive to professional-type youngsters. The Herter Committee rightly stressed the importance of improving the quality of recruitment, both at the junior level and through lateral entry at intermediate and higher levels.*

The basic guiding rule for the selection of Ambassadors, I believe, should be to find the most competent people for the jobs. As the quality of recruitment and career management in the Foreign Service are improved, career officers should in increasing proportion come to be the best qualified. In cases of close choice, I would give preference to the career man. I should be surprised, however, if 20 to 30 percent of the ambassadorial posts did not continue to be filled, under this criterion, by semiprofessional candidates.

Many competent career officers have emphasized to me the benefits which they themselves believe are brought to the career by the admixture of competent noncareer Ambassadors with a diversity of backgrounds and experience, and do not seem to resent their presence as unfair competition.

From the viewpoint of the noncareer Ambassador himself, there is the advantage of the greater sense of independence he feels through not having a vested interest in his own future within the career. If he carries this to the extreme of developing a policy of his own, at

---

* "Personnel for the New Diplomacy," report of the Committee on Foreign Affairs Personnel, Dec. 1962, pp. 65–80.

variance with the Government's policy, this independence can become counterproductive. But if he exercises it constructively to contribute to the formulation of policy jointly with his superiors in Washington, it may prove a real asset in the management of our foreign relations.

Case for Professional Diplomats

CHARLES W. THAYER

Nations, it has frequently been observed, are judged by their representatives abroad. For this if for no other reasons governments should take special pains in selecting their envoys. In the seventeenth century ambassadors were often selected from one of three professions: the church, the military, and the law. Today the first is seldom a source of recruits except for the Vatican. Though generals and lawyers are frequently appointed to diplomatic posts, most authorities agree that neither group is well suited to diplomacy.

Although on rare occasions brilliant generals have become excellent ambassadors, most have been failures. The military career has indeed little in common with diplomacy, and not only because one is directed toward war and the other toward peace. The headquarters atmosphere with its stress on procedures, channels of command, and external discipline is totally different from that of the chancellery, where individual methods are employed, informal relationships exist, and rank plays a lesser role.

There is an even greater difference in the subject matter of the military career and that of diplomacy. The one deals with weapons, logistics, and organization; the other deals with political concepts, the written word, and personal relations.

A diplomatic friend of mine, after reading in the papers of the appointment of a series of generals and admirals to diplomatic posts, asked facetiously: "Do you suppose that one day they will appoint Ambassador Smith to take command of the Sixth Fleet or Counselor of Embassy Jones to head the 45th Jet Fighter Squadron?"

Although it is quite commonly supposed that a legal career is an

SOURCE: "Our Ambassadors: An Intimate Appraisal of the Men and the System," *Harper's Magazine*, vol. 129 (September 1959), pp. 29–35.

advantage for diplomats and though many lawyers have been appointed to embassies, law in some respects is even less suited as training for a diplomatic career than the military profession. In fact Sir Harold Nicolson, the leading English authority on diplomacy, maintains that "the worst kind of diplomatists are missionaries, fanatics, and lawyers." "The training of a lawyer," said Callières, "breeds habits and dispositions of mind which are not favorable to the practice of diplomacy. The occupation of a lawyer," he added, "which is to split hairs about nothing is not a good preparation for the treatment of grave public affairs in the region of diplomacy."

Whether or not splitting hairs over nothing is the basis of a legal career, the superficial similarities between the law and diplomacy are perhaps one reason for their incompatibility. The lawyer, like the diplomat, deals in debate and compromise. A knowledge of law is essential to the diplomat, and ability to negotiate is essential to the lawyer, and a knowledge of human nature is essential to both.

But when the lawyer turns to international problems these similarities lead him to the false conclusion that diplomacy is a form of law. His whole training has accustomed him to presuppose a court where right is distinguished from wrong, legal from illegal, and where there are police and jails to enforce decisions. Moral as well as legal concepts govern his thinking.

When the lawyer faces a problem he attempts to solve it by legal agreements in which every contingency is foreseen and every detail is strictly defined. He seeks to regulate affairs by hard and fast formulas within a completely ordered system. None of these concepts apply to international affairs. Even international law, which covers only a tiny part of the field of diplomacy, has few sanctions. The World Court can regulate but a fraction of the daily disputes and differences which occupy diplomats because sovereign states refuse to submit to a higher sovereignty despite idealistic proposals that they should do so.

The traditions, customs, and histories of different countries, areas, and religions, on which their moral as well as their legal concepts are based, vary greatly. In Western countries Christian morality and principles prevail. In Arab lands the ethical rules of the Koran are the basis of law. In the East Buddhist ethics dominate. In England only a judge may condemn to death. In Germany not even a judge has the power of pronouncing death, but in Eastern lands a killer's life is at the disposal of his victim's family.

Nowhere is the difference more marked than between Western and Byzantine concepts of justice. In the Soviet Union a war to establish or defend a Communist dictatorship is a "just" war, a lie to the same purpose is a white lie, and what the West considers truth is often a bourgeois falsehood.

Diplomacy mediates not between right and wrong but between conflicting interests. It seeks to compromise not between legal equities but between national aspirations. Among nations, despite the efforts of statesmen since Grotius, no ordered system with a unified process of law enforcement exists. Furthermore, a nation's interests, aspirations, and the power to satisfy them vary from year to year, indeed from day to day. What yesterday was satisfactory may tomorrow be intolerable and unenforceable.

* * *

Tycoons in Striped Pants

To the church, the military, and the law the twentieth century has added a fourth potential reservoir of ambassadors—business. It is widely believed, particularly in America, that diplomatic negotiations are essentially business deals and that the best negotiator is therefore a shrewd Yankee horse trader operating under the cover of a pair of striped pants. As a result, a number of successful businessmen without diplomatic experience have found themselves pantless and shirtless at the end of a negotiation with experienced diplomats.

However, diplomatic negotiations differ fundamentally from commercial or business dealings. In the first place, business deals, like legal business, are conducted within the framework of a regulated system with self-enforcing powers. Business to a large extent is regulated by the laws of contracts. Even international business deals generally provide for arbitration in the courts of one or the other contracting party. Diplomacy has been defined as "commerce in mutual benefits" or the harmonizing of interests. Only as long as mutual benefits accrue or harmony prevails is there any real assurance that the agreements will be fulfilled.

The businessman who has concluded a "deal," whether to buy a factory or sell a shipload of coffee beans, knowing that the contract is binding, can often scarcely wait to announce his triumph to his stockholders and assure his associates of the profit he has made. The diplomat, however, never proclaims a diplomatic success. On the contrary, he will endeavor to advertise the benefits he has sacrificed to the other party.

In the second place, unlike the average businessman, the diplomat cannot pick and choose his associates. He must deal with the political power that rules. Nor can he ever be sure when power relationships will change and the government he rebuffed yesterday must be wooed as an ally today. Only the amateur or the Byzantine diplomat slams doors. The professional may say "perhaps" or "tomorrow" but he never says "no," whether to a treaty of alliance or a request for a loan to build a dam.

Thirdly, unlike the businessman's, a diplomat's negotiation is never finished. A treaty may be signed and sealed but it is seldom irrevocably delivered. So long as it remains in force it is subject to modification, renegotiation, or denunciation. For example, the United States may find it advisable to establish air bases in Spain. Delicate feelers are first put out by the ambassador in Madrid. If the Spanish government responds favorably, formal negotiations are begun. Long discussions and haggling follow on sites, payment for the final disposition of the fields, the labor terms and material costs to build them, and legal jurisdiction over the American airmen who will eventually man them.

Even when the treaty has been signed and ratified, the diplomat's job has scarcely begun. Differences of interpretation of the most precisely drafted text will arise. Unexpected obstacles will develop as construction crews go to work, equipment is imported, and finally the crews and their families move into their strange environment and start to adjust themselves to local customs and laws. Each of these problems must be ironed out in endless negotiations. Meantime the mutual benefits accruing to the Spanish and American governments will fluctuate with new political or economic conditions and the development of new weapons.

The North Atlantic Treaty Organization . . . is practically in a perpetual state of renegotiation. Scarcely a week passes without discussions between the diplomats stationed at NATO headquarters to smooth out difficulties, modify impractical commitments, or even occasionally to prevent the entire edifice from collapsing because of conflicting interests between the partners, whether Turkey and Greece or England and the United States.

Dilettantes Abroad

If churchmen, soldiers, lawyers, and businessmen make poor diplomats, Callières maintained, the dilettantes make the worst of all. Men of small minds, he said, should content themselves with jobs at home where their errors may be easily repaired; for errors abroad are too often irreparable. Acknowledging that there is always a temptation to use ambassadorships to pay old debts, he warned that the public interest must be supreme and that officials should steel themselves against the pressure of political friends or relatives seeking diplomatic posts.

Sometimes a host government may complain discreetly about the quality of the ambassador it receives. Some time ago, the Canadian prime minister is said to have complained that Canada had suffered her share of American dilettantes and hacks as ambassadors and pleaded that it be sent a professional diplomat. The President then sent a distinguished career officer.

After World War II the government of Luxembourg, having been host to a series of political party favorites as American ministers, let it be known in Washington that its patience was exhausted. If the next appointee was not a career official, it intimated, it would refuse to receive him. The United States again acceded.

Other governments have grown accustomed to non-professional American diplomats, tolerating them as part of the American system of conducting diplomacy. However, as Nicolson points out, the United States has suffered much from political appointments under the "spoils system." "The capitals of Europe and Latin America," he says, "echoed with the indiscretions of these amateur diplomatists and much damage was done to all concerned . . . by politicians whose intelligence and conduct were not consonant with the dignity of the United States."

Nevertheless, the spoils system continues to dispose of many diplomatic posts. Today only four of the fourteen American ambassadors in important Western European posts are professionals. Because many non-European posts, especially in out-of-the-way places, do not attract office seekers, the percentage of professionals on a global basis is somewhat higher. Even so, about half our embassies are still headed by amateurs whose previous experience has been as successful bankers, salesmen, race-horse breeders, and so on. Not all have been failures. Indeed some, like Douglas Dillon, have revealed the rare talents of a born diplomat.

It is popularly supposed that ambassadorships are bought by rich men with social ambitions or socially ambitious wives. This is only partly true. Aside from the professionals appointed from the career service, many ambassadors are selected by the President or the secretary of state because he genuinely believes that they possess the attributes of a good ambassador. They are good mixers. They make friends easily. They are conciliatory and have pleasing personalities or they have some special tie with a particular country that is expected to make them popular there.

President Roosevelt, who, according to John Gunther, shopped about for ambassadors like a housewife shopping for potatoes, selected Professor William Dodd as ambassador to Germany because he was a specialist in German history and a fanatical enemy of Nazism. Dodd was a great scholar but a disastrous diplomat. President Eisenhower appointed an ambassador to Southeast Asia because he knew the country well from the frequent big-game shooting expeditions he had made there.

Political Payoffs

Money nevertheless plays a prominent role in the distribution of diplomatic prizes. By making a substantial contribution to a political party, office seekers can enhance their chances for a diplomatic post, particularly if they or their backers can discover something in their background that passes for a diplomatic qualification: they have traveled abroad or know a lot of foreigners or are accomplished hostesses.*

An old friend of mine who had served for many years in the Foreign Service found promotions slow and anybody's chances of getting an embassy by way of the career ladder slight. Thereupon he resigned from the service and made a substantial contribution to the Republican party. Within months he had a good embassy.

In the roaring twenties a wealthy playboy was left a large fortune by his father, together with precise instructions about its disposition. One provision instructed him to make a heavy contribution to the Republican party. However, the elections of 1932 were in the offing and some of the playboy's Democratic friends persuaded him that the Republicans did not have a chance. His father, they argued, would have been just as pleased to back Franklin Roosevelt. He agreed and after the election found himself heading a choice embassy.

Contributions to parties need not be monetary. Editors who put their papers behind a political candidate can often count on an embassy for themselves or their wives. A lawyer may help a leading candidate to clear up a messy lawsuit and get a good appointment. Even mediocre journalists, by writing stories favorable to a candidate, can earn an embassy.

Exile to an embassy overseas has long been a way of sidetracking political opponents. Hitler thus got rid of former Chancellor Luther by sending him as ambassador to Washington.

---

* EDITOR's NOTE: In addition, because social functions may be expensive, wealth is often a necessary prerequisite for functioning effectively as an ambassador in certain capitals. See footnote 5 of the essay by Clare Boothe Luce, "Ambassadors: Professionals or Amateurs?"

Some years ago a novice Congressman from New York, having displeased his local party bosses, was offered by them either the embassy in New Zealand or the embassy in Portugal if he would step down and not run for re-election. Doubting their ability to dispose of embassies in this cavalier fashion, he made inquiries in the State Department and to his amazement learned that both posts had been put at their disposal. Nevertheless, he rejected the offer and is still a prominent member of Congress.

The national committees of both major parties supervise the disposition of political appointments to embassies through an informal system whereby the party in power maintains within the State Department and on its payroll a small group whose function it is to watch over the disposition of such patronage as becomes available within the department or the diplomatic service. They keep an eye out for possible openings for loyal party followers, check appointments with the patronage bosses of the state from which a candidate comes, and from time to time clean out the political appointees who have expended their patronage claims or dun them for further contributions.

Patronage bookkeeping is very informal, a circumstance that occasionally leads to misunderstanding and even bitter recriminations. An old friend of mine, a political incumbent of an embassy, was approached by his national committee chairman with the suggestion that he increase his annual contribution to the party or resign. The ambassador was well off, so he gladly upped his donation and settled back for another term in his pleasant embassy. However, the national chairman was suddenly replaced and the new man, searching for a vacancy for a prominent politician in need of a job, reneged on his predecessor's assurances and my friend found himself an ex-ambassador.

Since public-opinion polls are not perfect and elections are notoriously unpredictable, eager office seekers occasionally contribute to both major parties. This practice is considered unethical by some politicians and is frowned upon by patronage bosses. However, since the contributor usually uses his wife's name for one contribution and his own for the other, it is not always easy to check.

*　*　*

Although embassies are usually much sought after, it occasionally happens that a deserving party follower prefers his rewards in the form of a judgeship or a post office nearer to home. In the 'thirties a deserving claimant to party favors was asked whether he would like to be minister to a Baltic capital.

"Minister?" he asked incredulously, "hell, I've never even been in a pulpit let alone ordained." Nevertheless, he was induced to accept the post.

How to Fire a Diplomat

Before the establishment of the career service in 1924, all embassy officials were expected to submit their resignations when the Presidency changed hands. After that, career officers below chief of mission were considered permanent. In fact, several career ambassadors, assuming that they too were exempt, failed to submit their resignations. However, they were quickly put right by the White House and since then after every election all chiefs of mission whether career or political appointees submit their resignations.*

Partly as a consequence of this practice, professional diplomats who have risen to ambassadorial rank often find their careers suddenly terminated when their resignations are accepted by a party in power in need of patronage posts. Since there is no way for a career diplomat to remain an ambassador for more than a limited period without an embassy, he must thereafter retire. . . .

It has become a political tradition for Presidential candidates to pledge their support of the career principle and to promise not to replace career ambassadors. However, in view of the automatic resignation procedure, it is relatively easy to circumvent such pre-election pledges.

Whenever a new party comes to power it is customary to demonstrate statistically that the number of professional diplomatic incumbents has been increased or at least not decreased. The statistical game is fairly simple to play no matter what inroads the patronage committee has made on the embassies, since the number of embassies has in recent years steadily increased with the creation of new independent states, many of which political office seekers do not consider desirable.*

The most desirable diplomatic posts are generally those in Europe, especially London, Paris, Rome, and Madrid. The so-called "commuting embassies," Ottawa, Mexico City, and Havana, whence an incumbent can easily commute to his office in New York for the trans-

---

* EDITOR's NOTE: These formal, automatic resignations, known as "courtesy resignations," customarily are filed by all United States ambassadors serving as chiefs of mission when a new president takes office. The president may accept or reject each resignation as he decides. This practice often results in a chain reaction of resignations and appointments.

* EDITOR's NOTE: For statistics on U.S. practice in this regard since World War II, see pp. 303–4.

action of his personal business, also are highly in demand. Where climatic conditions are good outside Europe or where there is a special interest for an office seeker one also occasionally finds political appointees.

One office seeker accustomed to living in comfortable circumstances not long ago sought for and got an embassy in a far-off primitive post. Asked by a friend why he wanted to give up his comfortable existence in the U. S. for a squalid Asian city, he replied blandly, "My psychiatrist recommended it." Apparently the remedy for whatever problems ailed him was a success, for after serving several years there he applied for and got another embassy.

Not infrequently it becomes necessary to dismiss an ambassador to make room for an important politician who has lost an election or has been ousted from his job for other reasons. When the prospective victim is a political appointee it is relatively simple for a national committeeman or departmental patronage official to write him that the party deems its obligations to him fulfilled. Even this formality is not always observed. Not too long ago, an ambassador in Scandinavia read in the local morning paper that Washington had appointed a successor to him. Angrily he cabled for confirmation and shortly received it together with an urgent request for his resignation.

If the prospective victim is a career appointee, on the other hand, the procedure is more delicate. An old professional friend of mine with many years of service was happily serving out the last year or two before retirement in a not particularly pleasant post when suddenly a courier delivered an urgent letter from the State Department. It stated that it had been reconsidering his allegedly long-expressed wish for early retirement and reluctantly had decided to accept his resignation as ambassador. Since his successor, a New York lawyer, was planning to leave for his new post within a few days, it was suggested that he leave his embassy within the week. Sadly and bitterly the old diplomat wired his resignation, packed hurriedly, and retired on a substantially lower pension than he would have received had he been allowed to serve out his full career.

Although the Senate under the Constitution is empowered to pass on all diplomatic appointments, its responsibility has been fulfilled until recently with perfunctory regularity.* Only rarely has an appointment aroused such animosity that the appointee has withdrawn. When, for example, Edward J. Flynn, the retiring chairman of the Democratic National Committee, was turned out to grass as min-

---

* A recent exception was, of course, the argument over the appointment of Mrs. Clare Boothe Luce, which ended in her withdrawal as Ambassador to Brazil.

ister to Australia in 1943, the public reaction against him was such that he was persuaded to request that his nomination be withdrawn.

Breaking in the New Boss

Although, as we have noted, authorities on diplomacy have laid great stress on the prior training of an ambassador, the State Department has found it necessary to compress a political ambassador's briefing on the country to which he is assigned to a few weeks or even days. Largely because of the shortage of time, it frequently happens that an ambassador is not even able to pronounce the name of the country to say nothing of the name of its highest official, as Ambassador Gluck found to his sorrow.** One ambassador assigned to Yugoslavia boasted to his friends that he was on his way to Czechoslavia (*sic*) and constantly confused the Masaryks with the Karageorgeviches.

Once arrived at his new post, even a professional ambassador expects to spend weeks if not months familiarizing himself with conditions and making the acquaintance of its officials. For the political appointee a special and often costly routine has been established. As counselor or deputy chief of mission, an experienced professional officer is frequently designated as personal assistant to keep the ambassador informed of diplomatic usage and to reduce his diplomatic *gaffes* to a minimum. Against the weeks it takes a professional to work himself into a new post, it is an old axiom among career diplomats that an amateur often requires years.

It would be unjust to ascribe to pure cynicism this haphazard way of manning the key foxholes in the outer perimeter of our national defense. Whereas provincial party bosses and parochial National Committeemen may deliberately overlook national interests, the political leaders in whose name the appointments are made are frequently sincerely persuaded that the appointees foisted upon them actually possess qualifications popularly associated with "diplomacy" —affability, social grace, or Yankee shrewdness.

Furthermore, it is widely believed that the long-distance telephone and the cable have reduced the role of a diplomat to that of a Western Union messenger boy and that the risk of the irreparable damage, of which Callières warned, has been eliminated. Disregarded is the warning of Secretary of State Charles Evans Hughes. "It is perfectly idle," he said testily, "to believe that we can get along without diplomatic representatives. . . . We cannot rely on direct messages. We need the man in personal contact with other men in transacting

---

** EDITOR'S NOTE: This refers to Ambassador Maxwell Henry Gluck, appointed Ambassador to Ceylon (Sri Lanka) in 1957.

the business of their government." The French diplomat Jusserand was even more explicit. "Experience has already shown and will more and more show," he said, "that no invention, no telephone, no airplane, no wireless will ever replace the knowledge of a country and the understanding of a people's disposition."

Few statesmen or diplomatic authorities have argued that diplomatic posts should be filled exclusively from the trained career service. Callières urged that men of letters be enlisted. Others have warned against the incestuous habits of mind that a closed professional service inevitably induces.

Every political generation produces a half-dozen or more individuals capable of making a distinguished contribution to diplomacy without going through the long and arduous training of the professional service. If they are familiar with government practices and particularly foreign problems and have demonstrated their political sense, their appointment to diplomatic posts not only puts their talents to valuable use but also serves to refresh, invigorate, and inspire the career personnel. In recent years David Bruce, John Sherman Cooper, Chester Bowles, and Douglas Dillon have rendered outstanding service to the country in diplomatic posts. Great Britain, too, has frequently brought new blood into its career service through such men as Sir Oliver Franks.

Politicians have argued earnestly that the present method has for over a century adequately served our political system, providing the essential means for financing costly campaigns. For centuries, they point out, other countries also staffed their entire civil service by the same method. Indeed, up to the Crimean War the British Army was officered almost exclusively by the sale of commissions.

One of the most vigorous defendants of the present system, Mrs. Clare Boothe Luce, who has herself served as ambassador to Italy, has pointed out that despite occasional lapses the United States has not done too badly with it. "In 181 years of our diplomatic history," she has said, "America has not yet made the irrevocable diplomatic blunder."*

Could Lord Raglan, the British commander in the Crimea, have put the case for his officers more strongly as the Light Brigade charged into the Valley of Death?**

---

* EDITOR'S NOTE: See Clare Boothe Luce, "Ambassadors: Professionals or Amateurs?" above.

** EDITOR'S NOTE: Lord Raglan (Fitzroy J. H. Somerset), British General during the Crimean War (1854–56), participated in the Battles of Alma River and Balaklava; the latter was immortalized in Tennyson's Charge of the Light Brigade.

7

Functions of Diplomats

An American ambassador today is not the ambassador to the foreign office. He is the ambassador to the whole society.
HARLAN CLEVELAND in *The American Overseas*

An Ambassador has still the tedious round of official parties and entertainment. He must still participate in the pomp and ceremony of official life. But he must also hold the hands of newsmen, open doors for businessmen, and attend to visiting Congressmen. Besides, today's Ambassador is expected to get away from the capital and to acquire firsthand knowledge of the country's political, social and economic life. What the people are saying is often more important than the gossip of high society, and his business suits and even more informal attire may wear out sooner than his white tie and tails.
HENRY M. JACKSON in *Administration of National Security: The American Ambassador*

A study of diplomats and the nature of the diplomatic process would be negligent if it did not address the question, "What does the diplomat really do?" The essays in this chapter focus on some of his more obvious functions.

"A Day with the Ambassador," by Ellis O. Briggs, gives the reader a taste of an American envoy's daily routine. Briggs, who served as chief of mission in seven countries, presents a firsthand account of the envoy's diverse tasks, major and minor, as he follows an imaginary ambassador through his working day.

Lincoln Gordon, in "Expanded Foreign Relations Functions," explains that the new diplomacy produced a substantial increase in the volume and diversity of the American diplomat's pragmatic functions and duties. Traditional diplomatic responsibilities—representation of U.S. interests and policy, collection of information, negotiation, and protection of the interests of U.S. citizens and their concerns abroad—proliferated both quantitatively and qualitatively as American interests moved beyond political and military concerns into the realms of scientific, economic, social, cultural, and other matters. In addition, new responsibilities, such as the establishment and administration of U.S. information and aid programs and the coordination overseas of these new arenas of diplomatic activity, emerged to expand and complicate still further the diplomat's role in foreign relations.

Kingdon B. Swayne elaborates on the function of information gathering and reporting ("Reporting Function") from the perspective of both practitioner and analyst. Realizing that the decision maker and negotiator have a greater need for information and policy guidance as the arenas of diplomatic activity grow in size and number, Swayne stresses the importance of reliable diplomatic reporting. The intelligence agent, who serves a different purpose and clientele, cannot supplant the diplomat because he gathers raw data without the political analysis that the diplomat provides. Nor can the foreign correspondent serve as a dependable substitute, because he is not privy to certain types of information available to the diplomat, he writes for a general audience with different goals in mind, and he is constrained in his reporting by editorial guidelines and space limitations. Nevertheless, Swayne acknowledges a number of pressures that affect the diplomat's objectivity in reporting information, including the diplomat's own norms and values, the expected responses of his superiors, existing national policy, and the need to contribute to the production of specific foreign policy.

The negotiation function, one of the most fundamental to and characteristic of the diplomatic process, is elaborated in two essays. "Negotiating Effectively," by Fred Charles Iklé, defines negotiation as the "process in which explicit proposals are put forward ostensibly for the purpose of reaching agreement on an exchange or on the realization of a common interest where conflicting interests are present." Iklé analyzes various aspects of negotiation, such as introducing proposals and coming to terms, and discusses the skills necessary for the "compleat negotiator." In "Of Negotiation and Bargaining in the Modern World," Henry A. Kissinger discusses some of the problems besetting the negotiating function. Diplomacy has become intractable, he suggests, because of the destructiveness of modern weapons and the polarization of power relationships since World War II. Given this intractability, he cautions against flexibility and conciliation in negotiation as primary ends in themselves, indicating instead, in the case of dealing with a major adversary, the need for "a settlement which does not hazard our security and is consistent with our values. Only in the purposeful is flexibility a virtue."

Last but by no means least in the portfolio of basic diplomatic functions is the making and influencing of foreign policy. Dean Rusk, in "Formulating Foreign Policy," provides guidelines on important aspects of the policy-making process that are applicable to policy formulation in Washington and in the field. Among other things, he recommends the creation of a policy-making "check list" of questions that should be applied to each new initiative. This list would include queries such as: Is there, in a given situation, a question relating to United States interests, and if so, what is it? Who else has a stake in the matter? If action is indicated, what type of action is desirable? Will the public support it? By answering these and many other penetrating questions, the policy maker can clarify and systematize the "galaxy of utterly complicated factors" that are involved in each major policy decision and can create a more cogent and consistent foreign policy.

Finally, because it is important to the effective functioning of the diplomatic process, "Precedence and Protocol," by Charles W. Thayer, is added as a parting glimpse of the diplomat and his entanglements in the social and official subtleties of the modern international community. In this essay, replete with amusing anecdotes, Thayer communicates the complexities and the absurdities of protocol that confront an emissary in the execution of his duties. "Outside the local law," he states, "beyond the jurisdiction of the courts, the diplomatic corps would be a lawless community were it not for its self-imposed ethics and rules which together comprise protocol." While it seems extreme to assume the possibility of a Hobbesian war "of every man against every man" in the absence of common authority, the rules of diplomatic etiquette do nevertheless perform a necessary, though sometimes bewildering if not actually frustrating, function in the international community. To what extent these rules are critical, and how, if at all, the precepts of protocol might be altered, is a matter of continuing discourse in the diplomatic community worldwide.

A Day with the Ambassador

ELLIS O. BRIGGS

There is no such thing as a Typical Embassy. Therein lies some of the charm of diplomacy for professional diplomats, as well as some of its frustration. An Ambassador's life can be one of infinite variety, but what is effective procedure at Post A may have little relevance to operations at Post B, in a different continent. Or even at Post C on the same continent. The successful ambassadorial approach in one country may have to be abandoned in the next, where a whole new set of ground rules may be in operation.[1]

Moreover, an Ambassador, to a degree not approached by an executive of comparable responsibility in any other profession, can be at the mercy of forces over which he exercises little control—his own government, and the government of the country to which the Ambassador is accredited. Thus the host government, especially if it is an Emerging Nation, may suddenly wake up to find its treasury cupboard bare and demand of the Ambassador an X-million-dollar credit, to be available to the Minister of Finance by the following Wednesday. Or the State Department, prodded by an eager American representative at United Nations, may suddenly cable the Ambassador, directing him to twist the arm of the host government until the latter agrees to vote *yes* on some pending General Assembly item, even

---

[1] An effort was recently made by the State Department to divide diplomatic missions into those established in sophisticated countries, where traditional diplomacy is not yet in disrepute, and those functioning in countries dedicated to "internal development," where the United States is busy with "operational programs" calculated to ferment the yeast of rising expectations.

Ernest Hemingway put it more succinctly when he observed that "what you win in Boston, you lose in Brooklyn." But diplomats, unlike baseball players, play *all* their games away from home.

SOURCE: *Anatomy of Diplomacy: The Origin and Execution of American Foreign Policy* (New York: McKay, 1968), pp. 115–20, 130–36.

though the subject may have no more than marginal importance in the relations between the United States and the Ambassador's host country.

These events occur on weekends, when the Ambassador had planned to go fishing, or to catch up on his sleep, or to visit a hinterland province.

In the case of instructions dispatched by Washington, there is little awareness outside the geographic Bureau of the State Department of the mechanics of compliance abroad. There is no picture in the minds of other Potomac officials of the steps that have to be taken by an Embassy on the receipt of a message. Having dictated the phrase "you will accordingly seek an immediate interview with the Minister for Foreign Affairs, requesting an assurance on behalf of his Government that . . ." the task of the Washington bureaucrat is accomplished. He can then go home to his martinis, his backgammon, or his P.T.A. meeting, giving no further thought to the problem generated by his telegram until the Ambassador's reply reaches his Foggy Bottom cubicle.

But except in countries heavily dependent for survival on American bounty, and hence readily accessible to the American representative, getting an "immediate interview" with the head of the Foreign Office can be as difficult as it would be for the Washington representative of the country concerned to see on equally short notice the Secretary of State of the United States—even if the Secretary had not just flown off to attend a SEATO meeting in Canberra.

It may be revealing, therefore, to trace what happens to a message dispatched from Washington over the name of the senior member of the Cabinet, telling an Ambassador to take some kind of action.

The Embassy code clerk, having deciphered the telegram and having spotted the word "immediate," will have alerted the duty officer, noting the time—12:28 A.M.—in his log. But since the message is classified, the clerk will have been unable to describe its contents over the telephone; the duty officer, cursing, will accordingly read it in the code room at 1:30 A.M., as likewise recorded. Correctly refraining from waking up the Ambassador about something that cannot be tackled before daylight, the duty officer will appear at the Embassy Residence with the message at eight o'clock the following morning. He will be invited to share a cup of coffee with his Chief, who is already halfway through the local newspapers.

Most Foreign Offices do not open until ten in the morning, and the first question is whether the Ambassador should try to get through to a subordinate official before that hour, requesting an appointment with the Minister, or whether the Ambassador should make use of the Foreign Minister's private telephone number, communicating directly with him at home, notwithstanding the Minister's possible hostility to breakfast interruptions.

At that point there come into play factors that cannot be found in a rulebook: the Ambassador's assessment of the importance of the message, and its subject matter, in the scale of issues confronting the two countries. The Ambassador must weigh the message in terms of its impact on the host government. He will have to forecast the response of that government, and calculate how much of his own diplomatic ammunition is likely to be required, in order to produce the assurance demanded by Washington. He must decide whether—in the event that the cost in those terms may be considerable—the favorable reply of the foreign government is really an achievement commensurate with the expenditure of that much effort. (With Foggy Bottom bursting with bureaucrats, and all the bureaucrats supplied with paper, all sorts of messages reach foreign capitals demanding ambassadorial action.)

If he doubts the importance of the current project, the Ambassador can bounce back a message to Washington, setting forth his views and "requesting further instructions"—a gambit too frequent recourse to which can be irritating at home, especially if the majority of the Ambassadors receiving the same instruction act upon it without cavil.

In the case in point, the Ambassador concludes that an issue of substance is involved. The message deals with a proposed international conference on maritime jurisdiction, and the host country, possessing a seacoast and with appreciable fishery resources, should not only be interested in the project *per se*, but should be receptive to the views expressed by the United States. The Ambassador accordingly hunts up the Foreign Minister's unlisted phone number (given to him shortly after arrival, when the host government decided that the Ambassador knew his business). The Ambassador holds the receiver in one hand and his second cup of coffee in the other, while the Foreign Minister is wrapping a bath towel around his middle and pushing damp feet into bedroom slippers.

The Ambassador describes the situation set forth in the telegram, compressing it into its salient facts and expressing the belief that the interests of the two governments ought in this case to coincide. He bases the early approach to the minister on the unexpected United Nations action, scheduling with so little notice an Assembly debate on the issue.

After asking several pertinent questions, the Foreign Minister says on consideration that he agrees. He volunteers to cable his own UN representative in the sense desired, adding that he will tell his Ambassador in New York to get in touch with his American colleague. "No trouble, my friend. Your call has saved time for us both. I hope we can always settle our problems so quickly. . . ."

The Foreign Minister then returns to his bath. The American Ambassador, having scribbled his reply to Washington on a yellow pad, dismisses the duty officer and turns to the text of yesterday's White House press conference, received overnight in the Radio Bulletin. Mission accomplished.

The action described has taken place under optimum diplomatic conditions: a smoothly operating American Embassy Chancery with an efficient duty officer, an energetic Ambassador enjoying the confidence of the host Government and sharing a language with the Foreign Minister, and an issue soluble in terms of existing bilateral relations. Such conditions, in the troubled postwar period, are not always in conjunction. In Bolivia, Upper Volta, or Czechoslovakia, where interest in the law of the sea may be somewhat less than incendiary, the response will not be identical with that evoked in Japan, Great Britain, Peru, or Soviet Russia, even though all countries— landlocked or not—have the same vote in the General Assembly of [the] United Nations.

Furthermore, leaving aside the variety of the responses toward the substantive issues raised by that particular message, the circumstances in which a reply is obtainable can differ even more widely, country by country and capital by capital. The Foreign Minister might be out of town, leaving a Vice Minister unwilling to commit his chief. Or, having been found within the inadequate time limit, the Foreign Minister might wish to consult his Chief of State, or his legislative leaders, and then disappear again, remaining inaccessible, until after the clock has run out. Or the host Government might be going through a period of annoyance with the United States, and hence decline on principle to cooperate. Or the American Ambassador might himself be out of town when the telegram arrives, with his Deputy unable within the prescribed period to reach an official of sufficient authority to handle the problem.

All of which is illustrative of the desirability of leaving diplomatic representatives long enough at their posts for them to learn how to operate effectively in the special and distinctive atmospheres prevailing in their respective countries. No two capitals are alike, least of all (for example) the five neighboring capitals of Central

America, which share a common language and a common colonial heritage, but in no other particulars resemble each other.[2]

* * *

. . . Let us examine how this particular diplomat spends the rest of the day so auspiciously inaugurated.

At nine-thirty the Ambassador reaches his Chancery, having walked the mile and a half from his Residence, to the disgust of the Embassy chauffeur, who can imagine nothing more idiotic than going on foot, when there is a Cadillac automobile to ride in. The first half-hour is spent reading the incoming telegrams, as well as the pink copies of messages dispatched in his name overnight, and in exchanging views with his Deputy, who congratulates the Ambassador on the expeditious disposal of the United Nations matter. Arriving half an hour before his Chief, the DCM [Deputy Chief of Mission] will already have put the Chancery machinery in motion.

An informal ten o'clock meeting in the Ambassador's office will bring together the heads of the five sections,* together with the DCM and the CIA representative. Here the day's work is considered, positions adopted, and assignments made. It is the most important meeting of each day, although once a week the Ambassador will have a larger staff meeting in the Conference Room—a sort of weekly summary and orientation session, a principal purpose of which is to tie all the members of the organization together, including Defense and civilian Attachés, newly arrived officers, and juniors getting their first view of how an Embassy functions.

Likewise once a week, the Ambassador will meet with his so-called Country Team, a diplomatic adjunct dear to the heart of Washington which invented it. The Country Team is not a voting organization, but a device to get before the Ambassador the views of the different agencies operating in the country, the progress they think they are making, and the problems they think they are encountering. Participants are encouraged to urge on the Ambassador any course of action they favor, and the Ambassador may or may not go along with

[2] It is gratifying to report that in contrast to the Roosevelt, Truman, and Eisenhower Administrations, which played musical chairs with American diplomats with such abandon that both furniture and participants were exhausted, and the business of American diplomacy suffered, the average length of ambassadorial service during the 1960s has almost doubled. This has been accompanied by a marked increase in the effectiveness of American representation at a number of capitals.

* EDITOR'S NOTE: The author refers to the political, economic, public affairs, consular, and administrative sections as the usual components of a typical American embassy.

those recommendations. When he does not, the matter can be referred to Washington: the subordinate's view, plus the dissenting opinion of the Chief of Mission.

A main objective of the Country Team mechanism is the hoped-for elimination of conflicting reports reaching Washington, a source of never-ending confusion during the 1950s, when non-diplomatic personnel dominated the scene and each agency was the architect of its own floor in the Tower of Babel.[3]

If the Ambassador has a speech to make, he will discuss it at his ten o'clock staff meeting, outlining what he thinks ought to be said, calling for comment, and then assigning to his Public Affairs Officer and to the Chief of the Political Section the responsibility of producing a "first draft" for further consideration. The more experienced the Ambassador, the fewer public speeches he will make, knowing that of the ills afflicting diplomacy, the most painful are those that result from an Ambassador's not keeping his mouth shut. On the other hand, he recognizes that an occasional appearance before a local Chamber of Commerce, and of course shortly after arrival at a new post before the American Society, can represent a useful opportunity to emphasize some pertinent truth or to get across some profitable idea about the work of the mission. Generally speaking, however, the Ambassador concludes that there are too many speeches and too many public statements made by officials abroad, just as there is too much vaporing in the United States by everyone from the President and the Secretary of State down to the smallest sub-cabinet member: the great uninhibited American penchant for sounding off.

The remainder of the Ambassador's morning will be taken up by appointments. At eleven he receives the Minister for Public Works, an evasive little man who has difficulty in coming to the point, which is the possible availability of credit to finance a dam and accompanying power grid; the Ambassador has present the Chief of the Economic Section and the Treasury Attaché. If the Minister will kindly submit a memorandum outlining the project, it will receive careful and sympathetic consideration.

Encouraged by this reception and impressed by the knowledge-ability of the Treasury Attaché about his country's finances, the Minister for Public Works takes his departure, with the Ambassador as a mark of friendly respect accompanying his visitor to the elevator.

---

[3] In some of our larger Embassies, the Deputy Chief of Mission is chairman of all three of these Chancery meetings, thus leaving the Ambassador free to consort with the Prime Minister, to play golf with the heir apparent, and to brood about Larger Issues.

Then occurs the first untoward incident of the day. It involves the guardians of the Ambassador's outer office, which has been invaded by eight patriotic ladies from Texas, traveling together on a junket, and looking the part. Appearing at the Embassy without appointment but brandishing form letters furnished by their Congressmen, calling upon all comers to take notice, the ladies have been demanding to be received personally by the American Ambassador in order, so the spokeswoman declares, to bear witness.

The aforesaid guardians of the outer office, cognizant of their responsibility to protect the Chief of Mission from such hazards, have just completed a professional brush-off job, only to have it destroyed by the incautious and unexpected appearance in the hallway of the Ambassador himself, recognizable by the ladies even though he has a foreigner in tow and is not speaking English.

By the time the Ambassador is shaking hands with the Minister of Public Works, the eight ladies have surrounded the pair, while the spokeswoman leads her companions in rendering "Deep in the Heart of Texas" with sufficient volume to startle the jackrabbits into Mexico, if not to bring Sam Houston back from his Valhalla.

From the adjacent ambassadorial waiting room this scene is witnessed by the goggle-eyed Ambassador of Rwanda, whose eleven-thirty appointment to make a protocol visit to his American colleague is already twenty minutes past due.[4]

It takes the American Ambassador seven minutes to detach himself from the triumphant Lone Star ladies, and five additional minutes to explain to the bewildered and suspicious representative from Kigali what has happened. Meanwhile, the president of the American Chamber of Commerce, who heads an important American bank in the capital, and who has a twelve o'clock appointment with the Ambassador to discuss a piece of pending legislation, which if enacted might adversely affect American interests, is in turn entertained by the Ambassador's secretary.

Having finally had his talk with the banker, at twelve-thirty the Ambassador, accompanied by the Deputy Chief of Mission, the First Secretary for Political Affairs, and the Defense Attaché, in uniform, depart in the official limousine for the Peruvian Embassy, whose National Day it is. This consumes thirty-five minutes, which are by no

---

[4] In diplomatic practice, a new Ambassador notifies all other Chiefs of Mission of his arrival; thereafter, as rapidly as may be, he calls by appointment upon each of his ambassadorial colleagues. In capitals having large representation, these calls consume much time and are often tedious for the busy American representative, who will, however, incur substantial ill-will unless he is accessible to the representative of even the most implausible nation.

means wasted. The Ambassador has a brief talk with the Foreign Minister, who shows him the text of the telegram dispatched to his UN delegate in New York, pursuant to their telephone conversation that morning, and then thanks the Ambassador for his courteous treatment of the Minister of Public Works an hour before—thus discreetly confirming the interest of the host Government in the Minister's dam-and-power project. The Defense Attaché picks up a useful crumb of information from his opposite Polish number, who has been mixing slivovitz with pisco sours and is feeling patriotic. The DCM and the First Secretary, who between them command five languages, cruise about among the guests, exchanging impressions.[5]

At one-ten, the DCM reminds his Chief that he is attending a luncheon at the Italian Embassy in honor of a visiting atomic scientist. They offer a ride to the Dutch Ambassador, and with the glass partition raised, they discuss for the next quarter of an hour various pending NATO matters, plus the latest news from Indonesia.

The Ambassador returns to his Residence at twenty minutes to four that afternoon. He is about to take a short nap prior to the arrival of the Economic Counselor and the head of the AID mission, to consider their unreconciled views on a long circular from Washington

---

[5] Since World War II, and especially in the busier capitals, the interminable afternoon receptions to mark national holidays are being replaced by less costly and less painful twelve-to-one stag affairs, to which the foreign Ambassador invites officials of the host Government and members of the diplomatic corps, but not resident nationals, visiting compatriots, or members of the local society. This sensible arrangement results from the multiplication of countries and hence of national holidays. With as many as sixty or seventy separate countries represented in a single capital, officials would otherwise spend a disproportionate amount of their time rushing from party to party, congratulating each other on past revolutions.

Perhaps the next step may be for the host Government to encourage its diplomatic guests to join forces, on a monthly basis, and offer just one bang-up celebration every four weeks. Thus July, a month marked by a large number of national holidays, could witness a really rich and memorable affair, the cost shared among Canada, the United States, Venezuela, France, Belgium, Poland, and Peru, each of which could contribute according to its national specialty: truffles, champagne, bourbon, smoked ham, Caribbean crustaceans, pisco, and Canadian Club. The host Government, grateful to have seven celebrations compressed into one, with a corresponding saving in wear-and-tear on its own officials, would gladly contribute the free use of the foyer and reception rooms of the National Opera, or even the turf and lavatory facilities of the National Stadium; all seven national flags could be displayed, and seven national anthems could be rendered in rotation, alphabetically.

An even better arrangement might be to have national receptions limited to six per year, continent by continent plus Oceania—except that this might possibly ignite a new Cold War among the congested participants.

(The views of the State Department on these laborsaving devices are awaited with interest.)

demanding a study in depth of the relative merits of economic versus military aid on the social structure of the country to which they are accredited, when the DCM telephones from the international airport whither he has rushed to meet an unscheduled Senator, of whose pending arrival the mission has just been apprized by telephone from a neighboring capital. Although it is the height of the tourist season, a suite for the Senator has already been pried out of the leading hotel of the capital by the Administrative Officer. The DCM wants to know whether he should take on the visitor for the balance of the afternoon, or bring him to the Residence for cocktails, or invite him to dinner.

The Senator is not a member of the Foreign Relations Committee. Insofar as the Ambassador and his Deputy are aware, he has no special interest in their country. The Ambassador suggests cocktails at the Residence at six-thirty, with the DCM to convey the Ambassador's greetings and to say he hopes to have a luncheon or a dinner in the Senator's honor, as soon as the Embassy knows the duration of his visit.

The Senator proves to be an affable guest. He leaves the Residence at a quarter to eight, three bourbons the richer and still chaperoned by the faithful Deputy Chief of Mission, and then the Ambassador sits down to a belated family supper, the first he has enjoyed alone with his family in nine evenings, after which he retires to his study with the papers that accumulated in his Chancery desk between his departure that noon for the Peruvian reception and the arrival of the Deputy, Senator in tow, six hours later. Having disposed of the papers, they are returned to the waiting duty officer, successor to the one who called that morning before breakfast, some fifteen hours before.

The Ambassador presently finds himself falling asleep over the latest issue of *Foreign Affairs*, whose writers seem to be getting farther and farther away from center, if not from reality. That night he dreams that eight determined women, wearing sombreros and boots, are punching his chest and pounding his stomach. The Ambassador wakes up, bathed in sweat. He takes a nembutal, and as he drifts off to sleep again, he concludes that somewhere, in some incarnation, there ought to be an easier way to earn a living. . . .

Expanded Foreign Relations Functions

Lincoln Gordon

The impact of war and cold war, superimposed on a long-run trend toward increased involvement in world affairs, has vastly expanded the old dimensions, and introduced major new dimensions, into American foreign relations. International problems pervade the attention and interest of the public, the Congress, and wide sectors of the Executive Branch of the Federal government as never before in so-called time of peace.

On the administrative side, the war and postwar years have witnessed the creation and transformation of new agencies, and of new arms for old agencies, in bewildering variety. Some efforts have focused on strengthening the structure and staffing of long-established departments, but new methods and new institutions have also been improvised to handle critically urgent immediate tasks. With the changed position of the United States in the world, moreover, many policy areas once considered of exclusively domestic concern now have international repercussions which must be taken into account.

Traditional Functions

The traditional functions of overseas representation were fourfold: *negotiation* with foreign governments; *intelligence*—i.e., securing and reporting home information on foreign events, conditions, trends, and prospects of interest to the home government; *"representation"* in the narrow sense of informing foreign governments as to official United States views and interests and acting for the United States in formal

SOURCE: American Assembly, *The Representation of the United States Abroad* (New York: American Assembly, Columbia University, 1956), pp. 10–13.

and informal contacts with foreign officials, fellow diplomats, and influential private citizens; and performing *consular* activities concerning foreign trade, passports and visas, and the protection of American nationals abroad.

With respect to top-level negotiation, the combination of air travel and instantaneous communication may to some extent have reduced the responsibilities of permanent overseas missions. It is now common practice for foreign ministers to negotiate through direct personal contact, either bilaterally or in conferences of three, four, seven, fifteen, or sixty nations at a time. In a few cases, even the foreign ministers have been displaced by direct contact between heads of government. As the power and influence of the United States have grown, moreover, there is a tendency for crucial negotiations to be conducted more frequently in Washington rather than in foreign capitals. On questions of high policy, even where ambassadors participate, they are sometimes reduced to mere messenger boys whose every formal statement and almost every informal comment is controlled by cabled instructions. It is, indeed, a serious question whether this process has not been carried much too far.

With the sole exception of top policy negotiation, however, the functions of overseas missions have shown an almost continuous and geometric expansion in both size and scope. Even on the top policy questions, the ease of travel and communications, which works both ways, gives the overseas representatives opportunity to advise on policy and to appraise and report foreign reactions with a degree of immediacy not previously possible. Immediately below the highest level, there is a vast increase in the volume of negotiation handled by our overseas missions. As to intelligence and reporting on developments abroad, it no longer suffices for the home government to be informed of major political developments and the views of the foreign office on current international questions. Washington is necessarily concerned with every aspect of foreign happenings, whether they be domestic politics, military and strategic events, economic developments, or fluctuations in public opinion directly or indirectly affecting relationships with the United States.

The reporting function has shown most marked expansion in the economic, technical, and public opinion fields. The American business community needs and expects prompt and accurate official reporting on every aspect of every country's economy: production, trade, agriculture, employment and labor relations, finance, investment prospects and opportunities, and the maze of governmental controls which even in the most liberal countries affects foreign trade and investment.

347

Similar information is needed on technical developments, whether military, commercial, or purely scientific.

Sound policy-making requires the best possible insight into trends in the internal political affairs and public opinion of other nations. Moreover, the shrinkage of the world through transportation and communications improvements, together with the pressures of the cold war and the coming of independence to many formerly colonial areas, has meant that this sort of interest is world-wide in scope. There is no country anywhere about which we can afford to be officially ignorant.

It follows that the function of representation has also had to be expanded. It no longer suffices to have official contacts simply with the foreign offices and diplomatic communities in a foreign capital. Direct contact must be established with almost every department of a foreign government, including the treasury and central banks, the ministries of economics, commerce, labor, agriculture, transportation, fuel and power, and the military services. It must also extend to all types of organized and influential groups: labor unions, business and farm leaders; opposition as well as ruling political parties; journalists; editors and publishers; educators; religious leaders; and many others.

New Dimensions

All this is in essence an expansion of traditional functions, but so radical in size and variety as to make for differences in kind as well as degree. Over and above these are the new dimensions which create even more difficult problems of coordination. They are foreign program operations of various types. In many countries, they include the establishment of American military bases, with large numbers of uniformed personnel and the inescapable resulting problems of public impact and public relations, of economic repercussions, and of formal status and privileges. In a wider number of countries, there are military aid programs, with specialized missions engaged in providing equipment and training. In almost the whole free world, there are operating programs of economic aid and technical assistance, often requiring numbers of personnel dwarfing the regular diplomatic establishments, and there are programs of cultural and educational exchange. And in every country where diplomatic relations exist, and by shortwave radio to the rest, there are active and affirmative information programs designed to improve public understanding of the nature, purposes, and attitudes of the United States and to win support for our policies.

Yet another new dimension has been added by the growth of international organizations in which the United States plays an active part. There are the United Nations and its many specialized agencies; military alliances organized through the North Atlantic Treaty Organization, the Southeast Asia Treaty Organization, the Organization of American States, and the ANZUS Treaty (to which might be added the Middle East Treaty Organization, in which the United States has a major interest although not formal membership); and on the economic side the Organization for European Economic Cooperation, the regional commissions of the United Nations in Europe, Latin America, and Asia and the Far East; the Organization of American States, the International Bank for Reconstruction and Development, the International Monetary Fund, the U.N. Specialized Agencies in the fields of labor, agriculture, health, and child welfare, and the Colombo Plan, not to mention more technical agencies in such fields as telecommunications and aviation. Not only does our participation provide difficult problems of representation in itself, . . . but it also poses a problem of coordination between American viewpoints expressed to and through such bodies and our bilateral relations with the other member countries.

Reporting Function

KINGDON B. SWAYNE

* * *

The Reporting Function

. . . The reporting function consists of some or all of the following elements:

1. Identifying, often with the help of general or specific guidance from Washington, those aspects of the total life of the host country which may affect the interests of the United States or its citizens.

2. Collecting data—empirical data, estimates, attitudes—and establishing and maintaining the official and unofficial (overt or clandestine) contacts necessary to collect the needed data.

3. Analysis of the data collected.

4. Appraisal of the analyzed data in light of their impact on the interests of the United States.

5. Determination whether a policy recommendation is in order, and if so in what form to cast it to "sell" it to Washington.

The foregoing definition suggests that the reporting function can best be analyzed as a phased process. . . .

Uncle Sam's "Need to Know." It is commonplace observation that in any given capital the American Embassy is likely to be by far the largest. This is a relatively new phenomenon, unknown before World War II. It is in part the consequence of the *operational* needs of the new diplomacy, whose tools of military and economic assistance and

SOURCE: Paper, American Political Science Association, September 1971, in *An Introduction to Diplomatic Practice*, ed. John J. Hurley, Jr. (Washington, D.C.: Foreign Service Institute, Department of State, 1971).

propaganda (in a great variety of forms) require large operational staffs. It is in part the consequence of a vastly more complex pattern of relationships with other nations, which demands more people for the simple task of communication between governments. But it is also the consequence of a vastly increased "need to know." To a considerable degree this need is a necessary corollary of increasingly complex relationships, for one body of necessary knowledge is communications received from the host government. (The host government will often prefer to use its own embassy in Washington for official communications to the American government, though many non-European governments—for a variety of reasons—seem to prefer American Communication channels to their own.)

But to an even greater extent the "need to know" is based not on current operations but on future contingencies. In World War II we found ourselves conducting a variety of operations—combat by massed armies, civil government, economic warfare, guerrilla support, various "cloak and dagger" exercises—in a bewildering variety of foreign lands of whose very existence we had been but dimly aware (who ever heard of Guadalcanal?) before the war. Our isolationist stance of the 1920's and 1930's had left us miserably unprepared for global involvements. We had to start from scratch to build up stores of basic economic, demographic, and sociological data on remote areas while we were operating in them. We learned that detailed information on remote areas was a precious commodity, and that it could best be gathered in advance of a crisis.

The Cold War years confirmed the importance of good data on remote areas. (President Kennedy never did learn to rhyme Laos with "house" and not with "chaos," but his CIA probably knew more about the country than did its own prime minister.) It has therefore become an accepted article of faith that the U.S. Government's need to know penetrates into every aspect of the life of a foreign society that might remotely be of some use to us in the event we were called upon at some future date to conduct there any of a great variety of political, economic, military, or "intelligence" operations.

This definition of the need to know has resulted in a voracious appetite for information by the Washington bureaucracy. Large field staffs are needed to give it nourishment. In some countries where our motives are viewed with suspicion, the mere size of the reporting staff may be cause for alarm. Mutual restrictions on the size of embassies has been a characteristic Cold War expression of mutual hostility. But the very comprehensiveness of our need to know forms a more subtle basis for suspicion, for it tends to erase the fine line between the diplomat and the spy. This suspicion is reinforced by the practice of some nations of staffing their embassies in part with intelligence officers masquerading as diplomats.

In what might be called the classic period of European diplomacy —from Louis XIV to Clemenceau—it was clearly understood that diplomacy included a reporting function, but it was assumed that its scope would be quite narrow—the transmittal, analysis, and appraisal of official communications or other evidences of host government foreign policy; the identification of present and future "influentials" and their idiosyncrasies; the identification of domestic developments that would influence foreign policy. With the advent of popular government the task of identifying (and cultivating) future influentials became more subtle and complex, and the hallmark of the successful diplomat became the ability to maintain just the right degree of intimacy with both the "ins" and the "outs." But the overall scope of the diplomat's interest in the life of the host country remained quite narrow, and his role ordinarily remained distinct from that of the intelligence agent.

Data Collection, Analysis, and Appraisal. Given today's definition of his government's "need to know," the contemporary American diplomat's information gathering activities may at times seem indistinguishable from those of other individuals in the foreign intelligence field. But there are useful distinctions to be drawn, and perhaps the best way to define the diplomat's activities is to contrast them with the similar activities of the intelligence agent, the press correspondent, and the consul.

Diplomat vs. Intelligence Agent. It will be convenient to define the roles of the diplomat and the intelligence agent with the help of the accepted convention of roles analysis that recognizes that individuals play multiple roles. The diplomat may be forced by circumstances to play the role of intelligence agent. The intelligence agent may under some circumstances masquerade as a diplomat. But the roles can be kept distinct.

Both the diplomat and the intelligence agent depend to a substantial degree on published material, official and unofficial. Both have personal contacts with government officials, opposition leaders, influentials not in government positions, third country diplomats, and other knowledgeable observers. But we may define as diplomatic those contacts to which the policy makers of the host government would have no serious objection. (In a democratic country, the policy makers might be mildly annoyed by contacts with opposition leaders, but they can envision themselves in that role one day, so they are likely to be tolerant.) The intelligence agent undertakes the contacts of which the host government must remain unaware, or at least must be prepared to overlook.

* * *

The diplomat must also be distinguished from the intelligence agent with respect to documents of the host government. The diplomat can properly use only those documents which are either published or officially communicated to him in confidence. The intelligence agent seeks, of course, to beg, borrow, or steal key policy or military documents of the host country that the latter is seeking to preserve from prying foreign eyes.

In the area of data collection, there may be more similarities than differences between the diplomat and the intelligence agent. We must remind ourselves of the statements that emanate from the CIA from time to time that 90% of their intelligence material comes from published sources. When it comes to analysis and appraisal, however, the diplomat and the intelligence agent play far different roles.

The intelligence agent is discouraged from any effort to assess the significance of a piece of information that comes his way. He is duty bound to appraise the *source* of the information—reliable? impartial? trained observer?—but not the information itself. That task is left to the intelligence analyst in the home office. In the intelligence community there is a strict division of labor between gatherer and analyst.

Such is not the case with the diplomat. He usually refrains from reporting the odd, undigested bit of "raw" information until he has picked up enough other raw bits to form a pattern. . . .

This broadening and deepening find expression in the *kinds* of reports the diplomat writes. At the beginning of his tour of duty he may deal essentially in tidbits, whose isolated, episodic nature he will signal to his readers by casting them in the form of memoranda of conversation. As he grows in experience his reports will become more and more analytical, and more and more comprehensive. Toward the end of his tour of duty he may well become the officer in the embassy to whom his superiors look to pull together the periodic overall appraisals that are an important part of an embassy's reporting output.

We conclude this section on the diplomat and the intelligence agent with a brief note on the process of data gathering, American style, as viewed by the host country. . . . By and large, the nations of the traditional home of classic diplomacy in Western and Central Europe have accepted with good grace the new voraciousness of American data gathering. Their attitude stems in part from a basic sense of identity of interest with the United States and in part from the fact that in their open, sophisticated societies the needed economic, sociological, and demographic data are freely available. In Eastern Europe, on the other hand, the shame of relative backwardness and a sense of hostile intent combine with an inherited secretiveness to conceal as much as possible, and to view the prying foreigner with deep suspicion.

A careful survey of attitudes toward American data gathering in the rest of the world would probably reveal that the same basic variables will be the determinants: a sense of identity or conflict of interest, presence or absence of reliable data in the public domain, shame or pride in the country's state of development, xenophobia or xenophilia. The situation in a former British colony in Southeast Asia where I served in the mid-1960's is an example of extreme suspicion. It was the view of the host government that the proper role of the diplomat was to stay in the capital and deal with the Foreign Office. There should be no occasion for the diplomat to need any information other than that obtainable officially from the government or from the official English-language newspaper. Travel within the country should be for recreation purposes, not for data gathering. Efforts to learn the local language were viewed with suspicion. English was used in all official contacts. Why should the foreign diplomat learn the local language unless he planned to interfere in some way in the country's internal affairs?

What were the origins of this negative attitude? Outside of the capital and one or two resort areas, facilities for travelers were so primitive as to be a source of shame to the host government. Suspicion of foreigners is a conspicuous cultural trait. The host government lacked reliable economic, sociological, and demographic data. Above all, there existed a quasi-magical feeling that information gleaned by the foreigner would somehow be used against the host country. The host country had been a battleground between the Allied Forces and the power wielder on the China mainland (Japan) in World War II. The earth "scorched" by the retreating Allies and again by the retreating Japanese had not yet recovered. Much the same Allied Forces were now in hostile confrontation with the current power wielder on the China mainland (the People's Republic of China). Would the Allied Forces find the host country a convenient battleground once again? If they knew everything they wanted to know about it, perhaps so. If they were denied information about it, perhaps not. Is this reasoning magical? rational? a bit of both?

Dipomat vs. Consul. The consular officer who writes political reports stands somewhere between the diplomat and the intelligence agent with respect to analysis and appraisal. He is, in the American Foreign Service, indistinguishable from the diplomat by background and training. He is often a man accustomed to embassy assignments who finds himself for one tour of duty at a post outside the capital of the host country where he is in touch with developments of some political significance to the United States. Thus he is accustomed to analyzing and appraising as he writes, and is encouraged to do so. Yet he is often not in a position to see the total picture. . . . So his reporting is often fragmentary and episodic, a self-conscious effort to feed information into the embassy where the analyses may be completed and the significance for the United States appraised.

A few exceptions to this pattern of the consular reporting officer in the subordinate role should be noted. There are several consulates in the American Foreign Service that have taken on the character of embassies. Hong Kong is perhaps the most notable. For some years it has been a sort of embassy-in-exile from mainland China. Across the Taiwan strait the British have quietly maintained a consulate on Taiwan as the junior arm of their two-Chinas policy. In recent years a number of nations, after a break in diplomatic relations, have either maintained consular relations or restored consular relations first as a preliminary step to full diplomatic relations. Under those circumstances it can be assumed that the consular staffs include full-fledged political reporting officers performing their duties in a manner quite indistinguishable from their colleagues bearing formal diplomatic titles.

Diplomat vs. Foreign Correspondent. The reporting function of the American diplomat must justify its existence in a world in which the information flow into Washington from other sources is already so voluminous as to defy the bureaucracy's powers of digestion. Perhaps the question can best be put this way: The editorial writers of the *New York Times* obviously think that sound policy judgments can be made on the basis of information in the public domain. They do it every day, and in pontifical tones that leave no doubt of their self-confidence. *Why are they wrong?*

Before trying to answer that question, we should take note of a corollary challenge to the diplomatic reporting function from those who argue that diplomatic reporting is likely to be *less* reliable than press reporting. Those critics claim that bureaucrats create a little world of their own with its own "bureaucratic truths" that bear little relation to the real world. Bureaucratic truth, in this view, serves the interests of the bureaucracy that spawns it, or perhaps the interests of whatever lobby happens to dominate the part of the Washington scene in which the particular bureaucrats operate. . . .

To return to the American diplomat and the American foreign correspondent, several similarities and several differences in their reporting may be noted. Both seek to interpret foreign developments from the point of view of American interests. But each has a somewhat different concept of the American interest. The foreign correspondent cannot afford to ignore American interest in royal weddings, earthquakes, particularly juicy murders, human interest stories. The diplomat may also cover earthquakes, but as occasions for official American relief activities. His interest in royal weddings will not be in the bride's gown, but in the incidental meetings of heads of state or government who are in town for the occasion. But in the end it must be said that the correspondent's concept of the American interest includes everything the diplomat is likely to be interested in, plus a number of other things. The best that can be said for the diplomat is that the correspondent might be inclined to spread himself a bit thin.

So we must look elsewhere for a justification of the diplomat's reporting role. Here is a list of some of his advantages:

1. He does not have to sell newspapers, so his treatment of his subject will be more reasoned, less sensational. (Sometimes he does have to dramatize a bit to persuade a White House preoccupied with other problems that his host country demands attention. More on that later.)

2. Newspaper men supplement their daily chasing of headlines with year-end reviews and occasional thoughtful, analytical pieces. But the diplomat specializes in thoughtful, analytical pieces, which form the only proper basis for policy, and his specialization should make him more skillful.

3. The Washington policy maker has access to the diplomat's entire output. . . . Of the correspondent's output he sees only what the editor finds room for.

4. The diplomat takes orders from Washington; the correspondent does not. Washington cannot play a completely passive role in the data gathering operation. It has specific requirements, and needs a man in the field who is fully responsive to its demands.

5. Only the diplomat can report fully on his own activities as a negotiator. Lack of objectivity in reporting on oneself may be a problem (overcome to some degree by the presence of others in the negotiating "team"), but the key requirement is full, detailed reporting of every nuance of the negotiation. No newspaperman can attempt that kind of coverage.

6. Above all, the diplomat has access to information not available to the correspondent. Foreign heads of government may tell Cy Sulzberger everything they would tell the American Ambassador, but there is only one Cy Sulzberger, and he can't be everywhere at once. Government officials anywhere cannot be entirely candid with the press. Diplomatic officials in most places most of the time find it profitable to be candid with one another. Even when they are not, what they say to one another will often be somewhat different from what they say to the press.

The Reporting Officer and His Audience. A diplomatic reporting officer has five significant audiences:

1. Superiors and colleagues at his post of assignment.
2. The Washington bureaucracy.
3. Policy makers in the Executive Branch
4. Members of Congress, and behind them the rest of the American political elite.
5. Colleagues at other Foreign Service posts having an interest in the subject of the report.

His relationship to these audiences is extraordinarily complex. Perhaps the best way to begin to analyze it is to identify the kinds of pressures on an officer that cause him to report certain things in certain ways, and not other ways. There are seven sources of pressure, or determinants of behavior, that should be considered.

1. *The Reporter's Own Values and Norms*
2. *Professional Standards*

The first two determinants . . . are intimately intertwined. American diplomats, by and large, make the traditions of their profession part of their own values. Many were undoubtedly attracted to the profession by a perceived congruence between its values and their own. The internationalist outlook of the profession implies openness, tolerance, flexibility, and perceptiveness in dealing with others. Harold Nicolson would add the following "seven specific diplomatic virtues: (1) truthfulness, (2) precision, (3) calm, (4) good temper, (5) patience, (6) modesty, (7) loyalty." These add up to "Moral influence, the basis of good negotiation." Perhaps the first two and the last two might also be identified as the basis of good reporting.

But what happens when a conflict of values arises, when truthfulness seems in conflict with loyalty, or modesty takes a back seat because a promotion may be at stake? If the reporting officer can resolve or submerge or paper over the conflict in such a way that his immediate superior is not alerted to the presence of conflict (or is willing to connive at ignoring it), all is well. If not, the reporting officer may feel the weight of at least three other determinants of his output:

3. *Existing National Policy*
4. *Policy or Procedural Preferences of Superiors*
5. *Need for Specific Policy or Procedural Recommendation*
   (or absence thereof)

If a recommendation regarding policy or procedure is not obviously needed as a part of the report in question, a potential conflict may be avoided by simply making no recommendation, ending the report with an appraisal. But conflict may also arise over an appraisal. In that event one option is to back off still further, and drop the appraisal from the report. But professional standards dictate the inclusion of some kind of conclusion or assessment, so something has to be said. A common compromise is an appraisal that takes the form "on the one hand . . . on the other hand," the sort of thing that has given the State Department the nickname of "fudge factory."

* * *

A related, unresolved question in the Foreign Service is this: should an embassy speak always with one voice when it reports to Washington? . . . The problem is similar to that of a President's relationship to his advisers, which has been exhaustively analyzed by political scientists in recent years. The essence of the problem is this: should the decision maker demand, Eisenhower-style, that his subordinates resolve their differences among themselves, or should he expose himself, Kennedy-style, to all the minutiae and all the conflicting interpretations and appraisals? The problem may be similar, but the bureaucratic situation is not entirely comparable. Presidential advisers, by and large, have the same or similar status in the hierarchy. An ambassador and a second secretary do not. Can a hierarchical organization give an equal voice to individuals at all levels?

Those who argue for unanimity in an embassy's reporting to Washington claim that it is an essential condition for an effective embassy voice in policy making. This argument may not be taken seriously by those who see the ambassador as a mere messenger boy in an era of instant communications. But that view is oversimplified. It is true that an ambassador is not the free agent he necessarily was in the days of sailing ships. But the radio circuits do not flow only one way. They permit the ambassador's voice to be heard loudly, clearly, and frequently at the point of decision in Washington. In recent years strong ambassadors have been able to work themselves into positions of great influence in Washington decision making.

* * *

Ambassadors who want to play this role obviously want a unanimous embassy supporting them. It is also necessary for there to be close and confidential coordination between the embassy and the country director in Washington. Such coordination is commonly achieved by supplementing formal reporting with the so-called "official-informal" letter. Formal reporting, except on matters of the highest sensitivity, is routinely distributed all over Washington. When the ambassador or his political counselor wants to say something to the country director or regional assistant secretary alone, he writes an official-informal letter. This is a highly effective adjunct to the formal reporting media, used not only to maintain close working relationships over a span of thousands of miles but also to deal with sensitive matters of personnel assignments.

* * *

. . . Recruits to the Foreign Service whose *Weltanschauung* differs markedly from the American "Liberal Establishment" norm either fail to adjust to bureaucratic life and leave rather quickly, or submit to rapid socialization. Submission to bureaucratic socialization is the inevitable personal sacrifice of the "organization man," public or private, against which Consciousness III* cries out in such bitter rebellion. The spirit of Consciousness III appears to have gained something of a foothold in the Foreign Service, but by and large the Service remains staffed with thoroughly socialized individuals not inclined to think "dangerous thoughts" that might cause them to run afoul of the political level. . . . This prudence combines with the humility imposed by the essential unpredictability of political events to form the basic ingredients for "fudge," Foggy Bottom style.

---

* EDITOR'S NOTE: "Consciousness III" is a term created by Charles A. Reich in *The Greening of America* (Random House, 1970), which denotes the American counterculture mentality that emerged and grew in the late 1960s.

6. Formal Reporting Requirements

The time has come to describe with some specificity just exactly what kinds of reporting media are available to the Foreign Service reporting officer. They are:

1. The telegram.
2. The airgram.
3. The official-informal letter.
4. The memorandum of conversation.

Each has a number of significant variations.

Telegrams and airgrams are the basic reporting media. The latter, as the name implies, are sent to Washington by air mail rather than by electrical means, and have a correspondingly low priority in the eyes of the end-user. . . .

Most reporting telegrams or airgrams form part of a recognizable series of periodic required reports, occasional reports at the post's initiative, or exchanges of correspondence with Washington. Reporting on a negotiation with the host country would be an example of the latter, where the main thrust of the report would be an indication of progress, or lack of it, in carrying out the most recent negotiating instructions from Washington. It is customary in such cases to cite the most recent message in the series at the beginning of the report, so that the busy reader can quickly refer to his files and refresh his memory as to what has gone before. Messages without such a citation are presumed to be broaching a new subject.

For each report or series of reports, the originating officer must decide among a variety of available devices for calling his work forcibly to the attention of busy end-users in Washington. He must obviously keep in mind the fable of the boy who cried "Wolf!", and not shout at the top of his voice all the time. But he must also bear in mind the unwritten rule in the State Department that no one above the level of country director *ever* reads airgrams unless the country director takes pains to call a significant airgram to their attention. Even if one is content to address the specialists and opts for an airgram, if it is more than two pages in length it will receive more respectful attention if there is a brief summary at the top of the first page.

But let us assume that the nature of the event calls for a telegram. There is still a wide variety of attention-getting devices from which to choose, some legitimate and some not. An example of an illegitimate device would be the arbitrary reclassification to TOP SECRET of CONFIDENTIAL material, simply because readers always pay more attention to TOP SECRET items. One can also attract attention by instructing the distribution center to "limit distribution," thus implying that the subject matter is especially sensitive. Various indicators of urgency are likewise available for use or abuse. Top level State Department officers spend most of their working days willy-nilly as crisis managers, not as thoughtful, unhurried, far-seeing statesmen. They and those around them are conditioned to react quickly to telegrams with high urgency indicators.

Perhaps the most legitimate, and often the most effective, attention-getting device is the telegram that is addressed personally to an assistant secretary or under secretary. This is a privilege reserved to ambassadors, which they must use circumspectly lest they in turn [be] accused of crying "Wolf!". But ambassadors will sometimes lend their personal *imprimatur* to the reporting of a junior officer who has action responsibility on a subject of major significance.

7. *Professional Skills*

The skills required to perform the tasks of data gathering, analysis, and appraisal in diplomacy are a study in themselves. . . .*

Up to this point it has not been necessary to distinguish between the two groups of Foreign Service reporters who specialize in political and economic subjects. Most of what has been said so far has been written with the political reporting officer in mind, but it would apply with equal force to the economic reporting officer. In their day-to-day activities, however, the two groups of officers work within markedly different frames of reference.

It is a commonplace of modern social science analysis that politics and economics are intimately interrelated, yet must be separated for analytical purposes. The Foreign Service has found it convenient to use the distinction between politics and economics as an ordering idea underlying its administrative structure. . . .

The economic officer at work differs from his political counterpart in two major respects.

First, he has multiple bosses. The reader should be reminded at this point that we are talking about the Foreign Service of the United States of America, not about the foreign service of the State Department. It is explicitly the foreign service of the Departments of Commerce, Labor and Interior and to some extent the foreign service of the Treasury Department. It cooperates closely with the Foreign

---

* EDITOR'S NOTE: A companion essay develops this analysis; see Paul M. Kattenburg, "Some Comments on Observation, Analysis, and Appraisal in Diplomacy," paper, American Political Science Association, September 1971, in *An Introduction to Diplomatic Practice*, ed. John J. Hurley, Jr. (Washington, D.C.: Foreign Service Institute, Department of State, 1971).

Agricultural Service. Each of these bosses is a large bureaucracy with an insatiable lust for information. It is necessary to bring that lust under some kind of interagency control. The result is the Comprehensive Economic Reporting Program (CERP), drawn up for each Foreign Service post by interagency negotiation to carve up the time and energy of the economic officers in such a way that the basic information needs of all "end-users" will be met. For the officer in the field, the major consequence of this interagency arrangement is that he has much less scope for initiative and imagination than his political counterpart. The latter may be desperately busy, but he is busy responding to the demands of events rather than to an *a priori* work schedule.

Second, the economic reporting officer can count on having an audience in Washington that is made up in large part of sophisticated professionals who are undaunted by the arcane language of international trade and finance or development economics. The level of conceptual sophistication of Foreign Service economic reporting does not rival the learned journals in the field, but it has achieved a respectable degree of subtlety and precision. For some years the Foreign Service has placed a good deal of emphasis on skill in economics both in its recruiting and in its in-service training. The result is a general level of sophistication that can cope effectively with the analysis and reporting of economic developments around the world.

The political reporting officer, by contrast, is bound by a tradition that holds that a gentlemanly liberal education is quite sufficient background for political analysis and reporting. This is a tradition that should not be lightly dismissed. Political reporting officers are the elite of an elite (Foreign Service Officers in general), of an elite (the professional class in America). The clearest thinking, the most trenchant analysis, the most lucid writing from the embassies come from the political sections. Some of the most perceptive political analysis of all time has had its origins in this essentially dilletantish tradition. (Have you read Tocqueville lately?)

There are, I suppose, a few old hands still around who mourn the passing of the graceful style that characterized this dilletantish tradition at its best. It was not until after World War II that political reports dropped the theretofore obligatory "Sir: I have the honor to report. . ." that opened every "despatch," on the assumption that the Secretary of State himself would read them all. There remains to this day a sporadic war within the State Department between the writers who delight in long, involuted sentences (complex problems can only be elucidated with complex rhetoric, they say) and the busy readers who call for short, declarative sentences (get to the point!).

This war over style is only one phase of what promises to be a long range struggle between those who see diplomacy as the province of talented gentlemen and those who insist on its professionalization.

*   *   *

Negotiating Effectively

FRED CHARLES IKLÉ

* * *

When parties are interested in an exchange, they want *different* things. These they cannot obtain by themselves but can only grant to each other. The clearest examples are barters and sales. Similarly, commercial aviation agreements, where each country wants to have its planes fly to the other country, have the purpose of settling an exchange. So do agreements for mutual tariff concessions.

In reality, however, most negotiations embrace a combination of identical common interests and complementary interests. When the six European countries set up the European Economic Community, they had complementary interests in the exchange of tariff concessions and common interests in a large, unified European market. The nuclear test-ban treaty between the United States and the Soviet Union can satisfy the complementary interest in slowing down the opponent's development of new weapons and the common interest in preventing an increase in radioactive fallout or in discouraging the proliferation of nuclear weapons. Whether the identical common interests or the complementary interests dominate depends on how the purposes of the agreement are defined.

The process by which two or more parties relate conflicting to common interests is the warp and woof not only of international relations but of human society; individuals, groups, and governments engage in it all the time. We become aware of it only when we call it something special—like Molière's Monsieur Jourdain when he discovered that for forty years he had been speaking "prose." There seems to be no established term for all the ways in which parties with

SOURCE: *How Nations Negotiate* (New York: Praeger, 1967), pp. 3–6, 118–21, 193–96, 253–55.

conflicting and common interests interact—whether explicitly or tacitly —though "bargaining" is sometimes used that broadly.

"Negotiation" in a narrower sense denotes a process that is different from tacit bargaining or other behavior that regulates conflict. As used here, *negotiation is a process in which explicit proposals are put forward ostensibly for the purpose of reaching agreement on an exchange or on the realization of a common interest where conflicting interests are present.* Frequently, these proposals deal not only with the terms of agreement but also with the topics to be discussed (the agenda), with the ground rules that ought to apply, and with underlying technical and legal issues. It is the confrontation of explicit proposals that distinguishes negotiation (as here defined) from tacit bargaining and other types of conflict behavior. Beyond this confrontation appear other moves that the negotiating parties make to strengthen their own position, to weaken that of the opponent, or to influence the outcome in other ways. . . .

Only part of the frequent changes in relations between countries are the result of negotiation. Governments often revise their expectations and attitudes toward other countries as a result of unilateral actions or tacit bargains. Military and technological developments, growth or decline in economic strength, and internal political changes continually cause the rearrangement of conflicting and common interests between nations, and this happens whether or not diplomats negotiate.

There is no simple rule as to when negotiation is needed, and when tacit bargaining or even less conscious confrontations are more effective to restructure international relations. For certain arrangements negotiation clearly cannot be dispensed with; for others it is optional; and there are some issues which are better settled without it.

Negotiation is necessary for any arrangement that establishes complicated forms of collaboration, such as a joint war effort or Britain's attempted entry into the Common Market. (In contrast, the entry of, say, the Ivory Coast into the United Nations did not require significant negotiations.) Negotiation is needed for most exchanges, such as exchanges of prisoners or the granting of mutual consular facilities, and for all transactions involving monetary compensation, as in the payment of oil royalties or the leasing of air bases. Negotiation is, of course, necessary for the setting up of formal international institutions and for any arrangement where an *explicit* agreement is essential, such as a peace treaty or an alliance system.

On the other hand, certain undertakings are arrived at in such a delicate way that explicit proposals might interfere with the process.

The mutually observed restrictions in the Korean War (for instance, no attacks on the supply lines leading into North and South Korea) is an example of arrangements that would not have been facilitated or might even have been upset by negotiation. The very uncertainties of a tacit understanding may have made these restrictions more stable, because both sides were unwilling to probe and push toward the limits of the "bargain," lest it all be upset. The negotiation of an explicit *quid pro quo* might have given rise to new demands and invited more haggling and tugging than the arrangement which the parties never discussed and never explicitly settled. Furthermore, while soldiers were being killed fighting the enemy, negotiations to establish rules and restraints for the battle or on the interdiction of supplies would have clashed with domestic opinion and perhaps adversely affected the morale of the troops.

Likewise, if there is a deep-seated hostility between the populations of two countries, governments may be unable to negotiate because of public opposition but may work out some arrangements of mutual interest through tacit bargaining. The relationship between Jordan and Israel is an example.

In the field of arms control and disarmament, where we have become so accustomed to large and formal conferences, important understandings can at times be arrived at without negotiation. Formal talks might, in fact, make it more difficult to harmonize some arms policies insofar as they inevitably introduce political issues or questions of prestige and legal precedents.

Negotiation plays an important role in formalizing turning points in international relations, in catalyzing or at least clarifying changes that were caused by tacit bargaining or other processes, and in working out those finer shades in new arrangements between nations that the brute interplay of latent strength cannot define.

Although negotiation is necessary for any new relationship that is based on explicit agreement, an explicit agreement is usually only part of the outcome of negotiation. Negotiation may change the positions of the parties and their mutual relations in many other ways. The outcome may include, for example, tacit understandings between the parties, a clarification of the points of disagreement, a reorientation of national objectives, new commitments to third parties (allies, domestic groups, or world opinion), and propaganda effects. Many of these results may outweigh in importance whatever explicit agreement is arrived at. And even agreements themselves vary widely in their degree of specificity and the amount of disagreement that they leave unsettled.

* * *

The Community Spirit

Nations closely linked in a common effort sometimes develop a highly accommodating negotiating style, which resembles the decision-making process within an intra-governmental committee rather than the usual mode of bargaining between governments. The cooperation between the United States and Great Britain during World War II was conducted in this fashion, particularly on the highest level between Roosevelt and Churchill. More recently, the advocates of closer integration in the European Communities have been promoting such an accommodating style. In the negotiations among the six member states and within the Community organs, the participants are reminded regularly to act in accordance with the "community spirit," *l'esprit communautaire* as it is called in Brussels.

Back in 1950, when Jean Monnet chaired the negotiations for the formation of the Coal and Steel Community, he first taught his co-negotiators to see their task in the "community spirit." He wanted them to focus on the common interest, rather than on trades between conflicting interests, and to maximize the advantages of their joint undertaking, rather than to exchange separate gains and losses with each other. He discouraged compromises in which a party would barter a concession on one issue against some advantage on an entirely different issue. He felt logrolling or heterogeneous package deals would not be conducive to a constructive, joint effort in behalf of the common objectives. Monnet conducted the initial meetings, where the principles of the Coal and Steel Community were first discussed, without any verbatim records. The negotiators were not allowed to hold anyone else to his opinions or statements from earlier meetings. This facilitated the formation of a common view, based on a single conception of the joint undertaking, rather than on bartered compromises. Thus, in this setting a procedure proved fruitful which was the exact opposite of the rule that partial agreements should be adhered to.

* * *

A negotiating style in the "community spirit" is a necessary, but not a sufficient, condition for a successful integration of independent nations. Other conditions must, of course, be met, such as the formation of interest groups that cut across national boundaries, the absence of strongly conflicting objectives, and the existence of specific functions that are important to the member states and can be delegated to a supra-national level. A common external enemy also encourages integration.

What helps to preserve the "community spirit" is the interest of each partner in reciprocation. When nations are engaged in a long-term common effort, each government needs the future collaboration of its partners and remains dependent on their good will. This makes it possible to regard an act of generosity today as establishing a credit for tomorrow. And it makes it safe for negotiators to accept an agreement in principle—provided all partners have the same understanding of it—and to leave the details to the experts or technicians. The "community spirit" permits the negotiators to dispense with some of the more rigid rules of accommodation that may seem necessary between less friendly nations, such as the pettifogging concern about agendas, the objections to a revision of partial agreements, the one-to-one reciprocation of concessions, and the stickling equality of negotiating languages. Instead, there is a strong emphasis on the common objectives, there are no important hidden motives, and the discourse is free from the wasted verbiage to which the world has become so accustomed in East-West conferences or in the United Nations General Assembly.

* * *

The Function of Proposals

Proposals play a key role in the process through which the parties come to terms. Indeed, the confrontation, revisions, and final acceptance of proposals at the conference table is sometimes all that is meant by "negotiation." Even in the broader definition used in this book, explicit proposals are an essential feature of "negotiation," for they distinguish it from tacit bargaining. Certainly, if there is to be an explicit agreement, there must first be at least one explicit proposal.

Proposals, however, are not the whole story of negotiation; rather, they are markers on the surface which indicate more substantial developments underneath. It should also be recalled that governments prepare proposals in part or entirely for the purpose of producing certain side-effects: to spread propaganda, to maintain contact, to stave off violent actions, or for similar reasons that do not concern agreement. Here these side-effects will be ignored in order to concentrate on the ways in which governments use proposals to reach favorable terms of agreement.

Ostensibly, proposals *always* represent an offer; they give a description of the terms that are allegedly being made available to the opponent. But in fact, proposals are frequently meant as an offer only toward the final phases of a conference. And even then they are binding only to the extent that the parties observe the rule of accommodation according to which an accepted offer should not be withdrawn. In contrast to business negotiations, governments can always withdraw their offers after they have been accepted, albeit with some cost to their bargaining reputation.

If you are engaged in international negotiation, many of your proposals do not serve as offers. Instead they are meant to influence your opponent so that he will make better terms available to you than he was originally disposed to or, conversely, so that he will come to accept greater demands of yours. In other words, your proposals serve either as path-breakers for an eventual offer of yours or as stimuli to make your opponent produce an offer favorable to you.

Your proposals must change your opponent's expectations. They must make him believe that you will insist on certain demands. More than that, they must accustom him to the idea that he wants to reach agreement by meeting what seem to be your irreducible terms. Thus your proposals should accomplish two things with your opponent: they should change his expectations about *your* anticipated minimum, and they should change his anticipations concerning *his* minimum terms. As suggested earlier, the first change will help to bring about the second change. If your opponent changes his expectation as to what *you* intend to settle for, he may change his mind as to what *he* is trying to get.

In the nuclear test-ban conference, for example, the Western insistence early in 1963 on more than just three on-site inspections may have changed Khrushchev's expectations as to the minimum inspection arrangements that the Western powers would accept for banning underground tests. And this may have helped to change his mind about his accepting a partial treaty permitting underground tests, once he had become anxious to have a treaty.

To keep the opponent interested in negotiating, diplomats often formulate their proposals in a flexible fashion. The marked preference for flexibility among many Western diplomats results, in part, from the fear that the opponent might suddenly choose no-agreement if faced with a firm position. In part, Western diplomats keep their proposals flexible because they feel that this is the proper way to negotiate.

But this tactic is self-defeating if the diplomats on the opponent's side want to prove their mettle by showing that they pushed you as far as possible. They cannot satisfy themselves (or their government) that they have reached the limit as long as you offer them a menu of choices, particularly if the menu keeps changing. This is the reason why Westerners have been warned against trying out many variant proposals in negotiating with the Russians. Occasionally, though, a variant proposal may have helped to get a satisfactory agreement with the Soviet Union, for instance the Western proposal for a partial test ban.

However, if your opponent is under domestic pressure to reach agreement and to demonstrate his own flexibility, your flexibility can be used to hasten agreement. You may ensnare him into accepting one of your proposals by putting many alternatives before him.

Tacit bargaining moves may add firmness to negotiations that are otherwise conducted in a flexible manner. The reason is that the opponent usually cannot tell how flexible or firm a tacit move is meant to be as long as it does not become the subject of explicit negotiation. Statesmen who feel constrained by tradition or by domestic opinion to maintain an appearance of flexibility, therefore, can profit from tacit moves that they link to, but do not mention in, their proposals. Also, whereas rigid explicit proposals might antagonize the opponent and cause him to break off negotiations, tacit moves might be tolerated by him because he does not know whether the lack of flexibility is intentional or not.

Such effects of tacit moves may have helped to resolve the Cuba crisis in 1962. Many observers feel that what really compelled Khrushchev to withdraw his missiles was the intelligence he received of American military preparations suggesting that an air strike against his Cuban bases was imminent. Since this threat was tacit (as far as can be judged from the published exchange between Khrushchev and Kennedy), it gave Khrushchev no hint as to how firm or flexible it was. Therefore, it endowed the key American demand for the withdrawal of missiles (which was, of course, explicit) with particular firmness. All the other explicit positions—both the American and the Soviet ones—turned out to be so flexible that they practically melted away. . . .

Firmness in negotiating proposals can be a deliberate tactic, just like flexibility. It may be used to make the opponent think that one's proposal is close to one's anticipated minimum or, at any rate, that one firmly expects to have one's proposal accepted and will not make further concessions. A way of expressing firmness—though not always a successful one—is repetition. Communist diplomats never tire of reiterating the same position over and over again. Westerners, on the other hand, often try to convey firmness by using new arguments and minor variations; perhaps the feeling that the public is listening in makes sheer repetition of their proposals embarrassing to them. Westerners feel free to be repetitious only when asserting a governing principle, such as the need for verification of disarmament measures or the legality of Western rights of access to Berlin.

But firmness is not always a tactic deliberately chosen to impress the opponent. Negotiators may be firm and keep on repeating their demands simply because their government is unable to furnish them with new instructions. . . .

* * *

The Compleat Negotiator

The compleat negotiator, according to seventeenth- and eighteenth-century manuals on diplomacy, should have a quick mind but unlimited patience, know how to dissemble without being a liar, inspire trust without trusting others, be modest but assertive, charm others without succumbing to their charm, and possess plenty of money and a beautiful wife while remaining indifferent to all temptations of riches and women.

It is easy to add to this garland of virtues, but difficult in the real world to judge a good negotiator from a bad one. One cannot evaluate a negotiator merely by asking how close he came to realizing the aims of his government; for if he came close, he may owe his success to modest aims or favorable conditions rather than to his skill. Nor can one be sure that he has done well just because his gains and losses compare favorably with those of the opponent; for it is an essential task of negotiators to change the evaluation of gains and losses.

Frequently one judges a negotiator by comparing the results he obtained with results he might have obtained had he acted differently. In doing so, however, one should distinguish between errors in negotiation, on the one hand, and errors in prediction and foreign-policy planning, on the other. Furthermore, one has to allow for domestic constraints which limit the alternatives that the negotiator could have chosen. Even though a skillful negotiator will guide and strengthen his domestic support, he cannot escape these constraints completely.

On occasion, the outcome of an international conference seems predetermined by the balance of military strength, by economic factors, or by other forces beyond the negotiator's control. For example, George Kennan argued that the establishment of Soviet military power in Eastern Europe and the entry of Soviet forces into Manchuria did not result from the wartime conferences of Moscow, Teheran, and Yalta, but from the military operations during the concluding phases of the war when the Western democracies were not in a position to enter these areas first. One can surely agree with Kennan that only a limited range of alternatives was open at these conferences. But one should question how narrow this range actually was and whether the negotiators did not take for granted bounds that they drew themselves.

Imagine, for instance, a reverse of the situation in Iran and in Korea—that Iran was the country divided into a Communist North and a pro-Western South but that Korea was unified under a government friendly to the West. If this were the situation today, we would probably feel that the Western democracies could have done nothing to prevent the Russians from staying in Northern Iran (an area they occupied first, after all!) but that in Korea the West had a better chance to keep the country unified and friendly (obviously! Russia having entered the war against Japan so late and Korea being more accessible to American military strength than Iran).

Many of the clichés about the perfect negotiator might be revised rather than discarded. A good negotiator should be *realistic*, yes, but not in the sense of accepting an outcome as being determined by the balance of forces without trying to re-interpret this "balance" in his favor. Instead of taking a situation for granted, he should be realistic in recognizing that his opponent's evaluations as well as his own are constantly adrift, that issues are not created by Nature but by himself and by his opponent, and that there are ways of negotiating from weakness as well as from strength.

A good negotiator should also be *flexible*—not by being without a firm position but by utilizing both firm and flexible proposals. He should be flexible in his tactics by discriminating between occasions when it pays to adhere to rules of accommodation and when it does not. He must distinguish situations where it would be disastrous to make a threat from others where it is essential to threaten or even to bluff. He must know when to humor the personal quirks of his opponent and when to ignore them. He must be willing to disregard propaganda losses at one time and to negotiate merely for propaganda at another time. He must be prepared to follow domestic opinion at home as well as to encourage a new consensus both in his government and in his country.

And a good negotiator should be *patient*—though not primarily in order to sit in Geneva for months at a time hearing the opponent repeat speeches and repeating his own. He should be patient in working for seemingly lost causes, because by doing so he may slowly change the opponent's views and objectives. He should be patient to live with conflict and uncertainty and know that he may have succeeded even if (or precisely because) his negotiations failed. Above all, he must maintain the will to win.

Of Negotiation and Bargaining
in the Modern World

Henry A. Kissinger

* * *

What, then, has made the conduct of diplomacy so difficult [since World War II]? Why have tensions continued whether we negotiated or failed to negotiate? There are four basic causes: (1) the destructiveness of modern weapons, (2) the polarization of power in the contemporary period, (3) the nature of the conflict, (4) national attitudes peculiar to the West and particularly to the United States.

It is not an accident that the diplomatic stalemate has become more intractable as weapons have grown more destructive. Rather than facilitating settlement, the increasing horror of war has made the process of negotiation more difficult. Historically, negotiators have rarely relied exclusively on the persuasiveness of the argument. A country's bargaining position has traditionally depended not only on the logic of its proposals but also on the penalties it could exact for the other side's failure to agree. An abortive conference rarely returned matters to the starting point. Rather, diplomacy having failed, other pressures were brought into play. Even at the Congress of Vienna, long considered the model diplomatic conference, the settlement which maintained the peace of Europe for a century was not achieved without the threat of war.

As the risks of war have become more cataclysmic, the result has not been a universal reconciliation but a perpetuation of all disputes. Much as we may deplore it, most major historical changes have been brought about to a greater or lesser degree by the threat or the use of force. Our age faces the paradoxical problem that because the violence of war has grown out of all proportion to the objectives to

SOURCE: *The Necessity for Choice: Prospects of American Foreign Policy* (Garden City, N.Y.: Doubleday—Anchor Books, 1962), pp. 175–81, 210–17.

be achieved, no issue has been resolved. We cannot have war. But we have had to learn painfully that peace is something more than the absence of war. Solving the problem of peaceful change is essential; but we must be careful not to deny its complexity.

The intractability of diplomacy has been magnified by the polarization of power in the post-war period. As long as the international system was composed of many states of approximately equal strength, subtlety of maneuver could to some extent substitute for physical strength. As long as no nation was strong enough to eliminate all the others, shifting coalitions could be used for exerting pressure or marshaling support. They served in a sense as substitutes for physical conflict. In the classical periods of cabinet diplomacy in the eighteenth and nineteenth centuries, a country's diplomatic flexibility and bargaining position depended on its availability as a partner to as many other countries as possible. As a result, no relationship was considered permanent and no conflict was pushed to its ultimate conclusion. Disputes were limited by the tacit agreement that the maintenance of the existing system was more important than any particular disagreement. Wars occurred, but they did not involve risking the national survival and were settled in relation to specific, limited issues.

Whenever the number of sovereign states was reduced, diplomacy became more rigid. When a unified Germany and Italy emerged in the nineteenth century, they replaced a host of smaller principalities. This reflected the dominant currents of nationalism. But from the point of view of diplomatic flexibility, some of the "play" was taken out of the conduct of foreign policy. To the extent that the available diplomatic options diminished, the temptation to achieve security by mobilizing a country's physical strength increased. The armaments race prior to World War I was as much the result as the cause of the inflexibility of diplomacy. France and Germany were in fundamental conflict. And neither state could organize an overwhelming coalition. As a result, power had to substitute for diplomatic dexterity and the period prior to World War I witnessed a continuous increase of the standing armies.

World War I accelerated the polarization of power. By the end of World War II only two major countries remained—major in the sense of having some prospect of assuring their security by their own resources. But a two-power world is inherently unstable. Any relative weakening of one side is tantamount to an absolute strengthening of the other. Every issue seems to involve life and death. Diplomacy turns rigid, for no state can negotiate about what it considers to be the requirements of its survival. In a two-power world these requirements are likely to appear mutually incompatible. The area where diplomacy is most necessary will then appear most "unnegotiable."

* * *

Much of the diplomatic stalemate has therefore little to do with lack of good will or ingenuity on the part of the statesmen. Without an agreement on general principles, negotiations become extremely difficult. What will seem most obvious to one party will appear most elusive to the other. When there is no penalty for failing to agree and when at the same time the balance of power is so tenuous, it is no accident that the existing dividing lines are so rigidly maintained. For the *status quo* has at least the advantage of familiarity while any change involves the possibility of catastrophe. At the same time, since these dividing lines are contested, protracted tension is nearly inevitable.

This impasse has led either to long periods in which diplomacy has for all practical purposes abdicated its role; or else it has produced a form of negotiations which has almost seemed to revel in *not* coming to grips with the issues dividing the world. The reference which is often made to the coexistence achieved by Mohammedanism and Christianity or by Protestantism and Catholicism is not fully relevant to the contemporary problem. In both cases, coexistence was the result of protracted, often ruinous, warfare—the very contingency diplomacy is now asked to prevent. We must be aware that the factors that intensify the desire to resolve the impasse of the Cold War may also make a creative response more difficult.

These obstacles to serious negotiations are magnified by Western, and in particular American, attitudes towards negotiating with the Communists. A *status quo* power always has difficulty in coming to grips with a revolutionary period. Since everything it considers "normal" is tied up with the existing order, it usually recognizes too late that another state means to overthrow the international system. This is a problem especially if a revolutionary state presents each demand as a specific, limited objective which in itself may seem quite reasonable. If it alternates pressure with campaigns for peaceful coexistence, it may give rise to the belief that only one more concession stands in the way of the era of good feeling which is so passionately desired. All the instincts of a *status quo* power tempt it to gear its policy to the expectation of a fundamental change of heart of its opponent—in the direction of what seems obviously "natural" to it.

Were it not for this difficulty of understanding, no revolution would ever have been successful. A revolutionary movement always starts from a position of inferior strength. It owes its survival to the reluctance of its declared victims to accept its professions at face value. It owes its success to the psychological advantage which single-minded purpose confers over opponents who refuse to believe that some states or groups may prefer victory to peace. The ambiguity of the Soviet challenge results in part from the skill of the Soviet leadership. But it is magnified by the tendency of the free world to choose the interpretation of Soviet motivations which best fits its own preconceptions. Neither Lenin's writings, nor Stalin's utterances, nor Mao's published works, nor Khrushchev's declarations has availed against the conviction of the West that a basic change in Communist society and aims was imminent and that a problem deferred was a problem solved.

It is only to posterity that revolutionary movements appear unambiguous. However weak it may be at the beginning, a revolutionary state is often able to substitute psychological strength for physical power. It can use the very enormity of its goals to defeat an opponent who cannot come to grips with a policy of unlimited objectives.

The United States has had particular difficulty in this respect. From the moment in our national history when we focused our attention primarily on domestic development, we met very few obstacles that were really insuperable. We were almost uniquely blessed with the kind of environment in which the problems that were presented— those at least that we really wanted to solve—were difficult but manageable. Almost from our colonial infancy we have been trained to measure a man, a government, or an era by the degree of energy with which contemporary problems have been attacked—and hence by the success in finding a final, definite solution. If problems were not solved, this was because not enough energy or enough resolution had been applied. The leadership or the government was clearly at fault. A better government or a better man would have mastered the situation. Better men and a better government, when we provide them, *will* solve all issues *in our time*.

As a result, we are not comfortable with seemingly insoluble problems. There must be *some* way to achieve peace if only the correct method is utilized. Many of the erratic tendencies in American policy are traceable to our impatience. The lack of persistence, the oscillation between rigid adherence to the *status quo* and desire for novelty for its own sake show our discomfort when faced with protracted deadlock. We grow restless when good will goes unrewarded and when proposals have to be maintained over a long period of time.

When reality clashes with its anticipated form, frustration is the inevitable consequence. We have, therefore, been torn between adopting a pose of indignation and seeking to solve all problems at one fell swoop. We have been at times reluctant, indeed seemingly afraid, to negotiate. We have also acted as if all our difficulties could be removed by personal rapport among the statesmen. Periods of over-concern with military security have alternated with periods when we saw in a changed Soviet tone an approach to an end of tensions.

* * *

Another symptom of the formalistic nature of our view of negotiations has been the excessive concern with bargaining technique. Flexibility has been the insistent demand. But occasionally the impression has been left that the diplomatic deadlock is due at least in part to the inadequacy of the diplomatic method. It has been said that we have an obligation to make "acceptable" proposals. It has been urged that we must break diplomatic deadlocks with new offers. The frustration of the Cold War can be ended, so the argument goes, through willingness to compromise. When two sides take positions, each unacceptable to the other, it is said that the solution lies somewhere in between.

These maxims, unobjectionable in themselves, reflect the fact that the primary experience of our society with negotiations has been in the commercial field. In commercial negotiations, the rules of the game are known. Usually, there is an implicit understanding that an agreement will be reached. Restraints are imposed by the need for a continuing relationship. Both sides generally are in accord on what constitutes a "reasonable" argument. When each party believes that it has gained some advantage both will settle. The courts will interpret the agreement and enforce it.

Most of these factors are lacking to a greater or lesser degree in negotiations with Communist states. In contrast with most of our domestic experience, what has been at issue has been not the adjustment of disputes within a framework which could be taken for granted, but the framework itself.

In this situation, many "normal" bargaining rules of thumb become either irrelevant or dangerous. On the face of it, for example, the proposition that we should make "acceptable" proposals seems unexceptionable. However, if we can only offer what the Soviet leaders have indicated they will accept, the framework of every conference will be established by the other side and the terms of the settlement will be Soviet terms. Or else agreement will become an end in itself. Negotiations gravitate towards problems which seem "soluble"—often only because of their unimportance.

Pushed too far, such an approach implies the surrender of all judgment. It will cause us to fail in one of the major tasks of a revolutionary period: to make clear to the people of the free world the nature of the issues in dispute. While all possibilities of a settlement must be explored, it is equally necessary to develop conviction about the problems that are impossible to solve. It is important for us to be conciliatory if the Soviet leaders should be prepared to negotiate seriously. But it is no less crucial that we force them to bear the onus for their failure to accept responsible proposals.

Similar considerations apply to the proposition that we must always seek to break diplomatic deadlocks with new proposals. Such a "rule" deprives the Communist leaders of the incentive to accept *any* proposal. However moderate our offers, the Soviet leaders will be tempted to reject them in the hope that we will come up with even more favorable plans. The absurd lengths to which this method can be carried was demonstrated at the Geneva Foreign Ministers' Conference of 1959. Before the Western proposal had even been presented, a clamor arose in the British and American press for a fall-back position. It should have been obvious on purely pragmatic grounds that if a fall-back position is known to exist, any motive for accepting the first offer disappears. The only result can be to transform the fall-back position into the starting point of the negotiations and to raise the need for yet another fall-back position.

Implicit in the "principle" that we must break every deadlock with new proposals is the tentativeness of every position. In the long run, the conclusion will be inescapable that no issue is worth contending for and no Western proposal final. The people of the free world, or the Soviets for that matter, will never know whether a given offer is serious or simply a bargaining position. The result must be the confusion of all issues.

This becomes even more apparent when one considers another rule of thumb which is frequently heard: that the way to resolve disputes is to find a compromise somewhere between the initial positions. For the result of such a maxim again is likely to be the opposite of what is intended. If agreement is usually found between the two starting points, there is no point in making moderate offers. Good bargaining technique would suggest a point of departure far more extreme than what one is willing to accept. The more outrageous the initial proposition, the better is the prospect that what one "really" wants will be considered a compromise.

Such a method of negotiation is particularly difficult for a democracy. When the negotiators adhere to a maxim which makes compromise desirable in itself, effectiveness at the conference table depends on overstating one's demands. Yet extreme proposals make it difficult to muster public support. The dilemma is real. If we want to be perfectly flexible, we should start with a maximum program and offer "concessions" in the course of the conference. On the other hand, if we make proposals in which we really believe, we must inevitably be somewhat rigid about them. We cannot change our view about a just arrangement every year. At some point, our program must be settled or no American proposal will mean anything.

The emphasis on compromise for its own sake brings about an atmosphere of "damned if you do and damned if you don't." If the West develops a careful, serious program and maintains it over a period of years, it will be accused of inflexibility, no matter how moderate the original proposals. But if it starts with a bargaining program, it runs the risk of being accused of intransigence. And when it seeks to combine both approaches, it faces the dilemma that the program will not be precise enough to be maintained with conviction and yet will not have sufficient "play" in it to permit major concessions.

One result is that a double standard develops between our positions towards the uncommitted and the Communist worlds. It is often said that the uncommitted will judge us by the reasonableness and the moderation of our proposals. But towards the Communist world the recommended criteria are said to be "acceptability," "novelty," "compromise"—criteria which depend eventually on the Soviet willingness to settle. On the one side, the standard is substantive; on the other, largely formal. At the least, moderation and reasonableness come to be identified with accepting part of Communist demands.

This confusion of bargaining technique with purpose causes the diplomatic debate to be confined to issues of maximum embarrassment to the West, issues, that is, which the Soviet Union has raised and on which the West feels obliged to negotiate because, as the saying goes, no avenue of settlement must be neglected and because the mere readiness of the Soviet to talk about *anything* is considered "encouraging." Conversely, the West is prevented from raising issues of possible embarrassment to the Soviet Union because, it is said, we must not destroy the climate of confidence by making "unacceptable" proposals. On some issues an aura of unintended cynicism therefore surrounds Western proposals. . . .

*　*　*

The formalism of the Western approach to negotiations raises the question whether the real obstacle to a flexible and purposeful

Western diplomacy is not the absence of moral assurance. The impression is sometimes strong that too many in the West consider conviction incompatible with negotiation. Too often the laudable tendency to see the other point of view is carried to the extreme of refusing to make any moral distinctions. . . .

* * *

A lasting settlement is possible only if the Soviet leaders become convinced that they will not be able to use the West's desire for peace to demoralize it. If they are serious about their desire to avoid war, they must realize that negotiations can be used for purely tactical purposes only so often and that, measured against the dangers of such a course, the gains they may score are paltry. We in turn should strive to demonstrate to the Soviet leaders that they have a real policy decision to make which we will do everything possible to ease. They must face the fact that the policy of applying relentless pressures on the West creates untold perils for all the peoples of the world. On the other hand, they must be convinced that they can increase their security through negotiation. Should they seriously seek a settlement, they would find us flexible and conciliatory.

Negotiations are important. But it is essential to conduct them without illusions. We do not need to postulate a basic Soviet transformation in order to believe in the possibility of a settlement. Nor is it a prerequisite to successful negotiation to pretend that a relaxation of tensions is primarily within Western control. The West must have much more positive goals than to divine Soviet intent. We do ourselves an injustice if we make an issue of the desirability of relaxing tensions or of ending the Cold War. The test of conciliatoriness does not reside in interpreting Soviet trends in the most favorable manner. Nor does it consist of proving the desirability of peace—which should be taken for granted. Rather, the challenge which confronts the West is to determine what are the possibilities of a settlement which does not hazard our security and is consistent with our values. Only in the purposeful is flexibility a virtue.

Formulating Foreign Policy

Dean Rusk

* * *

It is quite true that the central themes of American foreign policy are more or less constant. They derive from the kind of people we are in this country and from the shape of the world situation. It has been interesting over the years to see how, in our democratic society based on the consent of the governed, movements off the main path of the ideas and aspirations of the American people have tended to swing back to the main path as a result of the steady pressures of public opinion.

Nevertheless we are today in a highly revolutionary world situation. Change is its dominant theme. I suppose that the central question before us is how we can properly relate ourselves to these fundamental and far-reaching changes. We are seeing a world in turmoil, reshaping itself in a way which is at least as significant as the breakdown of the Concert of Europe, or as the emergence of the national states in the Western system, or as the explosion of Europe into other continents of the world some three centuries ago.

* * *

With this enlarged role in mind, I should like to make a few suggestions: What we in the United States do or do not do will make a very large difference in what happens in the rest of the world. We in this Department must think about foreign policy in its total context. We cannot regard foreign policy as something left over after defense policy or trade policy or fiscal policy has been extracted. Foreign

SOURCE: Remarks made by secretary of state to Department of State policy-making officers, February 20, 1961, "The Formulation of Foreign Policy," Department of State, *American Foreign Policy: Current Documents, 1961* (Washington, D.C.: Government Printing Office, 1965), pp. 22–28.

policy is the total involvement of the American people with peoples and governments abroad. That means that, if we are to achieve a new standard of leadership, we must think in terms of the total context of our situation. It is the concern of the Department of State that the American people are safe and secure—defense is not a monopoly concern of the Department of Defense. It is also the concern of the Department of State that our trading relationships with the rest of the world are vigorous, profitable, and active—this is not just a passing interest or a matter of concern only to the Department of Commerce. We can no longer rely on interdepartmental machinery "somewhere upstairs" to resolve differences between this and other departments. Assistant Secretaries of State will now carry an increased burden of active formulation and coordination of policies. Means must be found to enable us to keep in touch as regularly and as efficiently as possible with our colleagues in other departments concerned with foreign policy.

I think we need to concern ourselves also with the timeliness of action. Every policy officer cannot help but be a planning officer. Unless we keep our eyes on the horizon ahead, we shall fail to bring ourselves on target with the present. The movement of events is so fast, the pace so severe, that an attempt to peer into the future is essential if we are to think accurately about the present. If there is anything which we can do in the executive branch of the Government to speed up the processes by which we come to decisions on matters on which we must act promptly, that in itself would be a major contribution to the conduct of our affairs. Action taken today is often far more valuable than action taken several months later in response to a situation then out of control.

There will of course be times for delay and inaction. What I am suggesting is that when we delay, or when we fail to act, we do so intentionally and not through inadvertence or through bureaucratic or procedural difficulties.

I also hope that we can do something about reducing the infant mortality rate of ideas—an affliction of all bureaucracies. We want to stimulate ideas from the bottom to the top of the Department. We want to make sure that our junior colleagues realize that ideas are welcome, that initiative goes right down to the bottom and goes all the way to the top. I hope no one expects that only Presidential appointees are looked upon as sources of ideas. The responsibility for taking the initiative in generating ideas is that of every officer in the Department who has a policy function, regardless of rank.

Further, I would hope that we could pay attention to little things.

While observing the operations of our Government in various parts of the world, I have felt that in many situations where our policies were good we have tended to ignore minor problems which spoiled our main effort. To cite only a few examples: The wrong man in the wrong position, perhaps even in a junior position abroad, can be a source of great harm to our policy; the attitudes of a U.N. delegate who experiences difficulty in finding adequate housing in New York City, or of a foreign diplomat in similar circumstances in our Capital, can easily be directed against the United States and all that it stands for. Dozens of seemingly small matters go wrong all over the world. Some times those who know about them are too far down the line to be able to do anything about them. I would hope that we could create the recognition in the Department and overseas that those who come across little things going wrong have the responsibility for bringing these to the attention of those who can do something about them.

If the Department of State is to take primary responsibility for foreign policy in Washington, it follows that the ambassador is expected to take charge overseas. This does not mean in a purely bureaucratic sense but in an active, operational, interested, responsible fashion. He is expected to know about what is going on among the representatives of other agencies who are stationed in his country. He is expected to supervise, to encourage, to direct, to assist in any way he can. If any official operation abroad begins to go wrong, we shall look to the ambassador to find out why and to get suggestions for remedial action.

It occurred to me that you might be interested in some thoughts which I expressed privately in recent years, in the hope of clearing up a certain confusion in the public mind about what foreign policy is all about and what it means, and of developing a certain compassion for those who are carrying such responsibilities inside Government. I tried to do so by calling to their attention some of the problems that a senior departmental policy officer faces. This means practically everybody in this room. Whether it will strike home for you or not will be for you to determine.

The senior policy officer may be moved to think hard about a problem by any of an infinite variety of stimuli: an idea in his own head, the suggestions of a colleague, a question from the Secretary or the President, a proposal by another department, a communication from a foreign government or an American ambassador abroad, the filing of an item for the agenda of the United Nations or of any other of dozens of international bodies, a news item read at the breakfast table, a question to the President or the Secretary at a news conference, a speech by a Senator or Congressman, an article in a periodical, a resolution from a national organization, a request for assistance from some private American interests abroad, et cetera, ad infinitum. The policy officer lives with his antennae alerted for the questions which fall within his range of responsibility.

His first thought is about the question itself: Is there a question here for American foreign policy, and, if so, what is it? For he knows that the first and sometimes most difficult job is to know what the question is—that when it is accurately identified it sometimes answers itself, and that the way in which it is posed frequently shapes the answer.

Chewing it over with his colleagues and in his own mind, he reaches a tentative identification of the question—tentative because it may change as he explores it further and because, if no tolerable answer can be found, it may have to be changed into one which can be answered.

Meanwhile he has been thinking about the facts surrounding the problem, facts which he knows can never be complete, and the general background, much of which has already been lost to history. He is appreciative of the expert help available to him and draws these resources into play, taking care to examine at least some of the raw material which underlies their frequently policy-oriented conclusions. He knows that he must give the expert his place, but he knows that he must also keep him in it.

He is already beginning to box the compass of alternative lines of action, including doing nothing. He knows that he is thinking about action in relation to a future which can be perceived but dimly through a merciful fog. But he takes his bearings from the great guidelines of policy, well-established precedents, the commitments of the United States under international charters and treaties, basic statutes, and well-understood notions of the American people about how we are to conduct ourselves, in policy literature such as country papers and National Security Council papers accumulated in the Department.

He will not be surprised to find that general principles produce conflicting results in the factual situation with which he is confronted. He must think about which of these principles must take precedence. He will know that general policy papers written months before may not fit his problem because of crucial changes in circumstance. He is aware that every moderately important problem merges imperceptibly into every other problem. He must deal with the question of how to manage a part when it cannot be handled without relation to the whole—when the whole is too large to grasp.

He must think of others who have a stake in the question and in its answer. Who should be consulted among his colleagues in the Department or other departments and agencies of the Government? Which American ambassadors could provide helpful advice? Are private interests sufficiently involved to be consulted? What is the probable attitude of other governments, including those less directly involved? How and at what stage and in what sequence are other governments to be consulted?

If action is indicated, what kind of action is relevant to the problem? The selection of the wrong tools can mean waste, at best, and at worst an unwanted inflammation of the problem itself. Can the President or the Secretary act under existing authority, or will new legislation and new money be required? Should the action be unilateral or multilateral? Is the matter one for the United Nations or some other international body? For, if so, the path leads through a complex process of parliamentary diplomacy which adds still another dimension to the problem.

What type of action can hope to win public support, first in this country and then abroad? For the policy officer will know that action can almost never be secret and that in general the effectiveness of policy will be conditioned by the readiness of the country to sustain it. He is interested in public opinion for two reasons: first, because it is important in itself, and, second, because he knows that the American public cares about a decent respect for the opinions of mankind. And, given probable public attitudes—about which reasonably good estimates can be made—what action is called for to insure necessary support?

May I add a caution on this particular point? We do not want policy officers below the level of Presidential appointees to concern themselves too much with problems of domestic politics in recommending foreign policy action. In the first place our business is foreign policy, and it is the business of the Presidential leadership and his appointees in the Department to consider the domestic political aspects of a problem. Mr. Truman emphasized this point by saying, "You fellows in the Department of State don't know much about domestic politics."

This is an important consideration. If we sit here reading editorials and looking at public-opinion polls and other reports that cross our desks, we should realize that this is raw, undigested opinion expressed in the absence of leadership. What the American people will do turns in large degree on their leadership. We cannot test public opinion until the President and the leaders of the country have gone to the public to explain what is required and have asked them for support for the necessary action. I doubt, for example, that, 3 months before the leadership began to talk about what came to be the Marshall plan, any public-opinion expert would have said that the country would have accepted such proposals.

The problem in the policy officer's mind thus begins to take shape as a galaxy of utterly complicated factors—political, military, economic, financial, legal, legislative, procedural, administrative—to be sorted out and handled within a political system which moves by consent in relation to an external environment which cannot be under control.

And the policy officer has the hounds of time snapping at his heels. He knows that there is a time to act and a time to wait. But which is it in this instance? Today is not yesterday and tomorrow will be something else, and his problem is changing while he and his colleagues are working on it. He may labor prodigiously to produce an answer to a question which no longer exists.

In any event he knows that an idea is not a policy and that the transformation of an idea into a policy is frequently an exhausting and frustrating process. He is aware of the difference between a conclusion and a decision. The professor, the commentator, the lecturer may indulge in conclusions, may defer them until all the evidence is in, may change them when facts so compel. But the policy officer must move from conclusion to decision and must be prepared to live with the results, for he does not have a chance to do it again. If he waits, he has already made a decision, sometimes the right one, but the white heat of responsibility is upon him and he cannot escape it, however strenuously he tries.

There is one type of study which I have not seen, which I hope we can do something about in the months ahead. The pilot of a jet aircraft has a check list of many dozen questions which he must answer satisfactorily before he takes off his plane on a flight. Would it not be interesting and revealing if if we had a check list of questions which we should answer systematically before we take off on a policy?

Perhaps this is a point at which to inject another passing comment. The processes of government have sometimes been described as a struggle for power among those holding public office. I am convinced that this is true only in a certain formal and bureaucratic sense, having to do with appropriations, job descriptions, trappings of prestige, water bottles, and things of that sort. There is another struggle of far more consequence, the effort to diffuse or avoid responsibility. Power gravitates to those who are willing to make decisions and live with the results, simply because there are so many who readily yield to the intrepid few who take their duties seriously.

*   *   *

Precedence and Protocol

CHARLES W. THAYER

"Protocol and striped pants," President Truman once wrote to me, "give me a pain in the neck." His sentiments would be virtually unanimously seconded by the American Foreign Service. Yet the fact is that American diplomats continue to observe the strictest protocol and don their striped pants to attend ceremonial affairs almost daily. Why?

Anthropologists claim that the more primitive the community the stricter are its conventions. Savage tribes are ruled largely by taboos and almost meaningless rituals. Nature's most primitive noblemen, whether in the trappers' camp or the trading post barroom, enforce their petty conventions at the point of a gun.

Most diplomats would perhaps resent being classified as anthropologically primitive, but in a sense their community is just that. Outside the local law, beyond the jurisdiction of the courts, the diplomatic corps would be a lawless community were it not for its self-imposed ethics and rules which together comprise protocol.

From its earliest origins, but especially after the emergence of national states in the Middle Ages, the diplomatic corps in every capital was a leaderless mob of inviolable representatives of sovereigns, each of whom considered himself at least the equal of his colleagues. Unlike barnyard fowl, they had no established pecking order. Occasionally the political or religious dominance of a Holy Roman emperor or a pope was universally acknowledged and his representative accorded precedence over other diplomats. But with these exceptions, the rivalry of diplomats for the place of honor was just as keen as the rivalry between the sovereigns themselves. The seventeenth-century struggle between the French and Spanish kings

SOURCE: "Protocol," *Diplomat* (New York: Harper, 1959), chapter 20.

for domination of Europe was, for example, reflected in miniature in every court where the Spanish and French ambassadors fought for precedence.

In 1661 the French and Spanish embassies in London both sent delegations, as was the custom at the time, to meet a newly arrived Swedish ambassador at London dock. As the cortege escorting the new arrival formed up for the return journey, the French contingent tried to squeeze into the place of honor behind the Swede's carriage. Thereupon the Spanish delegation, which had providentially brought an armed escort of about forty men, set upon the French delegates and hamstrung their horses, wounded the coachman, and generally raised havoc. When the smoke settled the French were out of action and the Spaniards were in the place of honor. When Louis XIV heard about the incident he was so incensed that he broke off diplomatic relations with Madrid.

A happier solution was found about the same time in The Hague when the Spanish and French ambassadors' carriages met in a narrow street and each solemnly refused to pull over for the other. After a long dispute it was finally decided to pull down a fence at the side of the road so that they might pass without either giving way to the other.

The Russians were no less assiduous in defense of their prerogatives. A century after the above incidents, at a court ball in London, the Russian ambassador, arriving early, sat down in the place of honor at the right of the Austrian ambassador of the Holy Roman Emperor. The Frenchman, arriving a few minutes later and finding what he considered his place taken by the Russian, leaped over the back of the bench on which the Austrian and the Russian were seated and managed to squeeze between them. The brawl that followed led eventually to a duel between the Frenchman and the Russian in which the Russian was wounded.

The great powers of the day were by no means alone in defending their seniority and place. The United States in its early history was constantly claiming that its dignity had been offended, and sent endless streams of protests to foreign governments.

Despite the efforts of Grotius and other authorities to establish order out of this chaos, nothing could be done until the Napoleonic Wars had so upset the hierarchical tables that some sort of international rule became essential. At the Congress of Vienna, therefore, a special convention was drawn up establishing precedence among diplomatic envoys. To overcome the pretensions of the various courts to first place the convention adopted the principle of "first come first served." Thus the ambassador who has served longest at a post is considered the senior and every other one takes precedence according to the date on which he presented his credentials. Ministers rank among themselves according to the same principle.

There are, of course, exceptions. For example, in Catholic countries the nuncio, the ambassador of the Vatican, is automatically the senior member of the diplomatic corps, known as doyen or dean. The Rules of Vienna, as the convention is called, cannot be considered international law and their observance is entirely a voluntary matter. However, most nations recognize it and enforce its practice in their capitals.*

The dean of the diplomatic corps and his wife, the doyenne, or, if he is a bachelor, the wife of the next senior ambassador, have certain special rights and duties. At some royal courts the doyenne must present the ladies of the diplomatic corps to the sovereign. At most posts the dean can convoke meetings of the corps and organize joint action involving the community. He may never, however, take a political lead in other than purely local questions and may never invoke the names of his colleagues without their consent.

As spokesman for the diplomatic corps the dean is not without influence. Partly because of this many smaller powers, including the Scandinavian countries, often keep their ambassador at a post for ten or twelve years as against the normal three or four. Their ambassadors thus are often deans of the corps and enjoy a precedence over those of larger countries because of their length of service.

The Vienna Rules solved the problem of seniority between diplomats but this, in most capitals, is only half the problem. Where, for example, does an ambassador rank in Washington vis-à-vis the Vice-President or the Chief Justice? Local ground rules, established by the host government, generally regulate these touchy problems. For this purpose governments employ a chief of protocol or master of ceremonies as the arbiter of local custom. What does a frustrated diplomatic hostess do when confronted by an insoluble seating problem: the senior guest at her dinner party is a woman ambassador, her other guests include the Vice-President's wife, and the host, her husband, has just come down with the mumps? Instead of calling the whole show off, the hostess can submit the list of guests to the local chief of protocol and he is obliged to come up with a solution. The chief of protocol's decision is not binding but is generally accepted lest some guest take offense and blame the hostess.

---

* EDITOR's NOTE: Matters of precedence are currently outlined in Articles 14–17 of the Vienna Convention on Diplomatic Relations; see Appendix A below.

In recent years husbands of ambassadors have created new problems to perplex protocol chiefs. Frequently a vigorous female ambassador will insist that her husband be seated above ministers. However, ministers represent sovereign states. Husbands represent something less. Husbands of ambassadors present other anomalies. When Winthrop Aldrich was American ambassador in London rumors spread that Mrs. Henry Luce, then in Rome, was to replace him. Meeting Mr. Luce in New York, Mrs. Aldrich is reported to have said to him: "Henry, I hear you are after my job."

The Rules of Vienna are fairly easy to apply when it comes to arranging ambassadors Indian file in a cortege. But how do you seat them around a square or rectangular table or on a reviewing stand? Universal protocol rules have largely solved the table problem but the rules for placing ambassadors on reviewing stands are less uniform. If there are only two to place, the order generally accepted is 2-1 (the senior on the right). With three, the order is generally 3-1-2 (senior in the center). With four, usage splits. The British claim 4-3-2-1; but other authorities argue it should be 4-3-1-2. With five, it becomes complicated: 5-3-1-2-4. However, even these rules have their exceptions: for example, in Scandinavia and Turkey and in certain religious ceremonies in Catholic countries, the left-hand place is the place of honor.

The rules of protocol are often based on plain common sense. For instance, at a formal banquet on which side of the table should the hostess sit? Since she is the last to enter the dining room, any parking lot attendant could tell you she should sit on the side nearest the door.

A newly arrived ambassador has his first taste of protocol when he prepares to present his letter of credence to the chief of state of the host government. This is not the prime minister but the sovereign or president or, as in Russia, the chairman of the ruling council. He will already have been met informally at the station or airport by the chief of protocol and will have sent the foreign minister a carbon copy of his letter of credence and of any speech he feels moved to make on the occasion.

On the morning set for the presentation the new ambassador, if he is an American, puts on his tails with a black waistcoat and white tie for reasons we shall discuss presently. His staff, including his military attachés in their dress uniforms, foregather in his parlor. At the appointed hour the chief of protocol of the host government arrives either in a state limousine or, in Madrid, for example, in a state carriage drawn by six horses for an ambassador but by only two for a minister. Usually extra coaches or cars are sent to take the ambassador's staff. At the palace, provided the country is a monarchy, he is greeted by the foreign minister and the court chamberlain and eventually taken to the throne room, where he bows once on entering, once when he is halfway across the room, and a third time as he stops before the King. He then hands him the letters and does or does not make a speech. Ordinarily the chief of state will carry on a few minutes of desultory chatter the length of which is severely prescribed lest he talk longer to one ambassador than to the next. At a signal the ambassador brings forward his staff and presents them individually and then, in royal ceremonies, makes his exit walking backwards at least part of the way. For those not accustomed to it, walking backwards can be the most awkward part of the ceremony. The King of Afghanistan requires an ambassador to take only three symbolic steps backwards, and then he may walk out like an ordinary human being.

The ambassador and his party are then escorted back to the embassy in the coaches or Cadillacs. There he can take off his wing collar and, if he wants to impress his new staff, break out some champagne.

Now begins what is probably the most burdensome of all diplomatic functions: the making of calls. Every new ambassador must personally call on every other ambassador in the capital and receive the first calls of all ministers, except the representatives of countries his government does not recognize. Each call must be returned in person. Since there are often sixty or seventy ambassadors to call on, the calls often last no more than ten minutes during which there is scarcely time to discover what one's colleague looks like.*

The custom of calls is probably one of the most anachronistic aspects of diplomatic protocol. When there were only a few embassies in a capital, when mails were slow and business was conducted leisurely, the call had a useful function in permitting an ambassador to get to know his colleagues and form at least a first impression of their personalities. Today it is an empty ritual which only consumes precious time.

In many capitals the calling routine is extended to members of the diplomatic staff. Even third secretaries are required on occasion to call not on ambassadors but upon their wives, this being the ceremonial manner of getting on the ambassadress's invitation list.

The calling card is an equally anachronistic auxiliary of the

---

* EDITOR'S NOTE: As noted earlier, the number of diplomats in a major capital, like Washington, now is double this quantity.

formal call. Before coming to a new post every ambassador and every secretary of embassy should be informed by his embassy how many calling cards he should have engraved. (Since protocol secretaries in embassies are invariably among the most snobbish of human beings, they almost instinctively run their thumbs over every card they receive to make sure it is engraved and not printed.)

The calling-card routine requires that every new arrival, including the least important member of the diplomatic staff, send his cards to every diplomatic member of every other embassy and legation. Ordinarily this is done automatically by the embassy's protocol secretary, who simply stuffs the required number of the newcomer's cards into an envelope and adds one card from the ambassador signifying that he is presenting (by messenger) his newest secretary. Thereupon the receiving embassy protocol secretary stuffs the required number of cards in another envelope and sends it back. The land-office business thus created for engraving companies has occasionally tempted secretaries to establish a calling-card clearinghouse, whereby the cards are returned to the owner for use on another occasion.

Calling-card lore is replete with quaint symbolic signs. A card with a dog-eared corner means that it was delivered in person by the owner and ranks above the unbent card in social if not in reissuance value. The letters "p.p.c.," "p.r.," "p.f.," and "p.c." penned in the lower left corner signify "pour prendre conger" (to take leave)—sent when the diplomat is leaving a post—or "pour remercier" (to thank) —sent after enjoying a colleague's hospitality—or "pour feliciter" (to congratulate) sent on national holidays and similar occasions—or "pour condoler" (to condole)—sent after a national or personal bereavement.

Diplomats had hardly been invented before host governments discovered they could be bribed to great advantage. Simultaneously the home governments discovered the same phenomenon. As a result it early became taboo for ambassadors to receive valuable gifts. Thereupon host governments began to resort to conferring valuable decorations as a form of bribe. Home governments retaliated by forbidding ambassadors to accept decorations without special permission. When two of her ambassadors violated these instructions, Queen Elizabeth I sent them both to jail.

The United States government today is particularly strict about refusing to let its diplomats receive decorations. The Constitution itself specifically forbids government officials to accept presents, titles, or decorations from foreign governments. This can cause embarrassment, especially when a foreign sovereign at a public ceremony unexpectedly pins a medal on an American diplomat's coat. In the past on such occasions the State Department agreed to take the medal in question and hold it in storage until the recipient had resigned or retired. Nowadays, however, this graceful escape is closed and the recipient of an honor must send it back by return messenger. Special exceptions have, however, been authorized by Congress in exceptional circumstances involving allied governments in time of war.*

An exception to the rule is also permitted in the case of small token gifts of no great value. In some countries, for example, it is the custom for guests to send flowers or small trinkets to a host after a formal party. These need not be returned. They do, however, pose a problem for diplomats and their wives who must scour the local market for suitable trinkets.

American business corporations have recently discovered what diplomats have known for many centuries—that wives are valuable auxiliaries. The Venetians, who were the first to establish permanent embassies, were initially skeptical on the subject of wives and required ambassadors to leave them at home—to avoid indiscretions. But they were required to take their own cooks—to avoid poisoners. When Ambassador Bullitt recruited his embassy to reopen diplomatic relations with the Soviets in 1933 he stuck to the old Venetian rule and with few exceptions took with him only bachelors as junior officers. However, as the Venetians doubtless discovered, the romantic attachments and resulting complications of the bachelors soon outmatched any indiscretions wives might have committed and today the recruiting policy for the Moscow Embassy is quite the reverse—preferably no bachelors.

Although the State Department has not gone as far as American businessmen in subjecting wives to intelligence, psychiatric, and social tests, it does take a good look at the spouses before the neophyte diplomat completes his probationary period. But this rule does not apply to wives of politically appointed ambassadors.

Before World War I the German government considered the social distinction of the ambassador's wife so important that when it

---

* EDITOR'S NOTE: Congress and the executive have regularized rules concerning the acceptance and disposition of gifts and decorations presented by foreign governments and other agencies. For current regulations consisting of legislation, executive orders, and Department of State regulations, see the current issues of *Legislation on Foreign Relations*, revised annually and published by the Government Printing Office for the Committee on Foreign Relations of the Senate and the Committee on International Relations of the House of Representatives.

wanted to name a certain Count von Hatzfeldt as ambassador to London, he was informed that before he could be appointed he would have to divorce his American commoner wife of Jewish extraction. Hatzfeldt refused, but eventually agreed to a legal separation for the duration of his assignment.

The social life of a diplomatic colony is carefully circumscribed by international and local protocol rules. Often the smaller and more primitive the host's country the more jealously are the rules observed. Even at the most informal parties the host will violate protocol in arranging the "placement" or seating order at his table at his own risk. Many a diplomat from a small country, finding himself improperly seated, has sent for his hat and coat and gone home.

The fact that the seating arrangement puts together people with no interests or even language in common makes no difference. During my year and a half in Kabul, my protocol rank followed the Iranian chargé d'affaires' and night after night I found myself seated beside his fat and jolly wife who could speak nothing but Persian. My knowledge of that language soon showed a marked improvement.

Local protocol often prescribes whom you may and may not invite to dinner. Sometimes the chief of state does not allow diplomats to invite him to dinner lest he be forced to spend his life on a round of diplomatic banquets. In some capitals diplomatic secretaries are not supposed to invite ambassadors to formal dinners.

When Ambassador Davies was in Moscow he wanted to give a dinner in honor of the newly arrived Italian Ambassador Rosso. He was much put out when told that he could not invite any other ambassador since all of them outranked Rosso and therefore automatically were entitled to the place of honor.

The forms of diplomatic entertainment, contrary to general belief, vary little from those in other walks of life. They include everything from the crowded cocktail party to the stiff "white tie" ball or reception where ancient aristocrats, their chests agleam with miniature decorations and their shirt fronts gaudy with bejeweled orders, dodder about gulping champagne.

Graham H. Stuart, in his authoritative *American Diplomatic and Consular Practice*, warns against "extravagant opulence" in diplomatic entertainment and cites as an example a Spring Festival given by Ambassador Bullitt in Moscow. In fairness to the ambassador it must be said that the arrangements for the festival were made in his absence by me as my first effort as a diplomatic impresario. It was never repeated. But in self-defense it might be added that at the Spring Festival there were no comedian waiters who intentionally spilled soup down the necks of indignant diplomatic guests as they did at a gala performance given by Ambassador Dawes in London. The worst that happened in Moscow was that a baby bear forgot himself on the gaudy tunic of a Soviet general, not by prearrangement.

Mr. Stuart warns also against "parsimonious frugality." After serving some years with Mr. Bullitt in the thirties I was transferred to Berlin under William Dodd, a professor of history whom Roosevelt had recruited as ambassador. At the first embassy reception I attended in Berlin Ambassador Dodd, taking his youngest vice-consul aside and with an air of admonition not unmixed with pride, confided that one could give a reception for two hundred people with only one bottle of gin if one was careful. The punch he served bore unmistakable evidence of the ambassador's carefulness.

At that time, when peoples were choosing sides between the dictators and the democratic world, it was sufficient to attend one of the glittering receptions of the Italian ambassador, arranged with impeccable taste by his wife Countess Atolico, and compare it to Ambassador Dodd's frugality to know who was setting the pace for the diplomats of the smaller uncommitted nations represented in Berlin. Dodd's frugality, in part due to his own lack of private means, demonstrated his and his compatriots' contempt for Nazi Germany, but it also contributed to the picture Hitler was attempting to paint of a miserly Uncle Sam indifferent to the good opinion or even to the fate of Europe.

When Dodd was eventually withdrawn his place was taken by Alexander Kirk as chargé d'affaires. Being a wealthy man, Kirk reversed Dodd's policy and entertained extensively. Each Sunday he invited several hundred people to a buffet luncheon. At that time, to save his food resources, Hitler had decreed that Sunday luncheons for Germans should consist of a single, simple dish. Kirk's lunches therefore became popular among not only his colleagues but German high officials as well, most of whom had standing invitations to come each week. On one occasion when Kirk was suddenly called to Paris for consultation on a Saturday afternoon he instructed his deputy, then George Kennan, to cancel the weekly luncheon. Upon his return from Paris he called Kennan and thanked him, but remarked that he had forgotten to notify two people of the cancellation—his chef and the Japanese ambassador.

Parsimony can take many forms. One American ambassador used to serve cheap local wines from bottles bearing the labels of famous Rhine or Burgundy vineyards. Once when entertaining a visiting foreigner known to most of the guests as a great authority on Rhine wines, the ambassador served a particularly ordinary native product in a Rhine wine bottle. As the distinguished guest took a sip and carefully rolled the liquid around his tongue, the other guests watched in awkward silence. Then the guest put down his glass and bowed to the ambassador. "Most unusual," he commented and ostentatiously reached for his water glass.

The same ambassador also invariably saved the place cards of his more frequent guests, including his staff. His daughter was charged with cleaning them up after each meal with an India-rubber eraser. As the cards grew grayer the ambassador's staff grew more indignant until they adopted the expedient of surreptitiously dunking their place cards in the red wine. No amount of rubbing could take out the stain and the cards were finally replaced.

The main occasion for entertaining is invariably an ambassador's national holiday—the Fourth of July for the Americans, the King's or Queen's Birthday for the British, Bastille Day for the French, and so on.* A generation ago it was more or less obligatory for diplomats to call on their colleagues on the national day and "sign the book"— a guest book prominently displayed in the embassy front hall—after which they were free to go home. Even today in royal courts it is the practice to put out the book on festive occasions—the marriage of a member of the royal family, the coming of age of an heir, or the birth of a prince—whereupon the diplomatic corps is notified that their signatures are awaited.

But nowadays, instead of putting out the book on national days, one usually gives a reception complete with cocktails and hors d'œuvres. Though essentially a national holiday reception is to receive the congratulations of one's colleagues, in the period between the wars it became customary for the American community in a foreign capital to expect the ambassador to entertain all his compatriots at a giant reception. The result was that gradually the Fourth of July became the occasion not to receive colleagues' congratulations but to alleviate the homesickness of the American colony. In Paris the Fourth of July became a monstrous free-loading operation to which even tourists temporarily in France flocked with or without invitation and often the number of guests reached several thousand.

Not to be outdone, American ambassadors in smaller capitals

---

* EDITOR'S NOTE: In Washington, for example, approximately 130 countries celebrate their national holidays each year; there are 10 or more such celebrations in each of seven months, with as many as 3 on July 1 and 9 on three days in mid-September. See Ellis O. Briggs's comments on this situation in his essay earlier in this chapter.

tried to emulate their Paris colleague by making their receptions as big as possible. An American ambassador in Prague once advertised his reception in the local papers, inviting "all Americans and friends of America." His staff was somewhat startled when a popular bargirl well known for the lavish manner in which she bestowed her affections on lonely foreigners appeared at the Fourth of July in a flashy low-cut dress and a huge picture hat. Asked by an acquaintance what she was doing at the embassy on the Fourth of July, she replied archly that she was the best friend of a lot more Americans in town than one might guess.

The Fourth of July is by no means the only occasion for diplomatic entertainment. As air travel has grown so has the number of important officials visiting foreign lands. Congressmen, prominent editors, assistant secretaries of departments, to say nothing of the secretary of state himself, all require luncheons or dinners or even business breakfasts. During his two years as ambassador in Paris David Bruce once complained that he'd had exactly one meal with his family—and that was a breakfast.

Then there are the parties one must give to repay one's colleagues for social obligations. Even when there are no visiting firemen to entertain, one's colleagues can force even the most retiring diplomat into throwing parties. In Moscow, between the wars, few officials came from abroad requiring entertainment, since the Soviets were frugal with visas and neither Moscow's business nor her pleasure attracted foreign firemen. Bored embassy wives made up for the lack by constantly giving dinners, dances, receptions, and cocktail parties, each one of which created a dozen more obligations on her guests to return the hospitality. Thus the breeding of social events became as prolific and incestuous as that of rabbits.

As Moscow between the wars demonstrated, a bored diplomatic colony is bad public relations. To avoid a bad name among diplomats, a host government will often go to great lengths to keep its guest ambassadors and their wives amused. Though the ambassadors of the larger countries are ordinarily kept busier than they care to be, other embassies are less put upon. Furthermore, their wives, including Americans, relieved of most of the household chores by adequate staffs of servants, often find time hanging heavy. Consequently, the host governments, if they are properly advised by their protocol chiefs, will make great efforts to organize entertainment. Gala performances at the theater or opera, concerts, and art exhibits are the commonest ways of keeping diplomatic colonies out of the mischief arising from idleness.

Other forms are wine-tasting expeditions to famous cellars, boat trips on famous rivers, and the oldest form of diplomatic entertainment—hunting stags, wild boar, pheasant, or other game. (Strangely enough, diplomatic fishing parties have never caught on. Perhaps it is because diplomats are usually too gregarious or garrulous to enjoy standing silent and alone by a trout stream.)

A generation ago the ability to shoot a gun was as important for the diplomat as being able to waltz. But today standards are lower and a diplomatic shoot is often regarded by experienced hunters as one of the more dangerous pastimes. I have spent the better part of several diplomatic shoots flat on my face in a ditch while bullets whistled above me. On one occasion at a state shoot in Germany I was "contained" behind the thick trunk of an oak by a colleague with a rifle on the next stand until I discreetly waved a white handkerchief on the end of a stick. My neighbor subsequently explained that he had seen something move and thought it was a stag hiding from him behind the tree.

Even the Soviets have not been able to remove all the traditional sport from diplomacy and will if pressed provide shooting for diplomats—at a fee. Under Socialism, they explain, one must pay for one's pleasures. Only when Communism has been fully established will everything be free. In capitalist countries the dogma is ignored and all state shoots for diplomats are on the cuff.

Since World War II, however, the Communist lust for respectability has grown, and shooting preserves and deer parks have once again come into their own as marks of distinction. A few years ago at a reception given by Marshal Tito for Mr. Khrushchev on the broad terrace of the White Palace outside Belgrade, guests were startled when, at the end of dinner, Tito leaped on a chair and clapped his hands. Suddenly several huge spotlights lit up the palace park beyond and a magnificently crowned stag blinked bewildered into the glare while the Eastern guests roared approval. A few months later Khrushchev, not to be outdone, was escorting some American diplomats around his estate outside Moscow. Approaching a grove of trees, he put two fingers in his mouth and let out a piercing whistle, whereupon an entire herd of stags leaped from behind a thicket and galloped off across the lawn.

Before the men's fashion market moved from Paris to London, where it was decreed that men should wear only the dullest clothing, the male of the human species, including the diplomats, delighted in appearing just as gorgeously attired as their brethren in the bird world. Since then on ordinary occasions only the military have been permitted to display their sartorial vanity.

Court dress was obligatory in all capitals and the smaller the capital the gaudier the costumes were supposed to be. Even today for gala occasions many countries provide a ceremonial uniform for their diplomats.

However, when the United States came on the world scene, young, self-conscious and imbued with its mission to propagate the republican ideology, it resented not only the pomp and pageantry with which royal courts surrounded themselves but also the "nonsense and flummery" of court dress.

Benjamin Franklin . . . made his first appearance at the court of Versailles dressed in an old coat, his balding head wigless, and supporting himself on a crooked crabapple cane. He soon discovered, however, that if he was to make any contribution to the preservation of the then frail American Republic he had better conform to local usage rather than combine an attack on European sartorial habits with the business of making allies for his country. He thereupon devised for himself what he described as a modest but elegant court uniform. Subsequent American envoys followed his example.

In 1817 the State Department prescribed as diplomatic court dress a blue, silk-lined coat, a cape embroidered with gold, white knee breeches with gold buckles, white silk stockings with gilt shoe buckles, a three-cornered hat "not so large as those used by the French nor so small as those of the English," a black cockade with an eagle attached, and a sword.

This remained the uniform until the Age of Jackson, when the Common Man decreed that the coat should be black. In 1853 Secretary of State Marcy issued instructions that American diplomats should show their devotion to republican institutions by discarding the three-cornered hat, sword, and knee breeches and appear in court "in the simple dress of an American citizen," which included long pants—then worn chiefly by workers and waiters.

Marcy's idea commended itself to a number of American diplomats struggling under the financial burden of maintaining the more elaborate wardrobe. However, when they tried out the idea they met with varying success if for no other reason than that monarchs disliked having their throne rooms used as fashion shows for dangerous republican propaganda.

The Swiss Republic welcomed the idea warmly. The Swedish King, however, told the American minister that he would receive him on business in any costume he wanted to wear but that when he appeared at court he would wear court costume or not come at all.

James Buchanan, the future President but then minister in London, had the most difficult time of all with Mr. Marcy's innovation. He started cautiously by sounding out Queen Victoria's master of ceremonies, Sir Edward Cust, a crabbed old general. Sir Edward curtly suggested that Buchanan either wear court dress to court or absent himself. He went so far as to say that, though the Queen was above such matters, "the people of England would consider it presumption" for him not to wear court dress. Buchanan retorted testily that he did not care whether he ever appeared at court or not. When he was subsequently invited to the opening of Parliament with an invitation reading "in full court dress" he simply stayed away. This was immediately picked up by the London press, including the *Times* which printed "an indiscreet and rather offensive remark."

Apparently Queen Victoria had more sense and tact than her master of ceremonies and sought to work out a compromise with the American minister. She sent word that if he should wear a small sword to distinguish himself from the court servants it would be all right with her. Buchanan did so and was greeted by the Queen with "an arch but benevolent smile." Thus the problem of appearing at the British court in "the simple dress of an American citizen" was settled for nearly a century until it was broached again by the singular attitude of Ambassador Charles G. Dawes. When asked whether he would wear the usual knee breeches at court occasions Dawes told the questioner, "You can go plumb to hell." The London protocol authorities and court officials humored Dawes with considerable understanding not only in the matter of dress but in his other peculiar manners.

Current regulations, backed by a federal law, require American diplomats to wear on formal occasions a tail coat and white tie and, instead of the normal white one, a black vest such as is worn by waiters in pretentious restaurants. In fact, except for the white napkin on the left forearm, there is often nothing to distinguish the waiters from the American diplomats, a circumstance that has given rise to confusion. On one occasion a testy old American minister was asked by a lady at a diplomatic reception whether he was the butler. "No," he answered angrily. "Are you the chambermaid?"

When Ambassador Choate was serving in London and attended a reception in the prescribed uniform he was approached as he was leaving by another guest resplendent in court uniform. "Call me a cab," the guest demanded imperiously.

"You are a cab, sir," Choate promptly replied. Then he added: "At least you had the courtesy not to ask me to call you a hansom cab."

The history of Soviet diplomatic costumes provides an interesting parallel to the American but has a slightly different ending. Immediately after the October Revolution the Bolsheviks were suffering from the same inferiority complex and sense of mission that the Americans had demonstrated after the Revolution of 1776. Their diplomats were required to appear in the simple dress of a Soviet citizen—a business suit, though dungarees would have been more logical. Furthermore, they were not called "ambassadors" but simply "plenipotentiaries," to avoid the stigma of bourgeois flummery. However, the unfortunate "plenpots," as the title was abbreviated, soon discovered that under the Rules of Vienna they thus lost their rank as ambassadors. Thereupon the Kremlin dropped its devotion to the common man and named its diplomats "ambassadors" as everyone else did but continued to refer to them for many years in their home press as "plenpots."

Toward the end of the thirties Stalin abandoned even these pretensions and formally renamed his envoys "ambassadors" both openly and privately. He also devised for them a most elaborate costume which closely resembled the full-dress Soviet military uniform except that crossed quill pens replaced the crossed swords or guns.

Nevertheless, in Moscow the Kremlin leaders continued to appear at official receptions in their business suits even when formal or informal (black tie) wear was prescribed for foreign guests. Thereupon several foreign ambassadors decided collectively that if their hosts were not going to bother to change for dinner they would not either, and appeared in business suits. The Communists were visibly miffed.

Since the October Revolution is only forty-odd years old it is too early to say whether the next generation of Bolsheviks will raid the Kremlin museum, where the old royal robes are still preserved, to add color to their diplomatic receptions.*

* Editor's Note: For some commentary on streamlining diplomatic protocol, see, for example, the essays of Angier Biddle Duke, "Perspectives in Protocol," *Department of State Bulletin*, vol. 44 (March 20, 1961), pp. 414–18; "Protocol and the Conduct of Foreign Affairs," *Department of State Bulletin*, vol. 49 (November 4, 1963), pp. 700–4; and "The Functions of Protocol in Today's World," *Department of State Bulletin*, vol. 50 (March 2, 1964), pp. 344–47.

APPENDIX A

Vienna Convention on Diplomatic Relations*

The States Parties to the present Convention,

Recalling that peoples of all nations from ancient times have recognized the status of diplomatic agents,

Having in mind the purposes and principles of the Charter of the United Nations concerning the sovereign equality of States, the maintenance of international peace and security, and the promotion of friendly relations among nations,

Believing that an international convention on diplomatic intercourse, privileges and immunities would contribute to the development of friendly relations among nations, irrespective of their differing constitutional and social systems,

Realizing that the purpose of such privileges and immunities is not to benefit individuals but to ensure the efficient performance of the functions of diplomatic missions as representating States,

Affirming that the rules of customary international law should continue to govern questions not expressly regulated by the provisions of the present Convention,

Have agreed as follows:

ARTICLE 1

For the purpose of the present Convention, the following expressions shall have the meanings hereunder assigned to them:

(*a*) the "head of the mission" is the person charged by the sending State with the duty of acting in that capacity;

---

* United Nations Conference on Diplomatic Intercourse and Immunities, Vienna, Austria, signed April 18, 1961.

SOURCE: TIAS 7502; 23 UST 3227; 500 UNTS 95.

(*b*) the "members of the mission" are the head of the mission and the members of the staff of the mission;

(*c*) the "members of the staff of the mission" are the members of the diplomatic staff, of the administrative and technical staff and of the service staff of the mission;

(*d*) the "members of the diplomatic staff" are the members of the staff of the mission having diplomatic rank;

(*e*) a "diplomatic agent" is the head of the mission or a member of the diplomatic staff of the mission;

(*f*) the "members of the administrative and technical staff" are the members of the staff of the mission employed in the administrative and technical service of the mission;

(*g*) the "members of the service staff" are the members of the staff of the mission in the domestic service of the mission;

(*h*) a "private servant" is a person who is in the domestic service of a member of the mission and who is not an employee of the sending State;

(*i*) the "premises of the mission" are the buildings or parts of buildings and the land ancillary thereto, irrespective of ownership, used for the purposes of the mission including the residence of the head of the mission.

ARTICLE 2

The establishment of diplomatic relations between States, and of permanent diplomatic missions, takes place by mutual consent.

ARTICLE 3

1. The functions of a diplomatic mission consist *inter alia* in:

(*a*) representing the sending State in the receiving State;

(*b*) protecting in the receiving State the interests of the sending State and of its nationals, within the limits permitted by international law;

(*c*) negotiating with the Government of the receiving State;

(*d*) ascertaining by all lawful means conditions and developments in the receiving State, and reporting thereon to the Government of the sending State;

(*e*) promoting friendly relations between the sending State and the receiving State, and developing their economic, cultural and scientific relations.

404

2. Nothing in the present Convention shall be construed as preventing the performance of consular functions by a diplomatic mission.

ARTICLE 4

1. The sending State must make certain that the *agrément* of the receiving State has been given for the person it proposes to accredit as head of the mission to that State.

2. The receiving State is not obliged to give reasons to the sending State for a refusal of *agrément*.

ARTICLE 5

1. The sending State may, after it has given due notification to the receiving States concerned, accredit a head of mission or assign any member of the diplomatic staff, as the case may be, to more than one State, unless there is express objection by any of the receiving States.

2. If the sending State accredits a head of mission to one or more other States it may establish a diplomatic mission headed by a *chargé d'affaires ad interim* in each State where the head of mission has not his permanent seat.

3. A head of mission or any member of the diplomatic staff of the mission may act as representative of the sending State to any international organization.

ARTICLE 6

Two or more States may accredit the same person as head of mission to another State, unless objection is offered by the receiving State.

ARTICLE 7

Subject to the provisions of Articles 5, 8, 9 and 11, the sending State may freely appoint the members of the staff of the mission. In the case of military, naval or air attachés, the receiving State may require their names to be submitted beforehand, for its approval.

ARTICLE 8

1. Members of the diplomatic staff of the mission should in principle be of the nationality of the sending State.

405

2. Members of the diplomatic staff of the mission may not be appointed from among persons having the nationality of the receiving State, except with the consent of that State which may be withdrawn at any time.

3. The receiving State may reserve the same right with regard to nationals of a third State who are not also nationals of the sending State.

ARTICLE 9

1. The receiving State may at any time and without having to explain its decision, notify the sending State that the head of the mission or any member of the diplomatic staff of the mission is *persona non grata* or that any other member of the staff of the mission is not acceptable. In any such case, the sending State shall, as appropriate, either recall the person concerned or terminate his functions with the mission. A person may be declared *non grata* or not acceptable before arriving in the territory of the receiving State.

2. If the sending State refuses or fails within a reasonable period to carry out its obligations under paragraph 1 of this Article, the receiving State may refuse to recognize the person concerned as a member of the mission.

ARTICLE 10

1. The Ministry for Foreign Affairs of the receiving State, or such other ministry as may be agreed, shall be notified of:

(*a*) the appointment of members of the mission, their arrival and their final departure or the termination of their functions with the mission;

(*b*) the arrival and final departure of a person belonging to the family of a member of the mission and, where appropriate, the fact that a person becomes or ceases to be a member of the family of a member of the mission;

(*c*) the arrival and final departure of private servants in the employ of persons referred to in sub-paragraph (*a*) of this paragraph and, where appropriate, the fact that they are leaving the employ of such persons;

(*d*) the engagement and discharge of persons resident in the receiving State as members of the mission or private servants entitled to privileges and immunities.

2. Where possible, prior notification of arrival and final departure shall also be given.

ARTICLE 11

1. In the absence of specific agreement as to the size of the mission, the receiving State may require that the size of a mission be kept within limits considered by it to be reasonable and normal, having regard to circumstances and conditions in the receiving State and to the needs of the particular mission.

2. The receiving State may equally, within similar bounds and on a nondiscriminatory basis, refuse to accept officials of a particular category.

ARTICLE 12

The sending State may not, without the prior express consent of the receiving State, establish offices forming part of the mission in localities other than those in which the mission itself is established.

ARTICLE 13

1. The head of the mission is considered as having taken up his functions in the receiving State either when he has presented his credentials or when he has notified his arrival and a true copy of his credentials has been presented to the Ministry for Foreign Affairs of the receiving State, or such other ministry as may be agreed, in accordance with the practice prevailing in the receiving State which shall be applied in a uniform manner.

2. The order of presentation of credentials or a true copy thereof will be determined by the date and time of the arrival of the head of the mission.

ARTICLE 14

1. Heads of mission are divided into three classes, namely:

(a) that of ambassadors or nuncios accredited to Heads of State, and other heads of mission of equivalent rank;

(b) that of envoys, ministers and internuncios accredited to Heads of State;

(c) that of *chargé d'affaires* accredited to Ministers for Foreign Affairs.

2. Except as concerns precedence and etiquette, there shall be no differentiation between heads of mission by reason of their class.

ARTICLE 15

The class to which the heads of their missions are to be assigned shall be agreed between States.

ARTICLE 16

1. Heads of mission shall take precedence in their respective classes in the order of the date and time of taking up their functions in accordance with Article 13.

2. Alterations in the credentials of a head of mission not involving any change of class shall not affect his precedence.

3. This article is without prejudice to any practice accepted by the receiving State regarding the precedence of the representative of the Holy See.

ARTICLE 17

The precedence of the members of the diplomatic staff of the mission shall be notified by the head of the mission to the Ministry for Foreign Affairs or such other ministry as may be agreed.

ARTICLE 18

The procedure to be observed in each State for the reception of heads of mission shall be uniform in respect of each class.

ARTICLE 19

1. If the post of head of the mission is vacant, or if the head of the mission is unable to perform his functions, a *chargé d'affaires ad interim* shall act provisionally as head of the mission. The name of the *chargé d'affaires ad interim* shall be notified, either by the head of the mission or, in case he is unable to do so, by the Ministry for Foreign Affairs of the sending State to the Ministry for Foreign Affairs of the receiving State or such other ministry as may be agreed.

2. In cases where no member of the diplomatic staff of the mission is present in the receiving State, a member of the administrative and technical staff may, with the consent of the receiving State, be

designated by the sending State to be in charge of the current administrative affairs of the mission.

ARTICLE 20

The mission and its head shall have the right to use the flag and emblem of the sending State on the premises of the mission, including the residence of the head of the mission, and on his means of transport.

ARTICLE 21

1. The receiving State shall either facilitate the acquisition on its territory, in accordance with its laws, by the sending State of premises necessary for its mission or assist the latter in obtaining accommodation in some other way.

2. It shall also, where necessary, assist missions in obtaining suitable accommodation for their members.

ARTICLE 22

1. The premises of the mission shall be inviolable. The agents of the receiving State may not enter them, except with the consent of the head of the mission.

2. The receiving State is under a special duty to take all appropriate steps to protect the premises of the mission against any intrusion or damage and to prevent any disturbance of the peace of the mission or impairment of its dignity.

3. The premises of the mission, their furnishings and other property thereon and the means of transport of the mission shall be immune from search, requisition, attachment or execution.

ARTICLE 23

1. The sending State and the head of the mission shall be exempt from all national, regional or municipal dues and taxes in respect of the premises of the mission, whether owned or leased, other than such as represent payment for specific services rendered.

2. The exemption from taxation referred to in this Article shall not apply to such dues and taxes payable under the law of the receiving State by persons contracting with the sending State or the head of the mission.

ARTICLE 24

The archives and documents of the mission shall be inviolable at any time and wherever they may be.

ARTICLE 25

The receiving State shall accord full facilities for the performance of the functions of the mission.

ARTICLE 26

Subject to its laws and regulations concerning zones entry into which is prohibited or regulated for reasons of national security, the receiving State shall ensure to all members of the mission freedom of movement and travel in its territory.

ARTICLE 27

1. The receiving State shall permit and protect free communication on the part of the mission for all official purposes. In communicating with the Government and the other missions and consulates of the sending State, wherever situated, the mission may employ all appropriate means, including diplomatic couriers and messages in code or cipher. However, the mission may install and use a wireless transmitter only with the consent of the receiving State.

2. The official correspondence of the mission shall be inviolable. Official correspondence means all correspondence relating to the mission and its functions.

3. The diplomatic bag shall not be opened or detained.

4. The packages constituting the diplomatic bag must bear visible external marks of their character and may contain only diplomatic documents or articles intended for official use.

5. The diplomatic courier, who shall be provided with an official document indicating his status and the number of packages constituting the diplomatic bag, shall be protected by the receiving State in the performance of his functions. He shall enjoy personal inviolability and shall not be liable to any form of arrest or detention.

6. The sending State or the mission may designate diplomatic couriers *ad hoc*. In such cases the provisions of paragraph 5 of this Article shall also apply, except that the immunities therein mentioned

shall cease to apply when such a courier has delivered to the consignee the diplomatic bag in his charge.

7. A diplomatic bag may be entrusted to the captain of a commercial aircraft scheduled to land at an authorized port of entry. He shall be provided with an official document indicating the number of packages constituting the bag but he shall not be considered to be a diplomatic courier. The mission may send one of its members to take possession of the diplomatic bag directly and freely from the captain of the aircraft.

Article 28

The fees and charges levied by the mission in the course of its official duties shall be exempt from all dues and taxes.

Article 29

The person of a diplomatic agent shall be inviolable. He shall not be liable to any form of arrest or detention. The receiving State shall treat him with due respect and shall take all appropriate steps to prevent any attack on his person, freedom or dignity.

Article 30

1. The private residence of a diplomatic agent shall enjoy the same inviolability and protection as the premises of the mission.

2. His papers, correspondence and, except as provided in paragraph 3 of Article 31, his property, shall likewise enjoy inviolability.

Article 31

1. A diplomatic agent shall enjoy immunity from the criminal jurisdiction of the receiving State. He shall also enjoy immunity from its civil and administrative jurisdiction, except in the case of:

(a) a real action relating to private immovable property situated in the territory of the receiving State, unless he holds it on behalf of the sending State for the purposes of the mission;

(b) an action relating to succession in which the diplomatic agent is involved as executor, administrator, heir or legatee as a private person and not on behalf of the sending State;

(c) an action relating to any professional or commercial activity exercised by the diplomatic agent in the receiving State outside his official functions.

2. A diplomatic agent is not obliged to give evidence as a witness.

3. No measures of execution may be taken in respect of a diplomatic agent except in the cases coming under sub-paragraphs (*a*), (*b*) and (*c*) of paragraph 1 of this Article, and provided that the measures concerned can be taken without infringing the inviolability of his person or of his residence.

4. The immunity of a diplomatic agent from the jurisdiction of the receiving State does not exempt him from the jurisdiction of the sending State.

ARTICLE 32

1. The immunity from jurisdiction of diplomatic agents and of persons enjoying immunity under Article 37 may be waived by the sending State.

2. Waiver must always be express.

3. The initiation of proceedings by a diplomatic agent or by a person enjoying immunity from jurisdiction under Article 37 shall preclude him from invoking immunity from jurisdiction in respect of any counter-claim directly connected with the principal claim.

4. Waiver of immunity from jurisdiction in respect of civil or administrative proceedings shall not be held to imply waiver of immunity in respect of the execution of the judgment, for which a separate waiver shall be necessary.

ARTICLE 33

1. Subject to the provisions of paragraph 3 of this Article, a diplomatic agent shall with respect to services rendered for the sending State be exempt from social security provisions which may be in force in the receiving State.

2. The exemption provided for in paragraph 1 of this Article shall also apply to private servants who are in the sole employ of a diplomatic agent, on condition:

(*a*) that they are not nationals of or permanently resident in the receiving State; and

(*b*) that they are covered by the social security provisions which may be in force in the sending State or a third State.

3. A diplomatic agent who employs persons to whom the exemption provided for in paragraph 2 of this Article does not apply shall

observe the obligations which the social security provisions of the receiving State impose upon employers.

4. The exemption provided for in paragraphs 1 and 2 of this Article shall not preclude voluntary participation in the social security system of the receiving State provided that such participation is permitted by that State.

5. The provisions of this Article shall not affect bilateral or multilateral agreements concerning social security concluded previously and shall not prevent the conclusion of such agreements in the future.

Article 34

A diplomatic agent shall be exempt from all dues and taxes, personal or real, national, regional or municipal, except:

(*a*) indirect taxes of a kind which are normally incorporated in the price of goods or services;

(*b*) dues and taxes on private immovable property situated in the territory of the receiving State, unless he holds it on behalf of the sending State for the purposes of the mission;

(*c*) estate, succession or inheritance duties levied by the receiving State, subject to the provisions of paragraph 4 of Article 39;

(*d*) dues and taxes on private income having its source in the receiving State and capital taxes on investments made in commercial undertakings in the receiving State;

(*e*) charges levied for specific services rendered;

(*f*) registration, court or record fees, mortgage dues and stamp duty, with respect to immovable property, subject to the provisions of Article 23.

Article 35

The receiving State shall exempt diplomatic agents from all personal services, from all public service of any kind whatsoever, and from military obligations such as those connected with requisitioning, military contributions and billeting.

Article 36

1. The receiving State shall, in accordance with such laws and regulations as it may adopt, permit entry of and grant exemption

from all customs duties, taxes, and related charges other than charges for storage, cartage and similar services, on:

(*a*) articles for the official use of the mission;

(*b*) articles for the personal use of a diplomatic agent or members of his family forming part of his household, including articles intended for his establishment.

2. The personal baggage of a diplomatic agent shall be exempt from inspection, unless there are serious grounds for presuming that it contains articles not covered by the exemptions mentioned in paragraph 1 of this Article, or articles the import or export of which is prohibited by the law or controlled by the quarantine regulations of the receiving State. Such inspection shall be conducted only in the presence of the diplomatic agent or of his authorized representative.

ARTICLE 37

1. The members of the family of a diplomatic agent forming part of his household shall, if they are not nationals of the receiving State, enjoy the privileges and immunities specified in Articles 29 to 36.

2. Members of the administrative and technical staff of the mission, together with members of their families forming part of their respective households, shall, if they are not nationals of or permanently resident in the receiving State, enjoy the privileges and immunities specified in Articles 29 to 35, except that the immunity from civil and administrative jurisdiction of the receiving State specified in paragraph 1 of Article 31 shall not extend to acts performed outside the course of their duties. They shall also enjoy the privileges specified in Article 36, paragraph 1, in respect of articles imported at the time of first installation.

3. Members of the service staff of the mission who are not nationals of or permanently resident in the receiving State shall enjoy immunity in respect of acts performed in the course of their duties, exemption from dues and taxes on the emoluments they receive by reason of their employment and the exemption contained in Article 33.

4. Private servants of members of the mission shall, if they are not nationals of or permanently resident in the receiving State, be exempt from dues and taxes on the emoluments they receive by reason of their employment. In other respects, they may enjoy privileges and immunities only to the extent admitted by the receiving State. However, the receiving State must exercise its jurisdiction over those persons in such a manner as not to interfere unduly with the performance of the functions of the mission.

ARTICLE 38

1. Except insofar as additional privileges and immunities may be granted by the receiving State, a diplomatic agent who is a national of or permanently resident in that State shall enjoy only immunity from jurisdiction, and inviolability, in respect of official acts performed in the exercise of his functions.

2. Other members of the staff of the mission and private servants who are nationals of or permanently resident in the receiving State shall enjoy privileges and immunities only to the extent admitted by the receiving State. However, the receiving State must exercise its jurisdiction over those persons in such a manner as not to interfere unduly with the performance of the functions of the mission.

ARTICLE 39

1. Every person entitled to privileges and immunities shall enjoy them from the moment he enters the territory of the receiving State on proceeding to take up his post or, if already in its territory, from the moment when his appointment is notified to the Ministry for Foreign Affairs or such other ministry as may be agreed.

2. When the functions of a person enjoying privileges and immunities have come to an end, such privileges and immunities shall normally cease at the moment when he leaves the country, or on expiry of a reasonable period in which to do so, but shall subsist until that time, even in case of armed conflict. However, with respect to acts performed by such a person in the exercise of his functions as a member of the mission, immunity shall continue to subsist.

3. In case of the death of a member of the mission, the members of his family shall continue to enjoy the privileges and immunities to which they are entitled until the expiry of a reasonable period in which to leave the country.

4. In the event of the death of a member of the mission not a national of or permanently resident in the receiving State or a member of his family forming part of his household, the receiving State shall permit the withdrawal of the movable property of the deceased, with the exception of any property acquired in the country the export of which was prohibited at the time of his death. Estate, succession and inheritance duties shall not be levied on movable property the presence of which in the receiving State was due solely to the presence there of the deceased as a member of the mission or as a member of the family of a member of the mission.

ARTICLE 40

1. If a diplomatic agent passes through or is in the territory of a third State, which has granted him a passport visa if such visa was necessary, while proceeding to take up or to return to his post, or when returning to his own country, the third State shall accord him inviolability and such other immunities as may be required to ensure his transit or return. The same shall apply in the case of any members of his family enjoying privileges or immunities who are accompanying the diplomatic agent, or travelling separately to join him or to return to their country.

2. In circumstances similar to those specified in paragraph 1 of this Article, third States shall not hinder the passage of members of the administrative and technical or service staff of a mission, and of members of their families, through their territories.

3. Third States shall accord to official correspondence and other official communications in transit, including messages in code or cipher, the same freedom and protection as is accorded by the receiving State. They shall accord to diplomatic couriers, who have been granted a passport visa if such visa was necessary, and diplomatic bags in transit the same inviolability and protection as the receiving State is bound to accord.

4. The obligations of third States under paragraphs 1, 2 and 3 of this Article shall also apply to the persons mentioned respectively in those paragraphs, and to official communications and diplomatic bags, whose presence in the territory of the third State is due to *force majeure*.

ARTICLE 41

1. Without prejudice to their privileges and immunities, it is the duty of all persons enjoying such privileges and immunities to respect the laws and regulations of the receiving State. They also have a duty not to interfere in the internal affairs of that State.

2. All official business with the receiving State entrusted to the mission by the sending State shall be conducted with or through the Ministry for Foreign Affairs of the receiving State or such other ministry as may be agreed.

3. The premises of the mission must not be used in any manner incompatible with the functions of the mission as laid down in the present Convention or by other rules of general international law or by any special agreements in force between the sending and the receiving State.

ARTICLE 42

A diplomatic agent shall not in the receiving State practise for personal profit any professional or commercial activity.

ARTICLE 43

The function of a diplomatic agent comes to an end, *inter alia:*

(*a*) on notification by the sending State to the receiving State that the function of the diplomatic agent has come to an end;

(*b*) on notification by the receiving State to the sending State that, in accordance with paragraph 2 of Article 9, it refuses to recognize the diplomatic agent as a member of the mission.

ARTICLE 44

The receiving State must, even in case of armed conflict, grant facilities in order to enable persons enjoying privileges and immunities, other than nationals of the receiving State, and members of the families of such persons irrespective of their nationality, to leave at the earliest possible moment. It must, in particular, in case of need, place at their disposal the necessary means of transport for themselves and their property.

ARTICLE 45

If diplomatic relations are broken off between two States, or if a mission is permanently or temporarily recalled:

(*a*) the receiving State must, even in case of armed conflict, respect and protect the premises of the mission, together with its property and archives;

(*b*) the sending State may entrust the custody of the premises of the mission, together with its property and archives, to a third State acceptable to the receiving State;

(*c*) the sending State may entrust the protection of its interests and those of its nationals to a third State acceptable to the receiving State.

ARTICLE 46

A sending State may with the prior consent of a receiving State, and at the request of a third State not represented in the receiving

State, undertake the temporary protection of the interests of the third State and of its nationals.

ARTICLE 47

1. In the application of the provisions of the present Convention, the receiving State shall not discriminate as between States.

2. However, discrimination shall not be regarded as taking place:

(*a*) where the receiving State applies any of the provisions of the present Convention restrictively because of a restrictive application of that provision to its mission in the sending State;

(*b*) where by custom or agreement States extend to each other more favourable treatment than is required by the provisions of the present Convention.

ARTICLE 48

The present Convention shall be open for signature by all States Members of the United Nations or of any of the specialized agencies or Parties to the Statute of the International Court of Justice, and by any other State invited by the General Assembly of the United Nations to become a Party to the Convention, as follows: until 31 October 1961 at the Federal Ministry for Foreign Affairs of Austria and subsequently, until 31 March 1962, at the United Nations Headquarters in New York.

ARTICLE 49

The present Convention is subject to ratification. The instruments of ratification shall be deposited with the Secretary-General of the United Nations.

ARTICLE 50

The present Convention shall remain open for accession by any State belonging to any of the four categories mentioned in Article 48. The instruments of accession shall be deposited with the Secretary-General of the United Nations.

ARTICLE 51

1. The present Convention shall enter into force on the thirtieth day following the date of deposit of the twenty-second instrument of

ratification or accession with the Secretary-General of the United Nations.

2. For each State ratifying or acceding to the Convention after the deposit of the twenty-second instrument of ratification or accession, the Convention shall enter into force on the thirtieth day after deposit by such State of its instrument of ratification or accession.

ARTICLE 52

The Secretary-General of the United Nations shall inform all States belonging to any of the four categories mentioned in Article 48:

(a) of signatures to the present Convention and of the deposit of instruments of ratification or accession, in accordance with Articles 48, 49 and 50;

(b) of the date on which the present Convention will enter into force, in accordance with Article 51.

ARTICLE 53

The original of the present Convention, of which the Chinese, English, French, Russian and Spanish texts are equally authentic, shall be deposited with the Secretary-General of the United Nations, who shall send certified copies thereof to all states belonging to any of the four categories mentioned in Article 48.

IN WITNESS WHEREOF the undersigned Plenipotentiaries, being duly authorized thereto by their respective Governments, have signed the present Convention.

DONE AT VIENNA, this eighteenth day of April one thousand nine hundred and sixty-one.

APPENDIX B

Convention on the Prevention and Punishment of Crimes against Internationally Protected Persons, Including Diplomatic Agents*

The States Parties to this Convention,

Having in mind the purposes and principles of the Charter of the United Nations concerning the maintenance of international peace and the promotion of friendly relations and co-operation among States,

Considering that crimes against diplomatic agents and other internationally protected persons jeopardizing the safety of these persons create a serious threat to the maintenance of normal international relations which are necessary for co-operation among States,

Believing that the commission of such crimes is a matter of grave concern to the international community,

Convinced that there is an urgent need to adopt appropriate and effective measures for the prevention and punishment of such crimes,

Have agreed as follows:

ARTICLE 1

For the purposes of this Convention:

1. "internationally protected person" means:

(a) a Head of State, including any member of a collegial body performing the functions of a Head of State under the constitution of the State concerned, a Head of Government or a Minister for Foreign Affairs, whenever any such person is in a foreign State, as well as members of his family who accompany him;

(b) any representative or official of a State or any official or other

---

* Annex to United Nations General Assembly resolution, adopted December 14, 1973.

SOURCE: *Department of State Bulletin*, vol. 70 (January 28, 1974), pp. 92–95; TIAS 8532.

agent of an international organization of an intergovernmental character who, at the time when and in the place where a crime against him, his official premises, his private accommodation or his means of transport is committed, is entitled pursuant to international law to special protection from any attack on his person, freedom or dignity, as well as members of his family forming part of his household;

2. "alleged offender" means a person as to whom there is sufficent evidence to determine *prima facie* that he has committed or participated in one or more of the crimes set forth in article 2.

ARTICLE 2

1. The intentional commission of:

(a) a murder, kidnapping or other attack upon the person or liberty of an internationally protected person;

(b) a violent attack upon the official premises, the private accommodation or the means of transport of an internationally protected person likely to endanger his person or liberty;

(c) a threat to commit any such attack;

(d) an attempt to commit any such attack; and

(e) an act constituting participation as an accomplice in any such attack

shall be made by each State Party a crime under its internal law.

2. Each State Party shall make these crimes punishable by appropriate penalties which take into account their grave nature.

3. Paragraphs 1 and 2 of this article in no way derogate from the obligations of States Parties under international law to take all appropriate measures to prevent other attacks on the person, freedom or dignity of an internationally protected person.

ARTICLE 3

1. Each State Party shall take such measures as may be necessary to establish its jurisdiction over the crimes set forth in article 2 in the following cases:

(a) when the crime is committed in the territory of that State or on board a ship or aircraft registered in that State;

(b) when the alleged offender is a national of that State;

(c) when the crime is committed against an internationally protected person as defined in article 1 who enjoys his status as such by virtue of functions which he exercises on behalf of that State.

2. Each State Party shall likewise take such measures as may

be necessary to establish its jurisdiction over these crimes in cases where the alleged offender is present in its territory and it does not extradite him pursuant to article 8 to any of the States mentioned in paragraph 1 of this article.

3. This Convention does not exclude any criminal jurisdiction exercised in accordance with internal law.

ARTICLE 4

States Parties shall co-operate in the prevention of the crimes set forth in article 2, particularly by:

(a) taking all practicable measures to prevent preparations in their respective territories for the commission of those crimes within or outside their territories;

(b) exchanging information and co-ordinating the taking of administrative and other measures as appropriate to prevent the commission of those crimes.

ARTICLE 5

1. The State Party in which any of the crimes set forth in article 2 have been committed shall, if it has reason to believe that an alleged offender has fled from its territory, communicate to all other States concerned, directly or through the Secretary-General of the United Nations, all the pertinent facts regarding the crime committed and all available information regarding the identity of the alleged offender.

2. Whenever any of the crimes set forth in article 2 has been committed against an internationally protected person, any State Party which has information concerning the victim and the circumstances of the crime shall endeavour to transmit it, under the conditions provided for in its internal law, fully and promptly to the State Party on whose behalf he was exercising his functions.

ARTICLE 6

1. Upon being satisfied that the circumstances so warrant, the State Party in whose territory the alleged offender is present shall take the appropriate measures under its internal law so as to ensure his presence for the purpose of prosecution or extradition. Such measures shall be notified without delay directly or through the Secretary-General of the United Nations to:

(a) the State where the crime was committed;

(b) the State or States of which the alleged offender is a national or, if he is a stateless person, in whose territory he permanently resides;

(c) the State or States of which the internationally protected person concerned is a national or on whose behalf he was exercising his functions;

(d) all other States concerned; and

(e) the international organization of which the internationally protected person concerned is an official or an agent.

2. Any person regarding whom the measures referred to in paragraph 1 of this article are being taken shall be entitled:

(a) to communicate without delay with the nearest appropriate representative of the State of which he is a national or which is otherwise entitled to protect his rights or, if he is a stateless person, which he requests and which is willing to protect his rights; and

(b) to be visited by a representative of that State.

ARTICLE 7

The State Party in whose territory the alleged offender is present shall, if it does not extradite him, submit, without exception whatsoever and without undue delay, the case to its competent authorities for the purpose of prosecution, through proceedings in accordance with the laws of that State.

ARTICLE 8

1. To the extent that the crimes set forth in article 2 are not listed as extraditable offenses in any extradition treaty existing between States Parties, they shall be deemed to be included as such therein. States Parties undertake to include those crimes as extraditable offenses in every future extradition treaty to be concluded between them.

2. If a State Party which makes extradition conditional on the existence of a treaty receives a request for extradition from another State Party with which it has no extradition treaty, it may, if it decides to extradite, consider this Convention as the legal basis for extradition in respect of those crimes. Extradition shall be subject to the procedural provisions and the other conditions of the law of the requested State.

3. States Parties which do not make extradition conditional on the existence of a treaty shall recognize those crimes as extraditable

offenses between themselves subject to the procedural provisions and the other conditions of the law of the requested State.

4. Each of the crimes shall be treated, for the purpose of extradition between States Parties, as if it had been committed not only in the place in which it occurred but also in the territories of the States required to establish their jurisdiction in accordance with paragraph 1 of article 3.

ARTICLE 9

Any person regarding whom proceedings are being carried out in connexion with any of the crimes set forth in article 2 shall be guaranteed fair treatment at all stages of the proceedings.

ARTICLE 10

1. States Parties shall afford one another the greatest measure of assistance in connexion with criminal proceedings brought in respect of the crimes set forth in article 2, including the supply of all evidence at their disposal necessary for the proceedings.

2. The provisions of paragraph 1 of this article shall not affect obligations concerning mutual judicial assistance embodied in any other treaty.

ARTICLE 11

The State Party where an alleged offender is prosecuted shall communicate the final outcome of the proceedings to the Secretary-General of the United Nations, who shall transmit the information to the other States Parties.

ARTICLE 12

The provisions of this Convention shall not affect the application of the Treaties on Asylum, in force at the date of the adoption of this Convention, as between the States which are parties to those Treaties; but a State Party to this Convention may not invoke those . Treaties with respect to another State Party to this Convention which is not a party to those Treaties.

ARTICLE 13

1. Any dispute between two or more States Parties concerning the interpretation or application of this Convention which is not settled by negotiation shall, at the request of one of them, be submitted to arbitration. If within six months from the date of the request for arbitration the parties are unable to agree on the organization of the arbitration, any one of these parties may refer the dispute to the International Court of Justice by request in conformity with the Statute of the Court.

2. Each State Party may at the time of signature or ratification of this Convention or accession thereto declare that it does not consider itself bound by paragraph 1 of this article. The other States Parties shall not be bound by paragraph 1 of this article with respect to any State Party which has made such a reservation.

3. Any State Party which has made a reservation in accordance with paragraph 2 of this article may at any time withdraw that reservation by notification to the Secretary-General of the United Nations.

ARTICLE 14

This Convention shall be open for signature by all States, until 31 December 1974 at United Nations Headquarters in New York.

ARTICLE 15

This Convention is subject to ratification. The instruments of ratification shall be deposited with the Secretary-General of the United Nations.

ARTICLE 16

This Convention shall remain open for accession by any State. The instruments of accession shall be deposited with the Secretary-General of the United Nations.

ARTICLE 17

1. This Convention shall enter into force on the thirtieth day following the date of deposit of the twenty-second instrument of ratification or accession with the Secretary-General of the United Nations.

2. For each State ratifying or acceding to the Convention after the deposit of the twenty-second instrument of ratification or accession, the Convention shall enter into force on the thirtieth day after deposit by such State of its instrument of ratification or accession.

ARTICLE 18

1. Any State Party may denounce this Convention by written notification to the Secretary-General of the United Nations.

2. Denunciation shall take effect six months following the date on which notification is received by the Secretary-General of the United Nations.

ARTICLE 19

The Secretary-General of the United Nations shall inform all States, *inter alia*:

(a) of signatures to this Convention, of the deposit of instruments of ratification or accession in accordance with articles 14, 15 and 16 and of notifications made under article 18.

(b) of the date on which this Convention will enter into force in accordance with article 17.

ARTICLE 20

The original of this Convention, of which the Chinese, English, French, Russian and Spanish texts are equally authentic, shall be deposited with the Secretary-General of the United Nations, who shall send certified copies thereof to all States.

IN WITNESS WHEREOF the undersigned, being duly authorized thereto by their respective Governments, have signed this Convention, opened for signature at New York on 14 December 1973.

APPENDIX C

Functions of Chiefs of Diplomatic Missions

The problem of coordinating the functions, responsibility, and authority of diplomatic chiefs of mission with those of other U. S. government representatives and agencies abroad has plagued the White House and Department of State since World War II. The documents included in this appendix represent selected presidential treatment of the central role of the American ambassador in the country to which he is accredited. These documents reflect several parallel progressions:

1. Form—from basic executive orders, to presidential communication to chiefs of government agencies, to presidential letters sent directly to American ambassadors in the field.
2. Functions—from simple "coordination," to "coordination and supervision," to "oversight and coordination," to "direction and coordination," to "direction, coordination, and supervision."
3. Responsibility and authority—from "responsibility," to "affirmative responsibility," to "authority and responsibility."

SOURCES: For commentary and selected documents covering the period from 1942 to 1961, see United States Senate, Committee on Government Operations, Subcommittee on National Security Staffing and Operations, *The Ambassador and the Problem of Coordination* (Washington, D.C.: Government Printing Office, 1963). The Truman, Eisenhower, and Kennedy documents appear at pp. 115–116, 147, 149–150, and 155–156; the Nixon letter is from the *Department of State Bulletin*, vol. 62 (January 12, 1970), pp. 30–31; and the Carter letter is from Department of State, *Digest of United States Practice in International Law, 1977* (Washington, D.C.: Government Printing Office, 1979), pp. 244–246.

Harry S. Truman (1952)

EXECUTIVE ORDER 10338, APRIL 4, 1952

By virtue of the authority vested in me . . . and as President of the United States and Commander in Chief of the armed forces of the United States, it is ordered as follows:

SECTION 1. *Functions of the Chief of the United States Diplomatic Mission.*—(a) The Chief of the United States Diplomatic Mission in each country, as the representative of the President and acting on his behalf, shall coordinate the activities of the United States representatives (including the chiefs of economic missions, military assistance advisory groups, and other representatives of agencies of the United States Government) in such country engaged in carrying out programs under the Mutual Security Act of 1951 . . . and he shall assume responsibility for assuring the unified development and execution of the said programs in such country. More particularly, the functions of each Chief of United States Diplomatic Mission shall include, with respect to the programs and country concerned:

(1) Exercising general direction and leadership of the entire effort.

(2) Assuring that recommendations and prospective plans and actions of the United States representatives are effectively coordinated and are consistent with and in furtherance of the established policy of the United States.

(3) Assuring that the interpretation and application of instructions received by the United States representatives from higher authority are in accord with the established policy of the United States.

(4) Guiding the United States representatives in working out measures to prevent duplication in their efforts and to promote the most effective and efficient use of all United States officers and employees having mutual security responsibilities.

(5) Keeping the United States representatives fully informed as to current and prospective United States policies.

(6) Prescribing procedures governing the coordination of the activities of the United States representatives, and assuring that these representatives shall have access to all available information essential to the accomplishment of their prescribed duties.

(7) Preparing and submitting such reports on the operation and status of the programs under the Act as may be directed by the Director for Mutual Security.

(b) Each Chief of United States Diplomatic Mission shall perform his functions under this order in accordance with instructions from higher authority and subject to established policies and programs of the United States.

(c) No Chief of United States Diplomatic Mission shall delegate any function conferred upon him by the provisions of this order which directly involves the exercise of direction, coordination, or authority.

* * *

Dwight D. Eisenhower (1960)

Executive Order 10893, November 8, 1960

(Extract)

Part II. Coordination and Supervision of Functions Abroad

Sec. 201. *Functions of Chiefs of United States Diplomatic Missions.*—The several Chiefs of the United States Diplomatic Missions in foreign countries, as the representatives of the President and acting on his behalf, shall have and exercise, to the extent permitted by law and in accordance with such instructions as the President may from time to time promulgate, affirmative responsibility for the coordination and supervision over the carrying out by agencies of their functions in the respective countries.

To the Heads of Executive Departments and Agencies, November 8, 1960

* * *

It is my desire that all appropriate steps be taken to assure that the Chief of the United States Diplomatic Mission is effective in discharging his role as the representative of the President. Therefore, I am instructing that, to the extent permitted by law and within the framework of established policies and programs of the United States, the Chief of Mission shall have and exercise affirmative responsibility for the coordination and supervision of all United States activities in the country to which he is accredited. It is expected that particular emphasis will be given to the following in the exercise of this authority: (1) the Chief of Mission will take affirmative responsibility for the development, coordination, and administration of diplomatic, informational, educational, and trade activities and programs; economic, technical and financial assistance; military assistance; and the disposal of surplus agricultural commodities abroad (2) the Chief of Mission will assure compliance with standards established by higher authority, and will recommend appropriate changes in such standards and suggest desirable new standards, governing the personal conduct and the level of services and privileges accorded all United States civilian and military personnel stationed in the foreign country and report to the President upon adherence to such standards, and (3) the Chief of Mission will establish procedures so that he is kept informed of United States activities in the country. He will report promptly to the President as to any matter which he considers to need correction and with respect to which is not empowered to effect correction.

In order that there be full understanding of the above, it is my desire that the Chief of Mission be made fully aware of his responsibilities and authority with respect to United States activities, in the country to which he is assigned, under today's order and this memorandum. Not only should instructions be issued to the United States Missions; provision should also be made for complete instruction in these matters before a new Chief of Mission assumes his duties at his post. It is the responsibility of each agency concerned to participate in the indoctrination of each Chief of Mission and take steps within the agency to instruct its personnel as to the authority of the Chief of Mission and as to the necessity of keeping him fully informed concerning current and prospective program and administrative activities.

* * *

John F. Kennedy (1961)

To Chiefs of Mission, May 29, 1961

Dear Mr. Ambassador: Please accept my best wishes for the successful accomplishment of your mission. As the personal representative of the President of the United States in . . . . you are part of a memorable tradition which began with Benjamin Franklin and Thomas Jefferson, and which has included many of our most distinguished citizens.

* * *

I have asked you to represent our Government in . . . . because I am confident that you have the ability, dedication, and experience. The purpose of this letter is to define guidelines which I hope may be helpful to you.

* * *

. . ., the manner in which you and your staff personally conduct yourselves is of the utmost importance. This applies to the way in which you carry out your official duties and to the attitudes you and they bring to day-to-day contacts and associations.

It is an essential part of your task to create a climate of dignified, dedicated understanding, cooperation, and service in and around the Embassy.

In regard to your personal authority and responsibility, I shall count on you to oversee and coordinate all the activities of the United States Government in . . . .

You are in charge of the entire United States Diplomatic Mission, and I shall expect you to supervise all of its operations. The Mission includes not only the personnel of the Department of State and the Foreign Service, but also the representatives of all other United States agencies which have programs or activities in . . . . I shall give you full support and backing in carrying out your assignment.

Needless to say, the representatives of other agencies are expected to communicate directly with their offices here in Washington, and in the event of a decision by you in which they do not concur, they may ask to have the decision reviewed by a higher authority in Washington.

However, it is their responsibility to keep you fully informed of their views and activities and to abide by your decisions unless in some particular instance you and they are notified to the contrary.

If in your judgment individual members of the Mission are not functioning effectively, you should take whatever action you feel may be required, reporting the circumstances, of course, to the Department of State.

In case the departure from . . . . of any individual member of the Mission is indicated in your judgment, I shall expect you to make the decision and see that it is carried into effect. Such instances I am confident will be rare.

* * *

I have informed all heads of departments and agencies of the Government of the responsibilities of the Chiefs of American Diplomatic Missions for our combined operations abroad, and I have asked them to instruct their representatives in the field accordingly.

As you know, your own lines of communication as Chief of Mission run through the Department of State.

Let me close with an expression of confidence in you personally and the earnest hope that your efforts may help strengthen our relations with both the Government and the people of . . . . I am sure that you will make a major contribution to the cause of world peace and understanding.

Good luck and my warmest regards,

Sincerely,

(Signed)　JOHN F. KENNEDY

Richard M. Nixon (1969)

To U.S. AMBASSADORS, DECEMBER 9, 1969

DEAR MR. AMBASSADOR: Your mission as American Ambassador to (country of assignment) is of the utmost significance to our country and to me personally. I wish you every success in this endeavor.

I attach the greatest importance to my Constitutional responsibilities for the conduct of our relations with other countries. As the personal representative of the President of the United States, you share these responsibilities in the country to which you are accredited.

You will, of course, report to me through and normally receive your instructions from the Secretary of State who has responsibility not only for the activities of the Department of State but also for the overall direction, coordination and supervision of the United States Government activities overseas.

I believe that all possible measures should be taken to improve and tighten the processes of foreign policy implementation abroad. I know I can count on your full support in directing the activities of all elements of the United States Mission to achieve this objective. To assure you and all concerned that you have my full personal backing, I want to make the following comments on your own authority and responsibilities.

As Chief of the United States Diplomatic Mission, you have full responsibility to direct and coordinate the activities and operations of all of its elements. You will exercise this mandate not only by providing policy leadership and guidance, but also by assuring positive program direction to the end that all United States activities in (the host country) are relevant to current realities, are efficiently and economically administered, and are effectively interrelated so that they will make a maximum contribution to United States interests in that country as well as to our regional and international objectives.

I am concerned that the size of our representation abroad be related to a stringent appraisal of policy and program requirements and that the number of personnel of all agencies be kept at the very minimum necessary to meet our objectives. I shall expect you to maintain a continuing personal concern on this matter and to inform the Secretary of State when you believe that the staff of any agency or program is excessive.

I shall expect you to assure the highest standards of personal conduct by all United States personnel, civilian or military; you have authority to take any corrective action which in your judgment is necessary.

* * *

With my best wishes,
Sincerely,
RICHARD NIXON

Jimmy Carter (1977)

To U.S. AMBASSADORS, OCTOBER 25, 1977

Please accept my personal best wishes for success in your mission. As my personal representative, you will share with me and with the Secretary of State the responsibility for the conduct of our relations with ——————.

I want to state clearly that, as Chief of the United States Diplomatic Mission to ——————, and my representative, you have the strongest mandate possible. As P.L. 93–475 [the State Department Authorization Act for Fiscal Year 1975] states, you have "full responsibility for the direction, coordination, and supervision of all United States Government officers and employees" in your country of accreditation. This authority includes all United States Government programs and activities in that country. The only exceptions to this rule are personnel under the Chief of a United States Mission accredited to an international organization, personnel detailed to duty with international organizations, and, as stated in P.L. 93–475, "personnel under the command of a United States area military commander." I expect you to provide positive program direction, assuring that all United States Government activities under the authority of your Mission reflect and support current United States policy, are effectively coordinated, and are economically administered.

I expect the highest standards of professional and personal conduct by the personnel from all agencies assigned to our missions abroad. As my personal representative you have the authority and my full support in taking actions required to assure that these standards are maintained. All United States Government personnel in your country of assignment should be made aware of your authority and responsibilities. It is their duty to keep you thoroughly and currently informed about all their activities so you can effectively direct, coordinate and supervise United States programs and operations under your jurisdiction and recommend missionwide policies to Washington.

* * *

I have notified all heads of departments and agencies of the Government concerning the authority and responsibilities of the Chiefs of American Diplomatic Missions, and I have asked them to inform their personnel in the field accordingly.

You have my personal confidence as you undertake your mission. I am sure that you will represent our country with the skill, dedication and goodwill which your post demands.

Literature on Diplomacy

Commentary

The French diplomatist Jules Jusserand wrote that the ancient art of diplomacy "reached, in the fifteenth and immediately following centuries, such prominence as to become the subject of numerous treatises in Latin, French, Italian, Spanish." An extensive diplomatic literature developed in English, German, Russian, and other languages during the nineteenth and twentieth centuries. Over the years the analysis of the subject was enriched by the commentaries of such eminent diplomatists as Francoise de Callieres (*De la Manière de Négocier avec les Souverains*, 1716), Jules M. Cambon (*Le Diplomate*, 1926; *The Diplomatist*, translated by C. R. Turner, 1931), Otto Krauske (*Die Entwicklung der Staendigen Diplomatie*, 1885), Vladimir Petrovich Potemkin (*Histoire de la Diplomatie*, translated by Xenia Pamphilova and Michel Emistor, 2 vols., 1946), Paul L. E. Pradier-Fodéré (*Cours de Droit Diplomatique*, 2 vols., 1881), and Abraham van Wicquefort (*The Ambassador and His Functions*, translated by Digby, 2 vols., 1681). Other substantial studies, largely in French, were written by Jean Dumont (8 vols.) in the eighteenth century, and by Ferdinand de Cussy, Guillaume de Garden (3 vols.), Charles de Martens (2 vols.), and August Heinrich Meisel (2 vols.) in the nineteenth century.

More recently, these have been augmented by the writings of such well-known British diplomatists as Sir Harold Nicolson (*Diplomacy*, 1939, and *The Evolution of Diplomatic Method*, 1954), Sir Ernest M. Satow (*A Guide to Diplomatic Practice*, 4th ed., 1957), William S. Strang (*The Diplomatic Career*, 1962), and Sir Charles K. Webster (*The Art and Practice of Diplomacy*, 1952); the more specialized monographs of Sir Douglas Busk (*The Craft of Diplomacy*, 1967) and Lord Maurice P. Hankey (*Diplomacy by Conference*, 1946); and the post–World War II essays of Sir Duff Cooper, Sir Ivone Kirkpatrick,

A. J. P. Taylor, Lord Robert F. Vansittart, and others. In the meantime, the library of general analyses in other languages has proliferated in the twentieth century; it is represented by Raoul Genet (*Traité de Diplomatie et de Droit Diplomatique*, 3 vols., 1931–32) and by such analysts of modern diplomacy as Farag Moussa (*Manuel de Pratique Diplomatique: L'Ambassade*, 1972), Jaime Peralta (*La Institucion Diplomática*, 1951), Leon van der Essen (*La Diplomatie*, 1953), and a good many other, similar treatises.

The record of contribution by U.S. diplomats, by comparison, is quite different. Not only is it of relatively recent vintage; it is also disappointingly meager. A few studies were published after World War I and the creation of the American career diplomatic service, including Hugh Robert Wilson (*The Education of a Diplomat*, 1938), Hugh S. Gibson (*The Road to Foreign Policy*, 1944), and William C. Bullitt (*The Great Globe Itself*, 1946). Only recently, however, have broad surveys been produced by American diplomats. These include Charles W. Thayer (*Diplomat*, 1959; in its preface Sir Harold Nicolson called this work "the first comprehensive report written by a professional United States diplomatist and from the American point of view"), Ellis O. Briggs (*Anatomy of Diplomacy*, 1968), and William Macomber (*The Angels' Game: A Handbook of Modern Diplomacy*, 1975). Other commentary includes essays by a number of practitioners, such as George W. Ball, Loy W. Henderson, George F. Kennan, Foy D. Kohler, Livingston T. Merchant, and Robert D. Murphy. Additional ventures, by noncareerists, include Thomas A. Bailey (*The Art of Diplomacy*, 1968; a collection of some 260 maxims with commentary) and Eric Clark (*Diplomat: The World of International Diplomacy*, 1974).

Some American studies, written largely by outside commentators, have concentrated primarily on diplomatic practitioners. These include, for example, Gordon A. Craig and Felix Gilbert, eds. (*The Diplomats, 1919–1939*, 2 vols., 1953), John Ensor Harr (*The Professional Diplomat*, 1969), Elmer Plischke (*United States Diplomats and Their Missions: A Profile of American Diplomatic Emissaries since 1778*, 1975), and E. Wilder Spaulding (*Ambassadors Ordinary and Extraordinary*, 1961). Careerists, government officials, and academics have devoted a good deal more literary attention to the more limited task of describing, assessing, criticizing, and reforming the career Foreign Service.

A few analysts, largely persons outside the professional diplomatic community, have written about diplomacy as an institution or function. Among these are E. A. J. Johnson (*The Dimensions of Diplomacy*, 1964), Stephen D. Kertesz (*American Diplomacy in a New*

Era, 1961), Arthur Ponsonby (*Democracy and Diplomacy*, 1915), Kenneth W. Thompson (*American Diplomacy and Emergent Patterns*, 1962), H. Bradford Westerfield (*The Instruments of America's Foreign Policy*, 1963), Henry M. Wriston (*Diplomacy in a Democracy*, 1956), and Charles W. Yost (*The Conduct and Misconduct of Foreign Affairs*, 1972).

These treatises and compilations have been supplemented by a series of textual volumes, broad in scope, on the conduct of American foreign relations. They include works by John W. Foster (before World War I) and by Malbone W. Graham, James L. McCamy, John M. Mathews, Elmer Plischke, Graham H. Stuart, Benjamin H. Williams, and Quincy Wright. These studies, listed in the bibliography, vary considerably in content and treatment, and most of them devote considerable attention to American constitutional and political practices, foreign policy making, and the bureaucratic and foreign relations personnel systems.

Systematic and comprehensive studies of the various categories of U.S. diplomatic envoys and other officials engaged in foreign relations activities are relatively rare. While E. Wilder Spaulding distinguishes various types of ambassadors (ranging from the "old masters" to "the female of the species" and from journalists, academicians, and "men of letters" to "the pros"), he tends to stress the background of emissaries rather than their pragmatic functioning. A number of other writers have chosen to address themselves to individual categories of diplomats and their activities. For example, Lee H. Burke analyzes the relatively recent position of the *Ambassador at Large* (1972), Maurice Waters surveys the activities of *The Ad Hoc Diplomat* (1963), Roy F. Nichols expounds on *Advance Agents of American Destiny* (1956), Henry M. Wriston deals with *Executive Agents in American Foreign Relations* (1929) and "The Special Envoy" (*Foreign Affairs*, 1960), Charles O. Paullin describes the *Diplomatic Negotiations of American Naval Officers* (1912), Alfred Vagts reviews the functions of *The Military Attaché* (1967), Jon L. Boyes addresses himself to the capacities of "The Political Adviser (POLAD)" as diplomatic counselor to U.S. military commanders (Ph.D. dissertation, 1971), and John C. Butner has produced a pilot study on the role of "Congressmen-Diplomats" (Ph.D. dissertation, 1977). Such literature is largely the production of persons outside the diplomatic profession.

This brief survey attests that interest in, and English language literature on, diplomatic affairs and envoys expanded in quantity and quality to a remarkable degree after World War II. The contribution of basic, comprehensive studies by American professionals, however, has been far from impressive. Much of the literary production, even if broad in scope and treatment, has been textual and monographic and, as might be anticipated, its growth and emphases were neither clearly planned nor systematically executed. Hundreds of specialized studies and essays supplementing the standard volumes and textual materials have focused more particularly on a small number of central functional issues or key agents and institutions in the foreign relations process. Writers have given special attention to the roles of the President, the Secretary of State, and the Foreign Service, together with foreign policy making, top-level interagency coordination (including the operation of the National Security Council system and other components of the federal bureaucracy), the coordination of the Department of State with other agency activities abroad, and the overseas "country team."

Writers have given equally generous literary attention to the roles in external affairs played by decision makers, the information media and public opinion, elites and special interest groups, the military, and the intelligence community and the foreign aid and other related administrative agencies. These have complemented some of the older, more traditional areas of concentration, such as treaty making, peace keeping and peaceful change, and the methods of settling international disputes amicably. Contemporary studies have refined the study of settling disputes into such specialties as "problem solving," "conflict resolution," "crisis management," and the more amorphous "peace research"; each of these categories has developed its own esoteric literature. Other studies have emphasized such matters as functional formalization, international integration, simulation, prediction, gamesmanship, cybernetics, and other forms of systematic analysis.

In the United States the principal literary expansion since 1945 has centered on three types of materials. The first of these, understandably attractive to both authors and readers, concerns the making and substantive nature of foreign policy, with more emphasis on policy essence or "policy science" than on diplomatic practitioners and the techniques of implementing foreign affairs. Second, also of widespread interest, is the literature that simply chronicles the concerns of the United States with particular foreign policy developments. There are dozens of volumes, often presented as diplomatic history, that may be loosely described as "case studies" of American policy and action in selected sets of international circumstances. The third category consists of the rich reservoir of autobiographies, biographies, commentaries, diaries, and memoirs by and about diplomats, consuls, presidents, secretaries of state, and other officials engaged in foreign affairs. Some of these are excellent, apperceptive, and penetrating studies. Others are largely public relations accounts motivated by visions of immortality and the best seller list and the remainder fall into the category of routine "I-was-there-when" reminiscences.

Portions of this literature are pedestrian, if not unconcerned with diplomacy as a profession or an art; much of it contributes positively to understanding the complex interrelations of nations. Nevertheless, writers in this field have neglected several important matters: an analysis of diplomacy as the primary process whereby governments conduct their official relations; the application of the "diplomatic" rather than some other perspective on foreign affairs; and the effects of various types of diplomatic mission structure and staffing. Even the memoirs of the professionals recount events or chronicle policy relations to a greater degree than they examine and assess their diplomatic profession. Moreover, their commentaries tend to be more concerned with the role of the United States in world affairs or with the Department of State and the career Foreign Service than with an analysis of the diplomatic art.

Selected Bibliography

This bibliography consists of books, monographs, and a few official reports on the art of diplomacy, the conduct of foreign relations, and diplomatic practice and practitioners. It does not emphasize American diplomatic history or materials on constitutional issues, the Presidency and Congress, the Department of State, the federal bureaucracy, or organizational and personnel reform. In addition to the bibliographies contained in individual entries listed below, further overall guidance may be found in:

Boyce, Richard Fyfe and Boyce, Katherine Randall. *American Foreign Service Authors: A Bibliography*. Metuchen, N.J.: Scarecrow, 1973. 321 p.

Conover, Helen Field, ed. *A Guide to Bibliographic Tools for Research in Foreign Affairs*. 2nd ed. Washington, D.C.: Library of Congress, 1958. 160 p.

Council on Foreign Relations. *Foreign Affairs Bibliography: A Selected and Annotated List of Books on International Relations*. New York: Harper or Bowker, several volumes covering sequential periods since 1919, published periodically since 1933. Compiled by various editors.

Harmon, Robert B., ed. *The Art and Practice of Diplomacy: A Selected and Annotated Guide.* Metuchen, N.J.: Scarecrow, 1971. 355 p.

Hart, Albert Bushnell. "A Trial Bibliography of American Diplomacy." *American Historical Review* 6 (1901): 848–66.

Plischke, Elmer. "Research on the Conduct of United States Foreign Relations." *International Studies Quarterly* 15 (1971): 221–50.

Rappaport, Armin. *Sources in American Diplomacy.* New York: Macmillan, 1966.

Simpson, Smith, ed. "Resources and Needs of American Diplomacy." *Annals of the American Academy of Political and Social Science* 380 (November 1968): 144 p.

Guidance to biographical, autobiographical, and memoir literature may also be found in:

Plischke, Elmer. *American Diplomacy: A Bibliography of Biographies, Autobiographies, and Commentaries.* College Park, Maryland: Bureau of Governmental Research, University of Maryland, 1957. 27 p.

Plischke, Elmer. "Bibliography on United States Diplomacy," Section entitled "Bibliography of Autobiographies, Biographies, Commentaries, and Memoirs." In *Instruction in Diplomacy: The Liberal Arts Approach,* edited by Smith Simpson. Monograph No. 13 of the American Academy of Political and Social Science, 1972, pp. 299–342.

A number of studies define and analyze basic concepts and theoretical considerations or provide glossaries of terminology important to diplomatic practice, including:

Bailey, Thomas A. *A Diplomatic History of the American People.* 9th ed. Englewood Cliffs, N.J.: Prentice-Hall, 1974. "Glossary of Diplomatic Terms," pp. 957–61, which defines 165 expressions used in American diplomatic history.

Gamboa, Melquiades J. *Elements of Diplomatic and Consular Practice: A Glossary.* Quezon City, Philippines: Central Lawbook, 1966. 489 p. A dictionary of some 950 terms and acronyms used in diplomatic practice.

Harmon, Robert B. *The Art and Practice of Diplomacy: A Selected and Annotated Guide.* Metuchen, N.J.: Scarecrow, 1971. "Glossary of Diplomatic Terms," pp. 160–74, which defines some 135 concepts.

Lerche, Charles O., Jr., and Said, Abdul A. *Concepts of International*

Politics. 3rd ed. Englewood Cliffs, N.J.: Prentice-Hall, 1979. Especially Chapters 2–6 and 10, which deal with diplomatic techniques and related matters.

Plischke, Elmer. *Conduct of American Diplomacy*. 3rd ed. Princeton, N.J.: Van Nostrand, 1967. "Glossary," pp. 643–51, which defines more than 100 terms and concepts employed in American diplomacy.

* * *

Akzin, Benjamin. *Propaganda By Diplomats*. Washington, D.C.: Digest, 1936. 22 p.

American Assembly. *The Representation of the United States Abroad*. New York: American Assembly, Columbia University, 1956. 217 p.

Armstrong, Hamilton Fish, ed. *Fifty Years of Foreign Affairs*. New York: Praeger, for Council on Foreign Relations, 1972. 501 p.

d'Auvergne, Edmund and Franck, Basil. *Envoys Extraordinary*. London: Harrap, 1937. 317 p.

Bailey, Thomas A. *The Art of Diplomacy: The American Experience*. New York: Appleton-Century-Crofts, 1968. 303 p. Bib.

Barnes, William and Morgan, John Heath. *The Foreign Service of the United States: Origins, Development, and Functions*. Washington, D.C.: Government Printing Office, 1961. 430 p. Bib.

Barnett, Vincent M., Jr., ed. *The Representation of the United States Abroad*. New York: Praeger, 1965. 251 p.

Bartos, Otomar J. *Process and Outcome of Negotiations*. New York: Columbia University Press, 1974. 451 p.

Baumann, Carol Edler. *The Diplomatic Kidnappings: A Revolutionary Tactic of Urban Terrorism*. The Hague: Nijhoff, 1973. 182 p.

Beichman, Arnold. *The "Other" State Department: The United States Mission to the United Nations—Its Role In the Making of Foreign Policy*. New York: Basic Books, 1967. 221 p.

Beloff, Max. *Foreign Policy and the Democratic Process*. Baltimore: Johns Hopkins Press, 1955. 134 p.

Blancke, W. Wendell. *The Foreign Service of the United States*. New York: Praeger, 1969. 286 p.

Bonner, Paul H. *Ambassador Extraordinary*. New York: Scribner, 1962. 306 p.

Borchard, Edwin M. *The Diplomatic Protection of Citizens Abroad: Or, the Law of International Claims*. New York: Banks, 1915; New York: Banks, 1928. 988 p. Bib.

Briggs, Ellis O. *Anatomy of Diplomacy: The Origin and Execution of American Foreign Policy*. New York: McKay, 1968. 248 p.

Buchan, Alastair. *Crisis Management: The New Diplomacy.* Boulogne-sur-Seine: Atlantic Institute, 1966. 63 p.

Buchanan, Wiley T., Jr. *Red Carpet At the White House: Four Years As Chief of Protocol in the Eisenhower Administration.* New York: Dutton, 1964. 256 p.

Burke, Lee H. *Ambassador At Large: Diplomat Extraordinary.* The Hague: Nijhoff, 1972. 176 p. Bib.

Burton, John W. *Systems, States, Diplomacy and Rules.* London: Cambridge University Press, 1968. 251 p.

Busk, Douglas. *The Craft of Diplomacy: How to Run a Diplomatic Service.* New York: Praeger, 1967. 293 p.

Cadieux, Marcel. *The Canadian Diplomat.* Toronto: University of Toronto Press, 1962. 113 p.

Calkin, Homer L. *Women In the Department of State: Their Role In American Foreign Affairs.* 2nd ed. Washington, D.C.: Government Printing Office, 1978. 307 p.

Callieres, Francoise de. *On the Manner of Negotiating With Princes.* Translated by A. F. Whyte. Boston: Houghton Mifflin, 1919. 145 p.

Cambon, Jules M. *The Diplomatist.* Translated by C. R. Turner. London: Allan, 1931. 151 p.

Childs, James Rives. *American Foreign Service.* New York: Holt, 1948. 261 p.

Clark, Eric. *Diplomat: The World of International Diplomacy.* New York: Taplinger, 1974. 276 p.

Claude, Inis L., Jr. *The Impact of Public Opinion Upon Foreign Policy and Diplomacy: Open Diplomacy Revisited.* The Hague: Mouton, 1965. 21 p.

Cleveland, Harlan; Mangone, Gerard J.; and Adams, John Clarke. *The Overseas Americans.* New York: McGraw-Hill, 1960. 316 p.

Cleveland, Harlan and Mangone, Gerard J., eds. *The Art of Overseasmanship: Americans At Work Abroad.* Syracuse, N.Y.: Syracuse University Press, 1957. 150 p.

Corbett, Percy E. *Law In Diplomacy.* Princeton, N.J.: Princeton University Press, 1959. 290 p.

Craig, Gordon A. and Gilbert, Felix, eds. *The Diplomats: 1919–1939.* 2 vols. Princeton, N.J.: Princeton University Press, 1953.

Creaghe, John S. "Personal Qualities and Effective Diplomatic Negotiation." Ph.D. dissertation, University of Maryland, 1965. 314 p. Bib.

Crosswell, Carol M. *Protection of International Personnel Abroad.* New York: Oceana, 1952. 198 p.

Davis, Nathaniel P. *Few Dull Moments: A Foreign Service Career.* Philadelphia: Dunlap, 1967. 158 p.

Delaney, Robert Finley. *Your Future In the Foreign Service.* New York: Richards Rosen, 1961. 158 p.

Dennett, Raymond and Johnson, Joseph E., eds. *Negotiating With the Russians.* Boston: World Peace Foundation, 1951. 310 p.

Do Nascimento e Silva, Geraldo E. *Diplomacy In International Law.* Leiden: Sijthoff, 1972. 217 p.

Dunham, Donald C. *Envoy Unextraordinary.* New York: Day, 1944. 162 p.

Dunn, Frederick S. *The Practice and Procedure of International Conferences.* Baltimore: Johns Hopkins Press, 1929. 229 p.

Eayres, James. *Diplomacy and Its Discontents.* Toronto: University of Toronto Press, 1971. 198 p.

Elder, Robert E. *Overseas Representation and Services for Federal Domestic Agencies.* New York: Carnegie Endowment, 1965. 106 p.

Eller, George. *Secret Diplomacy.* London: Swift, 1912. 214 p.

Etzold, Thomas H. *The Conduct of American Foreign Relations: The Other Side of Diplomacy.* New York: New Viewpoints, Watts, 1977. 159 p. Bib.

Eubank, Keith. *The Summit Conferences, 1919–1960.* Norman, Oklahoma: University of Oklahoma Press, 1966. 225 p.

Feller, Abraham H. and Hudson, Manley O., eds. *A Collection of the Diplomatic and Consular Laws and Regulations of Various Countries.* 2 vols. Washington, D.C.: Carnegie Endowment, 1933.

Fisher, Glen H. *Public Diplomacy and the Behavioral Sciences.* Bloomington: Indiana University Press, 1972. 180 p.

Foreign Policy Association. *A Cartoon History of United States Foreign Policy, 1776–1976.* New York: Morrow, 1976. 210 p.

Forgac, Albert T. *New Diplomacy and the United Nations.* New York: Pageant, 1965. 173 p. Bib.

Foster, John W. *The Practice of Diplomacy As Illustrated In the Foreign Relations of the United States.* Boston: Houghton Mifflin, 1906. 401 p. Bib.

Franck, Thomas M. and Weisband, Edward, eds. *Secrecy and Foreign Policy.* New York: Oxford University Press, 1974. 453 p.

Franklin, William M. *Protection of Foreign Interests: A Study In Diplomatic and Consular Practice.* Washington, D.C.: Government Printing Office, 1947. 328 p.

Graham, Malbone W. *American Diplomacy In the International Community.* Baltimore: Johns Hopkins Press, 1948. 279 p.

Graham, Robert A. *Vatican Diplomacy*. Princeton, N.J.: Princeton University Press, 1959. 442 p. Bib.

Gustavson, Milton O., ed. *The National Archives and Foreign Relations Research*. Athens, Ohio: Ohio University Press, for the National Archives, 1974. 292 p.

Hankey, Maurice P. *Diplomacy By Conference: Studies In Public Affairs, 1920–1946*. London: Benn, 1946. 179 p.

Hardy, Michael J. *Modern Diplomatic Law*. New York: Oceana, 1968. 150 p. Bib.

Harr, John Ensor. *The Anatomy of the Foreign Service: A Statistical Profile*. New York: Carnegie Endowment, 1965. 89 p.

———. *The Development of Careers In the Foreign Service*. New York: Carnegie Endowment, 1965. 104 p.

———. *The Professional Diplomat*. Princeton, N.J.: Princeton University Press, 1969. 404 p. Bib.

Henkin, Louis. *Foreign Affairs and the Constitution*. Mineola, N.Y.: Foundation Press, 1972. 553 p.

Hershey, Amos S. *Diplomatic Agents and Immunities*. Washington, D.C.: Government Printing Office, 1919. 218 p.

Hill, Martin. *Immunities and Privileges of International Officials*. Washington, D.C.: Carnegie Endowment, 1947. 281 p.

Hill, Norman L. *The Public International Conference: Its Function, Organization and Procedure*. Palo Alto, Cal.: Stanford University Press, 1929. 267 p. Bib.

Hilton, Ralph. *Worldwide Mission: The Story of the United States Foreign Service*. New York: World, 1970. 256 p.

Hoffman, Arthur S., ed. *International Communication and the New Diplomacy*. Bloomington: Indiana University Press, 1968. 206 p.

Iklé, Fred Charles. *How Nations Negotiate*. New York: Praeger, 1964. 272 p. Bib.

Ilchman, Warren Frederick. *Professional Diplomacy In the United States, 1779–1939: A Study In Administrative History*. Chicago: University of Chicago Press, 1961. 254 p.

Jenks, C. Wilfred. *International Immunities*. New York: Oceana, 1961. 178 p.

Johnson, E. A. J., ed. *The Dimensions of Diplomacy*. Baltimore: Johns Hopkins Press, 1964. 135 p.

Jones, Arthur G. *The Evolution of Personnel Systems for U.S. Foreign Affairs: A History of Reform Efforts*. New York: Carnegie Endowment, 1965. 136 p.

Joy, Charles Turner. *How Communists Negotiate*. New York: Macmillan, 1955. 178 p.

Jusserand, Jean A. A. Jules. *The School for Ambassadors, and Other Essays.* New York: Putnam, 1925. 355 p.

Kaufmann, Johan. *Conference Diplomacy: An Introductory Analysis.* New York: Oceana, 1968. 222 p.

Kelly, David Victor. *The Ruling Few: Or, the Human Background to Diplomacy.* London: Hollis and Carter, 1952. 449 p.

Kertesz, Stephen D. *The Quest for Peace Through Diplomacy.* Englewood Cliffs, N.J.: Prentice-Hall, 1967. 182 p.

Kertesz, Stephen D., ed. *American Diplomacy in a New Era.* Notre Dame, Ind.: University of Notre Dame Press, 1961. 601 p.

Kertesz, Stephen D. and Fitzsimons, M. A. *Diplomacy in a Changing World.* Notre Dame, Ind.: University of Notre Dame Press, 1959. 407 p.

Lall, Arthur S. *How Communist China Negotiates.* New York: Columbia University Press, 1968. 291 p.

————. *Modern International Negotiation: Principles and Practices.* New York: Columbia University Press, 1966. 404 p.

Lavine, David. *Outposts of Adventure: The Story of the Foreign Service.* Garden City, N.Y.: Doubleday, 1966. 84 p.

Lay, Tracy H. *The Foreign Service of the United States.* New York: Prentice-Hall, 1925. 438 p.

Lisagor, Peter and Higgins, Marguerite. *Overtime in Heaven: Adventures in the Foreign Service.* Garden City, N.Y.: Doubleday, 1964. 275 p.

McCamy, James L. *The Administration of American Foreign Affairs.* New York: Knopf, 1950. 364 p.

————. *Conduct of the New Diplomacy.* New York: Harper and Row, 1964. 303 p. Bib.

Macomber, William. *The Angels' Game: A Handbook of Modern Diplomacy.* New York: Stein and Day, 1975. 225 p.

Mathews, John M. *American Foreign Relations: Conduct and Policies.* 2nd ed. New York: Appleton-Century-Crofts, 1938. 766 p.

————. *The Conduct of American Foreign Relations.* New York: Century, 1922. 353 p.

Mattingly, Garrett. *Renaissance Diplomacy.* Baltimore: Penguin, 1955. 284 p. Bib.

Mayer, Arno J. *Political Origins of the New Diplomacy, 1917–1918.* New Haven, Conn.: Yale University Press, 1959. 435 p. Bib.

Mendershausen, Horst. *The Diplomat As a National and Transnational Agent: Dilemmas and Opportunities.* Santa Monica, Cal.: Rand, 1969. 28 p.

Mennis, Bernard. *American Foreign Policy Officials: Who are They and What are They?* Columbus: Ohio State University Press, 1971. 210 p. Bib.

Merli, Frank J. and Wilson, Theodore A. *Makers of American Diplomacy: From Benjamin Franklin to Henry Kissinger.* New York: Scribner, 1974. 728 p.

Michaels, David B. *International Privileges and Immunities: A Case for a Universal Statute.* The Hague: Nijhoff, 1971. 249 p. Bib.

Miller, Hope Ridings. *Embassy Row: The Life and Times of Diplomatic Washington.* New York: Holt, Rinehart, and Winston, 1969. 286 p.

Moore, John Bassett. *The Principles of American Diplomacy.* New York: Harper, 1918. 476 p.

Moreno Salcedo, Louis. *A Guide to Protocol.* 2nd ed. Manila: University Book Supply, 1959. 280 p. Bib.

Mowrer, Paul S. *Our Foreign Affairs: A Study in National Interest and the New Diplomacy.* New York: Dutton, 1924. 348 p.

Neal, Harry Edward. *Your Career in Foreign Service.* New York: Messner, 1965. 191 p.

Nichols, Roy F. *Advance Agents of American Destiny.* Philadelphia: University of Pennsylvania Press, 1956. 254 p.

Nicolson, Harold. *Diplomacy.* London: Butterworth, 1939. 255 p. Bib.
————. *The Evolution of Diplomatic Method.* New York: Macmillan, 1954. 93 p.

Nostrand, Howard Lee. *The Cultural Attache.* New Haven, Conn.: Hazen Foundation, n.d. 45 p.

Numelin, Ragnar J. *The Beginnings of Diplomacy.* New York: Philosophical Library, 1950. 372 p. Bib.

Ogdon, Montell. *Judicial Bases of Diplomatic Immunity.* Washington, D.C.: Byrne, 1936. 254 p.

Ostrower, Alexander. *Language, Law and Diplomacy: A Study of Linguistic Diversity in Official International Relations and International Law.* 2 vols. Philadelphia: University of Pennsylvania Press, 1965. Bib.

Oudenijk, Willem Jacobus. *Ways and By-Ways in Diplomacy.* London: Davies, 1939. 386 p.

Pastuhov, Vladimir D. *A Guide to the Practice of International Conferences.* Washington, D.C.: Carnegie Endowment, 1945. 275 p. Bib.

Paullin, Charles O. *Diplomatic Negotiations of American Naval Officers, 1778–1883.* Baltimore: Johns Hopkins Press, 1912. 380 p.

Pearson, Drew and Brown, Constantine. *The American Diplomatic Game.* Garden City, N.Y.: Doubleday, Doran, 1935. 398 p.

446

Perkins, Dexter. *The American Approach to Foreign Policy.* Cambridge, Mass.: Harvard University Press, 1952. 195 p.

Plischke, Elmer. *Conduct of American Diplomacy.* 3rd ed. Princeton, N.J.: Van Nostrand, 1967. 677 p. Bib. Reprinted Westport, Conn.: Greenwood, 1974.

―――. *Summit Diplomacy: Personal Diplomacy of the President of the United States.* College Park, Md.: Bureau of Governmental Research, University of Maryland, 1958. 125 p. Reprinted Westport, Conn.: Greenwood, 1974.

―――. *United States Diplomats and Their Missions: A Profile of American Diplomatic Emissaries since 1778.* Washington, D.C.: American Enterprise Institute, 1975. 201 p.

Ponsonby, Arthur. *Democracy and Diplomacy: A Plea for Popular Control of Foreign Policy.* London: Methuen, 1915. 198 p.

Poole, Dewitt C. *The Conduct of Foreign Relations Under Modern Democratic Conditions.* New Haven, Conn.: Yale University Press, 1924. 208 p.

Queller, Donald E. *The Office of Ambassador in the Middle Ages.* Princeton, N.J.: Princeton University Press, 1967. 251 p. Bib.

Radlovic, I. Monte. *Etiquette and Protocol: A Handbook of Conduct in American and International Circles.* New York: Harcourt, Brace, 1957. 240 p.

Regala, Roberto. *The Trends in Modern Diplomatic Practice.* New York: Oceana, 1959. 209 p.

―――. *World Order and Diplomacy.* Dobbs Ferry, N.Y.: Oceana, 1969. 205 p. Bib.

Reiff, Henry. *Diplomatic and Consular Privileges, Immunities and Practice.* Cairo, Egypt: Ettemad Press, 1954. 290 p.

Reinsch, Paul S. *Secret Diplomacy: How Far Can It Be Eliminated?* New York: Harcourt, Brace, 1922. 231 p. Bib.

Rinden, Robert W. and Nadler, S. I. *Life and Love in the Foreign Service.* Washington, D.C.: Foreign Service Journal, 1969. 60 p. (Pictorial spoof—photographs with humorous captions.)

Roetter, Charles. *The Diplomatic Art: An Informal History of World Diplomacy.* Philadelphia: Macrae Smith, 1963. 248 p.

Roudybush, Franklin. *Diplomatic Language.* Basle, Switzerland: Satz, 1972. 24 p.

―――. *Foreign Service Training.* Besancon, France: Press Comptoise, 1955. 279 p.

Rourke, Francis E. *Secrecy and Publicity: Dilemmas of Democracy.* Baltimore: Johns Hopkins Press, 1961. 236 p.

Satow, Ernest M. *A Guide to Diplomatic Practice.* 4th ed. Edited by Nevile Bland. London: Longmans, Green, 1957. 510 p.

————. *International Congresses.* London: H. M. Stationery, 1920. 168 p.

Sayre, Wallace S. and Thurber, Clarence E. *Training for Specialized Mission Personnel.* Chicago: Public Administration Service, 1952. 85 p.

Schulzinger, Robert D. *The Making of the Diplomatic Mind: The Training, Outlook, and Style of United States Foreign Service Officers, 1908–1931.* Middletown, Conn.: Wesleyan University Press, 1975. 237 p. Bib.

Schurman, Franz. *The Logic of World Power: Secrecy and Foreign Policy.* New York: Pantheon, 1974. 593 p.

Sen, Biswanath. *A Diplomat's Handbook of International Law and Practice.* The Hague: Nijhoff, 1965. 522 p. Bib.

Simpson, Smith, ed. *Instruction in Diplomacy: The Liberal Arts Approach.* Philadelphia: Monograph No. 13 of American Academy of Political and Social Science, 1972. 342 p. Bib.

Spaulding, E. Wilder. *Ambassadors Ordinary and Extraordinary.* Washington, D.C.: Public Affairs, 1961. 302 p. Bib.

Spector, Paul and Preston, Harley O. *Working Effectively Overseas.* Washington, D.C.: Institute for International Service, 1961. 179 p.

Strang, William S. *The Diplomatic Career.* London: Deutsch, 1962. 160 p.

Stuart, Graham H. *American Diplomatic and Consular Practice.* 2nd ed. New York: Appleton-Century-Crofts, 1952. 477 p. Bib.

Symington, James W. *The Stately Game.* New York: Macmillan, 1971. 256 p.

Thayer, Charles W. *Diplomat.* New York: Harper, 1959. 299 p. Bib.

Thompson, James Westphal and Padover, Saul K. *Secret Diplomacy: Espionage and Cryptography, 1500–1815.* New York: Unger, 1963. 290 p. Bib.

Thompson, Kenneth W. *American Diplomacy and Emergent Patterns.* New York: New York University Press, 1962. 273 p. Bib.

United States, Commission on the Organization of the Government for the Conduct of Foreign Policy. *Commission on the Organization of the Government for the Conduct of Foreign Policy, June 1975.* Washington, D.C.: Government Printing Office, 1975. 278 p. Bib. Report of the Murphy Commission, supplemented with 7 volumes containing 25 Appendixes (labelled A to X) published in 1976.

United States, Congress, House of Representatives, Committee on Foreign Affairs. *The Foreign Service: Basic Information on Organi-*

zation, Administration, and Personnel. Washington, D.C.: Government Printing Office, 1955. 178 p.

———. *Foreign Service of the United States*. Washington, D.C.: Government Printing Office, 1924. 226 p. (Hearings, 68th Congress, 1st Session, on Foreign Service Act of 1924.)

———. *The Future of United States Public Diplomacy*. Washington, D.C.: Government Printing Office, 1968. 175 p.

United States, Congress, Senate, Committee on Foreign Relations. *The American Overseas*. Washington, D.C.: Government Printing Office, 1959. 48 p.

———. *Recruitment and Training for the Foreign Service of the United States*. Washington, D.C.: Government Printing Office, 1958. 197 p.

———. *Study of United States Foreign Policy: Summary of Views of Retired Foreign Service Officers*. Washington, D.C.: Government Printing Office, 1959. 81 p.

United States, Congress, Senate, Committee on Government Operations, Subcommittee on National Security and International Operations. *Negotiation and Statecraft: A Selection of Readings*. Washington, D.C.: Government Printing Office, 1970. 59 p.

———. *Specialists and Generalists: A Selection of Readings*. Washington, D. C.: Government Printing Office, 1968. 71 p.

United States, Congress, Senate, Committee on Government Operations, Subcommittee on National Security Staffing and Operations. *The Ambassador and the Problem of Coordination*. Washington, D.C.: Government Printing Office, 1963. 159 p.

———. *Administration of National Security: The American Ambassador*. Washington, D.C.: Government Printing Office, 1964. 16 p.

———. *Administration of National Security: Basic Issues*. Washington, D.C.: Government Printing Office, 1963. 20 p. (Section IV on the Country Team.)

United States, Department of State. *The Country Team: An Illustrated Profile of Our American Missions Abroad*. Washington, D.C.: Government Printing Office, 1967. 70 p.

———. *Some Facts About the Foreign Service: A Short Account of Its Organization and Duties Together With Pertinent Laws and Regulations*. Washington, D.C.: Government Printing Office, 1950. 70 p.

Vagts, Alfred. *The Military Attache*. Princeton, N.J.: Princeton University Press, 1967. 408 p. Bib.

Van Dyne, Frederick. *Our Foreign Service: The "ABC" of American Diplomacy*. Rochester: Lawyers Cooperative, 1909. 316 p.

Walther, Regis. *Orientations and Behavioral Styles of Foreign Service Officers.* New York: Carnegie Endowment, 1965. 52 p.

Waters, Mourice. *The Ad Hoc Diplomat.* The Hague: Nijhoff, 1963. 233 p. Bib.

Webster, Charles K. *The Art and Practice of Diplomacy.* London: London School of Economics, 1952. 245 p.

Weil, Martin. *A Pretty Good Club: The Founding Fathers of the U.S. Foreign Service.* New York: Norton, 1978. 313 p.

Werking, Richard Hume. *The Master Architects: Building the United States Foreign Service, 1890–1913.* Lexington: University of Kentucky Press, 1978. 340 p.

Westerfield, H. Bradford. *The Instruments of America's Foreign Policy.* New York: Crowell, 1963. 538 p. Bib.

Wicquefort, Abraham van. *The Ambassador and His Functions.* 2 vols. Translated by Mr. Digby. The Hague: Steucker, 1681.

Wiggins, James R. *Freedom or Secrecy.* New York: Oxford University Press, 1956. 242 p.

Wilcox, Francis O. and Frank, Richard A. *The Constitution and the Conduct of Foreign Policy.* New York: Praeger, 1976. 145 p.

Williams, Benjamin H. *American Diplomacy: Policies and Practice.* New York: McGraw-Hill, 1936. 517 p. Bib.

Wilson, Clifton E. *Cold War Diplomacy: The Impact of International Conflicts on Diplomatic Communications and Travel.* Tucson: University of Arizona Press, 1966. 67 p.

————. *Diplomatic Privileges and Immunities.* Tucson: University of Arizona Press, 1967. 300 p. Bib.

Wise, David. *The Politics of Lying: Government Deception, Secrecy, and Power.* New York: Random House, 1973. 415 p. Bib.

Wood, John R. and Serres, Jean. *Diplomatic Ceremonial and Protocol.* New York: Columbia University Press, 1970. 384 p. Bib.

Wright, Quincy. *The Control of American Foreign Relations.* New York: Macmillan, 1922. 412 p.

Wriston, Henry M. *Diplomacy in a Democracy.* New York: Harper, 1956. 115 p.

————. *Executive Agents in American Foreign Relations.* Baltimore: Johns Hopkins Press, 1929. 874 p.

Yost, Charles W. *The Conduct and Misconduct of Foreign Affairs.* New York: Random House, 1972. 234 p.

Young, George. *Diplomacy Old and New.* London: Swarthmore, 1921. 105 p.

Young, Kenneth Todd. *Negotiating with the Chinese Communists: The United States Experience, 1953–1967.* New York: McGraw-Hill, 1968. 461 p. Bib.

CONTRIBUTORS

THOMAS A. BAILEY was Byrne Professor of American History at Stanford University, guest professor at Cornell and Harvard Universities, and staff member at the National War College.

WILLIAM BARNES was a career Foreign Service Officer and served abroad in a diplomatic and consular capacity and as Chief of the Reporting Staff of the Department of State.

ANDREW BERDING served as press representative abroad and in Washington, and as Assistant Secretary of State for Public Affairs, Public Relations Officer in the Defense Department, and Deputy Director of the U.S. Information Agency.

WILLIAM D. BLAIR, JR., former Director of the Office of Media Services of the Department of State, has been serving as Deputy Assistant Secretary for Public Affairs since 1970.

ELLIS O. BRIGGS was a career Foreign Service Officer for thirty-seven years and served as Ambassador to seven countries, including Korea, Brazil, Greece, and Spain.

WARREN CHRISTOPHER is Deputy Secretary of State and served as a member of United States delegations to several international conferences.

INIS L. CLAUDE, JR., is Edward R. Stettinius, Jr., Professor at the University of Virginia, and served as consultant to the Department of State and as a member and chairman of the Secretary of State's Advisory Committee on *Foreign Relations of the United States.*

HARLAN CLEVELAND is Director of International Affairs at the Aspen Institute, and served as Assistant Secretary of State, Ambassador to NATO, and Dean of the Maxwell School of Citizenship and Public Affairs at Syracuse University and President of the University of Hawaii.

HERMANN F. EILTS, Foreign Service Officer with the rank of Career Minister, served as Ambassador to Saudi Arabia and Egypt and as Diplomatic Adviser at the U.S. Army War College.

WILLIAM M. FRANKLIN, a career Department of State officer served in the management of the Historical Division of the Department of State from 1947 until his retirement as the Director of the Division in 1975.

HUGH S. GIBSON was a career diplomat and served as Ambassador or Minister to five countries, including Poland, Belgium, and Brazil, and as United States delegate to several arms limitation conferences.

LINCOLN GORDON is Senior Fellow at Resources for the Future, and served as William Ziegler Professor of International Economic Relations at Harvard University, and in an administrative capacity in the European Cooperation Administration and the Mutual Security Agency.

DAG HAMMARSKJÖLD, Swedish diplomat, served as Secretary-General of the United Nations and as Sweden's representative to the Organization for European Economic Cooperation and as a delegate to several international conferences; he also won the Nobel Peace Prize (1961).

FRED CHARLES IKLÉ, private consultant, served as Director of the Arms Control and Disarmament Agency, Professor of Political Science at the Massachusetts Institute of Technology, and head of the Social Science Department at the Rand Corporation.

GEORGE F. KENNAN is Professor at the Institute for Advanced Study, Princeton University, and a career Foreign Service Officer, retired; he served as Ambassador to the Soviet Union, the Philippines, and Yugoslavia, and as Director of the Policy Planning Staff of the Department of State.

HENRY A. KISSINGER is University Professor of Diplomacy in the School of Foreign Service at Georgetown University; he served as

Special Assistant to the President and Secretary of State and as Professor and Director of the International Seminar at Harvard University; he also won the Nobel Peace Prize (1973).

FOY D. KOHLER is Professor at the Center for Advanced International Studies, University of Miami (Florida) and a career Foreign Service Officer, retired; he served as Ambassador to the Soviet Union and as Deputy Under Secretary and Assistant Secretary of State.

CHARLES O. LERCHE, JR., was Professor and Dean at the School of International Service, American University, and Professor and Chairman, Political Science Department, Knox College.

CLARE BOOTHE LUCE, authoress and playright, was editor of *Vogue* and Managing Editor of *Vanity Fair;* she served as Ambassador to Italy.

JOHN HEATH MORGAN was a career Foreign Service Officer who served in various diplomatic and consular posts abroad and as faculty adviser at the U.S. Army War College.

SIR HAROLD NICOLSON was a British career diplomatist, historian, and biographer; he served in Spain, Turkey, Iran, and Berlin, as a British delegate to international conferences, and as a Member of Parliament.

ELMER PLISCHKE is Professor of Government and Politics at the University of Maryland, Adjunct Professor of Political Science at Gettysburg College, and Adjunct Scholar, American Enterprise Institute; he served as a Foreign Service Staff Officer and as a member and chairman of the Secretary of State's Advisory Committee on *Foreign Relations of the United States.*

ROBERT J. PRANGER is Director, Foreign and Defense Policy Studies at the American Enterprise Institute and Adjunct Professor at Georgetown University and Professorial Lecturer at George Washington University; he served as Deputy Assistant Secretary of Defense.

ELIHU ROOT, lawyer and statesman, served as Secretary of War, Secretary of State, United States Senator, presidential special emissary with rank of Ambassador Extraordinary to Russia, and participating architect of the League of Nations; he also won the Nobel Peace Prize (1912).

DEAN RUSK is Professor of Law at the University of Georgia; he served as Secretary of State and President of the Rockefeller Foundation.

ABDUL A. SAID is Professor at the School of International Service at the American University and the author of several books.

SIR ERNEST M. SATOW was a British diplomatist and historian; he served as Minister to several countries including Morocco, Japan, and China, as a delegate to a number of international conferences, and on the Permanent Court of Arbitration at The Hague.

J. ROBERT SCHAETZEL, career Department of State officer, retired, served as U.S. Representative to the European Communities and at the National War College.

MONTEAGLE STEARNS was a career Foreign Service Officer who served in the Department of State and the U.S. Information Agency, as Deputy Chief of Mission in Laos, and as Deputy Assistant Secretary of State.

KINGDON B. SWAYNE is Professor at Bucks County Community College and a career Foreign Service Officer, retired; he served in Britain, China, Japan, and Hong Kong.

CHARLES W. THAYER was a career Foreign Service Officer who served on the Secretariat of the European Advisory Commission and as Liaison Officer for the Office of the U.S. High Commissioner for Germany.

HARRY S. TRUMAN was U.S. Senator and Thirty-Third President of the United States (1945–1953).

HENRY M. WRISTON was President of Brown University and served as Chairman of the Secretary of State's Public Committee on Department of State Personnel, President of the American Assembly, and Trustee of the World Peace Foundation and the Carnegie Endowment.

ACKNOWLEDGMENTS

The publisher wishes to thank those who have given permission to reprint the following material:

"Diplomacy—Contemporary Practice." Reprinted by permission of author.

"Diplomacy—Political Technique for Implementing Foreign Policy." Reprinted by permission of Prentice-Hall, Inc., Englewood Cliffs, New Jersey. Copyright © 1970.

"Diplomacy/Diplomat—Derivation of the Concepts." Reprinted by permission of Longmen Group Limited, London. Copyright © 1957.

"Diplomacy—Search for Its Meaning." Reprinted by permission of the American Academy of Political and Social Science. Copyright © 1972, by the American Academy of Political and Social Science. All rights reserved.

"Titles of Diplomats." Reprinted by permission of Harper and Row, Publishers, Inc. Copyright © 1959 by Charles W. Thayer.

"Transition from the Old to the New Diplomacy." Reprinted by permission of author.

"The New Diplomacy." Reprinted by permission of *Virginia Quarterly Review*.

"Proliferating International Community and Changing Diplomatic Representation." Reprinted by permission of the World Future Society, Washington, D.C.

"Requisite for the Success of Popular Diplomacy," by Elihu Root. Reprinted by permission from *Foreign Affairs*, September 1922. Copyright © 1922 by *Foreign Affairs*.

"Democratic Diplomacy and the Role of Propaganda." Reprinted by permission of *Foreign Service Journal*.

"Quiet vs. Unquiet Diplomacy." Excerpted from *Foreign Affairs and You* by Andrew Berding. Copyright © 1962 by Andrew Berding. Reprinted by permission of Doubleday and Company, Inc.

"Secret vs. Open Diplomacy." Excerpted from *The Road to Foreign Policy* by Hugh S. Gibson. Copyright © 1944 by Hugh S. Gibson. Reprinted by permission of Doubleday and Company, Inc.

"[Ministerial Diplomacy—] The Secretary of State Abroad" by Dr. Henry M. Wriston. Reprinted by permission from *Foreign Affairs* (July 1956). Copyright © 1963 by Council on Foreign Relations, Inc.

"Summit Diplomacy—Diplomat in Chief." Reprinted by permission of *Virginia Quarterly Review*.

"Multilateralism." Reprinted by permission of the University of Wisconsin Press. Copyright © 1958 by the Regents of the University of Wisconsin.

"Crisis Management," from "Crisis Diplomacy" by Harlan Cleveland. Reprinted by permission from *Foreign Affairs* (July 1963). Copyright © 1963 by Council on Foreign Relations, Inc.

"Qualities of American Diplomats." Reprinted by permission of *Virginia Quarterly Review*.

"Advice for Diplomats." Reprinted by permission of author.

"Profiles of United States Diplomats: Bicentennial Review and Future Projection." Reprinted by permission of the American Peace Society.

"Foreign Service—Past and Future," from "The Future of Our Professional Diplomacy," by George F. Kennan. Reprinted by permission of *Foreign Affairs* (July 1955). Copyright © 1955 by Council on Foreign Relations, Inc.

EDITOR'S NOTE: Footnotes contained in the original essays included in this compilation are generally deleted—including documentary citations and references to additional information—although a few explanatory footnotes have been retained, and new content notes and cross-references have been added.